Europe TravelBook

The Guide to Premier Destinations

Twentieth Edition

Written by Des Hannigan, Sally Roy, Nia Williams.
Twentieth edition verified by Big World Productions Ltd, Sue Dobson,
Mary-Ann Gallagher, Mike Gerrard, Emma Levine, Melanie and Chris Rice,
Sally Roy, Dorothy Stannard.

Project Editor: Sheila McCarthy.

Published by AAA Publishing, 1000 AAA Drive, Heathrow, Florida 32746.
The *AAA Europe TravelBook* was created and produced for AAA Publishing by
AA Media Limited, Fanum House, Basing View, Basingstoke, Hampshire,
RG21 4EA, UK.

Text © AAA Publishing 2019, 20th edition.
AAA Editor: Michelle Palmer.

Maps © AA Media Limited 2019.
Contains Ordnance Survey data © Crown copyright and database right 2019.

Maps contain data available from openstreetmap.org © under the Open Database
License found at opendatacommons.org.

ISBN: 978-1-59508-603-7

Main cover photo and spine: The Colosseum, Rome, Italy
© istockphoto/vichie81.
Back cover: Extract from Europe map © AA Media Ltd 2019.

Cataloging-in-Publication Data is on file with the Library of Congress.

Color separations by Digital Department AA Publishing.
Printed and bound in Italy by G. Canale & C. S.p.A.

A05647

The Hungarian Parliament Building, Országház, on the eastern bank of the Danube, Budapest, Hungary

Foreword

A dream destination for countless travelers, Europe offers everything you could possibly want for an unforgettable vacation. The variety of places to explore and range of experiences to enjoy are dizzying. Feel the cool wind off a snow-capped peak on a hike in the Alps or bask on a sun-drenched beach along the French Riviera. Cruise among Venice's antique palazzos on an intimate gondola ride for two or gather friends for a group outing to a rowdy German beer hall. Ogle the pricey luxury goods in boutiques along Paris' Champs-Élysées or admire the priceless treasures crowding the Vatican Museums. Your choices are endless.

Each turn of a corner seems to bring you face-to-face with centuries of history, whether on a stroll among ancient ruins atop the Acropolis or the remnants of Roman splendor at the Coliseum or the notorious cells of the Tower of London. Walk in the footsteps of William Shakespeare in Stratford-upon-Avon, Wolfgang Amadeus Mozart in Vienna, Franz Kafka in Prague or James Joyce in Dublin. And the food! Each city seems to have its own specialty, and you could spend several vacations just sampling the cuisines of a single region.

Choosing where to go may not be easy, but this book will give you the information you need to fuel your dreams and give shape to your plans. Its wealth of practical information includes tips about what to bring and how to get around, maps to help you find your way, detailed descriptions of things to see and suggestions of where to stay and eat.

Contents

Map of Europe	**6–7**
Introduction to Europe	**8–16**

Before You Go	**8**
Passports and Visas	8
Travel and Health Insurance	9
Weather and When To Go	9
What To Pack	9

While You Are There	**10**
Emergencies	10
Health	10
Language	10
Media	10
Money and Valuables	10
Personal Safety	11
Phone Service	12
Travelers with Disabilities	12

Getting Around	**13**
City Transportation	13
Between Cities	13
Trains	13
Airlines	14
Ferries	14
European Customs and Immigration	14

Driving in Europe	**14**
European Automobile Clubs	14
Car Rental	15
Green Card	15
International Driving Permit (IDP)	15
Driving Regulations	15

Returning to the United States	**16**
Confirming Return Travel	16
Tax-free Shopping	16
U.S. Customs	16

Premier Destinations	**17–460**
■ **Austria**	**18**
Vienna	26
Innsbruck	34
Salzburg	40
■ **Belgium**	**48**
Brussels	56
Bruges	62
Ghent	70
■ **Britain**	**76**
London	86
Edinburgh	98
Oxford	106
Bath	112
■ **Czech Republic**	**118**
Prague	124
■ **Denmark**	**132**
Copenhagen	140
Odense	146
■ **Finland**	**152**
Helsinki	158
■ **France**	**164**
Paris	174
Lyon	186
Nice	194
Strasbourg	200
■ **Germany**	**206**
Berlin	216
Cologne	224
Munich	230
■ **Greece**	**238**
Athens	244
■ **Hungary**	**252**
Budapest	258

■ **Ireland** **266**
Dublin 274

■ **Italy** **282**
Rome 292
Florence 302
Naples 308
Venice 314

■ **Luxembourg** **322**
City of Luxembourg 328

■ **The Netherlands** **334**
Amsterdam 342
The Hague 350

■ **Norway** **356**
Oslo 364

■ **Portugal** **370**
Lisbon 378
Porto 386

■ **Spain** **392**
Madrid 402
Barcelona 410
Santiago de Compostela 418
Seville 424

■ **Sweden** **430**
Stockholm 436

■ **Switzerland** **444**
Geneva 450
Zurich 456

**Hotels and
Restaurants** **461–492**
Austria 463
Belgium 465
Britain 467
Czech Republic 470
Denmark 471
Finland 473
France 473
Germany 476
Greece 478
Hungary 479
Ireland 479
Italy 480

Luxembourg 483
The Netherlands 484
Norway 485
Portugal 486
Spain 487
Sweden 490
Switzerland 491

**Essential
Information** **493–569**
Austria 494
Belgium 498
Britain 502
Czech Republic 506
Denmark 510
Finland 514
France 518
Germany 522
Greece 526
Hungary 530
Ireland 534
Italy 538
Luxembourg 542
The Netherlands 546
Norway 550
Portugal 554
Spain 558
Sweden 562
Switzerland 566

**European Distance
Chart** **570–571**

Index **572–575**

Key to symbols

⊞ map page number and coordinates
⊠ address or location
☎ telephone number
🄾 opening times
🄼 nearest subway/overground train station
🚍 nearest bus/trolley bus/tram/funicular route
⛴ ferry
🍴 restaurant
💷 admission charge (per adult, unless
   otherwise stated)
🛈 information
For conversion charts, see the inside back cover

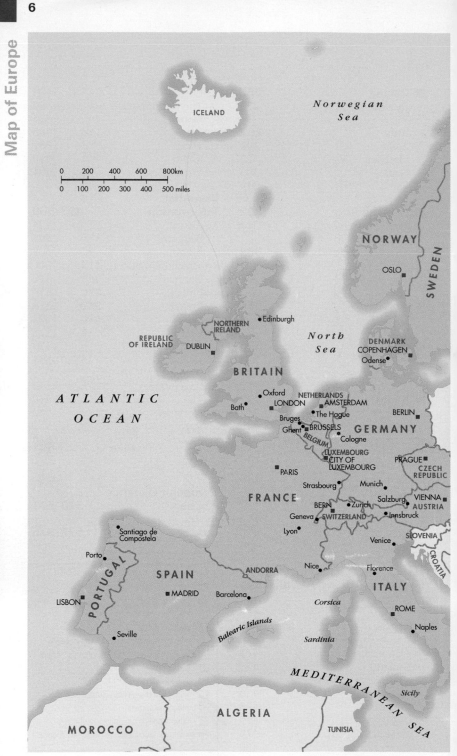

CONTENTS

Austria	**18**
Belgium	**48**
Britain	**76**
Czech Republic	**118**
Denmark	**132**
Finland	**152**
France	**164**
Germany	**206**
Greece	**238**
Hungary	**252**
Ireland	**266**
Italy	**282**
Luxembourg	**322**
The Netherlands	**334**
Norway	**356**
Portugal	**370**
Spain	**392**
Sweden	**430**
Switzerland	**444**

Before You Go

Passports and Visas

The most important document you'll need to arrange before you travel is a passport. Passport application forms can be obtained at any AAA office. They also are available from many federal, state and probate courts, post offices, some public libraries and county and municipal offices authorized to accept passport applications.

Passport information and downloadable application forms are available on the website for Passport Information at https://travel.state.gov. Travel warnings, consular information sheets, public announcements, publications information and information about individual countries also can be accessed.

If you need a passport urgently contact a passport agency located in major cities (see the *Yellow Pages* for the one nearest you). You also can request an application form from the National Passport Information Center (NPIC) at 1-877-487-2778. Automated information is available daily 24 hours; operators are available Mon.–Fri. 8 a.m.–10 p.m, Sat. 10 a.m.–3 p.m. (Eastern Time), excluding federal holidays.

U.S. CITIZENS

The information in this guide has been compiled for U.S. citizens who are traveling as tourists.

AAA recommends travelers consult online U.S. State Department travel advisories when planning travel abroad. Find this information at https://travel.state.gov/content/passports/en/alertswarnings.html.

Travelers who are not U.S. citizens, or who are traveling on business, should check with their embassies and tourist offices for information on the countries they wish to visit.

Entry requirements can be subject to change on short notice, and travelers are therefore advised to check the current situation before they travel.

Passport and consular/emergency services for Canadian citizens traveling abroad can be accessed at the Government of Canada internet site at https://travel.gc.ca.

Each person traveling must have a valid passport; apply early, since processing can take several months. Expedited service is available for an extra charge. Before departure, make sure your passport is valid for at least six months prior to the expiration date; some European countries require this.

You'll need your passport whenever you board an international flight, train or ferry. In some countries, you will be required to leave your passport with the hotel when you check in; this is to satisfy regulations requiring the hotel to register all foreign visitors with local police authorities. In addition, you may be required to show your passport whenever you cash a traveler's check.

Passports also need to be shown whenever national borders are crossed, although in practice border controls have been relaxed between many European Union (E.U.) member countries. In Geneva, the city transportation system crosses national borders and the airport also straddles the border, so you'll need a passport simply to get around.

Make two photocopies of the identification page; leave one copy with a friend in case of emergency and carry one with you in case your passport is lost or stolen while traveling. If this occurs, inform local police immediately and contact the nearest U.S. Embassy or consulate. The U.S. Department of State has a 24-hour travelers' hotline; phone 1-888-407-4747 (within the U.S.) or 1-202-501-4444 (from abroad).

Some countries require a visa also. Travel visas are not necessary when visiting the countries covered in this book, but if you'll be traveling to other nations, check their entry requirements; AAA offices have visa information.

AAA and CAA members will want to visit www.AAA.com before setting out on their international travels. Check for merchants who will accept your AAA or CAA membership card in order to obtain member savings at thousands of locations throughout the world. Members visiting their club's www.AAA.com website should look under "Benefits for AAA Members Traveling Overseas."

Travel and Health Insurance

Before leaving, make sure you are covered by insurance that will reimburse travel expenses if you need to cancel or cut short your trip due to unforeseen circumstances. You'll also need coverage for property loss or theft, emergency medical and dental treatment, and emergency evacuation if necessary. Before purchasing additional insurance, check to see whether your current homeowner's or medical coverage already covers you for travel abroad.

If you make a claim, your insurance company will need proof of the incident or expenditure. Keep copies of any police report and related documents, or doctor's or hospital bills or statements, to submit with your insurance claim.

Weather and When To Go

The European continent occupies a far more northerly location than its overall moderate climate would suggest. Different factors affect the weather at any given destination. The warming influence of the Gulf Stream affects all countries with an Atlantic coastline, from Spain and Portugal north through the British Isles into Scandinavia. The North and Baltic seas also affect temperatures and rainfall on the coastal areas they border.

Another definer is altitude, and Europe's great mountain ranges affect local temperatures and rainfall as well. The Pyrenees divide the Iberian Peninsula and France, while the Alps form an immense natural barrier across Austria, Switzerland and northern Italy south into France, where they descend to the Mediterranean Sea at Monaco. This entire region is popular with winter skiers, while summer visitors can expect clouds, mist and cool temperatures. The Apennines cut down the boot of Italy, also creating somewhat changeable conditions.

Destinations bordering the Mediterranean are ideal for summer vacations, with mostly sunny skies, warm temperatures and little rain. The flip side can be the heat – especially in southern Spain and Greece – so protect yourself from overexposure to the sun and carry drinking water for extended outdoor excursions. Winters in the Mediterranean region are cool and rainy, but temperatures are not usually severe and snow is rare in coastal areas.

Summer also is the main vacation season in central Europe, which has warm, mainly dry summers and cold winters with snow at higher elevations. The weather in spring is generally more unpredictable than in the fall.

The British Isles can have weeks of dry conditions in summer, although it's best to come prepared for rain. British winters are rainy, although temperatures can be extremely cold and snow is not uncommon. However, snow is most common in northern England and Scotland. In Ireland, rain is common year-round.

Scandinavia has varying weather and overall lower temperatures. Daytime highs in the summer months rarely exceed 75 degrees Fahrenheit, and the coastal locations of Copenhagen, Oslo, Stockholm and Helsinki increase the probability of unsettled conditions. Winters are uniformly severe, with significant snowfall the rule.

European school vacations are a factor in planning when to travel. Schools in most countries are in session from September until early July, making May, June and Spetember good months to visit.

What To Pack

Electrical appliances will require an adapter that changes the arrangement of the plug prongs, as well as an electrical voltage converter that will allow a normal 110-volt American appliance to take 220- to 240-volt European current. Two-in-one adapter/converters are available at some hardware stores and also at many AAA Travel Stores.

Bring a first-aid kit with adhesive bandages, sunblock, insect repellent and some over-the-counter remedies for minor ailments. Include written prescriptions for prescription medicines in case you need more or need to show the prescription to customs officials. Tissues will come in handy, as local restrooms in some areas may be ill-equipped or below U.S. standards. European hotel rooms provide towels but often no washcloth.

Check with your airline carrier prior to your flight to determine specific carry-on restrictions.

While You Are There

Emergencies

See the Essential Information section, pages 493–569, for information about a specific country.

Health

Take sensible precautions during hot weather. Wear a hat, sunglasses and sunblock, especially if you are on or near the water. Drink plenty of fluids, and remember that alcoholic beverages and the caffeine in coffee, tea and some sodas has a dehydrating effect.

The tap water in northern Europe is generally safe to drink, although its high mineral content can cause minor upsets if you're not used to it. Bottled water, still or carbonated, is inexpensive and widely available. In an area where the tap water is unsafe, avoid ice cubes and salads with ingredients that are likely to have been washed in water.

Pharmacists are a good first source for dealing with minor health problems; a pharmacist will be able to direct you to a doctor if necessary. For advice pertaining to specific topics, see the "Health" subheading under individual countries in Essential Information.

Language

Traveling is always more enjoyable if you can converse a bit in the local language. "Yes," "no," "please" and "thank you," accompanied by a pleasant smile and polite manner, will go far toward oiling social wheels. Refer to the "Useful Words and Phrases" subheading under individual countries in Essential Information for a helpful list.

English is most likely to be spoken in Scandinavia, The Netherlands, Belgium, Luxembourg, Germany, Austria and Switzerland. In Britain and Ireland you may encounter strong regional accents, as well as unfamiliar words and expressions.

To some Europeans – particularly the French and the British – good manners are a social necessity. "Please" and "thank you" should be part of every request in Britain; in France, anyone you don't know personally (including the staff in stores and restaurants) should be addressed as *monsieur* (sir), *madame* (madam) or *mademoiselle* (miss).

If you're really stuck with communications, remember that hotel receptionists very often speak English, and are invariably helpful and friendly; you can ask them to phone for taxis and arrange for cleaning and similar personal services on your behalf.

Media

Room televisions in the larger hotels have satellite or cable connections and broadcast BBC channels, the British Sky network or CNN. On the radio you may be able to pick up Voice of America, Radio Canada or BBC broadcasts.

In most major European cities, American newspapers (usually previous-day editions) and magazines are widely available; the most common publications are *USA Today*, the *New York Times International Edition* and *Time* magazine. They can be purchased at airports and central train stations, as well as at newsstands and tobacconists.

Money and Valuables

The euro (€) is the common currency of 19 European Union countries (Austria, Belgium, Cyprus, Estonia, Finland, France, Germany, Greece, Ireland, Italy, Latvia, Lithuania, Luxembourg, Malta, The Netherlands, Portugal, Slovakia, Slovenia and Spain). For additional information see the "Money" subheading in the Essential Information sections for the countries featured in this guide.

Currency exchange facilities are widely available in Europe. There are exchange offices at airport and central train and bus stations, in city central business districts, and at seaports and other internal border crossing points. Most hotel reception desks also will exchange currency. A fee is usually charged for each exchange transaction. Although the fee is likely to be a little higher at hotels, it may be worth paying extra for the convenience and safety while traveling. For lower commission rates, it is advisable to exchange currency at a travel office or a bank before you embark on your trip.

When traveling in highly developed countries or frequently visited tourist destinations, you will find ATMs abound. Prepaid travel/currency cards are recommended for use in these areas because they allow the withdrawal of useable amounts of local currency from ATMs without allowing access to checking or savings accounts. Your exchange and ATM fee is usually lower since it is set by your prepaid card provider, however, you may be charged an additional fee by the ATM provider. Most merchants prefer chip-and-PIN cards in Europe, instead of the old-style magnetic stripe cards. However, most merchants will accept the magnetic stripe cards with a little insistence by the cardholder.

It may be useful to travel with a second prepaid card in case your first card is lost or stolen. Keep a record of the card numbers and international phone numbers in order to report any lost or stolen cards, and always carry your second card in a separate place.

Credit cards are another method of payment when traveling abroad. American Express, MasterCard and Visa are the most widely accepted (Discover/Diners Club are accepted less often). Be sure to notify your credit card company before departure to let them know where and when you will be traveling. Often, credit card companies will block your card if the transaction is not a "usual and customary" transaction on your card.

You can get cash advances with your credit card from ATMs, but you will most likely incur cash advance charges in addition to your ATM and exchange fees.

Leave valuable jewelry at home; ostentatious displays mark you as a prospective target for theft. Make sure your luggage is lockable and labeled both outside and inside. Never leave your bags unattended. Train and bus stations normally provide lockers or check desks where you can leave a heavy bag while sightseeing. If you're traveling by car, keep your doors locked in slow-moving traffic or when driving through busy urban areas, and put everything in the trunk while the car is parked.

If you do have any belongings stolen, report the incident to the police immediately and obtain a police report or written statement to provide to your insurance company as evidence to support your claim.

Personal Safety

Most of the rules for personal safety constitute common sense. Keep valuables (passport, money, credit cards) hidden when you're on the move; a money belt or neck purse worn inside clothing is the safest option. Put money in different places so that if one bag is lost you have another source of funds. Fanny packs and pockets are not safe places to carry valuables. Any bag you'll be carrying with you during the day should have a secure fastener, with a sturdy strap that goes over your neck and crosses your body – not simply over the shoulder. This helps ensure that bulkier items (cameras, phones, tablets, etc.) will be safe from pickpockets and petty thieves in crowded urban areas or on buses or trains.

The big tourist attractions are prime territory for pickpockets, as are buses, trains, subways, markets and airports. Be on guard for people who "accidentally" bump into you, or watch while you use an ATM. In large cities, be on the lookout for gangs of youngsters who create a commotion and then steal bags from tourists while their attention is distracted.

Street beggars can be quite persistent; walk quickly away without responding or making eye contact. Contact a police officer if anyone becomes particularly aggressive or threatening.

In general, avoid walking alone after dark. In southern European city centers during the summer, however, you'll almost certainly find locals out walking and shopping late into the evening.

Phone Service

You can make international calls from most European telephones; for specific information see "Telephones" under individual countries in the Essential Information section (see pages 493–569). To place a call to another country, first dial the international code, then the country code, then the area code (minus any initial zero) and the local number. Sometimes you'll need to wait for another dial tone after dialing the international code. In some countries the telecommunications infrastructure is fragile, and it may take a few attempts to get through.

The least expensive way to make an international call is to use a prepaid calling card. Dialing the appropriate access number (numbers differ according to country) will connect you with an English-speaking operator who can place a collect call or a call credited to your card. To obtain a card and a list of country access numbers, contact your telephone service provider. Credit cards (American Express, Diners Card, MasterCard and VISA) are accepted in many public phones. If you use a pay phone, you may need to insert coins in the local currency (a minimum fee applies) to get an outside line to make the call.

The convenience of making a phone call from your hotel room will be offset by the hefty surcharges tacked onto the bill. It's always less expensive to use the pay phone in the lobby or even cheaper to use the phone on the street; ask the hotel staff for assistance if you can't figure out how the phone works.

Some cell phones may be adaptable for use in Europe, but the operating frequencies are different. Check with your service provider. You can rent cell phones for use during your trip. Check

with your AAA office for information). Most U.S. smartphones will not work if not configured to European networks, so you may have to use WiFi hotspots to access web-based services. WiFi is widely available in many cafés, bars and hotels as well as at airports and other public places.

If you're staying in one country for a few days, it may be worthwhile obtaining a local prepaid telephone card, which can be used with phones that accept them. They can normally be purchased at supermarkets and small stores called "tobacconists" that also sell cigarettes, candy, snacks, magazines and sometimes postage stamps.

Travelers with Disabilities

Facilities for visitors with disabilities in northern and central European countries are generally very good, but old castles, palaces, cathedrals and historic houses may not be adapted for special access. Facilities in the Mediterranean countries, the Czech Republic and Hungary are improving, but if you need help it is advisable to check in advance with local tourist offices. The old central cores of European cities are often difficult to change or adapt to make them suitable for those with special needs. Expect steps and stairways in city centers (some stairways have no handrails), in addition to cobbled and uneven street and sidewalk surfaces.

Almost all of the old buildings that you come across in Europe – including those that house hotels, restaurants and museums – are likely to contain stairways, narrow halls and doorways, and other access irregularities. Make certain that accessibility standards meet your requirements when reserving your accommodations.

In many instances hotels will be able to provide a room with adequate access if they know your needs in advance. Telephone ahead to museums, attractions and restaurants as well to ascertain the nature of their facilities and accessibility.

There are usually motorized carts at airports that will whisk you to and from arrival and departure gates – these can be quite far apart within an airport.

Getting Around

City Transportation

A good first stop when you arrive at your destination is either a central public transportation information center or the tourist information office (see the Essential Information boxes in the introduction to each featured city). Spend time here and obtain information on how to get around the city, including transportation maps and detailed city maps. You also may be able to purchase tickets for public transportation, including those valid for multiple rides or for one or more days; they will save you money and the inconvenience of having to buy a new ticket for every trip. The information office may be able to provide public transportation schedules also.

AAA has partnered with Gray Line to provide members with sightseeing tours in more than 700 destinations worldwide. Discounts are offered on tours lasting one day or less. Tours are available in Amsterdam, Dublin, Florence, Lisbon, Munich, Paris, Rome, Venice and Zurich, among other E.U. locations. In addition, there are a variety of public transportation options in Europe:

■ Subways (metros) are underground trains that travel beneath city centers, sometimes emerging to ground level in suburban areas, or to cross rivers.
■ Private bus companies operate along designated routes in city centers; double-decked buses are common for carrying larger numbers of passengers.
■ Long-distance buses are commonly known as "coaches" in Britain and Ireland.
■ Trams are vehicles that travel on rails set into the street surface. They are often powered by overhead electric cables that run along the route; be especially careful of trams since they have the right of way.
■ Trolley buses run on tires, but are powered by overhead electric cables running above the route, like trams. They have right of way and run quietly.
■ Funiculars are passenger cars that ascend and descend hills or cliffs on a track set into the ground, where there are steep inclines.

■ Cable cars are suspended from tension cables attached to the top of the cars. They are common at ski resorts, and in some cities.
■ Rack railways are a feature in Switzerland, where trains that climb steep mountains connect with a cog system between the rails and give extra power to get up the steep slopes.

In many continental European countries you buy a travel ticket at a ticket office, booth or ticket machine and validate it by pushing it into a special machine, either at the stop or on the vehicle, which will give the ticket a date and time stamp for the appropriate trip or time period. If you buy a tourist ticket valid for a number of days, you will usually need to validate it only once before you first use it.

Between Cities

Trains Most countries in Europe have a national train system, with trains operating across national borders. Service is generally efficient, although local routes with frequent stops can be slow. If your entire trip is going to be by train it may be worth obtaining a Eurail pass from your AAA travel agent in the United States before you go. It is important to note that they are not on sale in Europe and must be purchased before you travel. Passes are valid for periods from a few days to three months. In addition, many national rail systems have their own passes for travel within a country; these also are available from travel agents in the United States and Canada, and in Europe too. Some trains require reservations.

Tickets for most trains are available either in advance or just before travel. For special trains (some express trains – for instance, in Spain; overnight sleeper trains; the Orient Express; or the Eurostar trains between Britain, France and Belgium that travel through the tunnel beneath the English Channel) you may need to buy tickets a few days in advance to be sure of getting a seat. This is especially the case during busy vacation times.

Information about main city train stations is in the Essential Information panel for each city.

Airlines Most countries have a national airline, as well as independent operators and budget airlines that operate internationally, based on hub cities within the country. Smaller airlines serve smaller destinations, usually functioning within the country. Fares, schedules and availability are subject to frequent change.

If you have a specific itinerary in mind, your travel agent is the best place to start for flight information.

For the best choice of flights and prices, reserve your tickets well in advance. Airports in major cities such as Paris, London and Rome, will have the largest choice of flights, but are the busiest. For this reason it can be a good idea to begin your trip at a smaller destination within your preferred country.

Ferries Services transport individual passengers as well as cars, and in some cases trains (the cars of the train actually travel on the boat). Ferry companies offering longer-distance trips of two or three days have comfortable ships, and they promote these services as "mini-cruises" as a change to city sightseeing.

Ferries operate regularly in the Scandinavian archipelago and along the Norwegian fjords; among the Scottish islands; between Britain and Ireland, Scandinavia, Germany, The Netherlands, Belgium, France and Spain; and throughout the islands and coastal ports of Mediterranean countries and islands.

Generally speaking, transfers from ports to city centers are less straightforward than from airports and train stations. If you intend to carry a lot of luggage, it may be advisable to check ahead with the tourist information office about this when planning your trip.

European Customs and Immigration

Each country has its own customs import regulations; see the Essential Information section beginning on page 493. For the purposes of customs and duty-free allowances, the countries of the European Union are considered as one customs area, and there are no limits on goods for personal use when traveling between any of the member countries. However, customs restrictions do apply when traveling between E.U. countries and non-E.U. countries.

The current E.U. member countries include all the countries in this book, with the exception of Norway and Switzerland. The U.K.'s exit from the E.U. is scheduled to be March 2019.

At the immigration barrier in E.U. countries, travelers are separated into two lanes – one for E.U. citizens and one for non-E.U. citizens. Border controls between E.U. countries are relaxed but can be temporarily re-introduced in response to a crisis. You will probably pass through an immigration desk when arriving in a new country by plane, train or ferry. There are border controls still in place between the E.U. and the rest of Europe, however.

Driving in Europe

European Automobile Clubs

For the benefit of members traveling abroad, AAA maintains reciprocal agreements with motoring clubs in Europe. Presentation of your valid AAA membership card at participating motoring clubs allows you to receive services they provide to their own members. Operating philosophies and facilities differ from country to country, however, so services may not be the same as back home. AAA members will need to

AAA TRAVEL AGENCIES

AAA Travel Agencies offer various member services to help simplify the logistics of international travel planning, especially for the first-time visitor. They can make airline reservations, book accommodations, set up escorted tours and independent travel packages, offer passport and visa assistance, arrange for car rentals and an official International Driving Permit, and they also offer a VISA debit card.

AAA members also are eligible for discounts on selected hotels and motels and receive exclusive savings on cruising vacations.

visit their local club to obtain information about services that can be expected from a specific European motoring club.

Refer to the Essential Information pages for each country for motoring club contact details, as well as documentation requirements and driving regulations.

Car Rental

If you intend to drive through several countries, and therefore across national borders, you will need to tell the rental company as this will affect all the insurance documentation required. Some rental agencies may require advance notice to supply a car for travel to continental Europe. Most car rental companies in Europe limit car rental to persons over 25; few companies will rent to persons over 21 and some companies limit rental to drivers under 70 or 75.

To rent a car you will need a valid U.S. driver's license and preferably an International Driving Permit, necessary insurance and your passport. Some rental companies may require you to produce an additional credit card or further proof of identity for renting luxury cars.

European cars are generally small with manual transmissions; you will need to specify in advance if you want an automatic. Most rental companies offer vehicles equipped with air-conditioning. Rates vary, but a AAA travel agent should be able to give you an accurate estimate of cost. Reciprocal arrangements with European motoring clubs may not apply if you are driving a rental car (see the Driving section under Essential Information for each country). Be sure to inquire about local taxes; in France, for example, taxes increase rental rates by up to one-third. Find out exactly what insurance coverage is included, and check whether you need a collision damage waiver (CDW) – you might already be covered through your personal car insurance policy or credit card company. A CDW may not cover certain types of damage; for example, in Greece damage to the underside of a car caused by a rough road may not be covered.

AAA Travel Agencies can make rental car reservations, provide prepayment arrangements, or reserve a car for you for specified dates and destinations. Rates are generally lower if reservations are made in the United States prior to your departure. They also are guaranteed in U.S. dollars if you prepay; it is recommended that you reserve well in advance.

Hertz Europe offers discounts to AAA members in many European countries (including all those listed in this guide). Benefits include low competitive rates; free unlimited mileage; a 24-hour toll-free telephone information line; 24-hour emergency roadside assistance; enhanced computerized driving directions; and English-speaking personnel at every location. Hertz operates a fleet of more than 80,000 vehicles across Europe, including locations in 69 major airports. There are free drop-offs between major cities within the country of rental. For reservations contact a AAA Travel expert at www.AAA.com or Hertz at 1-800-654-3001 in the United States and Canada.

Green Card

If you drive a car in Europe you will need a Green Card (sometimes called an International Insurance Certificate) to prove that you have liability insurance. Most car rental agencies will provide this with the vehicle; most companies include it in the rental price.

A Green Card also is advised for motorists taking their own vehicle overseas; for additional information contact your automobile insurer.

International Driving Permit (IDP)

An International Driving Permit is a document containing your photograph and confirming that you hold a valid driver's license in your own country. It has a standard translation in several languages and is a useful document to carry if you plan to drive in Europe, even if it is not specifically required by the country. The permit is available from AAA Travel Agencies.

Driving Regulations

Driving in busy European cities can be challenging. If you are renting a car, ask the rental company for information on that country's driving conditions, including a chart of common road signs and an area road map. If you visit a city by car, park outside the city center, close to a public transportation link, and travel to the center by public transportation.

Check parking signs where you leave your car: Ensure that there are no restrictions, that you pay for and display a parking sticker if necessary, and check closing times if you use a multistory parking garage or a gated street parking area. Parking regulations are strictly enforced in city centers throughout Europe and penalties, including the immobilization or the removal of your vehicle, can be the consequence of leaving your car in an unauthorized place. Some European cities offer free evening and weekend parking, but always check before leaving your vehicle.

If you enter central London by car on any day between Monday to Friday you will incur a daily congestion charge of £11.50. Vehicles entering the charging zone (visit www.tfl.gov.uk to see the Congestion Charging zone map) must be registered; an area license permits drivers to enter and leave the zone an unlimited number of times within a particular day. The charging zone is clearly defined by signs and road markings at all central London entrance and exit points. The daily charge must be paid by midnight on the day of travel if not already prepaid; between midnight on the day of travel and midnight on the next charging day, the fee increases to £14. Payment can be made at pay stations, selected gas stations, retailers displaying the PayPoint logo and online. The charge is in effect Mon.–Fri. 7 a.m.–6 p.m. (excluding public holidays and Dec. 25–Jan. 1). For information telephone 0343 222 2222 (Mon.–Fri. 8–8) or go online to Transport For London at www.tfl.gov.uk.

Specific driving regulations for each country are provided in the Essential Information section (see pages 493–569). In some European countries, police can levy on-the-spot fines for serious offenses which can include speeding and drunk driving.

Returning to the United States

Confirming Return Travel

If you are flying, contact the airport the day before your departure to check flight details. Some carriers require you to reconfirm flights after an extended stopover of more than a few days. Allow plenty of time for check-in and clearing security. You may be able to check in online up to 24 hours in advance – check with your airline.

Tax-free Shopping

Some major stores offer "tax-free shopping" to tourists. Although specific procedures differ slightly between countries, this enables you to make purchases and have them either sent to the airport of your departing flight, or directly to your home address. Such shopping saves the (often substantial) sales tax, but these items are still subject to any applicable U.S. import duty, plus postage and handling charges.

U.S. Customs

During your flight or voyage returning to the United States, you will be required to complete a customs declaration form. Returning to the United States you are allowed up to $800 worth of personal goods and gifts (including items purchased in duty-free shops); keep sales slips and have them ready for inspection. The duty-free exemption can include 100 cigars and 200 cigarettes, as well as one liter of wine, beer or liquor if you are 21 or over. (Check the current situation with products originating from Cuba at www.cbp.gov.) Any purchases in excess of the $800 exemption will be subject to duty.

There is no restriction on the importing or exporting of currency, but any amounts exceeding the value of $10,000 must be declared.

For more information contact the U.S. Customs and Border Protection Info Center at (877) 227-5511 or (202) 325-8000 (Mon.–Fri. 8:30–4 Eastern Time) or visit www.cbp.gov where "Know Before You Go" has details.

Premier Destinations

- Austria 18
- Belgium 48
- Britain 76
- Czech Republic 118
- Denmark 132
- Finland 152
- France 164
- Germany 206
- Greece 238
- Hungary 252
- Ireland 266
- Italy 282
- Luxembourg 322
- The Netherlands 334
- Norway 356
- Portugal 370
- Spain 392
- Sweden 430
- Switzerland 444

Austria

Introduction and Map 20

Timeline 24

Survival Guide 25

Vienna 26

Feature: City of Composers 31

Feature: Viennese Flavors 33

Innsbruck 34

Feature: Winter Sports in Innsbruck 39

Salzburg 40

Feature: Mozart and the Salzburg Festival 45

Feature: A Day in Salzburg 47

Hotels and Restaurants 463

Essential Information 494

Opposite: Detail of cherubs on the Mozart memorial at the Hofburg (Imperial Palace) in Vienna

Austria

Small yet beautiful, Austria has unrivaled Alpine scenery, some of Europe's finest baroque architecture, and a long musical and cultural tradition. Straddling the center of Europe, the country has exerted a critical influence on the history of the European region through the centuries, becoming a major player in world politics.

Today, despite loss of territory and power after two world wars, Austria retains its status as the crossroads of modern Europe. The grandeur of the mountains draws visitors from all over the world, while the combination of efficiency and charm makes Austria one of Europe's most beguiling tourist destinations.

The Land

Austria is one of the most mountainous countries in Europe, with more than 70 percent of the land occupied by the Alps and Alpine valleys. This section of the eastern Alps is characterized by massive mountain chains with sheer rock faces and jagged ridges broken by deep valleys. The Tyrol region, bordering the Swiss and Italian Alps in western Austria, is renowned for its stunning scenery and is an extremely popular skiing and hiking area. Below the tree line the mountains are heavily forested,

giving way to lush Alpine meadows, grazed in summer by gentle-faced cattle and carpeted with vivid wildflowers.

Picturesque villages sit amid the pastures and along the valley bottoms, each with distinctive churches, clusters of traditional shuttered houses and wooden farm buildings. The Danube (Donau) river dominates northeastern Austria, and most of the country's people inhabit the rolling terrain around the river. The flat fields of the Vienna basin are intensely cultivated, producing grain, fruit and vines.

The Habsburg Legacy

Throughout six centuries of Habsburg rule, Austria dominated the politics of much of Europe. The Habsburg Empire spread from Spain to Hungary, with sons and daughters of the ruling families

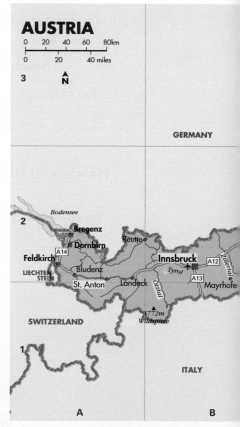

More Top Destinations in Austria

- Baden E2
- Bad Ischl C2
- Eisenstadt E2
- Eisriesenwelt C2
- Graz D1
- Grossglockner Hochalpenstrasse C1
- Hallstatt C2
- Kitzbühel B2
- Maria Saal D1
- Melk D2
- Mondsee C2
- Ötztal B1
- Riegersburg D1
- St. Anton A2
- Salzkammergut C2
- Stein D3
- Wachau D3
- Zillertal B2

marrying into other European ruling houses, thus furthering its influence. Vienna, with its grandiose architecture, splendidly illustrates Austrian prestige, and the entire country is rich in buildings from the days of the empire.

The Viennese Court sent administrators and army officials into the provinces; they brought along Viennese customs, attitudes and manners, as did the nobility who spent time both in the capital and on their country estates. The high-handed approach of these outsiders throughout the provinces has left a legacy of mistrust of the Viennese still discernible today. But, because of the terrain, the different areas of Austria were, and remain, immensely varied, each valley having its own dialect, dress, habits and way of life.

Crossroads of Europe

At the end of World War II, Austria was divided into four zones of occupation, with the Allied powers occupying most of the western half. With economic aid provided by the Marshall Plan after the war, this area was able to industrialize more efficiently than the Soviet-occupied zone, and the east–west divide continued even after the Second Republic was founded in 1945 and the country became independent 10 years later, in 1955.

Present-day Austria shares boundaries with eight European countries: Germany, Italy, the Czech Republic, Hungary, Slovakia, Slovenia, Switzerland and Liechtenstein. Its 8.5 million inhabitants are spread across nine distinctive provinces, each one with attractions for the visitor.

A view over the rooftops of Salzburg

manifests itself in an easy friendliness to everyone, and it's one of the first things visitors notice. Every region sees itself as the best, and people proudly wear regional dress and enjoy traditional music and festivals. So, if you encounter people wearing *Lederhosen* (leather pants) and *Dirndls* (bodiced dresses), it's for their benefit, not yours.

There's an elegance and ease to much Austrian life; cafés buzz with the chatter of people, a *Bierkeller* (tavern) is likely to be packed with young and old, and streets are full of strolling crowds. Manners are conservative, even old-fashioned; this is a country where children open doors for adults, and outside of the cities nearly every stranger is greeted with an amicable *"Grüss Gott."*

Environmental Issues

It's not only the magnificent tree-clad mountain slopes and verdant valleys that make Austria green; this is one of the most environmentally aware countries in Europe. Austria banned all nuclear power use in the 1970s, and since then its green policy has made giant strides.

Heavy investment in public transportation has considerably lessened the use of cars. This is a huge benefit to visitors, making travel in Austria, with its seamless connections between different forms of public transportation, very easy. Despite the Alpine terrain, Austrians cycle a lot, and every town has bike routes and parks.

Recycling is a way of life in Austria; there are many different types of garbage cans, each clearly labeled for the appropriate trash.

Sauerkraut and Strudel

Austrians take food seriously, and waiters are genuinely interested to know whether you've enjoyed a meal and are alarmingly downcast if you can't cope with the vast portions served. Mealtimes are closer to American schedules than elsewhere, with lunch around noon and dinner any time after 6 p.m.

More than half the working population is employed in the service sector: education, tourism, administration and health. Traditional agriculture continues thanks to large subsidies, and employs less than 10 percent of the workforce.

The vast majority of Austrians speak German or a German dialect. Austria was only slightly affected by the Protestant Reformation and is still a Catholic country. Its fine baroque churches still have congregations for Sunday Mass.

Proud Traditions

Despite sharing a common language, Austrians are very different from their German neighbors – more lighthearted, and generally more relaxed in their approach to life. They see themselves, correctly, as hospitable and cordial, thus defining the term *Gemütlichkeit*. This

Each region has its own specialties, but the emphasis everywhere is on heavy soups, plenty of meat, *Knödel* (a kind of dumpling) and noodles, and cream, cream, cream. The latter appears in sauces, soups, coffee and whipped mounds decorating just about every dessert. *Sauerkraut* (pickled cabbage) frequently accompanies main courses, along with piles of potatoes. Salads are drenched in creamy dressings.

Austrians indulge their passion for coffee and cakes between meals, and you should certainly sample *Apfelstrudel* (apple strudel), the delicious fruit dessert that is the hallmark of the country's pastry-making, and *Sachertorte,* a wickedly rich chocolate cake oozing apricot jam.

There are many different types of beer, and some excellent wines. Austria has been cultivating vines for thousands of years, particularly in Styria, Lower Austria and The Burgenland. *Veltliner,* made from the Grüner Veltliner grape, is the country's best-known white wine. You should also try *Schnapps,* a strong fruit or herb based liqueur, drunk as a digestive aid.

Coffee is the national drink, with cafés sometimes serving as many as 20 or more different variations; hot chocolate is good, too. And on the healthy side, there are outstanding fruit and vegetable juices.

Summer and Winter

Austria offers visitors as much in the winter as in the summer. For Europeans, the Austrian Alps have been a favorite skiing destination for many years, with impeccably organized facilities, trails ranging from gentle slopes to world-class diamond runs, and wonderful après-ski dining and nightlife.

Summer sees the Alpine pastures at their best, and the whole country is crisscrossed with hiking trails through glorious mountain scenery. It's in summer, too, that the cities come alive, with strolling crowds, colorful flowers

and a plethora of music and folk festivals. Spring starts late, so it's best to plan a visit in May or later.

In early spring and again in fall, you may experience the dreaded *Föhn* wind in western Austria; this is a fierce, warm, dry wind from the south that is notorious for making people generally tired and grumpy, so be prepared.

A quiet spot in Vienna's Schloss Schönbrunn

Timeline

15 BC to AD 50	Romans establish frontier provinces along the Danube and found the legionary fortress of Carnuntum.
500–700	After the final withdrawal of the Romans, Alamanni and Bavarian tribes settle lower Alpine regions.
966	Marcha orientalis (Ostmark), established as a bulwark against attacks from the east, is first referred to as Ostarrîchi.
1278	Founding of Habsburg Dynasty, beginning 640 years of power.
1493–1519	Foundations of the Habsburg world empire laid by marriage contracts of Maximilian I.
1683	Second Ottoman siege of Vienna is beaten back.
1699	Conquest of Hungary; Habsburgs gain hereditary right to the Hungarian throne in the male line.
1805–1806	Napoleon defeats the Austrians at Battle of Austerlitz; end of Holy Roman Empire.
1814–15	Congress of Vienna restructures the political map of Europe.
1905	Berta von Suttner is the first woman to receive the Nobel Peace Prize.
1914	Assassination of heir to Austrian throne at Sarajevo leads to outbreak of World War I; Austria fights on losing side.
1919	Dissolution of Austro-Hungarian monarchy; loss of territories.
1938	Hitler incorporates Austria into the German Reich.
1939–45	World War II; Austrians fight in German army; following defeat, Austria is divided into four zones of occupation.
1955	Full sovereignty and neutrality of Second Republic; Austria is admitted to the United Nations.
1995	Austria joins European Union.
1999	Austria enters European Monetary Union.
2010–11	Celebrations for the life of composer Gustav Mahler (1860–1911).
2012	The 150th anniversary of the birth of artist Gustav Klimt. Skydiver Felix Baumgartner sets multiple world records in his jump to earth from a balloon at an altitude of more than 128,000 feet.
2015	Thousands of migrants fleeing Syria's war zone arrive from Hungary and Slovenia and cross Austria's border into Germany.
2017	Austria hosts the Special Olympics World Winter Games, a sports and humanitarian event for people with intellectual disabilities.

The Last of the Knights

Maximilian I ruled from 1493 until 1519; these years saw the establishment of his family, the Habsburgs, as hereditary emperors of the Holy Roman Empire and rulers of Austria and far beyond, a dynasty that continued until 1918. Maximilian, through two strategic marriages, gained control over Burgundy (a region in eastern France) and the Low Countries. He married his son into the Spanish royal family, giving the Habsburgs rights over Spain, Naples and Spanish America and thus laying the foundations for the vast empire that was to come. Maximilian reformed the governmental administration, patronized the arts, loved hunting and jousting, and was known as "the last of the knights" who led Austria from the Middle Ages to the bright light of the Renaissance and the empire.

This street café on Kohlmarkt Square in Vienna offers welcome shade in summer

Survival Guide

- Always return greetings; hospitality is Austria's most important national characteristic. A polite reply to their welcoming "*Grüss Gott*," meaning "God's greeting." would be "*Guten Tag*," meaning "good day."
- For the opera, men should wear a jacket and tie; women, a dress, suit or fashionable pants.
- When going into churches, remember that it's disrespectful to show bare shoulders or upper arms.
- Take an umbrella; it can rain heavily, anywhere, at any time of year.
- For a day in the mountains, remember that the temperature drops as you gain altitude. Take water and food, and wear warm clothes and suitable footwear.
- Austrians are very litter-conscious and streets are immaculately clean; do your part to leave them that way.
- It's considered polite to stand in line when waiting for a bus or at an attraction, and to defer to the older members of society.
- Bedding in Austria generally consists of a large, puffy feather quilt in a cotton cover. This will be folded on your bed, waiting to be opened up.
- Austrians eat and drink with gusto, and spirits as well as the noise level will rise during the evening. Drunkenness, however, is always considered uncouth.
- All cafés, bars and restaurants have coat hooks and umbrella stands, and it's considered more respectful to leave coats and umbrellas there rather than on your chair.
- It's acceptable to spend up to an hour lingering over one or two drinks in a café.
- Public restrooms are free, numerous and spotless; you'll find them in most public buildings, and you also can use bathrooms in cafés and restaurants.
- Always cross the street at official crossings and wait for the green man signal. It's illegal, though seldom prosecuted, to cross anywhere else.

Vienna

For much of the 20th century, Vienna (Wien) had an air of fading grandeur, a city whose days of imperial glory had passed. But in the 1980s Vienna began to redefine itself, and continues to do so. In the last three decades the population has increased for the first time since 1919; a vibrant youth culture has emerged; and the imperial architecture of the 18th and 19th centuries has been joined by exciting modern designs, such as the huge museum quarter built on the site of the emperor's former stables. Now, in the 21st century, Vienna seems to be shaking off its torpor and styling itself, once again, as a vibrant, dynamic European cultural center.

Finding Your Way

Between 1857 and 1865 Emperor Franz Josef I had the bastions surrounding Vienna's Old Town (Innere Stadt) demolished, and laid out a vast boulevard known as the Ring. Within the Old Town and the Ring are Vienna's most important sights, including St. Stephen's Cathedral (Stephansdom, see page 32) and the Imperial Palace (Hofburg, see page 29).

It's possible to take in the main sights on foot, but the "Hop on, Hop off" buses are a flexible alternative, allowing you to hop on or off anywhere along their route. There also are trams and subway (U-Bahn), rapid transit and rail (S-Bahn) trains running through and around the area. A more expensive option is a horse-drawn carriage (*Fiaker*) at Stephansplatz, Heldenplatz or Albertinaplatz. Be sure to agree the price and route before your journey starts.

An outer ring road, the Gürtel (belt), links the city with major freeways. East of Vienna, the Danube (Donau) river and the Danube canal cut through some 23 Austrian districts, and on the

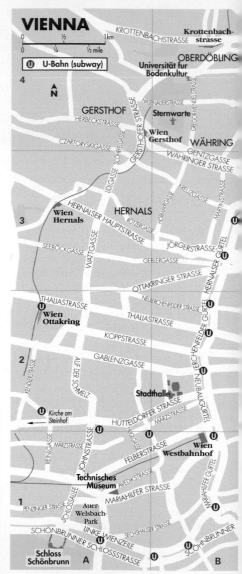

The Third Man

One of Vienna's favorite parks is the Prater, situated on the former imperial hunting grounds. It was opened to the public in 1766, and its attractions now include racing tracks, a fairground and a Ferris wheel built in 1897. This is where Joseph Cotten and Orson Welles had their confrontation high over the city in the 1949 film *Der dritte Mann (The Third Man)*.

southern outskirts are the Vienna Woods (Wienerwald). Maps showing walking routes through the woods are available from the efficient and helpful information center at the corner of Albertinaplatz and Maysedergasse.

Architecture

Wandering Vienna's streets is a treat for lovers of architecture. Styles range

from the Gothic pointed arches of St. Stephen's Cathedral and the neo-Gothic arcades of the New City Hall (Neues Rathaus) to the baroque of the 17th and 18th centuries.

Imperial 19th-century majesty is typified in buildings lining the Ring and also in the art nouveau edifices, known here as the "Secession" style because its practitioners seceded from the staid

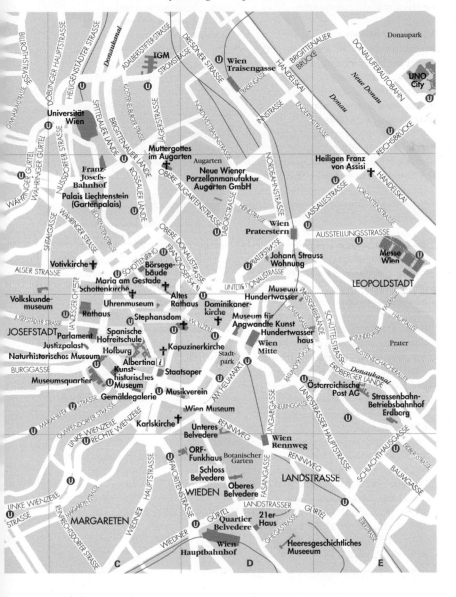

Association of Fine Artists in 1897. They later set up their own exhibitions in the Secession Building on Friedrichstrasse.

There also are modern styles, such as the 1990 Haas-Haus by Hans Hollein; and a postmodern housing block by Friedensreich Hundertwasser. The city has skyscrapers, like the Millennium Tower (663 feet) on the waterfront and Danube City (DC) Tower 1 (826 feet) on the north bank of the river.

Viennese Music

Vienna is proud of its long history as a center of classical music, and celebrates with a busy schedule of concerts, balls and café concerts. The grandest of the annual balls is the February's Opera Ball at the State Opera (Staatsoper).

Some classical music venues are worth seeing just for their decoration: the State Opera (on Opernring); the Konzerthaus (on Lothringerstrasse); the Musikverein (at Karlsplatz); and the Royal Chapel (Burgkapelle) where the Vienna Boys' Choir sings at Sunday Mass.

Viennese Shopping

Expect high prices. Clothes are especially expensive – the best options are chain stores such as Mango, H&M and Pimkie on Mariahilfer Strasse, the "shopping mile" that also features most major department stores.

Porcelain and glassware have been produced in Vienna for more than 200 years. Outlets on Kärntner Strasse (near central Stephansplatz), include J. & L. Lobmeyr (No. 26). Wieden district is noted for its hip stores and galleries. The section of Gumpendorfer Strasse closest to the MuseumsQuartier is known for its trendy style. The Old Town is great for window-shopping. Except for some museum shops, stores are closed on Sunday.

Essential Information

Tourist Information
Tourist-Info Wien (Tourist-Info Vienna)
Albertinaplatz, corner of Maysedergasse (daily 9–7) ☎ 01 24 555 (information and hotel bookings); www.wien.info

Urban Transportation
Vienna has a network of U-Bahn (subway) lines, tram (Strassenbahn) lines and buses. U-Bahn lines 1, 2 and 4 meet at central Karlsplatz/Oper. Subways are marked with a U on the city map. Rapid transit railroad, or S-Bahn, travels into the city center from the suburbs. Buses 1A, 2A and 3A stop near major Old Town sights. Pick up transportation maps at the Opern Passage/Karlsplatz U-Bahn

information counter (☎ 01 79 09 100; www.wienerlinien.at). Order taxis at: ☎ 01 31 30-0, 01 40 10-0 or check www.wien.info.

Airport Information
Vienna International Airport (☎ 01 7007 22233; www.viennaairport.com) is connected to the center by rail, the City Airport Train CAT (☎ 01 25250; www.cityairporttrain.com) running half-hourly between the airport and city center Wien Mitte station. The journey takes 16 minutes. High-speed Austrian Federal Railway (☎ 05 1717; www.oebb.at) trains also run regularly from the airport to the Main Train Station (Hauptbahnhof), with onward connections to destinations around Europe.

Climate – average highs and lows for the month

Jan.	Feb.	Mar.	Apr.	May	Jun.	Jul.	Aug.	Sep.	Oct.	Nov.	Dec.
2°C	3°C	9°C	14°C	19°C	22°C	25°C	24°C	20°C	14°C	7°C	4°C
36°F	37°F	48°F	57°F	66°F	72°F	77°F	75°F	68°F	57°F	45°F	39°F
-3°C	-2°C	2°C	5°C	9°C	13°C	15°C	15°C	12°C	6°C	2°C	-1°C
27°F	28°F	36°F	41°F	48°F	55°F	59°F	59°F	54°F	43°F	36°F	30°F

Vienna Sights

> **Key to symbols**
> ✚ map coordinates refer to the Vienna map
> on pages 26–27 🖫 admission charge:
> $$$ more than €10, $$ €3–€10, $ less than €3
> See page 5 for complete key to symbols

Albertina

Housed within the beautiful Hofburg (Imperial Palace), the Albertina is named for its founder, Duke Albert von Sachsen-Teschen (1738–1822), who lived in the palace at the end of the 18th century. The Albertina's collection of more than a million drawings, prints and engravings dates from the 14th century and includes exquisite pieces by Raphael, Michelangelo, Goya and Cézanne, plus studies of children by Rubens. Also here is the world's most important collection of work by German artist Albrecht Dürer, which includes his beautiful masterpieces *Young Hare* and *Praying Hands*. An ultramodern study and research center uses a state-of-the-art storage system to protect all of the invaluable works of art. There also is an interesting architecture collection.

✚ C2 ⬛ Albertinaplatz 1 ☎ 01 534 03-0, www.albertina.at ◎ Daily 10–6 (also Wed. and Fri. 6–9 p.m.) ⓠ U-Bahn: Stephansplatz or Karlsplatz 🚍 2A 🍴 Restaurant 🖫 $$$ 🚹 Guided tours; audio guide in English

Hofburg

Blue and gold domes top the magnificent Hofburg (Imperial Palace), which took more than six centuries to build. The original fortress, built in 1275, made way for the Schweizerhof (Swiss Courtyard), whose Schweizertor (Swiss Gate) was built in the 16th century. Other sections were added during the 17th and 18th centuries, including the gorgeously decorated Hofbibliothek (Library) and the world-famous Hofreitschule (Riding School), where white Lipizzaner horses perform for visitors (see page 32).

The Kaiserappartements (Imperial Apartments) were built in the 19th century, and new sections were added on as late as 1913 to create today's enormous complex of 18 wings, 2,600 rooms and 19 courtyards. Many of the Habsburg opulent trappings are on display, including the imperial crowns in the Kaiserliche Schatzkammer (Imperial Treasury). Located between the Kaiserappartements and the Silver Collection, the Sisi Museum is dedicated to the life of Empress Sisi (1837–98).

Kaiserappartements ✚ C2 ⬛ Michaelerplatz (entrance: beneath Michaelerkuppel cupola) ☎ 01 533 7570, www.hofburg-wien.at ◎ Daily 9–6, Jul.–Aug.; 9–5:30, Sep.–Jun. ⓠ U-Bahn: Herrengasse, Stephansplatz or Volkstheater 🚍 2A, 3A 🍴 Augustinerkeller restaurant, see page 463; café on site 🖫 $$$ 🚹 Guided tours

The Large Salon of Empress Elisabeth, a reception room in the Kaiserappartements of the Hofburg

A statue in the grounds of Schloss Schönbrunn

Kaiserliche Schatzkammer ✉ Schweizerhof
☎ 01 525 240; www.kaiserliche-schatzkammer.at
⏰ Wed.–Mon. 9–5:30 🚇 U-Bahn: Herrengasse,
Stephansplatz or Volkstheater 🚌 1, 2, 2A, 57A
🍴 Augustinerkeller restaurant, see page 463 💲 $$$
ℹ Guided tours; audio guide in English

Kirche am Steinhof

Huge copper angels guard the portico of
the eccentric, domed Kirche am Steinhof
(Steinhof Church), built between 1904
and 1907 for people suffering from
mental illness. Designed by esteemed
modern architect Otto Wagner, its white
interior is full of light, with colored
glass, and windows by Secessionist artist
Kolo Moser which brighten the vault
and side altar areas. A ceiling under the
cupola gives the effect of a starry sky.
➕ Off map at A2 ✉ Baumgartner Höhe 1, Penzing
☎ 01 91060 11007 ⏰ Interior Sat. 4–5 p.m., Sun.
noon–4; guided tour (in German only) Sat. 3 p.m.,
Sun. 4 p.m. 🚌 47A, 48A 💲 $$

Schloss Belvedere

The spectacularly baroque Schloss
Belvedere (Belvedere Palace) was built
for Austrian general and prince, Eugene
of Savoy, who led his army to many
victories over the French. Begun in
1714, building was in two phases: the
Unteres Belvedere (Lower Belvedere),
where Eugene's military triumphs are
celebrated in a ceiling fresco; and the
Oberes Belvedere (Upper Belvedere),
which housed his collection of paintings
and later became the Imperial Picture
Gallery. Archduke Franz Ferdinand,
whose assassination sparked the events
leading to World War I, lived here for
20 years until his death. The permanent
collection in the Upper Belvedere
displays Austrian art from the Middle
Ages to the present. Among the
highlights are Secessionist masterpieces
of the late 19th and early 20th centuries,
including *The Kiss* by Gustav Klimt and
superb French Impressionist paintings
by Manet, Renoir and Van Gogh. The
Lower Belvedere and Orangery are used
for special exhibitions.
➕ D1 ✉ Rennweg 6 (Unteres Belvedere);
Prinz-Eugen-Strasse 27 (Oberes Belvedere) ☎ 01 7955
7134; www.belvedere.at ⏰ Palace and gardens:
Upper: daily 9–6 (also Fri. 6–9 p.m.), Lower: 10–6 (also
Fri. 6–9 p.m.). Gardens closed in bad weather
🚇 Karlsplatz or Stadtpark 🚌 Tram 71 (Unteres
Belvedere) 🚌 69A; tram D, O, 18 (Oberes Belvedere)
🍴 Café 💲 $$$ ℹ Tours by appointment; audio
guide in English

Schloss Schönbrunn

Empress Maria Theresa's (1717–80)
dreams of creating a Habsburg Versailles
at Schloss Schönbrunn resulted in this
magnificent baroque palace with more
than 1,400 rooms. Nikolaus Pacassi
designed this imperial summer residence
between 1743 and 1749; the imposing
facade looks out onto peaceful
ornamental gardens, interesting
fountains and a park stretching into the
distance. Here you will find the world's
oldest zoo, the palm house and the
Children's Museum (for children aged
4–12 years). The main attractions are
the state rooms and private apartments,
inhabited by Maria Theresa and her 16
children, and later by Emperor Franz

City of Composers

Many 17th- and 18th-century Habsburg rulers were music lovers and musicians: Leopold I was a composer; Charles VI was a violinist; and Maria Theresa played the double bass. Royal patronage drew some of the world's greatest composers to Vienna, including Beethoven and Brahms. In 1762, at age six, Mozart gave a concert for the Empress Maria Theresa in Schönbrunn's Hall of Mirrors.

The waltz is inextricably linked to Vienna thanks to Johann Strauss, the "Waltz King," and every New Year's Day the Vienna Philharmonic Orchestra plays his waltzes to television viewers around the world. A statue of Strauss stands in City Park (Stadtpark).

In 1498 Emperor Maximilian I engaged 12 young male choristers to sing with the court orchestra. Over the centuries some of Austria's greatest composers served their apprenticeships with the Court Choir Boys, including Franz Schubert and Joseph Haydn. Beethoven and Mozart composed works especially for the choir. Today they are known as the Vienna Boys' Choir, and their naval-style dress dates back to the 1920s.

The elaborate and gilded Musikverein was built in the 19th century as a concert venue for the city's Society of the Friends of Music. (It's here that the Vienna Philharmonic performs its New Year concert.) In 1913 the hall was the scene of a brawl between conservatives and radicals of musical taste, at a concert conducted by Arnold Schönberg.

Schönberg was responsible for changing the face of modern musical composition by abandoning the standard eight-tone scale familiar to the Western ear and devising a complex 12-tone system. Together with his former pupils Alban Berg and Anton von Webern, he formed the Second Viennese School of Music. Their contemporary, Gustav Mahler (1860–1911), studied at the Conservatory and became artistic director at the Vienna State Opera House (Staatsoper).

The unassuming entrance of the Beethoven-Haus in a courtyard on Probusgasse in Vienna

Joseph and his consort, the Empress Elisabeth ("Sisi"). The opulent surroundings form a vivid backdrop for the displays of Indian and Persian miniatures, Gobelin tapestries, 18th-century porcelain and fine furniture.

✚ A1 ✉ Schönbrunner Schlossstrasse 47 ☎ 01 811 130 (palace); 01 81113 344 (Children's Museum); 01 877 9294-0 (zoo); www.schoenbrunn.at; www. zoovienna.at ⓖ Palace: daily 8–5:30, Apr.–Jun. and Sep.–Nov.; 8–6:30, Jul.–Aug.; 8–5, rest of year. Children's Museum: daily 10–5, mid-Mar. to early Nov.; Sat.–Sun. and public holidays 10–5, rest of year. Zoo: daily 9–6:30, Apr.–Sep.; 9–5:30, Mar. and Oct.; 9–4:30, Nov.–Jan.; 9–5, Feb. 🚇 U-Bahn: Schönbrunn 🚌 10A; tram 10, 60 🍴 Tyrolean Restaurant in grounds of zoo; cafés 💷 $$$ (palace, zoo and palm house); $$ (Children's Museum) ℹ Audio-guided tours

Spanische Hofreitschule

In a glittering white arena of the Imperial Palace the fine white Lipizzaner horses of the Spanische Hofreitschule (Spanish Riding School) strut to the gavotte, quadrille and waltz and show off the leaping, rearing and trotting of the high school of dressage. Originally the horses were brought from Spain and bred at a 16th-century stud farm at Lipica, Slovenia (hence the name).

Full performances, complete with music and uniformed riders, are booked well in advance, but same-day tickets for morning training sessions or a final rehearsal can be purchased at the visitor center, Michaelerplatz 1, daily 9–4.

✚ C2 ✉ Michaelerplatz 1 ☎ 01 533 9031; www.srs.at ⓖ Performance: selected Sat. and Sun. at 11 a.m., Feb.–Jun. and Aug.–Dec. Morning exercise: Tue.–Sun. 10–noon, Jan. to mid-Jun. and Aug.–Dec. 🚇 U-Bahn: Herrengasse, Stephansplatz or Karlsplatz/ Oper 🚌 2A 💷 $$$ ℹ Check times in advance

Stephansdom

Stephansdom (St. Stephen's Cathedral) is an unmistakable landmark, with its black-, yellow- and green-tiled roof and the 449-foot-tall Gothic South Tower, known to locals as "Steffl," or "Little Steve." Relics of earlier churches are incorporated into the building, including the Giant's Door and the Tower of Heathens, supposedly the site of a pagan shrine. Inside, St. Stephen the Martyr is represented on a baroque 17th-century altar painting by Tobias Pock. The catacombs house an ossuary containing the remains of plague victims.

✚ D2 ✉ Stephansplatz 3 ☎ 01 515 52-3054; www.stephanskirche.at ⓖ For tourists: Mon.–Sat. 6 a.m.–10 p.m., Sun. and public holidays 7 a.m.–10 p.m. 🚇 U-Bahn: Stephansplatz 🚌 2A, 3A ℹ Guided tours in English Mon.–Sat. 9–11:30 a.m. and 1–4, Sun. 1–4

Uhrenmuseum

In 1917 Vienna's city councillors set up a museum devoted to timepieces across the ages in the Obizzi Palace, once home to Count Ernst Rüdiger von Starhemberg, who defended Vienna against the 1683 Turkish siege; it is in a side street by the Am Hof Church. The Uhrenmuseum (Clock Museum) displays over 3,000 fascinating items.

✚ C2 ✉ Schulhof 2 ☎ 01 533 22 65; www.wienmuseum.at 🚌 2A, 3A ⓖ Tue.–Sun. 10–6 🚇 U-Bahn: Herrengasse or Stephansplatz 💷 $$ (free first Sun. of the month)

The nave of Stephansdom, looking to the high altar

Viennese Flavors

Coffeehouses and pastry shops (*Konditoreien*) are two pretty good reasons for visiting Vienna. At the turn of the 20th century, artists, musicians and writers gathered in cafés to swap ideas, work, read or just sit, and some of their old haunts are still going strong. Stop by Bräunerhof (Stallburggasse 2, ☎ 01 512 38 93); Central (Herrengasse 14, ☎ 01 533 37 63); or the grand old Imperial (Kärntner Ring 16, ☎ 01 501 10 389), in the former city mansion of the Duke of Württemberg. Customers are generally left alone to linger in the grandiose surroundings, sipping one of the many different types of coffee drinks on offer.

On average, Austrians consume almost 15 pounds of coffee a year, and the menu usually offers many different varieties. *Mocca* is strong black coffee; a *kleiner* or *grosser Brauner* has a little milk, a *Melange* has more; a *Fiaker* is mocca with rum or brandy; and an *Einspänner* is a mocca with whipped cream. The *Café-Konditorei*, or pastry-shop-cum-café, is a showcase for Vienna's pastry makers. The most famous is Demel at Kohlmarkt 14, a must for visitors who love these light, fluffy edibles.

Wine made from the most recent grape harvest is known here as *Heuriger*, and this also is the name for the Viennese taverns that serve it. These *Heurigen* stand in their own vineyards in the Vienna Woods, and serve food – usually roast meat, cheese and salad – to complement and soak up the wine. A small music band is more than likely to be playing rousing folk music, and in summer there are often long tables and benches set outside. A bunch of fir twigs is traditionally hung outside the tavern door to show that it's open.

Viennese cooking is plain, simple and filling. It's usually served in a tavern, locally called a *Beisl* – a Yiddish word introduced by traditionally Jewish tavern owners. Dishes might include boiled beef (*Tafelspitz*), steak with crispy onions (*Zwiebelrostbraten*), chopped calves' heart and lungs in sauce (*Beuschel*) and – perhaps the best-known export – *Wiener Schnitzel*, a fried veal cutlet coated with egg and breadcrumbs. For dessert the popular choice is *Strudel*, fruit-filled baked dough with raisins and cinnamon (a perfect choice with a Viennese coffee).

The Demel coffeehouse has a view toward the St. Michael's Gate entrance to the Hofburg

Innsbruck

Strategically and beautifully situated on the Inn river, at the heart of the Alps, Innsbruck stands on a great European crossroads. The 19th-century construction of the east–west railroad through the Arlberg valley, in combination with the city's historic control of the north–south trade route through the Brenner Pass, placed it firmly on the trans-European map. Today, travelers from across Europe pass this way, and Innsbruck, with its excellent tourist and winter sports facilities, is well worth more than a brief stop en route.

Innsbruck Through Time

Innsbruck has had a checkered past. By the 12th century a fortified town was growing up beside the bridge over the Inn river, close to the site of an old Roman garrison.

By the 1360s, when the Habsburgs had acquired the Tyrol region, the settlement had outgrown its original fortifying walls.

Under Maximilian I, Holy Roman Emperor from 1493 to 1519, Innsbruck was the administrative and cultural center of the Habsburg empire.

The next 200 years encompassed a golden age that continued through the reign of Empress Maria Theresa from 1740 to 1780. When Napoleon conquered Tyrol in 1806, Innsbruck became part of Bavaria, but was handed back to Austria in 1814.

After World War I Italy got the southern part of Tyrol (Bozen) and the Brenner Pass became the new frontier. The city suffered a great deal of damage during World War II, but since then it has prospered, and today it is a university city as well as a popular tourist destination.

Exploring Innsbruck

The center of Innsbruck is small, and it's likely your hotel will be within easy walking distance of the historic Old Town (Altstadt), a pedestrianized maze of picturesque streets.

Attractions outside the city are served both by regular local buses and special tourist shuttles that take you right to where the action is.

It's worth buying the Innsbruck Card, which gives you free entry to many museums and other attractions, plus free use of public transportation as well as four mountain cable-car systems – the latter can be otherwise very expensive. This discount card is valid for 24, 48 or 72 hours and available at the tourist office (www.innsbruck.info).

A Rich Culture

Due to its long history, Innsbruck is richly endowed with some marvelous buildings, churches and museums.

The Old Town is a tiny area packed with handsome houses and narrow arcaded streets.

Outside this fascinating, ancient core you'll find splendid Renaissance,

A street in the Old Town (Altstadt) area of Innsbruck, where tables have been set out on the sidewalk for sunny summer dining

baroque and rococo architecture. Many of these fine buildings house Innsbruck's museums, some devoted to history and the arts, others offering insights into such subjects as Tyrolean railroads, bells and hunting. The cathedral and churches are packed with interesting artistic treasures.

Landmarks along the 17th- and 18th-century street, Maria-Theresien-Strasse, include a column topped by a statue of the Virgin (the Annasäule, built 1706), and a resplendent arch, the Triumphpforte, built in 1765.

Nowadays, six bridges span the Inn river from which the city gets its name, leading to the riverfront houses of the Mariahilf neighborhood. This area also is home to a botanic garden.

You can stroll beside the river, with mountains towering in the background, to the Hofgarten – a colorful and attractive garden which was first laid out in 1410 but later refined by Archduke Ferdinand II in the 16th century.

Located southeast of the city center, in a wonderful position overlooking the

Inn valley, is Ferdinand's great palace, Schloss Ambras.

Mountain Scenery

Dramatic mountains encircle the city of Innsbruck, their lower slopes scattered with picturesque villages. The surrounding countryside offers year-round opportunities for fresh air and exercise amid some of Europe's loveliest upland scenery.The best way to experience this landscape is on foot, and the tourist office arranges good daily guided hikes outside the city in the summer; boots and a backpack can be rented. You can swim, ride, play golf, go rafting or summer skiing, or just enjoy the Alps from the comfort of a sightseeing airplane flight. Winter brings the skiing season, when sports fans flock to Innsbruck from all over the world and the city's architecture looks particularly beautiful under a fresh blanket of snow.

Tyrolean Tastes

Visitors can sample a wide range of Austrian and Tyrolean specialties at

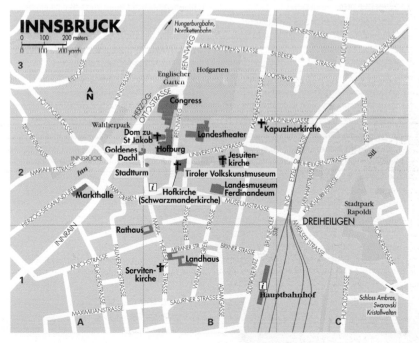

Innsbruck's restaurants, taverns and cafés (see pages 463–464). The food is good and portions are generous, and you'll find the warm welcome that is so common all over the country.

In the summertime, follow your dinner with a cable-car ride up the Seegrube mountain where you can enjoy a drink while watching the sparkling lights of the city far below, or you can take a lantern-lit hike to a party held inside a hillside hut.

Year-round you can take in a Tyrolean folklore evening, which includes traditional dances, yodeling and a performance on brass instruments; during the summer, *Schuhplattler* dancers and brass bands perform in the center of town.

Innsbruck's casino offers a more sophisticated evening, and there's always a choice of classical music, and often opera.

Woodcarvings and *Christkindlmarkt*

Some of Innsbruck's most appealing stores are tucked away in the narrow, winding streets of the Old Town, where you'll find ethnic Austrian souvenirs, clothes, knitwear, antiques and interior design pieces. Woodcarvings make ideal presents, as do dried-flower garlands and baskets – especially charming decorations for Christmas and Easter – and intricately made national costumes.

Maria-Theresien-Strasse has a range of department, home furnishing and linen stores. Excellent bookstores offer English-language illustrated books about Austria, as well as beautiful calendars that make good gifts.

The atmospheric Christmas market (*Christkindlmarkt*) sets up in the Old Town, its stalls brimming with gifts, traditional decorations, cookies and a range of tempting sweetmeats.

Essential Information

Tourist Information

Innsbruck Information and Reservation
Burggraben 3 ☎ 0512 59850/53560;
www.innsbruck.info
Ⓖ Daily 9–6

Urban Transportation

Many of Innsbruck's main sights are grouped together within walking distance in and around the Old Town (Altstadt); use the excellent tram and bus service (operated by IVB ☎ 0512 5307-500) to venture farther afield. You can buy a day-use ticket, book of tickets or weekly transportation card from the tourist information office, some tobacconists and other outlets. Validate your ticket when boarding the bus or tram. Press the illuminated button near the door to open the doors when you want to get off. There are taxi stands throughout the city center, or you can call a taxi (☎ 0512 238588, 0512 5311).

Airport Information

Innsbruck Airport (☎ 0512 22525-0; www.innsbruck-airport.com), with domestic and some European flights, is just 2 miles west of the city center; journey time by bus is 20 minutes. Bus F runs throughout the day to the central railroad station and the city center (journey time 20 mintes), or you can pick up a taxi outside the terminal.

Climate – average highs and lows for the month

Jan.	Feb.	Mar.	Apr.	May	Jun.	Jul.	Aug.	Sep.	Oct.	Nov.	Dec.
1°C	4°C	10°C	15°C	20°C	23°C	25°C	24°C	20°C	14°C	8°C	2°C
34°F	39°F	50°F	59°F	68°F	73°F	77°F	75°F	68°F	57°F	46°F	36°F
-7°C	-4°C	0°C	4°C	8°C	11°C	13°C	12°C	9°C	4°C	0°C	-4°C
19°F	25°F	32°F	39°F	46°F	52°F	55°F	54°F	48°F	39°F	32°F	25°F

Innsbruck Sights

> **Key to symbols**
> ✚ map coordinates refer to the Innsbruck map on page 35 ⑭ admission charge: $$$ more than €10, $$ €3–€10, $ less than €3
> See page 5 for complete key to symbols

The Golden Roof, Innsbruck's most famous sight

Goldenes Dachl

Innsbruck's Goldenes Dachl (Golden Roof) shimmers above a viewing balcony added onto the front of the previous ducal palace to commemorate Emperor Maximilian I's marriage to Bianca Maria Sforza of Milan in 1493. Beautifully decorated with reliefs of the Emperor, it is roofed with 2,657 gilt copper tiles – hence its name. The building now hosts a small museum of the life and times of Maximilian I, a heroic figure who was dubbed "the last knight."

✚ A2 ⊠ Herzog-Friedrich-Strasse 15 ☎ 0512 5360 1441; www.goldenes-dachl.at ⑥ Daily 10–5, May–Sep.; Tue.–Sun. 10–5, rest of year. Closed Nov. 🚊 A, C, J, O, TS, W; tram 1, 3 ⑭ $$

Hofkirche (Schwarzmanderkirche)

The Gothic Hofkirche (Court Church) was built by Ferdinand I in 1553 to house the mausoleum of his grandfather, Emperor Maximilian I. Considered the most important monument in the Tyrol region, the magnificent tomb is decorated with marble reliefs and flanked by 28 larger-than-life size bronze statues. See also the Silberne Kapell (Silver Chapel) and 1560 Ebert organ still used for concerts.

✚ B2 ⊠ Universitätsstrasse 2 ☎ 0512 5948 9514; www.tiroler-landesmuseen.at ⑥ Mon.–Sat. 9–5, Sun. 12:30–5 🚊 A, C, J, O, TS, W ⑭ $$

Hungerburgbahn and Nordkettenbahn

These connecting mountain transportation systems take you from Innsbruck city center up the Nordkette to 6,250-foot Seegrube; from here you can go to an even higher altitude, to the 7,400-foot Hafelekar.

The original Hungerburgbahn transportation system was a steep funicular, built in 1906 to link lower and upper Innsbruck. Designed by architect Zaha Hadid, the Hungerburgbahn/Nordkettenbahn lines opened at the end of 2007. The cable cars run up Hungerburg mountain over precipitous slopes to the Seegrube station, with ever-widening views over Innsbruck, the valley and the high Alpine peaks.

✚ Off map at B3 ⊠ Hungerburgbahn: Höhenstrasse 151; Nordkettenbahn: Rennweg 3 ☎ Hungerburgbahn and Nordkettenbahn: 0512 293344; www.nordkette. com ⑥ Sektion I Hungerburg (Alpenzoo–Hungerburg): Mon.–Fri. 7:15 7:15, Sat.–Sun. 8–7:15 (some seasonal variations). Sektion II Seegrube (Hungerburg–Seegrube): daily 8:30–5:30 (also Fri. 6 p.m.–11:30 p.m.). Sektion III Hafelekar (Seegrube–Hafelekar): daily 9–5 🚊 D, E, TS ⑪ Cafés and restaurants at top and bottom of cable car ⑭ Hungerburgbahn: $$; Nordkettenbahn: $$$

Schloss Ambras

Schloss Ambras (Ambras Castle) lies outside Innsbruck, a beautiful 16th-century conversion of a medieval castle standing in a landscaped garden above the Inn valley. It was the home of Archduke Ferdinand II from 1563 to 1595; an avid collector and patron of the arts, he built the superb Spanish Hall, with its colorful frescoes and beautiful ceiling, and amassed a collection of curiosities. They are displayed in the Chamber of Art and Curiosities, an early museum that offers great insight into the Renaissance mind.

The castle also contains an armory and a large portrait gallery dedicated to the imperial Habsburg family; many visitors also find interest in Ferdinand's wife's bathroom, a perfect and rare example of a 16th-century bathroom, complete with sunken copper bath.

🞣 Off map at C1 ✉ Schlossstrasse 20 ☎ 01525 24-4802; www.schlossambras-innsbruck.at
🞣 Daily 10–5. Closed Nov. 🚌 C, TS; tram 3 🍴 Castle restaurant and café 🎫 $$; children under 19 free

Stadtturm

For a bird's-eye view of Innsbruck, climb (148 steps, there's no elevator) the 167-foot-high Stadtturm (Town Tower), built between 1442 and 1450 as a watchtower. The bulbous cupola was added in the 16th century.

🞣 B2 ✉ Herzog-Friedrich-Strasse 21 ☎ 0512 58-7113 🞣 Daily 10–8, Jun.–Sep.; 10–5, rest of year 🚌 A, C, J, O, TS, W 🎫 $$

Swarovski Kristallwelten

One of the Innsbruck area's most visited attractions, Swarovski Kristallwelten (Swarovski Crystal Worlds) in Wattens, 9 miles east of Innsbruck, has to be experienced to be believed. This multimedia theme park centers around the magic of crystal and features moving walls, sculptures and sparkling crystals in underground caverns. You enter this experience through the Giant, a leafy face on the side of a hill.

🞣 Off map at C1 ✉ Kristallweltenstrasse 1, Wattens
☎ 05224 51080; http://kristallwelten.swarovski.com
🞣 Daily 8:30–7:30 (till 10 p.m. Jul.–Aug.). Last admission 1 hour before closing 🚌 Kristallwelten shuttle bus every 2 hours from the city railroad station
🍴 Restaurant and café 🎫 $$$

Tiroler Volkskunstmuseum

The Museum of Tyrolean Regional Heritage, next to the Hofkirche (see page 37), is a must for anyone interested in cultural history. Displays span traditional costumes to house interiors, with re-creations of lavish festivals and an informative multimedia show. Don't miss the charming nativity scenes depicted in busy Alpine villages.

🞣 B2 ✉ Universitätsstrasse 12 ☎ 0512 5948 9514; www.tiroler-landesmuseen.at 🞣 Daily 9–5
🚌 A, C, J, O, TS, W 🎫 $$; children up to 19 free

Ambras Castle stands in delightful landscaped grounds above the Inn valley

Winter Sports in Innsbruck

Innsbruck and its surrounding villages offer superb skiing amid beautiful Alpine landscapes. Winter sports enthusiasts will find something for every taste, and some excellent all-inclusive deals can be arranged through the Innsbruck tourist office.

Skiing and Snowboarding

You can ski at spots throughout the Innsbruck area as well as at surrounding resorts such as Kitzbühel and St. Anton am Arlberg, giving access to some 435 miles of well-maintained downhill runs served by 210 lifts. Every skill level is accommodated, from gentle runs of hard-packed snow for families and beginners to extreme slopes and off-run skiing for experts. Special areas are designated for snowboarding and carving, and for the truly tough and experienced backcountry skier there are superb high-altitude itineraries.

Cross-country skiing is very popular in Europe, and 12 different cross-country areas are accessible around Innsbruck, offering 186 miles of tracks. Ski and snowboard schools operate daily, and ski guides can be hired on a daily basis. Several areas have snowmaking equipment to supplement early winter snow. Access to the slopes is by a combination of bus, funicular, cable car, chairlift and surface lift. Free buses take skiers from the city center to their chosen ski area and collect them at the end of the day; these buses also run to Kitzbühel and St. Anton am Arlberg. Innsbruck's season runs from mid-December to mid-April.

Winter Fun

There are plenty of other activities on offer here besides hitting the slopes. With its Olympic facilities, Innsbruck offers skating and curling, or you can take a piloted bobsled ride down the Olympic run. Dog- and horse-drawn sleigh rides give you a chance to appreciate the natural beauty of the mountains, and tobogganing and winter walking provide a gentler pace. Events take place throughout the season, culminating on New Year's Day with torchlit celebrations in the Old Town and on the mountains.

🛈 Information on ski packages is available from the tourist information office (✉ Touristinformation Innsbruck, Burggraben 3, A-6021 Innsbruck, Austria ☎ 0512 53560; www.innsbruck.info)

Snowboarding is increasingly popular in Austria, and several schools run courses for novices

Salzburg

The beautiful little city of Salzburg, stretching along the Salzach river and tucked beneath the Mönchsberg hill, is a delightful combination of medieval, Renaissance and baroque architecture, the birthplace of Wolfgang Amadeus Mozart, its most famous son, and the gateway to some of Austria's most splendid landscapes. Add to this friendly people, a relaxed way of life and one of

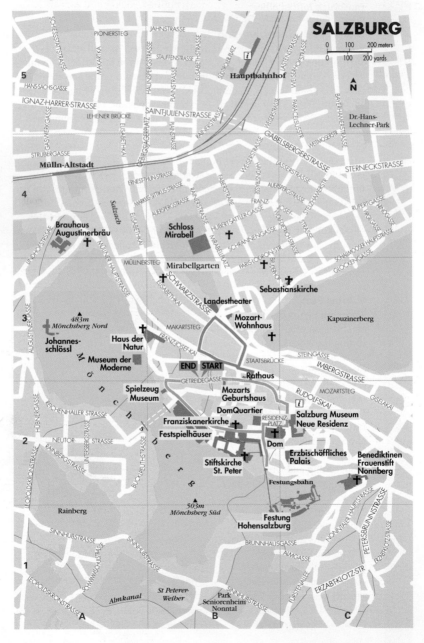

SALZBURG

0   100   200 meters
0   100   200 yards

N

Hauptbahnhof

Dr-Hans-Lechner-Park

Mülln-Altstadt

Brauhaus Augustinerbräu

Schloss Mirabell

Mirabellgarten

Sebastianskirche

483m Mönchsberg Nord

Johannes-schlössl

Haus der Natur

Landestheater

Mozart-Wohnhaus

Kapuzinerberg

Museum der Moderne

END START

Spielzeug Museum

Rathaus

Getreidegasse

Mozarts Geburtshaus

DomQuartier

Salzburg Museum Neue Residenz

Franziskanerkirche

Festspielhäuser

Dom

Erzbischöffliches Palais

Benediktinen Frauenstift Nonnberg

Stiftskirche St. Peter

Festungsbahn

Rainberg

503m Mönchsberg Süd

Festung Hohensalzburg

Almkanal

St Peterer-Weiher

Park Seniorenheim Nonntal

A   B   C

the world's greatest music festivals, and it's easy to see why Salzburg is popular year-round with tourists.

For fans of the movie *The Sound of Music*, there's the added bonus that the city was home to the Von Trapp family; you can find several of the movie's locations scattered around the city and various tour companies operate trips with English guides.

Mozart's Footsteps

For Mozart lovers, a visit to Salzburg is little short of a pilgrimage. You can see the composer's birthplace, the house the family rented when he was growing up, and the Residenz (see page 46) where he was literally kicked out by a steward for "getting above himself."

For classical music lovers, festivals are the other main draw (see pages 42 and 45); the city is packed during festival season and it's hard to find accommodations, so make reservations well in advance. Salzburg's charming cityscape, however, can be enjoyed any time of year. Late spring and autumn are good times to visit, but whenever you come it will probably rain: Salzburg has a reputation for being the country's wettest city.

Getting Your Bearings

Salzburg is an easy city to negotiate. The historic center on both banks of the Salzach river is pedestrianized. Although you can walk from end to end in roughly half an hour, you'll doubtless want to spend more time enjoying the medieval streets and spacious baroque squares. Most of what you'll probably want to see is on the left bank, with a few sights across the river.

Tourist offices sell the Salzburg Card, which is valid for 24 hours (€27 summer/€24 winter), for 48 hours (€36 summer/€32 winter) or 72 hours (€42 summer/€37 winter), and offers single admission to all museums and attractions, discounts on services and free access to public transportation.

Various companies will take you on city tours or farther afield to see the landscape of the Salzkammergut, one of the loveliest parts of Austria, with its shimmering lakes. There are fascinating walking tours around Salzburg, concentrating on different aspects of the city. If you just want to sit back and relax, you can take a trip in a horse-drawn carriage (*Fiaker*); pick one up on Residenzplatz.

Cosmopolitan Cuisine

You'll eat extremely well in Salzburg, which has dozens of restaurants, inns, taverns and cafés where you can enjoy anything from local and regional specialties to Japanese sushi. Traditional cooking is hearty and filling: plates of meat with dumplings, soups and spicy *Gulasch* (meat stew). The local specialty is *Salzburger Nockerl* (an egg dessert), and a variety of drinks and open wines (available by the glass) also are offered.

Make a point of lingering an hour or so in one of Salzburg's traditional cafés, which specialize in coffee and cream cakes served in elegant surroundings. Many cafés and restaurants have summertime beer gardens, some in beautiful settings.

Austrian Cafés

There's no better way to get the feel of the country than by spending an hour or so in a café, a quintessential Austrian experience. Café decor ranges from chandelier-hung baroque splendor to wood-paneled coziness, but the basic elements are always similar: excellent service, a vast range of coffees, and a wide choice of feather-light cream cakes and pastries, all indulged in by well-dressed locals chatting or reading the newspapers. Reading materials are provided by the establishment and hung on wooden poles. Cafés often serve beer and wine, and some offer savory snacks. Many have summertime terraces, the perfect place to write your postcards and rest your feet.

Salzburg Souvenirs

Salzburg is filled with tempting stores, many of them lining Getreidegasse (see page 44) and its surrounding streets, although there's a good cluster on the left bank of the river. Traditional women's clothes are appealing buys, but keep in mind that what looks lovely here might not look so good back home. Also look for wooden carvings, delicate porcelain and crystal, and bright china and linens, all with an Austrian theme, as well as big European designer names. Don't forget Austria's well-organized tax-free shopping service.

Music and Marionettes

Although classical music is the heart of the entertainment scene, it's not the only attraction. Folk, blues and jazz concerts take place year-round across the city or you can enjoy a traditional dinner in the largest preserved fortress in central Europe, the Festung Hohensalzburg (Hohensalzburg Fortress, see pages 43–44), followed by a Mozart serenade played by musicians in period dress. The main festival season runs from late July through August, but something happens most months. Tyrolean entertainments include a jazz festival in the fall and fairs in September and the weeks before Christmas.

To keep the whole family happy, adults can visit the city's casino, while children will enjoy watching one of the famous puppet performances at the Marionette Theater.

Essential Information

Tourist Information

Tourismus Salzburg
Mozartplatz 5 ☎ 0662 889 87-330; daily 9–7, Aug.; 9–6:30 Jul.; 9–6 Apr.–Jun., Sep. to mid-Oct. and Dec.; Mon.–Sat. 9–6, Jan.–Mar. and mid-Oct. to Nov.
Hauptbahnhof (Railroad Station): Südtiroler Platz 1 ☎ 0662 889 87-340; daily 9–6, Jan.–Apr. and Oct.–Dec.; 9–7, May and Sep.; 8:30–7, Jun.; 8:30–7:30, Jul.–Aug.; www.salzburg.info

change buses. To open the doors from either outside or inside the bus you must press the illuminated button beside the door. For service information contact Obus ☎ 0662 4480 1500; www.salzburg-ag.at. There are taxi stands outside the historic center, or you can call Taxi "2284" (☎ 0662 22 84) or Salzburger Funktaxi (☎ 0662 81 11). Parking is a problem in the city. If you are driving to Salzburg, park in one of the supervised parking lots outside the city and take a shuttle bus to the center.

Urban Transportation

Salzburg is easy to walk around but there are good bus and trolley bus services covering the city. Buy your ticket before boarding, at the main bus stops or from any tobacconist, and validate tickets as soon as you board the bus. Validation machines are marked *Entwerter*. There is no need to validate them again if you

Airport Information

Salzburg's W. A. Mozart Airport (☎ 0662 85 80-0; www.salzburg-airport.com), with domestic and some European flights, is 4 miles west of the city center. Bus No. 2 runs every 10–20 minutes throughout the day to the railroad station, journey time 20 minutes, and there is a taxi stand outside the terminal.

Climate – average highs and lows for the month

Jan.	Feb.	Mar.	Apr.	May	Jun.	Jul.	Aug.	Sep.	Oct.	Nov.	Dec.
2°C	4°C	10°C	14°C	19°C	22°C	24°C	24°C	20°C	14°C	7°C	2°C
36°F	39°F	50°F	57°F	66°F	72°F	75°F	75°F	68°F	57°F	45°F	36°F
-5°C	-4°C	-2°C	2°C	8°C	12°C	13°C	13°C	9°C	4°C	-2°C	-3°C
23°F	25°F	28°F	36°F	46°F	54°F	55°F	55°F	48°F	39°F	28°F	27°F

Salzburg Sights

Key to symbols

➕ map coordinates refer to the Salzburg map on page 40 💺 admission charge: $$$ more than €10, $$ €3–€10, $ less than €3

See page 5 for complete key to symbols

Dom

The ornate facade of the Dom (Cathedral) dominates Domplatz, its four marble statues indicating the magnificent interior splendors. There's been a cathedral here since the eighth century; today's structure is the third on the site. It was built between 1614 and 1628, damaged during World War II, and restored by 1959.

The huge interior is a riot of stucco, marble and gilding, whereas the simple 14th-century font provides a serene aesthetic contrast. In the crypt see the medieval foundations and remains of the original Roman church. The museum has superb treasures such as an eighth-century cross.

➕ B2 ✉ Domplatz 1a ☎ Dom: 0662 8047-7950; www.salzburger-dom.at ⏰ Cathedral: Mon.–Sat. 8–5, and Sun. 1–5, Jan.–Feb. and Nov.; Mon.–Sat. 8–6, Sun. 1–6, Mar.–Apr., Oct. and Dec.; Mon.–Sat. 8–7, Sun. 1–7, May–Sep. 🚃 3, 5, 6, 7, 8, 20, 25, 28 💺 Cathedral free; Museum $$$ 🚻 Guided tours on request; audio guides available

DomQuartier

The DomQuartier Salzburg is the city's newest cultural attraction. The quarter encompasses the buildings adjacent to and nearby the central Residenzplatz (see page 46), including the Archbishop's Palace, the stunning Cathedral (Dom) and the 12th-century St. Peter's Abbey. Highlights include the sumptuous interiors of the Archbishop's Palace, a new art gallery in the abbey and breathtaking city views.

➕ B2 ✉ Residenzplatz 1 ☎ 0662 8042-2109; www.domquartier.at ⏰ Wed. 10–8, Thu.–Tue. 10–5, Jul.–Aug.; Wed.–Mon. 10–5, rest of year 🚃 1, 3, 5, 6 🚈 S-Bahn, then short walk 💺 $$$ 🚻 Tours and audio guides in several languages available ($$$)

Festspielhäuser

The Festspielhäuser (Festival Theaters) are well worth visiting. They stand on the site of the old court stables, the winter riding school that was converted to form the Kleines Festspielhaus (Little Theater). The Grosses Festspielhaus (Large Theater) was built in 1960 and runs right into Mönchsberg hill; vast amounts of rock were removed during its construction. To see the theaters, unless you attend a performance, take a guided tour; this will allow you to experience the acoustics of the 2,000-seat Large Theater, among the best in the world.

➕ B2 ✉ Hofstallgasse 1 ☎ Ticket Office: 0662 804 5500; www.salzburgerfestspiele.at ⏰ Guided tours daily at 9:30 a.m., 2 and 3:30 p.m., Jul.–Aug.; at 2 p.m., rest of year 🚃 1, 4, 7, 8, 10, 22 💺 $$ 🚻 Entry is only with a guided tour; tour time is subject to change if rehearsals are in progress. Check before you visit

Festung Hohensalzburg

The massive Festung Hohensalzburg (Hohensalzburg Fortress) dominates Salzburg from atop Mönchsberg hill. This fortress was built and extended

The rooftops of the Dom (Cathedral)

between 1077 and 1681. Walk up or take the funicular to admire the views from the fortress before joining one of the guided tours. Within the building you'll see winding passages and ornate state rooms, including the Golden Room with its gilded tracery, and the Golden Hall, with a superb gold-and-blue coffered ceiling. The Rainer Museum displays a collection of weapons and coats of arms.

✚ C1 ✉ Mönchsberg 34 ☎ 0662 842 430-11; www.salzburg-burgen.at ◷ Grounds: daily 9–7, May–Sep.; 9:30–5, Jan.–Apr. and Oct.–Dec. Interior (by guided tour only): closes 30 minutes earlier. Rainer Museum: daily same hours as interior ◱ Festungsbahn funicular: daily 9–8, Apr.–Jun. and Sep.–Oct.; 9 a.m.–10 p.m., Jul.–Aug.; 9–5, rest of year ❚❚ Café and restaurant (see page 465) located in fortress ◱ Combination ticket $$$

Franziskanerkirche

A short distance from the cathedral stands the Franziskanerkirche (Franciscan Church), a peaceful and lofty building dedicated to the Virgin, which served as Salzburg's parish church until 1635. The nave, with its Romanesque details, is the oldest part, its dimness set off by the airy Gothic choir, built in the 15th century. Be sure to go behind the altar to admire the ring of baroque chapels that encircle it.

✚ B2 ✉ Franziskanergasse 5 ☎ 0662 843 629; www.franziskanerkirche-salzburg.at ◷ Daily 6:30 a.m.–7:30 p.m. ◱ 1, 4, 5, 22

Getreidegasse

The medieval street known as Getreidegasse runs through the center of old Salzburg and is lined with stores, each with a distinctive wrought-iron sign hanging above.

Most of the houses date from the 15th through the 18th centuries and were built by prosperous burghers for their businesses and to house their families. Passages run through the buildings to connect with picturesque courtyards and squares; these are called *Durchhäuser*, meaning "through the houses."

Crowds throng the street and its continuation, Judengasse, and there's no better place to come to soak up Salzburg's unique atmosphere.

✚ B3 ✉ Getreidegasse ◱ 1, 4, 5, 22

Haus der Natur

A few hours in Salzburg's Haus der Natur (Natural History Museum) provides a splendid antidote to an excess of fine architecture and Mozart.

The museum's more than 90 rooms house a wide range of scientific and nature displays, including a reptile zoo, European animal exhibits and an aquarium; among the fish here is a black-tipped reef shark. The Space Research Hall, with its mock-up of a future space city, is popular with kids.

✚ A3 ✉ Museumsplatz 5 ☎ 0662 842 653; www.hausdernatur.at ◷ Daily 9–5 ◱ 1, 4, 7, 8, 10, 22 ❚❚ Café in museum ◱ $$

Mirabellgarten

The beautiful Mirabellgarten (Mirabell Garden) spreads around the Schloss Mirabell (Mirabell Palace), built in 1606 by Archbishop Wolf Dietrich von Raitenau as a palace for his mistress, Salome Alt. The terraces and grounds around the house are a splendid example of baroque garden design, where trees and flowers contrast with statues and fountains to create a truly civilized landscape. Concerts of Mozart's music are held in the Marble Hall.

✚ B3 ✉ Mirabellplatz ☎ 0662 8072-0 ◷ Daily 6 a.m.–dusk ◱ 1, 2, 3, 5, 6, 20, 25, 28

Mozarts Geburtshaus

Wolfgang Amadeus Mozart was born in a modest middle-class apartment in the heart of Salzburg on January 27, 1756. These rooms are among Salzburg's most visited sights, a place of pilgrimage for music lovers from all over the world.

✚ B2 ✉ Getreidegasse 9 ☎ 0662 844 313; www.mozarteum.at/museen ◷ Daily 8:30–7, Jul.–Aug.; 9–5:30, rest of year. Last admission 30 minutes before closing ◱ 1, 4, 5, 22 ❚❚ Café on ground floor of museum ◱ $$$

Mozart and the Salzburg Festival

The facade of the Mozarts Geburtshaus in Salzburg where the composer was born in 1756

Although Mozart spent much of his adult life in Vienna, his name is inextricably linked with his birthplace, Salzburg. Considered by many to be the world's greatest composer, Mozart left a spiritual legacy to his native city that is exemplified by one of the world's greatest music festivals, the Salzburg Festival, an annual program of musical events.

Mozart

Wolfgang Amadeus Mozart was born in Salzburg in 1756, the son of a respected court musician, himself a fine violinist whose treatise on violin technique is still respected. The boy soon showed signs of genius, playing a variety of instruments by sight and ear and starting to compose at an early age. Mozart's father touted his talented son all around the European courts, keeping a stern eye on his behavior, spending and morals, and thus storing up trouble for the pair's future relationship.

Eventually the small-town atmosphere of Salzburg, with its reliance on the bishops for employment, proved too stifling, and Mozart moved to Vienna, where he married Constanze Weber. He composed prodigiously and was capable of writing scores as if by divine dictation, while chatting to his friends. Unfortunately, Mozart's genius did not extend to managing his finances; weighed down by money worries and stress, he died in 1791 and was buried in an unmarked grave.

The Salzburg Festival

The Salzburg Festival is held annually from late July through August. Founded in 1920 by poet Hugo von Hoffmannsthal and theater director Max Reinhardt, famous names associated with the festival have included composer Richard Strauss and conductors Arturo Toscanini, Bruno Walter and Herbert von Karajan, who became its artistic director in 1956. The music festival attracts audiences and renowned performers from all over the world. Its main venues are the Festspielhäuser (Festival Theaters) complex (see page 43), but performances are held in buildings around the city. The program always includes Mozart operas and orchestral works, but many other composers are featured, as well as plays – in particular *Everyman*, which is traditionally performed outside in the Domplatz.

If you want to attend the festival it is essential to book as far in advance as possible; reservations start in December, when you should also reserve your accommodations.

Salzburg Ticket Service ✉ Salzburg Information, Mozartplatz 5, A-5020 Salzburg, Austria
☎ 0662 840310; www.salzburgticket.com or www.salzburgerfestspiele.at

Mozart-Wohnhaus

In 1773 the Mozart family left their modest apartment on Getreidegasse and moved across the river to Makartplatz to occupy a far more spacious and elegant place, now the Mozart-Wohnhaus (Mozart's Residence). The building was badly damaged in World War II and was finally renovated and reopened in 1996 for the 240th anniversary of Mozart's birth. The result is a superb, state-of-the-art museum with evocative displays of Mozart memorabilia.

A true picture of the composer emerges – a man who loved games and jokes, who had an earthy sense of humor but who also had a difficult relationship with his father. Here are scribbled letters, musical manuscripts, books and instruments, all brought to life through an English-language commentary. Two rooms are devoted to audiovisual programs about Mozart's early life and his travels through Europe.

➕ B3 ✉ Makartplatz 8 ☎ 0662 874 227-40; www.mozarteum.at/museen ◉ Daily 8:30–7, Jul.–Aug.; 9–5:30, rest of year. Last admission 30 minutes before closing 🚇 1, 2, 3, 5, 6, 20, 25, 28 🚋 $$$ ℹ Audio guide

Residenzplatz

Residenzplatz is the triumphant architectural landmark of the inner city, splendidly adorned with an ebullient baroque fountain (the largest in central Europe) complete with water-spouting horses and dolphins and topped by a conch-blowing triton.

Opposite rises the Residenz (Archbishop's Palace), built between 1595 and 1619, and set around three courtyards. See the grandeur enjoyed by Salzburg's prince bishops via an audio-guided tour through rooms of ornate decoration with stucco, gilding, marble and astonishing painted ceilings. The palace also contains a gallery of European art. Concerts are held in the state rooms.

➕ B2 ✉ Residenzplatz 1 ☎ Palace: 0662 8042-2109; www.domquartier.at. Art Gallery: 0662 840 4510

◉ Palace and Art Gallery: daily 10–5, Jul.–Aug.; Wed.–Mon. 10–5, rest of year 🚇 3, 5, 6, 7, 8, 20, 25, 28 🚋 Palace $$; Art Gallery $$; reduced combination ticket $$$. See also DomQuartier page 43 ℹ Guided tours of Palace; audio guide

Salzburg Museum Neue Residenz/Spielzeug Museum

Salzburg's primary museum has collections housed in two buildings. The Neue Residenz specializes in antiquities, art and musical instruments. The Spielzeug Museum (Toy Museum) has a charming collection of toys, dolls and musical instruments.

You can trace Salzburg's history from Roman times and admire some lovely 17th-century paneled rooms. Among the highlights is a beautiful Celtic ewer (pouring vessel). The toys and dolls, some 250 years old, include train sets and puppet theaters.

➕ C2, B2 ✉ Neue Residenz: Mozartplatz 1. Toy Museum: Bürgerspitalgasse 2 ☎ Neue Residenz: 0662 620 808-700. Toy Museum: 0662 620 808-300; www.salzburgmuseum.at ◉ Daily 9–5, Jul.–Aug.; Tue.–Sun. 9–5., Sep.–Jun. 🚇 Neue Residenz: 3, 5, 6, 7, 8, 20, 25, 28; Toy Museum: 1, 4, 5, 22 🚋 $$ (each museum)

Stiftskirche St. Peter

The lovely Stiftskirche St. Peter (Abbey Church of St. Peter) was built between 1131 and 1147 but altered to its present rococo appearance in the 18th century. A simple Romanesque west door leads into a sumptuous interior, with 16 marble altars in its side chapels and decorated with green and pink molding and golden cherubs.

Make time to see the monument to Mozart's beloved sister Nannerl before leaving to explore the charming old Friedhof (cemetery), with its flower-bedecked graves.

➕ B2 ✉ St. Peter-Bezirk 1 ☎ 0662 844 576; www.stift-stpeter.at ◉ Church: daily 8–8; no admission during services. Catacombs: daily 10–12:30 and 1–6, May–Sep.; 10–12:30 and 1–5, rest of year 🚇 1, 4, 5, 22 🍴 St. Peter Stiftskeller, see page 465 🚋 Catacombs $

A Day in Salzburg

Although several companies offer a variety of tours in and around Salzburg, the city is small enough to find your way around easily, so it makes sense to plan your own day's sightseeing.

A view across Salzburg from Festung Hohensalzburg

A Mozart Morning

After a hearty breakfast, spend the morning concentrating on Wolfgang Amadeus Mozart, Salzburg's most famous son. His father, employed as a musician in the city, lived in a house on Getreidegasse, where Mozart was born in 1756 (see page 44). After visiting the house and its museum you may be ready for a cup of coffee and a break; head for the atmospheric Café Tomaselli on Alter Markt. It was here that Mozart's widow came with her second husband to write the composer's biography in 1820.

Next, cross the Staatsbrücke and walk along the river to Mozart's House (Mozart-Wohnhaus, see page 46) on Makartplatz, a far grander house where Mozart lived between 1773 and 1780 in a spacious apartment. Nearby you'll find the Mozarteum, the music university that holds the Mozart archives. The hut on the grounds is the Little Magic Flute House (Zauberflötenhäuschen) which once stood in Vienna. Here, Mozart composed the opera in less than five months.

An Afternoon in the Altstadt

Back across the river, have lunch in one of the cafés or restaurants and then spend the afternoon exploring the Old Town (Altstadt). Most sights are clustered around the trio of lovely squares known as the Residenzplatz, Domplatz and Mozartplatz. Behind the cathedral (Dom, see page 43), take the funicular up to the massive fortress of Hohensalzburg (see pages 43–44).

After this, visit the fine Salzburg Museum Neue Residenz (see page 46). En route, stop at the Pferdeschwemme (literally "horse-swim"), a frescoed fountain-cum-pool where horses were once led down sloping ramps in order to be washed. Leave time to enjoy the stores along Getreidegasse (see page 44) and in the alleys leading off it, where you'll find every imaginable Austrian souvenir.

A Salzburg Evening

No Salzburg visit would be complete without some music; many visitors enjoy special Mozart evenings, with dinner followed by a performance of the composer's works played by costumed musicians. Then wander back through the atmospheric streets to your hotel with music ringing in your ears. For details of the walk route, see the city map on page 40.

Belgium

Introduction and Map 50

Timeline 54

Survival Guide 55

Brussels 56

Feature: Grand' Place 61

Bruges 62

Feature: A Medieval Experience: The Burg 68

Ghent 70

Feature: *De aanbidding van Het Lam Gods –*

The Adoration of the Mystic Lamb 75

Hotels and Restaurants 465

Essential Information 498

Opposite: The striking facade of one of the beautiful guildhalls surrounding the Grand' Place, Brussels

Belgium

Belgium is a young country in terms of "old" Europe. Its name derives from a prehistoric tribe, the Belgae, but there is no racial or cultural link with such a distant past. The country has been in the melting pot of European history for centuries and only achieved true national identity in 1830 after the Belgian Revolution. Yet nowhere else on the continent will you be so close to such a powerful sense of European history.

Influential Neighbors

The Belgium of today is a nation born out of a divided Europe, surviving in spite of differences in politics, territory and language that remain within its own borders. Too often it is seen as the administrative focus of the European Union, a country preoccupied with international politics and commerce. Geographically, it is tiny (about the size of Maryland) relative to the size of Europe's larger nations. The Netherlands lies to the north; Germany to the east; France to the south; and Luxembourg, an independent Grand Duchy linked historically to Belgium, to the southeast.

The northwestern coastline of Belgium faces Britain across the narrow English Channel. The influences and interests of all of these European countries have had an impact on Belgium and, in the case of France and the Netherlands, have radically shaped the country's north–south linguistic and cultural divide.

Landscape of History

Apart from the canals in the north, Belgium has no outstanding landscape features that define it in the way that Norway is defined by its fjords, Greece by its islands or Switzerland by its Alps. Yet Belgium has a powerful identity expressed through historic cities and a peerless artistic legacy. You will be seduced by medieval Bruges and old Brussels; feel a sense of history in Ghent,

Antwerp and regional cities such as Leuven and Mechelen; and be enchanted by the castles in the Ardennes region. The dazzling works of art of early Flemish Masters and medieval painters will fascinate you: Prepare yourself for Jan van Eyck, Hans Memling and Peter Paul Rubens, as well as the Bruegels, Anthony van Dyck and Jacob Jordaens.

Belgium is about the landscape of history rather than of scenery. Yet outside the cities and towns lies a quietly charming countryside of fruitful

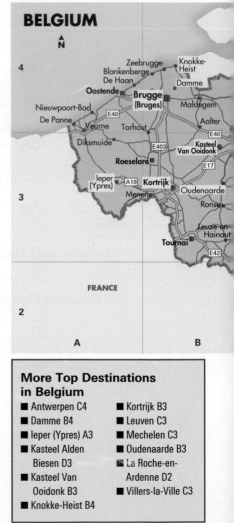

More Top Destinations in Belgium

- Antwerpen C4
- Damme B4
- Ieper (Ypres) A3
- Kasteel Alden Biesen D3
- Kasteel Van Ooidonk B3
- Knokke-Heist B4
- Kortrijk B3
- Leuven C3
- Mechelen C3
- Oudenaarde B3
- La Roche-en-Ardenne D2
- Villers-la-Ville C3

farms, serene waterways and flower-filled meadows. On the immediate outskirts of Brussels to the south is the Forêt de Soignes, a superb beech forest that is an oasis of peace. In the Haspengouw region to the west of Brussels are several historic castles, such as the stately Gaasbeek with its formal gardens and the 13th-century, moated Alden Biesen. A more somber yet compelling aspect of Belgium is enshrined in the poem *In Flanders Fields* by Canadian poet John McCrae

(1872–1918), who was a medical officer in World War I. Throughout Europe's turbulent history this northwestern corner of the continent has seen conflict, none so bitter as World War I. Towns such as Mons and Ypres still resonate with memories, and you will find many war memorials and graves in the now-healed landscape.

Beaches, Woodlands and Parks
Along Belgium's relatively short 42-mile coastline there are attractive sand dunes,

The Atomium is in Heysel, northern Brussels

(www.boudewijnseapark.be), situated just outside Bruges, is one of Europe's largest indoor dolphinariums.

Exploring Belgium

Public transportation in Belgium is universally efficient, but the railroad network is by far the best way to travel. It is well integrated with systems in neighboring countries, and trains are frequent. Intercity trains are fast and comfortable; local trains tend to be slower, and you may feel that some of the older equipment seems a little spartan and drab. However, the high standards that distinguish rail travel throughout northern Europe prevail.

City transportation systems also are well run. Trams are a northern European institution, and the larger cities in Belgium have good tram and bus services. Brussels and Antwerp have well-organized subway systems that visitors will find useful.

Renting a car will give you independence, but driving in Belgium can be a challenge due mainly to the small size of the country and, in part, to its congested urban nature. The road system is excellent, but because distances between built-up areas can be short, you are frequently faced with busy intersections. Traffic in Brussels and in many of the larger cities is hectic, and navigation can be complicated for visitors because road signs are in French and Flemish. Out on the road, along the east–west dividing line between French-speaking and Flemish-speaking Belgium, destination names on road signs change suddenly and confusingly between French and Flemish.

Diverse Foods

Food in Belgium is often characterized as being French in quality and German in quantity. The reality is more subtle. Wallonian cuisine shares the French penchant for wine-based sauces, but traditional Belgian cuisine focuses particularly on beef and pork, and

beaches and resorts, lively towns such as Oostende, quaint resorts like De Haan and stylish hangouts like Knokke Le Zoute, all connected by a tram line. There may be no dramatic mountains, but the hilly country of the Ardennes in southern Belgium offers a varied landscape of woods, rivers and soft moorland where you can walk or bicycle around Dinant and Rochefort.

Brussels has plenty of green spaces, such as the popular Bois de la Cambre, and the vast beech woodland of the Forêt de Soignes. For more gardens and floral displays, check out the Royal Greenhouses at Laeken or the National Botanic Garden in Meise, about 7 miles north of Brussels.

Belgium has a variety of theme parks to appeal to children and adults alike. At Wavre, near Brussels, is Walibi Belgium (www.walibi.com), a huge theme park with thrilling roller-coaster rides such as "Buzzsaw" and "Cobra," as well as a fabulous water park, Aqualibi, adjacent; at Boudewijn Seapark

The Last Post ceremony takes place at 8 p.m. daily at the Menin Gate war memorial in Ypres

specializes in seafood on the coast, and game in the Ardennes.

In most good hotels you will find the generous buffet breakfasts that are an international staple, consisting of a variety of cereals, cheeses and hams, along with fish and smoked meats. For lunch and dinner, be adventurous. Try *maatjes*, marinated raw herring swallowed whole, but not quite the raw experience it seems. Or settle for *mosselen/moules*, Belgian mussels in a variety of tangy sauces. For a truly filling meal, try *waterzooi*, the traditional Flemish stew of fresh vegetables with rabbit, chicken or fish, originating in Ghent, or *anguilles au vert/paling in 't groen*, freshwater eels in a green herb sauce, or *carbonnades*, beef stewed in beer. And do not miss Ardennes pâté, the region's excellent *jambon d'Ardennes* (smoked ham) or some of the many delicious local cheeses, little known outside Belgium.

In spring look for an asparagus dish with a butter-based sauce, as well as chopped boiled egg and chopped ham. This goes nicely with one of Belgium's many excellent beers, which tend to be rich, mellow and smooth. In the Flemish and the Liège regions of Belgium the specialty is *jenever (genièvre)*, a grain spirit like gin, flavored with juniper berries and other herbs and spices.

For those with a sweet tooth, Belgium's famous *chocolatiers* will be irresistible. The specialties are individually made pralines with liqueur or cream fillings, and truffles with the utterly indulgent ingredients of butter, cream and sugar. The shopfront displays are an art form in themselves and are guaranteed to tempt you inside. *Gaufres wafels*, tasty waffles, are a Belgian treat that you can buy from street vendors.

Traditional Courtesy

Throughout Belgium, visitors will find the local people unfailingly helpful. This is a conservative country with a strongly Roman Catholic religious tradition, factors that make people courteous yet reserved. The language divide (see page 54) lends a certain rivalry to relations between Flemings and Walloons, yet such cultural diversity seems to make most Belgians amenable to, and interested in, visitors. The people may seem busy and preoccupied, but they will respond politely if you ask for advice or information about their country, which is, after all, a distillation of the most significant aspects of old and new Europe.

Timeline

57 BC	Romans in northern Europe conquer Iron Age Belgae tribe territory.
AD 751	Carolingian Dynasty is formed; during reign of Charlemagne, Holy Roman Emperor, the Low Countries prosper.
993	King Baudouin I dies, and his brother, Albert II, becomes king.
1419	Central government established at Bruges; the city becomes a center of the cloth trade and a focus of early Flemish painters.
1519	Charles V of Spain is crowned Holy Roman Emperor; the Netherlands comes under Spanish control.
1581	The Netherlands divides into United Provinces of the Netherlands and Spanish Netherlands (Belgium).
1713	War of Spanish Succession ends; Austria controls Belgium.
1815	Congress of Vienna; Belgium and the United Provinces of the Netherlands form the Kingdom of the Netherlands, ruled from the Hague by the Dutch William of Orange.
1839	Belgian independence recognized by the (Dutch) Netherlands.
1914–18	World War I: most of Belgium is occupied by Germany.
1940–44	World War II: Belgium is again occupied by Germany.
1957	European Economic Community (now the European Union) establishes its headquarters in Brussels.
1967	NATO sets up headquarters in Brussels.
2006–present	Belgian politics is characterized by deep rifts based on Flemish/French language and cultural differences.
June 2010	A general election results in no overall majority for any one party. Negotiations begin to form a coalition government comprising the French- and Flemish-speaking parties.
October 2011	Agreement is reached on constitutional changes to allow a coalition government to take power.
December 2011	New Belgian government sworn in with Elio de Rupo as Prime Minister.
June/July 2013	King Alfred II abdicates. The crown passes to his son, Prince Philippe. King Philippe is sworn in as ruling monarch of Belgium.
October 2014	A new Federal government takes office headed by Reformist Movement party leader Charles Michel.
March 2016	Brussels Airport and the Metro system suffer terrorist attacks.

Language Divide

There is a dramatic linguistic divide between north and south Belgium, a legacy of the country's formation from a southern French-influenced area and a northern Flemish-influenced area. In northern Belgium the dominant language is Flemish, a Germanic language similar to Dutch. In southern Belgium, in the area known as Wallonia, the prevailing language is a French dialect. Brussels lies within the Flemish half of Belgium and is officially bilingual, but within the city French is the dominant language. Be careful in associating Flemish too closely with Dutch. Brugeans (residents of Bruges) will tell you that theirs is a far subtler language. And Antwerpenaars (residents of Antwerp) will tell you that they speak better Flemish than Brugeans; if you visit more remote rural districts you will find even more regional differences.

Survival Guide

- Flemish and French are both spoken in Brussels, where even street signs are in both languages. You can try out your French in Brussels and Wallonia and your Flemish in Ghent, Bruges and in the north, but to use either language in the wrong area may elicit a frosty reaction. However, many Belgians speak English, and this is often the wisest option, particularly in the city of Brussels, where it is now lingua franca.

- You will usually find that the Flemish and French proper names have similarities; for example, Bruges is Bruges (French) and Brugge (Flemish), Louvain is Louvain (French) and Leuven (Flemish). But there are problematic differences. For example, Ghent is Gand (French) but Gent (Flemish), and Mechelen is Malines (French) but Mechelen (Flemish). If in doubt, especially when checking train or bus destinations, confirm the destination with an English-speaking official.

King's House Café in Grand' Place, Brussels

- There are a few public restrooms in Belgian cities, but they are often not very clean. Railroad and bus stations, restaurants and the bigger cafés tend to have public bathrooms with attendants, where you are expected to pay about 20 to 50 cents per person.

- In restaurants, the *menu* usually signifies the dish of the day. If you want to choose from a selection of dishes, ask for the *kaart* (Flemish) or *la carte* (French).

- The cities of Brussels, Bruges and Ghent offer visitor cards with discounts to attractions and/or public transportation. The Brussels Card, available online (www.visitbrussels.be) costs €26 (24 hours), €34 (48 hours) and €42 (72 hours). The €28 Bruges Museum Pass offers access to 14 of the city's historic museums and monuments. Citycard Ghent costs €30

(48 hours) and €35 (72 hours) and is available at public transportation kiosks and participating museums. All of these discount cards are available to buy at tourist offices.

- For a quick snack there are numerous fast-food outlets and, in large shopping malls, café counter service. For a local snack try a *broodje*, a roll crammed with tasty fillings, or a *Gaufres wafels*, a vanilla-flavored waffle, spread with chocolate sauce and/or fresh cream.

- Beer brewing is a Belgian specialty, and there are hundreds of different Belgian brews to choose from. Have a beer at lunchtime or try a *bière/bier* with your meal at a restaurant. It is perfectly in keeping with the local cuisine, which incorporates beer in many dishes. Some of the best Belgian beers can be as distinctive as wine. There are many fruit-based varieties, but be aware that some have a high alcohol content.

Brussels

Brussels (Brussel or Bruxelles) takes most people by surprise. The city's name is so closely associated with the modern trappings of the European Union (E.U.) that for many it is synonymous with the world of suited bureaucrats.

The real Brussels is an exciting, modern city, yet rich in beautiful medieval and art nouveau buildings, outstanding museums and galleries, and a cultural life vibrantly international in character.

Life in the City

You may feel intimidated at first by the hectic pace of the busy streets, but Brussels is genuine "old Europe" at heart – open, friendly and welcoming. Life between the busy boulevards is engagingly relaxed. There is a wonderful variety about Brussels, a sense of its being several urban "villages" within a whole.

The heart of the city lies within a barrier of encircling main roads known as the *Petit Ring/Kleine Ring*. You should be able to reach the inner city's finest

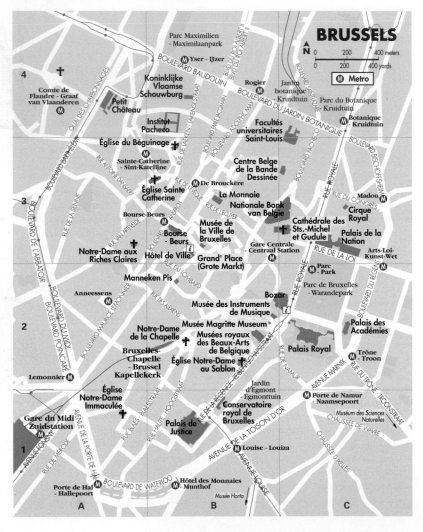

features easily, and you should have no difficulty finding your way around; another option is to join one of the many guided tours (check details with the tourist office; see page 58).

For areas outside the *Petit Ring/Kleine Ring*, use the city's subway system, one of the easiest ways of getting around greater Brussels.

Medieval Townscape

Historic Brussels is celebrated by the breathtaking Grand' Place (Grote Markt, see page 61), the best-preserved medieval townscape in Europe. North of here you will find the rue des Bouchers area, where narrow cobbled streets are lined with competing restaurants more reminiscent of Mediterranean cities. Nearby are the elegant, glass-roofed shopping malls of the 19th-century Galeries St.-Hubert.

A short distance west of Grand' Place, along rue au Beurre, is the massive neoclassical Bourse, the city's stock exchange, its front facing busy boulevard Anspach. Nearby is rue Neuve, a lively shopping street.

Head west from boulevard Anspach and discover Brussels' very old heartland of place St.-Géry, with its charming covered market, and atmospheric place Ste. Catherine and place du Béguinage, two old cobbled squares with slightly worn but still splendid baroque churches. Between St.-Gery and Ste.-Catherine lies rue Antoine Dansaert, a street which is home to many Belgian fashion stores.

Sightseeing and Shopping

Outside the Grand' Place area there are other atmospheric and stylish areas.

Le Sablon, near the southern edge of the *Petit Ring/Kleine Ring*, is convenient to the Royal Fine Arts Museums of Belgium (Musées royaux des Beaux-Arts de Belgique, see page 60). The leafy place de Grand Sablon is the center of Brussels' antiques trade, and it has some fine restaurants and antiques shops. Just south of Le Sablon is the busy and fashionable shopping street of avenue Louise, at the heart of the upscale area of Ixelles/Elsene. This is where many of the trendy shops and restaurants are located.

Brussels has much to see and you'll need to use your time efficiently to visit as many of the attractions as possible.

Branch out beyond the *Petit Ring/Kleine Ring* to places like Heysel, four miles north of Grand' Place. Here stands the striking Atomium (www.atomium. be), by architect André Waterkeyn, a vast model of a metal crystal, its steel spheres gleaming in the sun. At its foot, Mini-Europe (www.minieurope.be) presents scaled-down versions of Europe's most famous buildings.

Visit the Parc du Cinquantenaire, Leopold II's 1880 celebration of the Golden Jubilee of the Belgian State. The park has a central avenue, named after John F. Kennedy, that leads to a triumphal arch linking monumental halls. Several major museums are located here.

Petit Julien
South of Grand' Place on rue du Chène (reached via rue Charles-Buls and Stoofstraat) stands the famous *Manneken-Pis* (right), a bronze fountain statuette of a naked little boy happily urinating. *Petit Julien*, as he is properly called, dates from 1619 and has long been an irreverent and endearing symbol of "carefree" Brussels.

Belgium

Cuisine and Culture

Make sure you sample classic Brussels cuisine at gourmet restaurants such as Comme Chez Soi (see page 465), or try a less pricey local *geuze* or *kriek* beer in any of the café bars in and around Grand' Place and St.-Géry. Try mussels, of course, but also enjoy *anguilles au vert/paling in 't groen*, freshwater eels in sauce, or *waterzooi*, fish or chicken stew with vegetables and creamy sauce, and spoil yourself with Belgian chocolate.

Enjoy great music in the superb national opera house, Théâtre de la Monnaie (www.lamonnaie.be), or in one of the rock and jazz venues. There also are colorful street theaters, festivals and puppet theater events for kids.

Essential Information

Tourist Information
Brussels Tourist Information Office
Hôtel de Ville, Grand' Place (Grote Markt);
Brussels Info Place, rue Royale 2;
Station Europe, Place du Luxembourg
☎ 02 513 8940; www.visit.brussels
Flanders Region & Brussels Tourist Office
Marché des Herbes/Grasmarkt 61 ☎ 02 504 0300; www.toerismevlaanderen.be

Urban Transportation
Brussels has three main railroad stations: the Gare du Nord/Noordstation (Brussels North), Gare Centrale/Centraal Station (Brussels Central) and Gare du Midi/Zuidstation (Brussels South). Eurostar service from London's St. Pancras International station (1 hour 51 minutes) arrives at Brussels Midi station, as does the TGV/Thalys train (1 hour 25 minutes) from Paris. For international rail information call (toll call) ☎ 070 79 79 79 (Mon.–Fri. 8–8, Sat.–Sun. and public holidays 9–4:30); www.b-europe.com. For domestic services ☎ 02 528 2828 (daily 7 a.m.– 9:30 p.m.); www.belgianrail.be. There are metro (subway) stops at all three stations. Metro stations are marked on the map as "M"

and are identified at entrances by a white letter "M" on a blue background. Brussels has a metro, buses and an underground tram system (same ticket for all), and taxis. The metro lines have stations near major attractions. For general information about city transportation call (toll call) ☎ 070 23 2000 (Mon.–Fri. 7–7, Sat. 8–4); www.stib.be. Licensed, metered taxis can be hailed in the street or from a taxi stand at rue du Marche aux Herbes (Grasmarkt) for Grand' Place and at Gare Centrale; rates double when traveling outside the city. Call Taxis Bleus ☎ 02 268 0000; www.taxisbleus.be.

Airport Information
Brussels International Airport is located at Zaventem, 8 miles northeast of the city. There is an Airport City Express train that runs to/from all of Brussels' main stations at 15-minute intervals (journey time 17–30 minutes, depending on time of day), daily 4:35 a.m.–12:24 a.m. from the airport and 4:32 a.m.–11:34 p.m. from the city. For flight information call ☎ 0900 700 00 (toll call) within Belgium, 32 2 753 77 53 from outside Belgium (Mon.–Fri. 7 a.m.–10 p.m., Sat.–Sun. 7 a.m.–8 p.m.); www.brusselsairport.be.

Climate – average highs and lows for the month

Jan.	Feb.	Mar.	Apr.	May	Jun.	Jul.	Aug.	Sep.	Oct.	Nov.	Dec.
4°C	6°C	10°C	13°C	18°C	22°C	22°C	22°C	20°C	15°C	9°C	5°C
39°F	43°F	50°F	55°F	64°F	72°F	72°F	72°F	68°F	59°F	48°F	41°F
-1°C	0°C	2°C	5°C	8°C	11°C	12°C	12°C	10°C	7°C	3°C	0°C
30°F	32°F	36°F	41°F	46°F	52°F	54°F	54°F	50°F	45°F	37°F	32°F

Brussels Sights

Key to symbols

➕ map coordinates refer to the Brussels map on page 56 💵 admission charge:
$$$ more than €7.50, $$ €4–€7.50, $ less than €4
See page 5 for complete key to symbols

Cathédrale des Sts.-Michel et Gudule

Work began on the construction of the Cathédrale des Sts.-Michel et Gudule (Cathedral of St. Michael and St. Gudula) in the 13th century. Architecturally, the building shows the various forms of Brabantine Gothic that evolved over the 300 years it took to complete the work.

Inside, baroque style is lavishly celebrated by giant figures of the Apostles, while Renaissance influence shines from the fine stained glass of the 16th-century west window.

The Romanesque remains of an 11th-century church can be seen down in the crypt.

➕ C3 ✉ place Ste.-Gudule ☎ 02 217 8345; www.cathedralisbruxellensis.be 🕓 Cathedral: Mon.–Fri. 7:30–6, Sat. 7:30–3:30, Sun. 2–6. Treasure Museum: Mon.–Fri. 10–12:30 and 2–5, Sat. 10–3, Sun. 2–5. Crypt: by appointment only 🚇 Gare Centrale 💵 Cathedral free; Museum and Crypt $

Centre Belge de la Bande Dessinée

The unusual Centre Belge de la Bande Dessinée (Belgian Comic Strip Center) encompasses a dazzling celebration of the strip cartoon, the *bande dessinée*. The strip cartoon is closely associated with Belgium, not least in the shape of Hergé's (Georges Rémi's) character Tintin, created in 1929. The museum building is a delight, designed as a department store in 1906 by architect Victor Horta (see Musée Horta, right).

➕ B3 ✉ rue des Sables 20 ☎ 02 219 1980; http://www.comicscenter.net/en/home 🕓 Daily 10–6 🚇 Gare Centrale, De Brouckère, Botanique or Rogier 🚋 Tram 93 🍴 Museum restaurant 💵 $$$ (includes reading room); Library only $ ℹ Documentation Center of the library: visitors over age 16 only. "Tintin" themed walks available

Musée Horta

This is the house that Belgium's famed art nouveau architect, Victor Horta, built for himself. The art nouveau style, popular in Europe and especially in Brussels between 1893 and 1918, typically used industrial materials like steel and iron in the visible parts of houses. Art nouveau originated in England with the Arts and Crafts movement, and it became known as Jugendstil in Germany and Modernismo in Spain. The movement was inspired by nature, and was a reaction against growing industrialism.

From outside, Horta's house and studio look much like the neighboring terraced houses, but the interior is light and sensuous. The beautiful stained-glass ceiling floods the superb wrought-iron stairwell with light, and gives the house a wonderfully airy feel. At the top floor is a glass-roofed conservatory with a winter garden.

➕ Off map at B1 ✉ rue Américaine 23–25 ☎ 02 543 0490; www.hortamuseum.be 🕓 Tue.–Sun. 2–5:30. Last admission 30 minutes before closing 🚋 54; tram 81, 91, 92, 97 💵 $$$

Musée des Instruments de Musique

The excellent Musée des Instruments de Musique (Museum of Musical Instruments) is housed in a former department store, one of Brussels' most striking art nouveau buildings. The Old England store was built in 1899 by architect Paul Saintenoy in glass and steel. The well-adapted space holds one of the largest and most varied collections of musical instruments in the world. The galleries feature more than 1,000 of the 9,000 items in the museum's collection, dating from antiquity to modern day. Visitors are given infrared headphones that allow them to hear the sound of the musical instruments on display.

On the top floor is a pleasant tearoom-restaurant with a delightful terrace offering extensive views over Brussels.

✚ B2 ✉ rue Montagne de la Cour 2 ☎ 02 545 0130; www.mim.be Ⓖ Tue.–Fri. 9:30–5, Sat.–Sun. 10–5. Last admission 45 minutes before closing Ⓠ Gare Centrale, Porte de Namur 🚌 27, 38, 71, 95; tram 92, 94 🍴 Rooftop restaurant 💲 $$$; free first Wed. of the month after 1 p.m.

Musée Magritte Museum

Belgian artist René Magritte was a central figure in the Surrealist movement of the early 20th century, working with groups of artists in Brussels and in Paris until his death in 1967. The Magritte Museum, one of the Royal Museums of Fine Arts of Belgium, is home to the world's largest collection of the artist's work, with important and pivotal pieces including *The Secret Player* (1927), a canvas that propelled Magritte into Surrealism proper.

The museum is housed in the renovated former Hôtel Altenloh, with its neoclassical facade disguising a state-of-the-art gallery interior.

✚ B2 ✉ place Royale 1 ☎ 02 508 3211; www.fine-arts-museum.be Ⓖ Mon.–Fri. 10–5, Sat.–Sun. 11–6 Ⓠ Gare Centrale 🚌 27, 29, 38, 71, 95; tram 92, 94 🍴 Restaurant and café 💲 $$$; free first Wed. of the month after 1 p.m. Combined ticket available for all Royal Museums of Fine Arts ℹ Audio guide ($$)

Musées royaux des Beaux-Arts de Belgique

Three of the six Musées royaux des Beaux-Arts de Belgique (Royal Fine Arts Museums of Belgium) are housed within this former court of Charles Lorraine.

The Musée Oldmasters Museum concentrates on pieces from the 15th to 18th centuries, with Flemish Primitives, and Renaissance and baroque masterpieces. The collection by Pieter Bruegel the Elder is considered superb.

The Musée Fin-de-Siècle Museum displays works from the late 10th to early 20th centuries, during which time Belgium was at the very center of the exciting and important art nouveau and art deco movements.

The collections of the Musée Modern Museum span the 19th century to the present day (renovations are ongoing).

✚ B2 ✉ rue de la Régence 3 ☎ 02 508 3211; www.fine-arts-museum.be Ⓖ Tue.–Fri. 10–5, Sat.–Sun. 11–6 Ⓠ Gare Centrale 🚌 27, 29, 38, 63, 65, 66, 71, 95; tram 92, 93, 95 🍴 Museum café and brasserie/restaurant 💲 Individual museums $$$; combined tickets available; free first Wed. of the month after 1 p.m. ℹ English audio guide ($$) is available

Musée de la Ville de Bruxelles

The Musée de la Ville de Bruxelles (City of Brussels Museum) is a local celebration of Brussels. It merits a visit for its porcelain, pottery and tapestry collections as well as its paintings, including Bruegel the Elder's splendid piece *The Marriage Procession*.

The museum is on Grand' Place in the handsome building known as La Maison du Roi (The King's House). On the top floor there is a display of some of the more than 900 costumes comprising the "wardrobe" of the *Manneken-Pis* (see box page 57), which have been donated by heads of state and others since 1698.

✚ B3 ✉ rue du Poivre 1 (entrance from Grand' Place) ☎ 02 279 4350; www.brusselscitymuseum.brussels Ⓖ Tue.–Sun. 10–5 Ⓠ Bourse, Gare Centrale 💲 $$$; free first Sun. of the month ℹ Audio and tablet guides available in English

Muséum des Sciences Naturelles

Europe's largest dinosaur exhibition is the centerpiece of the Natural History Museum. Actual skeletons include nine of the many iguanodons discovered in the Belgian countryside in 1878. The state-of-the-art galleries shed light on the forces that have shaped the earth's history and explore the biodiversity that shapes the modern world.

✚ Off map at C1 ✉ rue Vautier 29 ☎ 02 627 4211; www.sciencesnaturelles.be Ⓖ Tue.–Fri. 9:30–5, Sat.–Sun. 10–6. Last admission 30 minutes before closing 🚌 34, 38, 80, 95 🍴 Café 💲 $$ ($$$ with temporary exhibition); free first Wed. of the month from 1 p.m.

Grand' Place

The late medieval Grand' Place, or Grote Markt in Flemish, is one of the most glorious sights of urban Europe. These are buildings that seem wrought from nature, yet their symmetry and elegance is ravishing. Any debate about the competing merits of traditional or Modernist architecture melts away in the face of such adventurous style.

What you see in Grand' Place today are some of the finest examples of Flemish Renaissance and Gothic architecture, most of which are 17th-century replacements of older wooden-framed guild houses. The originals were destroyed in 1695 during a devastating bombardment of Brussels by the troops of a spiteful Louis XIV. The citizens rebuilt the heart of their city in a bold act of defiance.

The late Gothic-style Town Hall (Hôtel de Ville), dating from the 15th century, is the focus of Grand' Place. Its soaring tower dominates the Brussels skyline; its facade is crammed with statues of dukes, duchesses, monks, saints and sinners.

The guild houses, which make up the remaining sides of the square, are named and represented by a collection of gilded statues, bas-reliefs, motifs and classical orders. They are a riot of exquisite forms and interesting symbols. Look for No. 7, Le Renard (The Fox), the Haberdasher's guild house; and No. 6, Le Cornet (the Horn), the guild house of the Boatmen, whose gable suggests the stern of a 17th-century sailing ship.

Opposite the Town Hall is La Maison du Roi (The King's House), known also as the Broodhuis (Bread House) and home to the City of Brussels Museum (Musée de la Ville de Bruxelles, see page 60).

On the east side of Grand' Place is the restored facade of the house of the Dukes of Brabant, six individual houses united by the cool elegance of a single Renaissance facade.

Finally, to the left of the Town Hall, is No. 10, L'Arbre d'Or (The Golden Tree). This is the headquarters of the Brewers' Guild, the Knights of the Mash Staff, which also houses a Brewery Museum. Next door is Le Cygne (The Swan), with its graceful swan motif.

🗺 B3 ✉ Grand' Place ☎ (Town Hall) 02 513 8940; www.brussels.be 🚹 Guided tours of Town Hall in English Wed. at 2, Sun. at 11, 3 and 4. Buy tickets ($$) from the Tourist Office in the Grand' Place on the day of the tour (sold on a first-come, first-served basis). Carpet of the Flowers mid-Aug. biennially on even numbered years; medieval festival, the Ommegang in early Jul.; Planting of the May Tree procession in Aug.

The biennial carpet of begonias in Grand' Place never fails to impress

Bruges

In Bruges (Brugge), the survival of exquisite medieval buildings provides a vivid architectural record of 16th-century Europe. Yet that survival is the result of a commercial decline that lasted for nearly 400 years. By the early 16th century, the Zwin river, which linked Bruges and its elegant canals to the North Sea, could not be navigated because of silting; the successful cloth trade had declined, and local and foreign traders moved their businesses to the flourishing port of Antwerp. There was no wealth with which to modernize the venerable townscape. We can thank the rough handling of history for a city that delights with the completeness of its medieval street plan and its ornate buildings, now a UNESCO World Heritage Site.

Finding Your Way

At Bruges railroad station you will find a small tourist information office on Stationsplein, outside the station to the right. It is only a short bus ride from Stationsplein to Bruges' grand central square, the Markt (see pages 66–67),

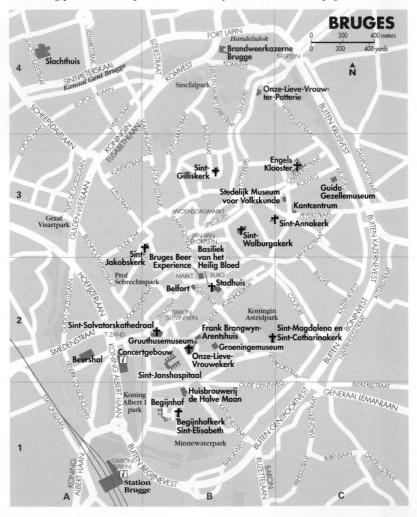

Sightseeing boats glide along a canal to pass under Groene Lei bridge

a good place to start sightseeing. A short walk along Breydelstraat, the street that begins at the southeast corner of the Markt, is the Burg (see pages 68–69), the historic heart of Bruges.

You can enjoy Bruges through guided tours, on foot, by bicycle, by bus or by canal boat (daily Mar.–Nov.). Trips on the famous horse-drawn carriages and trams of Bruges are enjoyable but more expensive. The city is easy to explore on your own, however.

A City of Canals

A few steps south of the Burg, along the narrow alley known as Blinde Ezelstraat (Blind Donkey Street), will bring you to the colonnaded Vismarkt (fish market), a lively scene Tuesday to Saturday mornings. From here proceed right to Huidenvettersplein, and then along Rozenhoedkaai (Rosary Quay) to the Dijver, a pretty, tree-lined walkway running alongside the canal. There is a splendid complex of museum buildings here, including the Groeningemuseum (see page 66), with a wonderful collection of paintings by the Flemish

Primitives, the Gruuthusemuseum (see page 66), which displays decorative arts, and the Church of Our Lady (Onze-Lieve-Vrouwekerk; see page 67). All are centered around Bonifaciusburg (St. Boniface Bridge), itself a reminder of medieval Bruges.

Across the road from the church is the Sint-Janshospitaal, the medieval St. John's Hospital, decorated by artist Hans Memling (see page 67). Also nearby is the old Begijnhof (Beguinage; see page 65), and from there you can explore the city's ancient walls and gates. The many canals lend Bruges the nickname "the Venice of the north."

Lace

Bruges has long been famous for its lace. Since the 16th century, lace-makers here specialized in bobbin lace, a method that used weaving and plaiting with thread-loaded bobbins, with the threads pinned to the pattern. In Italy, they made needlepoint lace, a method of embroidering with buttonhole and other stitches.

Cosmopolitan Tastes

Amid this historical splendor, modern Bruges has its own delights. The city's social life is centered on Markt (the Market Square) and 't Zand, both lined with sidewalk cafés and bars.

There is a Wednesday market on the first square and a larger Saturday Market on the latter. Between 't Zand and the Markt lie Bruges' busiest streets, Noordzandstraat and Zuidzandstraat, the latter leading into the shopping area of Steenstraat, with connecting squares and narrow streets harboring cafés and several bistros.

Eating out in Bruges is a diner's delight. You will find every type of international restaurant, but make sure you try Belgian specialties such as *kalfsblanket*, veal ragout, or *lapin à la gueuze*, which is rabbit cooked in *gueuze* beer. A warming winter specialty is *hutsepot*, a delicious hotpot made with vegetables (usually potatoes, carrots and onions) and lamb.

Lace, Chocolate and Music

If you like lace, make sure you do not miss the t'Apostelientje lace shop (www.apostelientje.be) on Balstraat for intricate, authentic work, or the many lace shops on Wollestraat, which is the street running south from the Markt.

For antiques and craft stores, Mariastraat running south from Simon Stevinplein on Steenstraat is the place to browse; and for mouthwatering chocolates, which make a good souvenir, try the locals' favorite store, Spegelaere at Ezelstraat 92 (see page 466), where all the chocolates and marzipan are made on the premises.

At night, Bruges spectacularly lights up; the buildings in the Markt and elsewhere are illuminated and there is plenty to keep you entertained. Find out what's happening at Cultuurcentrum (www.ccbrugge.be) in St. Jakobsstraat, or catch one of the summer concerts performed each year on the open-air stage on the Burg.

Essential Information

Tourist Information

Toerisme Brugge (Bruges Tourism)
Concertgebouw (Concert Hall), 't Zand 34
☎ 050 44 4646; www.visitbruges.be
◉ Mon.–Sat. 10–5, Sun. 10–2
Stationsplein, Bruges railroad station
◉ Daily 10–5. Contact details as above
Markt (Historium), Markt 1 ◉ Daily 10–5

Urban Transportation

Bruges railroad station is a mile southwest from the Markt. An efficient bus service caters to the city and its environs (☎ De Lijn bus company 070 220 200, toll call; www.delijn.be;

Mon.–Fri. 7–6, Sat. 10–6). Taxis: Rony's (☎ 050 344 344; www.ronystaxis.com). Stands at Markt and at Stationsplein.

Airport Information

The nearest airport to Bruges is Brussels International Airport at Zaventem (see page 58). For flight information ☎ 0900 700 00 (toll call) within Belgium, 32 2 753 77 53 from outside Belgium (Mon.–Fri. 7 a.m.–10 p.m., Sat.–Sun. 7 a.m.–8 p.m.); www.brussels airport.be. Train connections for Bruges are at Brussels' Nord/Noord (North), Centrale/Centraal (Central) and Midi/Zuid (South) stations.

Climate – average highs and lows for the month

Jan.	Feb.	Mar.	Apr.	May	Jun.	Jul.	Aug.	Sep.	Oct.	Nov.	Dec.
5°C	6°C	8°C	11°C	15°C	18°C	19°C	20°C	18°C	15°C	10°C	6°C
41°F	43°F	46°F	52°F	59°F	64°F	66°F	68°F	64°F	59°F	50°F	43°F
1°C	2°C	3°C	5°C	9°C	11°C	12°C	12°C	11°C	8°C	4°C	2°C
34°F	36°F	37°F	41°F	48°F	52°F	54°F	54°F	52°F	46°F	39°F	36°F

Bruges Sights

Basiliek van het Heilig Bloed

The Basiliek van het Heilig Bloed
(Basilica of the Holy Blood, see pages
68–69) has been a place of pilgrimage
for centuries. The basilica consists of
two chapels; the lower St. Basil's Chapel,
which displays a Romanesque style, and
the upper 15th-century Gothic-style
chapel with the famous Relic of the Holy
Blood. In the Middle Ages, this vial,
containing drops of Holy Blood, brought
to Bruges in 1150, was considered one of
the holiest relics in Europe.

Veneration (honoring worship) takes
place Thursday to Tuesday 11:30–noon
and 2–4, whereby a priest presents the
vial to the awaiting congregation so that
they may show their respects. The vial is
on display throughout the year.
➕ B2 ✉ Burg 10 ☎ 050 336 792; www.holyblood.
com ⏱ Basilica and museum: daily 9:30–12:30 and
2–5:30, Apr.–Oct.; Mon.–Tue. and Thu.–Sun. 2–5, rest
of year 🚌 All buses to station and market 💶 Chapels
free; museum $ ℹ Contact tourist office for
information regarding Ascension Day Procession

Begijnhof

The Begijnhof (Beguinage) complex, a
wonderful testimony to a more sedate,
spiritual age, has retained its tranquil
atmosphere. It was founded in 1245
to accommodate pious single women,
many of them lace-makers, who lived
reclusive lives. These inhabitants,
known as Beguines, abandoned the
complex in the 1920s, but Benedictine
nuns later settled in the Beguinage and
still live here today. The 17th-century
little whitewashed cottages surround a
peaceful square.

You can visit the Begijnhuisje
(Beguine's House), a museum house that
has old-style furnishings and a delightful
little cloister. The Begijnhof Church of
St. Elizabeth has a simple grace.
➕ B1 ✉ Wyngaardstraat ☎ 050 33 00 11
⏱ Beguinage: daily sunrise–6:30 p.m. Beguine's
House: daily 10–5. Church: daily 7–12:15 and 3–6 🚌 1
💶 Beguinage and church free; Beguine's House $

Belfort

Bruges' famous medieval Belfort (Belfry)
dominates the Markt. You can reach the
top of the 272-foot tower by climbing
the 366 steps. You may marvel at the
vast number of bricks and the tons of
mortar holding everything together,
including the 27 tons that the 47-bell
carillon weighs. Below the belfry is
the chamber containing the clock

After climbing the Belfort (Belfry) you can look down on the café-restaurants on the Markt

Groeningemuseum is housed on the former site of Eekhout Abbey

mechanism and copper carillon drum. The bells ring each quarter hour. You have time to watch the ingenious system whir and click into life, like a great mechanical beast, before the short climb to the belfry to enjoy the surprisingly muted peals and the view.

➕ B2 ✉ Markt ☎ 050 448 743; www.visitbruges.be ⏱ Daily 9:30–6. Last admission 1 hour before closing 🚌 All buses to station and market ✋ $$$ ℹ Only 70 people are allowed into the tower at a time. Check with the tourist office for carillon recitals

Bruges Beer Experience

Brewing has a long history in Belgium. This new interactive attraction celebrates the rich diversity of the drink, explains the brewing process and the different varieties available, and even explores food pairings. You can sample 16 different beers at the bar, which also is open to the public without a museum ticket.

There are two working breweries within downtown Bruges: Bourgogne des Flandres (www.bourgognedesfland res.be), and the historic Huisbrouwerij de Halve Maan (Half Moon Brewery, www.halvemaan.be), which has been producing beer since 1546.

➕ B2 ✉ Breidelstraat 3 ☎ 050 699 229; www.mybeerexperience.com ⏱ Daily 10–6 🚌 1 ✋ $$$

Groeningemuseum

The Groeningemuseum is housed in a former Augustinian monastery on the Dijver and contains Bruges' superb civic collection of 15th- to 20th-century Flemish, Dutch and Belgian paintings. There are exceptional works here, including Jan van Eyck's *The Madonna with Canon Joris van der Paele*, the works of Pieter Pourbus and Hans Memling, and the nightmarish *The Last Judgment* by Hieronymus Bosch.

➕ B2 ✉ Dijver 12 ☎ 050 448 743; www.visitbruges.be ⏱ Tue.–Sun. 9:30–5 🚌 11 ✋ $$$ (includes audio guide)

Gruuthusemuseum

The 15th-century city palace of the Gruuthuse family houses a collection of fine Flemish decorative arts, including a stunning display of 16th- and 17th-century tapestries. Its oratory overlooks the altar of the church next door and there is a collection of paintings by the Bruges-born British artist Frank Brangwyn. The vast kitchen is a revelation, with a large range of crockery, cutlery and pottery.

➕ B2 ✉ Dijver 17 ☎ 050 448 743; www.visitbruges.be ⏱ The museum is undergoing extensive renovation and is due to reopen spring 2019

Markt

The Markt (Market Square) is a superbly atmospheric square, the heart of Bruges. The Gothic buildings of the Provinciaal Hof, seat of the government of West Flanders, and the adjoining Central Post Office dominate the east side of the impressive square.

The Belfort (Belfry, see pages 65–66) is on the south side. The crow-stepped gables of a row of guild houses stand behind a statue of Jan Breydel and Pieter de Coninck, heroes of the 1302 uprising against French overlordship.

The west side of the Markt has a collection of handsome buildings, including the 15th-century Maison Bouchoute and the Craenenburg House (now the Café Craenenburg) flanking the entrance to Sint Amandstraat. At Markt 1, Historium is a walk-through attraction re-creating some of the medieval highlights of the city.

➕ B2 ✉ Markt 🚌 Most buses 🐴 Horse-drawn carriage trips ($$$) and mini-bus tours ($$$) start from the Markt

Historium ✉ Markt 1 ☎ 50 270 311; www.historium.be ⏰ Daily 10–6 💷 $$$

Onze-Lieve-Vrouwekerk

The brooding Onze-Lieve-Vrouwekerk (Church of Our Lady) plays host to several important objects. The superb Gothic stonework protects the gilded Renaissance mausoleum of Charles the Bold, the powerful ruler of the region as Duke of Burgundy. The pulpit designed by Bruges artist Jan Antoon Geramijn is a marvelous rococo extravaganza but the major artistic draw is Michelangelo's masterpiece sculpture *Madonna and Child*. Originally intended for a church in Siena, Italy it was bought by two wealthy Bruges merchants and brought to Belgium. The church is undergoing renovation but remains open. Michelangelo's sculpture is still on view, but some areas may be closed.

➕ B2 ✉ Mariastraat ☎ 050 448 711; www.visitbruges.be ⏰ Church and museum: Mon.–Sat. 9:30–5, Sun. 1:30–5. Last admission 30 minutes before closing 🚇 1 💷 Church free; Museum $$ (during renovation work). Combined ticket for all Bruges museum sites available

Sint-Janshospitaal

St. John's Hospital, founded in the 12th century, was one of Europe's oldest surviving medieval hospitals, but it has been renovated into a spectacular background for Hans Memling's work.

A German painter, Memling settled in Bruges in 1465 and soon was in great demand. The chapel, which contains magnificent 15th-century Memling decorative panels and the St. Ursula Shrine, is the highlight of the complex, but the fascinating old hospital pharmacy also is worth a visit. Look for masterpieces such as the *Madonna with Child* and the *Lamentation of Christ*.

➕ B2 ✉ Mariastraat 38 ☎ 50 448 711; www.visitbruges.be ⏰ Tue.–Sun. 9:30–5 (pharmacy closed 12:30–1:30) 🚇 1 💷 $$$ (includes audio guide)

Sint-Salvatorskathedraal

Bruges' churches reflect a sober Flemish style, but Sint-Salvatorskathedraal (St. Saviour's Cathedral) has many features to counteract its Gothic vastness. The high altar and the 15th-century choir stalls add a richly decorative note; the rood loft, beneath the organ case, contains a superb baroque sculpture of God the Father in white marble by Arthur Quellin the Younger. Visit the Cathedral Museum; among its treasures is the vivid realism of Dirk Bouts' 15th-century triptych *The Martyrdom of St. Hippolytus*.

➕ B2 ✉ Steenstraat ☎ 050 336 841; www.sintsalvator.be ⏰ Cathedral: Mon.–Fri. 10–1 and 2–5:30, Sat. 10–1 and 2–3:30, Sun. 11:30–12 and 2–5. Museum: Sun.–Fri. 2–5 🚇 1–5, 13, 89 and all buses to the Markt 💷 Cathedral free; museum $ 🎵 Major concerts held in cathedral

Stadhuis

The 14th-century Stadhuis (Town Hall) stands in the medieval Burg (see pages 68–69). It has undergone much renovation work over the years and has a superb carved Gothic facade. Inside is the splendid former council chamber, the Gotische Zaal (Gothic Hall), where local policies were once decided.

➕ B2 ✉ Burg 12 ☎ 050 448 743; www.visitbruges.be ⏰ Daily 9:30–5 🚇 All buses to the Markt 💷 $$. Combined ticket for all Bruges museum sites available

A Medieval Experience: The Burg

The Burg is medieval Bruges at its most tangible. Once it was a jealously guarded enclave, walled and with locked gates. Today it is the city's finest public square, an intimate space flanked by a series of exquisite historic buildings offering a unique perspective on the secular and religious importance of the city during its heydey. The northern side of this outstanding architectural complex contained the 10th-century Romanesque Church of St. Donatian, demolished in 1799 during the French occupation of the region. The only remaining element of the complex is the handsome facade of the Provost's House of St. Donatian.

On the east side of the Burg is the Paleis van de Brugse Vrije (Palace of the Liberty of Bruges; www.visitbruges.be; open daily 9:30–5), once the seat of the Bishop of Bruges and now the administrative headquarters of West Flanders, the westernmost province of the Flemish region of Belgium. This was once the ruling seat of the Bruges Vrije, a territorial precinct of Flanders. One wing harbors a magnificent Renaissance chimneypiece created in honor of Charles V, Count of Flanders and Holy Roman Emperor. The lower section is in black marble with an alabaster frieze depicting the biblical story of Suzanna and the Elders. The main section is in exquisitely carved wood and depicts the Emperor and members of the Habsburg family, the male contingent endowed with embellished Habsburgian codpieces.

To the right of the palace across narrow Blinde Ezelstraat (Blind Donkey Street) is the Stadhuis (Town Hall of Bruges, see page 67). This exquisite building dates from the 14th century but has been rebuilt and renovated over the centuries. The turreted, Gothic sandstone facade is a lyrical evocation of the mason's craft. Inside is the council chamber, the Gotische Zaal (Gothic Hall), with 19th-century romantic wall paintings that illustrate important events in the history of Bruges, and a handsome chimneypiece. Its glorious vaulted ceiling is all gilded wooden arches with slender ribs and hanging keystones. Fortunate couples are married here.

To the right of the Town Hall in the southwest corner of the Burg is the most medieval building of all, Basiliek van het Heilig Bloed (the Basilica of the Holy Blood; see page 65). In the building is a sacred vial believed to contain drops of Christ's blood, brought to Bruges in 1150 from the Holy Land by Diederik van den Elzas, count of Flanders. The Holy Blood is still venerated Thursday to Tuesday. Each Ascension Day in May or June, the relic is the focus of one of the most important events in West Flanders, the Heilig-Bloedprocessie (Holy Blood Procession), a colorful and theatrical costume pageant depicting religious events, where the relic is taken around the center of town.

There is something strangely compelling about the Basilica of the Holy Blood. It has a medieval authenticity that is irresistible, even to the ungodly. The building contains an upper and lower chapel. You enter the lower chapel through a modest doorway and it is as if you are stepping straight into the Middle Ages. The basilica dates from the 12th century and was built to house the relics of St. Basil. It has been partly restored, but is still one of the finest surviving examples of Romanesque architecture in Flanders. Wall carvings are simple, almost primitive. The air is dense and exterior sounds are muffled and resonant.

Gothic Mood

You reemerge into the daylight, pass through an enchanting Gothic doorway in the ornate facade of the main chapel and then mount a wide staircase beneath shallow vaults. The upper chapel is a breathtaking contrast to the somber Romanesque below the stairs. It is lavishly decorated in a late Gothic style that overlays original Romanesque themes. A rococo white marble altar, barrel roof, luminous stained glass, carved wood, and gold and silver artifacts all create a mood that is reminiscent of the heavy decoration of Orthodox churches.

There is a delightful spherical oak pulpit with disk canopy but with no visible access. The secret is a small door to the side of the Holy Blood altar, which opens onto hidden stairs. The Holy Blood is contained within a crystal sheath with a gold crown stopper and is supported by gilded copper and silver angels. Adjoining the upper church is a small museum with the gold and silver reliquary for the Holy Blood.

Above left to right: The Holy Blood Procession takes place in the town center on Ascension Day each year; outdoor café tables in Eiermarkt in the heart of the old city

Ghent

At first glance Ghent (Gent or Gand), the fourth-largest city in Belgium, may seem slightly rough around the edges, a city lacking the sparkle of Luxembourg or the carefully preserved splendor of Bruges.

Ghent has been an industrial and commercial center throughout its long history, and the fabric of the city has suffered because of this. But apart from the urban realities, this is Belgium's "City of Flowers," containing some of the finest historical and cultural artifacts in Europe, along with architecture that encompasses soaring towers and exquisitely decorative domestic buildings.

Its citizens, the friendly Gentenaars, are shrewd, down-to-earth and personable. Many speak some English and are always ready to oblige the visitor with guidance and advice.

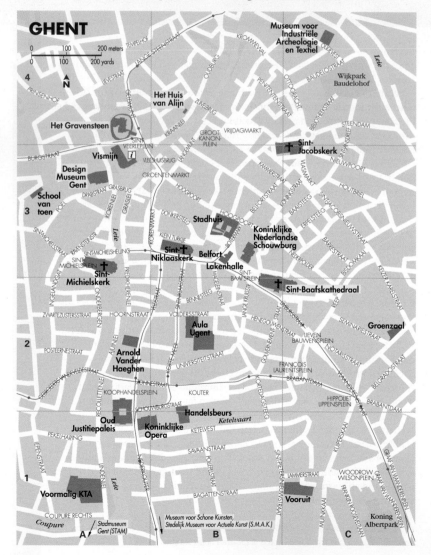

A tram on Korenmarkt makes its way through Ghent's busy historic center

First Impressions

Ghent's main railroad station, Sint-Pietersstation (St. Peter's Station), is just over a mile south of the city center. The station can be a sobering experience for the first-time visitor. It is a busy place and has reasonable facilities, including a digital information port offering tourist information. For comprehensive visitor information head to the heart of the city and the helpful tourist information center in Sint-Veerleplein, close to Het Gravensteen and just off Kraanlei.

Buses, trolley buses and trams leave regularly for Korenmarkt from a covered terminal on the east side of Sint-Pietersstation. Ghent's trams run along extremely narrow streets a mildly alarming experience at first – but they do so with great efficiency. Almost 75 acres of downtown Ghent is traffic free; the area encompasses some of the city's most important historical attractions.

The great central squares are the best places to get a handle on Ghent. Here are the powerful Gothic churches of Sint-Baafskathedraal (see page 74) and Sint-Niklaaskerk. Civic buildings between them include the Belfort (Belfry), the Lakenhalle (Cloth Hall) and the Stadhuis (Town Hall), with their distinctive mix of architectural styles. Take the glass elevator to the top of the Belfort (www.belfortgent.be) for superb views of this city of towers and steeples.

Old Ghent

For a taste of old Ghent, go west from Sint-Niklaaskerk, past the neo-Gothic, neo-Renaissance flamboyance of the 1910 former post office, to the bridge of Sint-Michielsbrug that spans the Leie river. Look back from the bridge for a breathtaking view of the skyline. North of the bridge is Tussen Bruggen, once a busy harbor and still lined by the gabled buildings of Graslei, a popular place for taking photographs, and Korenlei.

North of Graslei is Groentenmarkt, a tree-shaded square flanked by the sturdy 15th-century Groot Vleeshuis (Great Butchers' Hall), though meat is no longer sold there. Today the Groentenmarkt is the scene of a bio-produce market on Friday mornings, and an open-air art forum with displays by local artists and artisans, between 10 a.m. and 6 p.m. on Sundays.

A few steps farther is Sint-Veerleplein, with a monumental baroque archway to the old fish market and handsome gabled houses. However grand, these houses are all overshadowed by the brooding mass of Het Gravensteen, the 12th-century Castle of the Counts (see page 73).

Across the street, to the east of Het Gravensteen, is the narrow, waterfront street of Kraanlei, an attractive row of late medieval buildings lining a stretch of the Leie river. This is one of Ghent's finest streetscapes. From Kraanlei's far end, the Zuivelbrug (Zuivel Bridge) crosses the canal into the square of Vrijdagmarkt, where there is a popular and large market on Fridays.

Shopping in Ghent

Ghent's main commercial and shopping area lies to the south of Korenmarkt and Botermarkt. The busy Veldstraat has stores of all types, but if you walk through the network of little streets just east of here, including Mageleinstraat, Sint-Niklaasstraat, Kortedagsteeg and Koestraat, you'll find numerous specialty shops. These include chic fashion boutiques, delicatessens, *chocolateries*, antiques and crafts shops. At the heart

of the area is the Kouter flower market, held daily, but at its colorful best on Sundays, a vivid indication of Ghent's fame as the "City of Flowers."

Night Lights

Eating out in Ghent is an essential experience. Try such local specialties as *Gentse hazenpeper* (jugged hare) or *Gentse waterzooi van riviervis* (freshwater fish stew). There are many intimate restaurants in the Patershol area to the north of Kraanlei.

Enjoy Ghent by night, when the buildings are lit up and the streets hum with life. Spend an evening at the trendy and busy Handelsbeurs at Kouter 29 (www.handelsbeurs.be); at Opera Gent (www.operaballet.be) on Schouwburgstraat; or at the classical music venue Stedelijke Concertzaal De Bijloke (www.debijloke.be) on Josef Kluyskensstraat.

Essential Information

Tourist Information

Toerisme Stad Gent (Ghent Tourism)
Oude Vismijn Sint-Veerleplein 5
☎ 09 266 5660; www.visitgent.be

Urban Transportation

Ghent railroad station (Sint-Pietersstation) is 1 mile south of the city center. For international rail information ☎ 070 79 79 79 (toll call, Mon.–Fri. 8–8, Sat.–Sun. and public holidays 9–4:30); www.b-europe.com, domestic services ☎ 02 528 2828 (daily 7 a.m.–9:30 p.m.); www.belgianrail.be. Bus and tram stations adjoin the railroad station. Transportation service times are available from the tourist office or bus information offices, or

call Delijn ☎ 070 220 200 (toll call, Mon.–Fri. 7–6, Sat. 10–6); www.delijn.be. There are taxis at the Korenmarkt and Sint-Pietersstation or call ☎ 09 333 3333; www.taxigent.be.

Airport Information

The nearest airport is Brussels International Airport at Zaventem (see page 58). For flight information ☎ 0900 700 00 (toll call) in Belgium, 32 2 753 77 53 from outside Belgium (Mon.–Fri. 7 a.m.–10 p.m., Sat.–Sun. 7 a.m.–8 p.m.). Train connections to Ghent can be made at Brussels' Nord/Noord (North), Centrale/Centraal (Central) and Midi/Zuid (South) stations. The trip from the airport to Ghent takes 30 minutes.

Climate – average highs and lows for the month

Jan.	Feb.	Mar.	Apr.	May	Jun.	Jul.	Aug.	Sep.	Oct.	Nov.	Dec.
5°C	6°C	9°C	11°C	17°C	21°C	22°C	22°C	20°C	15°C	9°C	5°C
41°F	43°F	48°F	52°F	63°F	70°F	72°F	72°F	68°F	59°F	48°F	41°F
0°C	1°C	2°C	5°C	8°C	11°C	12°C	12°C	11°C	7°C	4°C	2°C
32°F	34°F	36°F	41°F	46°F	52°F	54°F	54°F	52°F	45°F	39°F	36°F

Ghent Sights

Key to symbols

➕ map coordinates refer to the Ghent map
on page 70 💷 admission charge:
$$$ more than €7.50, $$ €4–€7.50, $ less than €4
See page 5 for complete key to symbols

Het Huis van Alijn museum occupies several houses

Design Museum Gent

The Design Museum Gent is housed in
the handsome old Hotel de Coninck,
and its extension. The museum exhibits
international and Belgian decorative and
applied art, crafts and design from the
Renaissance to 20th-century art deco, art
nouveau and contemporary work.

➕ A3 ✉ Jan Breydelstraat 5 ☎ 09 267 9999;
www.designmuseumgent.be 🕐 Mon.–Tue. and
Thu.–Fri. 9:30–5:30, Sat.–Sun. 10–6 🚌 3, 17, 18, 22,
24, 38, 39; tram 1, 4 💷 $$$

Graslei en Korenlei

Graslei and Korenlei are the wharves
flanking the medieval harbor Tussen
Bruggen ("between the bridges") that
lies to the north of the bridge of
Sint-Michielsbrug. Their names relate
to their role in the grain trade; their
buildings were the trade and guild
houses of the medieval period, carefully
restored for the World Exhibition of
1913. The facades of these magnificent
buildings offer an impression of Ghent
in the days when the wharves were alive
with the bustle of medieval trade.

➕ A3 ✉ Graslei en Korenlei 🚌 All services for
Korenmarkt

Het Gravensteen

Magnificent Gravensteen (Castle of the
Counts) has all the authentic menace of
12th-century feudalism. A visit to this
well-restored building is irresistible,
made even better by the "movieguide"
visual tour companion (included in the
ticket price). The main castle is a series
of intriguing rooms linked by staircases.

In the upper rooms you will find
historical exhibitions, including the
Wapenmuseum (Weapons Museum)

and the rather grisly Museum voor
Gerechtsvoorwerpen (Museum of
Judicial Objects), which displays tools
of torture and execution.

➕ A4 ✉ Sint-Veerleplein ☎ 09 266 8500;
www.gravensteengent.be 🕐 Daily 10–6, Apr.–Oct.;
9–5, rest of year. Last admission 45 minutes before
closing 🚌 Tram 1, 4 💷 $$$ (includes museums)

Het Huis van Alijn

The intriguing and revamped (2017)
Alijn House owes much of its charm to
its location, set among the old buildings
of the 14th-century Kinderen Alijns
Hospitaal (Hospital of the Alijns
Children) on the canalside street of
Kraanlei. The collections are spread
throughout little houses surrounding
a central square. The domestic and
commercial life of Ghent through the
ages is represented in excellent set-piece
tableaux and displays combining once
common objects with high tech,
interactive content and video screens.

➕ B4 ✉ Kraanlei 65 ☎ 09 235 3800;
www.huisvanalijn.be 🕐 Mon.–Tue. and Thu.–Fri. 9–5,
Sat.–Sun. 10–6 🚌 Tram 1, 4 🍽 Café 💷 $$

Kraanlei

Kraanlei is one of Ghent's finest
canalside streets. Its name derives from
a wooden crane that unloaded cargoes.
The baroque facades of Kraanlei's
buildings, with touches of Gothic,
are survivors of an exuberant age of

Architectural gems along the Leie river in Ghent

prosperity and Flemish culture. Look for Ghent's version of Brussels' *Manneken-Pis* (see page 57), perched above a restaurant door at the beginning of the street. Halfway along is the Het Huis van Alijn (Alijn House, see page 73). Three of the finest facades are at the far end of Kraanlei and include the exquisite 17th-century house known as "The Flying Deer."

Lively Patershol, a few steps north of Kraanlei, is a warren of cobbled streets with art galleries and trendy restaurants. ✚ B4 ✉ Kraanlei 🚊 Tram 1, 4 🍴 Restaurants nearby

Museum voor Schone Kunsten

The Museum voor Schone Kunsten (Museum of Fine Arts) is one of Belgium's oldest art galleries. It offers an overview of local Flemish art from the Middle Ages to the first half of the 20th century. Exhibits also offer an insight into the tastes of the local bourgeoisie. The collection includes works by Flemish and other European masters from the 14th to mid-20th centuries. Of special note are the works by Hieronymus Bosch. Other superb pieces include Pieter Bruegel the Younger's *Wedding Feast* and Frans Hals' evocative *Portrait of a Woman*. ✚ Off map at B1 ✉ Fernand Scribedreef 1, Citadelpark 🕿 09 240 0700; www.mskgent.be 🕐 Tue.–Fri. 9:30–5:30, Sat.–Sun. 10–6 🚊 34, 35, 36, 55, 57, 58, 70, 71, 72, 73, 74, 76, 77, 78 🍴 Museum café 💲 $$$

Sint-Baafskathedraal

The tall four-stage tower of Sint-Baafskathedraal (St. Bavo's Cathedral) dominates the east end of Botermarkt. Externally, the cathedral is a mix of Gothic styles beneath a patina of city grime. Inside is one of the great art treasures of the world, the multipaneled *Het Lam Gods (The Mystic Lamb)*, known as the Ghent Altar (see page 75). Other treasures include the rococo pulpit in Carrara marble and Danish oak, with its carved staircases like twisted tree roots. ✚ B2–C2 ✉ Sint-Baafsplein 🕿 09 269 2045; www.sintbaafskathedraal.be 🕐 Cathedral and crypt: Mon.–Sat. 8:30–6, Sun. 11–6, Apr.–Oct.; Mon.–Sat. 8:30–5, Sun. 11–5, rest of year. *The Mystic Lamb*: Mon.–Sat. 9:30–5, Sun. 1–5, Apr.–Oct.; Mon.–Sat. 10:30–4, Sun. 1–4, rest of year 🚊 Tram 1, 4, 21, 22 💷 Cathedral and altar free; *The Mystic Lamb* $$ (includes audio guide) ℹ A panel may be missing due to renovation work

Stadmuseum Gent (STAM)

Take a walk through the history of Ghent at this interactive museum housed in a 14th-century abbey and contemporary annex. Follow the fortunes of the city through its medieval merchants to the present day. There are original wall paintings in the refectory. ✚ Off map at A1 ✉ Bijlokesite, Godshuizenlaan 2, 9000 🕿 09 267 1400; www.stamgent.be 🕐 Mon.–Tue. and Thu.–Fri. 9–5, Sat.–Sun. 10–6 🚊 6; tram 2, 4, 22 🍴 Café 💲 $$$ ℹ Audio guide $

Stedelijk Museum voor Actuele Kunst (S.M.A.K.)

Opposite the Museum of Fine Arts (see left) is the Stedelijk Museum voor Actuele Kunst (Municipal Museum of Contemporary Art), or S.M.A.K., Belgium's finest post-1945 art collection. It includes works by Andy Warhol, Francis Bacon, David Hockney and Belgian artist Marcel Broodthaers. The temporary exhibitions are excellent. ✚ Off map at B1 ✉ Citadelpark 🕿 09 240 7601; www.smak.be 🕐 Tue.–Fri. 9:30–5:30, Sat.–Sun. 10–6 🚊 34, 35, 36, 55, 57, 58, 70–74, 76, 77, 78 🍴 Museum café 💲 $$$

De aanbidding van Het Lam Gods – The Adoration of the Mystic Lamb

The famous Ghent Altar, *Het Lam Gods* (*The Mystic Lamb*), lives up to your highest expectations. A visit to Sint-Baafskathedraal (St. Bavo's Cathedral) and a view of the altar should not be missed. This luminous work unveiled in 1432 has an impact that can change lives and attitudes.

The Ghent Altar is a polyptych, a painting made up of many panels. It is allegedly the work of two 15th-century Flemish painters, brothers Hubert and Jan van Eyck. There are doubts over whether or not Hubert van Eyck even existed, although Jan van Eyck was unquestionably the most famous painter of his generation.

Two rows of paintings, one above the other, make up the altar. The centerpiece in the upper row is of Christ the King, who is flanked by the Virgin Mary, St. John the Baptist, singing angels, a musician and nude portraits of Adam and a pregnant Eve within the wing panels. The focus of the lower row is the Adoration of the Lamb of God. The flanking panels depict processions of the faithful, judges, knights, hermits and pilgrims. The painted wing panels fold over to enclose the central panels.

The altar has survived the meddling of history. Iconoclasts sought to destroy it. In the 1780s the panels showing the nude Adam and Eve were removed from view during a visit by Emperor Joseph II. In the late 1800s two panels showing the couple clothed in bear skins were displayed to take into account more prudish sensibilities of the times. Two panels were stolen in 1934. The panel depicting John the Baptist was found in Brussels Central railroad station. The panel of the Righteous Judges has never been traced and was replaced by a copy painted by a Belgian artist, Jef van de Veken. During World War II, German soldiers stole this particular work but it was later liberated by American troops.

A five-year restoration program of the Ghent Altar is under way and is scheduled to continue through 2019. One panel will be removed at a time for restoration but that section can still be seen through a window in the restoration room of the Museum voor Schone Kunsten (see page 74).

The complete Ghent Altarpiece *Adoration of the Mystic Lamb,* by Hubert and Jan van Eyck

Britain

Map 78

Introduction 80

Timeline 84

Survival Guide 85

London 86

Feature: Covent Garden Through Time 93

Feature: A Royal Stroll 97

Edinburgh 98

Feature: Stroll Down the Royal Mile 104

Oxford 106

Feature: Shakespeare's Stratford-upon Avon 111

Bath 112

Feature: Jane Austen 117

Hotels and Restaurants 467

Essential Information 502

Opposite: 13th-century Conwy Castle, North Wales

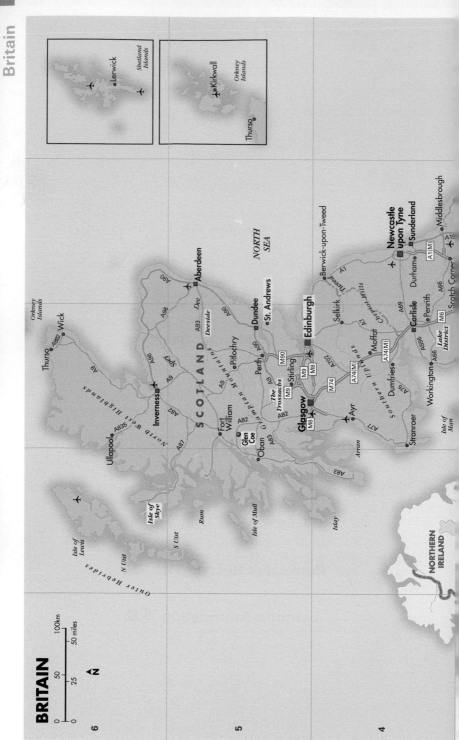

BRITAIN

N

0 — 25 — 50
0 — 50 — 100km
50 miles

Shetland Islands
Lerwick

Orkney Islands
Kirkwall
Thurso

Orkney Islands
Wick
Thurso
A882
A9

Ullapool
A835

North West Highlands

Isle of Lewis
Outer Hebrides
N Uist
S Uist
Run
Isle of Skye

Inverness
A82
A9
A96

SCOTLAND

Grampian Mountains
A9
Pitlochry

Aberdeen
A90
A96
Dee
Deeside
A93
A90

Dundee
St. Andrews

Perth
A9
A90
M90

The Trossachs
Stirling
M9
M9
M8

Fort William
A82
Glen Coe
Oban
A82
A83
A85

Isle of Mull
Islay
Arran
Isle of Man

Glasgow
M8
Ayr
A77
A71

Edinburgh
M8
M9
A702
M74
A74(M)
A74(M)

Selkirk
A7
Moffat
Southern Uplands
Dumfries
A75
Stranraer

Berwick-upon-Tweed
A1
Tweed
Cheviot Hills
A69

Newcastle upon Tyne
Sunderland
Middlesbrough
A11(M)
A19

Durham
A1
A66
Scotch Corner

Carlisle
Penrith
M6
A596
A66
Lake District
Workington
A66

NORTH SEA

NORTHERN IRELAND

6

5

4

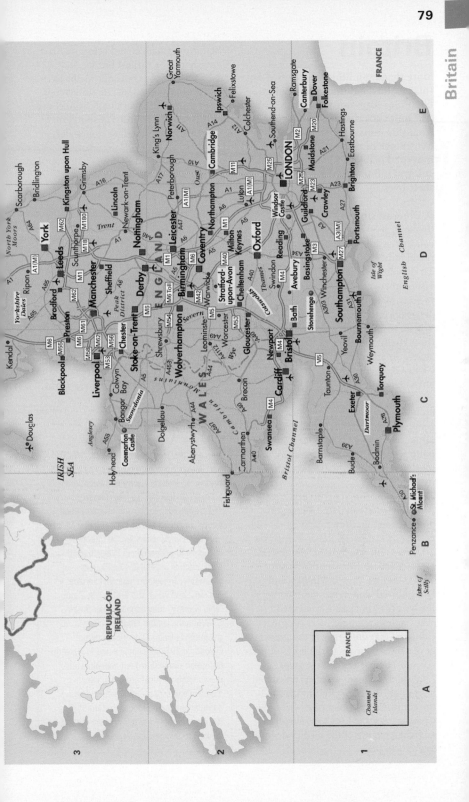

Britain

More than 65 million people live on this small island that spans only 600 miles from north to south and 275 miles at its widest point. But from this remarkable nation, a large percentage of the world's population inherited many of the linguistic and cultural influences that shaped their lives.

A Diverse Unity

England, Scotland and Wales – collectively known as Britain – each retain individual cultural characteristics. To complicate matters further for the visitor, there are distinct regions within regions, all reflecting the resilient and determined individuality that is typically British. If you spend any time traveling through Britain, you will find that the landscape and the customs of the people change dramatically, sometimes within only a few miles.

People have been arriving at all points around Britain's corrugated coastline for centuries, but London is now the focus of the country as a whole. Here history, politics and culture meet in one of the most invigorating and exciting cities in the world.

Beyond London lies provincial and rural England. You'll find a landscape of moors and meadows, hedgerows and woods, its earth relentlessly farmed for centuries. But much of the countryside has retained, in between the maze of roads and highways, a semblance of Old England, and in treasured corners the beauty of the past is preserved.

At Canterbury, in Kent, is the great cathedral that drew tens of thousands of medieval pilgrims to the relics of the revered Thomas Becket, the great English churchman who was murdered here in 1170. These pilgrims inspired the country's first great poet, Geoffrey Chaucer, to write his *Canterbury Tales*, as vivid a picture of the medieval world as you will find.

Yet before Chaucer and before Canterbury, the earliest Britons had raised their own pagan equivalents to the Christian cathedrals. At Stonehenge, and perhaps more hauntingly at Avebury in Wiltshire, in the heart of southern England, are the standing stones and burial chambers of Britons who commanded England centuries before Romans, Danes, Anglo-Saxons and Normans ever did.

Village Greens and Seaside

Throughout scores of picturesque villages in southern and western England, you will find the essence of the country; where people still play cricket on village greens, dance around maypoles on May Day and sell jars of local honey at village festivals – weather permitting, of course.

Yet England also boasts exciting cities and historic towns as well as great seaports such as Bristol and Portsmouth. The Georgian city of Bath, where warm

Britain Explained

The name "Britain" (or "Great Britain") refers to the countries of England, Scotland and Wales located on the main island of Britain. To include Northern Ireland, the correct name is the "United Kingdom." The United Kingdom is the official unified entity, governed by the central parliament in London and (nominally) by Queen Elizabeth II. Scotland and Wales have their own national assemblies and a degree of autonomy. Today, the legacy of London remains, and when the British talk about "this country" they usually mean Britain.

While the United Kingdom is geographically and historically part of Europe, in 2016 its people voted to leave the European Union (E.U.), an economic and increasingly political grouping, which includes some 28 member states. The political and legal process that the U.K. must go through in order to leave the E.U. is likely to take several years.

Stonehenge stone circle, on Salisbury Plain in Wiltshire, was built around 5,000 years ago

Cotswold stone and the elegance of 18th-century fashion conspired to create one of the world's most astounding cityscapes, seems consumed with golden light in the summer sun.

Miles of coastline fringe the English Channel. On the southern coast are the cliffs of Beachy Head, and famous resorts like Brighton and Bournemouth, as well as long stretches of undulating green and peaceful coast that run westward past Dorset's limestone cliffs and the rich red cliffs of Devon to the golden beaches of Cornwall.

From Oxford to the Lakes

North and west of London, in the counties of Oxfordshire and Warwickshire, are such cities as Oxford, university town par excellence (matched only by its rival Cambridge in the fen country of eastern England). Here, too, you will find the Cotswolds, with its honey-colored limestone villages and the historic town of Stratford-upon-Avon, birthplace of William Shakespeare.

Progress through the cultural heart of England is not an idyllic rural journey by any means. Yet the post-industrial cities of Manchester, Leeds, Birmingham and Liverpool are vibrant and exciting places, while historic cities such as Chester, on the Welsh border, and York in the east have managed to preserve their medieval townscapes.

Beyond the sprawling towns and cities large areas of an unspoiled England survive. Derbyshire's Peak District, the Yorkshire Dales, the exquisite Lake District of Cumbria and the lonely

---

More Top Destinations in Britain (see map pages 78–79)

- Avebury D2
- Caernarfon Castle C3
- Cambridge E2
- Canterbury E1
- Chester C3
- The Cotswolds D2
- Dartmoor C1
- Deeside C5
- Glen Coe C5
- Isle of Skye B6
- Lake District C4
- St. Andrews C5
- St. Michael's Mount B1
- Snowdonia C3
- Stonehenge D1
- Stratford-upon-Avon D2
- The Trossachs C5
- Windsor Castle D2
- York D3
- Yorkshire Dales D3

Urquhart Castle perches on the shores of the famous Loch Ness, near Inverness, in Scotland

heights of Northumberland appear like magic in the landscape.

Wild Wales

Wales is renowned as a land of poetry and song, and as a part of Britain that seems older than time. In the green borderlands, the ruined castles of Norman Britain survive, relics of a time when England failed to entirely subdue the Welsh communities. Strongholds of the Anglo-Norman conquerors, such as Caernarfon Castle, are reminders of a later age of determined feudalism. But in the beautiful countryside of central Wales, on the rugged west coast and in the great mountains of Snowdonia, the spirit of the ancient Welsh lives on, the powerful identity of modern Wales a token of that endurance.

North to the Highlands

North of Northumberland and Cumbria, the Southern Uplands guard Scotland's borderland, once infamous for its violent robber clans. It was this raw border country that gave courage to heroic Scottish patriots like Robert Bruce and William Wallace as they pitted themselves against England's might. And across these hills in 1745 marched Charles Edward Stuart – Bonnie Prince Charlie, the last of a moribund royal line – supported by the cream of the Highland clans in a doomed final gesture of defiance by Scotland against English domination.

North of the Southern Uplands are the Central Lowlands of Scotland, with the capital city of Edinburgh to the east and Glasgow, the great powerhouse of old industrial Scotland, to the west. Edinburgh is the historic distillation of all things Scottish, the political and cultural focus of the nation from a time when poet Robert Burns and novelist Sir Walter Scott graced fashionable 18th-century salons, to the vigorous and progressive Edinburgh International Festival of today.

Across the Forth river (Firth of Forth) from Edinburgh lies the region of Fife, often referred to as the "Kingdom of Fife," home to the university town and golfing mecca of St. Andrews. To the north and west are the Scottish Highlands, Britain's most dramatic landscape, and some of the last great wilderness areas of Europe.

At the edge of the Highlands are the Trossachs, Scotland's equivalent to England's Lake District, steeped in the history of real-life characters like Rob Roy Macgregor, inspiration for the classic novels of Sir Walter Scott. Farther north are the mountains of Aberdeenshire. Here, on Royal Deeside, sits Balmoral Castle, traditional summer retreat of the Queen and her family.

Scotland's most spectacular mountain country lies to the far west and north, at the Pass of Glen Coe, and then for more than 100 miles northward along the west coast to Kintail and Wester Ross. Out to sea lie the Isle of Skye and the misty Hebrides, romantic islands at Britain's far western edge.

Seeing the Country

Britain's essence lies in its diversity and in the hidden corners between the most popular places. Traveling independently by train or bus is one way to explore off the beaten track, but you will need to plan carefully. Britain's long-distance bus network is generally good, but away from major cities and main roads service can vary greatly. Organized bus tours, on the other hand, will whisk you efficiently to all the major tourist sights. Traveling by car is another option; Britain is so diverse that you can drive for a few hours on a main highway and then veer off onto quieter byways.

London is a year-round destination, but outside the main summer season and major vacation periods, Britain's hidden corners are quiet. May and June are good months to visit – the freshness of early June is invigorating in England's upland areas, northern Wales and the Scottish Highlands. Winter is quite another story, but even in December and January Britain's larger cities are vibrant; London, Manchester, Liverpool, Cardiff, Edinburgh and Glasgow all pulse with British fashion and style.

Great classical music can be savored year-round in London, Manchester and Edinburgh. Attend world-class theater in Cardiff and Glasgow. Outstanding choirs fill England's cathedrals with truly heavenly music, and the open-air performances by Welsh and Cornish choirs are enchanting. Enjoy folk music or a live rock band at a neighborhood pub, or discover a colorful local festival or time-honored custom in a Devonshire hamlet or Yorkshire town.

The Taste of Britain

The same variety applies to shopping. The British were dismissed by Napoleon as a "nation of shopkeepers," but the intended slight is actually a compliment. The British engaged in trade the world over, and today that spirit of enterprise, curiosity, good business sense and eclectic style is maintained. Fashion salons rival those in France and Italy. Britain has some of the finest antiques shops, art galleries and auction houses in Europe. Traditional and modern styles are blended to produce some colorful and out-of-the-ordinary clothing and craft items, and it is often in the provinces that the best examples are found.

Not so long ago, British food was seen as uninspired and overcooked. Today, British modern cuisine is exciting yet still essentially British, the ingredients fresh and flavorful. British beer and gin have rediscovered great traditions, too; every English region has a lively range of brewers and distillers. English wine also is well worth trying.

In Scotland, sample the best from the country's huge range of superb single malt whiskies.

Timeline

8000 BC	Mesolithic hunter-gatherers journey into southern Britain.
4000 BC	Neolithic people settle in southern Britain in the Stone Age.
circa 500 BC	Iron Age culture develops in Britain.
55–54 BC	Julius Caesar makes expeditions to Britain.
AD 43	Roman conquest of Britain begins, including a settlement of London.
circa 400	Roman army and administration withdraws from Britain.
1066	Battle of Hastings; Norman Conquest of Britain.
1314	Battle of Bannockburn, in which England suffers disastrous defeat at the hands of Scotland's Robert Bruce.
1534	Henry VIII appoints himself head of the Church in England; beginning of English Reformation.
1649	King Charles I executed; Commonwealth established until the restoration of the monarchy in 1660.
1707	Scotland and England unite by Act of Union.
1776	American colonies declare independence from Britain.
1815	Battle of Waterloo; Napoleon defeated by combined European force led by Duke of Wellington.
1914–18	Britain plays major part in World War I.
1939–44	World War II begins; Winston Churchill becomes Prime Minister of Britain; D-Day, Allied forces invade Normandy.
1945	War ends; Churchill loses in national elections.
1973	Britain joins European Economic Community, now known as the European Union.
1994	The Channel Tunnel opens.
2012	Britain hosts the Olympic Games and celebrates the Queen's Diamond Jubilee.
2013	The Duchess of Cambridge gives birth to a son, George.
September 2014	Scottish people vote "no" to independence in the historic Independence Referendum held on September 18.
2015	The Duchess of Cambridge gives birth to a daughter, Charlotte.
September 2015	Queen Elizabeth II becomes the longest reigning British monarch.
June 2016	Britain votes to leave the European Union – termed "Brexit."
2017	Formal negotiations begin for Brexit – set for March 2019.
2018	The Duchess of Cambridge gives birth to a second son, Louis. Prince Harry marries American actress Meghan Markle at Windsor Castle. The couple are entitled the Duke and Duchess of Sussex.

Protected by Sea

Britain's island location has protected it from invasion over the centuries. The country has experienced two definitive "invasions;" by the Romans in the first century AD and by the Normans in 1066. The Danes, or Vikings, steadily occupied eastern England during the ninth century but were later repulsed. The Anglo-Saxons did not invade in the sense of armed occupation, but by steady immigration and integration after Roman withdrawal left chaos within the country. In later centuries Britain developed a powerful military and naval force, and although constantly at war with various European powers during the medieval period was itself never invaded. In more recent times both Napoleon and Hitler tried and failed to conquer. The English Channel and the surrounding seas have been Britain's greatest strategic blessing.

Watch the Changing the Guard ceremony outside Buckingham Palace in London

Survival Guide

- If visiting London, try to see one of the city's pageants, such as Trooping the Colour on Queen Elizabeth II's "official" birthday in June, or the Lord Mayor's Show in November. For something far more informal, join the fun at the fantastic Notting Hill Carnival during the last weekend (Saturday to Monday) of August.
- In Bath, be careful where pedestrian zones end and traffic begins. As in all cities, watch out for pickpockets on crowded streets.
- Try Britain's various regional foods. The national dish – fish and chips – can be found almost anywhere. In London, seek out genuine East End whelks (chewy marine molluscs). In Cornwall, look for Cornish pasties (savory pastries), a true hand-held meal. In Wales, sample Caerphilly cheese; in Yorkshire, try roast beef and Yorkshire pudding; and don't miss steak-and-kidney pie in any English country pub. In Scotland, tackle haggis, tatties (potatoes) and neeps (turnips), or kippers (smoked herring) – all accompanied by a thick and creamy regional beer or a good strong cup of tea with milk.
- Be prepared for dramatic changes in the weather. They say that Britain has no climate, it just has weather. The truth is that the country is caught between the extremes of northern and southern Europe, while its island nature allows vast amounts of condensed Atlantic seawater to be deposited as wind-blown rain at regular intervals. Expect rain, and if it comes, enjoy it and carry on with your plans.
- Make sure you always know what county of England you are in, and try not to confuse counties, especially not Yorkshire and Lancashire. Never refer to Welsh or Scottish people as English.
- In southwest England especially, enjoy a cream tea. This grand traditional indulgence consists of a pot of tea and fresh scones (cakes) with jam and thick clotted cream. The elements of this treat are served separately; cut a scone in half and slather on the jam and cream.
- The strength of the summer sun can deceive, often because there are passing clouds. Guard against sunburn even if there is a breeze.

London

London is one of the world's great experiences, a city that is always exhilarating, sometimes bewildering, sometimes exhausting, but never disappointing. This political, financial and commercial center is a year-round tourist city. The excitement is palpable.

There is a feeling that something is always happening, that you are in one of a handful of truly great cities.

London needs to be taken very much on its own terms; if you do so, you will enjoy it. It is an expensive and sometimes stressful place; admission prices to major attractions are steep and the crowds of fellow visitors can be huge.

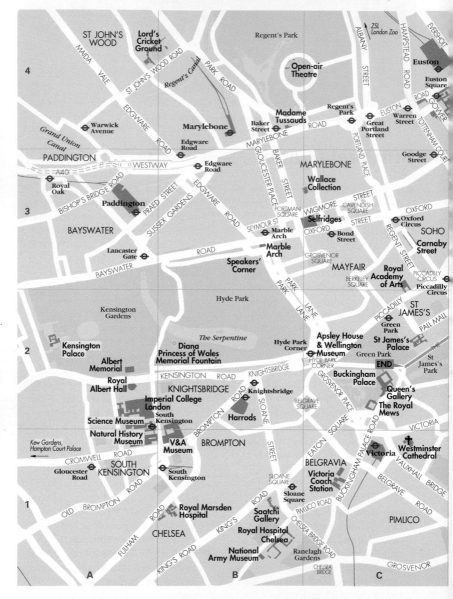

There are excellent guided tours, and bus tours are an easy way to sample all London (and beyond) has to offer. Exploring independently can be hugely rewarding, however, provided you plan well. Many attractions are some distance apart, and if you set out blindly determined to see everything you may end up frustrated and exhausted. Orient yourself by establishing two or three familiar focal points from which you can connect to other parts of the city.

Trafalgar Square to Big Ben

Trafalgar Square should be one of these focal points. It is the symbolic center of London; the towering pillar of Admiral Lord Nelson's column rises 169 feet into

the London sky. At the base of the column are fountains and monumental guardian lions. All around the central square a constant throng of people is besieged by fluttering pigeons. Trafalgar Square is overlooked from the north by the National Gallery. At the southwest corner of the square is Admiralty Arch, through which you reach The Mall and progress toward Buckingham Palace.

Whitehall, London's "political" street, runs due south from Trafalgar Square. You'll see such landmarks as the clock tower of the Palace of Westminster which contains the huge bell, Big Ben, as you walk past the Old Admiralty Building and the Horse Guards, where helmeted troopers in scarlet or blue sit immobile on their horses. Soon you pass the gates of Downing Street, where Britain's Prime Minister and Chancellor of the Exchequer have their homes. In the middle of Whitehall is The Cenotaph, a stark and simple memorial to the dead of two world wars. Beyond The Cenotaph, Whitehall merges with Parliament Street and then meets Bridge Street. To the left is Westminster Bridge and the River Thames; straight ahead are the Houses of Parliament and to the right is Westminster Abbey.

Piccadilly Circus to Covent Garden

Another focus of central London is busy Piccadilly Circus, with the elegantly poised statue of *Eros* at its center. You can reach Piccadilly from Trafalgar Square by walking along Pall Mall from in front of the National Gallery and then turning right up Haymarket. From Piccadilly you can plunge into London's world of great shopping. To the north lies Soho, the long-established heart of late-night London, slightly risqué but full of character. Here are some of the capital's best theaters, restaurants and cafés, offbeat and specialty stores, and a resident population that maintains a tradition of eccentricity, style and eclectic fashion. Soho spills eastward

through the small Chinatown area around Gerrard Street to reach Leicester Square, lined with movie theaters and restaurants. To the east, along Cranbourne and Garrick streets, is Covent Garden, a lively area with stores, cafés, restaurants and street entertainers.

Beyond the Center

Once familiar with central London, you can start to venture beyond the focal points. This is where the city's excellent subway network, the Underground or "Tube," comes in handy. Use of the subway does mean you lose some grip of how London lies above ground; sometimes it is more rewarding if you walk to your destination, and London buses also supply excellent service.

Head northeast from Trafalgar Square, by subway or on foot, along the Strand, Fleet Street and Ludgate Hill, to St. Paul's Cathedral. Then proceed east to the Tower of London and Tower Bridge. Or go west from Trafalgar Square, beyond Buckingham Palace, to the great green space of Hyde Park and exclusive Knightsbridge, where you will find Harrods department store and three great museums: the Victoria and Albert Museum, the Science Museum and the Natural History Museum.

Venture northwest for a stroll around Regent's Park, or continue on to ZSL London Zoo, still drawing crowds as it has done since it opened in 1847.

Crossrail

When it opened in 1863, London's Metropolitan railway was the world's first underground line, and the start of a complex transportation network beneath London's surface. The latest addition to this network is near completion: the Elizabeth line is part of Crossrail, the brand-new underground west–east rail link. It's a vast project, with new stations being built and some upscaling of older stations, as well as a designated fleet of high-tech trains. Some disruption to travel is likely until construction ends.

Essential Information

Tourist Information

Visit London www.visitlondon.com
Visit England
City Information Centre (CIC), St. Paul's
Churchyard, London EC4M 8BX
☎ 020 7332 3456; www.visitengland.com

Urban Transportation

The London Underground or "Tube" (subway) trains operate Mon.–Sat. 5 a.m.–12:30 a.m., Sun. 7 a.m.–12:30 a.m. (five Tube lines operate 24 hours Fri.–Sat.); Docklands Light Railway (DLR), connecting the Docklands (southeast London) with the Underground, runs Mon.–Sat. 5:30 a.m.–12:30 a.m., Sun. 7 a.m.–11:30 p.m. Services are every few minutes. The 11 Tube lines plus the DLR are named, color-coded and shown on maps divided into nine zones (Zone 1 is the central zone). Buy tickets from attended booths in some station entrance halls or from machines – contactless payment cards also are an option. For more than two trips, it is cheaper to buy a Travelcard or an Oyster card (an electronic smartcard) – both also are valid on suburban rail services and buses, and on Thames Clipper water buses. The subway symbol is a red circle crossed by a horizontal line. London's red buses cover central London and its suburbs and run from 5 a.m.–12:30 a.m.; many major routes operate 24 hours. London buses are cash free so you must have a valid ticket or Oyster card before you board a bus. For information on London's public transportation call Transport for London (TFL) ☎ 0343 222 1234 (24 hours daily); www.tfl. gov.uk. London's black cabs (various colors) are metered and can be flagged in the street or at designated taxi ranks.

Airport Information

London is served by two major airports; Heathrow (www.heathrow.com), 15 miles west of the city, and Gatwick (www.gatwickairport.com), 30 miles south. Rail services below operate Mon.–Sat. 5 a.m.–midnight, Sun. 6 a.m.–midnight; at night services will be less frequent. From Heathrow, the Heathrow Express (☎ 0345 600 1515; www.heathrowexpress.com) nonstop train goes to Paddington Station every 15 minutes; journey time is 15 minutes. The Heathrow Connect (☎ 0345 604 1515; www.heathrowconnect.com) makes the same journey every 30 minutes stopping at key stations en route; journey time around 35 minutes. The subway's Piccadilly line to central London departs every 5–10 minutes, Fri.–Sat. 24 hours, Mon.–Thu. 5 a.m.–11:45 p.m., Sun. 5:55 a.m.–11:28 p.m.; journey time is around an hour. National Express buses (www.nationalexpress.com) go to Victoria Coach Station, up to two buses an hour (but fewer overnight), travel time from 40 minutes. Taxis (expensive) are available 24 hours; travel time to central London is about an hour. From Gatwick, the Gatwick Express (☎ 0345 850 1530; www.gatwickexpress.com) and Southern trains (☎ 03451 272920; www.southernrailway.com) go to Victoria Station every 15–20 minutes; travel time 35 minutes. Thameslink trains (☎ 0345 026 4700; www.thameslinkrailway.com) go to four central London stations, including St. Pancras International, up to every 15 minutes; travel time is 30 minutes. National Express and EasyBus (www.easybus.com) buses go to Victoria Coach Station; travel time is around 90 minutes.

Climate – average highs and lows for the month

Jan.	Feb.	Mar.	Apr.	May	Jun.	Jul.	Aug.	Sep.	Oct.	Nov.	Dec.
6°C	6°C	10°C	13°C	16°C	20°C	21°C	21°C	18°C	14°C	10°C	7°C
43°F	43°F	50°F	55°F	61°F	68°F	70°F	70°F	64°F	57°F	50°F	45°F
2°C	2°C	3°C	5°C	8°C	11°C	13°C	13°C	11°C	7°C	5°C	3°C
36°F	36°F	37°F	41°F	46°F	52°F	55°F	55°F	52°F	45°F	41°F	37°F

London Sights

British Museum

The British Museum, founded in 1753, is a treasure house of global artifacts, many of them the riches of Britain's imperial past.

There are 8 million exhibits here, including the Parthenon Sculptures (Elgin Marbles), the fifth-century BC relief sculptures taken from the Parthenon in 1801, and still the subject of Greek demands for their return.

Other highlights are the Rosetta Stone, the key to the understanding of Egyptian hieroglyphics; the 2,000-year-old Lindow Man, whose preserved body was found in an English peat bog; the Mildenhall Treasure, a collection of Roman silver; and Anglo-Saxon artifacts from a ship burial discovered at Sutton Hoo on England's eastern coast during the outbreak of World War II. Don't miss the Egyptian Galleries, the finest collection outside Egypt itself.

The Queen Elizabeth II Great Court, enclosed by a massive glass roof, is the largest covered public square in Europe. It houses galleries, an education center, cafés, information desks and the fine Reading Room, resplendent in blue and gold. This is where Karl Marx wrote parts of *Das Kapital*.

➕ D3 ✉ Great Russell Street, WC1B 3DG ☎ 020 7323 8000; www.britishmuseum.org 🅚 Galleries: daily 10–5:30 (also selected galleries Fri. 5:30–8:30 p.m.). Great Court: Sat.–Thu. 9–6, Fri. 9–8:30 🯄 Holborn, Russell Square, Tottenham Court Road or Goodge Street 🚌 38, 59, 188 🍴 Restaurant and cafés 🅙 Free (also free tours); charge for special exhibitions ($$–$$$)

Houses of Parliament

The Houses of Parliament, also known as the Palace of Westminster, are mainly to be admired from the outside. The present building replaced an older palace dating from the 11th century. Most of this earlier building burned down in 1834. The structure's linear form is doubly enhanced by the vertical Elizabeth Tower which houses a giant bell called Big Ben.

Inside access is limited because it is the workplace of British government. You can attend debates in the House of Lords and House of Commons on a first-come-first-served basis; join the line for the "Strangers' Galleries" (public galleries) outside Cromwell Green Entrance. On Saturdays and during the Easter, summer and Christmas recesses, tours

The Houses of Parliament seen across the River Thames from the South Bank

of the Houses of Parliament are available to overseas visitors. Allow time for airport-style security checks. Advance reservations are recommended.
✚ D2 ✉ Parliament Square, SW1A 0AA ☎ 020 7219 3000; www.parliament.uk ◉ Public galleries Mon.– Thu. and some Fri. (times vary; phone for details), Sep. 15–late Jul. Closed 3 weeks at Christmas, 1 week in mid-Feb., 2 weeks at Easter and 1 week in late May; guided tours Sat. and during Easter, summer and Christmas recesses only 🚇 11, 24, 148, 159, 453 ⛴ Westminster Millennium Pier 🍴 Cafés nearby 🚇 Westminster 🎟 Free; tours $$$

Imperial War Museum

Two vast guns stand in front of the handsome Ionic portico of the Imperial War Museum, where the story of modern conflict is documented in a fascinating and varied collection. This includes more than 50 historic aircraft, tanks and other field weapons, some of which are displayed in the dramatic space of the atrium. The cruel lessons of conflict are not shirked, especially in the permanent exhibition on the Holocaust. Opened in 2014, the First World War Galleries are particularly evocative.

The museum was formerly the Bethlehem Royal Hospital, the notorious asylum for the insane that was known as "Bedlam."
✚ E1 ✉ Lambeth Road, SE1 6HZ ☎ 0207 416 5000; www.iwm.org.uk ◉ Daily 10–6 🚇 Elephant and Castle, Lambeth North or Waterloo 🚇 59, 148, 159, 188, 453 🍴 Café 🎟 Free; charge for some exhibitions

Kensington Palace

The traditional home of the Royal family from 1689, Kensington Palace was rebuilt and refurbished over the centuries by several monarchs. However, in 1837, Queen Victoria decided to make Buckingham Palace her London residence, and in 1898, she then opened the lavish Kensington Palace State Apartments to the public.

Kensington Palace rose to prominence once again when Prince Charles and Diana, Princess of Wales set up home there in 1981. Today, it is the official residence of many royals including the Duke and Duchess of Cambridge and their growing family, and newlyweds Prince Harry and Meghan Markle, the Duke and Duchess of Sussex.
✚ A2 ✉ Kensington Gardens, W8 4PX ☎ 020 3166 6000; www.hrp.org.uk ◉ Daily 10–6, Mar.–Oct.; 10–4, rest of year 🚇 Queensway or Notting Hill Gate 🚇 28, 52, 70, 328, 727, N28, N31 🍴 Café 🎟 $$$ ℹ Garden tours (free) in summer

Kew Gardens

A World Heritage Site, the Royal Botanic Gardens at Kew date from 1759 and represent one of the finest collections of plants in the world, all contained within a 300-acre site. The vast Temperate House contains plants from every continent, and the architectural wonders are just as fascinating. Highlights include the Palm House, a billowing pavilion in glass and wrought iron that is a classic expression of creative 19th-century design, and The Hive, a multisensory installation about bees.

Scattered throughout the gardens are such interesting buildings as a 10-story, 18th-century pagoda (closed to the public) and Kew Palace, used as a country retreat by George III. Also here is Queen Charlotte's Cottage, given by George III to his wife Charlotte and a superb example of "cottage ornée" style.
✚ Off map at A1 ✉ Kew Road, Kew TW9 3AE ☎ 020 8332 5655 (24-hour recorded information); www.kew.org ◉ Fri.–Sun. 10–8, Mon.–Thu. 10–7, May–Aug.; daily 10–7, Apr. and Sep.; daily 10–6, Oct. and Mar.; daily 10–5, Feb.; daily 10–4, Nov. and Jan.; daily 10–3:30, Dec. 🚇 Kew Gardens 🚇 65, 391 ⛴ Kew Pier (Apr.–Oct.) 🍴 Restaurants and cafés 🎟 $$$; Kew Palace: additional $$ (open Apr.–Sep. only) ℹ Kew Explorer land train tour ($). Guided and self-guiding walking tours

London Eye

Built as part of the city's millennial celebrations, the London Eye is a huge Ferris wheel-like structure. It rotates slowly (once every 30 minutes), giving visitors a bird's-eye view across London and up to 25 miles toward the horizon from within 32 glassed capsules. At 443 feet high, it is Europe's tallest cantilevered observation wheel.

➕ D2 ✉ Jubilee Gardens, South Bank, SE1 7PB ☎ 0333 321 2001; www.londoneye.com ◷ Daily 10–8:30, Jun.–Aug.; 11–6, rest of year (until 8:30 p.m. weekends and school vacations). Closed 2 weeks mid-Jan. 🚇 Waterloo 🚌 RV1, 59, 139, 188 🚢 London Eye Pier 💰 $$$ (includes 4D cinema experience)

Museum of London

This rewarding museum tells the story of London's history from prehistoric times to the present through set-piece galleries focusing on important periods.

The Roman section is superb; its reconstructed rooms, one with a fabulous mosaic floor, and its sculptures are not to be missed. Another highlight is the Lord Mayor's State Coach dating from the 1750s, a glittering golden extravaganza that is still used during the Lord Mayor's Show each November and for the coronation of a new sovereign.

The museum's second site, in Docklands, highlights London's growth as one of the world's great ports. Displays include the walk-through 19th-century "Sailortown" and a moving exhibition about slavery.

➕ E3 ✉ 150 London Wall, EC2Y 5HN; West India Quay, Canary Wharf, E14 4AL ☎ 020 7001 9844; www.museumoflondon.org.uk ◷ Daily 10–6; last admission at 5:40 p.m. 🚇 Barbican or St. Paul's; Canary Wharf for Docklands site 🚌 4, 8, 25, 100, 172, 242, 521 🍴 Cafés 💰 Free; charge for some exhibitions

National Gallery

London's National Gallery contains one of the finest collections of Western European art in the world. You may find most of the world here on a busy day, but "the National" seems able to absorb the crowds. The collection is displayed chronologically from 1250 to 1900. You will need a floor plan to navigate or join a free guided tour (daily 11:30 a.m. and 2:30 p.m., also Fri. 7 p.m.). Portable audio guides are available ($), with random-access commentaries about more than 1,200 paintings. They also can be used to follow a variety of thematic tours.

Among the highlights are: Leonardo da Vinci's *Virgin of the Rocks*; Sandro Botticelli's *Venus and Mars*; Titian's vivid and agile *Bacchus and Ariadne*; Jan van Eyck's *The Arnolfini Portrait*; Diego Velázquez's sensual *The Rokeby Venus*; Rembrandt's haunting *Self Portrait at the Age of 34*; Paul Cézanne's *Bathers*; and Vincent van Gogh's *Sunflowers*.

Head to Room 34, where you are surrounded by British paintings from the late 18th century to the early 19th century – the works of English masters such as Thomas Gainsborough, Sir Joshua Reynolds, George Stubbs and J. M. W. Turner.

➕ D3 ✉ Trafalgar Square, WC2N 5DN ☎ 020 7747 2885; www.nationalgallery.org.uk ◷ Daily 10–6 (Fri. to 9 p.m.) 🚇 Charing Cross, Embankment or Leicester Square 🚌 9, 11, 15, 23, 24, 139, 159, 453 🍴 Restaurant and cafés 💰 Free; charge for some temporary exhibitions

National Maritime Museum

A visit to the world's largest maritime museum offers insight into Britain's impressive past maritime expertise. The Nelson, Navy, Nation display celebrates the great admiral, with his bullet-pierced coat from the Battle of Trafalgar adding drama. In the superb glass-roofed Neptune Court is the gilded state barge created for Frederick, Prince of Wales in 1732. Themed galleries tell of early explorers, the age of ocean liners, lighthouses and Britain's historic maritime trade with Asia, Africa and the Americas. The restored *Cutty Sark* tea clipper ($$) lies close by, on King William Walk.

➕ Off map at F2 ✉ Park Row, Greenwich SE10 9NF ☎ 020 8312 6565; www.rmg.co.uk ◷ Daily 10–5, (to 6 p.m. during school vacations). Last admission 30 minutes before closing 🚇 Docklands Light Railway: Cutty Sark 🚌 177, 180, 188, 286, 386 🚢 Greenwich Pier 🍴 Restaurant and café 💰 Free; charge for special exhibitions

Covent Garden Through Time

London is an ever-changing city and, over the years, has evolved from surprising origins. A classic example of London's fascinating development is Covent Garden, today a lively and fashionable focus of entertainment, dining and shopping. The area gets its name from being the medieval-era "Garden of the Convent," when vegetables were grown here for the kitchens at Westminster Abbey.

During the 17th century it was laid out as the first and finest square in London, complete with the Church of St. Paul and arcaded houses. The architect was Inigo Jones, who planned it in Italianate style, with the square known as The Piazza. Then the owner of Covent Garden, the Earl of Bedford, decided to hold a market in the square. Commerce overcame culture; buildings were erected – first the older fruit and vegetable market and then the floral market. The Opera House is the third to be built on the site, after the previous two burnt down. It is now home to the Royal Opera and the Royal Ballet.

In 1974 the market moved to new premises in south London and the square's market halls were renovated and filled with new stores, cafés and restaurants that have transformed the old "Garden of the Convent" into a major leisure area.

From Covent Garden subway station, turn right and walk southeast, past the Cambridge Satchel Company store (renowned for its colorful, handmade leather satchels) on your right, into the heart of Covent Garden. This is a great place to browse and wander at your leisure. Fashion boutiques line the cobbled piazza, tastefully blending in with the Italianate architecture and elegant columns. Under the glass-and-iron roof of the renovated market building set in the middle of the square, you'll find stalls selling crafts, jewelry, different types of clothing and accessories. On the western side of the market, in front of St. Paul's Church, also known as the Actors' Church because of its long association with the acting profession, street performers often entertain the crowds with comedy or magic tricks, or you may see fire-eaters or even acrobats.

If you walk back toward the Covent Garden subway and head two blocks north, you will find yourself in the maze of small streets that intersect with Neal Street. Neal's Yard Dairy sells some of the best cheese in the country – it's all British or Irish made.

Covent Garden market extends across two levels, with stalls selling an eclectic mix of goods

The Millennium Bridge near St. Paul's Cathedral

Natural History Museum

The Natural History Museum shouldn't be missed and is a great favorite with children. The exhibitions display some fascinating specimens from the museum's incredible collection of more than 80 million items (not all on show), from the tiniest of preserved insects to the skeleton of a huge blue whale. The museum is divided into four zones (Blue, Green, Red and Orange). The Blue and Green zones cover life on Earth, the highlight of which is a huge, animatronic Tyrannosaurus rex, complete with smelly breath. The Red Zone deals with the world beneath our feet and is every bit as fascinating; the Orange Zone contains a wildlife garden. The Cadogan Gallery showcases a selection of 22 remarkable items spanning 4.5 billion years. At the state-of-the-art Darwin Centre visitors can share the experience of exploring the complex natural world.

🞡 A1 ✉ Cromwell Road, SW7 5BD (Blue, Green and Orange zones entrance), Exhibition Road (Red Zone entrance) ☎ 020 7942 5000; www.nhm.ac.uk
🕓 Daily 10–5:50. Last admission at 5:30 p.m.
🚇 South Kensington 🚌 14, 74 🍴 Restaurant and cafés 💷 Free; charge for special exhibitions

St. Paul's Cathedral

St. Paul's Cathedral is one of architect Sir Christopher Wren's greatest achievements, and is easily reached from the Tate Modern on the South Bank by a walk over the pedestrian Millennium Bridge. The twin towers and baroque elements of its facade and the crowning glory of its dome are still breathtaking. The bright interior is full of stately monuments, memorials and statues. You can descend to the crypt, where you will find the tomb of Sir Christopher Wren among others, or ascend heavenward up 528 steps, first to the famous Whispering Gallery, on to the Stone Gallery and then to the Golden Gallery for superb views over London. Choral Evensong is a daily service during school semester, featuring the famous choir (free).

🞡 E3 ✉ St. Paul's Churchyard, EC4M 8AD
☎ 020 7246 8357; www.stpauls.co.uk 🕓 Mon.–Sat. 8:30–4:30; closed during some services 🚇 St. Paul's
🚌 4, 11, 15, 23 🍴 Restaurant and café 💷 $$$
ℹ Guided tours (90 minutes) at 10, 11, 1 and 2, and multimedia guides (free); also shorter tours (15–20 minutes) throughout the day (free)

Science Museum

Every aspect of science and technology is covered in this vast collection, ranging from atoms to the *Apollo 10* command module. The museum's official guidebook will aid you around the seven floors, including the Information Age gallery and a state-of-the-art exhibit on Level 2 which is devoted to math. On display are George Stephenson's early locomotive, the *Rocket*, and Charles Babbage's enormous prototype computer. The huge Flight gallery contains ranks of aircraft, and in the Energy Hall great steam engines from the Industrial Revolution hiss and revolve. Many of the exhibits incorporate a hands-on element. Check for any special events on the day you visit. Wonderlab, on Level 3, is a complex of some 50 up-to-the-minute interactive scientific exhibits.

A2 ⊠ Exhibition Road, SW7 2DD ☎ 020 7942 4000; www.sciencemuseum.org.uk 🕐 Daily 10–6 (to 7 p.m. during school vacations) 🚇 South Kensington 🚌 14, 74 🍴 Cafés 🎫 Free; IMAX 3D cinema $$; flight simulators $; Wonderlab $$; charge for some exhibitions

Tate Britain

Tate Britain exhibits the world's greatest collection of British art, from 1545 to the present, in its chronological and thematic displays. Works by artists such as Barbara Hepworth, William Hogarth and David Hockney are on display.

The Turner Collection in the Clore Gallery includes oil paintings, sketches and watercolors by J. M. W. Turner.

D1 ⊠ Millbank, SW1P 4RG ☎ 020 7887 8888; www.tate.org.uk/visit/tate-britain 🕐 Daily 10–6. Last admission at 5:15 p.m. Selected Fri. 6–10 p.m. also 🚇 Pimlico 🚌 2, 36, 87, 88, 185, 436, C10 🛥 Tate Boat to Millbank Pier (from Tate Modern) 🍴 Restaurant and café 🎫 Free; charge for special exhibitions 🛈 Guided tours (free), talks and films

Tate Modern

Housed in the former Bankside Power Station, on the south bank of the River Thames, Britain's national museum of modern and contemporary art features an international collection from 1900 to the present, and draws around 5 million visitors each year. It includes works by major figures such as Salvador Dalí, Pablo Picasso, Henri Matisse, Edvard Munch, Piet Mondrian, Jackson Pollock, Andy Warhol and Roy Lichtenstein, as well as contemporary artists such as Damien Hirst. The collection is presented in themed groups rather than chronologically or by school. Often, controversial conceptual works and installations also are a feature.

You can reach Tate Modern from north of the Thames across the pedestrian-only Millennium Bridge. A fabulous new building, Switch House, to the south opened in 2016, extending the gallery further. From the roof terrace there are spectacular views of the London skyline.

E2 ⊠ Bankside, SE1 9TG ☎ 020 7887 8888; www.tate.org.uk/visit/tate-modern 🕐 Sun –Thu. 10–6, Fri.–Sat. 10–10. Last admission 45 minutes before closing 🚇 Southwark, Blackfriars or St. Paul's 🚌 RV1 🛥 Tate Boat to Bankside Pier (from Tate Britain) 🍴 Restaurant and café 🎫 Free; charge for special exhibitions $$$ 🛈 Guided tours (free), multimedia guides ($), events and talks

Tower of London

There are crowds of visitors at London's foremost historical sight most of the year, and you may find yourself being hurried through some of the sections – but it's worth it. Many of the nation's most daring personalities ended up here, as prisoners or as reluctant "guests," or, like Henry VIII's wives Anne Boleyn and Catherine Howard, on a final trip to the executioner's block. Tours conducted by the Yeoman Warders, or "Beefeaters," give an excellent introduction, after which you can wander at your own pace to see the Medieval Palace, White

The Tower of London was built in the 11th century

Tower, Bloody Tower, Traitors' Gate, the Jewel House (for the Crown Jewels), the Tower Ravens and the execution site at Tower Green.

✚ F3 ✉ Tower Hill, EC3N 4AB ☎ 020 3166 6000; www.hrp.org.uk/tower-of-london 🕐 Tue.–Sat. 9–5:30, Sun. and Mon. 10–5:30, Mar.–Oct.; Tue.–Sat. 9–4:30, Sun. and Mon. 10–4:30, rest of year. Last admission 30 minutes before closing 🚇 Tower Hill; DLR Tower Gateway 🚌 RV1, 15, 188 ⛴ Tower Pier 🍴 Restaurant and cafés 💷 $$$ (discount for online purchase) 🛈 Guided tours, every half hour, included in price of ticket; audio guide ($)

V&A Museum

The V&A is recognized as being the world's greatest repository of applied and decorative art, containing ravishing collections of jewelry, silverware, ironwork, glass, ceramics, textiles, costume and dress, furniture, sculpture, paintings, books, photographs and prints from all over the world.

The British Galleries (Levels 2 and 4), a chronological survey of British art and design from 1500 to 1900, are an attraction in themselves. The Medieval and Renaissance galleries alone are worth a whole day, and the Asia, Ceramics, Glass, Sculpture, Metalwork and Jewellery galleries, along with the superb art collection, are all worth seeing. The Fashion Collection (Level 1) is the biggest in the world, spanning from the 1750s to the present.

✚ B1 ✉ Cromwell Road, SW7 2RL ☎ 020 7942 2000; www.vam.ac.uk 🕐 Daily 10–5:45; selected galleries also Fri. 5:45–10 p.m. Last admission 15 minutes before closing 🚇 South Kensington 🚌 14, 74 🍴 Cafés 💷 Free; daily tours (free); charge for some exhibitions and events

View From The Shard

The coolest view over the city doesn't come cheap, but the experience of seeing London from 802 feet up, on the 72nd floor of Western Europe's highest building, is surely worth every penny.

Designed by Renzo Piano, the spectacular glass tower block dominates the skyline south of the Thames. There are viewing platforms on different levels, and the top one (level 72) is open-air. Security is strict, with airport-style scanners. Entry is by timed ticket, but stay as long as you like.

✚ F2 ✉ Railway Approach, SE1 9SG ☎ 0344 499 7222; www.theviewfromtheshard.com 🕐 Daily 10–10, Apr.–Oct.; Thu.–Sat 10–10, Sun.–Wed 10–7, rest of year. Last admission 90 minutes before closing 🚇 London Bridge 🚌 RV1, 43 🍴 Restaurants 💷 $$$ (buy e-tickets ahead online for discount and priority entry) 🛈 Children under 16 must be accompanied by an adult; audio guide (free)

Westminster Abbey

Westminster Abbey has been the ceremonial site of almost every British coronation, from William the Conqueror in 1066 to Queen Elizabeth II in 1953. Monarchs that are buried here include Elizabeth I and Mary, Queen of Scots. The abbey is full of monuments and memorials to famous people from Britain's history; in 2018, the ashes of renowned scientist, Stephen Hawking, were interred here. The Quire and Sanctuary are the ceremonial heart of the abbey, where Queen Elizabeth II was crowned and where Prince William married Katherine Middleton in 2011. The present abbey dates, in part, from the 13th century and is a powerful expression of English Gothic style.

Henry VII's chapel has a style of airy elegance that represents Gothic at its finest. Tiered sculptures line the walls, and there is exquisite fan vaulting in the roof. The Tomb of the Unknown Warrior is dedicated to the thousands of British servicemen killed in World War I. In the south transept is Poets' Corner, resting place of great writers including Geoffrey Chaucer and Alfred Tennyson.

✚ D2 ✉ Broad Sanctuary, SW1P 3PA ☎ 020 7222 5152; www.westminster-abbey.org 🕐 Mon.–Sat. 9:30–3:30. Last admission 1 hour before closing. Cloisters: daily 9:30–4:30. College Garden: Tue.–Thu. 10–4 🚇 Westminster or St. James's Park 🚌 11, 24, 148, 159, 453 🍴 Café 💷 Abbey $$$. Cloisters and College Garden free 🛈 Abbey tours ($); audio guide (free)

A Royal Stroll

Royal London begins at Admiralty Arch, at the southwest corner of Trafalgar Square. The arch dates from 1911 and was erected as part of a general celebration of Queen Victoria's life and reign. Beyond the arch is The Mall, a broad open avenue that runs southwest, directly toward Buckingham Palace. It was first laid out by Charles II in the 1660s as part of St. James's Park.

Keep to the sidewalk on the left of the avenue and you'll soon pass a statue of the seafarer Captain James Cook. St. James's Park spreads out to the left – a great sweep of open lawns, trees and gardens with a lake at its heart. The right (north) side of The Mall is lined with stately buildings. First is Carlton House Terrace, broken halfway by the Duke of York's Steps that lead up to the Duke of York's Column. At St. James's Palace, sentries guard the Tudor Tower. Next to the palace is Clarence House, the official London residence of the Prince of Wales and the Duchess of Cornwall. Five of the rooms are open to the public for guided tours Mon.–Fri. 10–4:30, Sat.–Sun. 10–5:30 in August (tickets must be reserved in advance; ☎ 0303 123 7303; www.royalcollection.org.uk; $$).

On your way to the large open area in front of Buckingham Palace is Lancaster House (now a government building). In front of the palace is the spectacular bronze and marble Victoria Monument, erected in 1911 and constructed with more than 2,300 tons of marble. The exuberant gilded bronze winged Victory crowns the monument.

Beyond the monument stands Buckingham Palace. The Royal Standard (the Queen's flag) flies when the Queen is in residence. Changing the Guard takes place daily at 11 a.m. from April through July and on alternate days the rest of the year (weather permitting).

Some 19 of Buckingham Palace's state rooms are open from late July through September (daily 9.30–7, late Jul.–Aug.; 9:30–6, Sep.) when the royal family is not in residence. Buy a ticket on the day of your visit ($$$), in advance at www.royalcollection.org.uk, or call ☎ 020 7766 7303.

The Royal Mews are worth a visit for their state carriages and splendid horses – the Ascot Landau royal carriage was used at the wedding in May 2018 of Prince Harry and Meghan Markle.

For the walking route, see the city map on pages 86–87.

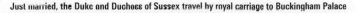

Just married, the Duke and Duchess of Sussex travel by royal carriage to Buckingham Palace

Edinburgh

Edinburgh is Scotland in microcosm. In this lively capital city, buildings do not overpower the spectacular landscape of hills and crags that march across the southeastern horizon. Yet Edinburgh's buildings – from the old houses of the Royal Mile to the elegant Georgian terraces and crescents of the New Town – are outstanding complements to the city's natural setting. Few other capitals seem to reflect the history and culture of their country so potently.

Edinburgh's famous castle sits high on a craggy promontory, Castle Rock, made inaccessible on three sides by steep cliffs and with a long descending ridge on its fourth side. The city's layout is linear, a pattern set by Castle Rock and Castle Ridge, down which the magnificent Royal Mile descends to the Palace of Holyroodhouse.

North of the Royal Mile lies a shallow valley once covered by swampy Nor' Loch, and now occupied by the lovely Princes Street Gardens, with Waverley Station, the city's main railroad station, at their eastern end. Above the gardens and to the north is Edinburgh's main thoroughfare, Princes Street, its south

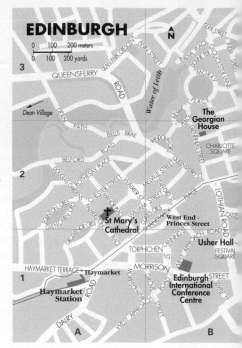

Greyfriars Bobby

This Skye terrier's devotion to his dead master is enshrined in Edinburgh folklore. The famous Greyfriars Bobby was a trained police dog who worked with his master, Constable John Gray, guarding livestock at Edinburgh's city market, the Grassmarket, during the 1850s. When Gray died at age 45 he was buried in Greyfriars churchyard, and his devoted terrier took up what began a 14-year vigil by his grave. Bobby was cared for and beloved by everyone in the neighborhood. A statue of Greyfriars Bobby stands at the intersection of Candlemaker Row and the George IV Bridge, near the church gate and opposite a pub named after the faithful dog.

side uncluttered by buildings and thus serving as a splendid place from which to view the castle and Old Edinburgh.

First Impressions

Many visitors arrive by train at Waverley Station. Perfectly located between the old town and modern Edinburgh, Waverley Station first opened in 1846, but then was rebuilt at the end of the 19th century. Some detail of the original structure can still be seen on the domed ceiling, which is adorned with cherubs amid the fine ironwork trusses.

From the station you emerge onto Waverley Bridge and get an immediate first impression of the city's visual drama. The castle and the dark soaring back walls of the buildings that enclose the Royal Mile rise to the south.

From the northern exit of the station, a stairway takes you to Princes Street. Here, the Scott Monument, a towering Gothic steeple, dominates one view while the bulk of The Balmoral Hotel, itself castle-like, dominates the other.

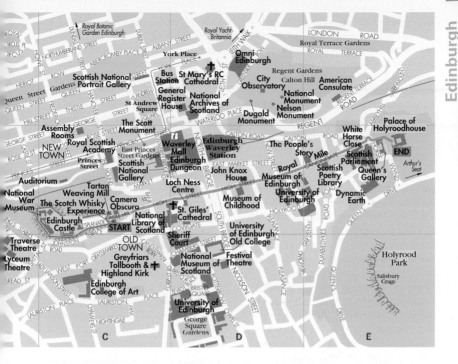

Up to the right looms Calton Hill, topped by neoclassical monuments.

From Waverley Bridge you can take an Edinburgh open-top bus tour that will introduce you to the city (Edinburgh Bus Tours, tel: 0131 220 0770; www.edinburghtour.com). You can find out about other guided tours from the Edinburgh and Scotland iCentre on Princes Street, close to Waverley Station. These include walking tours that take you through the Old Town's historic lanes and courtyards, and the entertaining ghost tours and murder and mystery walks around the city by Cadies and Witchery Tours (tel: 0131 225 6745 www.witcherytours.com).

Two Edinburghs

Exploring the city on your own is straightforward. Old Edinburgh is the southern part, encompassed by the castle and the Royal Mile; beyond them are the areas of Southside, the Grassmarket and Canongate. To the south of the Royal Mile you will find

the National Museum of Scotland (see page 102) and the Edinburgh Festival Theatre, a venue presenting fine drama, ballet and opera. Edinburgh Castle (see page 101) and the Royal Mile (see pages 104–105) are Old Edinburgh's main attractions.

You can easily spend an entire day here, and amid the souvenir shops and tourist spots there is a potent sense of history embodied by the splendid clutter of tall old sandstone buildings.

Also take time for a walk in Holyrood Park (see pages 101–102), a lovely green world of spectacular craggy hills, lochs and glens that is a genuine slice of Highland Scotland.

North of Waverley Bridge is Edinburgh's New Town, where Old Edinburgh expanded during the 18th century as part of a typically Georgian exercise in town planning. Above Princes Street is George Street, center of Scotland's financial district, with Charlotte Square and St. Andrew Square at either end. The elegance and unity of

Georgian architecture – an exhilarating contrast to the equally splendid Royal Mile – can be appreciated at such locations as Queen Street Gardens, the Royal Circus (a circular residential street), Great King Street and Drummond Place – all north of George Street – as well as around Moray Place, west of Queen Street Gardens.

Life in Edinburgh

George Street and Princes Street, and the short connecting streets between them, are Edinburgh's main shopping streets. On Princes Street you will find an Edinburgh institution, Jenners, a labyrinthine department store that sells luxury items and has a wonderful food hall. This street also has branches of Marks & Spencer as well as big-name brands like Gap. St. Andrew Square is the home of Harvey Nichols, the first Scottish outlet for the famous London store. For refreshment, visit Rose Street, which has more pubs than any other street in Scotland.

Edinburgh is crowded during the summer, but the cultural feast of the Edinburgh International Festival, spread over three busy weeks during August, is well worth taking in. There also are good alternatives outside the festival season – modern Scottish drama at the Traverse Theatre (www.traverse.co.uk), or musical performances at Usher Hall (www.usherhall.co.uk).

Stylish Edinburgh restaurants offer distinctive Scottish dishes such as wild salmon, Aberdeen Angus beef or game, such as grouse and venison.

Local residents are friendly and Scottish reticence is replaced here by a style that reflects sophistication without pretension, and by pride in the city's internationalism. And with a historic return to the Royal Mile by the Scottish Parliament, Edinburgh has renewed stature and optimism.

Essential Information

Tourist Information
Edinburgh and Scotland iCentre
3 Princes Street, EH2 2QP ☎ 0131 473 3868;
www.visitscotland.com
Edinburgh International Airport
International arrivals area

Urban Transportation
Waverley Station is on Princes Street (see National Rail Enquiries at www.nationalrail.co.uk). For bus information contact Lothian Buses City Centre Travelshops at Hanover Street or Waverley Bridge (☎ 0131 554 4494). For details of the city's tram system see www.edinburghtrams.com. Taxis can be hailed on the street, at Waverley Station or Waverley Bridge stands, or call Central Taxis (☎ 0131 229 2468; www.taxis-edinburgh.co.uk) or City Cabs (☎ 0131 228 1211; www.citycabs.co.uk).

Airport Information
Edinburgh Airport (www.edinburghairport.com) is 8 miles west of the city center. Airlink 100 buses go to Waverley Station every 10 minutes (20 minutes early morning), daily 4:30 a.m.–12:22 a.m.; travel time 30 minutes. Night Bus N22, departing every 30 minutes, operates daily 12:45 a.m.–4:15 a.m. The tram link to the city center runs 6:18 a.m.–10:48 p.m. and takes around 35 minutes.

Climate – average highs and lows for the month

Jan.	Feb.	Mar.	Apr.	May	Jun.	Jul.	Aug.	Sep.	Oct.	Nov.	Dec.
5°C	6°C	7°C	10°C	13°C	16°C	18°C	17°C	15°C	12°C	9°C	6°C
41°F	43°F	45°F	50°F	55°F	61°F	64°F	63°F	59°F	54°F	48°F	43°F
1°C	1°C	2°C	4°C	6°C	9°C	11°C	11°C	9°C	6°C	4°C	2°C
34°F	34°F	36°F	39°F	43°F	48°F	52°F	52°F	48°F	43°F	39°F	36°F

Edinburgh Sights

Key to symbols

➕ map coordinates refer to the Edinburgh map
on pages 98–99 🔲 admission charge: $$$ more
than £15, $$ £10–£15, $ less than £10
See page 5 for complete key to symbols

Edinburgh Castle

You can tackle Scotland's most visited attraction in several ways. There are official guided tours (included in admission), which are entertaining and informative, or a self-guiding audio tour ($) also is a good option.

You will need to brace yourself for the One O'Clock Gun, a 25-pounder that blasts off a single blank charge from the Half Moon Battery at 1 p.m. from Monday through Saturday.

Highlights of the castle are the tiny, 12th-century St. Margaret's Chapel (dedicated to Margaret, mother of David I); the Stone of Destiny; the Prisons of War exhibition in the Vaults; the mighty medieval siege gun, Mons Meg, which stands in grim splendor like some huge black beast; and the 16th-century Great Hall with its glorious hammerbeam roof and masses of weaponry. Take time also to see the interesting Honours of Scotland exhibition and Scotland's beautiful Crown Jewels.

➕ C2 🔲 Castlehill, EH1 2NG ☎ 0131 225 9846; www.edinburghcastle.gov.uk ⏰ Daily 9:30–6, Apr.–Sep.; 9:30–5, rest of year. Last admission 1 hour before closing 🚌 23, 27, 41, 42, 67 🍴 Cafés 🔲 $$$

ℹ The Royal Edinburgh Military Tattoo show takes place on the Castle esplanade every August. For more information see www.edintattoo.co.uk

The Georgian House

The Georgian House is the showplace of New Town's Charlotte Square and one of the most prestigious addresses in Scotland. Designed in 1791 by Robert Adam, this masterpiece of urban architecture was once home to the chief of the Lamont clan. Three floors are open, all full of 18th-century furnishings and beautiful paintings. The basement houses the wine cellar and kitchen.

➕ B2 🔲 7 Charlotte Square, EH2 4DR ☎ 0131 226 3318; www.nts.org.uk ⏰ Daily 10–5, Apr.–Oct.; 11–4 Mar. and Nov.; Thu.–Sun. 11–4, early to mid-Dec. Last admission 45 minutes before closing 🚌 3, 19, 41 🔲 $

Holyrood Park

Few cities are blessed with such a marvelous open space as Holyrood Park, or Queen's Park as it is also known. The park is dominated by the Salisbury Crags

Edinburgh Castle overlooks the city from atop the volcanic crag known as Castle Rock

The Royal Yacht *Britannia* remains a striking-looking vessel

and by Arthur's Seat, a high, rounded hill. You can enter the park from the bottom of the Royal Mile (see pages 104–105), just beyond the Palace of Holyroodhouse (see below). The high ground is encircled by a public road, the Queen's Drive, but the area is better enjoyed on foot. A slanting path slices up the slopes below Salisbury Crags, where the views are outstanding. Arthur's Seat can be climbed, but it is challenging. However, you can still enjoy the splendid sights if you keep to the low ground of the park.

🚹 E1 ✉ Queen's Drive, EH8 8HG ☎ Visitor center: 0131 557 4685; www.historicenvironment.scot 🚌 35 ♿ Free 🚹 Maps and exhibition at information center (open daily 9:30–3) by New Scottish Parliament

National Museum of Scotland
The National Museum of Scotland incorporates what used to be known as the Royal Museum in a bold space. The older part of the museum has retained its impressive Victorian ironwork Grand Gallery. In recent years, new galleries have opened up, showcasing design, fashion, science and technology.

Along with the dramatic modern buildings, in golden stone, the museum tells the story of Scotland from its geological beginnings to the 21st century, and the relationship between Scotland and the wider world. Historical highlights include the Lewis Chess Pieces and artifacts relating to Bonnie Prince Charlie and Robert Burns. The core of the complex contains several levels, each displaying a particular era

of Scotland's history. Pick up a copy of the floor plan from the information desk in the entrance hall. You also can check the plasma screens for information.

🚹 D1 ✉ Chambers Street, EH1 1JF ☎ 0300 123 6789; www.nms.ac.uk ⏰ Daily 10–5 🚌 23, 27, 41, 42, 67 🍴 Restaurant and cafés ♿ Free; charge for some exhibitions ($$$) 🚹 Free guided tours daily at 11 a.m., 1 and 3 p.m.

Palace of Holyroodhouse
Her Majesty Queen Elizabeth II's official residence in Scotland, Holyroodhouse was part of the Abbey of Holyrood, but much of the present palace was built during the reign of King Charles II. The severe neoclassicism of the courtyard block reflects the distinctly English fashion of the time; nevertheless it exudes Scottish history. The State Apartments are luxurious and grand, with artifacts and paintings elegantly displayed beneath superb stucco ceilings. Deep in the historic apartments is the bedchamber of Mary, Queen of Scots, and the adjoining closet where, in 1566, her secretary and confidante, David Rizzio, was stabbed to death by associates of the Queen's delinquent husband, Lord Darnley. The Queen's Gallery, in an adjacent building, has exhibitions of art from the Royal Collections. Behind the palace is Holyrood Park (see pages 101–102).

🚹 E2 ✉ Canongate, EH8 8DX ☎ 0303 123 7306; www.royalcollection.org.uk ⏰ Daily 9:30–6, Apr.–Oct.; 9:30–4:30, rest of year. Last admission 75 minutes before closing 🚌 35 🍴 Café ♿ $$ (includes audio tour) 🚹 Closed for state functions

Royal Botanic Garden Edinburgh

The Royal Botanic Garden Edinburgh is just a mile north of the New Town. Rhododendrons are the highlight here, at their colorful best from late April to early June. Other attractions are the glasshouses, where orchids and other exotics flourish, and the Chinese Hillside, a decidedly Scottish heath garden. The café's outdoor terrace has great views of the city.

Off map at C3 Inverleith Row, EH3 5LR 0131 248 2909; www.rbge.org.uk Daily 10–6, Mar.–Sep.; 10–5, Feb. and Oct.; 10–4, rest of year. Glasshouses: 10–5, Mar.–Sep.; 10–4, Feb. and Oct.; 10–3, rest of year. Last admission 30 minutes before closing 8, 23, 27 Restaurant and cafés Free. Glasshouses $ Guided tours Apr.–Oct. at 11 a.m. and 2 p.m. ($$)

Royal Yacht *Britannia*

See how the British royal family once traveled the world in this venerable queen of the seas, now permanently anchored in the harbor at Leith. The visitor center at Ocean Terminal will fill you in on the history of royal craft before you enter the historic ship itself, which was built in Scotland on the Clyde, and launched in 1953. It served as the ultimate floating royal residence for state occasions and holidays, before being decommissioned in 1997. Visit the State Apartments where celebrated guests were entertained, and the bedrooms where the Queen and her family resided. The other side of life onboard may be seen in the laundry and in the gleaming engine room.

Off map at D3 Ocean Terminal, Leith, EH6 6JJ 0131 555 5566; www.royalyachtbritannia.co.uk Daily 9:30–4:30, Apr.–Sep.; 9:30–4, Oct.; 10–3:30, Nov.–Mar. 11, 22 Café $$$ (includes self-guiding audio tour)

St. Giles' Cathedral

St. Giles' Cathedral (or the High Kirk of Edinburgh) is the mother church of Scottish Presbyterianism and a powerful feature of the Royal Mile (see pages 104–105). The Kirk is a mix of medieval Gothic and Georgian Gothic, the latter grafted on in the early 19th century; the interior reflects an enthusiastic Victorian restoration. There are some superb external features, including the 19th-century west door and the late medieval tower and spire. Inside, the cathedral has many fine features and memorials. The Thistle Chapel was built in 1911 as a private chapel for the Knights of the Most Ancient and Most Noble Order of the Thistle. Richly carved stonework enlivens the interior of the chapel. Look near the entrance door for the tiny bagpipe-playing angel.

D2 Royal Mile, EH1 1RE 0131 226 0674; www.stgilescathedral.org.uk Mon.–Fri. 9–7, Sat. 9–5, Sun. 1–5, Apr.–Oct.; Mon.–Sat. 9–5, Sun. 1–5, rest of year 23, 27, 41, 42 Café Free (donations requested) Rooftop tours ($$)

Scottish National Gallery

The Scottish National Gallery is a large, 19th-century neoclassical building with a good selection of works from the early Renaissance to the end of the 19th century, including Botticelli's *The Virgin Adoring the Sleeping Christ Child* and John Singer Sargent's *Lady Agnew of Lochnaw*. Most of the major names in 17th-century European art are represented; on display are landscapes by Claude Lorrain, and Nicholas Poussin's *Seven Sacraments*. There is a powerful work by Frederick Edwin Church, *Niagara Falls, from the American Side*. Scottish painting is well represented by Gavin Hamilton and Allan Ramsay. Sir Henry Raeburn's *The Reverend Dr. Robert Walker Skating on Duddingston Loch* and Alexander Carse's *The Penny Wedding* are lively and very typical Scottish narrative works.

C2 The Mound, EH2 2EL 0131 624 6200 or 0131 624 6336 (24-hour recorded information); www.nationalgalleries.org Daily 10–5 (also Thu. to 7 p.m.), Sep.–Jul.; daily 10–6 during Edinburgh Festival 23, 27, 41, 42 Restaurant and café Free; charge for some exhibitions The Gallery Bus links to the Scottish National Gallery of Modern Art ($)

Stroll Down the Royal Mile

Edinburgh's Royal Mile is the epitome of Old Edinburgh. Made up of four linked streets – Castlehill, Lawnmarket, High Street and Canongate – it descends the sloping back of a long, steep-sided ridge from Edinburgh Castle (see page 101) at the west end to the Palace of Holyroodhouse (see page 102) at the east end. On either side of the Royal Mile are tall buildings, riddled with courtyards and passageways known as "closes" and separated by narrow streets known as "wynds," all of it a delight to explore. All the way down the Royal Mile historic buildings punctuate the streetscape, and there are numerous stores, cafés, restaurants and pubs.

You can begin a relaxed descent of the Royal Mile from the entrance to the Castle Esplanade, starting with Castlehill. Attractions beckon from both sides. On the left is the Tartan Weaving Mill and Exhibition, with its masses of tartan cloth and working mill (free). On the right is the Scotch Whisky Experience, which offers a fun barrel-ride tour and tasting ($$). Next on the left and well worth a visit is the fascinating Camera Obscura and World of Illusions, where moving images of the surrounding area are projected onto a viewing table as part of five floors of fascinating optical illusions ($$$). The street is narrow here, but opens up just past the Highland Tolbooth, a handsome Gothic building with the tallest spire in Edinburgh. It is now The Hub, home of the Edinburgh International Festival and a focus of the city's cultural life. At this point, the Royal Mile becomes the much wider Lawnmarket, once the city's linen market.

Keep to the left side of the street, where steps rise from street level to the sidewalk. There are several stores here selling woolen and tartan goods. Soon you come to Gladstone's Land, a 17th-century merchant's house now restored by the National Trust for Scotland ($). The house's Painted Chamber is stunning. Just a bit farther is the entrance to Lady Stair's Close. A narrow alleyway leads to an open square and to Lady Stair's House, now The Writers' Museum (free), a quiet little corner housing memorabilia associated with Scotland's finest writers, including Robert Burns, Robert Louis Stevenson and Sir Walter Scott. The spiral stairs have an uneven step halfway up, a common trick in medieval houses aimed at tripping an intruder in the dark.

The Lawnmarket reaches an intersection with Bank Street and the street called George IV Bridge, where the Royal Mile becomes High Street. Here you will find a remarkable concentration of historic buildings. On the east

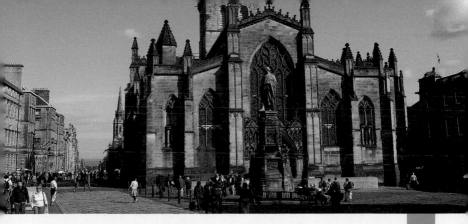

corner with Bank Street is the High Court, with a bronze statue of Scottish philosopher David Hume in front of it. Next to the High Court is Edinburgh City Chambers, with an arcaded entrance screen. Opposite is St. Giles' Cathedral (see page 103). Behind the cathedral is Parliament Square and the old Parliament House, seat of the Scottish Parliament until the union with England in 1707. Directly opposite St. Giles' is The Real Mary King's Close, a historically accurate interpretation of life in Edinburgh from the 16th to the 19th centuries ($$$).

High Street then descends gently to a junction with North and South Bridge streets. Stay on the north side of High Street, past the entrances to various alleys, and look for Chalmer's Close. Go through the entrance and down the steps to view the preserved apse of the 15th-century Trinity College Church.

On the other side of High Street, opposite Chalmer's Close, is the entertaining Museum of Childhood (free). Farther down High Street, just before an intersection is the John Knox House, a celebration of the 16th-century religious reformer who brought the Protestant Reformation to Scotland with more than a whiff of fire and brimstone. It is now part of the Scottish Storytelling Centre. Beyond Jeffrey Street the Royal Mile becomes Canongate and narrows once more.

Halfway down Canongate is the old Tolbooth, with its wonderful clock and conical-roofed towers. Canongate Tolbooth was once a courtroom and jail and is now The People's Story Museum, an exhibition of Edinburgh life (free). Just opposite is The Museum of Edinburgh, a beautifully restored late 16th-century building containing an excellent collection of artifacts of Edinburgh life (free).

Diagonally opposite the Museum of Edinburgh is the 17th-century Canongate Kirk and Kirkyard. The church has close royal connections; the royal family worship here when they are in residence at nearby Holyroodhouse, and the royal coat of arms can be seen decorating one of the church benches, or pews. Just past the church the Royal Mile passes The Scottish Parliament building to the right (free tours; see www.parliament.scot/visit-and-learn.aspx for details), and continues as Abbey Street to end at the gates of the Palace of Holyroodhouse (see page 102). For the walking route, see the city map on pages 98–99.

Above left to right: Lawnmarket is just one of the main streets linking with Edinburgh's Royal Mile; St. Giles' Cathedral, or the High Kirk (Church) of Edinburgh

Looking down onto the soaring spires of All Souls College from the Church of St. Mary the Virgin

Oxford

Oxford, 56 miles northwest of London, is a typical English market town at heart. It is located within a hollow amid low hills at the gentle confluence of the River Thames and River Cherwell.

What makes Oxford exceptional is its university, the oldest in the English-speaking world, an institution that consists of not one single campus but 38 independent colleges that are scattered throughout the city. They represent elegant seats of learning, but they also are blessed with beautiful, historic buildings.

The history of Oxford is said to have begun with the founding of a priory by the Saxon St. Frideswide, near where the River Thames and River Cherwell meet. Christ Church Cathedral supplanted the priory, and in time wealth from the medieval wool trade led to the founding of other religious houses, where learning was revered. Scholars were drawn to Oxford, and from these beginnings the university evolved.

Unless you're a student, Oxford is more of a journey through history and great architecture than through academia. For the visitor, the experience may seem faintly voyeuristic. You visit the colleges, picking your way through elegant quadrangles, chapels, arched passageways, gardens and libraries, and at times you may feel you are intruding on a select world of academic privilege and of cultural paradigms. Yet the physical integration of Oxford's colleges with the realities of Oxford as a city dispel any sense of intrusion. This is a living, working city that retains its own identity and commercial life.

Take a ride on an open-top bus to see the principal sights, leaving the bus where and when you like, or take a

The Original Alice

The children's books *Alice in Wonderland* and *Alice Through The Looking Glass* were inspired by Oxford life. Charles Lutwidge Dodgson, a writer, mathematician and ordained deacon at Christ Church, wrote the books during the latter part of the 19th century. Dodgson was the oldest of 11 children born to a clergyman father and he loved to entertain his siblings with stories and poems. He formed an intense friendship with Alice Liddell, the daughter of the Dean of Christ Church, and enjoyed entertaining her and her two sisters with his stories of Wonderland. Dodgson later published his stories under the pseudonym Lewis Carroll. Alice's Shop is where the real-life Alice bought her candy. It also sells Alice memorabilia.

✚ A1 ✉ 83 St. Aldates, OX1 1RA ☎ 01865 240338; www.aliceinwonderlandshop.com ⏲ Daily 9:30–6:30, Jul.–Aug.; 9:30–6, rest of year

guided walking tour of historic Oxford or of the colleges. Stroll by the Thames or take a river cruise.

Oxford's Colleges

You can walk around central Oxford in less than an hour, but it is the density and complexity of colleges and great buildings that is so absorbing. The heart of the university lies between High Street and Broad Street and is enclosed by the colleges of Brasenose, All Souls, Hertford and Exeter. The University Church of St. Mary the Virgin (see page 110) is on High Street. Behind St. Mary's is Radcliffe Square, which has the elegant 18th-century Renaissance rotunda of the Radcliffe Camera (chamber) at its heart. On the east side of the square is All Souls College. On the west side is Brasenose College, named after a traditional brass "mask" door

knocker and a treasured college possession; a replica can be seen on the great oak doors.

From Radcliffe Square you can walk into the Schools Quadrangle of the Bodleian Library, with its superb Jacobean entrance tower and decorative inner walls. Through the arch on the north side of the quadrangle is the Sheldonian Theatre, where the *Encaenia* (the ceremony to confer honorary degrees each June) and the degree ceremony for Oxford graduates are held.

The Radcliffe Square area is the heart of the university, but try to visit some of the colleges when their grounds are open to the public (get the free leaflet *Visiting the University of Oxford* from the Tourist Information Centre or check www.ox.ac.uk). Include Christ Church (see page 109), the largest and most famous of the colleges, and do not miss

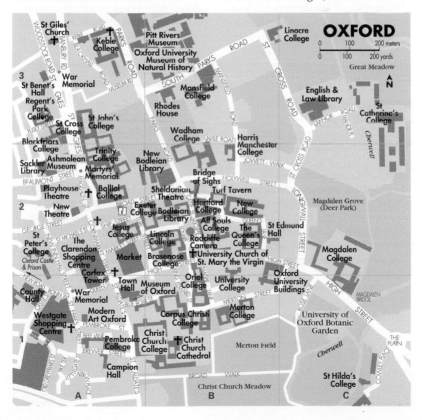

nearby Merton College ($), reputedly the oldest of them all and certainly one of the finest, with its delightful gardens, ancient quadrangle, medieval library and chapel. Adjoining Merton Street, cobbled and quiet, is one of the finest parts of the city. Merton counts among its alumni 14th-century religious reformer John Wycliffe, poet T. S. Eliot and actor-singer Kris Kristofferson. Then head east toward Magdalen (pronounced "Maudlin") and its superb tower, Cloister Quad, gardens and riverside walks ($). Magdalen alumni include playwright Oscar Wilde.

The Market Town

Oxford itself is famous for automobile manufacturing, and is the home of the Morris Oxford and the T-series MG sports car. They were produced at Oxford's Cowley factories, built up by William Richard Morris, later Viscount Nuffield, a self-made man who founded Oxford's Nuffield College among his numerous charitable acts. Visit the Museum of Oxford (see page 109) and discover the history of the city, and take in the Pitt Rivers Museum and the Oxford University Museum of Natural History (see page 110). Climb to the top of Carfax Tower for great views ($).

The streets radiating from Carfax constitute Oxford's main shopping area. Cornmarket has a range of well-known stores. Off Cornmarket's east side is Golden Cross, where Shakespeare's plays are said to have been performed. Just beyond is the celebrated covered market, with around 50 shops and outlets under one roof.

Oxford's university population and townspeople exhibit a fascinating contrast of lifestyles. In medieval times this duality led to occasional bloody battles, but although today's students are noted for their boisterous post-exam antics, Oxford is an eminently civilized place where the traditions of "town and gown" rest easily side by side.

Essential Information

Tourist Information
Tourist Information Centre
15–16 Broad Street, OX1 3AS ☎ 01865 686430; www.experienceoxfordshire.org

Urban Transportation
Oxford railroad station, Park End Street (☎ 03457 484950) offers regular train connections to and from London Paddington. Central Oxford is a 10-minute walk from the station. Local bus services in and around the city are frequent. Two companies provide all local services: The Oxford Bus Company (☎ 01865 785400; www.oxfordbus.co.uk)

and Stagecoach Oxford (☎ 01865 772250; www.stagecoachbus.com). Taxi stands are located at the railroad station, Carfax and the Gloucester Green bus station. Alternatively, try 001 Taxis (☎ 01865 240000).

Airport Information
The Airline buses (☎ 01865 785400; www. airline.oxfordbus.co,uk) depart every 20 or 30 minutes for London Heathrow Airport (every two hours at night), and every hour for London Gatwick Airport (every two hours at night). Birmingham Airport has daily rail (www. nationalrail.co.uk) connections with Oxford.

Climate – average highs and lows for the month

Jan.	Feb.	Mar.	Apr.	May	Jun.	Jul.	Aug.	Sep.	Oct.	Nov.	Dec.
7°C	7°C	10°C	13°C	16°C	16°C	21°C	18°C	18°C	14°C	10°C	8°C
45°F	45°F	50°F	55°F	61°F	61°F	70°F	64°F	64°F	57°F	50°F	46°F
3°C	3°C	4°C	5°C	8°C	10°C	13°C	13°C	11°C	8°C	6°C	4°C
37°F	37°F	39°F	41°F	46°F	50°F	55°F	55°F	52°F	46°F	43°F	39°F

Oxford Sights

> **Key to symbols**
> ✚ map coordinates refer to the Oxford map
> on page 107 💷 admission charge:
> \$\$\$ more than £15, \$\$ £10–£15, \$ less than £10
> See page 5 for complete key to symbols

Ashmolean Museum of Art and Archaeology

The Ashmolean is a fascinating museum of grand oddities and elegant art, housed in a neoclassical building dating from the 1840s. It is the oldest museum in Britain, founded in 1683, and its extensive collection includes much medieval material; Greek, Roman and Egyptian artifacts; and Asian porcelain.

Five floors of gallery space include the 2009 modern development that more than doubled the original space, around a central atrium and staircase. The state-of-the-art galleries of Ancient Egypt and Nubia, in which visitors are taken on a journey through 5,000 years of history, are just one highlight.
✚ A2 ✉ Beaumont Street, OX1 2PH ☎ 01865 278 000; www.ashmolean.org ◉ Tue.–Sun. and public holidays 10–5 (to 8 p.m. last Fri. of the month) 🚌 All city center buses 🍴 Restaurant and café 💷 Free; charge for some exhibitions

Christ Church College and Christ Church Cathedral

Oxford's largest college, Christ Church, is the most visited of all the university's colleges. It is recognizable to many as a location for the *Harry Potter* movies. Entry to Christ Church College is via the Meadow building, off St. Aldates.

Tom Quad is Christ Church's glorious central quadrangle; Mercury Pond, with Mercury Fountain at its center, adds an elegant accent. The figure of Mercury often sprouts neckties and other "outfits" donated by students. The entrance to Tom Quad and to Christ Church is the mighty gate tower, Tom Tower, that holds a massive seven-ton bell, Great Tom. Visit Christ Church's vaulted Great Hall, the Picture Gallery of Old Master works of art, and Canterbury and Peckwater quadrangles.

The present cathedral dates from the 12th century. Among its fine features are exquisite stained-glass windows.
✚ A1–B1 ✉ College and cathedral: St. Aldates, OX1 1DP. Picture Gallery, Canterbury Quad ☎ College and cathedral: 01865 276150. Picture Gallery: 01865 276172; www.chch.ox.ac.uk ◉ College and cathedral: Mon.–Sat. 10–5, Sun. 2–5, but phone ahead or check website as opening times are amended weekly. Picture Gallery: Mon.–Sat. 10:30–5, Sun. 2–5, Jul.–Sep.; Mon. and Wed.–Sat. 10:30–5, Sun. 2–5, Jun.; Mon. and Wed.–Sat. 10:30–1 and 2–4:30, Sun. 2–4:30, Oct.–May. Hall: Mon.–Fri. 10–12, 2–5, Sat.–Sun. 2–5 🚌 All city center buses 💷 College and cathedral \$; Picture Gallery \$ ℹ May close at short notice. Free gallery tours Mon. 2:30 p.m.

Museum of Oxford

The Museum of Oxford has well-arranged and interactive displays, and gives an excellent account of Oxford's history from prehistory through the Roman, Saxon and Norman periods to the present day. Highlights include Jan Wyck's painting of the Civil War *Siege of Oxford*, Alice Liddell's Red Cross medal (see page 106, panel) and a fascinating section of knucklebone pavement, once a common sight in the town. There is a program of changing exhibitions.
✚ A1 ✉ Town Hall, St. Aldates, OX1 1BX ☎ 01865 252334; www.oxford.gov.uk/museumofoxford ◉ Mon.–Sat. 10–5 🚌 All city center buses 💷 Free

Oxford Castle & Prison

Eleventh-century Oxford Castle, a place of incarceration for many souls from 1071 to 1996, was once as notorious as the German fortress of Colditz. Visitors can experience something of the austere confines of prison life over the centuries as people and events from the site's turbulent past are brought to life by costumed guides in character. Those who climb the 101 steps of the Saxon St. George's Tower (height restrictions apply) are rewarded with panoramic views of Oxford and beyond. The

19th-century wing of the prison has been converted to a hotel.
Off map at A2 44–46 Oxford Castle, OX1 1AY 01865 260666; www.oxfordcastleandprison.co.uk Daily 10–5 (last tour 4:20) 3, 5, 13, X3 Café $$ Opening times subject to change

Oxford University Museum of Natural History

This museum is housed in an Italianate-Gothic-style 19th-century building. The interior is a single open space, surrounded by an ambulatory and forested with slender iron columns that support a wrought-iron vault and glass roof. Exhibits range from dinosaur skeletons to minerals and fossils.

You can access the Pitt Rivers Museum from the rear of the building.
B3 Parks Road, OX1 3PW 01865 272950; www.oum.ox.ac.uk Daily 10–5 2, 7A, 27 Café Free

Pitt Rivers Museum

Founded in 1884, this fascinating museum is a marvelous example of 19th-century museum culture. It has a full program of changing exhibits and events, and houses more than half a million objects from many cultures around the world, including jewelry, pots, masks, boats, armor and weaponry, textiles, toys, and medical and musical instruments. The museum includes the often wildly eccentric collection of Lieutenant General Augustus Henry Lane Fox Pitt Rivers, who served throughout the British Empire and gathered many artifacts along the way.
B3 South Parks Road, OX1 3PP (enter through the Oxford University Museum of Natural History) 01865 270927; www.prm.ox.ac.uk Mon. noon–4:30, Tue.–Sun. 10–4:30 2 Free

University Church of St. Mary the Virgin

St. Mary the Virgin is both the parish church of Oxford and the university's church. It forms the southern side of Radcliffe Square. The early 14th-century tower rises above Oxford's dreaming

The splendid interior at the Pitt Rivers Museum

spires, domes and cupolas. The south porch, facing High Street, is a 17th-century addition that trumpeted Italian influence with its twisted columns and heavily decorated segmented arch.

For fantastic views over the city, climb up the tower's 127 steps as far as the base of the spire – there is a resting place halfway up, and it can be busy.
B2 High Street, OX1 4BJ 01865 279111; www.university-church.ox.ac.uk Daily 9–6, Jul.–Aug.; 9–5, rest of year. Tower: Mon.–Sat. from 9:30 a.m., Sun. from 11:30 a.m. All city center buses Café Church free; tower $

University of Oxford Botanic Garden

The University of Oxford Botanic Garden was founded as a "physic garden" in 1621 and is Britain's oldest botanic garden. This delightful enclave has a collection of around 5,000 plant species. The River Cherwell and Magdalen College's tower enhance the setting. There also are splendid greenhouses with 100-year-old cacti.
C1 Rose Lane, OX1 4AZ 01865 286690; www.botanic-garden.ox.ac.uk Daily 9–6, Jun.–Aug.; 9–5, Mar.–Apr. and Sep.–Oct.; 9–4, rest of year. Closed Mon. a.m. Sep.–May. Last admission 45 minutes before closing All city center buses $$ Guided tours ($$)

Shakespeare's Stratford-upon-Avon

Stratford-upon-Avon was the birthplace of William Shakespeare and today the town is something of a shrine to the poet-playwright, its numerous Tudor and Jacobean half-timbered houses enhancing the Shakespearean theme. Shakespeare's Birthplace on Henley Street has been restored with late 16th-century furnishings and is full of memorabilia. Another fine old building in the town is the Elizabethan Harvard House, which, although having no connection to Shakespeare, is interesting as the birthplace of John Harvard, who founded Harvard University in Massachusetts.

After an intriguing life, Shakespeare died in 1616 at the age of 52 in a house called New Place in Stratford. The original house no longer exists as it was demolished by the owner in 1759 because he found visitors a nuisance. The foundations remain and are adjoined by the Elizabethan-style Knott Garden and Nash's House, the superbly restored 17th-century home of Thomas Nash, husband of Shakespeare's granddaughter, Elizabeth Hall (admission with Birthplace Museum $$$).

Another famous Stratford building is the 13th-century Holy Trinity Church, where Shakespeare was baptized in 1564, located on the banks of the River Avon. Here you will see the remarkable alabaster bust of Shakespeare, modeled on a wax impression of the playwright's face at his death. Nearby is Shakespeare's tomb and those of his wife, Anne Hathaway, and their daughter, Suzanna. On the banks of the River Avon to the north of the church is the Royal Shakespeare Theatre, where the Royal Shakespeare Company performs the Bard's plays. Attending a performance here or at the more intimate Swan Theatre nearby is a highlight of any visit.

Arrange day trips to Stratford at the Oxford Tourist Information Centre.

Oxford Tourist Information Centre ✉ 15–16 Broad Street, Oxford OX1 3AS ☎ 01865 686430; www.experienceoxfordshire.org

Royal Shakespeare Theatre ✉ Waterside, CV37 6BB; www.rsc.org.uk 🛈 Theater tours ($)

Anne Hathaway's Cottage, just west of Stratford, was the childhood home of Shakespeare's wife

Bath

One of Britain's most delightful cities, Bath sits on the banks of the River Avon surrounded by the verdant, rolling countryside of the county of Somerset, 100 or so miles west of London.

With a population of only 88,000 this small city has a big reputation – recognized by UNESCO as a world heritage site for not just one but several criteria, Bath has a unique architectural heritage and authenticity, and a rich social history.

Nature's Bounty

If there's one feature that stands out above the rest as you wander around the city, it's Bath stone. A fine-grained, high-quality limestone which weathers to a golden hue, it's the unifying element that links the city's buildings throughout the ages. It is still quarried in the area.

Another welcome natural element that also comes from the ground is the city's famous hot spring. Gushing water at a constant temperature of 46 degrees Fahrenheit, the spring spews out 240,000 gallons each day. This natural wonder cemented the site of Bath as a sacred place from ancient times to today.

The Roman Era

Linked to *Londinium* (Roman London) along the Roman road known as the Devil's Highway, *Aquae Sulis* (Roman Bath) was a major settlement centered on worship of the goddess *Sulis Minerva* (the deity of healing and the spa). Her temple, built over the hot spring, was a place of worship, but pleasure has also played its part. Today, the temple forms the Roman Baths complex and is one of the country's finest ancient buildings.

Fashionable Bath: The Georgian Era

The hot springs played an important role in the renaissance of Bath during the Georgian period in the 1700s – so called because four kings named George came to the British throne in succession. The city received Royal patronage and became a social and cultural hub for the movers and shakers of the time, rivaling the country's capital, London.

During the Regency period (1811–1820) George III was deemed unfit, so his son, the Prince Regent ruled. The dashing, handsome and flamboyant Prince ushered in an era of style and an energy akin to the 20th-century Swinging 60s when socializing, fashion

The majestic Roman Baths attract visitors from across the globe

and modernism became major obsessions of the English upper classes. This also was the era of author Jane Austen (see page 117).

Money flowed and the city benefited from a building frenzy on a grand scale in the form of a planned town built of Bath stone – a series of interlinked streets, crescents and squares that you see today. Among the most beautiful and impressive are the Royal Crescent (see page 116) and The Circus, along with communal buildings such as the Assembly Rooms (see page 115) and the Sydney Hotel that houses the Holburne Museum (www.holburne.org). Standing alone, on the hill above the city, is the 120-foot-high Beckford's Tower, an eccentricity built by 18th-century landowner William Beckford.

21st-century Bath

But Bath is not just a historic relic of bygone days. The soothing waters remain a big draw today, and a modern spa complex, Thermae Bath Spa (www.thermaebathspa.com), can be found right in the heart of the city. The honey-hued Georgian buildings are no museum pieces either, preserved and sterile, but are still for the most part elegant, privately owned family homes brimming with life.

Commutable from London, Bath is once again a fashionable place to live for those who want to escape the capital, yet still yearn for culture and excitement. In the 21st century Bath is a vibrant and dynamic city full of excellent eateries, and is a good place to shop for one-of-a-kind items and antiques.

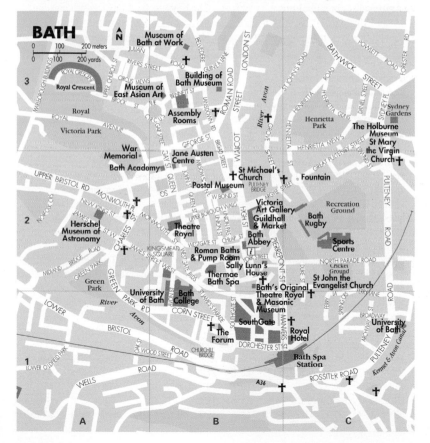

Visitors are happily welcomed and well-catered for, with small hotels, luxurious B&B's and numerous tea shops and cafés.

It's a compact city and you'll get immense pleasure from simply strolling the streets. It's easy to meander between tightly packed attractions, including the Beazer Maze. Alternatively, contact the Bath Information Office (see Essential Information panel, below) for details of guided walking tours of the city, or ask about audio-guided walks or cycle rides along the Kennet and Avon Canal which flows gently through Bath and beyond.

Bath's museums are well presented and informative. There's a full program of arts events and festivals throughout the year. And, if you have the chance to take a trip beyond the city, the surrounding countryside is breathtaking.

The Bath Bun

When is a bun not a bun? The answer is when it's a Bath Bun. The city is famed for this culinary creation, but there's a debate about what one should look and taste like. The story goes that in 1680 a young French Huguenot girl newly arrived in Bath started work in a bakery. Colleagues could not pronounce her French name – Solange Luyon – so she became known as Sally Lunn. Using her French baking skills, Sally created a light, sweet, brioche-like bun – an instant hit with fashionable society.

Later, during the Great Exhibition in London (1851), Bath Buns were served, but the need to mass produce them at a reasonable price caused changes to the Sally Lunn recipe to produce a smaller, sweeter and more doughy bun. Equally popular today, this bun is known as the London Bath Bun.

Essential Information

Tourist Information
Visit Bath Information Office
Bridgewater House, 2 Terrace Walk, Bath BA1 1LN ☎ 01225 614420; www.visitbath.co.uk; Mon.–Sat. 9:30–5:30, Sun. 10–4

Urban Transportation
Bath railroad station, Dorchester Street, Bath Spa, BA1 1SU (☎ 03457 484 950). Great Western Railways run frequent daily trains from Bath to London Paddington. First Group bus company (www.firstgroup.com) runs services to and from the city, around downtown and in the surrounding areas. A pack of five short zone tickets costs £7.50. Bath city center is easy to navigate on foot but several city sightseeing buses, including Bath Bus Company (www.bathbuscompany.com),

link the major sights. There are taxi stands at the railroad and bus stations. Abbey Taxis (☎ 01225 444 444; www.abbeytaxis.co.uk) have been in business in the area for more than 40 years.

Airport Information
International arrivals will land at the major London Airports. There are direct bus services from Bath to Heathrow Airport and Gatwick Airport run by Megabus (☎ 0900 1600 900 ticketline; 0141 352 4444 enquiries; www.megabus.com), journey time approximately 2 hours. Trains from London to Bath depart from London Paddington Station (www.gwr.com). There are trains on average every 30 minutes during the day, journey time 90 minutes.

Climate – average highs and lows for the month

Jan.	Feb.	Mar.	Apr.	May	Jun.	Jul.	Aug.	Sep.	Oct.	Nov.	Dec.
6°C	6°C	10°C	13°C	16°C	20°C	21°C	21°C	18°C	14°C	10°C	7°C
43°F	43°F	50°F	55°F	61°F	68°F	70°F	70°F	64°F	57°F	50°F	45°F
2°C	2°C	3°C	5°C	8°C	11°C	13°C	13°C	11°C	7°C	5°C	3°C
36°F	36°F	37°F	41°F	46°F	52°F	55°F	55°F	52°F	45°F	41°F	37°F

Bath Sights

The Assembly Rooms are built of mellow Bath stone

Assembly Rooms

Designed by John Wood the Younger
and completed in 1771, the Assembly
Rooms are the epitome of Georgian
architectural style. Described as "the
most noble and elegant of any in the
kingdom" they were at the center of
social life in the late 18th century and
used for the "assembly," an organized
form of socializing that was fashionable
at the time and described as "a stated
and general meeting of the polite
persons of both sexes for the sake of
conversation, gallantry, news and play."
Each of the four rooms had a purpose
– The Great Octagon (originally built for
card games), Tea Room, Ball Room and
the Card Room (added in 1777 to give
the card players more privacy). The
Assembly Rooms were restored to their
original style in the 1970s.

The Fashion Museum (www.
fashionmuseum.co.uk) on the lower
ground floor is a collection of historic
and contemporary dress, described by
CNN as being one of the top ten fashion
museums in the wold.

➕ 113 B3 ✉ Bennett Street, BA1 2QH ☎ 01225
477173; www.nationaltrust.org.uk 🕐 Daily 10–6,
Apr.–Oct., 10–5, rest of year. Last admission 1 hour
before closing 🚌 6, 6a, 7 🍴 Café 💷 Free. Fashion
Museum $$

Bath Abbey

The Abbey Church of St. Peter and
St. Paul is an impressive structure that
once stood at the heart of a wealthy
Benedictine monastery. There were
earlier places of worship on site, but the
present church was started in around
1499. Although not finished, the

building was badly damaged when King
Henry VIII dissolved the monasteries in
1539. The order handed the site over to
the British Crown and Queen Elizabeth
I, daughter of Henry VIII, paid for
restoration work to allow worship again.
In 1833 it was discovered that the
weight of the clock was causing
significant damage to the tower, so
architect George Manners was
commissioned to solve the problem. He
made a number of structural changes to
the building which included adding the
ornate parapets and buttress pinnacles
form such an important element of the
external decoration.

In the 1860s, George Gilbert Scott was
commissioned to renovate the interiors
whereupon he added several impressive
features including the fan-vaulted ceiling
in the chancel and the stained glass of
the Great East Window.

➕ 113 B2 ✉ 11a York Street, BA1 1LY ☎ 01225
422462; www.bathabbey.org 🕐 Sat. 9–6, Mon.
9:30–5:30, Tue –Fri. 9–5, Sun. 1–2:30 and 4:30–6
🚌 3, 4 🍴 Cafés nearby 💷 Free; donations welcome

Jane Austen Centre

In 1801, at the age of 25, the beloved
English author Jane Austen moved with
her family to Bath, where they lived for
five years. The informative Jane Austen
Centre in the city tells the story of the
author and the Regency era in which
she lived.

Knowledgeable costumed guides bring
the history to life, while a specially
commissioned waxwork figure of the
author, using accurate anatomical

information, presides over the bustle of local and international visitors.

➕ 113 B2 ✉ 40 Gay Street, BA1 3JN ☎ 01225 443000; www.janeausten.co.uk 🕐 Daily 9:45–5:30 🚌 No public transportation 🍴 Café 💲 $$ ℹ Walking tours available (free). Visitors can dress in the elegant Regency costumes fashionable at the time

Pulteney Bridge and Weir span the River Avon

Museum of Bath at Work

At the former Camden Works, this fascinating museum explores 2,000 years of Bath's industrial and commercial history and heritage, and the factors that helped these developments. There are galleries dedicated to an exploration of Bath stone, Bath Buns and what makes modern Bath such a successful city.

➕ 113 B3 ✉ Julian Road, BA1 2RH ☎ 01225 318348; www.bath-at-work.org.uk 🕐 Daily 10:30–5, late Mar.–Oct.; Sat.–Sun. 10:30–5, rest of year 🚌 6, 6a, 7, 8 🍴 Café 💲 $

Pulteney Bridge

The River Avon winds its way through Bath, and the city has developed and expanded along its shores. The city's most beautiful crossing point is Pulteney Bridge, which was designed by architect Robert Adam in Palladian style and completed in 1774. The bridge was commissioned and paid for by the aristocratic Pulteney family in order to create a link between the city and their lands on the far side of the river.

➕ 113 B2 ✉ Bridge Street, BA2 4AT 🚌 3, 4 💲 Free

Roman Baths

At the heart of Roman Bath was a sacred temple and the architecturally striking baths. The temple has not survived, but the Bath House, built for public bathing, is well preserved. The Great Bath at the center of the complex is still filled with natural, hot spring water. One of the finest Roman structures in Britain, it is 5.2 feet deep and is lead lined. The iconic columned hall above it once rose to 131 feet in height.

Finds from the Roman Baths include thousands of coins thrown into the ancient springs, pans used to make offerings of holy water and also curses thrown into the water to entreat the goddess to take revenge for injustices. Costumed actors roam the complex, adding character and energy to any visit.

The Pump Room restaurant (see page 470) within the complex is an elegant place for a daytime pitstop.

➕ 113 B2 ✉ Abbey Church Yard, BA1 1LZ ☎ 01225 477785; www.nationaltrust.org.uk 🕐 Daily 9 a.m.–10 p.m., mid-Jun. to Aug.; 9–6, Mar. to mid-Jun. and Sep.–Oct.; 9:30–6, rest of year 🚌 3, 4 🍴 Restaurant and café 💲 $$$ ℹ Audio guide (free)

Royal Crescent

Considered to be one of the finest architectural ensembles of any era in Britain, the 30 houses along Royal Crescent were designed by architect John Wood the Younger and built in the highly fashionable Palladian style (named after the Italian architect Andrea Palladio). Construction began in 1767, and on completion the houses were inhabited by Bath's most elite and fashionable residents. The exteriors have changed little since that time.

No. 1 Royal Crescent, whose foundation stone was the first to be laid, is now a museum and has been restored to the finest Regency style both inside and out. Each room in the house is furnished in period style, down to the smallest detail. In the Lady's Bedroom look for the little lapdog dog that would have been a companion for the mistress of the house, and the wig scratcher that was needed when the itching of head lice became too much to bear.

➕ 113 A3

Museum ✉ 1 Royal Crescent, BA1 2LR ☎ 01225 428126; www.no1royalcrescent.org.uk 🕐 Daily 10–5 🚌 No public transportation 💲 $

Jane Austen

Jane Austen is one of the world's best-known authors. Her works are international best sellers and film adaptations of her novels have raised her profile to stratospheric levels.

In her homeland of Britan she holds a special place in people's hearts. In 2002, on a national TV show, the British public voted her No. 70 in the 100 Greatest Britons, and she was chosen to feature on the redesigned £10 note which was introduced in 2017.

Jane was born in 1775, the seventh child and second daughter of an Oxford University-educated rector father. The Austen children were encouraged to learn and to be creative with words in stories and plays which they shared and performed in the family home.

At the age of seven, Jane was sent to boarding school with her beloved sister, Cassandra, but they were forced to return home after contracting typhus. Both the girls' schooling then ended because of lack of funds.

At age 25, Austen moved to Bath with her mother, father and sister but the death of her father in 1805 forced the family to uproot yet again, finally settling in Chawton, Hampshire. It was at this time that Jane began writing the novels which would become her lasting legacy.

Her brother helped secure a publisher and her books began to be published during her lifetime, though initially anonymously. The novel *Sense and Sensibility* was her first, published in 1811, followed by *Pride and Prejudice* in 1813, *Mansfield Park* in 1814, then *Emma* in 1816. *Northanger Abbey* and *Persuasion* – novels based in Bath – were both published in 1818, the year after her death. Her novels were re-published as a set in 1833, and this kick-started the rise to the author's global fame.

Jane's books continue to delight and fascinate us. Why? Perhaps because these well-written stories full of observations about life and society in the 1800s tell us much about a universal human nature that we can all identify with. Bath's Jane Austen Centre (see page 115) is a mine of Austen information.

The Jane Austen Centre is dedicated to one of England's most beloved authors

Czech Republic

Introduction and Map 120

Timeline 122

Survival Guide 123

Prague 124

Feature: Kafka 128

Feature: Excursion to Kutná Hora 131

Hotels and Restaurants 470

Essential Information 506

Opposite: The Astronomical Clock in Prague was installed in the 15th century

Czech Republic

Since November 1989, the people of this landlocked country have been embracing change and finding their footing as a new republic. In that year, the Velvet Revolution saw Czechoslovakia throw out 40 years of Communist rule without firing a shot. In 1993, Czechs and Slovaks amicably split into the Czech Republic and Slovakia. Today, the Czech Republic is a successful member of the European Union.

Bohemia and Moravia

Most visitors head straight for Prague, but there is plenty to enjoy in the country's diverse landscapes. Locked between Poland, Germany, Slovakia and Austria, the republic takes in two regions: Bohemia, surrounded by mountains, and the easterly highlands of Moravia. Both regions are filled with historical and cultural wonders, and boast areas of extreme natural beauty. Bohemia is considered beer country, while Moravians tend to favor wine.

In southern Bohemia, such medieval towns as České Budějovice (home of Budějovický Budvar or Budweiser beer) and Český Krumlov, with its 13th-century castle (one of Europe's largest), recall a time when kings and nobles were eager to build in one of Europe's richest regions. To the west are spa towns, best known by their German names: Franzenbad (Františkovy Lázně), Karlsbad (Karlovy Vary) and Marienbad (Mariánské Lázně).

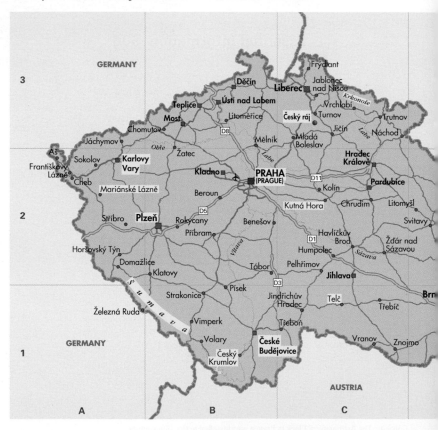

In Moravia, wedged between the western uplands and the eastern White Carpathian mountains, the city of Brno gives access to the Punkevní jeskyně (Punkva Caves).

Czech Culture

Despite the hijacking of the term "bohemian" by the West to mean "unconventional," the Czechs are generally rather reserved. Beyond this, though, is a friendliness and genuine interest in other cultures. Young Czechs often speak English, and are tuned in to Anglo-American pop culture. Love of arts and literature is also widespread. The late Václav Havel, the first post-Communist president, was better known among Czechs as a playwright.

Music has a special place in Czech life, too – from oompah-style brass bands to

A lovely way to explore Old Town Square in Prague

the classical tradition that produced such composers as Antonín Dvořák and Bedřich Smetana.

Generally speaking, most people who travel around the Czech Republic will be struck by the diversity of this small nation. As the republic embraces tourism, facilities for visitors continue to improve.

CZECH REPUBLIC

| 0 | 20 | 40 | 60 | 80km |
| 0 | 10 | 20 | 30 | 40 | 50 miles |

POLAND

↑
N

Jeseník
Krnov
Šumperk
Opava
Ostrava
Karviná
Sternberk
Frýdek-Místek
Olomouc
Nový Jičín
Punkevní jeskyně
Valašské Meziříčí
Vsetín
Vyškov
Kroměříž
Zlín
Slavkov u Brna
Uherské Hradiště
Hodonín
Mikulov
Břeclav
SLOVAKIA

D   E

More Top Destinations in the Czech Republic

- České Budějovice B1
- Český Krumlov B1
- Český ráj C3
- Karlovy Vary A2
- Krkonoše C3
- Mariánské Lázně A2
- Olomouc D2
- Plzeň B2
- Punkevní jeskyně D2
- Šumava A1–B1
- Telč C1

Timeline

AD **872**	The Přemysl Dynasty begins its 421-year rule of Bohemia.
929	"Good" King Wenceslas is assassinated by his brother, Boleslav, and made the country's patron saint.
1346	Devout Charles IV, Holy Roman Emperor, is crowned king of Bohemia and ushers in its Golden Age.
1415	Religious reformer Jan Hus is burned at the stake in Constance; four years later, in Prague, his supporters throw Catholic councillors from town hall windows and start the Hussite Wars.
1583	Emperor Rudolph I temporarily moves the seat of the Habsburg Empire from Vienna to Prague.
1620	Battle of White Mountain. Bohemia's Protestants are defeated and the Czech lands are formally annexed by the Austrian Habsburgs.
1848	The Habsburgs suppress an uprising of Czech nationalism.
1914	Czechs are forced to fight for Austria–Hungary in World War I, but thousands desert to the Russians.
1918	With the defeat of Austria–Hungary, the new state of Czechoslovakia is proclaimed.
1938	Czechoslovakia is forced to hand over the Sudetenland to Hitler. The country is occupied by Germany the following year.
1945	Slovakia and the Czech lands are liberated by the Red Army and the United States; the Communist Party seizes power in 1948.
1968	The First Secretary, Alexander Dubček, introduces "socialism with a human face" in the reforms of the "Prague Spring;" in August, Soviet troops invade Czechoslovakia.
1989	"Velvet Revolution;" Václav Havel becomes president of Czechoslovakia.
1993	Czechoslovakia splits into the Czech and Slovak republics.
1999	Czech Republic becomes a NATO member.
2004	Czech Republic joins the European Union.
2011	Václav Havel, former president, dies.
2013	The country holds its first direct, popular vote for the presidency, resulting in the election of Miloš Zeman.
2018	Zeman is re-elected as President of the Czech Republic to serve a second five-year term in office.

The Velvet Revolution

On November 17, 1989, a week after the fall of the Berlin Wall, there was an officially sanctioned demonstration in Prague to mark the 50th anniversary of the Nazi suppression of Czech universities. It soon turned into a protest march against the Communist authorities, and was forcefully put down by riot police. A rumor began that the police had killed one demonstrator. In fact, it wasn't true, but the story was enough to fuel public anger. People poured into the streets night after night, watched by television viewers across the world. Former leader Alexander Dubček was brought back from obscurity in Bratislava to address the crowds. Human rights activist and writer Václav Havel headed a newly established Civic Forum, and on December 10 a new government was formed, with the Communists reduced to a minority. Less than three weeks later, Havel was installed as president.

St. Vitus' Cathedral (Katedrála sv Víta) towers over Prague's historic buildings and the Vltava river

Survival Guide

■ Czech pronunciation is difficult, but worth mastering if only for place-names. Any attempt to speak Czech will be heartily appreciated, although many Czechs – particularly young city dwellers – may speak excellent English. The key is to stress the first syllable of a word. A grasp of German is also useful.

■ The cuisine here is heavily meat-based – dumplings with pork and duck are popular dishes – and can be quite flavorful. Czechs claim to have the world's best beer, and the products of České Budějovice (Budweis) and Plzeň (Pilsen) are the most famous among a multitude of local varieties.

■ It's worth looking through bookstores, as the illustrated books are a treat. For souvenirs, take home Bohemian crystal, porcelain, lacework, wooden toys and puppets, garnets and prints.

■ Easter is as important a holiday as Christmas, and is marked by the traditional fertility ritual of boys whipping girls' legs with birch twigs.

■ On St. Nicholas' Eve (December 5), trios in costume can be seen – St. Nicholas, an angel and a devil – walking the streets giving candy to good children and lumps of coal to "bad" ones. Christmas dinner is traditionally carp – sold live at street stalls to be eaten on Christmas Eve, fried, baked or cooked in a soup.

■ Prague is even busier than usual from mid-May to early June, when it hosts the Prague Spring International Music Festival (☎ 257 310 414; www.festival.cz): Reserve accommodations several weeks in advance for this period.

■ Public transportation (both buses and trains) is a good way of seeing the republic. Almost every town has a railroad station (*nádraží*), and side trips are cheap. The fast trains (*rychlík*) stop at major cities; local trains (*osobní vlak*) are slow, stop everywhere and usually have only second-class carriages.

■ Outside of Prague, the Czech Republic still suffers from a shortage of quality hotels and hostels, although this is fast changing. Many historic hotels have been overhauled and new accommodations built. A sign saying *Zimmer frei* ("room available" in German) indicates a bed-and-breakfast in a private home.

Prague

Nothing will prepare you for the beauty of Prague. Its title of "Golden Prague" barely conveys the color and elegance of its historic center: painted medieval, baroque and Renaissance facades glinting pink and green and silver in the sun; a jumble of rust-red rooftops; turquoise domes and gray Gothic spires. Prague's buildings and streets span 1,000 years. Wandering the cobbled alleys becomes the highlight of any visit.

Compass Bearings

Central Prague is made up of four towns, joined together in 1784. On the west bank of the Vltava river are Hradčany and the Lesser Quarter (Malá Strana); on the east bank are the Old Town (Staré Město) and New Town (Nové Město). In the 19th century the Jewish ghetto, Josefov, was also incorporated into the Old Town. Beyond this core is a circle of suburbs, but the main historic sights are within the substantially traffic-free center.

Charles Bridge and Prague Castle

The two banks of the Vltava are connected by a series of 15 bridges, the oldest of which, the Charles Bridge (Karlův most, see pages 127 and 129), is a magnet for tourists, performers and

vendors. On the west bank, Hradčany, the area around Prague Castle (Pražský hrad, see pages 129–130) and its hill, is the major attraction. It includes (along with the castle), St. Vitus' Cathedral (Katedrála sv Víta); Golden Lane (Zlatá ulička), with tiny 16th-century houses originally occupied by gatekeepers; the Gothic Mihulka Powder Tower (Prašná

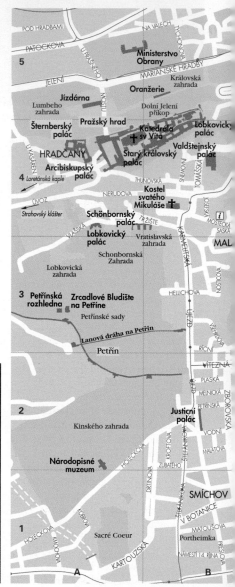

Nerudova

A steep street climbs from Malá Strana Square, in the Lesser Quarter, all the way up to Prague Castle. This street, Nerudova, was named after journalist and writer Jan Neruda. He wrote stories about daily life in 19th-century Prague, and was born at No. 47, near the top. Eighteenth-century houses line the street, identified by intricately crafted signs; numbers weren't introduced until the 1770s. Look for The Three Fiddles (No. 12), The Golden Cup (No. 16), The Green Lobster (No. 43) and Neruda's home, The Two Suns (No. 47).

věž Mihulka), where alchemists tried to create gold; and the palaces surrounding Hradčany Square (Hradčanské náměstí).

Old Town and New Town

Here, across the river, in the Old Town is the Old Town Square (Staroměstské náměstí), with the sprawling Old Town Hall (Staroměstská radnice; see page 130) and the dark towers of Týn Church (Týnsky chrám). This is a popular place for street artists to perform. The real hub of the New Town (Nové Město) is Wenceslas Square (Václavské náměstí), a thriving boulevard and the focus of the Velvet Revolution, the mostly peaceful protest that ended Communist rule here in November 1989.

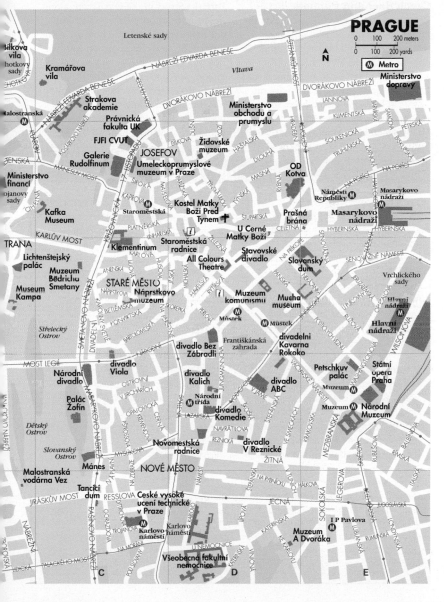

Czech Republic

Locals love their music – as Mozart found out, when he triumphed here after only moderate success in Vienna. Classical music seems to be everywhere in Prague, advertised in listings guides and on posters across the city. Tickets are reasonably priced and the performances can be superb.

Pražský hrad (castle) and the Malá Strana district

Czech Beer and Puppets

Restaurants and cafés fill up quickly in Prague, so it's a good idea to make reservations. You'll find a wide range of options as well as local cuisine, from American and Italian to Vietnamese and Japanese. Don't leave the city without tasting at least one Czech beer. Some of Prague's own brews include Staropramen and U Fleků.

The best shopping is along elegant Pařížská Street in the Old Town, along the pedestrian-only street Na Příkopě and also along Celetná. There are some interesting souvenir shops on Karlova, near the Charles Bridge. If you're looking for souvenirs, puppets make ideal gifts – they're works of art, not just playthings. For a huge selection of books, try Palác knih Luxor (Palace of Books) at Václavské náměstí 41.

Essential Information

Tourist Information

Prague City Tourism ☎ 221 714 714; www.prague.eu
Main Office: Staroměstská radnice (Old Town Hall), Staroměstské náměstí 1; daily 9–7
Branches: Staré Město (Old Town), Rytířská 12; daily 9–7
Václavské náměstí (Wenceslas Square), corner of Štěpánskou ulicí; daily 10–6
Prague Airport Terminals 1 and 2; daily 8–8

Urban Transportation

Prague has three metro (subway) lines: A (green), B (yellow) and C (red). Stations are indicated by the letter "M" (marked in a red circle on the city map). Trains run frequently every day between 5 a.m. and midnight. Trams and buses are frequent (4:30 a.m. to midnight, with some night services). Buses run outside the city center. One ticket can be used for the metro, buses and trams. For information ☎ 296 191 817 (daily 7 a.m.–9 p.m.; www.dpp.cz). Make sure a taxi has a meter registering the fare, or agree on a price before you get into the cab. Avoid taxi stands, especially near tourist spots or nightclubs, and at night. To hire a taxi call AAA Radio taxi (☎ 222 333 222).

Airport Information

Prague Airport (Václav Havel Airport Prague) (☎ 220 111 888; www.prg.aero) is 12.5 miles northwest of the city; bus Nos. 100 and 119 operate between the airport and central Prague. The Airport Express (AE) bus provides a direct service to Hlavní nádraží (Prague main train station).

Climate – average highs and lows for the month

Jan.	Feb.	Mar.	Apr.	May	Jun.	Jul.	Aug.	Sep.	Oct.	Nov.	Dec.
2°C	2°C	8°C	12°C	18°C	20°C	22°C	23°C	18°C	12°C	5°C	2°C
36°F	36°F	46°F	54°F	64°F	68°F	72°F	73°F	64°F	54°F	41°F	36°F
-4°C	-4°C	0°C	2°C	7°C	10°C	13°C	12°C	9°C	4°C	0°C	-2°C
25°F	25°F	32°F	36°F	45°F	50°F	55°F	54°F	48°F	39°F	32°F	28°F

Prague Sights

Josefov

Walls went up around Prague's Jewish
community in 1254, in keeping with a
church law dictating that Christians and
Jews should live apart. The inhabitants
of the ghetto suffered centuries of
persecution. In 1389, 3,000 inhabitants
were killed in a pogrom, and at regular
intervals, kings passed laws forcing Jews
to wear particular clothes or colors to
identify them.

Even in the face of such overt
discrimination, the ghetto developed as
a center of learning. In 1784 Joseph II
abolished residence restrictions (the area
was later named after him).

The ghetto survived until the end of
the 19th century, when the area was
cleared for residential housing, though
many of the most important buildings
were left standing. In the Starý židovský
hřbitov (Old Jewish Cemetery), some
12,000 tombstones are crammed into

Sculptures line both sides of Charles Bridge

the small but powerfully moving space,
now part of the Jewish Museum. Other
museum holdings are scattered
throughout the quarter. An exhibition
in the Pinkasova synagoga (Pinkas
Synagogue) remembers the 80,000
Czech and Moravian Jews who died in
concentration camps in World War II.

The oldest building in the ghetto is
the 13th-century Staronová synagoga
(Old-New Synagogue), where legend has
it the clay man, or Golem, created by
Rabbi Löw in 1580 to serve and guard
the ghetto, is still kept in the attic. The
Rabbi had to return his creation to clay
after it ran rampant through the streets.
This and other synagogues around the
cemetery survived World War II because
of Hitler's perverse plan to create a
museum dedicated to a vanished race.
The synagogues (apart from the
Old-New Synagogue) collectively form
the Židovské muzeum (Jewish Museum)
and can all be visited on one ticket.

🔋 C4 ✉ Jewish Museum: Information and
Reservation Center, Maiselova 15; Old-New Synagogue:
Červená 2 ☎ 222 317 191, www.jewishmuseum.cz
🅱 Jewish Museum sites: Sun.–Fri. 9–6, Apr.–Oct.;
9–4:30, rest of year. Old-New Synagogue: Sun.–Fri.
9–6, Apr.–Oct.; 9–5, rest of year. Closed Jewish
holidays 🚇 Staroměstská 🚊 Tram 17, 18
🍴 Restaurant 🅱 Jewish Museum $$$; Old-New
Synagogue $$$

Karlův most

Karlův most (Charles Bridge) is more
than just a river crossing. A walk across
the 1,700-foot span takes you past 30
sculptures and musicians, and offers
breathtaking views of the river and of
the city's domes and looming spires. It
was the work of Petr Parléř, who also
created much of St. Vitus' Cathedral,
and was built in 1357 to link the Old
Town with the Lesser Quarter. Known
until 1870 as the Stone or Prague Bridge,
it has 16 sandstone arches but was
originally quite plain. The first
ornament, a bronze crucifix, was added
in 1657. Over the following 60 years
more statues were erected, evenly spaced

Kafka

Franz Kafka wrote two of the 20th century's most significant novels – *The Trial* and *The Castle* – but he died practically unknown, having made his friend, Max Brod, promise to destroy all his writings. It's only because Brod broke his promise that Kafka is read throughout the world today.

His tales of helpless individuals caught in the workings of massive bureaucracy were inspired by the overgrown Habsburg administration. They came to represent the menace and detachment of authority in general, and the term "Kafkaesque" was coined to describe a seemingly ordinary but surreal and dangerous world of systems with their own life and logic.

Kafka was born in Prague, and moved with his family from house to house around Old Town Square, where his father was a haberdasher. He studied law and worked as an insurance clerk, writing his stories by night. The city appears throughout his writings. *The Castle* was inspired by Prague Castle; his story *The Great Wall of China* was based on the "Hunger Wall" on Petřín Hill, built as part of a 14th-century job-creation scheme and funded by money expropriated from Jews. Kafka rented a house between 1916 and 1917 on Golden Lane (Zlatá ulička) at No. 22, but his health was poor and he died of tuberculosis at the age of 41. His grave can be seen at the New Jewish Cemetery (Židovské hřbitovy) in the Vinohrady district. He left behind a third, unfinished novel, *Amerika,* and many short stories.

The most famous, *Metamorphosis,* related the story of Gregor Samsa, who awakens to find himself transformed into a giant insect and to his family becomes an object first of horror, then of pity and finally of contempt. The theme of a bewildered victim of inexplicable events is characteristic of Kafka's style.

The author also recorded his wanderings around Prague, his relationship with his father and with Felice Bauer (to whom he was twice engaged), and his tortured nights of writing in his diaries, which also were posthumously published.

The Communist regime subsequently suppressed Kafka's work, but he is now acknowledged and honored in the city he once described as "a little old mother with sharp claws: she won't let go."

Cobbled Golden Lane is built into the castle; Franz Kafka stayed here between 1916 and 1917

✚ B4 ⊠ Malostranské náměstí ☎ Church: 257 534
215; www.stnicholas.cz ⊕ Daily 9–5, Mar.–Oct.; 9–4,
rest of year. Tower: daily 10–10, Apr.–Sep.
⊜ Malostranská 🚊 Tram 12, 20, 22, 23 🎫 Church
$$; tower $

Loretánská kaple

As part of its campaign to win worshipers back to Catholicism after the Reformation, the Church made much of the cult of the Virgin Mary, and the ornate Loretánská kaple (Loreto Chapel) is one example of this time. It was built in 1626 around a replica of Mary's house, supposedly flown by angels from Nazareth to Loreto in Italy, and it soon became a site of pilgrimage. Don't miss the painting of St. Starosta, who grew a beard to repel a suitor and was crucified by her father.

✚ Off map at A4 ⊠ Loretánské náměstí 7 ☎ 220 516 740; www.loreta.cz ⊕ Daily 9–5, Apr.–Oct., 9:30–4, rest of year 🚊 Tram 22, 23 🎫 $$

Visitors in the vaulted Loreto Chapel

along the parapets; they include St. John of Nepomuk (with the spangled halo), who was allegedly thrown from the bridge in 1393 after taking the side of the church in a dispute with the king. You can visit the fortified towers at each end of the bridge – the Old Town Bridge Tower and Lesser Town Bridge Tower.

✚ C3 ⊠ Staré Město/Malá Strana ⊕ Old Town Bridge Tower: daily 10–10, Apr.–Sep.; 10–8, Mar. and Oct.; 10–6, Nov.–Feb. Lesser Town Bridge Tower: same as Old Town Bridge Tower times ⊜ Staroměstská 🚊 Tram 12, 17, 18, 20, 22, 23

Kostel svatého Mikuláše

Mozart played the 2,500-pipe organ here in 1787; he couldn't have chosen a more grandiose setting than the Kostel svatého Mikuláše (St. Nicholas' Church). It was constructed in the 18th century and is considered the city's best example of baroque style. The church is a frenzy of decoration: pink-and-green mock-marble pillars; a 16,146-square-foot fresco; a formidable copper statue of St. Nicholas; and huge sculptures of the four church fathers, including St. Cyril killing the devil.

Petřín

Woods and orchards cover this hill on the city's western bank, and a funicular railway (*lanová dráha na Petřín*) takes passengers up and down. The carriages were installed in 1891, the year that the Petřínská rozhledna (Petřín Lookout Tower) was built at the top. Steps (299 of them) lead to the viewing platform.

✚ A3 ⊠ Petrin Lookout Tower: Petřínské sady. Funicular railway: Újezd ☎ 257 320 112; www. muzeumprahy.cz ⊕ Lookout Tower: daily 10–10, Apr.–Sep.; 10–8, Mar. and Oct.; 10–6, rest of year. Funicular: daily 9 a.m.–11:30 p.m., Apr.–Oct. (to 11:20 p.m., rest of year) 🚊 Tram 9, 12, 15, 20, 22, 23 (then take funicular) 🎫 Tower $$; funicular $

Pražský hrad

Looming over the city and the river, Pražský hrad (Prague Castle – a UNESCO World Heritage Site) has been a symbol of Czech authority since the first fortress was built on this rocky site in the ninth century. The name refers to a complex of palaces, courtyards, churches and streets, all spread across the hill known as Hradčany. A flight of

Cafés in the square under the Astronomical Clock

broad steps climbs to the castle, a mixture of architectural styles spanning 450 years of restoration and guarded by a series of courtyards. At the entrance to the outer courtyard, two soldiers stand at attention under grotesque statues of the Titans. The guard detail is changed hourly on the hour (🕐 daily 5 a.m. – midnight, Apr.–Oct.; 6 a.m.–11 p.m., rest of year). In the second courtyard are the castle's excellent art gallery and information center.

Finally, you reach the third courtyard and Katedrála sv Víta (St. Vitus' Cathedral), which took 600 years to complete – it was only finished in 1929. Starý královský palác (Old Royal Palace), to the right, is a maze of rooms centered around the 15th-century Vladislav Hall, where mounted knights would trot down the Riders' Staircase to take part in indoor jousting matches.

➕ A4 ✉ Hradčany ☎ 224 372 423; www.hrad.cz 🕐 Castle precincts: daily 6 a.m.–10 p.m. Castle sights: daily 9–5, Apr.–Oct.; 9–4, rest of year. Castle gardens: daily 10–9, Jun.–Jul.; 10–8, Aug.; 10–7, May and Sep.; 10–6, Apr. and Oct. 🚇 Hradčanská 🚊 Tram 22, 23 🛈 Admission is by combined-entry ticket only which covers all of the sights $$$; gardens free 🛈 Tours in English ($$$). A valid passport or European Union ID is required to enter the castle grounds.

Staroměstská radnice

Since a merchant's house was earmarked for the city council in 1338, the Staroměstská radnice (Old Town Hall) has gradually expanded and taken over a row of houses. A tower and chapel were added to the original buildings; features range from the original carved facade to the 19th-century house to the late Gothic council hall inside. Its main attraction, however, is the huge, 15th-century Astronomical Clock, which gives the month, season, zodiac signs, course of the sun and Christian holidays. On the hour (9–9) a skeleton appears and chimes the bell, followed by a parade of the Twelve Apostles and, finally, a crowing gilded cock. Climb or take an elevator to the top of the tower.

➕ D4 ✉ Staroměstské náměstí 1 ☎ 236 002 629; www.staromestskaradnicepraha.cz 🕐 Tue.–Sun. 9 a.m.–10 p.m., Mon. 11–10 🚇 Staroměstská 🚊 Tram 17, 18 💰 $$$

Šternberský palác

In an alley off Hradčany Square is Šternberský palác (Sternberg Palace), a town house built for Count Sternberg in 1698, with a fine collection of Old Masters. Highlights include *The Feast of the Rosary* by German Renaissance painter and engraver Albrecht Dürer, and *Adam and Eve* by artist and woodcut-designer Lucas Cranach the Elder, both housed on the first floor.

➕ A4 ✉ Hradčanské náměstí 15 ☎ 224 301 122; www.ngprague.cz 🕐 Tue.–Sun. 10–6 🚇 Hradčanská 🚊 Tram 22, 23 🍽 Café 💰 $$$

Strahovský klášter

The baroque spires of Strahovský klášter (Strahov Monastery) dominate the hilltop west of Hradčany: the name means "to watch over." and it has guarded this site since the 12th century. Library halls store more than 130,000 books and manuscripts.

➕ Off map at A4 ✉ Strahovské nádvoří 1 ☎ 233 107 707; www.strahovskyklaster.cz 🕐 Daily 9–12 and 1–5 🚇 Malostranská 🚊 Tram 22, 23 🍽 Peklo restaurant (below ground) 💰 $$

Excursion to Kutná Hora

When silver and copper ore deposits were found on this hill 40 miles southeast of Prague, a town shot up virtually overnight, taking the appropriate name of Kutná Hora, which suggests "miners' mountain." That was in the late 13th century, and soon a royal mint was set up, hammering out the silver coin known as *pražské groše* in its workshops. Also constructed was a royal palace known as the Italian Court, a reference to the Florentine advisers of King Wenceslas II (1283–1305). The town flourished on its mining proceeds and by the 14th century was the country's

The Italian Court was once a royal palace

most important center after Prague. Kutná Hora even managed to recover after being taken over by one force after another during the Hussite Wars. But by the end of the 16th century the mountain was all mined out and the town fell into decay, suffering the final blow with a disastrous fire in 1770.

The handsome Cathedral of St. Barbara was paid for by miners and dedicated to their patron saint. For its design they turned to the prestigious architect of Prague's St. Vitus' Cathedral, Petr Parléř, who rose to the occasion with distinctive tent-like spires and flying buttresses.

Sculptures line Barborská ulice, a street leading to an impressive 15th-century house built for a profiteer who ran an illegal private mining operation. It's now the Mining Museum, and behind it is the medieval mine itself, consisting of 820 feet of tunnels; a horse-drawn winch at the entrance drew out the bags of ore. The royal mint is gone (although it is still possible to make out its outline); parts of the Italian Court – including the chapel, adorned with art nouveau frescoes – can be visited also. Kutná Hora is a UNESCO World Heritage Site. Some 2 miles north of town in Sedlec is the spooky *kostnice,* a chapel decorated with human bones, that was originally owned by Cistercian monks. During the 19th century its 40,000 human bones were put to artistic use by František Rint, who made them into bells and other items.

Contact Prague City Tourism (see page 126).

For an organized tour of Kutná Hora, contact:

Martin Tour ✉ Pařížská 1, 110 00 Praha 1 ☎ 224 212 473; www.martintour.cz

For more information contact: **Informační centrum Kutná Hora** ✉ Palackého náměstí 377, Kutná Hora ☎ 327 512 378; www.kutnahora.cz

Denmark

Introduction and Map 134

Timeline 138

Survival Guide 139

Copenhagen 140

Odense 146

Feature: Hans Christian Andersen 151

Hotels and Restaurants 471

Essential Information 510

Opposite: Designed in 1913, Copenhagen's famous *The Little Mermaid (Den Lille Havfrue)* statue in the harbor area is the most popular expression of Hans Christian Andersen's fairy-tale world

Denmark

Denmark

Denmark was the cradle of ancient Scandinavia. When you talk of the first Vikings you talk of Danes. It was from this fragmented mosaic of peninsulas and islands between mainland Europe and the Swedish-Norwegian landmass that those consummate seamen first struck out in search of plunder and new territory to conquer. Denmark is the smallest of the four Scandinavian nations, and yet the Danes have succeeded in making their country one of the most advanced and progressive in the world.

Danish Archipelago

The Kingdom of Denmark is just over 200 miles long, and the Jutland (Jylland) peninsula (the primary landmass) is only 75 miles wide. Nowhere in Denmark is much higher than 100 feet above sea level, and the country's highest point, Yding Skovhøj in central Jutland, only rises to 567 feet. Jutland's narrow southern border is with

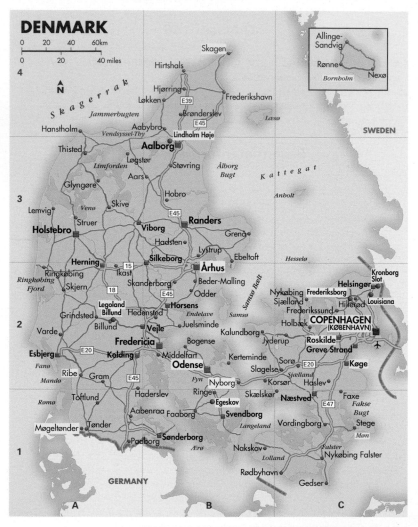

Germany, Denmark's only land frontier; its west coast adjoins the North Sea.

East of Jutland, and with barely a sliver of water in between, is Denmark's second-largest island, Funen (Fyn). East of Funen is Zealand (Sjælland), the largest island. Its northeastern tip is about 40 miles from the Swedish coast and home to the capital, Copenhagen (København), itself only a short drive or train journey across the Øresund bridge (see page 136) to Sweden. Zealand and Funen lie like natural fortresses across the Kattegat Sea. This position across the entrance to the Baltic Sea has always placed the country at the maritime heart of northern Europe.

The Jutland Peninsula

Houses on Bornholm, an island east of the mainland

Copenhagen is the magnet for visitors, but the rest of this disparate and fascinating country has much to offer. Far western Jutland has an invigorating coastal landscape of long, sandy beaches backed by broad dunes and moorland. This landscape is repeated in north Jutland beyond the dividing waters of the Limfjord and all the way to the Skagen peninsula, the beak of land that thrusts into the sea at Denmark's northern tip. In north Jutland, outside the city of Aalborg, are evocative traces of Scandinavia's Viking culture at the archeological site of Lindholm Høje, a remarkable Viking burial ground of nearly 700 excavated graves, many marked by stones in the shape of long ships.

The heathland of the west coast of central Jutland gives way in the east to a fertile, undulating countryside of small farms and woodland, interspersed with country towns and pretty villages. On the east coast is Århus, a sophisticated and historic university city and Denmark's second largest. Here you will find the mighty Århus Cathedral and the intriguing Den Gamle By, the Old Town and its dozens of restored, timber-framed buildings. South of Århus is a great stretch of woodland where you can enjoy peace and quiet along walking,

bicycling and horseback riding trails. Southwest of Århus is the town of Billund, overshadowed by Denmark's famous Legoland Billund, the country's most visited attraction outside of Copenhagen. Beyond all the plastic bricks is the farming country of south Jutland, which claims to be Denmark's oldest region with such fascinating towns and villages as Ribe, the oldest town in Denmark, established in the eighth century AD, with its handsome cathedral, cobbled streets and gabled houses. The little village of Møgeltønder, in the far southwest of the country, has a superb frescoed church and some charming thatched houses.

More Top Destinations in Denmark (see map page 134)	
■ Århus B2	■ Louisiana C2
■ Bornholm C4	■ Møgeltønder A1
■ Egeskov B1	■ Møn C1
■ Frederiksborg C2	■ Nyborg B2
■ Køge C2	■ Ribe A2
■ Kronborg Slot, Helsingør C2	■ Roskilde C2
■ Legoland Billund A2	■ Skagen B4
■ Lindholm Høje B3	

Country of Islands

More than 400 islands are scattered around Denmark's coasts and out across the Kattegat and the Baltic Sea. About 100 islands are inhabited. Funen (Fyn) is hailed as the "Garden of Denmark," a term probably first used by author Hans Christian Andersen (see page 151) because of its rich alluvial soils, a legacy of the glacial debris left by retreating ice sheets. The capital of Funen is Odense, birthplace of Andersen.

Funen has a timeless character, its lush farmland complemented by a pleasant southern coastline and by good beaches on the peaceful island of Langeland, off the southeast coast. Funen is connected to Denmark's largest island, Zealand, by a typically Danish feat of remarkable civil engineering. The 11-mile-long Storebælt (Great Belt) rail and road fixed-link bridge island hops, via Sprogø island, across the Store Bælt channel. The project took nine years to complete and the first rail passengers crossed the rail bridge in 1997, followed in 1998 by cars on the road link.

The ferry connection, used by visitors prior to 1998, was more romantic, but Scandinavian efficiency triumphed with this tunnel and bridge combination. A similar joint Danish-Swedish project, linking Copenhagen to Malmö across an artificial island built in the middle of the Øresund, was completed in 2000, laying the foundations for a new cultural and economic region.

Historic Zealand

Copenhagen may dominate Zealand, but the whole island is a treasure-house of Danish history. North Zealand has much to offer in terms of historic buildings: the lakeside setting of Frederiksborg Castle (Frederiksborg Slot), Denmark's magnificent Renaissance castle; and Elsinore Castle (Kronborg Slot) at Helsingør, thought to be the setting for Shakespeare's *Hamlet*, overlooking the Øresund and the Swedish coast.

Just west of Copenhagen is Roskilde, Denmark's medieval capital, with a splendid cathedral housing the decorated crypts of 38 Danish kings and queens. In southern Zealand is the city of Køge, whose medieval center survives; at Trelleborg, near Slagelse on the west coast where the new rail bridge slices across the Great Belt, are the remains of the finest Viking ring fort in Denmark. There are six circular forts in Denmark and Sweden called Trelleborgs – all named for this one, which was excavated first, between 1936 and 1941.

Little villages nestle amid lush greenery on the coastline of Denmark

Traditional painted houses in Odense, birthplace of Hans Christian Andersen, on the island of Funen

Finally, just off the south coast of Zealand are the islands of Møn, Falster and Lolland, Denmark's third-largest island, after Zealand and Funen, all linked to the main islands by bridges. Of these, Møn is the most interesting because of its green hills and chalk cliffs, a landscape in startling contrast to Denmark's almost uniform flatness.

Exploring Denmark

Denmark is one of the most accessible European countries. Its compact size and the smooth transition from island to island makes exploring various regions by car an easy option once you are clear of Copenhagen's urban center.

This compactness makes traveling by public transportation almost as convenient. Fast, comfortable trains can whisk you from Zealand to Funen, and then on to Jutland, in a few hours. The efficient and extensive rail network offers stiff competition to long-distance bus services in Denmark, although buses are less expensive than trains.

Denmark's climate is typical of a maritime environment, and the low elevation means there are no great extremes of temperature. Summers are pleasantly mild, but there can be wet spells; in winter snow is likely at times, but much less so than in the other Scandinavian countries.

In matters of food and drink Denmark remains engagingly Scandinavian. Danes relish the same hearty sandwich feast, here called the smørrebrød, that you find in Norway and Sweden, complete with its garnished mixes of delicious meat and seafood. Beer is a Danish specialty, and the famous Danish breweries of Carlsberg and Tuborg produce some of the most popular brews in the world.

You will find that Danes are generally helpful, friendly and speak good English. In rural areas and in provincial cities such as Odense, people are unfailingly polite, but in Copenhagen there may be a sharper edge to people's attitudes. At times you may detect an apparent reserve on the part of Danish people. It is not a negative sentiment; the Danes are supremely accomplished, and beneath the reserve is a fierce national pride in their country.

Timeline

4000 BC	Neolithic settlers begin developing a farming economy.
500 BC to AD 500	Iron Age people trade from Jutland and Funen.
AD 793	Danish Vikings raid England's east coast and penetrate deep into mainland Europe along the northern rivers.
circa 925	Gorm the Old becomes first king of a united Denmark.
1167	The founding of Copenhagen by Absalon, Bishop of Roskilde.
1588	Christian IV becomes king and promotes the construction of great Renaissance buildings, particularly in Copenhagen.
1611–60	Periodic wars with Sweden.
1814	Union with Norway ends after 278 years.
1849	New constitution establishes a two-chamber parliament.
1914–18	Denmark is neutral during World War I.
1940	Denmark is invaded by the German army in spite of its declared neutrality; the Danish Resistance carries out a vigorous campaign against Germany.
1945	Denmark is liberated. A postwar reconstruction program begins.
1949	Denmark joins NATO.
1973	Denmark joins the European Economic Community.
1998	Opening of the fixed-link rail and road bridge across the Store Bælt (Great Belt) Channel.
2000	Road and rail link opens to Malmö in Sweden.
2004	Prince Frederik marries Australian Mary Donaldson.
2011	Go-ahead given to build an underwater tunnel between Lolland Island and the German island of Fehmarn.
2012	Queen Margrethe II celebrates 40 years on the Danish throne.
2015	Denmark sends its first astronaut into space.
2017	Århus, Denmark's second city, shares European City of Culture status with Paphos, Cyprus.
2018	Prince Henrik, husband of Queen Margrethe II, dies at the age of 83.

A Talented Royal Lady

Denmark's current queen, Margrethe II, was born in 1940. She was the eldest daughter of King Frederik IX, who had no sons. After a favorable 1953 referendum, the Danish constitution, which allowed only for a male heir to the throne, was amended to enable female succession. Margrethe became queen at the age of 32, after Frederik's death in 1972. She is Denmark's first female monarch since the 15th century. Queen Margrethe qualified as an archeologist after studying at Copenhagen, Århus, Cambridge and Paris. She is a talented artist, who has illustrated an edition of J. R. R. Tolkien's fantasy *The Lord of the Rings* and designed stamps for the Danish postal service and theatrical costumes and stage settings for the Danish Royal Theatre. An accomplished linguist, Queen Margrethe has translated the work of the French novelist Simone de Beauvoir, a task in which she worked with her late husband and consort, French-born Prince Henrik.

Survival Guide

- If you drive or cycle through Denmark, ask the tourist office for details about the "Marguerite Route," which is a series of linked routes (2,170 miles long) along quieter roads that wind through the most scenic parts of the country. Distinctive signs display a daisy (marguerite) motif on a brown background.

- The Copenhagen Card, valid for 24, 48, 72 or 120 hours, costs 399, 569, 689 and 899 DKr respectively (half-price for 10–15 year olds, up to two children under 10 years free with a paying adult). It entitles you to unlimited travel by train, bus, harbor bus or metro, entry into more than 86 museums and attractions, and car rental, restaurant and shopping discounts in the city. Buy the Copenhagen Card online at www.copenhagencard.com.

- Danes celebrate Midsummer's Eve (*Sankt Hans*) on June 23. Bonfires are lit in celebration.

- In Denmark *morgenmad* is the word for breakfast, and *frokost* is lunch. *Smørrebrød*, the tasty Scandinavian open sandwich with a choice of toppings, including cheese, salami, smoked salmon and egg, remains a lunchtime favorite; but try *frikadeller*, fried meat or fish patties with salad and potatoes. For main meals, enjoy *kogt torsk*, poached cod in mustard sauce, or old-fashioned *Skipperlabskovs*, Danish stew.

- Danish pastries are called *wienerbrød* and come in all shapes and flavors.

- Amber is a Danish specialty, the "Danish gold." In Copenhagen, the House of Amber (Kongens Nytorv 2, ☎ 33 11 67 00; www.houseofamber.com) has an amber museum and is a good place to buy, but you will find also distinctive amber jewelry in stores throughout the country. If you're looking for Danish glass,

A soldier outside Amalienborg Palace, Copenhagen

porcelain and silverware, there are several shops on and leading off Strøget and also the Royal Copenhagen flagship store (Amagertorv 6, Copenhagen, ☎ 33 13 71 81; www.royalcopenhagen.com).

- Denmark, like Sweden, is noted for its distinctive furnishing designs. The style known as "Danish Modern" is a classic merging of the functional with the aesthetic. Visit Illums Bolighus (Amagertorv 10, Copenhagen, ☎ 33 14 19 41; www.illumsbolighus.com) store for some of the finest examples.

- Unlike some of the northern Scandinavian countries, Denmark has a relaxed approach to the sale of liquor. You can buy wines, spirits and beers in grocery stores.

- Traditionally formal, Danes are now more relaxed about dining attire. Stylish, casual clothes, especially during the summer, are acceptable for dining at most Danish restaurants.

Copenhagen

Copenhagen (København) is where the European experience becomes Scandinavian. This is a magnificent, vibrant city, far more a "Wonderful Wonderful Copenhagen" than even the Danny Kaye song implies. It is a city of towers and steeples that are elegant as well as monumental. It is a city that draws you in along pedestrian-only streets that lead in and out of delightful squares. It is a city with fine museums and attractions, restaurants, cafés and

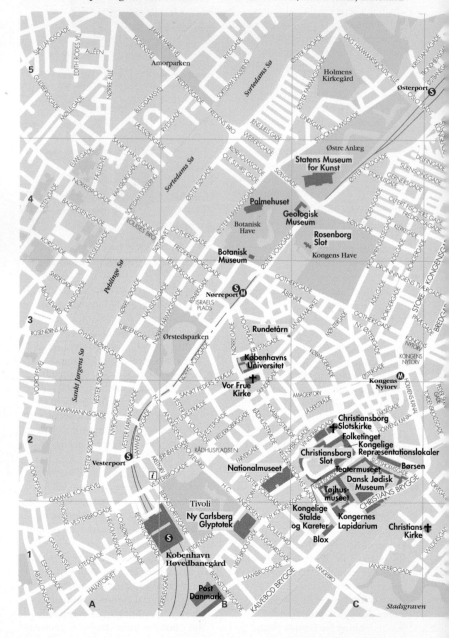

entertainment that place it among the finest of European capitals.

Copenhagen originated, like so many other Scandinavian towns and cities, as a small fishing village, its occupants taking advantage of the sheltered waters around Slotsholmen Island, the island

COPENHAGEN

that is now home to the Danish National Parliament (Folketing), and the Christiansborg Palace (Christiansborg Slot, see page 143). By the 12th century Slotsholmen had been fortified in keeping with the settlement's growing commercial status, a status signified by its name, Kømandshavn, "port of the merchants," later amended to København. By the middle of the 15th century, Copenhagen was the recognized capital of Denmark.

The city's status was enhanced by the construction of many fine buildings during the reign of Christian IV of Denmark (1588–1648) in the 16th and 17th centuries, and by the 19th century Copenhagen had emerged as a major European capital. Development continued during the 20th and 21st centuries, and today Copenhagen stands as a mature and hugely successful city.

First Impressions

To reach the central City Hall Square (Rådhuspladsen) from Copenhagen's 100-year-old central railroad station (Hovedbanegården), visitors pass Tivoli and then negotiate busy downtown streets. Hans Christian Andersen Boulevard, a broad thoroughfare, is as far removed from Andersen's fairy-tale world as can be imagined. Keep your eyes open for cyclists as well as cars. The broad expanse of City Hall Square, a relaxed, traffic-free environment dominated by the tower of the City Hall (guided visits for far-reaching views Mon.–Fri. 11 a.m. and 2 p.m., Sat. noon), leads to lively streets, colorful squares and hidden corners, where pedestrians are the priority.

Most attractions, including Rosenborg Castle (Rosenborg Slot, see page 145), which forms part of a museum quarter and the National Museum (Nationalmuseet; see page 144), are in the Old Town. The Waterfront is steadily being revitalized with arts centers, restaurants and museums springing up in new, striking buildings.

Getting around is easy, especially if you take advantage of the various guided walking tours that are available, or pick up a map from the tourist office. Other sightseeing tours go by bus and by harbor or canal boats. Copenhagen's bus service is very efficient, complemented by a system of electric S-trains and a metro (subway). However, it's fun to explore the city by bicycle. You can rent an electric one from Bycyklen (☎ 89 88 39 10; www.bycyklen.dk), and many hotels have bicycles available for guests.

Strøget and Beyond

Start at City Hall Square. Look up at the Nordea building, where you will see a bronze weathervane featuring a girl who appears on her bicycle in fine weather and with an umbrella when it rains.

The sequence of streets known collectively as Strøget (the Promenade) begins at Rådhuspladsen (City Hall Square), at narrow Frederiksberggade. Amid the many stores and restaurants, side streets lead to specialty outlets.

City on the Water's Edge

At the far end of Strøget, cross the large, bustling square of Kongens Nytorv (New Royal Market) to reach Nyhavn (New Harbor), the old harbor inlet, now a pretty area with trendy restaurants. Visit Amalienborg Plads (Amalienborg Square, see page 143), just to the north, then head east to waterside Larsens Plads; from this square a pleasant walk north takes you to the city's symbol, *Den Lille Havfrue (The Little Mermaid)*. Alternatively, hop aboard a sightseeing boat and see the city from the water.

Essential Information

Tourist Information

Copenhagen Visitor Center
Vesterbrogade 4A ☎ 70 22 24 42;
www.visitcopenhagen.com

Urban Transportation

Copenhagen's railroad station is København H/Central Station on Bernstorffsgade. For information ☎ 70 13 14 15 (there are free service phones at all stations); www.dsb.dk. The train system consists of S-trains (about 10 lines; trains every four to 20 minutes). Copenhagen has good bus routes leaving from Rådhuspladsen. There is a 24-hour driverless metro (light rail) system (M1 and M2). For all transportation information ☎ 70 15 70 00, or online at www.dinoffentligetransport.dk where there is a journey planner in English.

Taxis have fixed rates. Call Taxa 4X35
☎ 35 35 35 35; www.taxa.dk.

Airport Information

Copenhagen Airport (☎ 32 31 32 31 24 hours; www.cph.dk) is at Kastrup, 6 miles south of the city center. Trains run between København H/Central Station and Terminal 3 daily every 10 minutes during the day (travel time 13 minutes, plus five minutes on the free shuttle bus that runs every 15 minutes to or from other terminals). Metro line M2 trains run every four to six minutes from 5 a.m. to midnight, and every 15 to 20 minutes during the night, (travel time 15 minutes). Buses serve the airport; the 5A can be caught from Copenhagen Central Station, City Hall and Nørreport.

Climate – average highs and lows for the month

Jan.	Feb.	Mar.	Apr.	May	Jun.	Jul.	Aug.	Sep.	Oct.	Nov.	Dec.
3°C	3°C	5°C	10°C	15°C	19°C	20°C	20°C	16°C	11°C	7°C	4°C
37°F	37°F	41°F	50°F	59°F	66°F	68°F	68°F	61°F	52°F	45°F	39°F
-2°C	-2°C	0°C	2°C	7°C	11°C	13°C	12°C	10°C	7°C	3°C	0°C
28°F	28°F	32°F	36°F	45°F	52°F	55°F	54°F	50°F	45°F	37°F	32°F

Copenhagen Sights

Amalienborg Plads

The royal heart of Copenhagen is
the octagonal Amalienborg Plads
(Amalienborg Square), with a statue of
King Frederik V at its center, rococo
palaces on four sides, and broad avenues
leading off the other four. The Danish
royal family spends most of the fall and
winter in the palaces. The square has a
rather detached atmosphere except
during the changing of the guard, which
takes place daily at noon.

On the northwest corner of the square
is Christian VIII's Palace, containing the
Amalienborgmuseet (Amalienborg
Museum), with royal memorabilia and a
sequence of reconstructed private rooms
that illustrate what life was like for the
royal Glücksburg family between the
1860s and the 1970s.

 D3 Amalienborg Plads Museum: 33 15
32 86; www.kongernessamling.dk Museum: daily
10–5, mid-Jun. to mid-Sep.; 10–4, May to mid-Jun.
and mid-Sep. to Oct.; Tue.–Sun. 11–4, rest of year
(daily during school vacations) Kongens Nytorv
 1A, 26, 350S Museum $$$ Tours in English
available only by reservation 2 weeks ahead of visit

Christiansborg Slot

The monumental complex that makes
up Christiansborg Slot (Christiansborg
Palace) dominates the whole island of
Slotsholmen. It presents a rather stern
face to the city approaching across the
encircling canal from Strøget and Højbro
Plads. A visit to this complex may take a
whole day. The vast west wing houses
the Danish Parliament (Folketinget), the
Supreme Court and the Prime Minister's

Office, built between 1907 and 1928.
Here, too, are the lavishly decorated
Kongelige Repræsentationslokaler
(Royal Reception Rooms).

Below the palace are the Ruinerne
(Ruins) of Bishop Absalon's Castle,
dating from 1167, and its successor,
Copenhagen Castle, as well as the
Christiansborg Slotskirke (Palace
Chapel), built in 1826 and still used on
all royal and state occasions. Museums
around the royal riding grounds include
Museet Kongelige Stalde og Kareter
(Royal Stable and Carriages Museum),
the Teatermuseet (Theater Museum)
and the Tøjhusmuseet (Royal Danish
Arsenal Museum), which forms part of
the National Museum. The Kongernes
Lapidarium (Lapidarium of Kings), next
to the Tøjhusmuseet, displays statues of
various royal palaces within its interior.

Christiansborg Slot C2 Christiansborg
Slotsplads 33 92 64 92; www.christiansborg.dk
 Kongens Nytorv or Nørreport 1A, 2A, 9A, 26, 37,
66, 350S Combined ticket for Royal Reception
Rooms, Ruins, Kitchen and Stables $$$ (valid 30 days)
Folketinget 33 37 32 21; www.thedanish
parliament.dk Free Guided tours in English
Mon.–Fri. 1 p.m., Jul.–Sep.; Sun. 1 p.m., rest of year
Kongelige Repræsentationslokaler 33 92 64 92
 Daily 9–5, May–Sep.; Tue.–Sun. 10–5, rest of year
 $$$ Guided tours in English daily at 3 p.m.
Ruinerne 33 92 64 92 Daily 10–5, May–Sep.;
Tue.–Sun. 10–5, rest of year $
Christiansborg Slotskirke Tue.–Sun. 10–5, Easter,
Jul. and mid-Oct.; Sun. 10–5, rest of year Free
Museet Kongelige Stalde og Kareter Daily 1:30–4,
May–Sep.; Tue.–Sun. 1:30–4, rest of year $
Teatermuseet 33 11 51 76 Tue.–Thu. 11–3,
Sat.–Sun. 1–4 $
Tøjhusmuseet Tøjhusgade 3 33 11 60 37;
www.natmus.dk Tue.–Sun. 10–4 $$
Kongernes Lapidarium Frederiksholms Kanal 29
 33 92 64 92 Tue.–Sun. noon–4, Jun.–Aug.
 Café $$

Dansk Jødisk Museum

Designed by Daniel Libeskind and built
within the 17th-century Royal
Boathouse on Slotsholmen, the Danish
Jewish Museum is both an architectural

eye-opener and a fascinating exploration of the Jewish community's experience in Denmark over 400 years.

✚ C2 ✉ Proviantpassagen 6 ☎ 33 11 22 18; www. jewmus.dk 🕒 Tue.–Sun. 10–5, Jun.–Aug.; Tue.–Fri. 1–4, Sat.–Sun. noon–5, rest of year 🚇 Kongens Nytorv 🚌 1A, 2A, 9A, 26, 37, 66 💰 $$

Den Blå Planet

Northern Europe's state-of-the-art aquarium, Den Blå Planet (The Blue Planet) opened at Kastrup Havn, near Copenhagen Airport in 2013. The enormous steel-clad building, inspired by a whirlpool, contains 53 aquariums, including five giant tanks that re-create the world's great oceans and rivers. Birds and butterflies add to the colorful experience in the Amazon area, while sharks, sea turtles and rays patrol the wrap-around Great Ocean tank. Be prepared for long lines on weekends.

✚ Off map at D1 ✉ Jacob Fortlingsvej 1, 2770, Kastrup ☎ 44 22 22 44; www.denblaaplanet.dk 🕒 Daily 10–5 (until 9 p.m. Mon.) 🚇 Kastrup 🚌 5A. Also free shuttle bus Apr.–Sep. from København H/ Central Station 🍴 Restaurant 💰 $$$ 🎫 Tours

Inside Marmorkirken, or the Marble Church

Marmorkirken

With its great dome, Frederiks Kirke (Frederick's Church), known universally as Marmorkirken (Marble Church), seems out of place in a Copenhagen of slender steeples and towers. The church was begun in 1749 as a final flourish to the nearby Amalienborg Palace, but was not completed until 1894. Modeled on St. Peter's in Rome, its dome measures almost 100 feet in diameter.

The circular nave is surmounted by a walkway, above which is a whispering gallery with superb acoustics. A tour of the dome is available at certain times, subject to services. The paneled frescoes depicting the Apostles on the inside of the dome are painted and gilded.

✚ D4 ✉ Frederiksgade 4 ☎ 33 15 01 44; www.marmorkirken.dk 🕒 Church: Mon.–Thu. and Sat. 10–5, Fri. and Sun. noon–5 🚇 Kongens Nytorv 🚌 1A, 26 💰 Church free; Dome $ 🎵 Concerts are held on some evenings. Dome tours: daily at 1 and 3 p.m., mid-Jun. to Aug.; Sat.–Sun. at 1 p.m. rest of year

Nationalmuseet

Particular draws here at Copenhagen's National Museum are the burial possessions of two Bronze Age bog people and a collection of *lur* (horn instruments used for ceremony and communication). Other major collections cover the Middle Ages and the Renaissance, Egyptian and classical antiquities, and early human cultures. There is a children's museum and a theater. You also can visit the Victorian Home, the finely furnished apartment of a late 19th-century merchant, at nearby Frederiksholms Kanal.

✚ B2 ✉ Ny Vestergade 10 ☎ 33 13 44 11; www. natmus.dk 🕒 Museum: Tue.–Sun. 10–5. Children's Museum: Tue.–Sun. 10–4:30. Victorian Home: guided tour only (English language), Sat. 2 p.m., Jun.–Sep. 🚇 S-train København H 🚌 1A, 2A, 9A, 14, 26, 37 🍴 Restaurant and café 💰 $$; Victorian Home $$

Ny Carlsberg Glyptotek

A winter garden with huge palm trees is the unexpected focal point of the Ny (New) Carlsberg Glyptotek, one of the country's finest art museums. Highlights are the Etruscan collection and French sculpture (including a Rodin collection) and paintings by Paul Gauguin.

➕ B1 ✉ Dantes Plads 7 ☎ 33 41 81 41; www.glyptoteket.dk ⏰ Tue.–Sun. 11–6 (also Thu. 6–10 p.m.) 🚇 København H 🚌 1A, 2A, 9A, 12, 33, 37 🍴 Museum café 💰 $$$ (free on Tue. except special exhibitions)

Rosenborg Slot

The early 17th-century Rosenborg Slot (Rosenborg Castle) is an outstanding example of Renaissance architecture and style; it stands at the edge of the lovely Kongens Have (King's Gardens) and forms the center of the Parkmuseerne, a landscaped museum quarter that also includes the Statens Museum for Kunst.

The lavishly decorated rooms reflect the regal styles of Danish monarchs from Christian IV to Frederick IV. There are marbled ceilings, late 17th-century Dutch tapestries, gilded mirrors, silver lions, gold and enamelware, and beautiful ceiling paintings. The Danish Crown Jewels sparkle in the Royal Treasury, which is in the castle's basement.

➕ C4 ✉ Øster Voldgade 4A ☎ 33 15 32 86; www.kongernessamling.dk/rosenborg/ ⏰ Daily 10–5, mid-Jun. to mid-Sep.; 10–4, mid-Apr. to mid-Jun. and mid-Sep. to Oct.; Tue.–Sun. 10–3 (till 4 p.m. Dec. 26–30), Jan. to mid-Apr. and Nov.–Dec. 🚇 Nørreport 🚌 14, 42, 43, 150S, 173E, 184, 185, 350S 🍴 Restaurant 💰 $$$

Rundetårn

The Rundetårn (Round Tower) is a must for anyone fit enough to trek up the covered, cobbled ramp that winds its way through seven and a half turns to the top of the 114-foot landmark. Peter the Great of Russia is said to have ridden his horse up the ramp while the Czarina followed in a horse-drawn carriage. Today, everybody walks; keep to the outside for the easiest angle. From the top there are views of Copenhagen's red-tiled roofs and far-flung outskirts.

Christian IV built the tower as an observatory in 1642. It still functions as such and the public has access to the astronomical telescope. Concerts and exhibitions are held in the tower also.

➕ B3 ✉ Købmagergade 52A ☎ 33 73 03 73; www.rundetaarn.dk ⏰ Tower: daily 10–8, May–Sep.; 10–6, rest of year (10–9 Tue. and Wed.). Observatory: dependent on astronomical activity 🚇 Nørreport 🚌 5A, 6A, 11A, 14, 15E, 42, 150S, 184, 185, 350S 💰 $

Statens Museum for Kunst

A huge number of works are on display at the Statens Museum for Kunst (National Gallery). International and Danish art from the 13th century to 1900 includes superb 17th-century Dutch paintings by Pieter Bruegel, Rembrandt, Jacob Jordaens and Jacob van Ruisdael; 19th-century Danish painting is represented by Golden Age artists such as Christoffer Eckersberg and Christen Købke, and by the Skagen painters, Theodor Philipsen and the Funen Painters.

Twentieth-century art, displayed in the old building, includes works by Henri Matisse (*Odalisque*), Max Ernst, the CoBrA Group (*Springtime* by Asger Jorn), Georges Braque and Pablo Picasso, as well as other modern works.

➕ C4 ✉ Sølvgade 48–50 ☎ 33 74 84 94; www.smk.dk ⏰ Tue.–Sun. 11–5 (also Wed. 5–8 p.m.) 🚇 Nørreport, Østerport or Kongens Nytorv 🚌 6A, 11A, 14, 26, 42, 184, 185, 150S, 350S 🍴 Café 💰 $$$

Tivoli

At the heart of the city, Tivoli is given over to entertainment: flower gardens, lakes, theater, concert hall, carnival amusements – and people-watching.

There is an entrance fee, and separate charges for carnival rides and indoor attractions. Tivoli is never dull; it is lit brilliantly at night and there are shows and rock concerts during the summer.

➕ B1 ✉ Vesterbrogade 3 ☎ 33 15 10 01; www.tivoli.dk ⏰ Mon.–Fri. 11–11, Sat.–Sun. 11 a.m.–midnight, Apr.–Sep., 2 weeks mid-Oct., and mid-Nov. to Dec. (closed Dec. 24 and 25) 🚇 S-train København H 🚌 2A, 5A, 9A, 10, 12, 14, 26, 33, 34, 37, 66, 250S 🍴 38 food outlets 💰 $$$

Odense

Odense radiates a persuasive charm. Even factory chimneys on the outskirts of the city are gaily painted, and the surviving medieval buildings of the Old Town are enchanting. Above all, this city makes a refreshing change from the urban bustle of Copenhagen. Odense's wealth of museums and attractions is worthy of a city several times its size. This important regional capital and university town retains its provincial charm, and is celebrated as the birthplace of Hans Christian Andersen and the great composer Carl Nielsen.

The Modern City

The streets are busy here, but the city has invested heavily in pedestrianization and cycle routes throughout the city, and there are plans to ban motor vehicles from the center by 2020.

Directly across the road from the railroad station on Østre Stationsvej is Kongens Have, the old Royal Park. Laid out in the 1720s, the park provides a peaceful introduction to Odense and takes you along tree-shaded paths past the Odense Theater and Brandts 13 (see page 148) into the heart of the city.

The center of Odense is at Flakhaven, a pedestrian-only area in front of the red-brick Town Hall (Rådhus), the interior of which can be seen on a guided tour. The friendly and helpful VisitOdense (Odense tourist office) is to the left of the Town Hall.

Buses leave from stops near here, but you will have little need of public transportation unless you travel outside the city. Most attractions are just a short walk from the center, and it is easy to find your way around. From Flakhaven, turn left along the street Vestergade, which takes you into the pleasant,

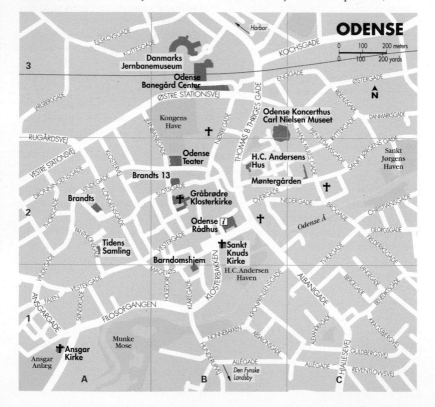

pedestrian-only heart of modern Odense. Here you will find a variety of stores, including top fashion boutiques. Visit Imerco Home (Vestergade 82–84, ☎ 66 12 96 93) for the best in Danish design and kitchenware. Vestergade is full of little cafés and restaurants, as is neighboring Jernbanegade where you can order a *smørrebrød,* the ubiquitous open sandwich consisting of a piece of rye bread topped with cold meats, cheese or fish and loaded with a variety of different garnishes.

The Old Town
Odense's Old Town spreads around Overgade and Nedergade, east of the Town Hall. Here in Hans Jensens Stræde is the Hans Christian Andersen Museum (closed until 2020 for extensive renovation), amid a little complex of cobbled streets and doll-like houses that was once the poor quarter of the city.

Nearby is the Odense Koncerthus (Odense Concert Hall; see page 149), home of the Odense Symfoniorkester and the site of an exhibition on Hans

Christian Andersen while the museum devoted to the author is closed. But the best of Old Odense is a couple of streets away, where the medieval thoroughfares of Overgade and Nedergade retain many of their detailed, interesting old buildings.

Pause at the entrance to Nedergade and look down the side street leading down to the river. This is Paaskestræde, location of the Old Poor House, with its rippled red-tile roof and scalloped cornice above the first floor. Hans Christian Andersen went to school here, and the wording on the wall is his touching comment: "Here I went with my wooden shoes to the poor school." At the bottom of Paaskestræde, along the footpaths beside the Odense river, you can rent rowing boats in summer.

The combination of old and new is what makes Odense such a delight. The city's human scale, its sense of healthy provincialism and its vigorous regional culture are all enhanced by the international cachet of Hans Christian Andersen and Carl Nielsen.

Essential Information

Tourist Information
VisitOdense
Rådhuset, Vestergade 2 ☎ 63 75 75 20; www.visitodense.com

Urban Transportation
Odense's railroad station (Odense Banegård Center) on Østre Stationsvej (☎ 70 13 14 15; for English press 3; www.dsb.dk) is a 10-minute walk from the city center, where most of Odense's main attractions are located. For bus information, ☎ 63 11 22 00;

www.fynbus.dk. The pink city buses are free. For taxis, call Taxafyn ☎ 66 15 44 15.

Airport Information
Odense Airport operates only charter flights to southern Europe. The nearest airport serving the U.K. and northern Europe is Billund Airport, on Jutland ☎ 76 50 50 50; www.bll.dk; Mon.–Fri. 8–5. There are no bus connections between Billund Airport and Odense. Call the airport for information or visit www.rejseplanen.dk.

Climate – average highs and lows for the month
Jan.	Feb.	Mar.	Apr.	May	Jun.	Jul.	Aug.	Sep.	Oct.	Nov.	Dec.
2°C	3°C	9°C	14°C	19°C	22°C	25°C	24°C	20°C	14°C	7°C	4°C
36°F	37°F	48°F	57°F	66°F	72°F	77°F	75°F	68°F	57°F	45°F	39°F
-3°C	-2°C	2°C	5°C	9°C	13°C	15°C	15°C	12°C	6°C	2°C	-1°C
27°F	28°F	36°F	41°F	48°F	55°F	59°F	59°F	54°F	43°F	36°F	30°F

Odense Sights

Brandts and Brandts 13

In 2013, the Fyns Kunstmuseum (Funen Art Museum) merged with Brandts Museum of Photographic Art to create two contrasting art spaces – Brandts, housed in part of an old garment factory, and Brandts 13, a stand-alone classical building on Jernbanegade. Brandts showcases the permanent collection, mostly works by Danish artists from the 17th century to the present day. Highlights include Jens Juel's vivid self-portrait and P. S. Krøyer's *Italian Field Workers*, with its preponderance of left-handed men – a little art puzzle. H. A. Brendekild's big painting *Outworn*, with its prostrate worker in a vast field,

portrays the hard life of peasant workers in old Funen. By contrast, a real charmer is Gustava Emilie Grüner's *Group Portrait of the Family Leunbach*, with its cheerful, inviting faces. The museum's sculptures and permanent collection of contemporary abstract art, includes pieces from the Danish CoBrA movement (1935–60).

Brandts 13, a short walk away, presents an exciting program of paintings, photography and installations by Danish and international artists.

➕ A2 and B2 ✉ Brandts: Brandts Torv 1; Brandts 13: Jernbanegade 13 ☎ Brandts and Brandts 13: 65 20 70 00; www.brandts.dk ⏰ Brandts: Tue.–Wed. and Fri.–Sun, 10–5, Thu. 12–9; Brandts 13: Wed. and Fri.–Sun. 10–5, Thu. 12–9 🖐 $$ (includes both galleries; free Thu. evening)

Danmarks Jernbanemuseum

Denmark's Railway Museum is ideally located next to Odense railroad station and is the biggest museum of its kind in Scandinavia. Small boys will be in heaven here. The museum features a reconstructed early 19th-century station

Den Fynske Landsby is an open-air museum, complete with a windmill

and locomotives, including luxurious royal carriages. Add to this a model train collection, trips on a mini train and a section dedicated to ferries and you might not even get out of the station.

➕ B3 ✉ Dannebrogsgade 24 ☎ 66 13 66 30; www.jernbanemuseum.dk ⏲ Daily 10–4

🍴 Café 💺 $$$ 🚂 Steam-train trips run during school vacations

Den Fynske Landsby

The open-air museum of Den Fynske Landsby (The Funen Village) gives an insight into rural life on the island of Funen during the 18th and 19th centuries. Around 30 thatched, timber-framed buildings are arranged like a farming village, with duck pond, smithy, water mill and windmill.

Imaginative tableaux detail the contrasting lives of a poor and a well-off 19th-century villager. In summer, visitors can watch harvesting, beer brewing and craftwork conducted as part of daily life by actors dressed as villagers, and from mid-July to mid-August the Hans Christian Andersen Players enact one of the famous fairy tales on the open-air stage.

➕ Off map at B1 ✉ Sejerskovvej 20 ☎ 65 51 46 01; www.museum.odense.dk ⏲ Daily 10–6, Jul.–Aug.; Tue.–Fri. 10–4, Sat.–Sun. 10–5, Apr.–Jun. and Sep.–late Oct. 🍴 Restaurant 💺 $$$ 🚂 Living history events in summer

H.C. Andersens Hus

The H.C. Andersens Hus (Hans Christian Andersen Museum) is being rebuilt and is closed until 2020. In the meantime, you can gain an insight into the author's humble beginnings by visiting the Barndomshjem – the writer's childhood home – in Munkemøllstræde, close to the museum. The two small rooms (only one of which was occupied by the Andersens; the other was home to a glovemaker's family) form part of a charming complex of old single-story houses, in what was once considered the "poor quarter" of Odense. It is said that Andersen gained inspiration for his fairy

tales from folktales that he heard on visits to the old people's home where his grandmother worked. Also, there is an exhibition about Odense's famous son in the Odense Koncerthus (see below).

➕ B2 ✉ Bangs Boder 29 ☎ 65 51 46 01; www.museum.odense.dk ⏲ Daily 10–5, Jul.–Aug.; Tue.–Sun. 10–4, rest of year 💺 $$$ (includes entry to Hans Christian Andersen's childhood home)

Møntergården

Housed in a marvelous old building, with red-brick, red-timber framing and a red-tiled roof, Møntergården tells the story of Odense's past with special emphasis on the Stone Age and the Viking era. Behind the main building is a lovely yard and on one side of the yard is a series of preserved domestic interiors from the 17th and 18th centuries right up to the 1950s.

➕ C2 ✉ Overgade 48 ☎ 65 51 46 01; www.museum.odense.dk ⏲ Tue.–Sun. 10–4 💺 $$

Odense Koncerthus and Carl Nielsen Museet

The Odense Koncerthus (Concert Hall) offers a packed program of classical music. Every two years, in June, it hosts the prestigious Carl Nielsen Competition for instrumentalists (violinists, flautists or clarinetists) under the age of 30. In addition to music of their own choice, the young musicians must perform a work by Nielsen.

The Carl Nielsen Museum (closed until 2020) is housed in an extension of the Koncerthus. Already blessed with Hans Christian Andersen, Odense also counts Denmark's most famous composer, Carl August Nielsen, as another native son. Born in 1865 at nearby Nørre Lyndelse, Nielson's most famous works are his six symphonies, his opera *Saul and David* and his beautiful choral works including the lovely *Springtime on Funen*.

➕ B3 ✉ Claus Bergs Gade 11 ☎ Odense Koncerthus: 70 20 20 96; www.odensesymfoni.dk. Call or check website for upcoming concerts Museum: 65 51 46 01; www.museum.odense.dk

Sankt Knuds Kirke

The elegant Gothic style of Sankt Knuds Kirke (St. Canute's Cathedral), reflects the importance of early medieval Odense and the homage paid to King Knud (Canute). Knud, with his brother Benedikt (Benedict) and 17 retainers, was slaughtered here on July 10, 1086 – having taken refuge in the church – by Jutland farmers in a protest against royal taxes (see below). The church has some impressive artifacts, including its splendidly detailed rococo pulpit and altarpiece, a dazzling wood triptych with exquisite carvings and gold leaf that is one of the finest pieces of religious art in northern Europe. In the atmospheric crypt are two reliquaries containing the alleged skeletons of Knud and Benedikt.

✠ B2 ✉ Klosterbakken 2 ☎ 66 12 03 92; www. odense-domkirke.dk ◷ Mon.–Sat. noon–5, Sun. 10–4, Apr.–Oct.; Sun.–Mon. noon–4, Tue.–Sat. 10–4, rest of year 🎫 Free

Tidens Samling

For a museum with a difference, Tidens Samling (Time Collection) is hard to beat. It displays a series of eight set-piece interiors from 1900 to the 1980s, each one crammed full with authentic artifacts and furnishings. The result is delightful – a unique look at changing domestic style and fashions in dress. One of the many charming aspects of the Time Collection is that you are able to step into the displays, relax in the chairs or, if it takes your fancy, do a bit of sock-mending. There is even a period-style coffee bar. Period fashion shows and temporary exhibitions with a cultural theme are sometimes staged. The museum is on the third floor (there is an elevator).

✠ A2 ✉ Farvegården 7, 3 sal ☎ 65 91 19 42; www.tidenssamling.dk ◷ Mon.–Sat. 10–4, first Sun. of the month 11–3 🍴 Café 🎫 $$

The Gothic cathedral of Sankt Knuds Kirke

The Martyred King

The violent death of the 11th-century Danish King Knud (Canute), a descendant of Canute, one-time king of England, did Odense a favor. The king and his brother, Benedikt, were slaughtered in Odense's old Church of St. Alban's on July 10, 1086, by Jutland peasant farmers angered by excessive taxes levied by the king to finance war with England. Fourteen years later Pope Paschalis II canonized the king as St. Knud the Holy. In an ironic twist, Benedictine monks from England settled in Odense and successfully promoted the town as a place of pilgrimage to the murdered ruler.

The reputed skeletons of Knud and Benedikt can still be seen in Sankt Knuds Kirke (see above).

Hans Christian Andersen

Odense's most famous son left his native city at an early age, yet Odense is still associated with Hans Christian Andersen. From quite humble beginnings – his mother was a washerwoman and his father was a shoemaker – Andersen's astonishingly fertile imagination and creativity led him on extensive travels throughout Europe and established him as Denmark's major literary figure. He was born in 1805 in Odense, but it is not certain in which location. By the age of seven Andersen was inspired after visiting the theater in Odense; by 14 he was in Copenhagen, where he tried unsuccessfully to join the Royal Theater Company.

Andersen was a man of complex sensitivities whose relationships were profound and often difficult, although he was never short of friends and benefactors. He was essentially a poet and dramatist, and his early works reflect this. He had the urge to travel, and his first, self-published book was about a journey he made on foot through Denmark. In 1835 he published *Fairy Tales, Told for Children*. Plays, novels and travel accounts followed, along with a continuing output of the fairy tales that were to make his name.

Andersen's fairy tales were far more profound than mere fantasy, however charming. He was a powerful moralist, an intensely humane man who understood the human condition and injected into his stories remarkable life lessons. Famous and popular tales such as *The Emperor's New Clothes, The Little Mermaid, The Ugly Duckling, The Tinder Box* and *The Nightingale* have entered the consciousness of generations of readers worldwide, for their literary elegance as much as their theatricality.

Andersen remained an intense and sometimes troubled man throughout his life. He was a friend and associate of kings and of the famous. He never married, though he was deeply in love at times, not least with the Swedish opera soprano Jenny Lind. He died at 70 in 1875, in a friend's house near Copenhagen. In the Denmark of his day Andersen was criticized and diminished for what was seen as his absorption with the wider European world. As always with genius, however, his work transcended time. In Odense the spirit of this remarkable man is vividly present, at the Hans Christian Andersen Museum and Childhood Home (see page 149) and also in quieter corners of the Old Town.

Hans Christian Andersen reads his story *The Angel* to a sick child

Finland

Introduction and Map 154

Timeline 156

Survival Guide 157

Helsinki 158

Feature: Imperial City: The Buildings of Helsinki 163

Hotels and Restaurants 473

Essential Information 514

Opposite: A sauna house at the edge of a forested lake near Jyväskylä

Finland

Finland, one of the world's great survivors, is a small nation that has had to contend with harsh nature and belligerent neighbors in an often hostile northern European world. For centuries Finland was trapped between the aggressive ambitions of Sweden and Russia, and then in the 20th century between the Eastern and Western protagonists of the Cold War.

The country's emergence as a self-confident, modern nation, with its historic identity intact, is a celebration of steady nerve, political shrewdness and tenacity.

A tall-masted vessel moored in Helsinki harbor

Land of Forests and Lakes

Finland is bordered on the east by Russia, on the northwest by Sweden and on the north by Norway. Most of Finland is less than 600 feet high, and over 70 percent of the country supports coniferous spruce and pine. The northern areas are covered with peat bog, and there are almost 188,000 lakes and nearly 180,000 islands. All of Finland is a seemingly endless blanket of trees, water and wide skies.

The main "lake district" of Saimaa in the east is a paradise of woodland and navigable rivers and lakes, punctuated by rugged cliffs and a glittering mosaic of islands and lakeside towns and villages. Apart from the special nature of the Finnish landscape, the main cities and towns – Helsinki, Turku (Åbo), Tampere, Porvoo, Savonlinna, Oulu and Rovaniemi – have much to offer the visitor. They are as modern as any other European urban center, yet retain a deep-seated Finnish identity.

The Islands and Lapland

The mirror image of the inland water world is Finland's coastal region. Off Finland's southwestern coast is the Saaristomeri archipelago, with its thousands of islands and little rock islets known as "skerries." Farther out lie the Åland Islands (Åland Ahvenanmaa), stepping stones to Sweden. You can explore the archipelago by ferry or steamship, or on land, visit the beaches of Yyteri, to the north.

In northern Finland, in the great wilderness of Lapland, you can learn about the life and culture of the Sami (Lapp) people in Rovaniemi's Arctic Center (Arktikum). The adventurous can go white-water rafting on the Tornionjoki river, follow one of the numerous hiking routes or head into the mountains of the northwest, where Finland's highest peak, Haltitunturi, reaches 4,300 feet. Up here in this wilderness, the Sami tend their reindeer herds and pursue the ever-hopeful prospect for gold.

Traveling in Finland

Traveling around the country by car is a good way to see rural Finland. There are excellent road systems around Helsinki and between the main towns, but in rural areas some roads may be poor or even just dirt tracks.

Finland's state railroad, VR (Valtion Rautatiet), serves all but the extreme north of the country, with the most frequent service in the south. There is an excellent bus service that runs

Scattered small islands on Lake Pielinen seen from the summit of Koli hill

throughout the country, and the east–west network in central and southern Finland is especially efficient.

FINLAND

The Finnish climate is far more amiable than you might expect. In spite of being in the same latitude as Alaska and Siberia, Finland and the whole Scandinavian peninsula enjoy a much milder climate owing to the influence of the Gulf Stream. There can be warm dry spells in summer; the southeast area of Finland has the highest summer temperatures throughout the Scandinavian region.

The Finnish people have a well-developed sense of irony, which may emerge in the form of jovial self-disparagement, especially among the young. The Finns know when to keep quiet and may appear to be unwilling to talk very much. But throughout the country you will be welcomed, and helped, with courtesy and kindness.

More Top Destinations in Finland

- Ahvenanmaa A1 (Åland)
- Helvetinjärven Kansallispuisto A1
- Lapland A2
- Loviisa B1
- Porvoo B1
- Rauma A1
- Rovaniemi B2
- Saimaa B1
- Savonlinna B1
- Tampere A1
- Turku A1
- Vaasa A2

Timeline

4000 BC	Sami peoples move into northern Finland from the east.
1600 BC	Development of Iron Age culture and the Finno-Ugric language.
1100	Finland is occupied by four tribal elements: the Sami in the north, Karelians in the east, Tavastians in the central lakes and Finns in the southwest.
1249	Swedish regent Birger Jarl establishes colonies in the southwest of Finland.
1290s	Invasions by Russia lead to Swedish–Russian conflicts.
1555	Finland is made a Swedish duchy.
1807	Czar Alexander I of Russia occupies Finland.
1906	Finland (although still part of the Russian Empire) is the first European nation to achieve universal suffrage.
1917	Finland declares its independence.
1919	Finland becomes a republic. Kaarlo Stahlberg is its first president.
1939–44	Finland declares neutrality but Russia invades; Finland declares itself a "co-belligerent" with Germany in resisting Russian attacks.
1992	The 1948 Treaty of Friendship, Cooperation and Mutual Assistance between Finland and Russia is dissolved.
1995	Finland becomes a member of the European Union.
2000	Tarja Halonen becomes the first female president of Finland.
2002	Finland adopts the euro as its national currency.
2010	Finland becomes the first country in the world to give its residents a legal right to broadband internet access.
2012	Sauli Niinisto of the National Coalition party becomes the first Conservative president since 1956.
2014	UNESCO awards Helsinki "City of Design" status.
2015	A right-wing coalition forms a new government.
2017	Finland celebrates the centenary of the country's independence.

A Bridge between East and West

Finland's 20th-century relationship with Russia has very often been misunderstood. The term "Finlandization" was used disparagingly by some to describe the country's carefully orchestrated policy toward its giant neighbor, but Finland's sensitive geographic position dictated this policy. For centuries, Russia competed with Sweden for domination over Finland. After 1807, Russian influence prevailed. Finland's declaration of independence in 1917 led to an uneasy relationship between the two countries, and resulted in bitter conflict during World War II. After the war, Finland was forced to tread a careful path between the Cold War policies of East and West. The Finnish politician who did the most to maintain national identity under these circumstances was Urho K. Kekkonen (president 1956–1981). Kekkonen's pragmatism and his careful balancing act between East and West earned him much criticism from Western politicians. But Finland remained essentially a Scandinavian country while maintaining "friendly coexistence" with Russia. Finland's rapid emergence, post-Cold War, as a democratic, pluralist and modern society is a testament to Kekkonen's strategy. It is said that he frequently conducted discussions with visiting Russian politicians in the relaxation of a traditional sauna.

Survival Guide

- Driving with dimmed headlights in the daytime is compulsory in Finland. When driving in rural Finland you will need to watch out for elk and reindeer on the roads.

- For Finnish and international fashion in Helsinki try Marimekko (www.marimekko.com), which has locations at Aleksanterinkatu 50, the Itis shopping mall and the Kamppi mall complex. For exclusive silkwear look for Marja Kurki's scarfs in Stockmann department store, Aleksanterinkatu 52. If you love Nordic design, visit the Design District, centering on Dianapuisto Park. Some 200 stores, workshops and galleries showcase the objects, furniture and clothes of many of Finland's top designers (www.designdistrict.fi).

- Consumer goods are generally more expensive in Finland than in the rest of Europe, and accommodations and restaurants also are more expensive.

- Many hotels have saunas, but most are electrically heated. The traditional Finnish "smoke" sauna is heated by a wood-burning stove and is said to be the real experience, an important cultural institution. For information on traditional saunas, including information on its own sauna, contact the Finnish Sauna Society (Suomen Saunaseura), Vaskiniementie 10, 00200 Helsinki ☎ 50 372 4167; www.sauna.fi.

- In Helsinki you will find numerous "grill kiosks," little huts selling fast food such as hamburgers, french fries, meat-filled pies and grilled sausages (*grillimakkara*).

- On the weekend that falls between June 20 and 26 there are midsummer celebrations throughout the country. After the long nights of winter, Finns celebrate Midsummer's Day with gusto.

- The useful Helsinki Card (www.helsinkicard.com) entitles you to entry to museums and major sights,

Elk can be a hazard for motorists in rural Finland

unlimited travel on local public transportation, a city sightseeing tour and a range of discounts. The cards are available for periods of 24 hours (€48), 48 hours (€58) and 72 hours (€68); for 4/6/6 euros more for each pass respectively, you can use it in the surrounding region.

- Other than in bars and restaurants, alcoholic drinks over 5.5 percent must be bought from state-controlled outlets known as Alko (stores closed on Sunday). Check information at www.visitfinland.com.

- Public restrooms in Finland are generally clean and modern. Signs are *Naiset* for ladies and *Michet* for men.

Helsinki

Helsinki (sometimes referred to in Swedish as Helsingfors) will take your breath away. It does so quite literally in the frozen winter, but even then it can have days of glorious weather. In summer, the city will delight you even more with its stunning architecture and its blue Baltic waters.

City of the Sea

The best way to approach Helsinki is by sea. The Lutheran Cathedral (Tuomiokirkko) and the Uspenski Cathedral (Uspenskin katedraali) stand out against the skyline behind the handsome waterfront buildings that include the 19th-century City Hall (Kaupunki aula) and Presidential Palace (Presidentin linna). In front of them is Market Square (Kauppatori), with vendors selling items from fish to crafts.

You miss this introduction to the city if you arrive by plane, bus or train, but the early 20th-century railroad station is a striking example of Helsinki's architecture. Bus and railroad stations are close to the heart of things and only a few streets from Senate Square (Senaatintori, see page 162) and the bustle of Mannerheimintie, the city's main street. Helsinki is easy to get around, with trams and buses serving all parts of the city.

The heart of summertime Helsinki is the tree-lined Esplanade (Eteläesplanadi) that runs west from Market Square and South Harbor (Eteläsatama) to Mannerheimintie. Kappeli restaurant (see page 473), located near the bandstand is a good place to sample Finnish specialties such as *lohikeitto* (salmon soup).

The streets bordering the Esplanade have many stylish boutiques, as well as colorful cafés and restaurants. Stop for coffee and pastries in the Swedish Theater (Svenska Teatern) at the west end of the Esplanade.

Uspenski Cathedral in Northern Harbor, Helsinki

Finlandssvenska

The form of Swedish spoken in Finland is *Finlandssvenska*, "Finland's Swedish." Today about six percent of Finnish residents speak Swedish exclusively, and everybody else has some knowledge. Swedish is a mandatory subject in schools. Most of Finland's signs and street names appear in Finnish and Swedish.

Quiet Corners

For green spaces and seashore walks go south from the Esplanade, past the University Observatory and the Russian Embassy, to reach Kaivopuisto Park, at the far end encircled by the seashore road, Ehrenströmintie, where moored yachts enhance the views of numerous islands. Alternatively, go north from the square in front of the railroad station to Kaisaniemi Park and the University Botanical Gardens (Kasvitieteellinen Puutarha), and on to the tree-fringed sea inlets beyond. Wander along and up Mannerheimintie to see the monumental Parliament House (Eduskuntatalo) and Finlandia Hall (Finlandiatalo), then go west to Temppeliaukio Church (Temppeliaukion Kirkko), a copper-domed church carved out of rock.

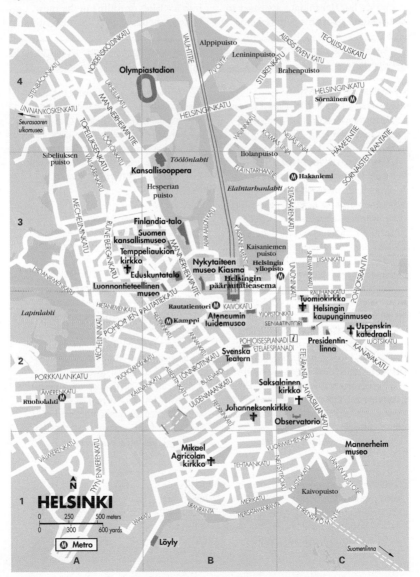

Despite Helsinki's reputation for long, dark winters, there is much to reward the visitor all year. Enjoy restaurants, listen to the music of Jean Sibelius in Finlandia Hall (☎ 09 402 41; www.finlandiatalo.fi) or attend a performance at the Finnish National Opera (☎ 09 4030 2211; www.opera.fi).

You will find fewer English speakers here than in other Scandinavian countries, but Helsinkians are eager to help visitors enjoy this cultured city.

"Smoke" Sauna

Sauna is a way of life for Finns. A sauna is an insulated room that is traditionally heated by a wood-burning stove. In a "smoke" sauna, steam is generated by throwing water on the hot stones of the stove, and the correct mix of steam and heat, known as *löyly*, fills the room in which you sit naked. Sometimes pine needles are added to the water. Plunging into icy lakes or rolling in the snow between bouts of *löyly* are other options.

Essential Information

Tourist Information

Helsinki City Tourist & Convention Bureau
Pohjoisesplanadi 19 ☎ 09 3101 3300; www.visithelsinki.fi

Urban Transportation

Helsinki's railroad station is located on Kaivokatu. It is the terminus for main train services throughout the country and to Russia. (St. Petersburg is just 3.5 hours by the high-speed Allegro service, which runs several times a day.) For information ☎ 0600 41 900 (358 9 2319 2902 from outside Finland; www.vr.fi/en). Helsinki's bus, tram and subway network is operated by Helsingforsregionens trafik or HSL (Helsinki Region Transport; ☎ 09 4766 4000, Mon.–Fri. 7–7, Sat.–Sun. 9–5; www.hsl.fi). Tram 2 is a useful route for visitors to take as it passes the main sights, while Tram 4 passes many of Helsinki's most striking buildings, and Tram 6 takes in the design district and food markets. Main tram stops are on Kaivokatu. The city bus terminal is in the Kampii Mall, from where connections to the rest of Finland also depart. For information on buses call Matkahuolto

☎ 0200 4000; www.matkahuolto.fi. Helsinki has a small metro (subway) system serving mainly suburban areas. Stations have a sign marked "M." Taxis have a yellow dome light and are available when it is lit. There is a taxi stand at the railroad station. Call the Helsinki Taxi Center at ☎ 0100 0700; https://taksihelsinki.fi.

Airport Information

Helsinki-Vantaa Airport is 12 miles north of the city. A train service between the Central Station and the airport runs every 10–30 minutes and takes about 30 minutes (www.hsl.fi). Finnair buses run to and from the airport to Helsinki railroad station (www.finnair.com/INT/GB/information-services/at-the-airport/transportation). The service is every 20 minutes, daily 5 a.m.–midnight (5:45 a.m.–1:05 a.m. from the airport) and the trip takes about 35 minutes. Slower, but less expensive, regular bus service No. 615 also runs between the airport and the city center (Rautatientori). For 24-hour flight information call the service center ☎ 0200 14636; www.finavia.fi.

Climate – average highs and lows for the month

Jan.	Feb.	Mar.	Apr.	May	Jun.	Jul.	Aug.	Sep.	Oct.	Nov.	Dec.
-3°C	-3°C	1°C	7°C	14°C	18°C	21°C	19°C	13°C	7°C	2°C	-1°C
27°F	27°F	34°F	45°F	57°F	64°F	70°F	66°F	55°F	45°F	36°F	30°F
-9°C	-9°C	-5°C	0°C	5°C	9°C	12°C	10°C	6°C	2°C	-2°C	-7°C
16°F	16°F	23°F	32°F	41°F	48°F	54°F	50°F	43°F	36°F	28°F	19°F

Helsinki Sights

Key to symbols

➕ map coordinates refer to the Helsinki map
on page 159 🎟 admission charge:
$$$ more than €10, $$ €5–€10, $ less than €5
See page 5 for complete key to symbols

Ateneumin taidemuseo

The Ateneumin taidemuseo (Ateneum
Art Museum) is housed in a handsome
19th-century building. Vincent van
Gogh, Amedeo Modigliani and Paul
Cézanne are represented, among many
other international figures from the
19th century to the 1960s. In addition,
a collection of Finnish art, from the
18th century to the mid-1960s, includes
powerful works by realist painters Fanny
Churberg and Albert Edelfelt, such as
Edelfelt's, *Women of Ruokalahti on the
Church Hill*. Finland's master Akseli
Gallen-Kallela dominates with works
such as the seductive *Aino-taru*, the *Aino
Myth* and the earthy *A New House*.
Gallen-Kallela pupil Hugo Simberg's
mildly disturbing and surrealistic *The
Wounded Angel* is another highlight.
➕ B2 ✉ Kaivokatu 2 ☎ 02 9450 0401; www.
ateneum.fi 🕐 Tue. and Fri. 10–6, Wed. Thu. 10–8,
Sat.–Sun. 10–5 🚇 Kaisaniemi 🚌 All buses to
Rautatientori Square bus terminus; tram 2, 3, 5, 6, 9
🍴 Café 🎟 $$$ 🎫 Guided tours in English. Reserve
in advance (☎ 02 9450 0500)

Helsingin kaupunginmuseo

The Helsingin kaupunginmuseo
(Helsinki City Museum) comprises a
cluster of historic buildings on or near
Senaatintori (Senate Square, see page
162). The interconnected buildings
bring the social history of Helsinki to
life with immersive experiences and
interactive displays and images. Enter
the Time Machine and be transported
to the cobblestoned streets of 1903, or
sit in a typical 1950s' interior.

One of the most popular parts of the
museum is the Sederholmin talo
(Sederholm House), otherwise known as

the Children's Town. Visitors of all ages
can visit the 18th-century shops and
workshops, sit in a 1930s classroom,
unload cargo from a ship or sit in
Grandma's kitchen.
➕ C2 ✉ Aleksanterinkatu 16 ☎ 09 3103 6630;
www.helsinkicitymuseum.fi 🕐 Mon.–Fri. 11–7,
Sat.–Sun. 11–5 🚊 Tram 1, 2, 3, 4 🍴 Café 🎟 Free

Löyly

This luxury public sauna on the
waterfront opened in 2016. The
sleek-looking structure contains three
saunas (one a smoke sauna), a
restaurant, a bar and a stunning sun
terrace suspended over the sea.
Eventually, the area surrounding the
sauna will form part of a coastal park.
➕ B1 ✉ Hernesaarenranta 4 ☎ 09 6128 6550;
www.loylyhelsinki.fi 🕐 Mon. 4–10 p.m., Tue.–Wed.
and Sun. 1–10 p.m., Thu. 8–10 a.m. and 1–10 p.m., Fri.
1–11 p.m., Sat. 8–10 a.m. and 1–11 p.m. 🚇 14; tram
6T, 9 🍴 Restaurant 🎟 $$$

Luonnontieteellinen museo

The venerable Luonnontieteellinen
museo (Natural History Museum) is
guarded by a very handsome bronze elk,
just one of the animals in the museum's
vast collection of mammals, birds,
insects and minerals. The mammal
collection is one of the best of its kind
in Europe, showing exotic beasts and
Finnish wildlife in their native habitats.
➕ B3 ✉ Pohjoinen Rautatiekatu 13 ☎ 09 1911;
www.luomus.fi 🕐 Tue.–Wed. and Fri. 9–4, Thu. 9–6,
Sat. 10–5, Sun. 10–4, Sep.–May; Tue.–Sun. 10–5 (also
Thu. 5–6 p.m.), rest of year 🚇 Kamppi 🚇 24; tram 1, 2
🍴 Museum café 🎟 $$$ (free first Fri. of the month
1–4 p.m., Sep.–May; first Fri. of the month 2–5 p.m.,
rest of year)

Nykytaiteen museo Kiasma

The Nykytaiteen museo Kiasma
(Museum of Contemporary Art Kiasma)
is housed in a bold, postmodern-style
building designed by American architect
Steven Holl. The changing exhibitions
of conceptual art and often radical
installations are at the forefront of
European contemporary art.

✚ B3 ✉ Mannerheiminaukio 2 ☎ 02 9450 0501;
www.kiasma.fi ◷ Tue. 10–5, Wed.–Fri. 10–8:30,
Sat. 10–6, Sun. 10–5 🚌 All buses to Rautatientori
Square bus terminus; tram 4, 7, 10 🍴 Museum café
🎟 $$$ (free first Fri. of the month)

Senaatintori

Senaatintori (Senate Square) is the focus
of Russian Imperial-style buildings. This
form of architecture was encouraged by
Tsar Alexander I in his bid to make
Helsinki a stylistically eastern capital
after it was annexed by Russia in 1809.

The square and its major buildings
were designed by C. L. Engel. Helsinki's
Lutheran Cathedral (Tuomiokirkko)
dominates Senate Square and the city
skyline. The cathedral, also by Engel
and completed in 1852, is essentially
Classical but has Byzantine elements.
Its domes are copper-sheathed and
gilded, the only accents in an otherwise
blinding whiteness. The square forms
part of the Tori Quarters, a lively area
with a vibrant art scene and one-off
shops and restaurants. In summer,
concerts, food fairs and exhibitions are
sometimes held in the inner courtyards
of the historic buildings; at Christmas,
you'll find a Christmas market and a
pop-up sauna.

✚ C2 ✉ Unioninkatu 29 ☎ Lutheran Cathedral:
09 2340 6120; www.helsinkicathedral.fi ◷ Lutheran
Cathedral: daily 9–6 (also 6 p.m.–midnight, Jun.–Aug.)
🚌 Tram 1, 2, 7 🍴 Cafe Krypta, daily 11–5, Jun.–Aug.
🛈 Summer events; organ recitals Wed. at noon

Seurasaaren ulkomuseo

The Seurasaaren ulkomuseo (Seurasaari
Open-Air Museum) is a collection of
Finnish regional buildings from the 17th
to the 20th century. On Seurasaari
Island, it is easily reached from central
Helsinki. Most of the 87 buildings on
the site date from the 18th and 19th
centuries and include a manor house,
traditional farmhouses and a church.

✚ Off map at A4 ✉ Seurasaari ☎ 0 40 649 3040;
www.seurasaarisaatio.fi ◷ Buildings: daily 11–5,
Jun.–Aug.; Mon.–Fri. 9–3, Sat.–Sun. 11–5, mid-May
to May 31 and in early Sep. Park: daily, all year

🚌 24, then a 10-minute walk 🍴 Café 🎟 $$
(park free) 🛈 Guided tours in English daily at
3 p.m., Jun. to mid-Aug.

Suomen kansallismuseo

Dating from the early 20th century,
the Suomen kansallismuseo (National
Museum of Finland) is a fine example of
the Jugend style of architecture. The
entrance is "guarded" by a large statue of
a bear by artist Emil Wikström.

The display galleries lead off a central
hall with a vaulted ceiling painted with
scenes from *Kalavela*, Finland's national
poetry epic. Highlights include a
sculpture of an elk's head from around
7000–6000 BC, the throne of Alexander
I, from which he proclaimed Finland's
"incorporation" with Russia in 1809,
and a hands-on area for children.

✚ B3 ✉ Mannerheimintie 34 ☎ 02 9533 6901;
www.kansallismuseo.fi ◷ Tue.–Sun. 11–5
🚌 Tram 4, 10 🍴 Museum restaurant 🎟 $$$
(free Fri. 4–6 p.m.)

Suomenlinna

The historic sea fortress of Suomenlinna,
a UNESCO World Heritage Site, is built
on six interconnecting islands. First
used by Sweden in 1748 under the name
Sveaborg ("Sweden's Fortress"), the
island was surrendered to Russia in
1808. It remained in Russian control
until 1918, when newly independent
Finland named it Suomenlinna
("Finland's Fortress").

Also here are the Suomenlinna
Museum, the Military Museum and
submarine *Vesikko*, a vessel that
operated in the Gulf of Finland during
World War II, as well as the Customs
Museum and a Doll and Toy Museum.

✚ Off map at C1 ✉ Suomenlinna ✉ Visitor Center:
02 9533 8410; www.suomenlinna.fi ◷ Visitor Center:
daily 10–6, May–Sep.; 10:30–4:30, rest of year
⛴ Ferries (summer waterbus) leave from the eastern
side of Market Square 🍴 Restaurants and cafés
🎟 Site, Visitor Center and Custom Museum free; other
museums $–$$ 🛈 Guided tours ($$) in English daily
at 11 a.m., 12:30 and 2:30 p.m., Jun.–Aug.; Sat.–Sun. at
1:30 p.m., rest of year

Imperial City: The Buildings of Helsinki

Helsinki has some of the finest buildings in northern Europe, with the architectural heart of the city being Senate Square. Here, in the early 19th century, Berlin-born Carl Ludvig Engel was commissioned to create a new Helsinki in neoclassical Russian Imperial style. On its high podium, the gleaming white Lutheran Cathedral (Tuomiokirkko) is the focus of the square. Leave the square at its northeastern corner and take a stroll up Snellmaninkatu a short distance to where the Bank of Finland (Suomen Pankki) faces the regal-looking House of Estates (Säätytalo), built in the Classical style with beautiful gilded Corinthian capitals.

Another great architectural theme in Helsinki is art nouveau, or Jugend as it is known in Finland. This style drew its motifs from Finnish culture and tradition; its materials are the timber and rough-faced granite of the country used in naturalistic ways. Jugend architecture is best seen in residential areas such as Eira, on the southern peninsula of the city, and on the little island to the east of the harbor, Katajanokka. The island is guarded by the magnificent Uspenski Cathedral (Uspenskin katedraali), the most impressive expression of orthodoxy you are likely to find in northern Europe.

Jugend architecture is characterized by turrets, castellated features and carved motifs. Yet the buildings remain elegant and restrained. Take a walk down Eira's streets of Huvilakatu and Laivurinkatu. On Laivurinkatu, look for No. 25, the Villa Johanna. Walk down Luotsikatu and Kauppiaankatu, a short distance east of the cathedral, where there are numerous examples of Jugend to compare with Senate Square's Classicism and with the city's more modern buildings. Finlandia Hall and the Museum of Contemporary Art Kiasma maintain Helsinki's international reputation for architectural excellence.

Helsinki's dramatic white Lutheran Cathedral (Tuomiokirkko) is the focal point on Senate Square

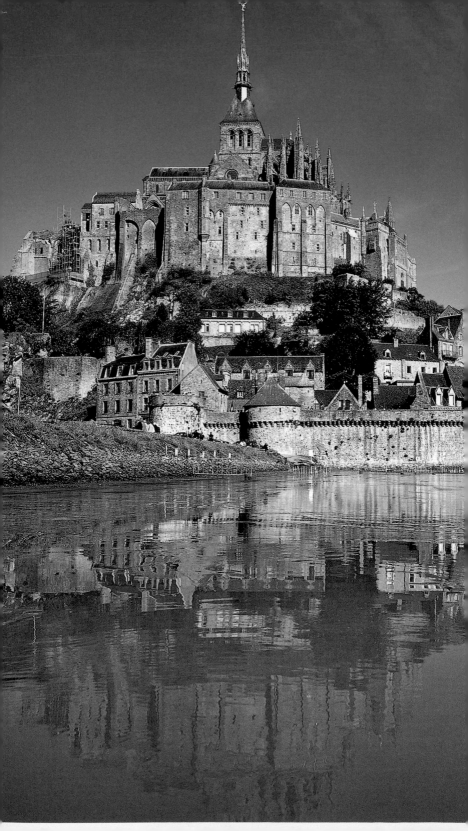

France

Introduction and Map 166

Timeline 172

Survival Guide 173

Paris 174

Feature: The French Revolution 181

Feature: Eating and Drinking in Paris 185

Lyon 186

Feature: La Cuisine Lyonnaise 192

Feature: Lyon and the Silk Tradition 193

Nice 194

Feature: Parks, Gardens, Trees and Flowers 199

Strasbourg 200

Feature: A Day in Strasbourg 205

Hotels and Restaurants 473

Essential Information 518

Opposite: Le Mont-St.-Michel is one kilometer off of France's Normandy coastline

France

France is the largest country in western Europe, geographically one of the most diverse, and among the most beautiful. Its cities contain some of the greatest treasures in Europe; its countryside is prosperous and well tended. The French combine practicality with romance; they lead a stylish life, eat delicious food and bask in a pleasant climate.

Historically, France has developed the notion of equality for all and, while retaining its sense of tradition, remains a forward-looking country. Over the past half-century, for instance, the French have forged ahead in modern technology. France is a country of contrasts, making it a delight to explore.

France Today

France was among the first European countries to dispense with its monarchy. Apart from a couple of brief periods, it has been a republic almost as long as the United States. The French Revolution gave a tremendous sense of patriotism to all French men and women, which continues to the present day.

Despite the apparently never-ending political ups and downs, French people have a strong sense of national pride and

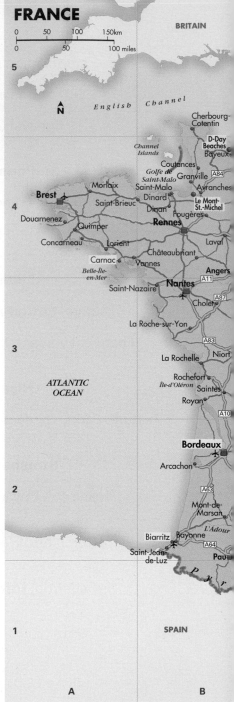

More Top Destinations in France

- Avignon D2
- Beaune D3
- Biarritz B2
- Bordeaux B2
- Carcassonne C1
- Carnac A4
- Château de Versailles C4
- Cirque de Gavarnie B1
- D-Day Beaches B4
- Grasse E2
- Grotte de Lascaux C2
- Honfleur C4
- Le Mont-St.-Michel B4
- Pont du Gard D2
- Rocamadour C2
- Sarlat C2
- Toulouse C2

The Château d'Azay-le-Rideau is built on an island on the Indre river in the heart of the Loire Valley

unity; they are essentially one people and one country. Every town and village in France flies the flag (*tricolore*) with pride, and displays in its town hall a bust of Marianne, the beautiful woman who epitomizes the spirit of the country.

The French despair of their politicians, grumble at their government and taxation, and are quite capable of unruly demonstrations against the most surprising things, but *au fond*, at heart, they remain proud and devoted admirers of their country.

La belle France

La belle France – beautiful France – is indeed truly beautiful. Hexagonal in shape, each of its six sides acts as a natural boundary. The English Channel and the rolling Atlantic guard the west coast; the Pyrenees and Alps, the southwest and southeast borders; the Mediterranean laps along the southern coast; and the mighty Rhine river forms a barrier against Germany in the northeast. Within this area lies a huge variety of landscapes, with plains, arable flatlands, forested hills, vine- and olive-growing terraces, lush river valleys, inhospitable mountain massifs and a combined coastline stretching for almost 2,000 miles.

As you travel around France you'll notice how sparsely populated the land is compared to most other European countries. Miles go past without a sign of a town or village, yet the land is mostly cultivated, forested or tended in some way. France has always been an agricultural country, and today is the largest agricultural producer in the European Union.

Cities, Towns and Villages

In a country as geographically varied as France there is bound to be a diverse range of architecture, as styles evolved to suit the environment. In southern rural areas, the population lived in easily defensible communities and worked the fields daily, leaving a legacy of picturesque hilltop villages, with narrow streets for shelter against the fierce sun. In the mountains the design was dictated by the climate, and cozy wooden chalets evolved, with steep or flat roofs depending on the region.

The whole country in general enjoyed great prosperity during the 17th and 18th centuries, and in most of the major cities there are architectural reminders of this time, in the shape of churches, fine civic buildings, spacious squares and well-planned streets.

Before the French Revolution, the aristocracy spent several months a year on their estates and built fine fortified houses and beautiful châteaux in which they lived.

This wonderful mixture of styles still exists, and the French have been far more successful than some other European nations at preserving the historic centers of their towns. The second half of the 20th century saw some truly imaginative and innovative civic building projects in major cities, which you'll certainly notice.

The French Character

Other Europeans have a peculiar relationship with the French people, in which there may be more than a touch of envy. The French have much to boast about, and are rightly proud of their culture. As a result, they have gained a reputation with their neighbors for being arrogant. They are often accused of seeing themselves as decidedly superior to every other nation.

For years the French have been criticized and stereotyped for their attitude. But the minute a foreigner steps on French soil he or she is once more seduced: by the country, the overwhelming charm of the people, the way of life.

Lifestyle

The French strike a happy balance between the work-driven culture of northern Europeans and the wonderfully alluring, but sometimes frustratingly relaxed, southern European approach to life. This is a prosperous country with a high standard of living, where both men and women hold down prestigious and influential jobs in every sector. It also is a highly efficient country with an excellent infrastructure, making things very easy for visitors.

Public transportation is first-rate, with Europe's best and fastest train system. If you're driving, you'll find the roads fast and in good condition; the country's speeding and drunk-driving laws are strictly enforced.

Hotels are comfortable, restaurants provide good value, and tourism is a well-organized, thriving industry.

All this is augmented by the innate French sense of style, which is obvious the minute you arrive. This is evident in everything from the way produce is artfully stacked in market stalls to the sensible layout of an airport.

You'll find the French have a relaxed approach to most problems, but note that the wheels of daily life are oiled with a high level of politeness. Even if you don't speak the language, bear in mind that courtesy is extremely important in everyday dealings.

People work hard in France, but indulge in relaxation as well. In the evenings they enjoy themselves over a lengthy meal or sit for hours in cafés. French citizens have always backed their country's achievements in culture and

The Vieille Ville (Old Town) area of Nice in Provence

The national game of *boules* is taken very seriously by its devotees, and is fun to watch

the arts, so there's a lively arts scene everywhere. You'll also find that almost everyone has strong views on a wide range of artistic, political and economic events, which they're eager to share.

Religion

France is nominally a Catholic country, with the church separated from the state in 1905.

More than 80 percent of its 65 million inhabitants have been baptized into the Catholic church, although only a small percentage regularly attends services.

There are approximately 1 million Protestants, who for historical reasons tend to be more active churchgoers. Immigrants from France's former colonies make up a large proportion of the considerable number of Muslims, while the Jewish population in France never recovered its numbers after World War II.

Every large town has one or more churches with Sunday services.

Pastimes

The French take relaxation seriously. They enjoy sports, both as spectators and participants, with soccer the national favorite, closely followed by rugby. Cycling is popular with the Tour de France rolling through the streets around the country in July, watched by millions. Tennis and golf also are popular sports, both with good facilities for tourists, and you'll find challenging golf courses all over France. Resort areas offer a huge range of pastimes, from tennis to sailing to organized hiking.

With the Alps on their doorstep, many people ski, especially during early February when children are out of school and families head for the slopes. As well as the Alps, the Pyrenees and the Massif Central at Le Mont-Dore also are destinations for French skiers.

You may often see *boules* being played. This is a game where players attempt to surround a small target ball on the ground by throwing larger, heavier balls

Les Aiguilles (literally "The Needles") is a mountain range in Chamonix, a popular skiing area

from a specified distance. A game local to the Basque area is *pelota*, where two teams hit a ball against a wall.

Pleasures

Food and drink are among the national pleasures of France, and much time is spent shopping for and preparing food. Although modern life has taken its toll, fast food, frozen meals and "grazing" items are not considered mealtime options. If the French can't be bothered to cook, they can pick up fresh dishes from a *traiteur*, a type of delicatessen. Desserts are rarely homemade, bought instead from a *pâtisserie* (cake shop), ensuring the highest quality.

Every region has its own particular food specialties and these are taken so seriously that some foodstuffs have an *appellation controlée* label, similar to the labeling used for wine, meaning that the product must be from the area for which it is known. Well-known regional dishes include *pot au feu de la mer* (seafood stew) from Brittany, *salade Niçoise* (Niçoise salad, made with fresh tuna, anchovies and eggs) from Provence and quiche Lorraine from the north.

French wines need no introduction, and visitors can enjoy winery visits and tastings in all the wine-producing areas. Champagne is kept for special occasions, while alongside wine, everyday drinks include many varieties of beer and the *pastis* family – an aniseed-flavored spirit diluted with water so it turns milky.

Material pleasures are important in France, where shopping is an art form. This is the country that produces cognac, internationally famous scents, and some of the world's most desirable clothes and accessories. Prices may vary little from those back home, but the satisfaction is great from buying luxuries in their native land.

Expect a wealth of experience and pleasure in France: natural beauty, historic cities and good value despite the relatively high cost of living.

Timeline

15,000 BC	Lascaux cave paintings; first works by tribal group in area now covered by modern France.
3000 BC	Carnac stones erected.
58 BC	Julius Caesar invades Gaul.
AD 500	Frankish King Clovis unites tribes to form France.
800	Charlemagne crowned first Holy Roman Emperor.
1431	Joan of Arc burned at the stake; resulting patriotism gives France national identity.
1763	France loses North American possessions to England at end of Seven Years War.
1789	Start of French Revolution; monarchy overthrown and republic established.
1804	Napoleon proclaimed emperor; Napoleon defeated at Waterloo in 1815.
1889	Eiffel Tower, at the time the world's tallest man-made structure, built for Paris Exhibition; beginning of *belle époque* era.
1914–18	France allies with Britain, Russia and United States against Germany and Austro-Hungary to fight World War I.
1939–45	France swiftly defeated by Germans in World War II; Charles de Gaulle leads Free French Army from England.
1957	France is a founder member of European Economic Community.
1968	Student and Trade Union unrest almost bring down the government of President de Gaulle.
2003	The French government votes against military intervention in Iraq.
2007	Nicolas Sarkozy is elected as the French President.
2012	Socialist François Hollande is elected as the French President.
2014	Parisian's vote in their first female mayor, Anne Hidalgo.
2015	Paris suffers deadly terrorist attacks. December: The Government loses votes to the center and right parties in regional elections.
2016	January: A review of the metropolitan administrative regions of France sees the number reduced from 22 to 13. July: Horrific terrorist attacks in Nice and Rouen result in many deaths.
2017	Pro-E.U. Emmanuel Macron is elected president. At 39, he is France's youngest head of state since Napoleon. Macron's centrist La République En Marche (LRM) party also wins a majority of seats in the National Assembly.
	Regional elections show President Sarkozy is losing popularity.
	France wins the 2018 Soccer World Cup.
	Paris is awarded the 2024 Summer Olympic Games.

Impressionism

In the 1870s a group of Parisian artists shunned traditional painting methods and became obsessed with light and its effects. Among these artists were Monet, Manet, Pissarro, Renoir, Dégas and Sisley. In 1874 they held their first public exhibition, where their work was ridiculed. One critic was scathing about Monet's painting *Impression of a Sunrise*, and so the name of the movement was born. Literary figures such as Zola and Flaubert supported Impressionism, mirroring in words this new artform, and public opinion was gradually won over.

Chateau de Villandry, in the Loire Valley, has splendid ornamental gardens

Survival Guide

- Many French people speak some English and young people in particular are keen to practice their language skills. It's polite to master the phrase "*parlez-vous anglais?*" to use before asking a question.
- Politeness is highly regarded in France, so preface requests with "*bonjour monsieur/madame*" (hello) and always say "*merci*" (thank you).
- French people can be among the world's best dressed, with a casual style that's difficult to emulate.
- Smoking is banned in all public buildings. This includes all cafés, bars and restaurants. However, smoking is still allowed on terraces attached to restaurants and bars, and smoking is still a popular habit with French people of all ages.
- Make sure taxi meters are set at zero when starting a trip.
- Restrooms in most places are generally modern, but in some rural areas the toilet may consist of two floor-level porcelain plaques, on which the user squats. This often flushes automatically at high pressure causing splashes, so watch out for your shoes.

- Most French cities offer tourism passes through the tourist office which, once purchased, offer free or reduced admission and/or fast-track access into attractions. Some offer public transportation, river cruises or hop-on, hop-off bus tours. In Paris, the tourist office offers the Paris Passlib' pass, while the Leisure Pass Group offers the very popular Paris Pass (www.parispass.com).
- Parisians can be inconsiderate drivers, giving little leeway to other road users, but elsewhere you'll encounter few problems. If you are driving long distances, use the toll (*péage*) highway system. It's faster and less crowded.
- Sodas and soft drinks are very expensive in France; a beer (*bière*) often costs less than a Coke.
- Ice water and ice in drinks is not served routinely in France. Ask for *des glaçons* if you want ice. Legally, restaurants are obliged to serve tap water if you ask for it.
- French coffee is strong, so if you want a weaker cup ask for a *café américain*. Unless you ask for milk (*lait*) or cream (*crème*), it will always be served black (*noir*).

Paris

It's hard to be indifferent to historic, hectic, elegant Paris. With all its moods, this is a city that can exhilarate you, exasperate you and leave you speechless with wonder, but it won't leave you cold. Paris is beautiful no matter when you visit: the quality of light ranges from crystalline brilliance to mellow gold; distant sounds mingle with bustling main streets; and with each season a new scent blows in to announce its arrival.

Getting Your Bearings

It would take months to explore all of Paris, so resign yourself to the idea that you're not going to be able to see everything on just one trip to this great city. Some people prefer to familiarize themselves with the city by wandering the different neighborhoods; others will try to see as many attractions as possible. Consider which style best suits you and then plan ahead.

You will probably be surprised by the compressed scale of the city; the 2.2 million inhabitants of inner Paris all live within an area bounded by the 21-mile boulevard Périphérique that encircles the city. Even so, be prepared to walk considerable distances, even within the museums, some of which are on a grand scale.

Your first stop should be at one of the three city tourist offices, the main office being at rue des Pyramides (open daily). Here you can get excellent maps, leaflets and information on excursions and events. Ask about tourist passes, which may reduce entry fees into the city's many museums and attractions and offer discounts on eating and shopping.

Tours and Excursions

Taking a city tour is an excellent way to get your bearings. Most tours cover the main sights on either side of the Seine river and take about two hours. An alternative is to take a bus run by Paris L'Open Tour (www.paris.opentour. com). There is a choice of four routes covering the city center, Bastille-Bercy, St.-Germain and Montmartre with stops along the way, allowing you to get on and off to do your own sightseeing. Tickets are valid for one, two or three days, and there's English commentary. You may want to take a tour outside Paris; obvious choices are the fabulous

Palace of Versailles built for Louis XIV, or the old royal hunting lodge of Fontainebleau and its surrounding forest, a favorite retreat of the kings of France. If you'll be spending your entire stay in Paris, consider taking a day trip to the châteaux of the Loire Valley, Chartres and its fine cathedral, or to the magical island of Le Mont-St.-Michel in Normandy.

Parisian Neighborhoods

Most Parisians mentally split their city into two neat halves – Left Bank (Rive Gauche) and Right Bank (Rive Droite) – with the sinuous curve of the Seine dividing them. Traditionally, the Right Bank has stood for order and elegance, typified by the monumental architecture running from the Louvre up to the Arc de Triomphe; while the Left

A sightseeing boat heads toward Pont Notre Dame, soon to pass the cathedral on the Île de la Cité

Bank is an altogether more raffish place. This is too simplistic, however. Paris, in fact, is a series of extremely individual *quartiers* (districts), each with its own personality, style and charm.

Riverbanks and Bridges

More than 30 bridges crisscross the Seine, and the banks, known as *quais*, offer lovely views of the city. The best stretch of riverside for walking lies between the Pont de la Concorde (Concorde Bridge), leading to the place de la Concorde, and the Pont de Sully (Sully Bridge), at the eastern end of the Île St.-Louis. Browse in the *bouquinistes* (secondhand booksellers') stalls that line the riverbank, or simply revel in the subtly blended colors of sky, river, trees and stone. Several companies operate cruises on the Seine, an ideal way to enjoy the river.

Parisians

As inhabitants of a capital city, Parisians are surprisingly able to combine the inevitable pace of big-city life with the ability to switch off and spend hours strolling, window-shopping or endlessly chatting in a café. This is the quintessential image of the chic Parisian. To get a good taste of another side of life in the city, however, you should visit a neighborhood market: Food shopping is a serious business.

One characteristic you will notice is how much people seem to read: There are countless bookstores and newsstands selling French and international publications. Your overall impression may be that the pace of life here is hurried, and the people can seem brusque, but they can also be charming, particularly to those who love their city.

Shopping

The selection in the stores makes shopping irresistible for some. Haute couture stores cluster mainly around the Faubourg St.-Honoré and avenue Montaigne, with boutiques selling ready-to-wear (*prêt-à-porter*) designer outfits. Paris has a number of department stores; the best known are Galeries Lafayette and Printemps, on the monumental boulevard Haussmann. Both buildings are an architectural tour de force and purveyors of high-quality merchandise.

Visit some of the covered shopping arcades, built in the 18th and early 19th centuries; Galerie Colbert and Galerie Vivienne are among the most attractive. Food stores are a must. Head for the ultramodern emporium of Fauchon, 26 place de la Madeleine; Androuët, 134 rue Mouffetard, the ultimate cheese shop; and Lionel Poilâne, 8 rue du Cherche-Midi, Paris' most famous baker.

Essential Information

Tourist Information
Office de Tourisme et des Congrès de Paris (Paris Convention and Visitors Bureau)
25 rue des Pyramides (daily);
Gare du Nord (daily);
Reception du Carrousel du Louvre (daily);
www.parisinfo.com (Note: no phone service)

Urban Transportation
The easiest way to get around Paris is by the métro (subway), which runs Sun.–Thu. 5:30 a.m.–12:45 a.m., Fri.–Sat. 5:30 a.m.–1:45 a.m. Métro maps (free) are available at métro stations. The RER (Réseau Express Régional), a suburban express train, connects with the métro inside Paris. Tickets are available singly or in *carnets* (books) of 10; they are available at the stations and from tobacconists *(tabacs)* and must be validated before boarding. Keep your ticket, as there are heavy fines for travelers without tickets. The Paris Visite card, valid for 1, 2, 3 or 5 consecutive days, is interchangeable with the métro, bus and SNCF (main line) trains within the Île-de-France. Buses run daily 6:30 a.m.–8:30 p.m. (Noctilien night routes until 5:30 a.m.); tickets are interchangeable with the subway. For transportation information in English ☎ 34 24 from within France; www.ratp.info. Taxis can be hailed on the street or from stands around the city. From early Feb. to early Jan. you can take the Batobus (☎ 0825 050 101; www.batobus.com); this boat runs between the Eiffel Tower and the Jardin des Plantes daily 10–9:30 every 25 minutes, late Apr. to early Sep.; 10–7 every 30 minutes, early to late Apr. and mid-Sep. to early Nov.; Mon.–Thu. 10–5, Fri.–Sun. 10–7 every 40 minutes, rest of year. Paris operates a bike rental system, Velib' Metropole (☎ 01 76 49 12 34; www.velib-metropole.fr), with some 600 terminals around the city. Go online to register and pay a subscription fee before you rent a bicycle. No need to book.

Airport Information
Paris has two international airports, Roissy-Charles-de-Gaulle and Orly (both aiports ☎ 3950 within France; 33 1 70 36 39 50 from outside France; www.adp.fr). Most U.S. visitors arrive at CDG. It is 14 miles north of Paris; taxis are available at both terminals (terminal 2 serves Air France only). Roissybus buses run every 15–20 minutes, daily 6 a.m.–12.30 a.m. into central Paris, and RER trains every 12–15 minutes daily 4:30 a.m.–11:50 p.m. (travel time 45 minutes); buses may replace some trains). Orlybus buses (for Roissybus and Orlybus ☎ 34 24) run from Orly, 8 miles south of Paris into the center, every 15 minutes, 6 a.m. 12:30 a.m. Bus transfers to RER trains leave every 25–35 minutes, daily 5:12 a.m.–12.27 a.m.

Climate – average highs and lows for the month

Jan.	Feb.	Mar.	Apr.	May	Jun.	Jul.	Aug.	Sep.	Oct.	Nov.	Dec.
2°C	3°C	9°C	14°C	19°C	22°C	25°C	24°C	20°C	14°C	7°C	4°C
36°F	37°F	48°F	57°F	66°F	72°F	77°F	75°F	68°F	57°F	45°F	39°F
-3°C	-2°C	2°C	5°C	9°C	13°C	15°C	15°C	12°C	6°C	2°C	-1°C
27°F	28°F	36°F	41°F	48°F	55°F	59°F	59°F	54°F	43°F	36°F	30°F

Paris Sights

> **Key to symbols**
> ➕ map coordinates refer to the Paris map on pages 174–175 ⛔ admission charge: $$$ more than €12, $$ €5–€12, $ less than €5
> See page 5 for complete key to symbols

Arc de Triomphe

At the western tip of the Champs-Élysées, the Arc de Triomphe is a splendid starting point for a day's sightseeing. Commissioned by Napoleon, the 164-foot-high Arc is now dedicated to the Unknown Soldier of World War I; the eternal flame burns beneath. Twelve avenues radiate from it, giving the surrounding square its original name of place de l'Étoile (the star); today it's called place Charles-de-Gaulle, in memory of the famous general. There are 284 steps to the top of the arch, and no elevator.

➕ A3 ✉ place Charles-de-Gaulle ☎ 01 55 37 73 77; www.paris-arc-de-triomphe.fr 🕐 Daily 10 a.m.–11 p.m., Apr.–Sep.; 10 a.m.–10:30 p.m., rest of year. Last admission 45 minutes before closing 🚇 Métro/RER Charles de Gaulle-Étoile ⛔ $$

Cathédrale Notre-Dame

The great Gothic Cathédrale Notre-Dame (Cathedral of Our Lady), built between 1163 and 1345, stands on the Île de la Cité, the oldest part of Paris. The outside elevation is as impressive as the lofty interior; admire the twin towers, buttresses and facade.

Arrive early to climb one of the towers, and to view the paintings and the rose window at each end of the transept.

➕ D2 ✉ 6 place du Parvis de Notre-Dame ☎ Cathedral: 01 42 34 56 10; www.notredamedeparis.fr. Towers: 01 53 40 60 80; www.tours-notre-dame-de-paris.fr 🕐 Mon.–Fri. 7:45–6:45, Sat.–Sun. 7:45–7:15 (no visits during religious services). Towers: Sun.–Thu. 10–6:30, Fri.–Sat. 10 a.m.–11 p.m., Jul.–Aug.; daily 10–6:30, Apr.–Jun. and Sep.; daily 10–5:30, rest of year. Last admission 45 minutes before closing 🚇 Cité; RER Châtelet or St.-Michel Notre-Dame ⛔ Cathedral free; Tower $$ ℹ Organ recitals Sat 8 p.m. and before Vespers. Guided tours in English Mon.–Tue. and Sat. 2:30 p.m., Wed.–Thu. and Fri. 2 p.m. (free)

Centre National d'Art et de Culture Georges-Pompidou

This controversial 1970s-built art center quickly earned the nickname "the refinery in the center of the city," due to its similarity to an oil refinery. The architectural team of Richard Rogers and Renzo Piano designed it as the first postmodernist public building to show its structural elements on the outside.

It's home to a movie theater, library and exhibition space, and the Musée National d'Art Moderne (National Modern Art Museum), which displays art from 1905 to the present day, including work by Salvador Dalí, Pablo Picasso's early Cubist *Femme Assise dans un Fauteuil*, and pop art by Andy Warhol.

France's capital covers an area in excess of 40 square miles

D3 ✉ place Georges Pompidou ☎ 01 44 78 12 33;
www.centrepompidou.fr ⏰ Wed.–Mon. 11–9
(museum and exhibitions close at 9 p.m. but Galeries 1,
2 and the Level 6 exhibition close at 11 p.m. Thu.).
Ticket counter closes an hour before galleries 🚇 Hôtel
de Ville or Rambuteau; RER Châtelet-Les-Halles
🍽 Restaurant 🎫 Centre $; Musée $$–$$$ (free first
Sun. of the month)

Champs-Élysées

The stately and much-loved Champs-Élysées (Heavenly Fields) runs from the place de la Concorde (see page 184) up to the Arc de Triomphe, and divides neatly into two sections, with the Rond-Point standing at the halfway mark. The lower section is bordered with grass and chestnut trees, behind which stand the Grand and Petit Palais, both devoted to the arts. Along the upper section from bustling Rond-Point are stores, offices, movie theaters and sidewalk cafés.

B3 ✉ avenue des Champs-Élysées ⏰ Concorde,
Champs-Élysées-Clémenceau, Franklin D. Roosevelt,
George V or Charles de Gaulle-Étoile 🍽 Le Cinq,
see page 474

Conciergerie et Ste.-Chapelle

The Conciergerie, so called because it was administered by a "concierge" or governor, gained a sinister reputation during the 1790s, when Marie Antoinette, queen of France, and the infamous revolutionary Robespierre were imprisoned here. It is the only remaining part of the royal complex on the Île de la Cité, a superb Gothic building with twin round entrance towers and a distinctive roofline. Inside, its huge vaulted hall is the highlight, along with reconstructed prison cells.

Nearby stands Ste.-Chapelle, commissioned by Louis IX in 1245 to house the Crown of Thorns and a fragment of the True Cross. Built as two chapels, the upper was reserved for the royal family. Slender pillars divide the 13th-century, 50-foot-high stained-glass windows showing scenes from the Old and New testaments.

The glowing interior of the church of Ste.-Chapelle

Conciergerie D2 ✉ 2 boulevard de Palais
☎ 01 53 40 60 80; www.paris-conciergerie.fr
⏰ Daily 9:30–6. Last admission 30 minutes before
closing 🚇 Cité; RER St.-Michel Notre-Dame 🎫 $$;
combined ticket with Ste.-Chapelle ($$$) ℹ Audio
guide in English (free)
Ste.-Chapelle D2 ✉ 8 boulevard du Palais ☎ 01
53 40 60 80; www.sainte-chapelle.fr ⏰ Daily 9–7,
Apr.–Oct.; 9–5, Nov.–Mar. Last admission 30 minutes
before closing 🚇 Cité; RER St.-Michel Notre-Dame
🎫 $$; combined ticket with Conciergerie $$$
ℹ Audio guide ($), guided tours for visitors without
reservation, daily 11 a.m. and 3 p.m. Security (overseen
by the National Police) will confiscate any sharp
metal objects

Île de la Cité

One of the loveliest parts of Paris, the Île de la Cité is the ancient heart of the city; in medieval times it was the monarch's capital and a religious and intellectual center. Among its pretty streets and squares you'll find famous monuments, including Notre-Dame (see page 178) and Ste.-Chapelle (see left), as well as impressive civic buildings.

D2 ✉ Île de la Cité ⏰ Cité

Île St.-Louis

Pont St.-Louis will lead you straight from the Île de la Cité onto the Île St.-Louis, ideal for a peaceful stroll,

The Cathédrale Notre-Dame is one of the world's greatest churches

a light lunch and some expensive shopping. Once two islands, this largely residential area was developed in the 17th century, when most of its lovely streets and houses were built.

🚇 D2 ✉ Île St.-Louis 🚇 Pont Marie

Jardin des Tuileries

The Jardin des Tuileries (Tuileries Gardens) is a good place to recharge your batteries after the rigors of a visit to the Louvre. Designed by Le Nôtre, it's an excellent example of a 17th-century formal garden, its long central *allée* (alley) carrying the eye from the Louvre buildings and fountains to the expanse of the place de la Concorde.

🚇 C3 ✉ place de la Concorde ☎ 01 40 20 90 43 🕐 Daily 7:30–7:30, Oct.–Mar.; 7 a.m.–9 p.m., Apr.–May and Sep.; 7 a.m.–11 p.m., Jun.–Aug. 🚇 Concorde or Tuileries 🎟 Free

Le Marais et place des Vosges

For many people, le Marais is the loveliest part of Paris. Its charm lies in the combination of architecture, atmosphere, the crowds that wander its streets, and its restaurants and shops. In the early 17th century Henri IV launched development by building the place des Vosges, Paris' oldest square. Its brick-and-stone facades, arcades and central garden make it one of the world's most beautiful areas of city planning.

Surrounding it are mansions built along streets that form an enclave of superb architecture. The area has excellent museums, including the Carnavalet Museum (see page 182), Picasso Museum and Victor Hugo's House.

Musée Picasso 🚇 D2 ✉ 5 rue de Thorigny ☎ 01 85 56 00 36; www.museepicassoparis.fr 🕐 Tue.–Fri. 10:30–6, Sat.–Sun. 9:30–6 🚇 St. Paul; RER Châtelet-Les Halles 🍴 Café 🎟 $$$ ℹ Guided tours in English Tue. 11 a.m.

Maison de Victor Hugo 🚇 E2 ✉ 6 place des Vosges ☎ 01 42 72 10 16 🕐 Tue.–Sun. 10–6. Last admission at 5:40 p.m. 🚇 Bastille or St.-Paul 🎟 Free (charge for exhibitions) ℹ Audio guide $$

Montmartre

Over-commercialized and crammed with tourists, Montmartre still draws thousands of visitors daily. The neighborhood, once famous for its 40 or more windmills, gained a bohemian reputation in the late 19th century when artists and writers moved in, among them Pierre-Auguste Renoir, who portrayed the area in some of his liveliest and most popular paintings. Later came a new wave of talent, when Montmartre became home to Pablo Picasso and fellow Cubist painters. The place du Tertre is the hub of the quarter; nearby is the Basilique du Sacré-Cœur (Sacred Heart Basilica), an ornate 19th-century church built of brilliant

The French Revolution

All over Paris there are reminders of France's 1789 Revolution, when the monarchy was swept away and equal rights for all citizens were established under the law. America's own Revolutionary War served as the catalyst for events in France.

By the end of Europe's Seven Years War in 1763, France had lost all its North American possessions. Louis XVI of France, thirsting for revenge, was happy to offer arms and troops to help American colonists during their struggle against the English. These soldiers came home inspired by the American ideals of liberty and equality, taking what was, in France, an intellectually led and tiny movement to a larger grass-roots level.

France had enjoyed a Golden Age during the 17th and much of the 18th centuries; power became centralized in the hands of the monarchy, the country prospered and Paris became a center of art and sophistication. But this was at the expense of most of the population, whose standard of living dropped lower and lower. Meanwhile the nobility, deprived of any real political power, threw itself into a reckless and hedonistic lifestyle. The divide between the rich and the poor grew ever wider; time was ripe for republican ideas to bear fruit.

In 1789, the Third Estate, representing some 96 percent of France's commoners, declared itself a National Assembly and demanded social and constitutional reform. On July 14, a Parisian mob attacked Les Invalides to procure arms then stormed the Bastille prison, a hated symbol of royal power. Matters moved quickly, and within weeks France was in the grip of revolution as peasants across the country rose in revolt against the nobility and clergy.

In August, the Declaration of the Rights of Man was signed and the cry "Liberté, égalité, fraternité" (liberty, equality, brotherhood) was heard all over France. These high ideals soon degenerated into a bloodbath resulting in more than 40,000 people being executed. This period, aptly known as the "Terror," was halted only by Napoleon's rise to power.

The excesses of royalty who built Versailles while peasants starved led to the Revolution

white stone, whose domes are a familiar landmark on the skyline of the city.

✚ C4 ✉ Montmartre ☎ Basilique du Sacré-Cœur: 01 53 41 89 00; Welcome Center: 01 53 41 89 09; www.sacre-coeur-montmartre.com ◉ Basilique du Sacré-Cœur: daily 6 a.m.–10:30 p.m. Last admission at 10:15 p.m. Dome: daily 8:30–8, May–Sep.; 9–8, rest of year. The crypt is currently closed for security reasons ◉ Anvers, Abbesses or Lamarck-Caulaincourt ◉ Basilique du Sacré-Cœur free; crypt and dome $$

Musée d'Art Moderne de la Ville de Paris

The Musée d'Art Moderne begins where the Musée d'Orsay (see page 183) ends its artistic journey, with collections leading on from Fauvism and Cubism through Surrealism to some of the wonderful abstract art of today. Don't miss the Salle Dufy (the Dufy Room) with *La Fée Electricité (The Electricity Fairy)*, a wraparound vista created by Raoul Dufy in 1937.

✚ A3 ✉ 11 avenue du Président Wilson ☎ 01 53 67 40 00; www.mam.paris.fr ◉ Tue.–Sun. 10–6 (also Thu. 6–10 p.m.). Last admission 45 minutes before closing ◉ Alma-Marceau or Iéna ◉ Free

Musée Carnavalet

The Musée Carnavalet (Carnavalet Museum) is of one of the finest houses in the Marais (see page 180). Built in 1540 and remodeled in the 17th century, this beautiful Renaissance mansion was the home of Madame de Sévigné, a famous hostess and literary figure during the reign of Louis XIV. The interior of the museum is undergoing a major renovation program until the end of 2019. However, some of its collections are on show at other venues in Paris (see website for details).

✚ D2 ✉ Public access via 16 rue des Francs-Bourgeois ☎ 01 44 59 58 58; www.carnavalet.paris.fr ◉ St.-Paul or Chemin Vert

Musée du Louvre

The Musée du Louvre (Louvre Museum) started life as a palace in the 1190s. Demolished, rebuilt and extended over the centuries, this vast royal residence on the Seine assumed its present form by the 18th century, when the court of Louis XIV moved to the palace at Versailles. The Revolutionary government of 1793 transformed it into a museum to house the royal collections, which were augmented by subsequent donations and purchases.

In the 1980s President François Mitterrand launched the "Grand Louvre" project to renovate and extend the existing museum space. Chinese-born U.S. architect I. M. Pei was commissioned to design a new entrance in the Cour Napoléon. Below his now-famous stunning glass Pyramide lies a vast foyer giving access to the main museum areas, named Richelieu, Denon and Sully.

The museum is divided into eight departments, ranging from Egyptian,

The 20th-century Pyramide contrasts sharply with the 18th-century architecture of the Musée du Louvre

Greek, Etruscan, Roman and Oriental antiquities through a huge painting collection, to sculpture, objets d'art, prints and drawings. Signage in the museum is excellent. Most visitors head straight for the most famous pieces, with Leonardo da Vinci's enigmatic and mysterious *Mona Lisa* topping the list (now in a prominent position in the Salle de la Jaconde, room 6 in the Denon Wing). Another great work of art to admire is the *Virgin of the Rocks*, also by Da Vinci, a work in better shape and just as representative of his genius. The Louvre also has wonderful paintings by Georges de la Tour, the 17th-century French painter famous for his depictions of candlelit night scenes. Take time, too, for Jan Vermeer's light-infused *Lacemaker*; Veronese's *Marriage Feast at Cana*, the largest single piece of work in the Louvre and full of fascinating detail; and Raphael's *Beautiful Gardener*, one of the sweetest of all his paintings of the Virgin Mary.

Two classical sculptures draw the crowds: the *Winged Victory of Samothrace*, a second-century BC marble figure, full of movement and tension and positioned at the top of a grand staircase, and the *Venus de Milo*, a Hellenistic figure of the goddess Aphrodite from the fourth century BC. Contrast these two with Michelangelo's *Slaves*, sculpted almost 2,000 years later but clearly inspired by Classical work.

✚ C3 ✉ rue de Rivoli (main entrance: Pyramide, Cour Napoléon) ☎ 01 40 20 53 17; www.louvre.fr Ⓒ Main museum and collections: Mon., Thu. and Sat.–Sun. 9–6, Wed. and Fri. 9 a.m.–9:45 p.m. Note: rooms begin closing 30 minutes before museum closing time Ⓜ Palais-Royal Musée du Louvre 🍽 Restaurants 🖐 $$$ (free first Sun. of the month Oct.–Mar. and Jul. 14 – does not include Salle Napoleon); temporary exhibitions $$; combined tickets for permanent collection and temporary exhibitions $$$ ℹ Self-guiding audio tours ($$) are available daily. Guided tours ($$) in English are available daily 11 a.m. and 2 p.m., apart from on the first Sun. of each month (☎ 01 40 20 52 63). Sections may be closed; check ahead of your visit

Musée d'Orsay

The architecturally controversial Musée d'Orsay (Orsay Museum) was opened in 1986 in what was the old railroad station, the Gare d'Orsay. Whatever your artistic preference, the art collection inside cannot fail to impress. The whole field of visual arts – painting, sculpture, architecture and design – from 1848 to 1914 is represented.

The major draw is the excellent Impressionist and Postimpressionist collection. Here hangs Edouard Manet's *Olympia*, a portrait of a naked prostitute that caused a sensation when it was painted in 1863. Also in the gallery is a series of countryside scenes by Alfred Sisley and Camille Pissarro. You'll find also world-famous paintings such as Manet's *Déjeuner sur l'Herbe*, and Claude Monet's radiant images of glorious Rouen Cathedral and paintings of his water gardens at Giverny. In the gallery too are James Abbott McNeill Whistler's portrait of his mother, examples by Renoir, and Edgar Degas' controversial little dancers.

✚ C7 ✉ 62 rue de Lille ☎ 01 40 49 48 14; www.musee-orsay.fr Ⓒ Tue.–Wed. and Fri.–Sun. 9:30–6, Thu. 9:30 a.m.–9:45 p.m. Ⓜ Solférino; RER Musée d'Orsay 🍽 Restaurant and snack bar 🖐 $$ (reduced fee after 4:30 p.m. Tue.–Wed., Fri.–Sun. and after 6 p.m. Thu.; free first Sun. of the month); combined ticket with Musée de l'Orangerie or Musée Rodin ($$$) ℹ Guided tours in English ($$); contact the museum for details. Audiotape ($$) available in English.

Musée du quai Branly – Jacques Chirac

Housed in an innovative and elevated glass structure set around trees and vegetation, this museum is a center of excellence for non-Western arts, with collections from cultures throughout Africa, the Americas, Asia and Oceania.

✚ A3 ✉ 37 quai Branly 75007 ☎ 01 56 61 70 00; www.quaibranly.fr Ⓒ Tue.–Wed. and Sun. 11–7, Thu.–Sat. 11–9 Ⓜ École Militaire or Alma-Marceau 🚌 42 🍽 Restaurant and café 🖐 $$; free first Sun. of the month ℹ Downloadable audio guides available

Place de la Concorde

Nothing better epitomizes the wealth and flair of 18th-century France than the place de la Concorde, scene of Louis XVI's execution in 1793. From this elegant square there are sweeping views up the Champs-Élysées (see page 179) and down to the Louvre (see pages 182–183), and from the Madeleine to the Assemblée Nationale across the river. The octagonal square is decorated with statues, while in the center rises a slender 3,000-year-old Egyptian obelisk, flanked by two fountains.

➕ B3 ✉ place de la Concorde 🚇 Concorde

Quartier Latin and vicinity

The area around the Sorbonne, Paris' ancient university, has long been known as Le Quartier Latin (The Latin Quarter) because until the 1789 Revolution, Latin was the language spoken by students. Cross the boulevard to admire the Jardin du Luxembourg (Luxembourg Garden), then move on to the Panthéon, where great Frenchmen, including Voltaire and Victor Hugo, are buried.

Jardin du Luxembourg ➕ C2 ✉ rue de Medicis/rue de Vaugirard 🕿 01 42 64 33 99; www.senat.fr/visite/jardin 🕐 Daily from 7:30 a.m., Mar.–Oct. (then 15 minutes later each fortnight thereafter) and closes 4:30–9:30 p.m. 🚇 Odéon; RER Luxembourg
Panthéon ➕ D2 ✉ place du Panthéon 🕿 01 44 32 18 00; www.paris-pantheon.fr 🕐 Daily 10–6:30, Apr.–Sep.; 10–6, rest of year. Last admission 45 minutes before closing 🚇 Cardinal-Lemoine or Jussieu; RER Luxembourg 💶 $$

What's On Where

Brochures published weekly and monthly help you track down evening entertainment in Paris. English-language publications include *Where Paris, Gogoparis* and *Time Out* (monthly) and the weekly *Pariscope*, which has an English section. These list an enormous selection of entertainment, including temporary events, shows and festivals. You can find them at tourist offices and many English-language bookstores.

Tour Eiffel

When it was built by engineer Gustave Eiffel in 1889, the Tour Eiffel (Eiffel Tower) was, at almost 1,000 feet, the world's tallest man-made structure. Part of the World Exhibition, it became the symbol of Paris. You can take an elevator to each of its three levels for spectacular city views. Mail a letter from the first-floor post office and the postmark will be "Paris Tour Eiffel."

➕ A2 ✉ Champ de Mars 🕿 08 92 70 12 39 (toll call); www.toureiffel.paris 🕐 Daily 9 a.m.–12:45 a.m., mid-Jun. to Aug. (final elevator to top floor at 11 p.m., steps close at midnight); 9:30 a.m.–11:45 p.m., rest of year (final elevator for top floor 10:30 p.m., steps close at 6:30 p.m.). Last admission 45 minutes before closing 🍴 Restaurants and bar 🚇 Bir-Hakeim; RER Champ de Mars Tour Eiffel 💶 Elevator: 2nd floor $$$; top floor $$$; Staircase: 2nd floor $$

La Villette

On the northeast edge of Paris stands a large modern park which has been transformed into a cultural landmark. La Villette has two main zones: Cité des Sciences et de l'Industrie (City of Sciences and Industry) and Cité de la Musique – Philharmonie de Paris (City of Music – Philharmonie of Paris) where you'll find the sparkling and futuristic Philharmonie de Paris auditorium, designed by Jean Nouvel. The Cité des Sciences et de l'Industrie has several family friendly science-based attractions, including Explora, focusing on life, natural resources and technological development, and the Géode, a movie theater with a hemispheric screen. Tour L'Argonaute, a real submarine from the 1950s; or let the kids enjoy interactive games in the Cité des Enfants (Children's City).

➕ Off map at E4 ✉ 211 avenue Jean Jaurés 75019 🕿 01 40 03 75 75; www.lavillette.com 🕐 Ticket office: daily 9:30–6:30 🚇 Porte de la Villette or Porte de Pintin 🍴 Restaurants and cafés 💶 $–$$$
Cité des Sciences et de l'Industrie 🕐 Sun. 10–7, Tue.–Sat. 10–6 💶 $$$
Cité de la Musique – Philharmonie de Paris 🕐 Sat.–Sun. 10–6, Tue.–Fri. noon–6 p.m. 💶 $$$

Eating and Drinking in Paris

Your hotel will probably provide you with breakfast (normally at an extra charge), usually consisting of fruit juice, freshly baked baguettes and a selection of croissants and *viennoiseries* (assorted pastries). However, a basic Continental breakfast can be purchased at most street cafés for a fraction of the price charged in many hotels, and usually with a genuine Parisian atmosphere.

Main Meals

Lunch is generally served from midday until 2:30, and dinner from 7:30 until after 10 p.m. For an earlier meal, head for a brasserie where you'll get simple, freshly cooked meals, and drinks and snacks throughout the day. Bistros are more modest than restaurants, although not always cheaper. You'll get the best value anywhere by choosing from the menu (often called *la formule*), where there's a choice of three or four courses for a fixed price. Some restaurants also serve a *menu gastronomique*, which will include small portions of many of the famous house specialties, an excellent way to sample a wide range of dishes. If you order water, you'll probably get bottled mineral water (still or carbonated), for which you'll be charged. Wine can be fairly expensive, but all restaurants serve their own house wine in bottles and carafes, which is often good value. A typical meal will include a starter, frequently some type of salad; a main course with vegetables; and cheese, followed by the dessert.

Snacks, Fast Food and Picnics

If you want a light lunch head for the cafés, which usually have tables outside when the weather's nice. They serve sandwiches and other snacks, and hot, cold and alcoholic drinks. Many of the museums in Paris have very reputable cafés, where you can take stock of your visit and rest your feet after exploring the galleries. A popular lunch place in Paris is the *bar à huîtres* (oyster bar), where other seafood also is available. There also are plenty of burger joints, as well as the *boulangerie* (bakery), where you can get a variety of savory pastries to take out. For those with a sweet tooth, a *pâtisserie* (cake shop) is the place for a mouthwatering range of cakes and pastries. Summer weather may tempt you to plan a picnic: you can put together a wonderful feast at any of the many food markets that are scattered throughout the city.

French *pâtisseries* are famous for their beautifully crafted cakes and delicate pastries

Lyon

France's second-largest city, once a hub on a vital trade route, has much to offer. It's a fascinating place where history and tradition, excellent civic facilities and architectural merit combine with commercial importance to give a real big-city feel on a very human level.

The City and the Presqu'Île

Lyon's sprawl may be daunting if this is your first visit, but the city's major tourist attractions are in a surprisingly compact area. Public transportation is excellent, so it should take little time for you to get your bearings.

Lyon's name is derived from the Latin *Lugdunum*, the capital of Roman Gaul, which was founded at the top of the hill called Fourvière in 43 BC, from where the settlement spread to above the confluence of two great rivers known today as the Rhône and the Saône. After Rome fell, the medieval town gradually established itself, spreading out slowly to occupy the narrow spit of land immediately above the rivers' junction. This became known as the Presqu'Île (the isthmus), and here the city grew in

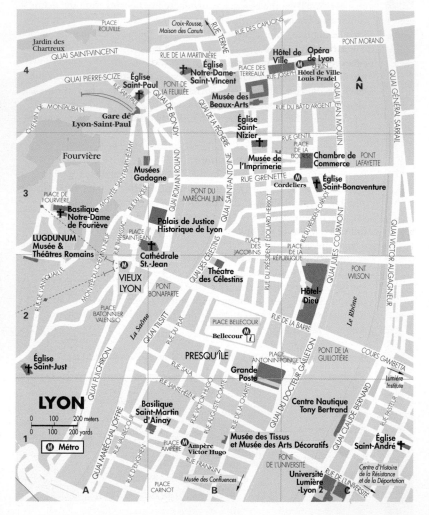

the 17th and 18th centuries; it was only later that it expanded farther to the north and east. For visitors, the main sights are almost all either along the west bank of the Saône river or on the Presqu'Île, the oldest parts of the city.

Exploring Lyon

Most visitors use the métro system, or subway, to travel around. Although it will get you from place to place effortlessly, you'll get a better sense of the city's layout if you set out on foot, and walking can actually be quicker. The hill of Fourvière (see pages 189–190) is a useful landmark; if it's on your left you're heading north, right and you're walking south. For orientation purposes remember that the Saône is the river immediately below Fourvière, while the Rhône lies on the other side of the Presqu'Île. Lyon is remarkably hilly, especially the climb up Fourvière and the slopes of the Croix-Rousse district (see pages 189 and 193), so a trip to these places probably merits the short métro or bus ride.

The tourist office offers an excellent one-, two- or three-day pass called the Lyon City Card (www.lyoncitycard. com). This moderately priced ticket gives you unlimited travel on the bus, trolley bus, tram and métro network, a river cruise (April through October), admission to Lyon's best museums, a guided tour, a self-guiding audio tour of the Fourvière Basilica, access to the observatory, a performance at the Théâtre le Guignol and discount entrances to the aquarium and several other sights, as well as literature to help you make the most of your stay.

The Lyonnais – with their reputation for common sense, wit and kindness – are helpful and friendly, and are usually happy to assist strangers.

Enjoying the Sights

Lyon, like so many historic cities, really needs to be explored at leisure. Get a flavor of the city by wandering through its picturesque neighborhoods, sit in cafés, pause in the lovely squares and linger on the bridges to admire the river scene. If pressed for time, consider taking a tour. The tourist office can provide details for both bus and walking tours, and cruises run during summer.

This prosperous city is well endowed with museums, some of which are remarkably esoteric. If you're an avid old-film fan, period automobile fanatic or if medical history or the discovery of electricity rivets you – you'll not be disappointed. Lyon also has many child-friendly attractions, including a museum of automation history, a puppet museum and a huge and well-presented natural history museum.

La Cuisine

Ask any French citizen what he or she thinks is Lyon's main attraction and the answer will probably be "la cuisine" (the food). This is a city where eating is taken very seriously indeed. There are hundreds of restaurants, ranging from very simple, family-run places to world-class establishments, and then there is the wine.

North of Lyon, miles of famous vineyards produce quality reds and

A view of Lyon from Notre-Dame de Fourvière

France

whites, with names to excite a wine lover – Mâcon, Pouilly, Fleurie and Beaujolais, to name but a few. Wine enthusiasts may consider an excursion to the wine country; the tourist office can help with this.

Souvenirs of Silk

Lyon has all the shopping you would expect from a city of its size and importance. The most fashionable stores lie in and around rue Président Edouard Herriot, and in the streets near place Bellecour and place des Terreaux, on the Presqu'Île. All the big international names are here, from jewelers, fashion designers and interior decorators to the best of shoe, leather, china and glass stores. The modern city center, around Part-Dieu railroad station, is home to downtown malls and chain stores, and there also are branches of France's top department stores, such as Galeries Lafayette. Lyon has its own specialties, with silk topping the list, and you'll find lovely silk goods to take home. Silk has been produced in Lyon for hundreds of years and the history and craft can be seen still in workshops in Passage Thiaffait as well as on the slopes of the Croix-Rousse (see pages 189 and 193).

On the Town

Lyon has plenty to offer in the way of evening entertainment. Opera, ballet, classical concerts, theater, jazz, rock and movies all thrive, with constantly changing programs; listings are available from the tourist office. There are dozens of bars playing live music; cabaret restaurants; nightclubs and floor shows; discos and karaoke bars; English, Irish and Australian pubs; a casino – the list goes on and on.

Essential Information

Tourist Information
Office du Tourisme et des Congrès du Grand Lyon (Lyon Convention and Visitors Bureau) place Bellecour ☎ 04 72 77 69 69; www.lyon-france.com

Urban Transportation
Central Lyon has bus, trolley bus, tram and métro (subway) systems. The métro runs daily 5 a.m.–12:25 a.m. Transportation maps are available from station service booths and tourist offices. Métro stations are marked with an "M" on the city map. Tickets, single (valid for one hour or one journey) or in *carnets* (books) of 10, can be used on the métro, bus and tram systems. A two-hour ticket (Ticket 2 Heures) or a one-day travel pass (Ticket 24 Heures) give unlimited access to the transportation system and are good value. For information ☎ 04 26 10 12 12; www.tcl.fr. Validate tickets before boarding. Taxis can be hailed or called. Try Taxilyon ☎ 04 72 10 86 86; www.taxilyon.com. Lyon Prestige Limo (www.lyonprestigelimo.com) offers chauffeur-driven tourist routes.

Airport Information
Lyon-Saint Exupéry Airport (☎ 08 26 80 08 26, toll call; or 33 426 00 70 07 outside France; www.lyonaeroports.com) is 13 miles from the city. Rhonexpress runs a tram service between the airport and Part-Dieu train station, 4:25 a.m.–midnight, ☎ 04 79 75 92 79 (toll call); www.rhonexpress.fr.

Climate – average highs and lows for the month

Jan.	Feb.	Mar.	Apr.	May	Jun.	Jul.	Aug.	Sep.	Oct.	Nov.	Dec.
5°C	8°C	12°C	14°C	20°C	23°C	27°C	26°C	22°C	17°C	10°C	7°C
41°F	46°F	54°F	57°F	68°F	73°F	81°F	79°F	72°F	63°F	50°F	45°F
0°C	1°C	3°C	5°C	10°C	14°C	17°C	16°C	12°C	8°C	4°C	2°C
32°F	34°F	37°F	41°F	50°F	57°F	63°F	61°F	54°F	46°F	39°F	36°F

Lyon Sights

Cathédrale St.-Jean

Post-Roman Lyon grew up around the site of the Cathédrale St.-Jean (St. John's Cathedral), a serene building with a flamboyant Gothic facade, flanked by a Romanesque 11th-century choir school. Much of the interior dates from the 14th and 15th centuries. The rose windows in the transept date to the 1200s.

Due to renovation work, some parts of the cathedral are not accessible, but the cathedral remians open for worship.

✚ A3/B3 ✉ place St.-Jean ☎ Cathedral: 06 60 83 53 97; www.cathedrale-lyon.ccf.fr 🕐 Cathedral: Mon.–Fri. 8:15–7:45, Sat.–Sun. 8–7 🚇 Vieux Lyon 💵 Free

Centre d'Histoire de la Résistance et de la Déportation

World War II saw a highly organized, fearless and active resistance movement in Lyon, so it's fitting that the city should have created the fascinating Centre d'Histoire de la Résistance et de la Déportation (Center of the History of the Resistance and Deportation) here. Permanent and temporary displays, documents, audiovisual guides and videos commemorate the past as well as educate the young.

✚ Off map at C1 ✉ 14 avenue Berthelot ☎ 04 72 73 99 00; www.chrd.lyon.fr 🕐 Wed.–Sun. 10–6 (ticket office closes 5:30) 🚇 Jean Macé 🚋 Tram T2 (Centre Berthelot) 💵 $$

Croix-Rousse

The slopes of the Croix-Rousse (Red Cross) area rise at the north end of the Presqu'Île, the neck of land between the Saône and Rhône rivers.

This area was mainly occupied by religious institutions before the French Revolution, but these were dissolved in 1789, leaving the area open to redevelopment by the silk industry. Today it is a UNESCO World Heritage Site and one of the liveliest areas of Lyon.

✚ Off map at B4 ✉ Croix-Rousse 🚇 Croix-Rousse
ℹ You can arrange a guided tour at the tourist office

Fourvière

One of your first impressions upon arriving in Lyon will be the hill of Fourvière, the site of Roman *Lugdunum* (see page 190).

The Roman Catholic Cathédrale St.-Jean stands at the center of the old city of Lyon

The hill rises above the Saône river, topped by the 19th-century Basilique Notre-Dame de Fourvière and what looks like a copy of the Eiffel Tower – actually the Tour Metallique (Metal Tower), built in 1894 and now housing a radio and television transmitter.

Take the funicular to the top and enjoy the fabulous views across the city.

✚ A3 🚇 Vieux Lyon then Fourvière funicular 🍴 Jérémy Galvan, see page 475 💲 Free

LUGDUNUM Musée & Théâtres romains

The remains of Roman Lugdunum offer a fascinating insight into life in the ancient Roman province of Gaul. Set into the hillside of Fourvière is France's oldest amphitheater begun in 15 BC, a second-century odeum (a small covered theater) and other city remains.

After exploring the huge structures, make your way to the museum to see the striking collection of excavated artifacts from the site. The modernist, underground structure was designed by French architect Bernard Zehrfuss and features objects ranging from important items relating to the running of the Roman Empire to domestic items that shed light on everyday life in the city. Highlights include the "Claudius Tablet," part of a speech given by Emperor Claudius to the Senate in AD 48, and the Circus Mosaic, which vividly portrays a chariot race.

✚ A2 ✉ Museum: 17 rue Cléberg. Amphitheater: 6 rue de l'Atlantiquaille ☎ 04 72 38 49 30; www. museegalloromain.grandlyon.com 🕐 Museum: Tue.–Fri. 11–6, Sat.–Sun. 10–6. Theaters: daily 7 a.m.–9 p.m., mid-Apr. to mid-Sep.; 7–7, rest of year 🚇 Vieux Lyon 💲 $$ ℹ Audio guide free

Maison des Canuts

The Silk-weavers' House is a museum-cum-workshop devoted to the history of silk and silk-weavers (*canuts*) in the heart of the Red Cross area.

Here you can enjoy an informative video, browse through old machinery displays and watch silk-weaving demonstrations on traditional looms. On a clear day you can enjoy wonderful views right across to the Alps.

✚ Off map at B4 ✉ 10–12 rue d'Ivry ☎ 04 78 28 62 04; www.maisondescanuts.com 🕐 Guided tours in French only Mon.–Sat. 11 a.m. and 3:30 p.m. Guided tours in English Mon. and Sat. 11 a.m., May–Sep. 🚇 Croix-Rousse 🚌 C13, S4 💲 $$

Musée des Beaux-Arts

The elegant building of the Musée des Beaux-Arts (Museum of Fine Arts) dominates one side of the spacious place des Terreaux, with the impressive Hôtel de Ville (Town Hall) at right angles to it.

The building was formerly the Benedictine convent of St.-Pierre, rebuilt between 1659 and 1685, and it opened as a museum in 1803. The museum has exhibits from Egypt and the ancient world, and collections of pottery, porcelain, glass and sculpture. Especially good are the Lalique glass display and paintings by Bacon, Degas, Dürer, Gauguin, Monet, Picasso and Veronese.

In the entrance foyer Pietro Perugino's *Ascension of Christ* is a fitting introduction to what's in store.

✚ B4 ✉ 20 place des Terreaux ☎ 04 72 10 17 40; www.mba-lyon.fr 🕐 Wed.–Thu. and Sat.–Mon. 10–6, Fri. 10:30–6 (some galleries close during lunch between 12:30 and 2) 🚇 Hôtel de Ville 🚌 C1, C3, C5, C13, C14, C18, C19, S1, S6, S12 🍴 Museum restaurant 💲 $$ ℹ Audio guide free

Musée des Confluences

The Confluence Museum is set in an astonishing contemporary edifice designed by Coop Himmelb(l)au and located at the point where the Rhône and Saône rivers meet. It illustrates the story of mankind across the globe through a thought-provoking exploration of the theories of the origins of Man – both in science and theology – our relationship with other species, how societies worldwide have evolved, and our different approaches to life after death.

✚ Off map at B1 ✉ 86 quai Perrache ☎ 04 28 38 12 12; www.museedesconfluences.fr 🕐 Tue.–Wed. and Fri. 11–7, Thu. 11–10, Sat.–Sun. 10–7. Last admission 45 minutes before closing 🚻 C7, C10, C15, C63; tram T1 🍴 Restaurant and café 🏷 $$ ℹ️ No guided tours in English

Musées Gadagne

The Musées Gadagne (Gadagne Museum) consists of two museums, the Musée d'Histoire de Lyon (Lyon Historical Museum) and the Musée des Arts de la Marionette (Museum of the Art of Puppetry). Both are housed in the 15th-century Hôtel de Gadagne, one of Old Lyon's stateliest Renaissance mansions. The building has undergone extensive renovation work.

The history museum galleries display over 80,000 objects explaining Lyon's long and fascinating history.

➕ A3 ✉️ 1 place du Petit Collège ☎️ 04 78 42 03 61; www.gadagne.musees.lyon.fr 🕐 Wed.–Sun. 11–6:30 🚇 Vieux Lyon and short walk 🚌 31, 40 🍴 Café 🏷 $$

Musée des Tissus et Musée des Arts Décoratifs

The Musée des Tissus (Fabric Museum) is appropriately located in Lyon – home of some of the industry's most beautiful silk and innovative production methods. An impressive 18th-century mansion houses the collection; fabrics date from as early as the fifth century.

The Far Eastern silks and embroideries are exquisite, but the Lyon silk and costumes steal the show. These intricate pieces – including designs by Philippe de Lassalle – are still stunningly vivid. Also exhibited are articles of clothing,

An equestrian statue of Louis XIV in place Bellecour

featuring Mariano Fortuny's Greek-influenced 1920s gowns.

The Musée des Arts Décoratifs (Museum of Decorative Arts) displays examples of all types of French craftsmanship in chronological order.

➕ B1 ✉️ 30–34 rue de la Charité ☎️ 04 78 38 42 00; www.mtmad.fr 🕐 Both museums: Tue.–Sun. 10–6 🚇 Ampère Victor Hugo 🚌 S1 🏷 $$ (includes both museums)

Place Bellecour

The sweeping expanse of the place Bellecour – the old place Royale – is one of Europe's biggest squares.

In the center is a bronze equestrian statue of Louis XIV. Elsewhere within the park are meandering gravel paths and large shady trees, making this a splendid oasis of calm in the heart of the busy Presqu'Île.

➕ B2 ✉️ place Bellecour 🚇 place Bellecour

Vieux Lyon

Until the 1960s, Vieux Lyon (Old Lyon) was a run-down, derelict area. Happily, both the French government and the city of Lyon stepped in with the funds to save this historic quarter, the largest Renaissance-era urban area in France and a UNESCO World Heritage Site.

The medieval cathedral town grew and prospered as an international trade and banking center. Merchants and bankers built ornately detailed houses along the narrow streets that included the St.-Paul, St.-Jean and St.-Georges neighborhoods, and they still stand today. Many streets are linked by the passages known as *traboules*, which wind through courtyards and under other buildings; the name is derived from the Latin words *trans ambulare*, meaning "to walk through."

Today Old Lyon hums with new life; there are studios, boutiques, bars and restaurants, thronged in summer with both locals and visitors.

➕ A2 ✉️ Vieux Lyon 🚇 Vieux Lyon 🍴 Jérémy Galvan, see page 475 ℹ️ Guided walking tours available with audiocassette or English-speaking guides. Apply at the tourist office

La Cuisine Lyonnaise

Lyon is said to have more restaurants per capita than any other city in the world; no wonder that even other French people will admit, "*on mange bien à Lyon*" ("you eat well in Lyon").

Geography helps: The city stands at an agricultural crossroads, benefiting from prime beef from Charolles, excellent wines from Beaujolais and superb dairy products from the Dauphiné. The commercial fruit and vegetable gardens of France supply the freshest ingredients, and better *boulangers* (bakers) and *pâtissiers* (cake-makers) than the Lyonnais are hard to find. Here you can spend happy hours practicing the art of *lèche-vitrines*, literally "licking the windows," but in reality window-shopping for food. Have a look in the *boucheries* (butchers), *traiteurs* (delicatessens) like you've never seen before, and *épiceries* (grocer shops) piled high with olive oil, vinegar, honey and jam. Afterward, go to the morning markets (except Monday) on the quai St.-Antoine along the river and drool over the gleaming vegetables, glistening fish and mounds of fruit. Then you can find a restaurant and eat – *bon appetit!*

Lyon has a long tradition of professional kitchens being managed by women, a legacy from times when all restaurants were family-run and *Maman* (mother) did the cooking. Such restaurants, known as *bouchons*, still exist, and are usually small and friendly, with visible kitchens. You can count on authentic Lyonnaise dishes accompanied by straightforward wines, which are served in small jugs called *pots*, holding a standard amount. Some restaurants are renowned, and it's often necessary to book ahead to secure a table.

What should you eat? The cooking is classic French, with quality ingredients, subtle sauces, properly aged meat and perfectly ripe cheeses. *Boudin blanc*, a veal sausage, is a specialty, as are *quenelles*, lighter-than-air poached fish dumplings served with Lyon's classic crayfish-based *sauce Nantua*. Tripe, pigs' feet and brains may not be what you're used to, but don't rule them out. *Pommes Lyonnaises* (potatoes fried with onions) are eaten worldwide, but try *gratin dauphinois* (a satisfying dish of potatoes baked in butter, cream, garlic and mustard) as well.

Leave room for a dessert, such as a luscious fruit tart; *île flottante*, a dish with floating islands of meringue on a custard lake; sinful chocolate mousse; or the simplicity of *fromage blanc* – a fresh cream cheese eaten with sugar and cream; or tasty *crêpes* with different flavorings.

Lyon is famous for its food – the biennial *Bocuse d'Or* (world cooking competition) is held here

Lyon and the Silk Tradition

Nearly 5,000 years ago the Chinese discovered that the cocoon of an insignificant moth, *Bombyx mori,* could be gently unraveled in a continuous thread and woven to produce a light and luxurious fabric. This fabric is silk, still one of the softest and most desirable of all textiles.

Silk thread made its way overland from China to Europe by the 12th century, and by the 1600s Lyon had become the center for European silk textile production. (The silkworm also came to Europe and is now a domesticated insect with a ravenous appetite for mulberry leaves, which grow well in southern France and elsewhere.) The industry thrived, producing sophisticated weaves to supply France's rich and demanding upper classes. Sumptuous designs in dazzling colors were achieved on hand looms; silk damask, patterned silks and brocades, and figured silk velvets poured out of the workshops of Lyon.

In 1804, Joseph-Marie Jacquard invented the mechanical loom, which enabled patterns to be programed using a punch-card system. These very large looms were moved from the Old Town into special buildings designed to accommodate their size in the Croix-Rousse (Red Cross) area (see page 189). The silkweavers *(canuts)*, who also moved, were paid an abysmally low price for each pattern, with the middleman scooping the profits. Social unrest finally erupted in 1831, after a three-year struggle by the *canuts* to get better pay and conditions.

By 1870 the industry had recovered and Lyon silk was considered to be among the best fabrics in the world. The creation of artificial silk and other man-made fibers in the 20th century brought an end to large-scale silk production. Numbers of Lyon's 30,000 weavers dwindled, and today there are only a handful of workshops where people still weave manually; hand-woven weaves are in high demand and are used to help restore the interiors of France's historic buildings.

If you're interested, follow the silk trail in Lyon, from the Old Town to the slopes of the Red Cross district, where you can visit silk workshops and working hand looms. Be sure not to miss the Fabric Museum (Musée des Tissus, see page 191), keeping in mind that the most a skilled worker could hope to weave was three to four inches a day.

Ties, scarves and colorful fabrics make excellent souvenirs to take back home (see page 188).

Skilled workers in Lyon continue to create delicate items using manual silk looms

Nice

Nice, France's fifth-largest city and its biggest tourist resort, is perfectly situated on the sweeping Bay of Angels (Baie des Anges). With hills as its backdrop, it is blessed with gorgeous surroundings, a superb climate, a historic past and friendly people. Until 1860 Nice belonged to the County of Savoy, which became part of Italy in 1870, and to this day both the way of life and the inhabitants seem to combine Italian charm and flair tempered with a strong dash of Gallic sophistication.

The City

The Greeks built their settlement on the hills above the bay, and 300 years later the Romans settled here. The modern city stands on the same spot and has spread down to the flat land along the sea. Sheltered to the east and west by substantial promontories, and with the Maritime Alps to the north, Nice has its own microclimate, with mild winters and perfect summers. Over the centuries city planners have taken advantage of these conditions, resulting in one of the most graceful and flower-filled cities in Europe – the average Frenchperson's retirement-home fantasy. In recent years, Nice has marketed itself as a convention center and vacation hotspot. It has more museums than any other French city outside of Paris, including the new Musée National du Sport (National Museum of Sport). A ticket that gives entry to all Nice municipal museums costs €10 for 48 hours and €20 for seven days (www.nicetourisme.com).

Getting Around

Nice is a big city, with several districts. The best way to orient yourself is to take a bus or taxi to an area, then explore on foot. Start with the atmospheric and picturesque Old Town (Vieille Ville, see page 198), which you'll probably want to visit more than once. The seafront stretches nearly 4 miles west of the Old Town, with the famous promenade des Anglais running along much of it. Behind the promenade and situated around the place Masséna is the commercial and business center, punctuated by peaceful gardens. The upscale residential suburb of Cimiez lies on the hill behind the old port and is home to excellent museums. As you explore, notice how the ambience varies, from the earthy gaiety in the streets of the Old Town to the haute couture you'll find along the Promenade des Anglais. You can see the different parts of Nice by taking the tourist train

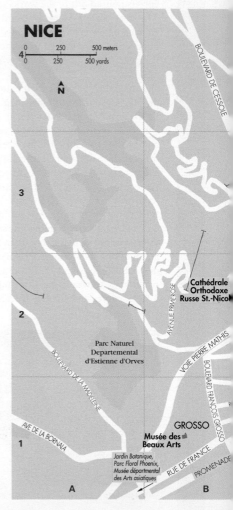

around the old quarter. For those who wish to explore the greater Côte d'Azure area, there is a useful tourist pass, the French Riviera Pass, available from tourist offices, which offers reduced admission to attractions in the region.

Flavors of the South

The French- and Italian-influenced cuisine of Nice is complemented by the sunny flavors of southern France. Look for fish and seafood. Vegetable dishes include *ratatouille* (Mediterranean vegetable stew), which was created here. Also try *mesclun*, a bitter selection of wild leaves. *Estocaficada* is a Niçois dish made from dried Norwegian cod and tomatoes. The area produces several wines, including the historic Château de Bellet. The main wine from the region, often offered as house wine in restaurants and cafés, is Côtes de Provence AOC.

Local Wares and Souvenirs

Nice combines the temptations of big-city chain stores and designer outlets with local markets, antiques shops and souvenir stores. Department stores and big-name labels are found around place Masséna, while local products are sold

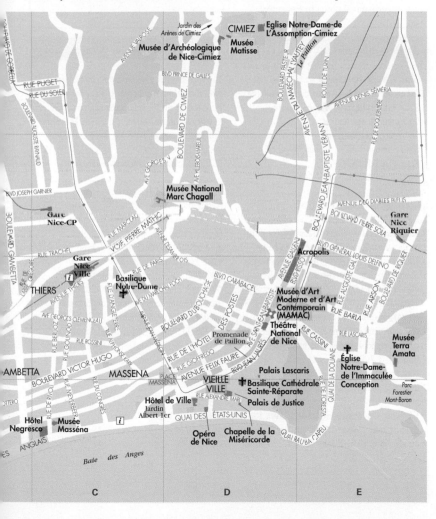

in the Old Town. Traditional cotton goods, scents from around Grasse, oils and wines make lovely gifts, but the best souvenirs from Nice are traditional carved figurines, known as *santons*.

Carnaval

Nice has dynamic theaters, concert halls and an opera, as well as movie theaters, nightclubs, a casino and cabaret restaurants, live-music bars and discos. Enjoy the local festivals, the biggest and most colorful of which is the *Nice Carnaval et Bataille de Fleurs* (Nice Carnival and Battle of Flowers; www.nicecarnaval.com) in February.

Beaches

Nice has some public beaches, but to spend a day in the sun as the Niçois do, go to one of the city's 15 private beaches (open April through October). A fee is payable, but included in the fee is use of an outdoor lounge chair and sun-shade umbrella, changing rooms, freshwater showers, a range of activities and access to a private bar/restaurant.

The beaches are covered in pebbles here, not sand. Topless sunbathing is accepted on the French Riviera though it's falling out of fashion with the younger generation.

Essential Information

Tourist Information

Office de Tourisme et des Congrès de Nice (Nice Convention and Visitors Bureau)
5 Promenade des Anglais;
www.nicetourisme.com
SNCF railroad station, avenue Thiers,
Promenade de Paillon
Tourist information line ☎ 04 92 14 46 14

Urban Transportation

Ligne d'Azur operates all over the city; maps are available from 1 rue d'Italie (☎ 08 10 06 10 06; www.lignedazur.com ⓦ Mon.–Sat. 7 a.m.–8 p.m., Sun. 8–6); ✉ boulevard Jean Juarès ⓦ Mon.–Fri. 8–7 or from tourist offices. Buy your ticket – SOLO, Multi or Pass 1 Jour (valid for 24 hours), Pass 7 Jours (valid for 7 days) or books of tickets valid for different numbers of days – at a kiosk before you board; don't forget to validate your ticket. Only SOLO (single journey ticket) and Pass 1 Jour are available for sale on board. Buses run until around 8 p.m. with limited night service.

The Nice tram system links the city center with the northern suburbs. Ticket prices are the same as for the bus. Taxis can be found at city-center cab stands (Esplanade Masséna, Promenade des Anglais and place Garibaldi are convenient), or call Taxi Riviéra (☎ 08 91 03 93 92 toll call; www.taxis-riviera.fr).

Airport Information

Aéroport Nice-Côte d'Azur (☎ 08 20 42 33 33 for inquiries in English; www.nice.aeroport.fr) is west of the city. International flights generally leave from Terminal 1; Paris and other French destinations are served by Terminal 2. Shuttle bus services from both terminals, linking the airport to the city center, are 98 (to main bus station and city center every 16 minutes 5:40 a.m.–11:45 p.m.) and 99 (to train station every 30 minutes 7:53 a.m.–8:53 p.m.). Taxis are available at airport exits, and take about 20 minutes to reach the city.

Climate – average highs and lows for the month

Jan.	Feb.	Mar.	Apr.	May	Jun.	Jul.	Aug.	Sep.	Oct.	Nov.	Dec.
13°C	13°C	14°C	17°C	20°C	24°C	25°C	27°C	24°C	20°C	17°C	13°C
55°F	55°F	57°F	63°F	68°F	75°F	77°F	81°F	75°F	68°F	63°F	55°F
5°C	6°C	8°C	9°C	13°C	17°C	19°C	20°C	17°C	13°C	9°C	6°C
41°F	43°F	46°F	48°F	55°F	63°F	66°F	68°F	63°F	55°F	48°F	43°F

Nice Sights

This Genoese-style villa houses the Musée Matisse

Cathédrale Orthodoxe Russe St.-Nicolas

The Cathédrale Orthodoxe Russe St.-Nicolas (St. Nicholas' Russian Orthodox Cathedral) is a pink-and-gray concoction of a church building with six green-and-gold onion-shaped cupolas and an excessively ornate exterior.

Tzar Nicolas II had it built from 1903 to 1912 for the Russian nobility in Nice, a city favored for its climate.

✚ B2 ✉ avenue Nicolas II ☎ 09 81 09 53 45; www.sobor.fr ⦿ Daily 9–12 and 2–6. The church may be closed during religious services 🚌 64, 71, 75 ⦿ Free ⓘ Respectful dress required

Cimiez

Cimiez is an elegant residential area of the city packed with attractions, including the Matisse Museum, a 16th-century Franciscan church and monastery, a small museum and cloister devoted to St. Francis, and the cemetery where artists Henri Matisse and Raoul Dufy are buried.

A Roman site has been excavated here, revealing the remains of an amphitheater and public baths. The attached museum holds the treasures uncovered.

Franciscan Church, Monastery and Museum

✚ D4 ✉ place du Monastère ☎ 04 93 81 00 04 ⦿ Mon.–Sat. 10–12 and 3–5:30 🚌 17, 25 ⦿ Free ⓘ Concerts in monastery cloisters in Aug.

Musée d'Archéologique Nice–Cimiez

✚ D4 ✉ 160 avenue des Arènes de Cimiez ☎ 04 93 81 59 57; www.nice.fr ⦿ Wed.–Mon. 10–6, late Jun. to mid-Oct.; Wed.–Mon. 11–6, rest of year 🚌 15, 17, 22, 25 ⦿ $$ (24-hour combined ticket for all municipal museums $$, 7-day ticket $$$)

Jardin des Arènes de Cimiez

✚ D4 ✉ avenue des Arènes ⦿ Daily dawn–dusk 🚌 15, 22, 25 ⦿ Free

Musée d'Art Moderne et d'Art Contemporain (MAMAC)

The Museum of Modern and Contemporary Art, or MAMAC, is an impressive museum constructed of four gray marble towers linked by glass walkways. The collection, founded by Nice artist Yves Klein, includes New Realism, Minimalism and Pop Art, with works by Roy Lichtenstein and Andy Warhol. Look for Klein's innovative *Mur du Feu* (*Wall of Fire*).

✚ D2 ✉ place Yves Klein, Promenade des Arts ☎ 04 97 13 42 01; www.mamac-nicc.org ⦿ Tue.– Sun. 10–6, late Jun. to mid-Oct.; 11–6, rest of year 🚌 All routes for Garibaldi/Promenade des Arts; tram 1 (Garibaldi) ⓘ Café ⦿ $$ (24-hour combined ticket for all municipal museums $$, 7-day ticket $$$)

Musée départmental des Arts asiatiques

Japanese architect Kenzo Tange designed this exciting glass-and-marble building that houses a huge collection of exquisite arts and objects from Asia.

✚ Off map at A1 ✉ 405 Promenade des Anglais ☎ 04 92 29 37 00; www.arts-asiatiques.com ⦿ Wed.–Mon. 10–6, Jul.–Aug.; Wed.–Mon. 10–5, rest of year 🚌 9, 10, 23 ⦿ Free

Musée Matisse

The whole range of artworks covering the working life of this remarkable artist forms the collection, along with personal possessions and photos.

Bequeathed to the city by Henri Matisse (and then his heirs), it traces the artist's evolution through Impressionism and Fauvism. The artworks are housed in a 17th-century Genoese-style villa with a stunning modern extension.

➕ D4 ✉ 164 avenue des Arènes de Cimiez ☎ 04 93 81 08 08; www.musee-matisse-nice.org ⏰ Wed.–Mon. 10–6, late Jun. to mid-Oct.; 11–6, rest of year 🍴 Café/restaurant 🚆 15, 17, 25 💰 $$ (24-hour combined ticket for all municipal museums $$; 7-day ticket $$$) ℹ Guided tours $$ ☎ 04 93 53 40 53; 04 97 13 55 06 for booking information

Musée National Marc Chagall

The Marc Chagall National Museum is a dramatic modern gallery that houses Chagall's donations to the city and is the world's most important single collection of his work. The 17 canvases that make up the Biblical Message were painted between 1954 and 1967 and depict the artist's interpretation of the Bible's story. Other rooms display the 39 gouaches, 105 etchings and copper plates, and 200 original sketches by Chagall.

➕ D3 ✉ avenue Dr. Ménard ☎ 04 93 53 87 20; www.musees-nationaux-alpesmaritimes.fr ⏰ Wed.–Mon. 10–6, May–Oct.; 10–5, rest of year 🚆 15 💰 $$ (includes audio guide); free first Sun. of the month

Place Masséna and Promenade de Paillon

The Niçois regard the elegant, arcaded place Masséna as the heart of their city. Around the square, with its sparkling

Lido Plage is near the Promenade des Anglais

fountain representing the planets, are broad boulevards and gardens. The manicured garden known as the Promenade de Paillon links place Masséna and the sea with the Théâtre National de Nice and is an outdoor focus for the town.

➕ D1/D2 ✉ Promenade des Anglais ⚙ Gardens: 7 a.m.–11 p.m. Apr.–Sep.; 7 a.m.–9 p.m., rest of year 🚆 3, 7, 8, 10, 11, 14, 17, 27, 38, 52, 59, 62, 70, 98, 217; tram Masséna 💰 Gardens free

Promenade des Anglais

Early in the 19th century the English discovered that France's sheltered Mediterranean coast had mild winters, and soon they flocked here in large numbers. Afternoon strolls were fashionable, but the rocky, 6-foot-wide path along the shore was hardly suitable for gentle walks. In 1820 the Reverend Lewis Way organized the construction of a sweeping promenade, planted with palm trees and decked with flowers. The locals soon called it the Promenade des Anglais (the Englishmen's Walk). Today a busy highway cuts between the sea and the ornate exteriors of the *belle époque* luxury hotels. Even amid the sprawl of apartment blocks, the palms, flowers and strolling crowds remain unchanged.

➕ B1 ✉ Promenade des Anglais 🚆 3, 8, 9, 10, 11, 12, 22, 23, 52, 59, 60, 62, 70, 94 ℹ *Nice Carnaval et Bataille de Fleurs* (Feb.); *Fête Nationale* fireworks display (Jul. 14); *Les Soirées estivales*, music evenings (Jul. and Aug.)

Vieille Ville

Until the 1970s Nice's Vieille Ville (Old Town) was a decaying slum, but today it's one of the liveliest neighborhoods in the city, with shops, bars, fine old houses, baroque churches and splendid civic buildings. The cours Saleya is the hub of the area, an elongated square that is home to Nice's markets.

➕ D1 ⚙ Fruit and vegetable markets: Tue.–Sun. morning. Antiques market: Mon. Flower market: Tue.–Sat. all day, Sun. morning. All on cours Saleya 🚆 Any bus for the Gare Routière; tram Opéra–Vieille Ville and Cathedral–Vieille Ville 🍴 Illia Pasta, see page 475

Parks, Gardens, Trees and Flowers

Many Mediterranean cities have lovely *parcs* (parks) and *jardins* (gardens), but none more so than Nice, and every street is decked with tubs, planters and window boxes filled with colorful flowers.

Formal parks lie within the city center, forming a green oasis for locals and visitors; the newly reopened Promenade de Paillon (see page 198), incorporating several once separate smaller parks, is the best example. Also in the city center, the wooded Parc du Château features winding paths and cascading water. The wilder Jardin des Arènes de Cimiez (see page 197) is a beautifully tended olive grove, the wind rustling the silver-gray foliage on the shapely trees.

Lovely, aromatic Aleppo pine trees, planted in 1866, abound in the Parc Forestier du Mont-Boron; they line almost 7 miles of trails that are edged with wild carnations and tiny orchids. Views from this park are spectacular: to the east is St.-Jean Cap Ferrat, and to the west is Nice's own Bay of Angels.

Avid gardeners should head for Nice's Jardin Botanique (Botanic Garden) at the west side of Nice, which has a comprehensive collection of Mediterranean flora as well as some tropical plants. The Parc Floral Phoenix is another garden attraction focusing on tropical plants and fruit trees. A vast greenhouse, one of the largest in Europe, dominates the 17-acre site and is packed with numerous exotic and rare orchids among other delights. There also is an aviary and beautifully colored butterflies.

Most of Nice's trees and flowers are common to all Mediterranean countries, where this vegetation thrives in lime-rich, sandy or poor soil, can withstand months of summer heat and drought, and can endure an occasional wet or cold spell in winter. Olives, palms and pines are native; citrus trees, bougainvillea, mimosa, gerbera and many succulents have been introduced. Roses love Mediterranean conditions, which is why you'll see bigger and brighter ones here than anywhere else.

If you're in the countryside – nature's own glorious garden – in April, May or June, you'll find spreads of wildflowers to rival any city park.

Detail of a fountain in Promenade de Paillon, the green artery in downtown Nice

France

Strasbourg

Strasbourg's tiny historic center, circled by arms of the Ill river, could easily lull a visitor into thinking that there was little more to the city than picturesque streets, a breathtakingly beautiful cathedral and a huge number of restaurants. But beyond its medieval core lie grandiose 19th-century civic buildings, an ancient university and the gleaming buildings housing European institutions, since Strasbourg is the seat of the European Parliament.

It's a prosperous, cosmopolitan city, a beguiling blend of ancient and modern, Teutonic and French.

A Visitor's Strasbourg

For tourists, modern everyday Strasbourg need not intrude upon enjoyment of the old city. Aim to stay within the old, mostly pedestrian quarter; it's a delightful place to walk around, with an impressive choice of hotels, bars and restaurants.

There's a large presence of European parliamentary officials, many of whom speak English, and the range of available English-language tourist literature is excellent.

Strasbourg's appeal lies in its combination of history, architecture and culture. First impressions are of a very German city, the timbered houses and cobbled streets reminiscent of villages across the Rhine river, a little to the east. But the atmosphere is definitely French, with the style and way of life that it implies. Lying so near the German border, however, Strasbourg is a favorite destination for day and weekend visits, and you'll see and hear many Germans.

Exploring the City

Undoubtedly, it's best to explore Strasbourg on foot. Apart from visiting the wonderful cathedral, museums and fine churches, most visitors spend time simply strolling the streets. You'll find hidden corners and buildings waiting to be photographed around every turn, so take your time. Water plays a large part in the city's layout; the center is encircled by water, divided into different channels and crossed by graceful bridges. Old mills and fortifications along the river bear witness to the city's

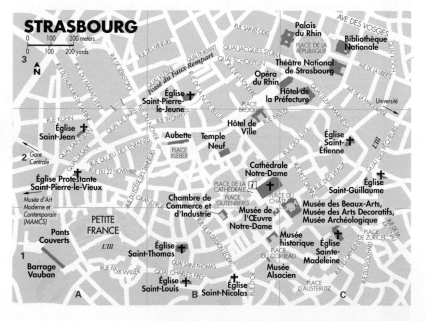

The medieval Ponts-Couverts, a fortified bridge in the heart of old Strasbourg

historic importance, while the mighty Rhine, the German border, lies only a stone's throw away.

If you're interested in architecture, you could follow one of several marked routes through the heart of the old city center (see Petite France, page 204). The tram can be useful for saving your legs, and taxis are easily available. There's also the peaceful boat trip around the center (see page 205).

Eat, Drink and Enjoy

The Strasbourg and Alsace area is one of the few regions in Europe that produces both notable wines and beers, and it also is home to some of the finest cooking in France. There are strong German influences here, giving the cuisine a different character from typical French fare. The popular French dish *choucroute*, for instance, is really the same thing as sauerkraut.

But don't be fooled. There's much more to the cuisine in Strasbourg than German cooking; you'll find Italian, Chinese, Lebanese, Tex-Mex, Moroccan and others. Don't overlook the opportunity to try some real Strasbourg specialties (see page 476). Stop in a *winstub*, a small family-run restaurant often housed in a historic building, where you'll be able to sample the best of local cooking and flavors in a cozy setting with a friendly atmosphere.

Alsace produces some notable wines, mainly whites, which are similar in character to the best of German wines. They are traditionally labeled with the name of the grape rather than the place of origin. Riesling, Gewürztraminer, Pinot Blanc and Muscat are all reliable varieties to look for. Beer also is big in Alsace, the home of Heineken and Kronenbourg. Other smaller local breweries produce excellent beer.

Evening Diversions

Strasbourg has a rich cultural life, with its own orchestra participating at the renowned International Music Festival in June; in late September through early October there's the annual *Musica* (www.festivalmusica.org), a festival of contemporary music. Opera, theater, jazz and dance performances are held year-round and are widely advertised. In summer, most tourists are drawn to the nightly folklore displays of music and dance held in some of the old city's most picturesque squares.

Malls and Markets

Shopping in Strasbourg is a real pleasure, with an excellent choice of designer names, jewelers, antiques shops and international bookstores clustered around the center of the old city. Across the river, the place des Halles (www.placedeshalles.com) is a fair-sized shopping mall housing France's familiar chain stores.

The weekly farmer's market takes place on Saturday mornings on rue de la Douane, where stalls of fresh produce, cheese and meat jostle with inexpensive and cheerful clothes and household goods. Souvenir shops sell Alsatian handicrafts; pottery, lace and carved wood are worth looking at. Strasbourg is famous for its colorful Christmas market, *Christkindelsmärik*, first held in 1570 in the cathedral (www.noel. strasbourg.eu). Each year, from late November to late December, the festive market attracts shoppers from across Europe (see page 203).

Essential Information

Tourist Information

Office de Tourisme de Strasbourg (Strasbourg Tourist Office)
17 place de la Cathédrale
☎ 03 88 52 28 28;
www.otstrasbourg.fr

Urban Transportation

Buy tickets for the trams from machines located at stops, and validate them before boarding. Outer Strasbourg is served by an efficient bus service, which you can use to visit the European institutions. The Trio ticket is valid for one day across the public transportation network for up to three people. Transportation maps are available at the railroad station and the tourist office (call Compagnie des Transports Strasbourgeois

☎ 03 88 77 70 70; www.cts-strasbourg.eu). Taxis are reasonably priced; find them at the station, place Kléber or place Gutenberg, or call Taxi 13 ☎ 03 88 36 13 13; www.taxi13.fr.

Airport Information

Strasbourg-Entzheim International Airport (☎ 03 88 64 67 67; www.strasbourg.aeroport. fr). operates flight connections to most major European cities, and is 10 minutes south of the city by car. A train service links the central train station to the airport. Trains run daily, every 15 minutes, from 5:20 a.m. to 10:35 p.m.

Climate – average highs and lows for the month

Jan.	Feb.	Mar.	Apr.	May	Jun.	Jul.	Aug.	Sep.	Oct.	Nov.	Dec.
4°C	5°C	10°C	15°C	19°C	22°C	24°C	24°C	20°C	14°C	8°C	4°C
39°F	41°F	50°F	59°F	66°F	72°F	75°F	75°F	68°F	57°F	46°F	39°F
-2°C	-2°C	1°C	5°C	9°C	12°C	14°C	13°C	10°C	6°C	2°C	0°C
28°F	28°F	34°F	41°F	48°F	54°F	57°F	55°F	50°F	43°F	36°F	32°F

Strasbourg Sights

The red sandstone facade of the cathedral

Cathédrale Notre-Dame

A superb example of Gothic architecture, the Cathédrale Notre-Dame (Cathedral of Our Lady) dominates old Strasbourg, its single steeple soaring to 466 feet. Imposing by day, the cathedral is a striking sight by night when it is lit.

Built between 1176 and 1439, the cathedral stands in a cobbled square on the site of an earlier basilica. A team of masons from Chartres worked on it in the 13th century, creating superb statuary and a harmonious interior, subtly lit by fine stained-glass windows. The main facade, a riot of biblical figures and saints, was completed half a century later. A platform constructed in the late 14th century to connect the two towers is reached by 330 stairs.

The astronomical clock in the south transept is a huge timepiece with a planetary dial constructed in the 1540s. Its automated figures perform daily at 12:30 (see below), when figures of the Apostles appear, a cock crows and beats its wings, and the seven ages of man can be seen.

The cathedral's loveliest sculpture is the *Pilier des Anges* (*Pillar of the Angels*), a wondrously carved pillar entwined with the four evangelists and trumpeting angels, all heralding the Last Judgment.

➕ B2 ✉ place de la Cathédrale ☎ 03 88 21 43 34; www.cathedrale-strasbourg.fr ⊙ Cathedral: daily 9:30–11:15 and 2–5:45; Platform: daily 9–8, Apr.–Sep.; daily 10–6, rest of year. Last entrance to platform 30 minutes before closing. Cathedral closed during Mass ⛲ Tram A, B, C, D, F 💷 Cathedral free; platform $$; clock $ (free Sun.) – ticket holders enter by porte St.-Michel. A recording is shown Mon.–Sat. 11:35 a.m. before clock performs ℹ Daily allocation of clock tickets on sale 9:30–11 a.m.

Les Grandes Places

Strasbourg is scattered with *grandes places* (large squares). The main three – place Kléber, place Gutenberg and place de la Cathédrale – are all within a five-minute walk of each other. The cathedral square, with its cobblestones and timber-framed houses, is distinctly medieval; 18th-century place Kléber has an elegant spaciousness; and attractive Renaissance-style place Gutenberg nicely bridges the architectural time gap. From late November through December, all three squares are the backdrop for Strasbourg's famous *Christkindelsmärik* (Market of the Child Jesus), a month-long street market dating from 1570.

➕ B2 ✉ place Kléber, place Gutenberg, place de la Cathédrale ⛲ Tram A, B, C, D, F ℹ *Christkindelsmärik*, last week in Nov. through Dec.

Musée Alsacien

If you have time to visit only one museum in Strasbourg, it should be the Musée Alsacien (Alsatian Museum), housed in a disorderly canalside building. Not only does it offer a chance to see the interior courtyards and inside of a 15th-century house, but it's crammed with displays illustrating traditional Alsatian life. Look for the votive pictures – naive religious paintings commissioned as prayer and thanks to God, and illustrating farm animals, children and loved ones.

➕ B1 ✉ 23–25 quai St.-Nicolas ☎ 03 68 98 51 60; www.musees.strasbourg.eu ⊙ Wed.–Mon. 10–6

🚊 10; tram A, D 🎟 \$\$, 1-day ticket for nine museums in Strasbourg \$\$, 3-day ticket \$\$\$ (free to all first Sun. of the month)

Musée Archéologique

Strasbourg is proud of the Musée Archéologique (Archeological Museum), one of the most important museums of its kind in France. Imaginatively laid out, it's housed in the basement of the Palais Rohan (Rohan Palace) and takes visitors through the history of Alsace from 600,000 BC to AD 800. There are interesting prehistoric sections, but more appealing are the reminders of everyday life in Roman Gaul.

➕ C2 ✉ 2 place du Château ☎ 03 68 98 51 60; www.musees.strasbourg.eu ⊙ Wed.–Mon. 10–6 🚊 Tram A, B, C, D, F 🎟 \$\$, 1-day ticket for nine museums in Strasbourg \$\$, 3-day ticket \$\$\$ (free to all first Sun. of the month)

Musée d'Art Moderne et Contemporain (MAMCS)

The Musée d'Art Moderne et Contemporain (Modern and Contemporary Art Museum) is an airy building across the water from the Old Town. The collection covers painting and sculpture from 1870 to the present day. The room devoted to Gustave Doré gives a fine introduction to his many works of art.

➕ Off map at A2 ✉ 1 place Hans-Jean Arp ☎ 03 68 98 51 60; www.musees.strasbourg.eu ⊙ Tue.–Sun. 10–6 🚊 10; tram B, F 🍴 Museum restaurant 🎟 \$\$, 1-day ticket for nine museums in Strasbourg \$\$, 3-day ticket \$\$\$ (free to all first Sun. of the month)

Musée des Beaux-Arts

The elegant first-floor rooms of the Palais Rohan (Rohan Palace) house the Musée des Beaux-Arts (Fine Arts Museum), a comprehensive provincial collection covering European paintings from the Middle Ages to 1870. Memling's *Polyptych of Earthly Vanity and Heavenly Redemption* steals the show, although the museum is justly proud of *La belle Strasbourgeoise*, by Nicolas de Largillière – a portrait of an enigmatic local lady. The ground floor of this same Renaissance building is home to the Musée des Arts Décoratifs (Decorative Arts Museum) and the Musée Archéologique (see left).

➕ C2 ✉ 2 place du Château ☎ 03 68 98 51 60; www.musees.strasbourg.eu ⊙ Wed.–Mon. 10–6 🚊 Tram A, B, C, D, F 🎟 \$\$, 1-day ticket for nine museums in Strasbourg \$\$, 3-day ticket \$\$\$ (free to all first Sun. of the month) **Musée des Arts Décoratifs** ➕ C2 ✉ 2 place du Château ☎ 03 68 98 51 60; www.musees.strasbourg.eu ⊙ Wed.–Mon. 10–6 🚊 Tram A, B, C, D, F 🎟 \$\$, 1-day ticket for nine museums in Strasbourg \$\$, 3-day ticket \$\$\$ (free to all first Sun. of the month)

Musée de l'Œuvre Notre-Dame

The Musée de l'Œuvre Notre-Dame (Museum of the Works of Our Lady) occupies a building used from the 14th to 16th centuries for cathedral maintenance. In addition to the rambling warren of fine rooms and staircases, there are courtyards, one of which is planted with medicinal herbs and plants similar to a 13th-century garden. Some of the cathedral's most precious sculptures are kept here, including examples of 14th-century Gothic sculpture. The streamlined *Seven Wise Virgins* is a highlight, as is the group of singularly unintimidating lions from the cathedral's main facade.

➕ B1 ✉ 3 place du Château ☎ 03 68 98 51 60; www.musees.strasbourg.eu ⊙ Tue.–Sun. 10–6 🚊 10; tram A, B, C, D, F 🎟 \$\$, 1-day ticket for nine museums in Strasbourg \$\$, 3-day ticket \$\$\$ (free to all first Sun. of the month)

Petite France

On the banks of the Ill river, at the west end of the town's historic center, cobbled streets of picturesque Little France are lined with medieval and Renaissance timbered houses, shaded by ancient trees. The area got its name in the 16th century, when sufferers of syphilis were isolated here, to keep them well away from "worthier" citizens.

➕ A1 ✉ place Benjamin-Zix 🚊 15; tram A, B, D, F 🍴 L'Epicerie, see page 476

A Day in Strasbourg

You awake early in the morning, and your time in this wonderful old city is limited. Here's what to do: Spend an hour or so strolling around the historic center, visiting one of the daily produce markets, taking some photos in the morning light and nibbling on something delicious from one of the tempting *pâtisseries* (cake) shops. Around mid-morning head for the Ill river, near the Palais Rohan, and buy your ticket for one of the 70-minute boat tours of Strasbourg. On the tour you can sit back and listen to the English commentary about the city's history and important monuments. The tour circles the central island, passing churches, fine buildings and flower-hung, timber-framed houses before heading upstream to give you a glimpse of the modernistic glass-and-steel palaces housing the buildings connected with the European Union.

Head next for the cathedral, timing your visit so that you'll be there at 12:30, when the marvelous astronomical clock (see page 203) swings into action. For lunch there is a wide choice of pretty outdoor eating places serving local specialties, such as *tarte flambée* (onion tart).

If you enjoy museums, the afternoon's the time for checking out two of the best. At the top of the list is the Alsatian Museum (Musée Alsacien, see pages 203–204), closely followed by the Gothic treasures in the Museum of the Works of Our Lady (Musée de l'Œuvre Notre-Dame, see page 204). After this, you may be ready for a drink at a sidewalk café.

Evenings in Strasbourg feature a special dinner in one of the dozens of superb restaurants; be sure to eat a local dish, or follow the set menu, which is bound to be good. Afterward you can go to the movies (in English), a concert, enjoy a folklore display or simply stroll through the atmospheric old streets and have a nightcap at a music bar. For night owls, there are discos and clubs that stay open into the early hours.

🚶 Boat tours leave from the landing stage near the Palais Rohan on two different tours daily. There are many departures daily between 9:30 a.m. and 9:15 p.m. in July and August, and several departures between 9:45 a.m. and 5 p.m. in December. There are few sailings in January and February. Call Batorama (☎ 03 69 74 44 04; www.batorama.fr) for details 🎫 $$–$$$. Consult the tourist office about the 3-day inclusive "Strasbourg Pass" and for evening events

This half-timbered house is characteristic of the older houses in the center of the city

Germany

Introduction and Map 208

Timeline 214

Survival Guide 215

Berlin 216

Feature: The Berlin Wall 222

Feature: An Excursion to Potsdam 223

Cologne 224

Feature: An Excursion to Bergischer Dom 229

Munich 230

Feature: Hofbräuhaus 235

Feature: A Walk Along Prinzregentenstrasse 237

Hotels and Restaurants 476

Essential Information 522

Opposite: Pleasure craft on the Mosel river at Cochem

Germany

Germany is not easily summed up. Before 1871 there was no single, unified German state: The area was made up of several territories, loosely knit together in alliance. Their local languages and loyalties still have first claim on many Germans' hearts.

After World War II, the country was split between two opposing powers: the West, whose territory was known as the Federal Republic of Germany; and the Soviets, who created the German Democratic Republic (GDR). In 1989, faced with popular protests and a retreating Soviet authority, the GDR's government opened the Berlin Wall, which had divided the city's eastern and western zones since 1961.

A year later the country was reunited, and a new Germany was born. But within its unified political boundaries this is still a nation of diversity, where the people and cultures vary as dramatically as the landscapes.

Traveling in Germany

Germany's 16 federal states (*Bundesländer*) extend from the tail of Denmark south to the Swiss and Austrian Alps; the Netherlands, Belgium, Luxembourg and France border on the

More Top Destinations in Germany

- Bamberg C2
- Berchtesgaden D1
- Bodensee C1
- Dresden D3
- Freiburg im Breisgau B1
- Goslar C3
- Hamburg C4
- Heidelberg B2
- Lübeck C5
- Mecklenburgische Seenplatte D4
- Regensburg D2
- Rheintal B3
- Sächsische Schweiz D3
- Trier B2
- Tübingen B1
- Ulm C1

DENMARK

BALTIC SEA

Nordfriesische Inseln

Flensburg
Schleswig · Kieler Bucht · Puttgarden
Rügen · Sassnitz
A7
Kiel
Mecklenburger Bucht · Stralsund
Heide · Neumünster · Bad Doberan · **Rostock** · Greifswald
A23 · A20
Brunsbüttel · Itzehoe · A21 · **Lübeck** · Wismar · Güstrow
Cuxhaven · A7 · A1 · A20 · Waren · Neubrandenburg
A27 · Stade · Schwerin · (Müritz)
Bremerhaven · Parchim · Neustrelitz
Hamburg · A24 · Ludwigslust · Prenzlau
A1 · A39 · Lüneburg · Mecklenburgische Seenplatte · Oder · A11
Oldenburg · Soltau · Wittenberge · Neuruppin · Eberswalde
Bremen · Uelzen · Elbe · POLAND
Weser · Salzwedel · A24
Nienburg · Celle · Stendal · Brandenburg · **BERLIN**
(Weser) · an der Havel · A10 · Frankfurt (Oder)
Hannover · **Wolfsburg** · A2 · **Potsdam** · A12
Herford · A2 · **Brunswick** · Treuenbrietzen · A13 · Lübben
Hildesheim · [Braunschweig] · **Magdeburg** · (Spreewald) · Guben
Bielefeld · Hameln · Wolfenbüttel · A9 · Lutherstadt · Luckau · **Cottbus**
Gütersloh · **Salzgitter** · Halberstadt · Wittenberg · A15
Paderborn · Goslar · Harz · Dessau- · Lauchhammer
Lippstadt · A7 · Northeim · Quedlinburg · Rosslau · Elbe · Neisse
Göttingen · A14 · A13
Nordhausen · **Halle (Saale)** · Bautzen
Kassel · A38 · Mühlhausen/ · **Leipzig** · Meissen · Görlitz
Thüringen · Naumburg · Colditz · **Dresden** · Zittau
Eisenach · Gotha · **Erfurt** · (Saale) · Freiberg · Sächsische
Marburg · A7 · A4 · Weimar · Gera · **Chemnitz** · Schweiz
Arnstadt · **Jena** · Erzgebirge
A45 · A5 · Alsfeld · Thüringer Wald · Zwickau · A72
Wetzlar · Giessen · Fulda · Saale · A9 · Plauen
Bad Neustadt · Hof
Frankfurt · A66 · Bad · an der Saale
am Main · Kissingen · Coburg · Bayreuth · CZECH REPUBLIC
Offenbach am Main · A73
Wiesbaden · Aschaffenburg · Schweinfurt
Mainz · **Darmstadt** · Bamberg
Worms · Michelstadt · A3 · **Würzburg** · A9 · Weiden in
Mannheim · A7 · **Erlangen** · der Oberpfalz
Bad · **Fürth** · Amberg
Heidelberg · Mergentheim · **Nürnberg**
Heilbronn · Ansbach · A93
Karlsruhe · Schwäbisch · Dinkelsbühl · **Regensburg**
A8 · **Pforzheim** · Hall · Eichstätt · Donau
Baden- · Nördlingen · **Ingolstadt** · A3
Baden · **Stuttgart** · A92 · Passau
Tübingen · **Reutlingen** · A7 · Isar · Landshut
Freudenstadt · Lech · A9 · A94
A81 · Hechingen · **Ulm** · A8 · Dachau
Triberg · **Augsburg** · **München** · Burghausen
Villingen- · Donau · (Munich) · A8
Schwenningen · A96 · Rosenheim · Chiemsee
Überlingen · Kempten · A95 · Berchtesgaden · AUSTRIA
Konstanz · (Allgäu) · Oberammergau · 2713m
Bodensee · Lech · Garmisch-Partenkirchen · Watzmann-
Lindau · Füssen · 2962m · Mittelspitze
(Bodensee) · Zugspitze · Mittenwald

SWITZERLAND

C · D · E

west, Poland and the Czech Republic on the east. Each state has enough of interest to warrant a vacation in its own right, and Germans are themselves often tourists in their own country.

Traveling in Germany – by automobile or by public transportation – is not a problem, despite the country's size. The road network here is excellent, from the highways (*Autobahnen*) to minor roads.

The biggest culture shock to drivers is likely to be the speed of traffic. There is no official upper limit on some sections of German highways, and many drivers ignore, and drive in excess of, the recommended 130 k.p.h., the equivalent of which is 80 m.p.h. Driving etiquette is taken seriously, though: You can be stopped and fined for swearing or making rude gestures.

Taking the train is a convenient way to cover large areas. The quickest and most comfortable trains are the high-speed InterCityExpress (ICE) trains, and the somewhat slower InterCity (IC) and EuroCity (EC) trains linking major centers. Even the InterRegio (IR) trains connecting smaller towns are quite fast.

The North and the Baltic

Northern Germany has a maritime character. Schleswig-Holstein, a state Germans and Danes have often fought over, is made up of two former dukedoms and shares the coastline with Lower Saxony. Together they take in a shore ranging from the fjords and hills of the Baltic coast to wind-lashed North Sea beaches. Inland, the countryside is rolling farmland and peat bogs; offshore, the East Frisian, North Frisian and Baltic islands are favorite summer destinations, with beaches and brisk sea air. The inhabitants of coastal Friesland have their own culture and language.

Northern Germany's cities were a force to be reckoned with in the Middle Ages. In the interests of trade and power, they banded together to form the Hanseatic League, a federation of trading towns and seaports that monopolized trade between the North and Baltic seas. The league's merchants made huge fortunes and had impressive houses and churches built in seaports such as Hamburg, Lübeck and Bremen.

Some of their legacies have survived – or at least have been rebuilt after the heavy bombing raids of World War II. The Gothic/Renaissance architecture of Bremen's Town Hall and Lübeck's Music Academy, both converted from merchant homes, still suggest the affluence and style of the region's medieval heyday.

Lower Saxony has many features that are quintessentially German. Its historic center, Hannover, is a thriving commercial city; towns such as Celle, Brunswick, Hildesheim and Wolfenbüttel, the latter with its painted, half-timbered facades, have been partly restored after wartime damage.

The winter sports resort of Goslar, once a silver- and lead-mining town, has picture-book streets and squares lined with Gothic, Renaissance and baroque buildings, some inscribed with gold lettering, others featuring curving, sinuous slate roofs. To the east are the Harz Mountains, on the old East–West border, where witches are said to celebrate their Sabbath on *Walpurgisnacht*, the eve of May Day.

The Rhine

The great 765-mile Rhine flows from the Swiss Alps across the western regions of Germany, through the ancient city of Koblenz and the former seat of West German government, Bonn, and through the industrial country of the Ruhr toward Rotterdam. Its valleys and those of its tributaries, the Mosel, Main, Nahe and Neckar, have been wine-producing (mainly white wines) areas since Roman times. Castles with fairy-tale Gothic towers loom over the river, built for their powerful princes' protection and profit, which was gleaned from tolls on passing river traffic.

Gilded statuary sits at the center of a pond in the grounds of Schloss Linderhof, built for Ludwig II

On the Lorelei rock, above a twisting Rhine gorge, the beautiful siren Lorelei is said to lure sailors to their death with her enchanting song. This is a myth-laden part of the country, and a river cruise is a popular way of seeing it.

The East

More than 25 years after German reunification, some parts of the old East Germany are still blighted to some degree by industrial decay, unemployment and depopulation. Many other parts, though, are booming and have regained much of their pre-War and pre-division cachet. Among the winners are Baltic seacoast islands, resorts and cities that can trace their upscale lineage back to the days of the Kaisers (19th century) and the Hanseatic League.

These include places like Rügen, Germany's largest island; the tiny resort of Heiligendamm; and former Hanseatic powerhouses like Rostock, Wismar and Stralsund. Inland from the seacoast, aristocratic towns like Schwerin and Güstrow, national parks, and the

many hundreds of lakes in the state of Mecklenburg-Lower Pomerania, exert a magnetic pull on vacationers.

One of eastern Germany's highlights is Dresden, which re-created itself after devastation by more than 2,000 Allied bombers in 1945. Fine 18th-century buildings surround its Brühlsche Terrace, an elevated section on the bank of the Elbe river, and the nearby baroque Zwinger pavilions house a marvelous collection of museums. Leipzig is a vibrant university town with elegant shopping malls, beautifully restored squares and gardens, and a rich cultural heritage.

Weimar, once the home of the poet and dramatist Johann Wolfgang von Goethe, composer Franz Liszt and philosopher Friedrich Nietzsche, has a core of lovely historic buildings, parks and boulevards.

The gentle hills and red-roofed villages of the Thüringian Forest form a stretch of popular walking country. This attractive region has a flourishing industry of family-run lodgings and restaurants to attract visitors.

The gilded clockface on the exterior of the Altes Rathaus (Old Town Hall) on Marienplatz in Munich

The Black Forest and Bavaria

Two states make up southern Germany: Baden-Württemberg in the southwest and Bavaria in the southeast. As the name suggests, Baden-Württemberg is itself made up of two distinct areas: mainly Catholic Baden, where the inhabitants are said to be amiable and easy-going, and traditionally Protestant Württemberg (Swabia), where the work ethic is strongly established and the Swabian dialect is spoken.

Lovers of the outdoors flock to the Black Forest (Schwarzwald), a swath of highlands reaching over 4,800 feet and encompassing attractive villages, lush valleys, orchards and meadows, as well as woods. Clock-making has been a successful industry here since the 1660s, and cuckoo clocks are on sale at every gift shop. The other notable local product is Black Forest cake – the authentic and superior original is called *Schwarzwälder Kirschtorte.*

East of the Black Forest there is an impressive range of limestone cliffs and hills known as the Swabian Jura, where castles peer down at the Danube

(Donau) river as it begins its long journey to the sea. Pleasant resorts surround the "Swabian Ocean," Lake Constance (Bodensee), which straddles the German-Austrian-Swiss border. The Neckar river flows through Swabia's vineyards and past romantic Heidelberg, where students and tourists really do raise huge beer tankards over tavern tables, as they did in Sigmund Romberg's operetta *The Student Prince.*

Clichés also come true in southern Bavaria. Here the people are characterized by their detractors as loud and brash, and by their admirers as humorous, warm and fun-loving. People are often seen dressed in traditional leather trousers (*Lederhosen*) or embroidered dresses, and are primarily Catholic and conservative: the standard daily greeting here is "*Grüss Gott,*" or "God's greeting."

Between the Bavarian capital, Munich (München), and the magnificent Alpine peaks lie the wooded hills, pretty villages, lakes and castles that attract so many visitors from all over the world to this part of the country. The spectacular

Deutsche Alpenstrasse (German Alpine Road) takes in the mountain scenery and passes the theatrical 19th-century castles of Linderhof, Herrenchiemsee and Neuschwanstein.

Northern Bavaria has its own character. In fact, not everyone here appreciates being labeled "Bavarian." This is the region known as Franconia (Franken), and its main city is Nuremberg (Nürnberg). Architecture and art come into their own here. During the late Middle Ages and early Renaissance, artists such as Lucas Cranach and Albrecht Dürer were prominent in Germany, and Nuremberg's wonderful German National Museum displays some of their best work. A more sinister aspect of the city's past is recalled in the giant stadium and Hall of Congress, built for Hitler's mass rallies, and preserved as chilling memorials to that era.

The hugely popular Romantische Strasse (Romantic Road), running from ancient Würzburg and the Franconian wine country all the way to the Alps, 255 miles south, links several unspoiled medieval towns. On the way, it passes Rothenburg ob der Tauber, one of the loveliest old towns in Germany.

Also along this route are the old walled, half-timbered town of Dinkelsbühl and the wonderful Renaissance city of Augsburg.

Spa Towns

Health and fitness are national preoccupations, apparent in the German love of soccer, skiing and tennis, and in the spa towns that thrive all over the country. At these spas Germans reap the benefits of the medicinal waters and enjoy the other facilities, which can include mud baths, saunas and steam treatments.

Germany's oldest casino is one of the features of Baden-Baden, a celebrated spa town with graceful 19th-century hotels. Other spas also are worth investigating. Bad Ems, in the

Rhineland's picturesque Lahn valley, was 19th-century ruler Kaiser Wilhelm's personal favorite. A steam train travels from Bad Doberan, near Rostock in eastern Germany, to the country's oldest seaside resort, Ostseebad Heiligendamm, founded in 1793. Bad Kissingen, Bavaria's most popular spa, is on the banks of the Saale river.

A view of Freiburg in the Black Forest region

Timeline

800–700 BC	Celtic tribes settle around the Rhineland.
AD **9**	The Roman Empire is defeated in its campaign to conquer Germania east of the Rhine.
AD **800**	Franks overrun the territory; Charlemagne, the Frankish king, is crowned Emperor of the West.
1241	Hamburg and Lübeck form an alliance, from which the Hanseatic League federation of trading cities evolved.
1273	Rudolf of Habsburg is elected king, founding the 600-year Habsburg dynasty.
1517	Martin Luther precipitates the Reformation.
1740	Frederick the Great is crowned king of Prussia.
1871	Franco-Prussian War ends with states united under the Prussian King and German Kaiser Wilhelm and chancellor, Otto von Bismarck.
1914–19	Germany sides with Austro-Hungarian Empire in World War I; the Treaty of Versailles demands huge war reparations and surrender of territories from defeated Germany.
1933	Adolf Hitler becomes chancellor; under Hitler's dictatorship, millions of Jews and minorities are persecuted and killed.
1939	Hitler invades Poland; Britain and France declare war on Germany.
1945	Allied forces enter Berlin; Hitler kills himself.
1949	Western occupying powers create the Federal Republic of Germany; the Soviet Union forms the German Democratic Republic.
1961	The Berlin Wall is built.
1989	Radical political change in East Germany leads to the opening of the Berlin Wall and jubilation on the streets.
1990	East and West Germany reunite.
1999	Government moves to Berlin. Parliament meets in the Reichstag.
2005	Angela Merkel is elected as the first woman Chancellor.
2009	Celebrations mark the 20th anniversary of the fall of the Berlin Wall.
2011	Compulsory military service is abolished.
2014	Germany's soccer team wins the 2014 World Cup in Brazil.
2015/ 2016	Germany receives more than a million refugees from the ongoing Syrian refugee crisis.
2017	Germany celebrates 500 years since the Reformation. Political elections result in the return of a Grand Coalition government.

Mad King Ludwig

Ludwig II of Bavaria lost all interest in running his kingdom after it was drawn first into war and then into the German Empire by the Prussian Chancellor, Otto von Bismarck. The late 19th-century ruler was left with nothing to do so he amused himself by having three flamboyant castles built – Herrenchiemsee, Linderhof and Neuschwanstein. Ludwig found other ways to spend his money, too, supporting Richard Wagner while he wrote his operas, but eventually he ran out of cash altogether. This, and his eccentric manner, made him an increasing liability to the Bavarian government. Its ministers plotted with Ludwig's uncle Luitpold to depose him and certify him insane. Only days later, Ludwig and his doctor drowned in the Starnberger See, a boating lake near Munich – whether by accident or design, no one knows.

Survival Guide

- Formality is important to Germans. Don't address people by their first names unless invited to; always use *Herr* (Sir) or *Frau* (Madam) at first.
- Job titles are used frequently in social exchange; doctors, for example, are addressed as *Frau Doktor* or *Herr Doktor*.
- Local dishes, particularly in southern Bavaria, use the classic German ingredients of sauerkraut (pickled cabbage), *Wurst* (sausage), dumplings, pork and potatoes. German cooking (*Gutbürgerliche Küche*) can be sampled at a *Gasthaus*, a restaurant serving simple meals.
- German wine is mainly white. *Tafelwein* is table wine, less expensive and harsher than the quality wines; *Deutscher Tafelwein* is guaranteed to be wholly German, rather than a mix of different countries' grapes. *Qualitätswein* is the better product, from a specified range of vineyards. Some of the best grapes are Riesling, the fruity Müller-Thurgau and the spicy Gewürztraminer.
- Brewing is big business in Germany. *Bock* is a strong beer, light or dark, popular in Bavaria; *Weissbier* is pale wheat beer; and *Malz*, an unfermented black malt beer.
- *Imbiss* (snack) stands are found everywhere and sell fast food.
- Stores in cities are usually open from 9 or 9:30 a.m. until 7 or 8 p.m., sometimes until 10 p.m. A few close on Saturday afternoons; most stores are closed on Sunday.
- Germany has a long tradition of toymaking, particularly china dolls and the famous Steiff teddy bears.
- Beer and wine festivals take place all over the country. Munich's *Oktoberfest* (September/October) is the best known, and the *Weinfeste*, celebrations held in the Rhine-Mosel area also are worth attending.
- Dinkelsbühl's 10-day *Kinderzeche* festival (July), recalls the Thirty Years War, when local children persuaded Swedish soldiers not to ransack their town. It features plays, a pageant and the *Knabenbataillon* (boys' battalion) in 18th-century military garb.
- The music of Richard Wagner is performed in the summer *Bayreuther Festspiele* (Bayreuth Festival), northeast of Nuremberg near the composer's former home. Tickets are snapped up a year in advance, and must be reserved online or by mail; for information and an application form contact Bayreuther Festspiele, Kartenbüro, Postfach 100262, D-95402 Bayreuth, Germany, ☎ 0921 7878-780; www.bayreuther-festspiele. de. If you want to order a ticket for the first time, you must request an application form or complete an online application. All orders must be received by mid-October.

The Berliner chocolate shop inside the huge KaDeWe department store in Berlin

Berlin

Berlin has had its highs and its lows, but while not everything in today's Berlin is idyllic, there's no doubt that this time is one of the highs. As a visitor here, you'll encounter a city that's going places, that's filled with a vibrant creative energy, and that holds a natural place as one of Europe's great capitals.

Berlin Flavors

The numerous restaurants, cafés and bars in the city cater to a wide range of tastes, and the cuisines on offer are more diverse than ever – Indian or Thai, Australian or Moroccan, Croatian or Lebanese, the choice is yours.

The Italian community has been running restaurants in Charlottenburg since the 1960s, especially around Savigny Platz and on Kurfürstendamm (Ku'damm), and Berlin has the largest Turkish community of any other city outside Turkey. There is a Turkish community in Kreuzberg, where inexpensive meals are served in dozens of restaurants and fast-food outlets, especially in the neighborhood of Kottbusser Tor. In Mitte, commercial artists rub shoulders with diners in the renovated courtyards (Höfe) around Hackescher Markt. Gentrified Prenzlauer Berg has a thriving eating-out culture; start at Schönhauser Allee or Kollwitzplatz.

Kaffee und Kuchen (coffee and cakes/pastries) is a tradition indulged in each day at around 4 p.m., but it doesn't come cheap. The custom came from Vienna in the 19th century. To experience a traditional coffeehouse today, visit Café Einstein Stammhaus (Kurfürstenstrasse 58, Mon.–Sun. 11–8).

Though vegetarians and vegans are well catered to, Berlin home-style cooking is heavily meat based. Representative dishes include Eisbein (pork knuckle), usually served with sauerkraut (pickled cabbage) and potatoes, and Leber Berliner Art (liver

Berlin-style) which comes with mashed potatoes, onions and apple sauce. To sample new German cuisine (neue Deutsche Küche), visit one of the 20 or so restaurants that have gained Michelin-star status.

Beer is, of course, a favorite beverage here and has been for hundreds of years. Craft beer (some locally produced) is available in pubs and bars all over the city. Berliner Weisse mit Schuss is a light wheat beer, turned pink with a dash of raspberry syrup or green with some extract of woodruff.

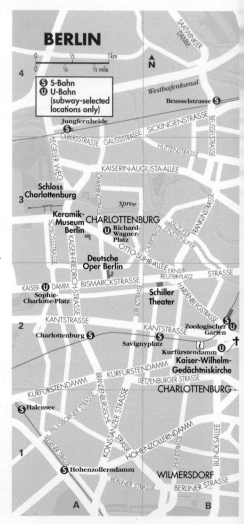

Nightlife

Berliners love live music in all its forms – folk, jazz, musical theater, variety, classical and some cabaret. To find out what is on, consult listings available from tourist offices, or the English-language Berlin magazine *ExBerliner* (www.exberliner.com).

The Berlin Philharmonic has its home at the Philharmonie, in the Kulturforum (see page 220), a large complex of concert halls and museums near Potsdamer Platz. The Berlin Symphony Orchestra performs at the Philharmonie

and in the 19th-century Konzerthaus Berlin (Berlin Concert House), on Gendarmenmarkt. Berlin's oldest opera house (built 1743) is the recently, and extensively, renovated Staatsoper (State Opera), a fine neoclassical concert hall on Unter den Linden – its glittering list of past directors includes big names such as Felix Mendelssohn Bartholdy.

Store of the West

One of Europe's biggest department stores is Berlin's KaDeWe (Kaufhaus des Westens, or Store of the West),

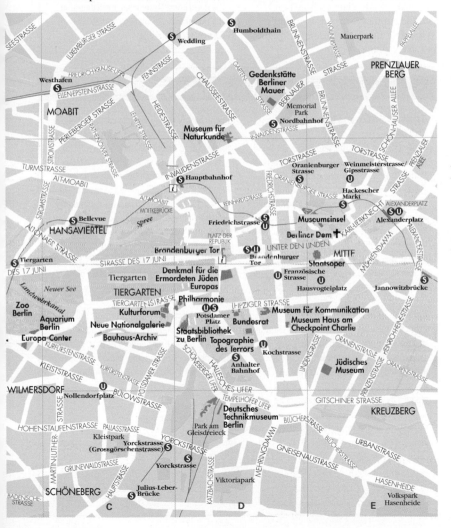

on Tauentzienstrasse. Potsdamer Platz Arkaden is another vast shopping mall with more than 130 stores, cafés, bars, restaurants and a cinema.

Berlin porcelain makes a perfect souvenir. It has been produced here since 1763, when the Royal Porcelain Manufactory opened (KPM, Wegelystrasse 1; tours, in German, Sat. 3 p.m. Call to book ☎ 030 390 090; www.kpm-berlin.com).

Street markets flourish in Berlin; on weekends try Strasse des 17. Juni (Tiergarten), Am Zeughaus (Mitte), John F-Kennedy Platz (Schöneberg), and the popular Saturday-morning Winterfeldtmarkt on Winterfeldtplatz is a lively affair.

Berlin Classicism

Sculptor, painter, set designer and architect Karl Friedrich Schinkel (1781–1841) left his mark all over Berlin. After designing the Prussians' military medal, the Iron Cross, he was commissioned to create a series of civic buildings, including the National Theater, the Old Museum on Museum Island and St. Nicholas' Church in Potsdam. He mixed his own Romantic tastes with the royally approved Classical style to form "Berlin Classicism," and gave his undivided attention to every detail, right down to the doorknobs. Despite his involvement in the movement, Schinkel moved away from Classicism in later life.

Essential Information

Tourist Information

Visit Berlin

Service Center ☎ 030 25 00 23 33, 00 49 30 25 00 23 33 (from abroad); www.visitberlin.de

Berlin Tourist Information offices

☎ 030 25 00 25

Hauptbahnhof (Central Station), Floor 0, North entrance, Europa Platz 1, daily 8 a.m.–10 p.m. Brandenburger Tor (Brandenburg Gate) South Wing, Pariser Platz, daily 9:30–7, Apr.–Oct.; 9:30–6, rest of year

At Berlin Airports: Tegel, daily 7 a.m.–10 p.m.; Schönefeld Terminal A, daily 7 a.m.–10 p.m.

Urban Transportation

There are two city rail networks: the U-Bahn (subway) and the city S-Bahn (railroad). Tickets are interchangeable. U-Bahn stations are identified by a white "U" on a blue background (often a circle), and S-Bahn stations by a white "S" in a green circle.

Buy tickets (valid for all transportation) in the station foyer; validate them in the machine on the platform. Trains run daily 5 a.m.–12:30 a.m. and all through the night Fri.–Sat. Bus route 100 runs through the center from Bahnhof Zoo (Zoo station) in the west to Unter den Linden in the east. The long-distance bus terminal is the ZOB, on Messedamm (Charlottenburg). Information on all Berlin transportation is available from BVG ☎ 030 19 449; www.bvg.de; for the S-Bahn, ☎ 030 297 43 333; www.s-bahn-berlin.de. For taxis call ☎ 26 10 26 or 20 20 20 or at city stands.

Airport Information

Berlin has two airports, Tegel and Schönefeld. The new Berlin Brandenburg Airport, will not open before 2020. For information on airports ☎ 030 609 11150; www.berlin-airport.de.

Climate – average highs and lows for the month

Jan.	Feb.	Mar.	Apr.	May	Jun.	Jul.	Aug.	Sep.	Oct.	Nov.	Dec.
2°C	3°C	8°C	12°C	18°C	21°C	23°C	23°C	18°C	13°C	7°C	3°C
36°F	37°F	46°F	54°F	64°F	70°F	73°F	73°F	64°F	55°F	45°F	37°F
-3°C	-3°C	0°C	2°C	7°C	11°C	13°C	13°C	10°C	5°C	2°C	-1°C
27°F	27°F	32°F	36°F	45°F	52°F	55°F	55°F	50°F	41°F	36°F	30°F

Berlin Sights

The Brandenburg Gate on Pariser Platz

Alexanderplatz

Germany's largest square, and known to Berliners as "Alex," was the heart of the old city and the center of former East Berlin. Two old buildings have survived: the Rotes Rathaus (Red City Hall), built from 1861 to 1869 in Italian Renaissance style; and the St. Marienkirche (St. Mary's Church), built from 1270 to 1340 and Berlin's second-oldest parish church.

At the center of the square, the iconic Fernsehturm, a 1,207-foot television tower, has a revolving restaurant and a viewing platform at the top.

➕ E3 ✉ Alexanderplatz ☎ Fernsehturm: 030 2475 75875; www.tv-turm.de. St. Marienkirche: 2475 9510; www.marienkirche-berlin.de 🕐 Fernsehturm: daily 9 a.m.–midnight, Mar.–Oct.; 10 a.m.–midnight, rest of year. St. Marienkirche: daily 10–9, Apr.–Sep.; 10–6, rest of year 🚇 U-Bahn/S-Bahn to Alexanderplatz 🚌 100, 200, 248, N2, N42, TXL; tram M2, M4, M5, M6 🍽 Restaurant in Fernsehturm 🏛 Fernsehturm $$$; St. Marienkirche free 🚹 St. Marienkirche. guided tours by appointment (☎ 030 247 595 10)

Bauhaus-Archiv

After World War I Walter Gropius founded an architectural movement in Weimar known as "form follows function," stressing function above beauty and encouraging collaboration between art and industry.

The Bauhaus (Building House) school's theory greatly influenced 20th-century design, but the school was closed in Berlin by the Nazis in 1933. The Gropius-designed Bauhaus-Archiv (Bauhaus Archive), built between 1976 and 1979 (and now being extended), shows the style and explains the aims of the Bauhaus artists.

➕ C2 ✉ Klingelhöferstrasse 14 ☎ 030 254 0020; www.bauhaus.de 🕐 Wed.–Mon. 10–5 🚇 U-Bahn to Nollendorfplatz 🚌 100, 106, 187, M29 🍽 Café 🏛 $$

Berliner Dom

Berliner Dom, Berlin's Protestant Cathedral, completed in 1905, is a monument to imperial wealth and power, and contains approximately 90 sarcophagi and some tombs of the royal Hohenzollern dynasty in its vault.

➕ E3 ✉ Am Lustgarten ☎ 030 202 6913C; www.berlinerdom.de 🕐 Mon.–Sat. 9–8, Sun noon–7, Apr.–Sep.; Mon.–Sat. 9–7, Sun noon–7, rest of year 🚇 U-Bahn/S-Bahn to Alexanderplatz; S-Bahn to Hackescher Markt 🚌 100, 200, N2; tram M4, M5, M6 🍽 Restaurants and cafés nearby 🏛 $$ 🚹 Guided tours 🕐 030 202 69119 for reservations

Brandenburger Tor

Built from 1788 to 1791 as an "arch of peace," the Brandenburger Tor (Brandenburg Gate) was modeled after the entrance to the Acropolis temple in Athens. A sculpture of the goddess Victory and her chariot, added to the top of the gate between 1789 and 1793, was stolen by Napoleon in 1806. After it was returned, Karl Friedrich Schinkel added a triumphal wreath and iron cross to the goddess' staff. During the East–West split, it stood in the area known as No Man's Land. Now a symbol of reconciliation, the city's historic landmark is a key tourist destination.

➕ D3 ✉ Pariser Platz 🚇 U-Bahn/S-Bahn to Brandenburger Tor 🚌 100

Denkmal für die Ermordeten Jüden Europas

A powerful and moving monument to the 6 million Jews who were victims of the Nazis, the somber Memorial for the Murdered Jews of Europe – also known as the Holocaust-Denkmal (Holocaust Memorial) – occupies a rectangular space covering 2 square miles, filled with 2,711 gray concrete stelae of varying heights. The maze looks from a distance like a vast field of headstones. In an underground information center, the Holocaust's terrible human cost is carefully documented.

➕ D2 ✉ Cora-Berliner-Strasse 1 ☎ 030 263 9430; www.stiftung-denkmal.de 🕐 Memorial open permanently; Information Center Tue.–Sun. 10–8, Apr.–Sep.; 10–7 rest of year 🚇 U-Bahn/S-Bahn to Brandenburger Tor 🚌 100, 200, M85, TXL 🎫 Free

Kaiser-Wilhelm-Gedächtniskirche

The ruined Kaiser Wilhelm Memorial Church has become a monument to peace and reconciliation. The 19th-century Romanesque hall was all that remained of Kaiser Wilhelm II's church after the World War II air raids in 1943; it has been left as it was, with an octagonal chapel and hexagonal blue stained-glass tower which were added to it from 1957 to 1963. Inside, the church displays a cross of nails donated by Coventry, in Britain – another city devastated by bombs.

➕ B2 ✉ Breitscheidplatz ☎ 030 218 5023; www.gedaechtniskirche-berlin.de 🕐 Church: daily 9–7; guided tours start in the Memorial Hall in the Ruined Tower: daily at 12:15, 1:15, 2:15 and 3:15 p.m. Mon., Fri. and Sat. also at 10:15 and 11:15 a.m.
🚇 U-Bahn/S-Bahn to Zoologischer Garten; U-Bahn to Kurfürstendamm 🚌 100, 109, 145, 200, 204, 245, M19, M29, M46, X9, X10, X34 🎫 Free

Kulturforum

World-class museums, art galleries and concert halls cluster in modernist buildings edging Potsdamer Platz. Highlights include the Gemäldegalerie (Picture Gallery) displaying European masterpieces from the 13th to the 18th centuries; the Kunstgewerbemuseum (Museum of Decorative Arts), and the Kupferstichkabinett (Museum of Prints and Drawings). The Neue Nationalgalerie is closed until 2020. Music lovers shouldn't miss the Philharmonie and Kammermusiksaal (Philharmonic and Chamber Music Hall), home to the Berlin Philharmonic Orchestra and Musikinstrumenten-Museum (MIM; Museum of Musical Instruments).

➕ C2 ✉ Gemäldegalerie, Kunstgewerbemuseum, Kupferstichkabinett: Mattäikirchplatz. Philharmonie: Herbert-von-Karajanstrasse 1. Musikinstrumenten-Museum (MIM): Ben-Gurion-Strasse
☎ Gemäldegalerie: 030 266 424242; www.smb. museum. MIM: 030 254 81139; www.sim.spk-berlin.de
🕐 Gemäldegalerie: Tue., Wed. and Fri. 10–6, Thu. 10–8, Sat.–Sun. 11–6. Kunstgewerbemuseum, Kupferstichkabinett: Tue.–Fri. 10–6, Sat.–Sun. 11–6. MIM: Tue.–Fri. 9–5, Thu. 9–8, Sat.–Sun. 10–5
🚇 U-Bahn/S-Bahn to Potsdamer Platz; S-Bahn S1, S2, S25 to Potsdamer Platz 🚌 200, M29, M41, M48, M85 🍴 Cafés on site 🎫 Kulturforum area ticket $$$, 3-day Museum Pass Berlin $$$

Museum Haus am Checkpoint Charlie

The crossing point of the Berlin Wall, known as Haus am Checkpoint Charlie (House at Checkpoint Charlie), is now a tourist attraction. The Eastern border guards' hut was taken down and moved to the Deutsches Historisches Museum on Unter den Linden (see page 221).

Displays at the site's Mauermuseum illustrate the effects of the wall and some escape attempts. A video on the history of the wall includes a look at the graffiti artists who decorated the Western side.

➕ D2 ✉ Friedrichstrasse 43–45 ☎ 030 253 7250; www.mauermuseum.de 🕐 Mauermuseum: daily 9 a.m.–10 p.m. 🍴 Café on site 🚇 U-Bahn to Kochstrasse 🚌 M29 🎫 $$$

Museumsinsel

This group of five imposing buildings (now a UNESCO World Heritage Site), was begun on an island in the Spree river in 1830. In 1841, Frederick William IV designated the area a "sanctuary for art and science." Ravaged by war and the East–West divide, restoration of the museum complex is ongoing and expected to continue for several more years. The Alte Nationalgalerie (Old National Gallery), modeled on the Acropolis in Athens, displays 19th-century German art and French Impressionist paintings. The baroque Bode Museum is renowned for its sculpture collection and Byzantine art, and the Neues Museum (New Museum) displays 6,000 years of human history; its showstopper is a bust of Egyptian Queen Nefertiti. Work continues on the neoclassical Altes Museum (Old Museum), housing Greek and Roman antiquities, and on the monumental Pergamonmuseum, which attracts over a million visitors a year (the Pergamon Altar may open in 2019).

➕ E3 ✉ Museumsinsel, Am Lustgarten/Bodestrasse ☎ 030 266 424242; www.smb.museum ◷ Tue., Wed. and Fri.–Sun. 10–6, Thu. 10–8 Ⓤ U-Bahn/S-Bahn to Friedrichstrasse; S-Bahn to Hackescher Markt; U Bahn to Weinmeisterstrasse/Gipsstrasse 🚌 100, 200, TXL; tram M4, M5, M6 to Hackescher Markt; M1, M12 to Am Kupfergraben 🍴 Cafés on site 🎟 $$$

Schloss Charlottenburg

When work started on the Schloss Charlottenburg (Charlottenburg Palace) in 1695, it was designed as a rural home for Sophie-Charlotte, wife of the future King Frederick I of Prussia. Over the next 100 years it grew into a vast palace with dazzling rooms such as the White Hall and Golden Gallery, and gardens in both French and English styles.

➕ A3 ✉ Spandauer Damm 10–22 ☎ 0331 969 4200; www.spsg.de ◷ Tue.–Sun. 10–5:30, Apr.–Oct.; 10–5, Nov.–Dec., 10–4:30, Jan.–Mar. Ⓤ U-Bahn to Richard-Wagner-Platz or Sophie-Charlotte-Platz; S-Bahn to Westend 🚌 109, 309, M45, X21 🍴 Café on site 🎟 Combination ticket for all buildings $$$

Tiergarten

Once a well-stocked hunting ground, the Tiergarten (Animal Garden) is a 524-acre park in the center of the city, with woodlands, lakes and waterways, gardens and a network of walking and cycling paths. Landscaping first began in 1818. The park is divided by the Strasse des 17. Juni, where the 1873 Siegessäule (victory column) commemorates military campaigns against Denmark, Austria and France.

➕ C2 ✉ Around Strasse des 17. Juni Ⓢ S-Bahn to Tiergarten 🚌 100, 123, 200, 248, 341, TXL

Topographie des Terrors

The grim Topography of Terror occupies the site of the former Nazi secret police headquarters in the Government Quarter. Photographic displays trace the history of Nazism in Germany and throughout Europe, including the extermination of the Jews, and an outdoor walkway overlooks the remains of the former cells.

➕ D2 ✉ Niederkirchnerstrasse 8 ☎ 030 254 509-50; www.topographie.de ◷ Daily 10–8 Ⓤ U-Bahn to Potsdamer Platz or Kochstrasse; S-Bahn to Anhalter Bahnhof or Potsdamer Platz 🚌 M29, M41 🍴 Café on site 🎟 Free

Unter den Linden

Unter den Linden (Under the Lime Trees) was laid out in 1648 as a route to the Tiergarten. It runs from the Brandenburg Gate to Museum Island and the river, and is lined with baroque and neoclassical buildings. The 1695 Zeughaus (Arsenal) houses the Deutsches Historisches Museum (German History Museum). An equestrian statue of Frederick the Great at the eastern end was turned by the Communist regime to ride toward the East rather than the West.

➕ D3 ✉ Deutches Historisches Museum: Unter den Linden 2 ☎ Museum: 030 203 04-0, www.dhm.de ◷ Museum: daily 10–6 Ⓤ U-Bahn to Französische Strasse, Hausvogteiplatz or Friedrichstrasse; S-Bahn to Hackescher Markt or Friedrichstrasse 🚌 100, 200, TXL 🎟 Museum $$; children under 18 free

Germany

The Berlin Wall

On August 13, 1961, shortly after East German leader Walter Ulbricht had stated that there was "no intention of building a wall," the German Democratic Republic began work on an "Anti-Fascist Protection Wall." Relations between the Eastern and Western sectors of Berlin had never been easy. The Soviets closed off their routes out in 1948, so supplies had to be flown in from the West in a year-long airlift. There had been popular protests against the Soviet authorities, and a steady exodus of East Berliners to the West. Finally the Eastern government decided to mark its boundary with bricks and barbed wire.

The houses on Bernauer Strasse (Bernauer Street), which were on the route, became part of the barrier, and their exits were bricked up. Residents tried to jump to freedom from the upper windows; 20 people were shot down. Even a guard tried to leap to freedom when the wall was under construction. Those who didn't make it across were cut off from the West as the 70 miles of 12-foot-high barricade took shape.

After the escape of 30 people through a tunnel from a bakery cellar in 1964, a large part of Bernauer Street was demolished, and a No Man's Land, or "death strip," was created, guarded by dogs and 302 watchtowers, and wide enough for tanks and vehicles to patrol. Booby traps were sunk into the Teltow canal, at the point where the border crossed the Spree river, after Günter Litfin was shot trying to swim his way to the West, on August 24, 1961. As the restrictions increased, the escapes grew more daring. One steamship's crew got the captain drunk and shut him in his cabin before sailing to the western bank. A homemade hot-air balloon was used to float over the wall. But the risks were very high: 239 people were killed in these attempts, including 25 guards.

At 9:15 p.m. on November 9, 1989, under pressure from an impatient crowd, border guards finally lifted the barriers and Easterners crossed the border freely for the first time for more than 40 years. Fittingly, the first to cross the divide were residents of Bernauer Street.

The Gedenkstätte Berliner Mauer – the Berlin Wall Memorial (Bernauer Strasse 119, www.berliner-mauer-gedenkstaette.de. Visitor Center: Tue.–Sun. 10–6; open-air exhibition, daily 8 a.m.–10 p.m.) tells of the creation of the barricade and contains the last remaining piece of the wall.

Souvenir pieces of the Berlin Wall that were gathered after its destruction in 1989

An Excursion to Potsdam

Visits to several palaces can be combined on a trip to Potsdam, southwest of Berlin. The setting for the 1945 Potsdam Conference, at which Allied leaders redrew the European map, was Cecilienhof Palace (Schloss Cecilienhof), a 1916 mock-Tudor building now partly used as a hotel.

It was built for Kaiser Wilhelm II; although his nation was two years into a war with Britain, the Kaiser chose to have it built in the style of an English country house. Those of the imperial Hohenzollern family not in exile lived here until 1945. The conference hall, delegates' studies and the reception rooms used by Churchill, Truman and Stalin are unchanged and can all be seen.

The palace that really draws crowds to Potsdam is the Sanssouci Palace (Schloss Sanssouci). This summer retreat was where Frederick the Great could enjoy life "without care" (*sans souci*).

A green dome tops the single-story, yellow rococo facade; inside, the richly furnished rooms are full of artworks and ornaments. Sanssouci Park has lovely gardens, an 18th-century Chinese teahouse and the third Potsdam palace – Frederick's New Palace (Neues Palais), with its vast marble hall and indoor grotto beautifully decorated with shells.

The town of Potsdam also is worth seeing. St. Nicholas' Church (Nikolaikirche) is one of Karl Friedrich Schinkel's classical monuments. In the Old Town, sculptures of rearing horses mark the site of the former royal stables, and the 17th-century Marstall building is now a movie museum. Built in 1732, the New Town became the focus of Potsdam's exiled French Huguenot (Protestant) community. Some of the original redbrick, gabled houses survive in what became known as the Dutch Quarter, as it was home to the many Dutch construction workers.

🏠 Cecilienhof Palace, Sanssouci Palace and New Palace: 0331 969 4200; www.spsg.de
🕐 Cecilienhof and Sanssouci: Tue.–Sun. 10–5:30, Apr.–Oct.; 10–5, Nov. Dec.; 10–4:30, Jan.–Mar. Sanssouci Park: daily, dawn–dusk. New Palace: Wed.–Mon 10–5:30, Apr.–Oct.; 10–5, Nov.–Dec.; 10–4:30, Jan.–Mar. 🚌 614, 650, 695 or the S-Bahn (Potsdam Stadt) from Berlin to Potsdam; from there bus 605, 606, 695 to Neues Palais. Tour operators in Berlin offer day trips by bus (inquire at the tourist office) 🎫 Cecilienhof Palace $$; Sanssouci Palace $$$ (guided tour only); New Palace $$

The Neues Palais (New Palace) was built for Frederick II on the western side of Sanssouci Park

Cologne

The skyline of Cologne (Köln) is dominated by the 515-foot-tall twin spires of the Cathedral that soar above the Rhine, reminders of its past glory as a center of pilgrimage and the biggest city in medieval Germany. Despite the destruction of most of its central core through heavy bombing during World War II, the city has retained and restored considerable evidence of its long and distinguished past. Today Cologne is thriving again, in business, trade, the arts and education, and its inhabitants' renowned sense of fun adds to the character that makes it one of Germany's most attractive cities.

Old Town

Cologne's Old Town (Altstadt) forms a vast semicircle on the west bank of the Rhine (Rhein) river, hemmed in by the Ring, a long boulevard that changes names along its route. The Old Town extends along the line of the former city fortifications and passes the old city gates of Eigelsteintor, Hahnentor and St. Severinstor.

Within this area, the Cathedral (Dom, see page 227) is the main attraction and, among the most visited monuments in Germany. The railroad station and a group of major museums are within easy reach of it.

Passenger barges on the Rhine near the cathedral

The Gothic-Renaissance Town Hall (Rathaus, see page 228) stands at the heart of the Old Town, just south of Alter Markt (Old Market Square); to the east, toward the river, is the 12th-century church of Gross St. Martin (see page 227), one of 12 wonderful pre-Gothic churches still standing in the city. These sights form the old core.

Head across the river via the bridges Deutzer Brücke (100 feet wide) or Hohenzollern Brücke for a look back at an unrivaled view of historic Cologne.

Cafés and Taverns

There are more breweries here than in any other German city. All produce the refreshing local beer, *Kölsch*, which is light and clear and served in tall, slim glasses. (*Kölsch* is also the name of the dialect spoken by natives of Cologne.) Beer halls, known in the local dialect as *Weetschaften*, also serve food at very reasonable prices. Specialties at these establishments include rolls with cheese (*Halve Hahn*) or rye bread with black sausage (*Kölsche Kaviar*).

You will find a wide variety of restaurants in the historic center, ranging from the traditional *Gasthaus* (tavern) to trendy bistros, and the range of cuisines includes Japanese, French, Burmese, Chinese, Turkish and East European. Wine bars and cellars are another source of refreshment, serving some of the excellent wines from the Rhine valley. There are many cafés in which to stop for the ubiquitious *Kaffee und Kuchen* (coffee and cakes).

Karneval and Concerts

To see Cologne at its most boisterous, come to the city before Easter for Carnival (*Karneval*) week. Precise dates change every year, but the celebrations and fun always reach a peak before Ash Wednesday, in time for the abstinence of Lent.

On the Thursday before the seventh Sunday prior to Easter, the festival begins in a morning ceremony at Old

Market Square, and everyone gears up for the three "Crazy Days" *(Tolle Tage)* – Thursday, Sunday and Monday.

There are costume balls at night, and more informal revelry on the streets and in the taverns. On Sunday there's a procession of floats, and on Rose Monday a spectacular parade provides the lively and colorful climax.

For the rest of the year, there is a choice of calmer entertainment at the city's main cultural centers. Concerts are performed at the Philharmonie, beside the Wallraf-Richartz/Ludwig museums building, which is located on Bischofsgartenstrasse.

Other concerts take place regularly in the city's churches and are usually free. Opera is staged at the Opernhaus. Cologne has a famous puppet theater – the Puppenspiele – but dialogue is in the local *Kölsch* dialect.

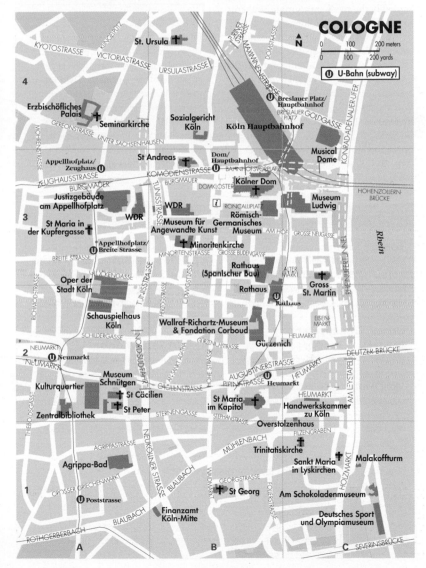

COLOGNE

U U-Bahn (subway)

Listings for movies, theater and concerts are published in the magazines *Kölner Illustrierte, StadtRevue* and *Cologne In Your Pocket.*

Nightclubs and discos are concentrated on the streets around Gross St. Martin; in the St. Severin quarter, Südstadt; and in the university quarter – the Kwartier Lateng, in the southwest part of the city.

Eau de Cologne

Probably the most appropriate souvenir to take home from Cologne is a bottle of the world's most famous fragrance, *eau de Cologne,* first distilled from flower blossoms by an Italian immigrant in the 18th century and intended as an aphrodisiac. Known here as *Kölnisch Wasser,* it's made by about 20 local businesses, including one of the originals, Farina, which has been in operation since 1709. Stores all over the city sell it, but the Old Town is the best place to browse around for gifts.

An all-day market takes place each Friday in the Old Market Square. On spring weekends, during April and May, the same square is completely taken over by hundreds of flower stalls. Wine markets set up in New Market to sell their wares in May and late June. Just before Lent Cologne celebrates *Karneval* (Carnival), and all shops close during the "Crazy Days."

Crazy Days

On the first of the *Tolle Tage* (Crazy Days) of Carnival, a procession takes place based on the local legend of Jan and Griet. Jan von Werth worked for a farmer and was very much in love with Griet, who refused him, hoping to find a wealthy husband. In desperation, Jan went off to fight in the Thirty Years War. However, he came back many years later as a highly honored hero who went on to become a general.

Essential Information

Tourist Information

KölnTourismus (Cologne Tourist Office)
Kardinal-Höffner-Platz 1, in front of the cathedral ☎ 0221 346430; www.koeln tourismus.de; www.cologne-tourism.com

Urban Transportation

Cologne has an integrated transportation system. Trams travel through the Old Town, some above ground (east–west lines), some underground (north–south lines). U-Bahn (subway) stations are identified by a white "U" on a blue background. Tickets are sold individually or for groups of up to five people *(Tages Ticket)* and are valid 9 a.m.–3 a.m.; you

also can buy a 7-day travel card *(Wochen Ticket)*. The bus and railroad stations are next to the Cathedral. Information is available from Cologne transportation company, KVB ☎ 0221 5470; www.kvb-koeln.de. For a taxi, call TAXI RUF Köln ☎ 0221 2882.

Airport Information

Köln Bonn Airport (www.koeln-bonn-airport. de) is 20 minutes by taxi from the city center. Suburban (S-Bahn) trains operate from the airport to the city center, and InterCity Express (ICE) trains take passengers to destinations across Germany. Call for flight information ☎ 02203 40 4001 (24 hours).

Climate – average highs and lows for the month

Jan.	Feb.	Mar.	Apr.	May	Jun.	Jul.	Aug.	Sep.	Oct.	Nov.	Dec.
3°C	4°C	10°C	14°C	19°C	22°C	24°C	24°C	20°C	14°C	8°C	3°C
37°F	39°F	50°F	57°F	66°F	72°F	75°F	75°F	68°F	57°F	46°F	37°F
-2°C	-2°C	0°C	4°C	8°C	12°C	14°C	13°C	10°C	6°C	3°C	0°C
28°F	28°F	32°F	39°F	46°F	54°F	57°F	55°F	50°F	43°F	37°F	32°F

Cologne Sights

Detail of reliquary busts in St. Ursula's church

Gross St. Martin

From its consecration in 1172 until the 19th century, the church of Gross St. Martin was the most distinctive feature of Cologne's skyline. Its tower, with four turrets at the corners, makes an interesting contrast to the lacy stonework of the spires.

Originally this was a monastery church, built for Benedictine monks from Ireland and Scotland.

➕ C3 ✉ An Gross St. Martin ☎ 0221 2508 4900 🕐 Tue.–Sat. 9:30–5:30, Sun. noon–7:15 p.m. 🚇 Lines 5, 12, 16, 18 to Dom/Hbf 🚊 Tram 1, 7, 9 to Heumarkt 💶 $

Kölner Dom

It took more than 600 years to complete the Kölner Dom (Cathedral), a Gothic masterpiece that incorporated all of the original architects' plans. The purpose of the project (begun in 1248) was to provide a grand setting for the relics of the Three Magi, which were snatched from Milan and kept here in a golden shrine. The final result is majestic, with intricately worked masonry serving to lighten the great mass of the facade and the two 515-foot spires, which, at the time that they were built, were the tallest structures in the world.

The golden shrine is the main focus of the interior, but there are many other treasures. In the south ambulatory chapel, the altarpiece of the *Adoration of the Magi* is a superb work by Stefan Lochner, one of the 15th-century artists of the Cologne School.

In the north chapel is the 10th-century Gero Crucifix, one of the largest sculptured crucifixes of its time. Another of the church's inspiring features is the stained glass, ranging from the intricately detailed 13th-century Bible Window in the ambulatory to the Bavarian windows in the nave, donated by King Ludwig I in the 19th century.

➕ B3 ✉ Am Hof ☎ Cathedral: 0221 9258 4730; www.koelner-dom.de 🕐 Cathedral: Mon.–Sat. 6 a.m.–9 p.m., May–Oct.; 6 a.m.–7:30 p.m., rest of year. Treasure Chamber: daily 10–6. Tower: daily 9–6, May–Sep.; 9–5, Mar.–Apr. and Oct.; 9–4, rest of year 🚇 Lines 5, 12, 16, 18 to Dom/Hbf 🍴 Brauhaus Sion, see page 477 💶 Cathedral free (guided tours $$); Treasure Chamber $$; Tower $$

Museum für Angewandte Kunst

Founded in 1888, the Museum für Angewandte Kunst (Museum of Applied Art), known as the MAKK, is mostly closed for restoration until 2020, but it continues to display temporary exhibitions, drawing on its exquisite collections of paintings, fashion and textiles, jewelry and porcelain.

➕ B3 ✉ An der Rechtschule ☎ 0221 2212 3860; www.museenkoeln.de/museum-fuer-angewandte-kunst 🕐 Tue.–Sun. 10–8 (also 10–10 first Thu. of the month) 🚇 Lines 5, 12, 16, 18 to Dom/Hbf 🍴 Café 💶 $$$

Museum Ludwig

Many great 20th-century artists are represented in the Ludwig Museum, among them Otto Dix and Max Ernst; the section on Pop Art has works by Andy Warhol and Roy Lichtenstein.

➕ C3 ✉ Heinrich-Böll-Platz ☎ 0221 221 26165; www.museum-ludwig.de 🕐 Tue.–Sun. 10–6 (also 10–10 first Thu. of the month) 🚇 U-Bahn to Hauptbahnhof 🍴 Café 💶 $$$

Museum Schnütgen

Some fine medieval religious art and furnishings can be seen at the Schnütgen Museum, which occupies the deconsecrated church of St. Cäcilien (St. Cecilia).

Among the treasures here are original carvings from the cathedral altar. The carved *memento mori* (reminders of mortality) are chilling depictions of human bodies in a state of decay.

🚩 A2 ✉ Cäcilienstrasse 29 ☎ 0221 2213 1355; www.museum-schnuetgen.de ⏰ Tue., Wed. and Fri.–Sun. 10–6, Thu. 10–8 (also 10–10 first Thu. of the month) 🚇 Lines 1, 3, 4, 18 to Neumarkt 🚊 Tram 1, 3, 4, 9, 16, 18 to Neumarkt 🍴 Brauhaus Sion, see page 477 🎟 $$ ℹ Guided tours; audio guide

Rathaus

The Rathaus (Town Hall) is a Cologne landmark at the heart of the Old Town. A flamboyant, octagonal, 15th-century tower tops off the 14th-century main body of the building. The Renaissance loggia (porch) was added sometime in the 1570s.

Under a glass pyramid in front of the hall is a 12th-century Jewish bathhouse, the *Mikwe*. There was once a ghetto on this land, where the city's Jewish community lived until they were expelled in 1424.

🚩 B2 ✉ Rathausplatz ☎ 0221 2210 ⏰ Mon.–Thu. 9–3, Fri. 9–noon 🚇 Lines 5, 12, 16, 18 to Dom/Hbf; 5 to Rathaus 🚊 Tram 1, 7, 9 to Neumarkt 🍴 Restaurant in Ratskeller ℹ Contact Tourist Office to book guided tours (see page 226)

Römisch-Germanisches Museum

For hundreds of years Cologne was under Roman rule; city status was granted in AD 50 by Emperor Claudius. The Römisch-Germanisches Museum (Roman-Germanic Museum) depicts daily life in the Roman Empire through locally excavated items.

The main exhibit is the impressive 230-foot Dionysus Mosaic, once part of a third-century Roman villa: it features Dionysus, god of wine, indulging in drunken revelry. An older exhibit is the 49-foot-high tomb of a legionnaire called Poblicius, who died about AD 40.

A combined ticket gives visitors access also to exciting finds from the Archeological Zone located near the Town Hall.

🚩 B3 ✉ Roncalliplatz 4 ☎ 0221 2212 4438; www.museenkoeln.de/roemisch-germanisches-museum ⏰ Tue.–Sun. 10–5 (also 10–10 first Thu. of the month) 🚇 Lines 5, 12, 16, 18 to Dom/Hbf ℹ Admission and hours may vary for exhibitions. Guided tours available

St. Ursula

To the north of the city center is the Romanesque church of St. Ursula, named for the daughter of a fourth-century king of Britain, who was said to have been killed in the city by Huns, along with her 11,000 virgin companions. The popularity of the cult of St. Ursula contributed to the city's development as a center of pilgrimage, and she appears in the Cologne coat of arms. The church sacristan can provide visitor access to the baroque Goldene Kammer (Golden Chamber).

🚩 B4 ✉ Ursulaplatz 24 ☎ 0221 133 400 ⏰ Mon.–Sat. 10–12 and 3–5, Sun. 3–4:30 🚇 Lines 5, 12, 16, 18 to Dom/Hbf 🎟 $

Wallraf-Richartz-Museum & Fondation Corboud

Here you will find a fabulous collection of German and international art, including the finest examples of Impressionist and neo-Impressionist painting in Germany. Also at this gallery you can study the work produced in Cologne in the 15th century, when the city was at the forefront of artistic development. In particular, make time to look for the triptychs by the artist known as the Master of St. Bartholomew, whose interesting, brightly colored paintings resemble carvings.

🚩 B2 ✉ Obenmarspforten ☎ 0221 2212 1119; www.wallraf.museum ⏰ Tue.–Sun. 10–6 (also 6–10 p.m. first and third Thu. of the month) 🚇 Lines 5, 12, 16, 18 to Dom/Hbf 🎟 $$ ℹ Special exhibitions

An Excursion to Bergischer Dom

Bergischer Dom (Altenberger Dom), about 11 miles northeast of Cologne, is set on the Dhünn river in the woods of the hilly country called Bergisches Land. The original church of this former Cistercian monastery was built using stone from the manor of the Count of Berg, who left it to the monks after moving his headquarters elsewhere in 1133. It took a little more than 100 years to finish building the present monastery, which was begun in 1259 – only seven years after work had started on the cathedral in Cologne (which took more than six centuries to complete). In medieval times it was a stopping-off place for pilgrims on the way to Santiago de Compostela in Spain.

The end result is one of Germany's best examples of 13th-century Gothic style: no elaborate embellishments and no tower, but a marvelous sense of space and light, enhanced by the simple, silvery stained-glass windows in the chancel. The west window representing *Das Himmlische Jerusalem (Holy Jerusalem)* is the biggest stained-glass window in the country. You will find tombs of the past counts, princes and abbots of Berg in the north transept.

During the Napoleonic Wars in the late 18th and early 19th centuries, the church fell into disuse and disrepair. Luckily, King Frederick William IV took an interest in its restoration, and it was opened to worshipers on the condition – decreed by the king – that both Catholics and Protestants could attend. This holds true today, and on Sundays both Catholic and Protestant congregations attend services. The outbuildings house various restaurants; at any of these, you can ask for the key to the oldest standing part of the monastery, the 13th-century Markuskapelle (chapel). An exquisite feature of the complex is the choir surrounded by chapels, viewed most rewardingly from the slope east of the monastery.

It takes an hour to reach Bergischer Dom from Cologne's center: The underground trams (U-Bahn lines 4, 15, 16, 18, 19) take you to Wiener Platz for a connection with bus 434.

Guided excursions from Cologne can be arranged by the Cologne Tourist Office (KölnTourismus, see page 226) ⊙ Daily 8–6. No visits during services and concerts ℹ For information about free guided tours ☎ 02174 4199-36; www.altenbergerdom.de

Fine stonework dominates the light, airy interior of Bergischer Dom

Munich

The capital of Bavaria, just an hour from the Alps, is one of Germany's most appealing and popular cities. Although Munich (München) is the country's third-largest city, with a cosmopolitan society and culture, it has retained a village-like atmosphere with parks, a pedestrian-only center and an easygoing feel. Even on the briefest German tour, Munich is a city not to be missed.

Munich on Foot

Central Munich is compact and attractive and the easiest way to explore is on foot. Long pedestrian-only streets (Kaufingerstrasse and Neuhauser Strasse) run from the main railroad station and from Karlstor, one of the city gates, to Marienplatz, the square at the heart of the Old Town. Here you can watch the mechanical characters of the carillon (*Glockenspiel*) at the front of the Neues Rathaus (New Town Hall, see page 234) and visit the twin-towered cathedral. To the north of the square is the tree-lined Maximilianstrasse, which leads to the Bavarian Parliament building and the Residenz (palace, see page 236). Great art collections – the Alte Pinakothek (Old Picture Gallery, see page 233), the Neue Pinakothek (New Picture Gallery, see page 234) and the Pinakothek der Moderne (Modern Art Picture Gallery, see page 236) – are northwest of the city center; to the south are the history museum and, on an island in the Isar river, one of the world's foremost museums of science and technology, the Deutsches Museum (German Museum, see page 233).

Bavarian Eateries

Munich has a vibrant restaurant and café culture, and its large foreign population ensures a wide range of cuisines. At specifically Bavarian cafés, the Munich *Weisswürste* (white veal sausage with parsley) is a staple. This delicacy is usually eaten before noon. Meals are generally early in Munich, as people start work at 7 or 8 a.m. Lunch can begin at 11:30 but is often substantial, and the "lunch hour" can last until 2 p.m. Dinner is served between 6:30 and 11 p.m., but locals tend to stick to a light supper (*Abendbrot*). The Schwabing district, north of the city center, is a busy area of sidewalk cafés and taverns. Snack bars (*Lokal* or *Schnellimbiss*) and even butcher shops (*Metzgereien*) sell tasty meatloaf and sausages all day.

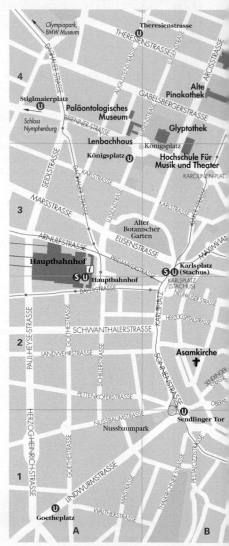

Music and Film

Munich is a major European cultural center, with thriving movie and publishing industries and a proud musical tradition. Four symphony orchestras are based here, and the Residenz provides an impressive venue – either in the concert hall or, in summer, in the courtyard. Opera and ballet are staged at the Bavarian State Opera, where the July Opera Festival is the highlight of the city's calendar. The main cultural center is the modern Gasteig, home of the Munich Philharmonic Orchestra; students from the Richard Strauss Conservatory give free lunchtime or early-evening recitals in the Small Concert Hall during the week. The annual International Film Festival takes place across the city in late June and early July – the high point of a series of festivals devoted to the movies.

Munich tends to shut down early, but Schwabing has many cabarets, theaters

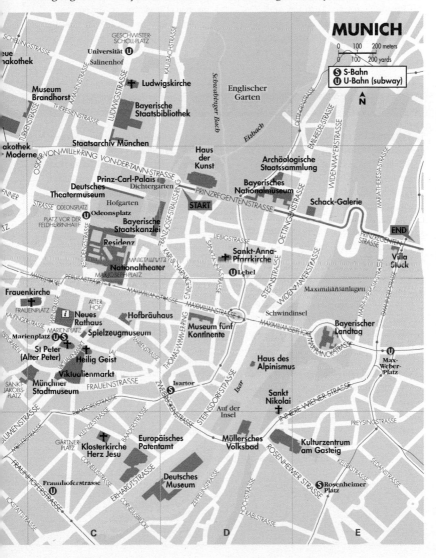

MUNICH

0   100   200 meters
0   100   200 yards

S S-Bahn
U U-Bahn (subway)

N

Universität **U**
Salinenhof
Ludwigskirche
Museum Brandhorst
Bayerische Staatsbibliothek
akothek Moderne
Staatsarchiv München
Prinz-Carl-Palais
Deutsches Theatermuseum
Dichtergarten
Hofgarten
PLATZ VOR DER FELDHERRNHALLE
Odeonsplatz **U**
Bayerische Staatskanzlei
Residenz
Nationaltheater
MAX-JOSEPH-PLATZ
Frauenkirche
ALTER HOF
i Neues Rathaus
Hofbräuhaus
Marienplatz **U S**
Spielzeugmuseum
St Peter (Alter Peter)
Heilig Geist
Viktualienmarkt
Münchner Stadtmuseum
Isartor
Klosterkirche Herz Jesu
Europäisches Patentamt
Deutsches Museum
Fraunhoferstrasse **U**

Schwabinger Bach
Englischer Garten
Eisbach
Haus der Kunst
Archäologische Staatssammlung
Bayerisches Nationalmuseum
Schack-Galerie
START
Sankt-Anna-Pfarrkirche
U Lehel
END
Villa Stuck
Schwindsel
Museum fünf Kontinente
Bayerischer Landtag
Haus des Alpinismus
Sankt Nikolai
Max-Weber-Platz **U**
Auf der Insel
Müllersches Volksbad
Kulturzentrum am Gasteig
S Rosenheimer Platz

and live music venues ranging from rock to folk and jazz, including Jazzclub Unterfahrt at Einsteinstrasse 42.

Boutiques and Markets

There's good window-shopping all over the old center, especially along Neuhauser Strasse and Kaufingerstrasse. Maximilianstrasse is a browser's paradise, lined with designer boutiques, art galleries and jewelers. More stores abound in the arcades and lanes leading off Residenzstrasse. Antiques and secondhand stores are concentrated in the student area of Schwabing, and Bavarian crafts are sold in the streets that run off Max-Joseph-Platz.

Munich's open-air Viktualienmarkt, with its formidable vendors and fresh goods ranging from local cheese to Alpine flowers, sets up south of Marienplatz every day except late Saturday afternoon and Sunday.

City of Monks

Munich's city emblem is the *Münchner Kindl*, or "little monk," recalling its origins as a monastic settlement. The first recorded mention of *Munichen*, or "the home of monks," was in AD 777. The city itself was founded nearly 400 years later by Henry the Lion, Duke of Saxony.

Essential Information

Tourist Information

München Tourismus
(Munich Tourist Office)
Sendlinger Strasse 1
☎ 089 23 39 65 00;
www.muenchen.de
Hauptbahnhof, Bahnhofplatz 2
Neues Rathaus (New City Hall), Marienplatz 8

Urban Transportation

A U-Bahn (subway) and S-Bahn (suburban) train network covers the city center and beyond. U-Bahn stations are identified by a white "U" on a blue background, and S-Bahn stations by a white "S" on a green background. Trains run daily 5 a.m.–1 a.m. Buy tickets from machines at Münchner Verkehrs und Tarifverbund (MVV) stations, MVV sales desks, newsstands and on buses and trams. Purchase tickets individually, in strips or for 1 or 3 days: multiple tickets are valid for buses and trams, too. Validate your ticket in the machine as you board, except for tickets bought from machines on trams (these will stamp automatically). One ticket is good for up to four bus/tram or two train stops; two tickets for additional stops. For MVV information ☎ 089 41 42 43 44; hotline: 0800 344 22 66 00; www.mvv-muenchen.de (Mon.–Fri. 7–5). Taxi stands can be found all over the city. Call Taxi-München ☎ 089 21610 or 089 19410, or IsarFunk Taxizentrale ☎ 089 45 05 40.

Airport Information

The international airport, Flughafen München Franz Josef Strauss (www.munich-airport.de), is 19 miles northeast of the city center. S-Bahn trains (lines 1 and 8) run 4:04 a.m.–1 a.m. to the main railroad station (Hauptbahnhof), a 40-minute trip; airport buses run to the station from outside Terminals 1 and 2, daily 6:30 a.m.–10:30 p.m., a 45-minute trip. For flight information ☎ 089 97 500.

Climate – average highs and lows for the month

Jan.	Feb.	Mar.	Apr.	May	Jun.	Jul.	Aug.	Sep.	Oct.	Nov.	Dec.
2°C	3°C	9°C	14°C	19°C	22°C	25°C	24°C	20°C	14°C	7°C	4°C
36°F	37°F	48°F	57°F	66°F	72°F	77°F	75°F	68°F	57°F	45°F	39°F
-3°C	-2°C	2°C	5°C	9°C	13°C	15°C	15°C	12°C	6°C	2°C	-1°C
27°F	28°F	36°F	41°F	48°F	55°F	59°F	59°F	54°F	43°F	36°F	30°F

Munich Sights

Alte Pinakothek

The huge Alte Pinakothek (Old Picture Gallery), built in 1836 to store the expanding royal art collection, exhibits about 700 paintings chosen from its collection of 14th- to 18th-century art. Among the treasures are works by Albrecht Dürer, Raphael, Rembrandt and the world's best collection of work by Peter Paul Rubens.

An ongoing and ambitious renovation program here may cause some disruption, but extensive areas of the museum will remain open.

🔡 B4 ✉ Barer Strasse 27, door on Theresienstrasse 🕾 089 23 80 52 16; www.pinakothek.de 🕐 Tue. 10–8, Wed.–Sun. 10–6 🚇 U-Bahn to Königsplatz 🚌 100; tram 27 🎗 $$ ($ on Sun.)

Asamkirche

The tiny Asamkirche (Asam Church) is a fine example of baroque architecture. Built as a private chapel (1733–46) by architect and sculptor brothers, Egid Quirin Asam and Cosmas Damian Asam, it is dedicated to St. John Nepomuk. Squeezed in between two houses, the richly decorated interior includes the Asams' frescoes, stucco and gilding.

🔡 B2 ✉ Sendlinger Strasse 32 🕾 089 2360 7909 🕐 Mon.–Thu. 7:30–6, Fri. noon–6, Sat. 8–6, Sun. 8–3 🚇 U-Bahn to Sendlinger Tor; S-Bahn to Marienplatz 🚌 Tram 16, 17, 18, 27 🎗 Free

BMW Museum

This stylishly revamped museum is now five times bigger than before and celebrates nine decades of BMW technology and expertise. There are plenty of vehicles to see, of course, along with themed areas and displays relating to automobile design, media design and architecture. A central route leads visitors along a historical timeline.

🔡 Off map at A4 ✉ Am Olympiapark 2 🕾 089 1250 16001; www.bmw-welt.com 🕐 Tue.–Sun. and public holidays 10–6 🚇 U-Bahn to Olympiazentrum or Petuelring 🚌 50; tram 27 🍴 Café on site 🎗 $$$ ℹ Guided tours, audio guide

Deutsches Museum

One of the biggest science and technology museums in the world, the German Museum has more than 100,000 items on display, and deals with everything from lightning demonstrations to space travel to hydraulics to the first German submarine. Audiovisual displays and hands-on exhibits add to the fun.

🔡 D1 ✉ Museumsinsel 1 🕾 089 21 79-1; www.deutsches-museum.de 🕐 Daily 9–5; closed some holidays 🚇 U-Bahn to Fraunhoferstrasse; S-Bahn to Isartor 🚌 132; tram 16, 18 🍴 Cafés on site 🎗 $$$ ℹ Guided tours; audio guide

Englischer Garten

The landscaped park Englischer Garten (English Garden) was created in 1789 and is a beloved city green space. Boats can be rented at the Kleinhesseloher See and there is a beer garden, the Seehaus, near the lake. Enjoy good city views from the circular "temple," the *monopteros*; other attractions include the Chinesischer Turm (Chinese Tower). In summer, surfers ride the waves on the Eisbach river that runs through the park.

🔡 D4 ✉ Northeast Munich 🕐 Daily 24 hours

Englischer Garten offers surprising sports options

Germany

🚇 U-Bahn to Universität or Giselastrasse 🚌 54, 154 to Chinesischer Turm; tram 18 to Tivolistrasse 🍴 Beer gardens, cafés and restaurants

Frauenkirche

Munich's twin-towered cathedral (Church of Our Dear Lady) was built between 1468 and 1488, but was left without a roof. In 1524 its Italian Renaissance, green onion domes were "temporarily" added – and have been there ever since. Near the entrance is a footprint in the floor, said to be that of the devil, who stamped with glee thinking that the architect had forgotten to put in the windows. In fact, the windows can't be seen from where the devil was standing – but they are there.
➕ C2 ✉️ Frauenplatz 1 ☎️ 089 29 00 82-0; www.muenchner-dom.de 🕐 Church: daily 7:30 a.m.–8:30 p.m., May–Oct.; 7:30 a.m.–8 p.m., Nov.–Apr. 🚇 U-Bahn/S-Bahn to Marienplatz 🚌 52, 132; tram 19 💰 Church free 🛈 South Tower may be closed due to building work

Haus der Kunst

Opened by the Nazis in 1937 as "Haus der Deutschen Kunst" (House of German Art) the large white columned building was immediately mocked by its detractors as "Weisswurstallee" (White Sausage Boulevard). The gallery was part of Hitler's campaign against modern so-called *entartete Künstler* (degenerate artists). Today it presents sophisticated thematic exhibitions and retrospectives.
➕ D3 ✉️ Prinzregentenstrasse 1 ☎️ 089 211 27-113; www.hausderkunst.de 🕐 Daily 10–8 (also Thu. 8–10 p.m.) for exhibitions only; closing times are extended for special exhibitions 🚇 U-Bahn to Odeonsplatz or Lehel 🚌 100; tram 18 🍴 Café in gallery 💰 $$$; exhibition admission varies

Lenbachhaus

Built in 1887 as the home of aristocratic painter Franz von Lenbach, the Lenbachhaus is now an art gallery. It shows the progression of art in Munich from the 15th and 16th centuries to the 19th-century Romantics. Highlights of the collection are works by the Munich Expressionists, the so-called *Blaue Reiter* (Blue Rider) group of the 20th century, with more than 90 abstract paintings and 900 other works by Wassily Kandinsky – the world's largest assemblage of his art.

The spectacular new wing reflects this museum's continuing acquisition of international contemporary art.
➕ A4 ✉️ Luisenstrasse 33 ☎️ 089 2333 2000; www.lenbachhaus.de 🕐 Wed.–Sun. 10–6, Tue. 10–8 🚇 U-Bahn U2, U8 to Königsplatz 🚌 100; tram 27 to Karolinenplatz 🍴 Café 💰 $$$; children under 18 free

Neue Pinakothek

Across the street from the Renaissance-style Alte Pinakothek (Old Picture Gallery, see page 233) is the Neue Pinakothek (New Picture Gallery), a modern building featuring art from the late 18th to the 20th centuries.

It has examples of the French and German Impressionists, Romantic and rococo paintings, and the art nouveau style known in Germany as *Jugendstil*.
➕ B4 ✉️ Barer Strasse 27, entrance on Theresienstrasse ☎️ 089 23 80 51 95; www.pinakothek.de 🕐 Wed.–Mon. 10–6 (also Wed. 6–8 p.m.) 🚇 U-Bahn U2 to Königsplatz 🚌 Tram 27 to Pinakotheken 🍴 Café 💰 $$ ($ on Sun.)

Neues Rathaus

A forest of neo-Gothic turrets, towers, spurs and gargoyles, the 19th-century Neues Rathaus (New Town Hall) sprawls around six courtyards on the north side of Marienplatz.

On its central tower is a 43-bell clock (*Glockenspiel*), which comes to life every day at 11 a.m. (also at noon and 5 p.m., Mar.–Oct.) as life-size figures from Munich's history come dancing out to its four melodies. The *Schäfflertanz*, a dance which celebrates the end of the plague in 1517, is performed by dancers in the city streets every seven years (the next is due in 2019).
➕ C2 ✉️ Marienplatz 8 ☎️ 089 23 300 🕐 Tower: daily 10–7, May–Sep.; Mon.–Fri. 10–5, rest of year 🚇 U-Bahn/S-Bahn to Marienplatz 🚌 52, 132 🍴 Ratskeller, see page 478 💰 Tower $

Hofbräuhaus

Wilhelm V, Duke of Bavaria, founded Munich's Hofbräu brewery in 1589 to brew a dark ale more to his liking than the local beer. At this time, beer was a drink restricted to the Bavarian upper classes: they had made it their own preserve after losing their vineyards in a series of severe winters. In 1828, the brewery became an inn, and the delights of its beer were made accessible to all townspeople.

The huge beer hall and its lovely tree-shaded courtyard (⊞ C2) have been the scene of political upheaval and violence in modern history. The Nazi party held its early mass meetings here, and a fight that became known as the Battle of the Hofbräuhaus broke out among the crowd during one of Adolf Hitler's speeches.

Nowadays, there is nothing sinister about the hall's fame: tourists flock to the long benches, listen to the Bavarian brass bands and drink beer served by traditionally dressed waitresses. They no longer practice the customary quality test for *Bock* beer, though, which is probably just as well. The test apparently consisted of drinkers sitting at one of the Hofbräuhaus' beer-soaked benches and consuming *Bock* beer for hours at a time, staying put even while nature took its course. If, at the end of the session, they stuck to the benches when they tried to get up, the beer was reckoned to be thick enough and ready to sell.

The Hofbräuhaus is the city's most popular beer hall and fills up very quickly, especially during the annual and world-famous, 16-day *Oktoberfest*, a beer festival that traditionally ends on the first Sunday in October and takes place on the fairground at Theresienwiese, west of the city center. Barbecues, processions and music all play their part in this annual jamboree, but beer is the main ingredient.

At all times of the year, if the Hofbräuhaus is too crowded – as it is often – there are many other options all over the city, plus numerous beer gardens where you are allowed to bring and eat your own food.

Hofbräuhaus ✉ Platzl 9 ☎ 089 290 136100; www.hofbraeuhaus.de 🕓 Daily 9 a.m.–midnight 🚇 U-Bahn U3, U6; S-Bahn to Marienplatz

Musicians perform traditional Bavarian music in Munich's Hofbräuhaus (beer hall)

A detail of the ceiling in the fabulous Residenz

Odeonsplatz

This regal square was laid out for Ludwig I early in the 19th century and marks the beginning of Ludwigstrasse and Prinzregentenstrasse. The Feldherrnhalle (Military Commanders' Hall) was added as a tribute to the Bavarian army, and is guarded by two marble lions. Overlooking Odeonsplatz is the lovely baroque, golden-stone Theatinerkirche, the church where members of the ruling Wittelsbach family were laid to rest. The gardens of Hofgarten are next to the square.

✚ C3 🚇 U-Bahn to Odeonsplatz 🚌 100 🍴 Halali, see page 478

Olympiapark

The park built for the 1972 Summer Olympics has become a venue for sporting and music events and a focus for joggers, strollers and swimmers. Its television tower, the 995-foot-high Olympiaturm, has a platform and revolving restaurant with Alpine views. The Rock Museum, on the platform, features memorabilia from famous rock groups. A tour train takes visitors around Olympic Lake; Olympic Hill, made of wartime debris; and the Olympic Village. You also can visit the Olympiastadion (Olympic stadium).

✚ Off map at A4 ✉ Spiridon-Louis-Ring 21 ☎ 089 30 67-0; www.olympiapark.de ⊙ Olympiapark: daily 9–8, May–Sep.; 9–4, rest of year. Olympiaturm: daily 9 a.m.–midnight. Last admission at 11:30 p.m. 🚇 U-Bahn to Olympiazentrum 🚌 144, 173, 175, 177, 178; tram 20, 21, 27 🍴 Revolving restaurant, Olympiaturm (beer garden in summer) 💲 Olympiapark free; Olympiastadion $$; Olympiaturm $$

Pinakothek der Moderne

This is one of the most important contemporary art museums in Germany. The building, innovative in design and architecture, displays 20th- and 21st-century art.

✚ B4 ✉ Barer Strasse 40 ☎ 089 2 38 05 3-60; www.pinakothek.de ⊙ Tue.–Wed. and Fri.–Sun. 10–6, Thu. 10–8 🚇 U-Bahn to Königsplatz 🚌 100, 154; tram 27 💲 $$$ ($ on Sun.)

Residenz

The 130 rooms of the Wittelsbach dynasty's dazzling palace are a treasure trove of art and, despite ongoing renovation, 80 of the rooms remain open. Highlights include the vaulted Antiquarium, built between 1568 and 1571; the exquisite crown jewels in the Treasury; and the Ahnengalerie (Ancestral Portrait Gallery).

✚ C3 ✉ Residenzstrasse 1/Max-Joseph-Platz 3 ☎ 089 29 06 71; www.residenz-muenchen.de ⊙ Daily 9–6, Apr. to mid-Oct.; 10–5, rest of year 🚇 U-Bahn to Odeonsplatz; U-Bahn/S-Bahn to Marienplatz 🚌 100 to Odeonsplatz; tram 19 to Nationaltheater 🍴 Spatenhaus an der Oper, see page 478 💲 $$$

Schloss Nymphenburg

For centuries the mighty Wittelsbach family ruled Bavaria. Schloss Nymphenburg (Nymphenburg Palace) was built as their summer villa by Agostino Barelli between 1664 and 1674, and later generations of Wittelsbachs added to his creation. In the central section is the Schönheitsgalerie, or Gallery of Beauties – 36 paintings of beautiful women produced between 1827 and 1850 for Ludwig I. The former palace stables house the Marstallmuseum, a museum of porcelain and a collection of state carriages and sleighs, and in the 1734 Amalienburg hunting lodge there is a Hall of Mirrors.

✚ Off map at A4 ☎ 089 17 90 8-0; www.schloss-nymphenburg.de ⊙ Palace: daily 9–6, Apr. to mid-Oct.; 10–4, rest of year. Gardens: daily dawn–dusk 🚇 U-Bahn to Rotkreuzplatz 🚌 51; tram 12, 17 💲 $$$

A Walk Along Prinzregentenstrasse

This grand boulevard runs east from the 17th-century Court Garden (Hofgarten), with its beautiful fountains and Renaissance arcades. A startling modern addition, the steel-and-glass Neue Staatskanzlei, houses the Bavarian State Chancellery. Prinzregentenstrasse was laid out at the end of the 19th century and named for Prince Luitpold, who ruled as regent after his nephew, Ludwig II, had been declared mad and deposed.

Today it takes visitors through one of the city's main museum and gallery quarters. Running past the southern end of the English Garden (see pages 233–234), the boulevard first reaches the Haus der Kunst (House of Art, see page 234), formerly a gallery of Nazi-approved art. It exhibits the kind of work the Nazis had condemned.

Next door is the Bavarian National Museum (Bayerisches Nationalmuseum), in an early 20th-century building incorporating different architectural styles.

The next notable monument is the former Prussian Embassy, now the Galerie Schack (Prinzregentenstrasse 9), named for one of the 19th century's great patrons of the arts, Count Schack. His own collection of paintings is represented by such artists as Franz von Lenbach and Arnold Böcklin, who relied on the count for their livelihoods. The gallery is open Wednesday–Sunday 10–6.

Prinzregentenstrasse continues across the Isar river and past the *Angel of Peace (Friedensengel)*, a golden monument to peace, erected to commemorate the end of the Franco-Prussian War. Nowadays citizens gather on New Year's Day to enjoy fireworks displays and the view of Munich. Farther along, past Europaplatz, is the Villa Stuck (Prinzregentenstrasse 60), a 19th-century house built in a mix of styles by artist Franz von Stuck. Von Stuck was part of the 1890s *avant-garde* school known as the Munich Secession, and his own work is displayed inside. There also are exhibitions by such modern artists as Brian Jungen from Canada. For guided tours in English ☎ 089 45 55 51-0. The boulevard continues east to the Prinzregententheater (☎ 089 218 502), which stages drama, concerts and musicals. It was designed in 1900–01 to emulate the neoclassic Wagner Festival Theater in Bayreuth and sits on Prinzregentenplatz 12, where there is a U-Bahn station; trains travel back to Odeonsplatz and the Hofgarten. For the walking route, consult the city map on pages 230–231.

The Diana Temple stands at the heart of the Hofgarten (Court Garden); musicians often entertain visitors here

Greece

Introduction and Map 240

Timeline 242

Survival Guide 243

Athens 244

Feature: An Excursion To Delphi 251

Hotels and Restaurants 478

Essential Information 526

Opposite: The narrow streets and old white-painted houses that are typical of the Pláka area in Athens

Greece

Subconsciously, we all feel we have a stake in Greece. The language, political systems, values and ethics of the Western world are inextricably connected to this country's ancient civilization. Visitors often arrive with high expectations and romantic notions, snippets of myths, history and hearsay mingled in their minds. However, the country and its people have endured economic strife in recent years and face yet more difficult times ahead in order to realize a level of political and economic stability.

The Land

Greece's landscape is as dramatic as the people who inhabit it. There are about 200 inhabited islands in Greece, scattered on three sides of the mainland. Some are lush and studded with pine and eucalyptus, and others are arid or mountainous. Most are blessed with idyllic sand beaches and picturesque villages, and many have superb ancient sites, Frankish castles or Venetian fortifications.

You could spend years discovering them all, so spare at least a few days to visit one or two. Greek islands are a vital part of the country and have bedazzled travelers for centuries. There are regular ferry services to the main islands in summer, but services to more remote islands are less regular and can be challenging – though worth the effort – to organize. Check the website www.gtp.gr, which lists monthly ferry routes.

Much of mainland Greece is very mountainous. The slopes of Olympus and Parnassus are carpeted with wildflowers in spring, offering superb vistas and rewarding hiking, as do the eerie and stony landscapes of the Máni, a region of rugged mountains and isolated villages, and the steep-sided gorges and wild coastline of Crete.

Public transportation, especially by bus, is usually regular and reliable in mainland towns.

If you prefer to be more independent, car rental is simple to arrange. If you do rent a car, be prepared for some poorly surfaced roads, and avoid driving in cities and some of the larger rural towns if possible.

Traditional Culture

Greece has one of Europe's most vigorous cultures, perpetuated through architecture, crafts, music and dance. Traditional customs permeate everyday life, despite the growing impact of Western consumer values. If you can, see traditional dancing and listen to the music – the real thing is often easier to find in rural areas.

As in many other Mediterranean countries, much of life is lived in the full gaze of the public eye, hence the strolling crowds and packed cafes.

The worldwide recession sparked riots in Athens in the last few years.

The Greeks and You

Tourism is not a slick operation in Greece; everything works, things eventually happen, but not necessarily with streamlined efficiency. So relax, slow down and you'll get much more out of your trip.

The Greeks have been dealing with foreign incursions for centuries, so they took the late 20th-century tourist influx in their stride. The classical Greek tradition of hospitality to strangers is still strong, which makes for a relaxed attitude toward visitors, particularly when you go off the beaten track.

Greek is the official language, but English is widely spoken, though in remote areas it is likely that only Greek will be understood.

Hospitality often takes the form of innumerable personal questions, among which "How much do you earn?" is usually near the top of the list. Don't be offended, as this is considered an acceptable and friendly exchange. If someone offers you something – a drink, some fruit, a flower – accept it graciously, as the donor is acting out a tradition that goes back thousands of years.

Greeks have a strong code of honor, which makes Greece a safe country to visit. It's highly unlikely you'll be cheated in any way, and you can still safely walk most streets at night without worrying.

Society has changed beyond recognition in the last 40 years, and young Greeks are far more emancipated than their parents. Female virtue – especially in rural areas – is still held in high regard. As a consequence young Greek males may occasionally pester foreign girls in the often mistaken belief that they will respond more readily to their advances.

There's still a large rural class in Greece, and outside cities and tourist areas you'll see black-garbed figures laboring in tiny fields. This traditional way of farming has been going on for centuries, a lifestyle that is a million miles from that of city dwellers.

More Top Destinations in Greece (see map page 240)

■ Chaniá B1	■ Monemvassía B1
■ Delfoí B2	■ Mykínes B2
■ Ídra B2	■ Náxos C2
■ Kefalloniá A2	■ Óros Píndos A3
■ Léros C2	■ Samothráki B3
■ Máni A1	■ Skópelos B2
■ Metéora A3	■ Thíra/
■ Mikonos B2	Santorini B1

Greece

Timeline

776–700 BC	City-states established; first Olympic Games.
499–400 BC	Persian Wars; Golden Age of classical Greek culture; Peloponnesian Wars against Sparta.
336–323 BC	Alexander the Great conquers the known world.
146 BC	Greece becomes a Roman province.
AD **394**	Christianity established throughout the Roman Empire; the Olympic Games finish and the Delphic Oracle is closed.
476–1453	Greece ruled from Constantinople; fall of Constantinople in 1453; Greece ruled by Turks for next 400 years.
1821–29	Greek War of Independence; Greece becomes an independent modern state.
1917–18	Greece sides with Allies in World War I.
1920–23	Greece continues a misjudged war against Turkey, ending in defeat.
1940–44	Axis occupation during World War II.
1945–60	Many Greeks emigrate to the United States and Australia; others flood into Athens from the countryside.
1974	Conflict with Turkey over Cyprus; situation remains tense into the 21st century.
1975	Tourist boom begins.
1981	Greece joins the European Economic Community; community funding catapults much of the country into mainstream Europe.
1996	Macedonian claims by former Yugoslavs seen as implicit threat to northern Greek region of Macedonia.
2001	Greece adopts the euro as its new national currency.
2004	Athens hosts the 2004 Olympic Games.
2009	George Papandreou of the PASOK party is elected as Prime Minister.
2010–2014	Widespread protest marches take place against austerity measures.
January 2015	Alexis Tsipras, of the left-wing SYRIZA Party, is elected Prime Minister. Greece's debt crisis leads to the country needing an emergency financial bailout in order to remain in the Eurozone.
August 2015	Prime Minister Alexis Tsipras resigns. Refugees and migrants fleeing Syria's war zone reach Greek Islands by sea from Turkey.
2016/2017	Despite its problems, tourism remains strong in Greece. In 2016 around 30 million people visited the country, four million up on 2015 and 14 million more than in 2005.
2017	The Greek island of Kos is hit by an earthquake of 6.4-magnitude.

The Golden Age of Classical Greece

The peace following the defeat of the Persians in the fifth century BC marked the start of a cultural, artistic and intellectual blossoming for Athens and the other city-states. Much of what truly epitomizes "the glory that was Greece" dates from this era. The great architectural triumphs, the start of drama and comedy, and the first steps in philosophical thought can all be traced to Athens at this time. The Acropolis took the form whose remains are seen today, decorated by Pheidias' sublime marbles, and harmonious temples were built everywhere. The names Sophocles, Euripides, Aristophanes, Socrates and Plato are familiar worldwide, yet they lived and worked in this tiny state in the eastern Mediterranean more than 2,500 years ago.

Survival Guide

- Athens is best avoided during the sweltering summer months, when temperatures can soar above 90 degrees Fahrenheit, noise levels are high around the clock, and the ever-present pollution is at its worst.

- Head for restaurants and tavernas where the locals eat; the food will be good. If you don't understand the menu in a taverna you may be invited into the kitchen for a look – choose what you want and point!

- In some areas of Greece there is an enduring belief that hot food harms the stomach, and food may therefore be served lukewarm. However, the preference for hot food is normally accommodated.

- Remember to *never* flush toilet tissue down the toilet – it goes in the basket provided. You'll flood the bathroom if you put paper down the narrow pipes. The only exceptions are modern, luxury hotels. Public restrooms are few and far between, and many of them leave much to be desired. Carry your own toilet paper as it is not always available.

- Greeks prefer to be cool and comfortable rather than stylish, but usually don't wear shorts in the city. It's respectful to cover bare shoulders and upper arms when visiting churches or religious establishments. Topless and nude sunbathing are widely but discreetly practiced.

- Taxis outside main cities are fairly inexpensive, but in Athens drivers may hike rates for foreign visitors. Ask what the destination fare is before getting into a taxi or compare fares before deciding which one you'll use. On arrival by ferry or plane, if you already have a hotel reserved, resist being talked into going to another hotel.

- Don't rent a scooter; more tourists have accidents on them than by any other means.

Guarding the Tomb of the Unknown Soldier, Athens

- At important sites you may be approached by guides wanting to be paid for their services; some are good, others barely speak English. If you want guide service, use an official one or take a tour.

- There's a plethora of attractive, handmade items to buy in Greek stores and markets. Most prices are fixed, but you can try a little gentle haggling in markets.

- Be careful after it rains, when marble-surfaced walkways in Athens become very slippery. Also look out for unmarked holes on sidewalks, especially in poorly lit areas at night.

Athens

Athens is one of the Mediterranean's great cities, boasting some of the world's most treasured relics; it's also noisy, crowded, traffic-clogged and polluted, with sprawling, unattractive suburbs. Summertime heat and the lack of shady spots can be oppressive, but the city is exhilarating, fascinating and stimulating, as much for its past as its present. Enjoy it for the colorful place it is.

Tackling Athens

You'll probably spend most of your visit in Athens' tiny historical center. Base yourself near Syntagma Square (Platéia Syntágmatos, see page 250) or Pláka (see page 250), which are a short walk from most of the main tourist sights. Plan your day carefully; get an early start to avoid the heat of the afternoon.

If you need information or advice, you will find that most people connected with tourism speak English, ranging from a few words to polished and idiomatic speech.

Moving around the historic center on foot is easy, but is occasionally challenging at busy street crossings. Be aware that where there are no traffic lights local drivers rarely take note of

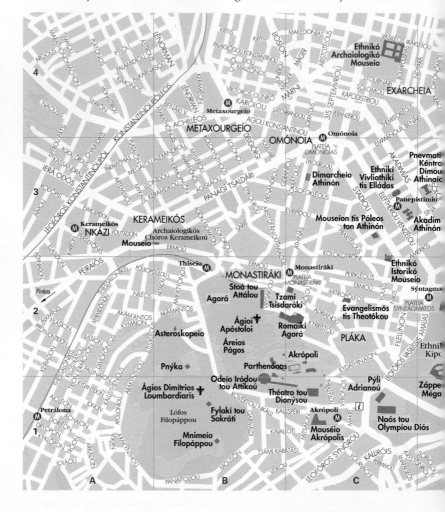

pedestrian crossings; wait for a clear gap in the traffic before crossing. In the last few years there has been an expanding pedestrianization program in the center.

City buses and trolley buses are often packed and may be delayed by traffic jams. Taxis are convenient for excursions out of the city, as is the greatly improved metro (subway) system. The main road systems into the city also have been improved.

Athenian Flavors

Sitting at a shady café table, lingering over a gargantuan lunch, munching sunflower seeds, melon, pistachios and pine nuts, or eating ice cream as you stroll on balmy evenings are true Athenian pleasures.

In a country where hospitality to strangers is one of the bedrock rules of society, it's not surprising that eating and drinking socially play an important role. Eating establishments are known as *estiatorio* (restaurants) or tavernas (less expensive, simpler and often family run). Greek food is delicious and healthy – fresh salads with feta cheese and olives, fantastic *mezédhes* (hors d'ocuvres), grilled meats, moussakas, and tasty stews and vegetables, perhaps washed down with one of the increasingly good selections of Greek wines. Dessert is normally fresh local fruit; if you want something sweeter, head for a *zaharoplastío*, a café serving the honey-soaked pastries much loved by the Greeks.

Festivals and Theater

Athens has theater, movies, dance, galleries and nightlife; everything changes rapidly, so pick up a free copy of one of the English-language newspapers to find out schedules.

In summer, the main tourist attraction is the Hellenic Festival (www. greekfestival.gr/en/), which runs from June through mid-August. The festival offers a wonderful program of excellent cultural events, although it's most famous for classical Greek theater, some taking place at the Odeon of Herodes Atticus on the slopes of the Acropolis.

The Greek Alphabet

At first it may be daunting to see Greek script everywhere, but it won't be a major inconvenience. All street signs are in both Greek and Roman letters, as are signs to museums and most restaurants and shops. Public transportation is usually displayed in Greek. However, you'll get the hang of deciphering Greek letters and you'll feel a real sense of achievement when you do.

Ceramics and Honey

There's a wide range of shopping in Athens, from international labels to traditional Greek products. In Kolonáki and on and around Ermoú Street, the most fashionable retail areas of the city, you'll find familiar merchandise.

Ethnic buys are another matter, with much to hunt down around Pláka and its vicinity. Leather and woolen goods, ceramics and tapestries, felt slippers, olive oil, honey and pistachio nuts are all excellent buys. For something that bit more special, check out jewelry or religious stores; Greece has a long tradition of gold craftsmanship, and traditional icons are still made.

Keep a look out for Athens' *períptera* (street kiosks) – much more than newsstands, they sell everything from

A view of Lycabettus Hill from the Acropolis, Athens
Opposite: The Acropolis Museum, Athens

snacks and drinks to bus tickets, simple medicines and telephone cards. In central Athens you will find that some *períptera* open 24 hours a day.

Essential Information

Tourist Information

Tsoha 24, Ambelokipi ☎ 210 870 7000; www.visitgreece.gr
At the Acropolis ☎ 210 331 0529

Urban Transportation

The metro (subway) system is being expanded, but it's a long-term project and for now the easiest way to get around Athens is to walk or take one of the numerous yellow taxis. Taxis are hailed on the street and often shared; you pay for your segment of the trip, so check the meter when you get in. Alternatively, your hotel can arrange a taxi for you. Buses, trolley buses and the metro (subway) operate daily 5:30 a.m.–12:30 a.m. (Fri.–Sat. metro lines 2 and 3 operate until 2:30 a.m.); tickets are available at kiosks and are interchangeable with metro tickets, which can be bought at stations. Validate bus and trolley bus tickets on board, and validate metro tickets at entrances to the platforms. The Athens Urban Transport Organization's (OASA) website, www.oasa.gr, is useful for finding bus, trolley bus and metro routes.

Airport Information

Athens International Airport (Eleftherios Venizelos) is at Spáta, 17 miles east of Athens (☎ 210 353 0000; www.aia.gr). The metro line 3 linking the airport to the city is the easiest way into Athens. There are four 24-hour express bus lines, connecting the airport with Athens and Piréas: the X93 to the Kifíssos Coach Station, X95 to Syntagma Square, X96 to Piréas and X97 to the Dafni metro station. Tickets cost €6 one way. For details see the airport's website: www.aia.gr.

Climate – average highs and lows for the month

Jan.	Feb.	Mar.	Apr.	May	Jun.	Jul.	Aug.	Sep.	Oct.	Nov.	Dec.
13°C	13°C	15°C	19°C	24°C	30°C	31°C	32°C	28°C	23°C	17°C	14°C
55°F	55°F	59°F	66°F	75°F	86°F	88°F	90°F	82°F	73°F	63°F	57°F
6°C	6°C	7°C	11°C	15°C	20°C	22°C	22°C	19°C	15°C	11°C	8°C
43°F	43°F	45°F	52°F	59°F	68°F	72°F	72°F	66°F	59°F	52°F	46°F

Greece

Athens Sights

Agorá

The stately civic center and marketplace of ancient Athens is at the foot of the Acropolis, to which it was once linked by the Panathenaic Way.

Today, the site is an atmospheric jumble of tree-shaded ruins, and you'll need to use your imagination to visualize how much of it looked in its glorious heyday. However, dominating one end is the virtually reconstructed, fifth-century BC Doric temple known as the Thieío.

Opposite, the two-story Stoá Attálou, a second-century BC arcade, has been restored by the American School of Archeology to give an idea of the glory of these ancient public buildings. It contains a museum with archeological finds from within and around the site.

➕ B2 ✉ Adrianou or Theorias ☎ 210 321 0185 🕓 Daily 8–7:30. Last admission at 7 p.m. 🚇 Thiseío or Monastiráki 🎟 $$

Akrópoli

The Akrópoli (Acropolis) should top your sightseeing list. This naturally defensible rock was the sacred focal point of ancient Athens. What you see today dates mainly from the fifth century BC, an era of peace and prosperity thought of as the true "Golden Age" of Greece.

You reach the summit through the Propylaia, a magnificent stepped gateway, with the graceful little temple of Athena Nike to your right. Ahead rises the great Doric temple of the Parthenón, one of the world's most beautiful buildings; built using no perpendicular lines, its columns actually taper, giving the whole structure a feeling of lightness. It was decorated by Athenian sculptors and dedicated to the goddess Athena Parthenos, whose statue by the sculptor Pheidias stood inside.

To the left of the Parthenón stands the Erechtheion, shrine to Athena and Poseidon, and said to be the place where the goddess created the first olive tree. The roof of the south portico is supported by six caryatids, stately maidens dressed in pleated tunics.

At the foot of the Acropolis you can see two Roman theaters, and visit the Acropolis Museum (see page 250).

Looking toward the Acropolis on its rocky setting, as the sun sets across the city

🚻 C2 ✉ Akrópoli ☎ 210 321 0219; www.acropolisofathens.gr ⏰ Daily 8–7. Last admission 6:30 p.m. Ⓜ Akrópoli 🍴 $$

Ethnikó Archaiologikó Mouseío

For lovers of Classical art the Ethnikó Archaiologikó Mouseío (National Archeological Museum) is one of the world's top sights. This vast and varied collection covers all the finest art from ancient Greece, with the added bonus of an exceptional Egyptian collection.

The best approach is to concentrate on only the prime examples. Head first for the treasures from the royal tombs at Mycenae, dating from 1500 BC; they include exquisite gold funerary masks, necklaces and filigree flowers. Next, take in the sixth-century BC *kouros*, vibrant statues of nude male athletes; Aristodikos' superbly tactile athlete is one of the finest ever carved. Move on to admire the huge statue of Poseidon and the little jockey urging on his horse, both found in the sea off Cape Artemision on the island of Evvoia in 1927. There's also a stunning bronze by the famous sculptor Praxiteles in room 28.

Upstairs you'll find frescoes from Santorini (Thíra), buried 3,500 years ago during a volcanic eruption, showing riverside scenes. Rooms 49–56 house the pottery collections; look for the rare *lekythoi* (white-ground clayware), and the exquisite red and black Attic vases.
🚻 C4 ✉ 44 Patission ☎ 210 821 7724; www.namuseum.gr ⏰ Tue.–Sun. 8–8, Mon. 1–8, Sun. 8–3 Ⓜ Omónoia 🚌 2, 3, 11, 13, 15, 022, 224, 226 🍴 Café in museum 🍴 $$

Ethnikós Kípos

The green and somber Ethnikós Kípos (National Gardens) provide a wonderful oasis of cool off noisy Leóforos Amalias. Laid out in the 19th century by Queen Amalia, wife of King Otto, this is a true southern Mediterranean garden – no colorful flowerbeds, but deep shade and sylvan green. With plenty of cafés, the gardens are a good place for lunch.

Within the grounds is a botanical museum with samples of all the gardens' plants, many of them rare.
🚻 D2 ✉ Amalias ☎ Museum: 210 721 1178 ⏰ Daily dawn to 30 minutes before dusk (museum: Tue.–Sun. 9–3) Ⓜ Syntagma 🚌 1, 2, 4, 11, 12, 022, 025, 026

Goulandris Mouseío Kykladikís Téchnis

The beautifully presented Goulandris Mouseío Kykladikís Téchnis (Museum of Cycladic Art) houses a superb collection of prehistoric artifacts from around the Aegean islands. The collection, once the private property of the shipowning Goulandris family, dates from the Cycladic civilization, which flourished on the Greek islands from 3000 until 2000 BC. The marble figures displayed could be taken for 20th-century work, elegant and minimalist, yet full of powerful feeling.
🚻 D2 ✉ 4 Neophytou Douka ☎ 210 722 8321; www.cycladic.gr ⏰ Mon., Wed. and Fri.–Sat. 10–5, Thu. 10–8, Sun. 11–5 Ⓜ Sýntagma or Evangelismós 🚌 3, 7, 13, 224, 235 🍴 Café in museum 🍴 $$

Lykavittós and Kolonáki

From Kolonáki Square, the hub of one of Athens' most fashionable shopping areas, the slopes of Lykavittós (Lycabettus Hill) rise steeply to the 912-foot-high summit, one of the city's great vantage points. You can walk up or take the funicular for panoramic views over the city, from the Acropolis down to the sea at Piréas. Get there for sunset, and visit the whitewashed chapel of Agios Giorgios (St. George), which crowns the top of the hill.
🚻 D2–D3 ✉ Kolonáki ⏰ Funicular: daily 9 a.m.–midnight (times may vary) 🚌 022, 060 🍴 Terrace restaurant at top 🍴 $$ (funicular)

Monastiráki

This bustling area surrounds Monastiráki Square, named for a former monastery on this site. Today the square's focal point is the 18th-century Tzistarakis Mosque, a relic of Turkish rule, which houses the Keramiki Silogi (Museum of Greek Ceramics). Most people head straight for Monastiráki's famous flea market, selling anything from clothes and kebabs to icons and CDs. Sunday is the big day here.

➕ B2 ⊠ Monastiráki ☎ Museum of Greek Ceramics: 210 324 2066 🕙 Market open daily, but largest on Sun. Museum: Wed.–Mon. 9–2:30 Ⓜ Monastiráki 🐾 $ (free to all some Sun. in winter)

Naós tou Olympíou Diós and Pýli Adrianoú

Along with the Tower of the Winds in the Roman Agora, Naós tou Olympíou Diós and Pýli Adrianoú (Temple of Olympian Zeus and Hadrian's Arch) are Athens' most impressive Roman legacy. Both of these structures were completed around AD 130 by the Emperor Hadrian; the temple as a shrine to this paramount Roman god, and the arch to mark the boundary between the old Greek city and Hadrian's new one. Fifteen massive columns remain of what was once the largest temple in Greece.

➕ C1 ⊠ 2 Vasilissis Olgas ☎ 210 922 6330 🕙 Daily 8–6 Ⓜ Akrópoli 🚌 1, 4, 11, 040, 057 🐾 $$

Piréas

Piréas is a town in its own right, although it's only five stops on the subway from Athens' city center. It's a noisy, bustling port, one of the biggest in the Mediterranean, and many of the interisland boats leave from its harbor. Piréas boasts a magnificent cathedral, rebuilt after World War II; a fine archeological museum with some striking exhibits; and Greece's national naval museum.

Come here on a Sunday for a leisurely browse in the flea market.

➕ Off map at A2 Ⓜ Piréas

Pláka

Visitors return time and again to the pretty Pláka neighborhood, at the foot of the Acropolis. The maze of colorful narrow streets, flower-bedecked squares and huge range of stores and tavernas may be touristy, but they also radiate timeless charm. Bustling Kidhathineon and Adrianoú, the main thoroughfares, teem with noisy street life and are lined with mainly 19th-century, colorfully painted houses.

Don't miss the dazzling white alleys that make up Anafiotika, on the northern slopes of the Acropolis. This area was built in the 1840s by masons from the Cycladic islands, and it still retains a village atmosphere.

➕ C2 ⊠ Pláka Ⓜ Syntagma or Monastiráki 🚌 9, 11, 15, 025, 026

Plateía Syntágmatos

Noisy, crowded, Plateía Syntágmatos (Constitution Square) is at the heart of modern Athens, where you'll find a variety of hotels, offices, banks, restaurants and myriad jostling Athenians. The neoclassic edifice at the top is the Voulí (Parliament Building), which was once the royal palace. In front of it is the Tomb of the Unknown Soldier, patrolled around the clock by the Evzones, a guard of honor whose dress uniform features a short pleated kilt and pom-poms on their shoes.

The central area is pleasantly pedestrianized, with several cafés.

➕ C2 ⊠ Syntágmatos Ⓜ Syntagma 🚌 1, 2, 4, 5, 022, 025, 026 🎖 Changing of the guard at varied times Mon.–Fri., at 11 a.m. on Sun.

Acropolis Museum

The stunning Mouséio Akrópolis was built at a cost of €130 million. The interior of the building is phenomenal with its superbly designed galleries, subtle lighting and spectacular views of the Acropolis. The museum exhibits some 4,000 artifacts.

➕ C1 ⊠ Dionysiou Areopagitou 15 ☎ 210 900 0900; www.theacropolismuseum.gr 🕙 Fri. 8 a.m.–10 p.m., Tue.–Thu. and Sat.–Sun. 8–8, Mon. 8–4, Apr.–Oct.; Fri. 9 a.m.–10 p.m., Sat.–Sun. 9–8, Mon.–Thu. 9–5, Nov.–Mar. Last admission 30 minutes before closing. Closed public holidays Ⓜ Akropoli 🐾 $$

An Excursion To Delphi

The sacred site of Delphi (Delfoí), 93 miles northwest of Athens, is the obvious choice for a day trip. The greatest shrine of the ancient Greek world, the center of their earth, lies in an unrivaled position below the great peaks of Mount Parnassós. Dedicated to the god Apollo, in ancient times Delphi was independent – belonging to no state – so enemies could worship there together. It was famed for its oracle, which gave enigmatic and prophetic advice through the medium of a priestess.

In return for this, petitioners brought gifts and erected treasure-houses to hold them; ancient writers referred to the marble and precious stones of the sanctuary. For centuries, pilgrims trudged through the mountains to bathe in the sacred Castalian spring and worship here, but in the fourth century Christianity triumphed and the last oracle slipped away. Below the site, olive groves spread down to the sea, the ground is carpeted with flowers and the sky is full of birds.

The French excavated Delphi in the 1890s, and today it lies on a series of terraces below Parnassós. The paved Sacred Way leads past treasure-houses – one has been sensitively reconstructed – to the remains of the Temple of Apollo. Six columns still stand, giving an idea of the ancient ruin's former size and grandeur.

Up the hill you'll find the 5,000-seat theater and the marvelously evocative and well-preserved athletic stadium, set amid pine trees. To visit the ruins of the Sanctuary of Athena, you will need to leave the main site and cross the modern road. Use the columns of the fourth-century BC Tholos, undoubtedly the most photographed of all Delphi's wonders, as your guide.

The adjacent museum contains the finds from Delphi, some of the finest in Greece. Sculptures from the Temple of Apollo, two superb examples of archaic kouroi (statues), ivory, jewelry and pottery are all here. The highlight of the collection is the striking bronze sculpture of a charioteer, which dates from 478 BC and is an artistic and technical masterpiece.

✚ See page 240, B2 ✉ Delphi ☎ 226 508 2312 or 226 508 2346 🕓 Daily 8–8.
Museum: daily 8–7 💶 Delphi $$$; Museum $$$ 🛈 A guided excursion is the easiest way to visit Delphi

Excursion Operators Chat Tours (✉ 9 Xenofontos Street, off Amalias Avenue ☎ 210 323 0827; www.chatours.gr) is an experienced tour operator in Athens

The Sacred Way leads past this well-reconstructed Treasury building at Delphi

Hungary

Introduction and Map 254

Timeline 256

Survival Guide 257

Budapest 258

Feature: Excursion to Esztergom 265

Hotels and Restaurants 479

Essential Information 530

Opposite: Hősök tere (Heroes' Square), Budapest, with statues of the ancient leaders who founded Hungary

Hungary

Hungary is situated at the heart of Europe. Surrounded by Austria, Slovakia, Ukraine, Romania, Serbia, Croatia and Slovenia, it has absorbed the cultures of such peoples and conquerors as the Romans, Magyars, Turks and Habsburgs. Its majestic capital, Budapest, sits on the broad Danube river, which has brought trade and settlers through the country on its course from southern Germany to the Black Sea.

For centuries Hungary has been a nation in flux, its territories gaining or diminishing through much invasion, occupation and liberation.

It is today undergoing yet further change after emerging from more than 40 years of life behind the Iron Curtain and transitioning to a modern democracy and member of the European Union.

Landscape of History

Northern, western and southern Hungary are different worlds. In the north, beyond the architecturally beautiful capital of Budapest and the industrial city of Miskolc, are the uplands and their wide, rolling, forested hills. The vineyards in this region produce the famous Tokay (Tokaj) and Bull's Blood (Egri Bikavér), the "wine of kings and king of wines."

In the west there continue to be strong links with Western European culture. The rich farmlands are punctuated with historic towns that have many examples of both fine Renaissance and ornate baroque buildings.

In the south and east the landscape changes completely. Vast, flat grasslands form the *puszta* of the Great Plain (Alföld), dotted with farmsteads and presided over by the regional capital, Debrecen. In the far south, the medieval city of Pécs, provincial capital of the county of Baranya, preserves many relics of its 143 years under Turkish rule.

Making Contact

The Hungarian language, distantly related to Finnish and Estonian, can be daunting for visitors. English may be spoken in the main tourist areas, but German is more frequently used. When you find a common language, however, you will discover that Hungarians are courteous and generous, but formal.

Hungary is a multiethnic nation, and despite its close proximity to the Balkan region, it considers itself West European.

Hungarian Heritage

Hungarians have strong folk traditions and customs, especially when it comes to music and dance. You can enjoy them at a dance house (*táncház*); there are several in Budapest. Bands usually

include bagpipes, cimbalom (a stringed instrument) and a hurdy-gurdy, and the dancing is fast and furious.

At Bugac in Kiskunság National Park, between the Danube and the Tisza rivers, a horse-drawn buggy takes visitors to see farmsteads, long-horned cattle and curly-horned Podokan sheep. There also are farming displays at Hortobágy National Park – Hungary's first national park – with its vast expanses of grasslands.

In the Cserhát hills of the north, the village of Hollókő sits at the foot of a 13th-century castle. The village is home to the Palóc people, who speak a distinct regional dialect and wear vibrant, colorful embroidered costumes and elaborate headdresses.

For another insight into Hungary's heritage, visit the famous Király thermal baths in Budapest and enjoy the luxury of a Turkish-style bath or massage.

More Top Destinations in Hungary

- Balatonfüred B2
- Bugac-Puszta C2
- Eger D3
- Fertőd A2
- Gödöllő C2
- Hollókő C3
- Hortobágyi Nemzeti Park D2
- Kecskemét C2
- Mátra C3
- Pécs B1
- Sopron A3
- Szabadtéri Néprajzi Múzeum C2
- Szentendre C2
- Tihany B2
- Tokaj D3
- Visegrád C3

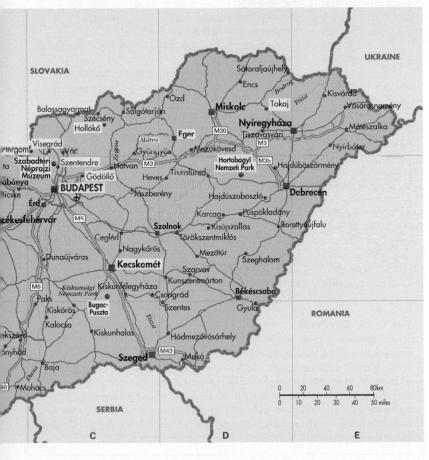

Timeline

13 BC	The Roman province of Pannonia is established on the west bank of the Danube; nomadic tribes occupy the east.
AD 896	Seven Magyar tribes cross the Carpathian Mountains and invade the Hungarian plains.
1000	King Stephen is crowned and makes Hungary a centralized, Christian state.
1443	King Matthias I, considered the greatest Hungarian king, is born in Cluj-Napoca, in modern-day Romania.
1526	The Turkish army of Sultan Suleiman I defeats the Hungarians at Mohács.
1686	Habsburg troops recapture Buda, on the west bank of the Danube (later united with Pest, on the east).
1896	The Great Exposition celebrates the 1,000th anniversary of the Magyar Conquest.
1919	Hungary briefly becomes a Bolshevik republic.
1920	Under the Treaty of Trianon, Hungary loses two-thirds of its territory to Czechoslovakia, Yugoslavia and Romania.
1939	Hungary enters World War II as a German ally.
1944	German occupation; most Jews are deported to concentration camps.
1948	Communists take power.
1956	Rebellion against Communist rule is crushed by Soviet troops.
1989	Hungary opens its borders to Austria and the Iron Curtain begins to lift.
1990	Free elections are won by a center-right coalition.
1999	Hungary officially joins NATO.
2004	Hungary joins the European Union.
2006	Danube floods to record levels.
2010	Pécs is the European Capital of Culture.
2011	Celebrations mark the 200th anniversary of the birth of composer Franz Liszt.
2014	Center-right Prime Minister Viktor Orbán wins reelection.
2015–16	Hungary's European border crossings come under pressure as thousands of Syrian refugees and migrants try to cross Europe.
2017	Events mark the 50th anniversary of the death of Zoltán Kodály, the classical composer and collector of Hungarian folk music.
2018	Hungarians reelect right-wing premier Viktor Orbán for the third time.

The Good Old Days

Hungary enjoyed two "golden ages" – one in the 15th century and another in the 19th. Under 15th-century ruler King Matthias, the nation expanded its borders and established its court in Vienna. Matthias patronized Europe's most brilliant scholars, and employed the best Italian artists to work on his palace in Visegrád. His reign became a byword for good government. In the 19th century, Count István Széchenyi, the man known as "the greatest Hungarian" ushered in a second age of achievement. He modernized the country, laying surfaced roads, introducing steamships and founding an academy of sciences. He also linked Buda and Pest with the Chain Bridge, and stopped the cycle of floods around the Tisza river by building dams.

Survival Guide

- Hungary's best-known export is *gulyás* (goulash), a soup made with beef, onions, potatoes, paprika, tomatoes, garlic and caraway seeds. Salami is a familiar item, as is *lecso*, a mix of peppers, tomatoes, onions and bacon fried in pork fat. Pastries are specialties, sold in the *cukrászda* (pastry shop). Try *palacsinta*, pancakes stuffed with sweet or savory fillings.

- Rural Hungarians produce and sell beautifully crafted items such as embroidered blouses and carved wood furniture. Purchase these in city stores, at national parks and from street sellers like the costumed Transylvanian (Romanian) Hungarians.

- Wine is a good Hungarian buy, sold by dealers in the main wine regions such as Eger. The vineyards on the slopes of Lake Balaton are delightful and many give tastings in their cellars.

- Go to street markets in the main towns and cities, such as the popular flea market on the southwest outskirts of Pécs. This is one of the biggest open-air markets in the country, selling antiques, crafts and food on Fridays and Saturdays. On Sundays it also sells livestock, and the place is packed with country people.

- Some of Hungary's ethnic communities have become big tourist magnets. Hollókő is filled with visitors for the summer Palóc festivals and especially for Easter – an important countrywide celebration.

- Summer festivals attract crowds to Pécs and Sopron in June and July. On St. Stephen's Day, August 20, there are fireworks all over Hungary.

- A Budapest Card, valid for 1–5 days (24 hours/6490Ft, 48 hours/9990Ft, 72 hours/12,990Ft, 96 hours/15,990Ft, 120 hours/18,900Ft), can be purchased from tourist offices and includes unlimited travel on public transportation, walking tours and entry to many of the city museums.

- The state railroad, Hungarian Railways (operating passenger trains as MÁV-Start), travels throughout the country, though the service may be reduced in some rural areas. Special Eurail One Country tourist passes offer unlimited use of the network for 3 to 8 days. Make advance reservations at www.eurail.com.

- Accommodations are not limited to city hotels. The Danube bend, a spectacular deep gorge north of Budapest, is lined with attractive towns such as Szentendre and Visegrád, where many private homes offer rooms. The resorts around Lake Balaton are another option.

- For overnight stays on the Great Plain, try the Sarlóspuszta Club Hotel near Dabas (H-2375 Tatárszentgyörgy-Sarlóspuszta ☎ 29 319 118; www.sarlospuszta.hu). It is a good base for hiking and horseback riding in the Kiskunság National Park, just 37 miles from Budapest.

Detail of the entrance of National Széchenyi Library

Budapest

Until the 19th century, two communities faced each other across the Danube. Royal, medieval Buda, with its majestic architecture, stood on the hilly western bank; and modern Pest, a flat area of busy boulevards, was on the east bank. Then the Chain Bridge (Széchenyi lánchíd) was built and Budapest, "Queen of the Danube," was created, linking the green uplands behind Buda, and the flat fields of the Great Plain beyond Pest.

Crossing the Divide

The best place to get a feel for the capital's character and history is at Buda. Here you will find the oldest and grandest architecture, museums and galleries, and cafés and bars. You can

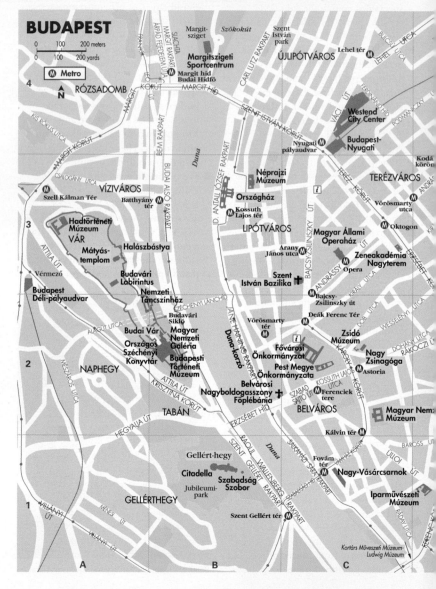

survey the whole city from Gellért Hill (Gellért-hegy, see page 261), and visit Castle Hill (Várhegy), a renovated medieval quarter which is reached by funicular railroad from the Buda end of Chain Bridge (Budavári Sikló). This is where you'll find the Buda Castle (Budai Vár, see page 261) and the Fisherman's Bastion (Halászbástya, see page 262).

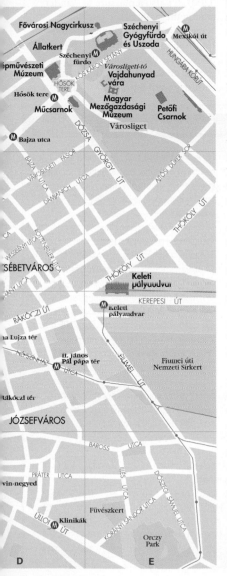

Pest has a much more contemporary feel; its main landmark is the neo-Gothic, many turreted parliament building (Országház, see pages 263–264) on the riverbank. Also worth visiting are the Hungarian State Opera House (Magyar Állami Operaház, see page 262) and the Hungarian National Museum (Magyar Nemzeti Múzeum, see page 263). Between the riverbanks is tranquil Margaret Island (Margit-sziget), named after St. Margaret, a medieval nun of royal birth.

Local Flavors

In the late 19th and early 20th centuries Budapest ranked with Vienna and Paris as part of European café society, drawing artists and intellectuals to its great coffeehouses. At the end of World War II, few of these hubs of creative life remained. The Café Restaurant New York, (Erzsébet körút 9–11, ☎ 1 886 6167; www.newyorkcafe.hu) manages to preserve the aura of those days.

Traditionally, Hungarian meals rely on the staples of spices, meat and cream and include intriguing specialties such as *túrós csusza* (pasta with cheese curd and sour cream). Since 1989 the range of international restaurant options has increased immeasurably.

Budapest at Night

The main home of opera and ballet is the Hungarian State Opera House (Magyar Állami Operaház, see page 262), a massive neo-Renaissance confection. Classical concerts occasionally take place in the Liszt Academy of Music (Zeneakadémia, Liszt Ferenc tér 8, ☎ 1 462 4600; www.zeneakademia.hu). There are many clubs, rock venues, bars and discos. Since the mid-1990s Hungary has been included in the mainstream of European pop and rock. There are several English-language websites that give extensive entertainment listings, including www.budapest.com and www.budapestbylocals.com.

Halászbástya (Fisherman's Bastion) in Budapest

Shopping

Pedestrian-only Váci utca, on the Pest side of the river near Erzsébet bridge, is the perfect place to begin shopping trips. In Buda, there's an excellent browsing area around Móricz Zsigmond körtér, south of the Citadella.

A well-known flea market (Ecseri bolhapiac) sets up daily (mornings on Sunday) at Nagykőrösi út 156 (☎ 1 348 3200). It's also a pleasure to wander among the stalls of the renovated Nagy-vásárcsarnok (Central Market Hall) on Vámház körút 1–3 (☎ 1 366 3300; www.piaconline.hu). The market is open all day Monday to Friday, and Saturday until 3 p.m.

Essential Information

Tourist Information

Budapestinfo (Tourism Office of Budapest)
All offices ☎ 1 438 8080; www.budapest.
com/travel/tourist_information.en.html
Deák Ferenc tér, Sütő utca 2 (daily 8–8)
Olof Palme sétány 5 (daily 9–7)
Budapest Ferenc Liszt International Airport:
Terminals 2A and 2B, daily 8 a.m.–11 p.m.

Urban Transportation

Metro (subway) lines are color coded: yellow (M1), red (M2), blue (M3) and green (M4). Buy tickets from the counter (pénztár) until 8 p.m., then from the section called forgalmi ugyelét. Trains run daily 4:30 a.m.–11 p.m. Buses with red or black numbers and no letter stop all over the city; avoid the express buses, which have a letter "E." The trams and trolley bus networks run daily 4:30 a.m.–11 p.m. Buy tickets from transport terminals, metro stations, vending machines or newsstands.

For public transportation information ☎ 1 461 6500; www.bkv.hu. Metro stations are marked with an "M" on the city map. The biggest city taxi company here is Fötaxi (☎ 1 222 2222; www.fotaxi.hu).

Airport Information

Budapest's Ferenc Liszt International Airport is 12 miles southeast of the center: Terminal 2A serves flights within the European Union's Common Schengen border, while Terminal 2B serves other international flights. For details: ☎ 1 296 7000; www.bud.hu. Bus 200E runs from Terminal 2 to the city center and via the Kőbánya–Kispet metro station, 4 a.m.–11 p.m.; a new airport shuttle bus, 100E, connects the airport with the city center (Deák tér) every 30 minutes from 4 a.m.–11:30 p.m. Airport minibuses depart regularly; go to the miniBud desk (☎ 1550 0000; www.minibud.hu).

Climate – average highs and lows for the month

Jan.	Feb.	Mar.	Apr.	May	Jun.	Jul.	Aug.	Sep.	Oct.	Nov.	Dec.
2°C	4°C	10°C	15°C	22°C	24°C	26°C	26°C	22°C	15°C	7°C	3°C
36°F	39°F	50°F	59°F	72°F	75°F	79°F	79°F	72°F	59°F	45°F	37°F
-4°C	-3°C	1°C	5°C	10°C	14°C	15°C	15°C	11°C	6°C	1°C	-3°C
25°F	27°F	34°F	41°F	50°F	57°F	59°F	59°F	52°F	43°F	34°F	27°F

Budapest Sights

Budai Vár

Part of the UNESCO World Heritage Site, Budai Vár (Buda Castle) looks down over the Danube from the southern end of Várhegy (Castle Hill). Little is left of the earliest castle, built in the 13th century under Béla IV, but what remains is in the underground cellars, now part of the Budapesti Történeti Múzeum (Budapest History Museum), in Wing E. Here there are displays of Roman and medieval finds and a collection of historical paintings and prints. After destruction in World War II, the palace was rebuilt in the second half of the 20th century. The interior now houses important museum collections.

Statue of the Turul at Budai Vár (Buda Castle)

The Magyar Nemzeti Galéria (Hungarian National Gallery) collection of Hungarian art occupies Buildings A, B, C and D, under the dome. A walk from here past the Matthias Fountain takes you to the West Wing (F) and the Országos Széchenyi Könyvtár (National Széchenyi Library), with its 2 million books.

Statues outside the palace include Prince Eugene of Savoy, who routed the Turkish armies; King Matthias; and a mythical bird called the Turul.

➕ B2 ✉ Várhegy 🖥 www.budacastlebudapest.com 🚍 For all attractions: Várbusz 16 from Szell Kálmán tér or Deák Ferenc tér; funicular from west end of Chain Bridge 🔧 Free access to courtyards around the castle **Budapesti Történeti Múzeum** ✉ Szent György tér 2 ☎ 1 487 8854; www.btm.hu 🕐 Tue.–Sun. 10–6, Mar.–Oct.; 10–4, rest of year 📖 $$ 🔧 English audio guide $$

Magyar Nemzeti Galéria ☎ 1 201 9082; www.mng.hu 🕐 Tue.–Sun. 10–6; Dome 10–5 🍴 Gallery café 📖 $$; dome $$ 🔧 Guided tours (book in advance); English audio guide $

Országos Széchényi Könyvtár ☎ 1 224 3700; www.oszk.hu 🕐 Tue.–Sat. 10–8 📖 $

Gellért-hegy

Bishop Gellért failed to convert the pagan Magyars to Christianity; legend has it they stuck him in a barrel and threw him into the river from this 771-foot-high limestone cliff. His statue, best viewed from Elizabeth Bridge, stands at the bottom of Gellért-hegy (Gellért Hill).

Offering fine views at the top is the Citadella (Citadel), a stronghold built after the 1848–49 War of Independence to watch over the restive citizens. Inside the fortifications are a war museum ($), an exhibition, hotel and restaurant. The Szabadság szobor (Liberation Monument), also at the top, was erected by the Russians in 1947. Before the fall of Communism, the monument featured a Soviet soldier as well as the now lone woman brandishing a palm leaf.

➕ B1 ✉ Between Erzsébet híd (Elizabeth Bridge) and Szabadság híd (Freedom Bridge) 🚍 7; tram 41, 47, 49 🍴 Panoráma, see page 479

The columned entrance to Magyar Nemzeti Múzeum

Halászbástya

Halászbástya (Fisherman's Bastion) is one of the city's greatest tourist draws: a fairy-tale, seven-towered rampart in pale stone wedged into Castle Hill and with great river views. The architect, Frigyes Schulek, designed the fortress as part of the city's millennial celebrations of Magyar nationhood in 1895.

✚ A3 ✉ Hess Andràs tér, Várhegy ☎ 1 458 3000; www.fishermansbastion.com 🕐 Upper towers: daily 9–7, mid-Mar. to Apr.; 9–8, May to mid-Oct. Terrace: daily, open access 🚌 Várbusz 16 from Szell Kálmán or Deák Ferenc tér 💲 $. Terrace free 🍴 Alabárdos, see page 479

Hősök tere

At the end of the grand Andrássy út and at the entrance to Városliget (City Park) is magnificent Hősök tere (Heroes' Square), which was designed to mark the city's 1896 millennial celebrations. On either side of the square are the Műcsarnok (Palace of Arts) and the newly renovated Szépművészeti Múzeum (Museum of Fine Arts); between these two buildings is a monument to Hungarian successes. Perched on a 118-foot-high column is the Archangel Gabriel; guarding the foot of the column are statues of the seven fierce and triumphant Magyar chiefs,

with Árpád, their leader, in the center. They are flanked by colonnades bearing the figures of Fame, Knowledge, Peace and War; between the columns there are more Hungarian icons, including King Stephen (who would later be sainted).

✚ D4 ✉ Andrássy útca 🚇 M1 Hősök tere

Kortárs Művészeti Múzeum – Ludwig Múzeum

The Ludwig Museum is dedicated to contemporary art and includes works by Andy Warhol, Roy Lichtenstein, Jasper Johns and Malcolm Morley as well as Eastern European works. The gallery is part of the dazzling modern MÚPA (Művészetek Palotája) complex.

✚ Off map at C1 ✉ Komor Marcel útca 1 ☎ 1 555 3444; www.ludwigmuseum.hu 🕐 Tue.–Sun. 10–8 🚋 Tram 2 to Millenniumi Kultrális Központ 🍴 Café and restaurant 💲 $$; temporary exhibitions $$$ ℹ Deposit coats and bags at the cloakroom

Magyar Állami Operaház

The Hungarian State Opera House building has beautiful marble-work, gold leaf and frescoes. Opened in 1884, it celebrates the musical world with statues of Beethoven, Mozart, Verdi and Wagner on the stone cornice of the front terrace. Pride of place goes to Hungarians Franz Liszt and opera composer Ferenc Erkel, whose statues flank the entrance. Inside the building an enormous bronze chandelier hangs over the auditorium, which is decorated with dazzling frescoes of the Greek gods by Károly Lotz. Tours may include a "mini-concert" of live singing.

✚ C3 ✉ Andrássy útca 22 ☎ 1 332 7914 (box office) or 1 332 8197 (tours); www.opera.hu 🕐 Tours daily from Hajós útca entrance at 2, 3 and 4 p.m. (duration 45 minutes) 🚇 Opera 🚋 4 🍴 Művész Kávéház, see page 479 💲 Tour $$$; mini-concert $$$

Magyar Nemzeti Múzeum

Five collections form this, the Hungarian National Museum and cover an area of 861,111 square feet. They include Roman artifacts, medieval and modern displays, a numismatic

Spires and turrets characterize the Országház, the parliament building

collection and historical portraits. The prize among the exhibits is the bejeweled and embroidered silk coronation mantle worn by King Stephen, dating to around AD 1030. Along with other items from the royal regalia now held in the parliament building (Országház, see below) it was recovered at the end of World War II and held for safekeeping in the U.S. until President Jimmy Carter ordered its return in 1978.

Other curiosities are the inscribed brick from a 13th-century monk's tomb, and the tent of a Turkish commander taken at the siege of Vienna in 1683. ✚ C2 ✉ Múzeum körút 14–16 ☎ 1 327 7773; www.mnm.hu 🕒 Tue.–Sun. 10–6 🚇 Astoria or Kálvin tér 🚌 9, 15, tram 47, 48, 49; trolleybus 83 🍴 Café ♿ $$ ℹ Audio guides $; tours (reserve in advance)

Mátyás-templom

Fifteenth-century King Matthias was married twice in the Roman Catholic Mátyás-templom (Matthias Church), which had already been in existence for two centuries. It later served the Turks as a mosque, and was remodeled in the 19th century in striking neo-Gothic style. Medieval touches have been reproduced in the interior, along with dramatic features such as the soaring bell tower (197 steps to climb!). The tombs of 12th-century monarch Béla III and his wife, Anne of Châtillon, are in the Trinity Chapel near the main door. ✚ A3 ✉ Szentháromság tér 2 ☎ 1 355 5657; www.matyas-templom.hu 🕒 Mon.–Fri. 9–5, Sat. 9–noon, Sun. 1–5 🚌 16, 16A ♿ Religious visits free; tourists $$; bell tower $$

Nagy Zsinagóga

Budapest's Great Synagogue marks the site of the former Jewish quarter and is one of the largest Jewish houses of worship in the world. It's home to the city's excellent Jewish Museum, as well as a Holocaust Memorial. ✚ C2 ✉ Dohány utca 2–8 ☎ 1 343-0420; www.greatsynagogue.hu/gallery_syn.html 🕒 Sun.–Thu. 10–8, Fri. 10–4, May–Sep.; early closing rest of year 🚇 M2 Astoria ♿ $$$ (combined entrance for synagogue, museum and memorial garden) ℹ Call ahead for guided tours

Országház

Bristling with neo-Gothic spires and turrets, the Országház (parliament building) sits on the eastern bank of the Danube, and covers 200,000 square feet. Its red dome is 315 feet high and rises above a 16-sided hall between the upper and lower houses of parliament. ✚ B3 ✉ Kossuth tér 1–3 ☎ 1 441 4415; www.parlament.hu 🕒 Daily 8–6, Apr.–Oct.; 8–4, rest of year. Guided tours in English daily at 10 a.m., noon, 1, 2, and 3 p.m. (subject to parliamentary sessions)

🚇 15; tram 2; trolley bus 70, 78 🍴 Café 🏛 $$$
(tickets available from the visitor center or in advance
online) 🔒 Strict security rules apply

Széchenyi Gyógyfürdő és Uszoda

Budapest's famous Széchenyi Baths
include 15 indoor and three outdoor
pools, plus thermal baths and steam
rooms. The bathing complex dates from
the early 20th century, but has been
thoroughly modernized and is clean and
safe. It is within Budapest's large City
Park (Városliget). For something
different, try the Thermal Beer Spa.
➕ E4 ✉ Állatkerti körút 9–11 ☎ 1 363 3210;
www.szechenyibath.com 🕐 Pools: daily 6 a.m.–10 p.m.
Thermal baths: daily 6 a.m.–7 p.m. 🚇 Széchenyi fürdő
🚌 Trolley bus 72 🍴 Café 🏛 $$$

Szent István Bazilika

Budapest's biggest church, Szent István
Bazilika (St. Stephen's Basilica), took 55
years to finish, and its dazzling interior
includes 90 pounds of 24-carat gold.
Transylvanian and Hungarian heroes are
represented by 88 statues, and the most
cherished item – the mummified right
hand of St. Stephen – is displayed in a
glass case. The 315-foot-high dome
(accessed by elevator) provides views
of the city.
➕ C3 ✉ Szent István tér 1 ☎ 1 338 2151 (tours);
www.bazilika.biz 🕐 Church: Mon.–Fri. 9–5, Sat. 9–1,
Sun. 1–5. Dome: daily 10–6:30, Jun.–Sep.; 10–5:30,
Apr.–May and Oct.; 10–4:30, rest of year. Tours in
English (Mon.–Fri. 10–3) 🚇 M3 to Arany János útca
🚌 15; trolley bus 70, 72, 78 🏛 Free (donations
welcome); dome $; tour $$ 🔒 Regular concerts and
organ recitals ($$$), see www.organconcert.hu

Szépművészeti Múzeum

Emerging in 2018 from a three-year
renovation, the Museum of Fine Arts is
one of Europe's top art museums. There
are works by Old Masters, including
Raphael, Titian, Tintoretto and
Caravaggio, and the Spanish painters
Velázquez and Goya. The post-1800
galleries include a good sprinkling of
works by the French Impressionists.
Many of the paintings were acquired by
the art-loving Esterházy family, whose
fortune was even greater than that of the
Habsburg emperors.
➕ D4 ✉ Andrassy útca ☎ 1 469 7100; www.
szepmuveszeti.hu 🕐 See website 🍴 Café and
restaurant 🚇 M1 Hősök tére 🚌 Tram 4, 6 🏛 $$$

Városliget

Beyond the boulevards of Pest is
Városliget (City Park). It was laid out
in the 18th century and has acquired
several "extras" over the years. The
oddest is Vajdahunyad vára
(Vajdahunyad Castle), built for the 1896
World Exhibition and based on a
Transylvanian fortress, with an artificial
moat that doubles as an ice-skating rink
in winter. Inside the walls is the Magyar
Mezőgazdasági Múzeum (Hungarian
Agricultural Museum). The Állatkert
(zoo) is another park favorite, as is the
Fővárosi Nagycirkusz (circus).

Magyar Mezőgazdasági Múzeum ➕ E4
✉ Vajdahunyad vára ☎ 1 422 0765; www.
mezogazdasagimuzeum.hu 🕐 Tue.–Fri. 10–4, Sat.–
Sun. 10–5 🚇 M1 to Széchenyi fürdő 🚌 Trolley bus
70, 72, 75, 79; tram 1 🍴 Café 🏛 $$
Állatkert ➕ D4 ✉ Állatkerti körút 6–12 ☎ 1 273
4900; www.zoobudapest.com 🕐 Mon.–Thu. 9–6, Fri.–
Sun. 9–7, May–Aug.; Mon.–Thu. 9–5:30, Fri.–Sun. 9–6,
Apr. and Sep.; Mon.–Thu. 9–5, Fri.–Sun. 9–5:30, Mar.
and Oct.; daily 9–4, Nov.–Feb. 🚇 M1 to Széchenyi fürdő
🚌 Trolley bus 72, 75, 79 🍴 Cafés 🏛 $$$
Fővárosi Nagycirkusz ➕ E4 ✉ Állatkerti körút 12
☎ 1 343 8300; www.fnc.hu 🕐 Shows Mon.–Fri. 3
p.m., Sat.–Sun. 11 a.m. and 3 p.m., Apr.–Aug.
🚇 Széchenyi fürdő 🚌 Trolley bus 72, 75, 79
🏛 $$–$$$ 🔒 Performances last around 2.5 hours

The Danube Esplanade

Running alongside the river on the Pest
bank, between Chain Bridge (Széchenyi
lánchíd) and Elizabeth Bridge (Erzsébet híd),
is the broad, tree-lined Danube Esplanade
(Duna-korzó). In the 19th century, this was
the place to be seen. The elaborate Pesti
Vigadó (Pest Concert Hall) is a legacy of that
era, and still a venue for exhibitions and
classical music concerts (www.vigado.hu).

Excursion to Esztergom

Hungary's largest cathedral towers over the stunning scenery of the Danube Bend at Esztergom, former royal city and the birthplace of King Stephen I (975–1038). There has been a settlement here, guarding the western approach to the gorge, since Roman times. Medieval Esztergom was destroyed by the Turks in 1543, but the city rose again, and it now boasts a center full of ornate baroque buildings.

The cathedral (*bazilika*) is the seat of the Catholic Church in Hungary and by far the most imposing structure: It is 328 feet from the floor to the top of its huge dome, which is visible for miles around. It includes one of the world's biggest paintings – an altarpiece based on the work of 16th-century Italian artist Titian. The white marble altar itself was designed in 1519 and made by expert craftsmen from Florence, Italy.

Among other treasures are the impressive Renaissance interior of the Bakócz Chapel, dedicated to Archbishop Tomás Bakócz, and a gold and enamel Gothic cross, studded with pearls and precious stones, known as the Calvary of Matthias Corvinus. The dome offers a spectacular view over Esztergom and its surroundings (20 268 1553; www.bazilika-esztergom.hu; free, dome $).

The present version of the cathedral was begun in the 1820s: Hungarian composer Franz Liszt celebrated its reconsecration in 1856 with a Mass. Long before this second lease of life, Esztergom was the seat of the Hungarian Primate and an important royal base. King Stephen was crowned in a church on the site in AD 1000, and the remains of a royal palace are housed in the Castle Museum (Vármúzeum) next door.

Two other museums are worth a visit. The Museum of Christian Art (Keresztény Múzeum; www.keresztenymuzeum.hu) has a superb collection of medieval religious paintings and works by Italian artists such as Duccio di Buoninsegna, Lorenzo di Credi and Giovanni di Paolo. The Danube Museum (Duna Múzeum; www.museum.hu) features displays that clearly illustrate (despite Hungarian-only captions) the role of the river and its effects on the life of the town.

Map page 255, C3 Esztergom is 41 miles north of Budapest. To travel by bus, take metro M3 to Árpád hid, then the Vólanbusz intercity bus (line 800) direct to Esztergom (www.volanbusz.hu). There also is a regular service from Nyugati (Western) railroad station. In summer, boats leave from Vigadó tér landing stage (journey time 70 minutes). Call Mahart 1 484 4013; www.mahartpassnave.hu.

Hungary's largest cathedral, begun in the 1820s, dominates Esztergom

Ireland

Introduction and Map 268

Timeline 272

Survival Guide 273

Dublin 274

Feature: James Joyce 278

Feature: Dublin's Pubs 281

Hotels and Restaurants 479

Essential Information 534

Opposite: Giant's Head in County Antrim, with Dunluce Castle on the clifftop

Ireland

People long for Ireland in a way that they pine for few other countries. Call it romantic, call it sentimental, but there is something about this remarkable country that tugs at the heartstrings of even those who have no Irish blood.

The beauty of the country, its powerful Gaelic traditions and the irrepressibly romantic and creative nature of the Irish people underscore this potent appeal.

Ireland is a country that is not without problems, however, and its political and religious divide has had far-reaching, universal impact.

Mists of Time

Ireland claims with pride that it was a "land of saints and scholars" when the rest of Europe was deep in the Dark Ages. It is often described as a Celtic country, with all the myth-making that goes along with that term.

The Celts are seen as being a distinctive lost race of Iron Age people who, in the face of first Roman and then Anglo-Saxon aggression, retreated into Scotland, Ireland, Wales and Cornwall in England, from which they passed down the cultural values of their time. They did not call themselves Celts, and the term may be only a convenient label, but what is certain is that the influence

of the earliest Bronze Age and Iron Age cultures survives on the peripheries of the British Isles. This is especially true in Ireland, where the Gaelic language, still heard today and experiencing a revival, is its greatest expression.

There are thousands of prehistoric sites in Ireland, including megalithic tombs, stone circles and cairns littering the countryside: on the remote western seaboard, on the Beara Peninsula, in County Kerry, and at exceptional places such as the Brù na Bòinne burial complex, in County Meath, north of Dublin. Together with evidence of primitive dwellings such as *crannógs* (island settlements) and ring forts, Ireland's heritage is everywhere to be seen. Even where they are ruinous and vestigial, these ancient sites are hauntingly evocative.

You will find within the same landscape the music, poetry, wit and drama of Ireland that have been enshrined in hundreds of films, songs, dances and stories. A sense of the past is intense here; it has shaped Ireland in a seminal way, for better or for worse.

From Dublin to Kerry

Dublin is the boisterous heart of Ireland, the "family home." It should not be missed, of course, but Dublin will only whet your appetite for the rest of the country. Save time to explore other areas for the essential Irish experience. South of the capital lie the Wicklow Mountains, with the popular Glendalough at their heart – half religious site, and wholly spectacular from a scenic point of view.

Farther south lies the fascinating Viking town of Wexford, from where the long, rambling southern coast of Ireland runs through endless great bays toward the distant west (and the most spectacular scenery).

The western coast stretches for nearly 180 miles from north to south, but measures much more if all the many sinuous indentations, bays, river

More Top Destinations in Ireland (see map page 269)

- An Daingean (Dingle) A1
- Beara Peninsula A1
- Blarney Castle B1
- Brú na Bóinne (Newgrange) C3
- The Burren A2
- Clifden A3
- Galway B2
- Giant's Causeway C4
- Glendalough C2
- Kilkenny B2
- Killarney A1
- Oileáin Árann (Aran Islands) A2
- Rock of Cashel B2
- Titanic Belfast (Belfast) C4

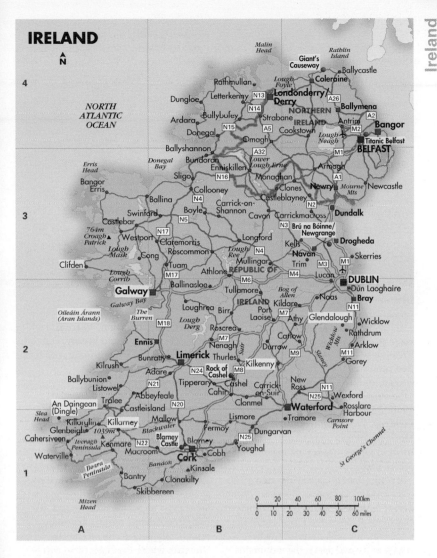

mouths, peninsulas and islands are taken into account.

Try to visit the far southwest. Take in the charming historic city of Kilkenny on the way; and visit Cork, the Irish Republic's second largest city, where you can kiss the nearby Blarney Stone.

Heading to the West

Beyond Cork lies the Beara Peninsula. The bigger Iveragh Peninsula is part of County Kerry to the north, land of the mountains of Macgillycuddy's Reeks. The town of Killarney, with its scenic lakes, is the gateway to the romantic Dingle Peninsula (Corca Dhuibhne) and County Clare. County Clare's southern half is mundane, but becomes spectacular the farther north you go, past the huge, echoing Cliffs of Moher and into the limestone country of the Burren, with its karst landscape (natural limestone pavement), dramatic stone burial chambers and hill forts.

Clifden, Connemara, on Ireland's west coast, enjoys a reputation for good food

In the pubs of Clare you are likely to encounter the foot-tapping essence of Irish music and song, in an environment that preserves the best of the past with energy, vitality and lyricism.

Off Clare's northwestern coast are the stunning Aran Islands (Oileáin Árann), the magic names of Inishmore (Inis Mór), Inishmaan (Inis Meáin) and Inisheer (Inis Oírr) resonating with all things Irish.

Beyond Clare is Galway Bay and Galway City (known as "The City of the Tribes"), the latter a lively, unfailingly charming place on the threshold of the Gaeltacht, the major area of Gaelic-speaking Ireland. Here, the mountains of Connemara and the broad waters of Lough Corrib and Lough Mask match an astonishing coastline of raw, rocky wilderness that lies to either side of the romantic town of Clifden.

Inland, Ireland also has much to offer. The heart of the country is a green bowl of rich farmland, of lakes, rivers and isolated ranges of rounded hills. These regions of Ireland may be outshone by the stupendous coastline of the far west, but it is a charming country full of character and tradition, where you will hear talk of horses and history, and where lakes and rivers throng with fish.

Traveling North

Farther north is the remote county of Mayo, where you can follow the pilgrims' route up the Holy Mountain of Croagh Patrick, if you feel fit enough for the grueling four-hour clamber over rough rocks to the place where St. Patrick is said to have banished the snakes. Beyond Mayo are Sligo and Donegal, and golden beaches and tumbling Atlantic surf. Lakes and remote peninsulas enhance north Donegal, where the coast turns east toward the beautiful City of Derry (Londonderry), gateway to Northern Ireland, and Antrim, Armagh, Down, Londonderry, Fermanagh and Tyrone – the six (of a total of nine) counties of Ulster known as Northern Ireland.

This British-ruled area was riven for decades by sectarian violence, but the Good Friday Agreement of 1998 began the slow process of peace. Ulster's image has suffered from "the Troubles" (the resumption of political violence since

The unusual "organ-pipe" cliffs of the Giant's Causeway, County Antrim

1969), yet the beauty of its coast and countryside is of classic Irish quality.

The Giant's Causeway, on County Antrim's north coast, is Northern Ireland's most famous landmark, an astonishing landscape of perfectly formed hexagonal rock sections. Farther east lies the seaside town of Ballycastle, beyond which are the towering cliffs of Fair Head and then the green and peaceful Glens of Antrim.

South of Antrim lies Belfast, Northern Ireland's capital, a city that in the past has shown a grim face but is now welcoming a new generation of tourists. Belfast has rediscovered its waterfront and invested in redevelopment. Victoria Square is now a contemporary shopping center, the old Gasworks site has been replaced with hotels and offices, and redevelopment of the Titanic Quarter on Belfast Harbour has quickened its pace. All this new building has brought an exciting dynamic to the city.

The Gaelic Lifestyle

In Dublin you will find museums, stores, theaters and restaurants to match those anywhere else in Europe, all suffused by the richness of Irish culture and by a modern sophistication.

In parts of rural Ireland things are different. You may come across an easygoing attitude, a relaxed approach reflecting the fact that the Irish have been around for a long time and often see no reason to rush things. At the same time, you may find yourself swept off your feet in places like beautiful Galway City, where a vigorous student population adds a contemporary note to the Gaelic culture that most young people continue to embrace.

If you travel through Ireland, you will find the Irish a particularly hospitable and friendly people. Often, if you ask a local for the way to a nearby site or place in town, you will be taken there rather than given directions.

The Irish are fired by an all-consuming curiosity and have an almost total lack of pretension. They are a people whose history has often been terrible, bleak and unforgiving. Yet they have survived as the inheritors of a bewitching country that lies off the western edge of Continental Europe but is also an integral part of it.

Timeline

circa 3000 BC	Neolithic burial chambers constructed at Brú na Bóinne.
circa 500 BC	Celtic tribes arrive from Europe.
AD 432	St. Patrick brings Christianity to Ireland.
circa 840	Vikings found Dublin, Waterford, Wexford and Limerick.
1170	Powerful Anglo-Irish hegemony established in Ireland.
circa 1610	Large areas of Ulster are confiscated by the English Crown.
1845–51	The Great Famine; a million Irish people die and a million emigrate, chiefly to America.
1916	Easter Rising.
1921	Anglo-Irish Treaty partitions Ireland into the Irish Free State and Northern Ireland, which remains under British rule.
1948	Irish Free State is declared a republic.
1969	Beginning of "the Troubles" in Northern Ireland.
1972	Republic of Ireland joins the European Economic Community.
1985	The Anglo-Irish Agreement promises cooperation on Northern Ireland's future.
1994	Main paramilitary groups in Northern Ireland call a ceasefire.
1997–2007	Ireland enjoys rapid economic growth, known as the "Celtic Tiger."
1998	Good Friday Agreement paves the way for a Northern Ireland Assembly.
2007	Devolved government returns to Northern Ireland with an historic power-sharing agreement.
2008–10	The global financial crisis causes Ireland's booming property bubble to burst, resulting in a bailout by the EU/IMF in 2010.
2011	Queen Elizabeth II and the Duke of Edinburgh visit the Republic of Ireland. This is the first such visit by a British monarch since 1911.
2015	Ireland becomes the first country to approve same-sex marriage.
2018	A referendum in the Republic of Ireland results in a repeal of the country's eighth amendment which will liberalize Ireland's strict abortion laws.

Divided Ireland

Ireland has been a divided country for centuries. The reasons are complex and lie in historical developments over hundreds of years. The largest part of modern Ireland is the Republic of Ireland, Poblacht na hÉireann – mainly Roman Catholic, with a small minority of Protestants and a strong Irish Gaelic culture and identity. After years of economic stagnation the nation enjoyed a period of great success and modernization until 2008 when the global economic crisis took effect. There are signs now that the "Celtic Tiger" may well roar again. Six counties in the province of Ulster in the northern part of Ireland are called Northern Ireland, and remain part of the United Kingdom. Its majority Protestant community is traditionally Unionist and wishes to maintain the union between Great Britain and Northern Ireland. The smaller, but substantial, Catholic community is traditionally Republican and wishes to break the union with Great Britain and establish an all-Ireland republic. The political differences and the lack of civil rights for Northern Ireland Catholics gave rise to some 30 years of violent conflict. Through the peace process, the 1998 Good Friday Agreement created a devolved legislative Assembly for Northern Ireland and a framework for multiparty power-sharing. Violence was largely eliminated, and following a temporary reversion to direct British rule, the Northern Ireland Assembly reconvened in 2007 and continues to strive for peace.

Survival Guide

- If you visit the city of Dublin in the early spring, try to be there on March 17, St. Patrick's Day, when the city celebrates with song and dance, culminating in a parade, all-night parties and fireworks displays.
- If you're interested in shopping for Celtic crafts, don't miss the Kilkenny Design Centre in Kilkenny. This is the city's finest showcase for stylish Irish housewares, glass, books, fashion and jewelry. The upstairs restaurant serves delicious homestyle food.
- Ireland is rapidly modernizing its road system, but there are still some poor public roads, especially in rural parts of the country and the farther west you travel. Here, roads are narrower, so passing oncoming traffic (vehicles and animals) requires patience.
- One of the best ways to learn a little about the complexities of Irish politics is to take a tour. Coiste Political Tours provides walking tours of Belfast's historical and political sites, led by ex-prisoners, and Blue Badge Guides take visitors on tours of Derry City and the Bogside. In Dublin, there are tours covering the Great Famine, the 1916 Easter Rising, the War of Independence and Partition.
- Be aware that there is a no-smoking policy throughout the Republic of Ireland in all public places.
- Visit the local pubs in rural Ireland, especially in County Clare, where in towns like Ennis you will find some of the greatest Irish music of all and the wholehearted Irish *craic* (good times, enjoyment and fun).
- Visit popular places such as Glendalough in County Wicklow, Killarney in County Kerry and the Cliffs of Moher in County Clare outside of peak season (July and August). Glendalough, especially, can become jammed with traffic.
- Enjoy the beautiful and often remote beaches of Ireland's west coast, but

A statue of James Joyce at Dublin's Merrion Hotel

take great care if you go swimming. The tides are very strong here and there can be unexpected sea currents.
- Irish road signs began to appear in both Gaelic and English in the Republic of Ireland shortly after partition and today they must appear in both languages by law, the Irish first in italics with the English underneath. In the Gaeltacht (Irish-speaking) areas only the Irish name is written.
- Ireland's Roman Catholic churches are extremely important places to the communities they serve, and you'll usually find someone praying if you visit. Be as discreet as possible when walking around church interiors, especially in front of the altar. Please refrain from taking photographs during Mass and other services.

Dublin

All roads seem to lead to Dublin; it is a homecoming city where the visitor will feel as welcome as the Irish do. Dublin is celebrated today as one of Europe's most vibrant, colorful cities. It is a rich distillation of all things Irish – music, conversation and laughter amid the city's lively streets, buzzing pubs and magnificent Georgian buildings.

Finding Your Way

The main Dublin tourist office can be found in a new building close to the handsome old church of St. Andrew's,

at 25 Suffolk Street, just west of Trinity College in the city center. Here you can obtain information about guided walking tours.

Central Dublin is a reasonably easy place to explore on foot. The main museums and notable buildings are concentrated in south Dublin, but there are must-see attractions across the River Liffey in north Dublin.

A good starting point is the famous O'Connell Bridge. Take time to adjust to the breezy pace of it all. To the north is O'Connell Street, one of the broadest streets in Europe. Lively shopping streets such as Abbey Street Lower and

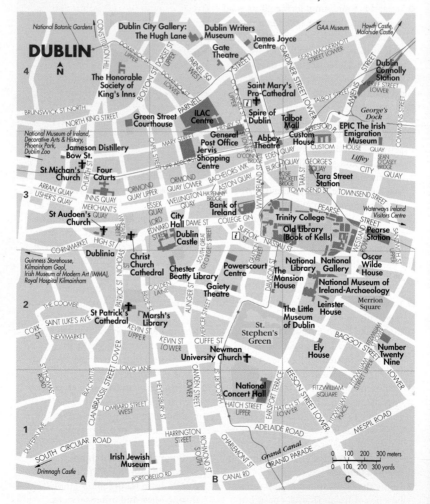

Earl Street North lead off to either side. On Earl Street you will find a statue of James Joyce, Ireland's most famous writer and chronicler of Dublin life. Go down Earl Street and then turn left onto Marlborough Street to visit St. Mary's Pro-Cathedral, a magnificent neoclassical building.

Opposite Earl Street is busy Henry Street, with the huge Ilac and Jervis shopping centers and the adjoining fruit and vegetable market on Moore Street. This whole area leading down to Smithfield Village has been the subject of much renovation work. Here you'll find Jameson Distillery Bow Street, which offers tours and tastings at the 200-year-old whiskey distillery (open Mon.–Thu. 9:30–5:30, Fri.–Sat. 9:30–7, Sun. 10–5:30; www.jamesonwhiskey.com).

On O'Connell Street is the General Post Office. This is a landmark site of the 1916 Easter Rising, when Irish nationalists mounted an uprising against British rule and occupied the building. Still a working post office, it is home also to the GPO Witness History permanent exhibition (open Mon.–Sat. 10–5:30, Sun. 12–5:30; www.gpowitnesshistory.ie). Opposite is the dramatic Monument of Light, a stainless-steel needle unveiled in 2002. At the north end of O'Connell Street, Parnell Square is home to Dublin City Gallery: The Hugh Lane (see pages 277 and 279) and the Dublin Writers Museum (see page 279).

The Heart of Dublin

South of O'Connell Bridge is the buzzing heart of Dublin. From the south side of the bridge, walk down Westmoreland Street to College Green to admire the neoclassical splendor of the Bank of Ireland and the elegant entrance to Trinity College (see page 280).

Otherwise, cross College Green to the south and then continue past the works for the Cross City Luas. This is the original spot for the statue of Molly Malone, heroine of the famous "Cockles and Mussels" refrain. The statue can now be found on Suffolk Street.

Ahead lies pedestrian-only Grafton Street, with interesting stores and delightful side streets, plus a variety of street performers. Stop at Bewley's Oriental Café, a Dublin institution (renovated in 2017). Head east and make for Leinster House, seat of Irish government, and to the National Museum of Ireland – Archaeology (see page 280) and the National Gallery (see page 280). Beyond these lie the 18th-century Georgian splendors of Merrion Square and Fitzwilliam Street.

Alternatively, go west from Grafton Street along store-lined Wicklow Street, then on to Dublin Castle (see page 277) and Christ Church Cathedral (see page 277); or head back north across Dame Street and into lively Temple Bar, the rejuvenated old riverside district that is the exciting focus of Dublin by night.

A view along the sun-drenched River Liffey toward the Ha'penny Bridge and Bachelors Walk area of Dublin

Vary your Dublin experiences. Enjoy Temple Bar's restaurants and lively lanes, visit St. Patrick's Cathedral on Patrick Street or the rejuvenated Docklands district. Cross the Liffey via the modern Samuel Beckett and Sean O'Casey bridges and book theater tickets for the Bord Gáis Energy Theatre on the south side. Enjoy outstanding drama at Dublin's Abbey Theatre on Lower Abbey Street, or classic Irish entertainment at the Olympia on Dame Street. Above all, visit Dublin's famous pubs (see page 281) for great music and the "craic."

The Ha'penny Bridge

Dublin's famous Ha'penny Bridge, over the River Liffey, is best reached from Temple Bar by going down the narrow Merchant's Arch – look closely for the symbols of nearby stores carved into the street.

The bridge dates from 1816 and is made of cast iron; its elegant arches are lit up at night. It was officially named the Wellington Bridge after the British Duke of Wellington, but gained its popular name from the halfpenny toll once charged for crossing it.

Essential Information

Tourist Information

Discover Ireland Information Office
14 Upper O'Connell Street ☎ 01 850 230 330; www.visitdublin.com. Also at Terminal 1 and Terminal 2, Dublin Airport
Visit Dublin
25 Suffolk Street ☎ 01 850 230 330; www.visitdublin.com

Urban Transportation

Dublin has two main railroad stations: Heuston Station, St. John's Road West, and Connolly Station, Amiens Street. The Dublin Area Rapid Transit (DART) railroad line runs north to Malahide and Howth, and south to Greystones. Connolly Station, Pearse Station and Tara Street Station are city-center stops. For intercity train and DART information ☎ 01 836 6222; www.irishrail.ie. The LUAS tram system has two lines. The Red Line runs from Connolly and The Point to Tallaght and Saggart; the Green Line, connecting the suburbs to the city center, runs from Broombridge to Bride's Glen, via St. Stephen's Green. For LUAS ☎ 01 850 300604; www.luas.ie. The citywide bus service

is run by Dublin Bus (Bus Átha Cliath), 59 Upper O'Connell Street (☎ 01 873 4222; www.dublinbus.ie); buses daily 7 a.m.–11:30 p.m. Nitelink service Fri.–Sat. midnight–4 a.m. The Leap card is a prepaid smartcard for use on public transportation in Dublin, Cork, Limerick, Waterford and Galway, and is available to buy at places displaying the Payzone logo or online at www.leapcard.ie. Countrywide services leave from the main bus station, Busáras, on Amiens Street (www.buseireann.ie). Dublin taxis are on stands at O'Connell Street, St. Stephen's Green, Dawson Street and Westmoreland Street, or phone National Radio Cabs (NRC ☎ 01 677 2222).

Airport Information

Dublin Airport (www.dublinairport.com) is 7 miles north of the city. Aircoach runs a bus service (No. 700) to the city center every 15–30 minutes, 24 hours a day; the trip takes 30 minutes (☎ 01 844 7118; www.aircoach.ie). The Dublin Bus Airlink Express services 747 and 757 run to/from Busáras and the railroad stations/Harcourt Street.

Climate – average highs and lows for the month

Jan.	Feb.	Mar.	Apr.	May	Jun.	Jul.	Aug.	Sep.	Oct.	Nov.	Dec.
8°C	8°C	9°C	11°C	14°C	17°C	19°C	18°C	16°C	13°C	10°C	8°C
46°F	46°F	48°F	52°F	57°F	63°F	66°F	64°F	61°F	55°F	50°F	46°F
3°C	3°C	4°C	5°C	7°C	10°C	12°C	12°C	10°C	8°C	5°C	4°C
37°F	37°F	39°F	41°F	45°F	50°F	54°F	54°F	50°F	46°F	41°F	39°F

Dublin Sights

Key to symbols

➕ map coordinates refer to the Dublin map on page 274 🏛 admission charge:
$$$ more than €10, $$ €5–€10, $ less than €5
See page 5 for complete key to symbols

The State Drawing Room in Dublin Castle

Christ Church Cathedral

Dublin's great cathedral was originally founded around 1030 under Dunan, its first bishop. The building dates from the 12th century, but much of it is now a 19th-century Gothic Revival renovation.

The oldest remaining parts of the cathedral include the late 13th-century transepts and crypt, one of the largest medieval crypts in Europe. Rare church silver, manuscripts and artifacts feature in the fine Treasures of Christ Church exhibition alongside audiovisuals of the cathedral's history.

Linked to the cathedral by a stone bridge is Synod Hall, where the interactive Dublinia heritage center explores Dublin's Viking and the city's medieval history.

Christ Church Cathedral ➕ A3 ✉ Christchurch Place
☎ 01 677 8099; www.christchurchcathedral.ie
🕐 Mon.–Sat. 9:30–7, Sun. 12:30–2:30 and 4:30–7, Apr.–Sep.; Mon.–Sat. 9:30–6, Sun. 12:30–2:30 and 4:30–6, Mar. and Oct.; Mon.–Sat. 9:30–5, Sun. 12:30–2:30, rest of year 🚌 13, 27, 40, 49, 77A, 123
🏛 $$ ℹ Guided tours Mon.–Fri. at 12:10, 2 and 4 p.m., Sat. 2, 3 and 4 p.m. ($); specialist belfry tours Sat. 11:30 a.m., 1:15 p.m., Sun. 1:15 p.m. ($)
Dublinia ➕ A3 ✉ St. Michael's Hill ☎ 01 679 4611; www.dublinia.ie 🕐 Daily 10–6:30, Mar.–Sep.; 10–5:30, rest of year. Last admission 1 hour before closing
🚌 49, 49A, 54A, 123 🍴 Café 🏛 $$

Dublin Castle

Dublin Castle was built by King John in 1204 on the site of a former Gaelic ring fort and Viking fortress. Today only one of the medieval towers remains, the rest destroyed by fire in the 17th century. Most of what can be seen today dates from the 18th century, including the opulent state apartment rooms.

However, restoration work in the 1980s uncovered 10th-century Viking defences alongside medieval castle walls.

The state apartments open to the public include St. Patrick's Hall, the Throne Room, the State Drawing Room and the Portrait Gallery, all of which have sumptuous decorations and furnishings. The castle's Chapel Royal is a glorious neo-Gothic indulgence dating from 1814.

Within the castle grounds is the Chester Beatty Library (free) which holds a superb collection of books from around the world.

➕ B3 ✉ Dame Street ☎ 01 645 8813;
www.dublincastle.ie 🕐 Daily 9:45–5:45.
Last admission at 5:15 p.m. 🚌 27, 49, 56A, 77A, 123
🍴 Café 🏛 $$ ℹ Guided tours. State apartments may be closed for official functions

Dublin City Gallery: The Hugh Lane

The gallery is located in Charlemont House, an elegant Georgian mansion. The collection, bequeathed by Hugh Lane in 1908, features 19th- and 20th-century Irish and international painters, including Claude Monet, Edouard Manet and Edgar Degas. Notable Irish artists include Jack B. Yeats, and there are contemporary Irish works and exhibitions. The gallery also

James Joyce

Ireland's most controversial novelist, James Joyce, was one of world literature's most important figures. Joyce was an innovator of the highest order, a writer of dazzling intellect.

He was born in 1882 into a Dublin Catholic family of some gentility, although poverty overtook the family while Joyce was in his teens. He was educated at Ireland's leading Jesuit schools and then at University College Dublin (UCD).

Joyce rebelled early against the tenets of his class and religion and against Ireland's prevailing politics and culture, both of which he felt were too "nationalistic." He left Ireland in 1904 with Nora Barnacle, who became his lifelong partner. After a visit in 1912, Joyce never returned to Ireland and remained in Europe until his death in Zurich in 1941.

Joyce wrote several books of poetry and novels; his most famous novels were *Ulysses* and *Finnegans Wake*. *Ulysses* was a monumental work, an allegorical saga describing the daylong wandering of its central character, Leopold Bloom, through the streets of Dublin. The novel developed new literary forms in its exploration and use of language and in its epic structure. It was published in Paris in 1922 but was banned for obscenity in Britain and in the United States until 1936. *Finnegans Wake* was published in 1939 and carried the "stream of consciousness" style of writing to revolutionary limits.

Joyce is a national hero in Ireland, something that would have amused this complex and essentially solitary man. The James Joyce Centre is at No. 35 North Great George's Street in north Dublin (www.jamesjoyce.ie, open Mon.–Sat. 10–5, Sun. noon–5; closed Mon., Oct.–Mar; $$). Each year on June 16, Dublin celebrates Bloomsday, a week-long festival with guided walks, readings and numerous events based on Leopold Bloom's progress through the Dublin of *Ulysses*. Visits to famous Dublin pubs play a lively part in the festivities; participants dress in Edwardian clothes from the period featured in the novel, and readings of *Ulysses* are staged.

The Bloomsday festival captures the imagination of many James Joyce fans

displays examples of stained glass by Dublin illustrator Harry Clarke. The new wing houses a collection of Sean Scully paintings. Francis Bacon's studio was gifted to the gallery in 1998, painstakingly removed from its London home and reconstructed here.

B4 ⊠ Charlemont House, Parnell Square North ☎ 01 222 5550; www.hughlane.ie Ⓒ Tue.–Thu. 9:45–6, Fri. 9:45–5, Sat. 10–5, Sun. 11–5 🚌 7, 11, 13, 16, 38, 40, 46A, 123; LUAS Abbey Street 🍽 Gallery café Free

Dublin Writers Museum

Literary Dublin in all its glory is represented by this museum's large collection of documents, portraits and memorabilia of famous Irish writers, including Oscar Wilde, James Joyce and Samuel Beckett. The museum is housed in an 18th-century Georgian property – look for well-preserved period detail such as the stuccowork downstairs. The colonnaded main salon has busts, paintings, a decorative ceiling and various boisterous friezes. Next door is The Irish Writers' Centre, while Chapter One restaurant (see page 480), is located below the museum.

B4 ⊠ 18 Parnell Square North ☎ 01 872 2077; www.writersmuseum.com Ⓒ Mon.–Sat. 9:45–4:45, Sun. 11–4:30 🚌 7, 11, 13, 16, 46A, 123 🍽 Café; Chapter One restaurant (see page 480) in basement (separate entrance) $$ Self-guiding audio tour lasts about 40 minutes

EPIC The Irish Emigration Museum

This digital museum, housed in the vaults of the former Customs House, tells the story of centuries of emigration from Ireland. Interactive screens recount 1,500 years of the country's history.

C3 ⊠ The CHQ Building, Customs House Quay ☎ 01 906 0861; www.epicchq.com Ⓒ Daily 10–6:45. Last admission at 5 p.m. 🚌 14, 15, 27; LUAS Georges Dock 🍽 Café $$$

Guinness Storehouse

Dublin without Guinness is like the earth without air. You can sample the

EPIC Ireland can be found on the banks of the Liffey

brew in its creamy, lip-smacking originality in the city's multitude of pubs (see page 281), but to reach the heart of things visit the enlightening and entertaining Guinness Storehouse, located in a huge original hop store at the brewery. The admission charge includes a pint of the famous stout in the upstairs Gravity Bar.

Off map at A2 ⊠ St. James's Gate ☎ 01 408 4800; www.guinness-storehouse.com Ⓒ Daily 9–8, Jul.–Aug.; 9:30–7, rest of year. Last admission 2 hours before closing 🚌 123; LUAS St. James's Hospital 🍽 Bars and restaurant $$$

Kilmainham Gaol

This notorious gaol (prison) has been the scene of great misery. Kilmainham opened in 1796 and until 1924, when it closed, just about every famous name in the struggle for Irish independence was incarcerated here, including Robert Emmet, Charles Stewart Parnell and Eamon DeValera. Fourteen leaders of the bloody 1916 Easter Rising, pivotal in Ireland's history, were executed in the prison yard. A major exhibition set out a graphic picture of Irish history.

Off map at A2 ⊠ Inchicore Road ☎ 01 453 5984; www.kilmainhamgaolmuseum.ie Ⓒ Tours daily 9–4:45; 9–5:15, May; 9:30–4:45, Oct.–Mar. 🚌 13, 40, 69; LUAS Suir Road 🍽 Café $$ (includes guided tour; booking essential)

National Gallery

Ireland's national art collection contains works that represent all major schools of European art. The historic wings of the gallery have reopened after major renovation, revealing architectural features including a new light-filled courtyard. Highlights include the European Masterpieces collection in the Millennium Wing, and a rotating exhibition of highlights plucked from the European collection. Painters represented include Francisco de Goya and Caravaggio, Thomas Gainsborough and J. M. W. Turner, and Irish artists Jack B. Yeats and Sir John Lavery.

➕ C2 ✉ Merrion Square; entrances via Millennium Wing on Clare Street and Merrion Square West ☎ 01 661 5133; www.nationalgallery.ie 🕐 Mon.–Sat. 9:15–5:30 (also Thu. 5:30–8:30 p.m.), Sun. 11–5:30. Closure of the galleries begins 15 minutes before final closing time 🚌 4, 7, 8, 39A, 46A; LUAS Dawson Street 🍽 Café 💷 Free; charge for some exhibitions ℹ Self-guiding audio tours, free

National Museum of Ireland – Archaeology

This museum occupies buildings that date from the 1890s. Together with the National Library opposite, the complex forms the approach to Leinster House, the seat of the Irish Government. Exhibits dating from 7000 BC onward feature examples of Celtic and medieval art and the finest collection of prehistoric gold artifacts in Europe. Highlights of the collection include the Tara Brooch, the Cross of Cong, the Ardagh Chalice and Viking discoveries from Dublin itself.

➕ C2 ✉ Kildare Street ☎ 01 677 7444; www.museum.ie/Archaeology 🕐 Tue.–Sat. 10–5, Sun. 2–5 🚌 25, 33, 41, 51, 66, 67, 84; LUAS St. Stephen's Green 🍽 Café 💷 Free; guided tours $

St. Stephen's Green

Delightful St. Stephen's Green has been a public park since 1664, when Dublin Corporation set aside 27 acres of open ground for the gentry. Access was by payment only until 1880, when the park was made free to all. There are statues and busts of famous Irish men and women, including James Joyce, Robert Emmet, Constance Markiewicz and Sir Arthur Guinness.

The park is surrounded by some fine buildings including the Shelbourne Hotel and the Royal College of Surgeons. Here also the Little Museum of Dublin contains a fascinating collection donated by the city's people.

➕ B2 ✉ St. Stephen's Green ☎ 01 475 7816; www.ststephensgreenpark.ie 🕐 Mon.–Sat. 7:30 a.m.–dusk, Sun. 9:30 a.m.–dusk 🚌 All city center buses; LUAS St. Stephen's Green
The Little Museum of Dublin ☎ 01 661 1000; www.littlemuseum.ie 🕐 Tours daily 9:30–5 (till 7 p.m. Thu.) 💷 $$ (includes guided tour)

Trinity College

Dublin's Trinity College is an outstanding architectural and cultural oasis at the heart of the city. It was founded in 1592 on the site of an Augustinian monastery, but all of the present buildings date from after 1700. Enter from College Green, between statues of poet Oliver Goldsmith and orator Edmund Burke, and then go through the Corinthian facade of the Palladian Regent House. This leads into cobbled Parliament Square, which is dominated by a tall campanile.

Trinity's Old Library and its Long Room contain some outstanding artifacts, including the ninth-century *Book of Kells*, an illuminated manuscript of the four gospels of the New Testament. The "Turning Darkness into Light" exhibition in the Old Library leads you up to the beautiful *Book of Kells* and offers a historical perspective on the manuscript.

Campus ➕ B3–C3 ✉ College Green ☎ 01 896 1000; www.tcd.ie 🕐 Daily 🚌 All cross-city buses 💷 Free ℹ Student-led guided walking tours (last 35 minutes, $$$) depart from inside the Front Gate. Check the schedules posted there for times and availability
Old Library ✉ College Green 🕐 Mon.–Sat. 8:30–5, Sun. 9:30–5, May–Sep.; Mon.–Sat. 9:30–5, Sun. noon–4:30, rest of year 💷 $$$

Dublin's Pubs

Irish pubs are fueled by good drink, but they are rooted in the gregarious nature of the Irish. Many pubs also are outstanding folk music venues, inevitable in a country so well suited to such spontaneous music.

A local favorite is the Brazen Head, at 20 Bridge Street Lower, hailed as the oldest pub in Ireland. Davy Byrnes, on Duke Street, just off busy Grafton Street, is associated with James Joyces' *Ulysses*, as it was here that the book's main protaganist, Leopold Bloom, stopped for refreshment. For Victorian authenticity try the Stag's Head, on Dame Court, with its stained-glass windows and wood paneling. Very popular with Dubliners in the 1890s, the pub was another favorite of author James Joyce.

You can hear great Irish music with your Guinness in some of the busy Temple Bar pubs like Oliver St. John Gogarty's, on the corner of Fleet and Anglesea streets.

One of the best Dublin music pubs is O'Donoghue's, on Merrion Row, down from St. Stephen's Green. This was the favored haunt of the Dubliners folk group in its 1960s heyday, and the city's best folk musicians regularly raise the roof here.

Other good traditional pubs are Doheny & Nesbitt on Baggott Street Lower; O'Neill's, on Suffolk Street, opposite the tourist information office; and old-fashioned Mulligan's on Poolbeg Street, a last outpost of Joycean Dublin amid the modern office blocks. South of St. Stephen's Green at the corner of Camden Street Upper and Harcourt Road is The Bleeding Horse, formerly a blacksmith's shop and a church; it is a warren of little rooms called "snugs." North of the Liffey, The Cobblestone is a traditional, down-to-earth bar that has regular traditional music sessions.

If you want a more modern vibe, try Café en Seine on Dawson Street, where a trendy crowd drinks in extravagant surroundings. For a fusion of old and new, go to the Chophouse gastro pub at 2 Shelbourne Road. For a down-to-earth atmosphere, visit the Foggy Dew on Fownes Street in Temple Bar, with music memorabilia behind the bar, a laid-back crowd and regular live music. The George, on South Great George's Street, is one of Dublin's best-known gay pubs and has regular club nights.

At the heart of Dublin's lively nightlife scene is the Temple Bar area

Italy

Introduction and Map 284

Timeline 290

Survival Guide 291

Rome 292

Feature: The Vatican 299

Feature: Excursion to Tivoli 300

Florence 302

Feature: A Day in Florence 307

Naples 308

Feature: Excursion to Capri 313

Venice 314

Feature: The Lagoon Islands 321

Hotels and Restaurants 480

Essential Information 538

Opposite: Santa Maria della Salute, Venice, illuminated at night

Italy

Few countries have as much to offer as Italy, with its warm and passionate people, varied and beautiful landscape, a rich artistic, historic and cultural heritage, some of the world's best food and wine, and a stylish and relaxed philosophy on life.

Italy has something for everyone, whether the visitor is seeking great cities, tiny villages, idyllic countryside or beautiful beaches.

Bell' Italia

Of all European countries, Italy is the one to which many travelers return time and again, their love affair blossoming with each trip. Whether your visit is a chance opportunity or the dream of a lifetime, Italy will fulfill and exceed your expectations, capture your heart and senses, and leave you longing to return.

From the Alps in the north, through the prosperous and fertile heartland to the stark beauty of the deep south, Italy is blessed with some of the world's most beguiling landscapes. The northern half features Tuscany's classic olive, vine and cypress-studded rolling countryside; the dramatic peaks of the Dolomites (Dolomiti); pine-clad white cliffs and turquoise seas; and the eerie loveliness of mist-laden mornings in the great river valleys. The south is equally lovely, with an arid and fierce beauty during the

More Top Destinations in Italy

- Agrigento C1
- Amalfi Coast D2
- Assisi C4
- Cinque Terre B4
- Dolomiti C5
- Gargano Peninsula D3
- Lago di Garda B5
- Mantova B4
- Milano (Milan) B5
- Ravenna C4
- San Gimignano B4
- Siena B4
- Urbino C4
- Verona B5
- Vicenza C5

AUSTRIA

HUNGARY

hluderns-
sluderno   Meran-
            Merano
    Bolzano
    Bozen
Molveno   Belluno   A23   Cividale
    Trento   del Friuli   SLOVENIA
            Asolo   A27   A4   Monfalcone
    Vicenza   A4   Treviso   **Trieste**   SERBIA
erona   CROATIA
    Padova   ■**Venezia**
                   (Venice)
antova   Po   A13   Rovigo
Reggio   **Ferrara**
nell'Emilia
Modena   **Bologna**
                ■**Ravenna**   BOSNIA &
    A1   Faenza   HERZEGOVINA
cca   Prato   **SAN**   ■**Rimini**
    Firenze   **MARINO**   A14   Pesaro
    (Florence)
Arno   San Gimignano   Urbino   ■**Ancona**
sterra   Siena   A1   Loreto
            Cortona   Gubbio
    Perugia   Assisi   A14   MONTENEGRO
        Todi   Orvieto   Ascoli Piceno   Adriatic
Sovana   Spoleto   Sea
    Viterbo   **Terni**   Rieti   A24   ■**Pescara**
Civitavecchia   A1   L'Aquila   A25   Chieti
            A12   Tivoli   Avezzano   Vasto
                   Subiaco   A14   Gargano   Vieste
        ROMA   Frosinone   San Severo   Peninsula
        (ROME)   A1   Campobasso   ■**Foggia**
    Latina   Cassino   Volturno   Barletta
        Terracina   Caserta   Benevento   A16   Molfetta
                Napoli   1281m   Altamura   ■**Bari**
                (Naples)   Vesuvius   A14
        Ischia   Pompei   Matera   Ostuni
    Tyrrhenian Sea   Sorrento   ■**Salerno**   Brindisi
            Capri   Ruvello   A3   ■**Taranto**   Lecce
                Amalfi   Paestum   Potenza
                Coast   Gallipoli
                    Custrovillari   Santa Maria
                                              di Leuca
                        Rossano
                    Cosenza
                        Crotone
                    Catanzaro
                        A3
                    Palmi   N
        Palermo   Cefalù   **ITALY**
    Trapani   A19   A20   **Messina**
                A18   **Reggio di**
        A29   A19   Enna   **Calabria**   0   100   200km
    Marinella   Caltanissetta   3329m   Taormina
    di Selinute   Enna   Etna   0   50   100 miles
            Piazza   ■**Catania**
    Agrigento   Armerina
                        ■**Siracusa**
        Pantelleria   Sicilia   Ragusa   A18
                        Noto

    C   D   E

long hot summers, when the intense color of the sea offsets the bleached ocher of the mountains.

Most of Italy is mountainous, the long spine of the Apennines (Apennini) running almost from top to bottom and stretching virtually from coast to coast. Some hilly areas are immensely fertile, as in Tuscany and Umbria in central Italy, while in other places, such as Basilicata and Calabria in the south, the combination of altitude and extreme climate can make the land unproductive.

The largest area of flatland is the great plain of the Po river valley in the north, which extends down the eastern seaboard, an agriculturally rich and productive swath. Much of upland Italy is wooded, and there is a wide variety of indigenous plants.

Diverse Regions

Until 1870 Italy was a collection of separate and disparate states with a complex history, which does much to explain the diversity of people and attitudes. Camillo Cavour (statesman and first prime minister of a united Italy) remarked after unification in 1860, "We have made Italy, now we must make Italians." This aim still seems to await fruition, such is the gulf between the different regions. Italy has been a republic since 1946, the 20 regions (regioni) enjoying a large degree of self-government; some, such as Sicily and Sardinia, are semiautonomous.

Italians would be the first to agree that there is no such thing as "an Italian." Ask an Italian where he or she is from and the answer will be "from Tuscany", or Rome, or Naples, or Sicily, but rarely "from Italy." Primary loyalties are firmly local and regional. The Italian character, attitudes, outlook and prejudices have been formed by the native region, not by the country as a whole. So the fiery Sicilians are light years away from the Milanese and their urbane efficiency,

the cool and rational Tuscans or the abrasive Romans.

Language also has played a part. Modern Italian, rich, elegant and musical, derives from Tuscan, a medieval dialect used by Dante and Petrarch and firmly based on Latin. But throughout Italy there are some 1,500 diverse dialects, which were in daily use until widespread literacy and access to television. There are still some elderly people who have difficulty speaking modern Italian, although mass media are rapidly weakening dialects.

The considerable geographic differences between the north and south have produced another element of regionalism – a very real economic and cultural divide between the halves of the country. The cooler, more fertile north is richer, more advanced and more successful than the arid and impoverished south.

The People

All Italians do seem to share the same attitude toward life, one that is instantly apparent to foreigners. Life is for living, for enjoying, for savoring. There's always time to pause to chat, time for kindness, time to laugh; passions run high but anger is quickly over and forgotten. Watch the way Italians treat children or the elderly, without condescension but with respect for their age. Problems are solved with little fuss on a personal level, although the labyrinth of Italian bureaucracy might drive visitors crazy.

Despite having one of the world's lowest national birthrates, family ties are exceptionally close, with children often living with their parents into their 30s, and elderly people are still mainly cared for at home. The mother's role is pivotal; Italian men, it is said, search for a woman who lives up to their mother.

If you want to attract the opposite sex, you have to do your best to look good.

Opposite: Siena's narrow winding streets seen from the town's 14th-century campanile (bell tower)

This helps explain the importance of the *bella figura*, literally "beautiful form," but meaning infinitely more. Italians have an innate sense of style, and it matters greatly that their clothes, cars and other personal possessions are stylish and contemporary.

Bella figura dictates that these must all be admired, and what better way to display them than during that fine Italian tradition, the *passeggiata*? This nightly outdoor perambulation occurs in every village, town and city, when citizens exit en masse from their homes, strolling through the streets, exchanging news and gossip, but above all admiring and hoping to be admired in return.

Landscapes and Townscapes

A rich historical and cultural past has shaped the townscapes in Italy. Cities, towns and villages are crammed with fine buildings, churches and works of art, a legacy of pre-Unification days. But over the past century, and notably since World War II, there has been huge development and growth in urban areas, with unattractive spreads of industrial buildings and blocks of soulless

The evening stroll around Piazza Rotonda, Rome

apartments on the outskirts of countless towns. Every town still retains its central piazza, with civic buildings and a church grouped around or near it.

In many rural areas, people have traditionally lived in villages rather than on the land they work, traveling daily to the fields, so in some areas isolated country farmhouses are rare. There has sometimes been a huge gulf between the urban and rural populations, possibly due to the very early development of Italian towns.

The middle class was a late arrival in Italy and only really emerged during the great economic boom of the 1950s and 1960s. Even now there are agricultural workers and small shareholders working the land as it has been worked for centuries, while their cousins may be employed in high-tech industries.

Exploring Italy

Despite the enduring financial woes affecting the country as a whole, as well as other parts of Europe, Italy has a comfortable standard of living, making traveling easy and pleasurable. Tourism is a major industry, so you'll find English widely spoken in city hotels and restaurants, although less so away from the main tourist areas.

Italian engineering prowess has produced an excellent road network, with both toll roads and good highways. Minor roads are often unpaved. Italians drive fast and aggressively but mostly safely; once you're accustomed to the style of driving you should have no problems. All major cities have an airport, with frequent internal flights. Trains are cheap and punctual, although cross-country routes can be slow and complicated; it's safer to stick to the intercity services. Buses connect even the smallest villages.

Italian hotels are rated and inspected by regional authorities; regardless of the price range, they are spotlessly clean. Bathtubs are rare except in deluxe establishments, and showers frequently

A *traghetto* (ferry) crossing the Grand Canal in Venice; it's customary to stand

dribble when turned on; water is precious in many parts of the country. Air-conditioning is becoming more widespread but is by no means universal, and buildings can be stifling in summer. Laws govern the date when public places turn their heat on or off.

Culinary Traditions

Italian cooking is regional and simple, relying on the superb quality of the ingredients, and you'll find wonderful dishes wherever you go. In a country where frozen food is only now becoming widespread, menus are dictated by the seasons, with a rich variety of dishes punctuating the different months.

The various types of restaurant can be confusing. The terms *ristorante*, *osteria* and *trattoria* are fairly interchangeable; *tavola calda* and *pizzeria* imply something a bit more humble. Lunch has traditionally been the main meal, but there is a trend toward making dinner the extravaganza. The evening menu often consists of *antipasto* (hors d'oeuvre), the first course (*primo*) of pasta, soup or rice, the meat or fish second course (*secondo*) with its accompanying *contorni* (vegetables) or *insalata* (salad), followed by *formaggio*, *dolce* or *frutta* (cheese, dessert or fruit). If a meal this size seems a bit daunting, choose just a couple of courses.

The perfect accompaniment to Italian food is a locally produced wine. *Denominazione d'Origine Controllata* (DOC) is a method of classification that guarantees the origin of the wine, and that it has been made following the guidelines for a particular area. However, it is no indication of quality.

Pastimes

The favorite Italian pastimes are probably eating, drinking and talking; preferably all together. Immensely sociable people, they tend to relax en masse, making group activities of every type very popular. Soccer is the national sport, but since Italy's early defeat in the 2014 World Cup and failure to qualify for the 2018 tournament, the Italian team's world ranking has fallen to nineteenth place. Many Italians are extremely passionate about soccer.

Deeply traditional, Italians prefer their pleasures to be family-oriented; a Sunday drive, a day at the beach or a gentle stroll, accompanied by a nonstop stream of chatter, constitute most people's idea of leisure.

Timeline

3000–1800 BC	First traces of migratory peoples in peninsula.
700–300 BC	Etruscan federation exists alongside Roman republic.
264–146 BC	Punic Wars against Carthage.
AD 200–400	Decline of Roman Empire.
550–770	Peninsula fragmented with different areas under Byzantine, Papal, Lombard and Frankish influence.
1300–1400	Emergence of the city-states in north; Renaissance era.
1500–1848	Fragmentation of peninsula under foreign domination.
1848–61	Struggle for unification, with brief republic established in 1848; kingdom of Italy proclaimed in 1861.
1870	Rome and the Papal States become part of a unified Italy.
1890	Emergence of Fasci Siciliani movement to help the poor and exploited – which was to evolve into the Mafia.
1915–18	Italy sides with Allies during World War I.
1940	Italy enters World War II on Axis side.
1943	Fall of Mussolini and armistice with Allies; Mussolini reinstated by Germany as head of puppet republic; Rome liberated in 1944.
1946	Italian Republic established.
1957	Treaty of Rome; Italy becomes a founding member of European Economic Community, now called the European Union.
1985–2005	Corruption is rife, but Italy flourishes as desire for political and institutional reform grows.
2011	Prime Minister Silvio Berlusconi steps down in midst of scandal; technocrat government, led by Mario Monti, is put in place.
2013	Pope Benedict XVI abdicates. Cardinal Jorge Mario Bergoglio of Argentina is elected as Francis I.
2014	Matteo Renzi (Democratic Party) becomes Prime Minister.
2015	Sergio Matarella, Matteo Renzi's nomination, is elected President.
2016	Virginia Raggi of the anti-establishment Five Star Movement is elected (the first female) Mayor of Rome.
2018	General election see antiestablishment Five Star Movement win most votes; they form governing alliance with League, who hold the majority of seats.

The Etruscans

For centuries historians have questioned exactly who the Etruscans were. This enigmatic race preceded the Romans and were at the height of their power from 800 to 400 BC. They formed a confederacy of 12 cities, built towns, passed laws, traded overseas and believed firmly in an afterlife. A lively and imaginative people, they also had highly developed cultural, political and social systems. The Romans, admirers of Etruscan culture, absorbed much of it as they rose to power. By the third century BC the Romans had virtually assimilated the entire nation, along with much of its language, customs and religious beliefs. Today only the monuments remain, particularly those to the Etruscan dead. Wonderful finds have been made in these tombs – jewelry, vases, sculpture and frescoes. They are preserved in museums all over ancient Etruria, the name given to the area they inhabited. You can visit Etruscan sites at Tarquinia and Cerveteri, both a short distance north of Rome, and see the finest Etruscan collection in the world at the Museo Nazionale Etrusco di Villa Giulia in Rome (see page 298).

People viewing paintings displayed on a street stall in Rome

Survival Guide

- The fashion-conscious Italians spend much time and thought on looking good. Dressing appropriately means no shorts in cities. If you do show too much leg or arm, you won't be allowed to enter churches.
- Inevitably, Italy's star attractions in Rome, Venice, Florence and other major cities become packed during the hot summer. Get out early to avoid the main rush or, better still, visit in the late fall or winter when it's quieter and cooler.
- Nowadays, many of the stores and major sights in larger cities throughout the country stay open all day, but in rural towns everything closes from around 12:30 until 4:30 or 5, while in high summer most of the population eats a large lunch and has a siesta. Plan your day around this, remembering that most museums, churches, galleries and stores will all be closed for several hours too.
- Italians love their wine, which they drink with meals, but they disapprove of people who drink to excess.
- It is typical to go out to eat lunch from around 12:30 to about 2:30 p.m., and dinner at around 7:30 or 8 p.m.

- Vegetarians will find plenty of choices in most restaurants. As for children, Italians genuinely love them, and most restaurants – even upscale ones – welcome them. Italian coffee is extremely strong, so if you want it weaker just ask for a *caffè americano*.
- Bars are often much more than the name suggests. They are open from dawn until midnight or later, and offer coffee, tea, soda, snacks and pastries, as well as alcohol. All bars have restrooms.
- Many Italians are enthusiastic smokers, but smoking is prohibited in all public places, including bars, cafés and restaurants. The law is generally well observed.
- One of the joys of Italy is shopping in local stores and at the colorful street markets. However, Italian shopping habits are slowly changing and out-of-town shopping centers are becoming more common. All shop and market prices are fixed.
- Facilities for visitors with disabilities are improving, but are not yet as good as those back home. If you need help it's best to check ahead with local tourist offices and with hotels and sights themselves.

Rome

There's almost too much to Rome (Roma); too much history, too much art, too much noise, confusion, traffic.

This is an overwhelming city in every way, with splendors and frustrations in equal measure. Nowhere else in the world will your senses be assaulted by such a glorious mélange of ancient,

medieval, Renaissance, baroque and modern sights.

Expectations run high, and every visitor comes with preconceptions of sun-filled days of *dolce vita* and romantic strolls through ancient streets. Put them aside, take it slow, accept Rome not as you think it should be, but as it is, and you'll discover a city that is virtually impossible to describe.

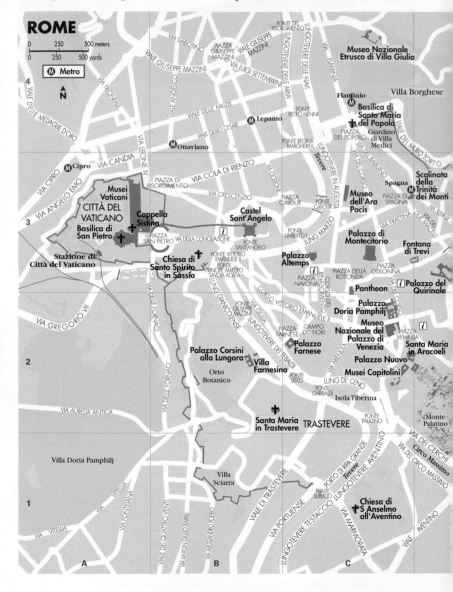

Mapping the City

It's a good idea to stay as centrally located as you can, but avoid the unwholesome area around the central railroad station, Stazione Termini, and keep in mind that few areas of the city offer peace and quiet.

You'll quickly realize that Rome has no discernible center, although Piazza Venezia, dominated by the vast, wedding cake-like monument of Victor Emmanuel II, is a good place to orient yourself. From here, the Via del Corso stretches north, and to the south lies the Forum (Foro Romano, see page 297), the heart of classical Rome.

Between the Corso and the Tiber (Tevere) river lies the *centro storico*, or historic center, a maze of medieval streets and Renaissance squares and one of the city's most beguiling areas.

On the other side of the Corso are Rome's most elegant shopping streets, more sun-dappled piazzas, some lovely green spaces and the Via Vittorio Veneto, with its luxury hotels and galaxy of upscale cafés.

Across the river lies Trastevere, filled with charming streets and squares and noted for its excellent restaurants.

To the north is Vatican City (Città del Vaticano, see page 299), home of the Pope and St. Peter's Basilica (Basilica di San Pietro, see page 296).

Seeing the Sights

It would take months to see all of Rome, so before you arrive, decide where your priorities lie. It's a mistake to rush out, exhausted from travel, and see the Vatican on your first day; instead wander around the back streets or linger over a cup of coffee before you plunge into serious sightseeing. If you're not a sightseer, enjoy the street life and the stylish stores and restaurants.

It's best to tackle the highlights early in the day, before the crowds and heat intensify and while you're still fresh. Make a point of resting during the early afternoon; most stores and attractions are closed then anyway, and you can venture out again refreshed and relaxed in the late afternoon.

If time is short and you want to see a lot, think about taking a tour; your hotel will be able to advise you.

Other options include walking tours with local experts to explore off-the-beaten-track areas, or a boat trip on the Tiber river.

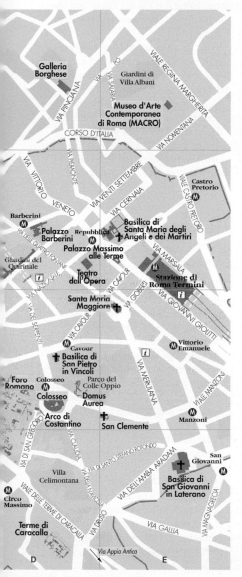

Peace and Quiet

Tranquility is in short supply in Rome, but there are moments when it seems within reach. In addition to the Villa Borghese (see page 301), other green spaces exist around the city, where the roar of the traffic is at least muted.

One of the best is the Palatine Hill (Palatino, see page 297) above the Forum, a good place to picnic after a morning's sightseeing, with scattered ruins, cypresses and wildflowers. The Botanical Garden (Giardino Botanico) in Trastevere provides cool shade amid the 7,000 species of plants, while the park Colle Oppio, with its strolling mothers and babies, is a good bet after a morning at the Colosseum.

Roman Cuisine

Romans enjoy dining out, and there are plenty of restaurants to choose from. Trastevere and the streets around Piazza Navona are packed with eateries; as always in Italy, look for places that locals patronize.

Roman specialties center around the less attractive parts of animals, such as offal, brains and tripe, but staples like grilled meat and the delicious *saltimbocca alla Romana* (veal scaloppine cooked with prosciutto and sage) are easy to find. Pasta dishes include spicy *rigatoni all'amatriciana* (pasta with bacon, chili and tomato), and the delicious and familiar *spaghetti alla carbonara*, made with bacon, egg and fettuccine. Artichokes are a great Roman specialty, eaten either deep fried or raw; look also for asparagus in early summer. Pizzas are excellent too.

Desserts are simple, but Roman ice cream is mouthwatering, and it's worth forgoing restaurant desserts and opting instead for a *gelateria*.

Local wines come from the hills outside Rome, in an area known as the Castelli Romani; Frascati is the best known. You'll also find wines from all over Italy, as well as herbal aperitifs and liqueurs.

Boutiques and Markets

Shopping can be a pleasure in self-indulgent Rome, where there is a superb range of luxurious silk, linens, leather and accessories. Shoes, bags, handmade evening wear and exquisite china and porcelain are found in the very chic stores clustered around the Via Condotti and the Via Frattina, just off the Piazza di Spagna. You'll find moderately priced shops along the Via del Corso and the Via Nazionale; knitwear and sweaters are good buys.

Rome also has several department stores, including the upscale La Rinascente, with its flagship store on Via del Tritone and a branch at Piazza Fiume; Upim and OVS are inexpensive chain stores with plenty of stylish buys.

If you enjoy markets, head for the popular daily food and vegetable market in the lovely Campo dei Fiori, or the many smaller street markets dotted around the city.

Nightlife

Romans consider having a meal in a restaurant the pinnacle of evening

Roman Fountains

Lovely fountains are scattered around Rome, and their beauty will stick in your mind when much else has faded. They provide cool places for a few minutes of rest, and the soothing sound of splashing water somehow manages to make itself heard over the noise of Rome's frenetic traffic. Be sure to pause at the Fontana delle Naiadi in Piazza della Repubblica, with its bronze nymphs; the dolphin-decorated Fontana del Tritone in Piazza Barberini; and the charming tortoise fountain, the Fontana delle Tartarughe, in Piazza Mattei.

The city's most famous fountain is the Fontana di Trevi in the small Piazza di Trevi (see page 297). This awesome baroque masterpiece of carved figures flanking the central figure of Neptune is the most photographed fountain in Rome.

entertainment, but there are many other options and events going on. Pick up a copy of *Trovaroma* or go online at www.trova-roma.com for information on where to go and what to do in Rome.

There are plenty of music bars and discos to satisfy music lovers. Opera is a good option, either at the Teatro dell'Opera or outdoors in summer at the Terme di Caracalla.

Rome has a clutch of movie theaters showing films in their original language. Concerts and recitals are frequently held in the city's churches.

Essential Information

Tourist Information
Call Centre ☎ 06 0608 (for all offices)
Daily 9:30–7 (English speaking)
Fiumicino Airport: International arrivals, Terminal 3
Castel Sant'Angelo: Piazza Pia
Ciampino airport: arrivals hall
Minghetti: Via Marco Minghetti
Navona: Piazza delle Cinque Lune
Nazionale: Via Nazionale, near Palazzo delle Esposizioni
Fori Imperiali: Via dei Fori Imperiali
Sonnino (for Trastevere): Piazza Sydney Sonnino
Termini: Termini Railway Station. Inside station at Binario 24 (Platform 24)
www.turismoroma.it or www.060608.it

Urban Transportation
Public transportation in Rome consists of red-gray, orange or green buses and trams and a two-line metro (subway) system. Metro stations are marked on the Rome city map by the letter "M" in a red circle. Bus tickets must be purchased from machines before boarding, or from shops and newsstands displaying an ATAC or COTRAL sticker. They are valid for multiple bus trips plus one metro trip within a 100-minute period, and must be validated on the vehicle when boarding. The éRoma 24/48/72 is valid for 1,2 or 3 days unlimited travel on buses, trams, the metro and the suburban train service. A weekly pass, the

Carta Integrata Settimanale, also is available. The useful bus 40 takes in the main sights between Stazione Termini (Termini Station) and San Pietro (Vatican). Taxis are white and park at stands with a blue-and-white sign; they do not stop on the street. Call a taxi from Radio Taxi (☎ 06 3570); the meter will start running straight after your call. The meter should be at zero if you begin your ride at the taxi stand. Do not get in a "private" taxi.

Airport Information
Rome has two airports (http://www.adr.it): Leonardo da Vinci, at Fiumicino (west of the city); and Ciampino, south of Rome. The easiest link from Leonardo da Vinci to the city center is by train to Stazione Termini (the central railroad station); trains leave every 30 minutes between 6:23 a.m. and 11:53 p.m., and 17.53 and 22:53; every 15 minutes between 12:53 and 17:53 (precise times may vary). Buses also run to Termini and Tiburtina stations (check Terravision online at www.terravision.eu; no night bus services). Tickets cost €10 return. Travel time is 70 minutes, with four stops. Taxis cost a fixed €48 to central Rome. Only take official white or yellow taxis with meters, numbers and names. Ciampino airport: Terravision buses leave from outside the terminal every 20 minutes until midnight. Return fare €10, journey time 40 minutes; www.terravision.eu.

Climate – average highs and lows for the month

Jan.	Feb.	Mar.	Apr.	May	Jun.	Jul.	Aug.	Sep.	Oct.	Nov.	Dec.
13°C	14°C	16°C	19°C	23°C	27°C	31°C	31°C	27°C	23°C	18°C	14°C
55°F	57°F	61°F	66°F	73°F	81°F	88°F	88°F	81°F	73°F	64°F	57°F
3°C	4°C	7°C	8°C	12°C	15°C	18°C	18°C	14°C	11°C	9°C	5°C
37°F	39°F	45°F	46°F	54°F	59°F	64°F	64°F	57°F	52°F	48°F	41°F

Rome Sights

> **Key to symbols**
> ➕ map coordinates refer to the Rome map on pages 292–293 💵 admission charge: $$$ more than €10, $$ €5–€10, $ less than €5
> See page 5 for complete key to symbols

Basilica di San Pietro

The spiritual heart of Catholicism, the Basilica di San Pietro (St. Peter's Basilica) stands on the site of the saint's burial place.

This is architectural grandeur on a triumphant scale, from the sweeping colonnades branching away from the structure's magnificent facade to the soaring dome high above the twisted columns of Giovanni Bernini's High Altar *baldacchino*.

There's much that dates from 1506 to 1626, when Donato di Angelo, Bramante and Bernini were the basilica's principal architects.

Near the end of his life, Michelangelo designed the dome, from which there are superb views; inside you can see the sublime *Pietà*, one of his earliest works. The right nave contains a bronze statue of St. Peter, his right foot worn away by pilgrims' caresses. Other artists who worked on the decoration of this exquisite basilica include Antonio Canova and Pietro da Cortona.

➕ A3 ✉ Piazza San Pietro, Città del Vaticano ☎ 06 6988 3229; www.vaticanstate.va ⏱ Daily 7–7, Apr.–Sep.; 7–6, rest of year. Dome: daily 8–6, Apr.–Sep.; 8–5, rest of year 🚇 Ottaviano 🚌 62 to Piazza San Pietro; 23, 32, 49, 81, 271, 590, 982, 990 to Piazza del Risorgimento 💵 Admission free ($$ for elevator to terrace and steps to dome)

Colosseo

The massive Colosseo (Colosseum) dates from AD 72, and this original design has never been bettered. Today, it is still a functional stadium yet it once seated 55,000 and the sophisticated "backstage" facilities allowed the arena to be flooded for mock sea battles. Most ancient entertainment featured animals, slaves and gladiators, but few Christians were martyred here.

During the Middle Ages the Colosseum was a source of building stone, which explains the missing sections.

➕ D2 ✉ Piazza del Colosseo, Via dei Fori Imperiali ☎ 06 3996 7700 or www.coopculture.it for advance reservations ⏱ Daily 8:30 a.m. to 1 hour before dusk 🚇 Colosseo 🚌 75, 81, 673, 175, 204; tram 3 💵 $$$ (includes Palatino and Foro Romano; valid 48 hours)

The arena and arcades in the Colosseum – the world's largest surviving structure from Roman antiquity

Fontana di Trevi

Among Rome's delightful fountains, none is more famous than the Fontana di Trevi (Trevi Fountain), a baroque creation tucked into a tiny piazza. There's been a fountain here since Roman times; the present example dates from 1732 and takes its name from the three roads – *tre vie* – that converged here. With your back to the fountain throw two coins over your shoulder into the water; legend claims that the first coin grants a wish, the second guarantees that you will return to Rome.

➕ C3 ✉ Piazza di Trevi Ⓜ Spagna or Barbarini 🚌 52, 53, 61, 62, 63, 71, 80, 85, 160, 492, 850

Foro Romano e Monte Palatino

Heart of the Roman Empire, the Foro Romano (Roman Forum) contained all of the ancient city's most important political, religious and municipal buildings. Today it's a romantic jumble of tumbled columns and walls set amid cypresses and wildflowers. Spend time here, tracking down the second-century Arch of Septimius Severus, the Temple of Antoninus and Faustina (AD 141), the stately columns of the fourth-century Portico of the Dei Consentes, and the House of the Vestal Virgins, home of the guardians of the sacred fire. On the Palatino (Palatine Hill), overlooking the Roman Forum, there are ruins of the homes of rich Romans and emperors.

➕ D2 ✉ Via dei Fori Imperiali, Largo Romolo e Remo 1 ☎ 06 3996 7700; www.coopculture.it (advance reservations) Ⓖ Daily 8:30 a.m. to 1 hour before dusk Ⓜ Colosseo 🚌 81, 673, 175, 204, tram 30 💰 $$$ (includes Foro Romano, Colosseo and Palatino; valid 48 hours)

Galleria Borghese

The Galleria Borghese (Borghese Gallery), housed in the 17th-century summer palace of Cardinal Scipione Borghese, is a treasure-house of sculpture, mainly collected by the cardinal. He greatly admired Giovanni Bernini, whose works dominate – the *David* is said to be a self-portrait.

Look for Antonio Canova's *Paolina Borghese*; this beautiful little minx was Napoleon's sister, married off to a later Borghese. Stunning paintings include Caravaggio's *Boy with a Fruit Basket*.

➕ D4 ✉ Villa Borghese, Piazzale del Museo Borghese 5 ☎ 06 32810; www.galleriaborghese.it Ⓖ Tue.–Sun. 9–7 Ⓜ Spagna 🚌 5, 19, 52, 53, 63, 86, 88, 92, 95, 116, 204, 217, 231, 360, 490, 491, 495, 630, 910, 926 🍴 Museum/gallery restaurant 💰 $$$ (advance reservations necessary ☎ 06 328 10, Mon.–Fri. 9–6, Sat. 9–1, or online at www.tosc.it)

Musei Capitolini

The two *palazzi* housing the great classical collection of the Musei Capitolini (Capitoline Museums) are set on either side of a square designed by Michelangelo. Look for the *Dying Gaul* and the tautly muscled *Discobolus* (Discus Thrower). Bronzes include the famous fifth-century BC *Capitoline Wolf Suckling Romulus* and *Remus* and, finest of all, the superb equestrian statue of *Marcus Aurelius*. Paintings feature major works by Titian, Paolo Veronese, Van Dyck and Caravaggio.

➕ C2 ✉ Piazza del Campidoglio 1 ☎ 060608; www.museicapitolini.org Ⓖ Daily 9:30–7:30 Ⓜ Colosseo 🚌 40, 63, 70, 81, 87, 95, 160, 170, 271, 628, 630, 716 💰 $$$

Musei Vaticani

The Vatican Museums make up the world's largest museum complex, with around a dozen self-contained museums in 1,400 rooms. Plan your visit to pick out some highlights, however, do not miss the Cappella Sistina (Sistine Chapel), with world-renowned frescoes by Michelangelo covering the ceiling and the altar wall, showing scenes from the Old Testament, and the powerful *Last Judgment*. The Stanze di Raffaello (Raphael Rooms), among the artist's masterpieces, were started in 1508. Classical sculpture, an Egyptian collection and modern religious art are among the other features at this venue.

➕ A3 ✉ Viale Vaticano 100, Città del Vaticano ☎ 06 6988 4676; www.museivaticani.va Ⓖ Mon.–

Sat. 9–6, (last ticket 4 p.m.). Also last Sun. of the month 9–2 (last ticket 12:30 p.m.). Closed major religious holidays ☒ Ottaviano, Cipro-Musei Vaticani 🚌 49 (to front of museums), 32, 81, 982 to Piazza del Risorgimento or 492, 990 to Via Leone IV, both 5 minutes' walk 💰 $$$; free to all last Sun. of the month ℹ️ Individual tickets and a wide range of guided tour tickets are available online by following the links at www.museivaticani.va

Museo d'Arte Contemporanea di Roma (MACRO)

An imaginative conversion of a former brewery houses the Rome Museum of Contemporary Art. The original building was extended with a 108,000-square-foot purpose-built area, large enough for multimedia installations by cutting-edge young artists as well as established international names. The permanent collection concentrates on Italian modern artists from the 1960s on, while changing exhibitions highlight the work of Italian and world artists.

➕ E4 ☒ Via Nizza 138 (corner of Via Cagliari) ☎ 06 696 271; www.museomacro.org ⏰ Tue.–Sun. 10:30–7:30 🚌 38, 90 💰 $$$

Museo Nazionale Etrusco di Villa Giulia

Visit this enlightening museum to learn more about the Etruscans (see page 290). The collection is housed in a late Renaissance villa; its architects included Michelangelo. Highlights are the Castellani exhibits and fine Greek vases. Be sure to see the Sarcofago degli Sposi, sixth-century BC figures of a reclining married couple, and the terra-cotta Hercules and Apollo.

➕ C4 ☒ Piazzale di Villa Giulia 9 ☎ 06 322 6571; www.villagiulia.beniculturali.it ⏰ Tue.–Sun. 9–8 ☒ Flaminio 🚌 3, 19, 30,52, 926 💰 $$$

Pantheon

The superb Pantheon, erected between AD 118 and AD 128 and still in use today, gives a better idea of the splendor of ancient Rome than any other surviving monument. Built as a temple, it became a Christian church in AD 609 and now

The interior of the Pantheon, seen from the doorway

houses Raphael's tomb and those of two Italian kings. Its dome was the largest ever built before the introduction of the building material reinforced concrete in the 20th century.

➕ C3 ☒ Piazza della Rotonda ☎ 347 820 5204; www.pantheonroma.com ⏰ Mon.–Sat. 9–7, Sun. 9–5:45 ☒ Spagna 🚌 64, 70, 81, 86, 87, 90, 119, 170 and all services to Largo di Torre Argentina 💰 Free

Piazza Navona

Piazza Navona owes its shape to the Roman racetrack that once stood here. Pope Innocent X, who commissioned Giovanni Bernini to design the focal point, the Fountain of the Four Rivers, rebuilt the piazza in 1644. The 17th-century church of Sant'Agnese is a good example of Francesco Borromini's work.

➕ C3 ☒ Piazza Navona ☒ Spagna 🚌 30, 56, 60

Piazza di Spagna e Scalinata della Trinità dei Monti

The Scalinata della Trinità dei Monti (Spanish Steps), situated at the heart of Rome's trendiest shopping area and curving gracefully up from Piazza di Spagna to the church of Trinità dei Monti, attract myriad visitors. The steps, built in 1723, get their name from the

The Vatican

The Città del Vaticano, and all it stands for, has had its detractors through the ages, among them Thomas Paine, the English-born American revolutionary, writer and inventor, who likened the influence of the Papacy to "a dagger through the heart of Italy." Even he, though, would have to admit that architecturally it remains perhaps the world's greatest monument to beauty. The Vatican, an area covering some 109 acres around the Basilica of St. Peter (Basilica di San Pietro), in the heart of Rome, is the world's smallest independent sovereign state. Until Italian unification in 1870, the Papacy had held territory covering a large part of central Italy, known as the Papal States. These became part of the new united Italy, and the Pope, Pius IX, retreated to the Vatican, a virtual prisoner, until in 1929 the Lateran Treaty recognized the Vatican State.

The Pope, as well as being head of the Catholic church, is also Europe's only absolute monarch, ruling over the 400-plus inhabitants of the Vatican. In March 2013 Cardinal Bergoglio, Archbishop of Buenos Aires, was elected Pope (Francis I) following the surprise abdication of Benedict XVI. The Argentinian son of Italian immigrants, he grew up in Buenos Aires and became a Jesuit priest. Francis I has maintained a modest lifestyle and preaches a simple message of love and hope. Many of the world's Catholics are hopeful that this Pontificate will see the Church return to Christianity's basic tenets and teaching.

The Pope has been defended by the Swiss Guard since 1506. Their distinctive, colorful striped red, yellow and blue dress uniform, said to have been designed by Michelangelo, is instantly recognizable. The 110 members are Swiss, young men recruited between the ages of 19 and 25, from Switzerland's four Catholic cantons. They are Swiss rather than Roman because it was unthinkable that the army of the Church of Rome should take up arms against Romans in defence of the Papacy.

The Pope gives a weekly audience on Wednesdays at 11 a.m. in the Papal Audience Chamber, and very occasionally in the Basilica of St. Peter or in the piazza. These occasions, for up to 7,000 people, are open to everyone and tickets are free. The Pope also gives a blessing from the windows of his rooms overlooking the piazza on Sundays at midday.

Audience tickets are available by writing to Prefettura della Casa Pontificia, 00120 Città del Vaticano, online at www.papalaudience.org or by visiting the office through the bronze doors in the right-hand colonnade of Piazza San Pietro (open Mon. 9–1, Tue. 9–6; ☎ 06 6988 3114).

The Biblioteca Vaticano (Vatican Library) holds more than 1.5 million books

Excursion to Tivoli

Most visitors to Rome seize the chance to escape the city by taking an excursion to Tivoli, a small town in a lovely wooded location 19 miles northeast of Rome. Its main attractions are the gardens of the Villa d'Este, among the world's most beautiful, and the vast Classical site of Villa Adriana (Hadrian's Villa), about 4 miles southwest of Tivoli.

It's easy to make an independent trip to Tivoli, either by train from the central railroad station, Stazione Termini, then local bus, or by bus from central Rome. There are guided excursions from the city, while an English-speaking guide tells you all you need to know.

Villa d'Este

The Villa d'Este is famous not so much for the villa itself, built by Cardinal Ippolito d'Este in 1550, but for the stunning gardens, terraces and fountains that belong to it. The main attractions are two Giovanni Bernini fountains, the elegant Fontana di Biccierone and the Fontana dei Draghi, and the breathtaking Avenue of a Hundred Fountains (Viale delle Cento Fontane), a wooded walkway. Nearby lies the lovely Villa Gregoriana, where a pair of waterfalls cascades into a deep-cut gorge.

Villa Adriana

Many prosperous Romans built retirement villas at Tivoli, and in AD 125 the Emperor Hadrian embarked on the construction of his own. The villa and its gardens grew and grew, eventually covering as much ground as Imperial Rome itself. The site is vast and romantic, and you'll need a map to make sense of it all. Don't miss the Maritime Theater (Teatro Marittimo), a colonnaded palace on an island in the middle of a lake.

Villa d'Este ✚ Off map ✉ Piazza Trento 5 ☎ Toll-free in Italy 199 766166 or 00 39 041 271 9036; www.villadestetivoli.info ◷ Tue.–Sun. 8:30 to 1 hour before dusk. Last admission 1 hour before closing 🚌 COTRAL bus from metro station Ponte Mammolo (Line B) 🚆 Train to Tivoli 🍴 Refreshments available in gardens ⬛ $$$

Villa Gregoriana ✉ Largo Sant'Angelo ☎ 0774 332650 (entrance and ticket office); www.visitfai.it/parcovillagregoriana ◷ Daily 10–6:30, Apr.–Oct.; Tue.–Sun. 10–4:30, Nov.–Dec. and Mar. ⬛ $$

Villa Adriana ✉ Largo Marguerite Yourcenar 1 ☎ 06 3996 7900 or www.coopculture.it (reservations); www.villaadriana.beniculturali.it ◷ Daily 9 a.m. to 1 hour before dusk 🚌 COTRAL bus from metro station Ponte Mammolo (Line B) to Tivoli, stop approximately a mile from site. Train Stazione di Tivoli from Roma Termini then take bus CAT 4 🚆 Train to Tivoli 🍴 Refreshments at villa site ⬛ $$

The Avenue of a Hundred Fountains in the gardens at Villa d'Este

piazza, which once housed the Spanish Embassy. The eccentric-looking "sunken boat" fountain dates from 1627, while on the right of the steps (at No. 26) is the Museo Keats-Shelley, in the lodgings where poet John Keats died in 1821.

➕ C3 ✉ Piazza di Spagna 26 ☎ Museo Keats-Shelley: 06 678 4235; www.keats-shelley-house. org 🕒 Museum: Mon.–Sat. 10–1 and 2–6 🚇 Spagna 🚌 116, 117, 119, 590 🎟 Museum $$

San Clemente

No church in Rome gives a better idea of history than San Clemente, a multilayered structure whose newest part dates from the 12th century. In its dim interior, the apse mosaics glitter above the marble panels of the choir screen and pulpits. From here, descend to the fourth-century lower church, with its ghostly traces of 8th- to 11th-century frescoes, before plunging deeper to examine the fine altar of the Roman Mithraic temple (the Mithraic cult was most popular in Rome from 67 BC to the late second century).

➕ E2 ✉ Via Labicana 95 ☎ 06 774 0021; www.basilicasanclemente.com 🕒 Mon.–Sat. 9–12:30 and 3–6, Sun. 12–6 🚌 3, 85, 87, 117, 186, 571, 810, 850 🎟 Church free; Templo $$$

Santa Maria Maggiore

Mass has been said daily in Santa Maria Maggiore (St. Mary the Major) since the fifth century, when it was built on a site marked by a summer snowfall, as predicted by the Virgin when she

The beautiful apse of Santa Maria in Trastevere

appeared before the reigning Pope. The mosaics in the nave date from the fifth century, those in the apse from the 13th century. The gilding on the ceiling reputedly comes from the first gold to arrive from the New World.

➕ E2 ✉ Piazza di Santa Maria Maggiore 42 ☎ 06 698 86800; www.vatican.va 🕒 Daily 7–6:45 🚇 Cavour, Termini 🚌 5, 16, 75, 84, 105, 360, 590, 649 🎟 Free

Santa Maria in Trastevere

The facade of Santa Maria in Trastevere, with its lustrous 12th-century mosaics, overlooks an atmospheric fountained piazza. The charming portico, added in 1702, leads to an interior with nave columns that once supported Roman buildings. The 12th-century, Byzantine-style mosaics of the apse represent the glorification of the Virgin.

➕ B2 ✉ Piazza Santa Maria in Trastevere ☎ 06 581 4802 🕒 Daily 7:30 a.m.–9 p.m (may close 12:30–3:30 in Aug.) 🚌 H, 23, 44, 75, 170, 181, 280, 630, 780

Via Appia Antica

A short bus ride from central Rome takes you to the Via Appia Antica (Old Appian Way), built in 4 BC to link Rome with Brindisi in southern Italy. Here, Spartacus and his men were executed, and St. Paul marched to prison. This cobbled way, shaded by pine trees, is lined with monuments and tombs; you can visit the catacombs, with their mementos of early Christian life.

➕ Off map at E1 ✉ Catacombe di San Sebastiano: Via Appia Antica 136 ☎ 06 785 0350; www.catacombe.org 🕒 Catacombs: Mon.–Sat. 10–4:30 🚌 118, 218, 660 🎟 $$$

Villa Borghese

If you long for some cool green grass, head for the extensive grounds of the Villa Borghese gardens, central Rome's largest park, an oasis of verdant lawns, umbrella pines, lakes and fountains. The adjoining Pincio Gardens offer views across the rooftops to St. Peter's.

➕ C4 ✉ Porta Pinciana 🕒 Daily dawn–dusk 🚇 Flaminio, Spagna 🚌 52, 53, 88, 116, 120, 150, 490

Florence

More than six million tourists visit Florence (Firenze), the capital of Tuscany, annually, totally outnumbering the resident population of around 380,000. It is a city of great beauty, stunning art and is steeped in history. However, in summer, the heat, crowds, noise and cultural overload can be overwhelming. When touring Florence, it pays to plan ahead.

Choose the time you visit carefully. If art and architecture are the main purpose of your trip, try to come off-season, when Florence is quieter and the heat in this largely non-air-conditioned city won't wipe you out. Be prepared for crowds, try to time gallery visits for early and late in the

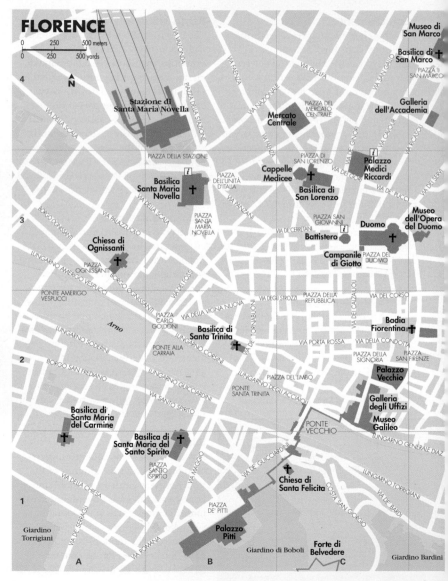

FLORENCE

0 250 500 meters
0 250 500 yards

N

Museo di San Marco
Basilica di San Marco
Galleria dell'Accademia
PIAZZA DI SAN MARCO
VIA GUELFA
VIA FAENZA
VIA NAZIONALE
VIA VALFONDA
PIAZZA DELLA STAZIONE
Stazione di Santa Maria Novella
PIAZZA DEL MERCATO CENTRALE
Mercato Centrale
PIAZZA DI SAN LORENZO
Cappelle Medicee
Palazzo Medici Riccardi
VIA DE' SERVI
VIA DE' PUCCI
PIAZZA DELL'UNITÀ D'ITALIA
Basilica Santa Maria Novella
Basilica di San Lorenzo
PIAZZA SAN GIOVANNI
Duomo
Museo dell'Opera del Duomo
VIA PANZANI
PIAZZA SANTA MARIA NOVELLA
VIA DE' CERRETANI
Battistero
Campanile di Giotto
PIAZZA DEL DUOMO
BORGO OGNISSANTI
VIA PALAZZUOLO
VIA DELLA SCALA
Chiesa di Ognissanti
PIAZZA OGNISSANTI
LUNGARNO AMERIGO VESPUCCI
PONTE AMERIGO VESPUCCI
Arno
LUNGARNO SODERINI
BORGO SAN FREDIANO
LUNGARNO GUICCIARDINI
VIA SANTO SPIRITO
PIAZZA CARLO GOLDONI
VIA DELLA VIGNA NUOVA
Basilica di Santa Trinita
PONTE ALLA CARRAIA
LUNGARNO CORSINI
VIA DE' TORNABUONI
VIA DEGLI STROZZI
PIAZZA DELLA REPUBBLICA
VIA DEL CORSO
Badia Fiorentina
VIA PORTA ROSSA
VIA DELLA CONDOTTA
VIA DE' CALZAIUOLI
PIAZZA DELLA SIGNORIA
PIAZZA SAN FIRENZE
Palazzo Vecchio
PIAZZA DEL LIMBO
PONTE SANTA TRINITA
LUNGARNO DEGLI ACCIAIUOLI
Galleria degli Uffizi
Museo Galileo
Basilica di Santa Maria del Carmine
Basilica di Santa Maria del Santo Spirito
PIAZZA SANTO SPIRITO
VIA MAGGIO
VIA DE' GUICCIARDINI
PONTE VECCHIO
LUNGARNO GENERALE DIAZ
Chiesa di Santa Felicita
COSTA SAN GIORGIO
LUNGARNO TORRIGIANI
VIA DE' BARDI
VIA DELLA CHIESA
VIA DE' SERRAGLI
VIA ROMANA
PIAZZA DE' PITTI
Palazzo Pitti
Giardino Torrigiani
Giardino di Boboli
Forte di Belvedere
Giardino Bardini
VIA SAN GIORGIO

A   B   C

day, and check opening times for museums and churches before you visit to avoid disappointment. Reserve accommodations before you come, and don't plan to use Florence as a base for touring the rest of Tuscany.

Florence and Florentines

Florentines are Tuscans – generally restrained and rational, and less given to

fiery displays. They also are more reserved. Accustomed to huge numbers of visitors, they do not go out of their way to befriend tourists but are courteous and professional in their everyday dealings.

Florence at first glance is not as instantly appealing as Rome or Venice – let it grow on you and experience it as a living city, not merely as a vast treasure-house of art. Get away from the major sights and their crowds of sightseers, and explore the quieter areas, with atmospheric streets and traditional activities. Vary the artistic glories with a bit of hedonism, and take time to relax.

The best way to see Florence is on foot. Most of the main attractions are clustered together in the largely pedestrian central core, making walking easier (but watch out for enthusiastic scooter riders).

Eating in Tuscany

There are all types of restaurants in Florence, from fast-food joints to world-class establishments. Many are specifically aimed at tourists and have prominently displayed fixed-price (but mediocre) menus. To ensure a memorable meal, eat where the Italians themselves eat and be prepared to pay somewhat high prices. For a simple lunch, try a slice of fresh-baked pizza to go or a quick snack in a *vinaio* or *fiaschetteria*, traditional wine bars.

Food markets are particularly tempting, where you can put together the makings of a picnic – bread, salami, cheese, fruit and a bottle of wine. Tuscan food is simple and excellent, centered around basic ingredients such as olive oil, fresh vegetables and meat, with plenty of soups, superb pork dishes, grilled meats and vegetables. Bean dishes are especially popular (Tuscans are fondly nicknamed *mangiafagioli*, or "bean-eaters"). The most famous wine is Chianti, a delicious red wine, but look also for Brunello di Montalcino, a superb red from Tuscany.

Pucci, Gucci and More

Intriguing stores, markets and boutiques are scattered throughout the center of Florence. Shoes and leather goods are famous, as are fine china, exquisite bed and table linen, and jewelry. Designer-label fans can visit Pucci and Gucci on their home ground; other tempting gifts include glazed majolica pottery, marbled paper, prints and antiques.

Via de'Tornabuoni and surrounding streets house the most elegant stores; less expensive fashion is found around Piazza della Repubblica and Via dei Calzaiuoli, while jewelers line the Ponte Vecchio. There are many leather factory outlets near Santa Croce. Be sure to spend time browsing in a market; you'll find tempting food in the Mercato Centrale. Most stores will ship to the United States.

Festivals Galore

A summer visit is likely to coincide with one of the cultural festivals, the *Estate Fiesolana* or the *Maggio Musicale Fiorentino*, which run from May through August, with concerts, opera and ballet – often outdoors in an historic setting.

Excursions

Even if your time in Tuscany is limited, try to fit in an excursion outside Florence, viewing the timeless landscape en route to another of the region's superb historic towns. Possibilities include Pisa, Siena, San Gimignano and the wine country of Chianti, all easily reached by tour bus or public transportation. Nearer still lies Fiesole, a picturesque hill town just above Florence, the perfect escape from noise and heat.

Essential Information

Tourist Information

Go online at www.firenzeturismo.it or go to one of the city's tourist offices at: Piazza della Stazione 5; Via Cavour 1r; Piazza San Giovanni 1; Aeroporto Amerigo Vespucci, Peretola phones; www.ataf.net). Stamp tickets, as you board, in the orange box on the bus. Hail taxis at central locations, or call Radio Taxi FIRENZE 4242 (☎ 055 4242).

Urban Transportation

Buses, both regular and electric, run from Santa Maria Novella station all over town. Buy tickets (€1.20) before boarding: passes are available from machines and tobacconists and are valid for unlimited trips within a period of 90 minutes; a 24-hour (€5), a 3-day (€12) or a 7-day pass (€18), or an electronic Carta Agile (10 or 20 90-minute tickets), also are available. Maps and timetables can be found at the ATAF office (✉ Piazza della Stazione ☎ 800 424500 toll free or 199 104 4205 from cell

Airport Information

Most visitors use Pisa's Galileo Galilei Airport (☎ 050 849 111; 050 849 300 for flight information; www.pisa-airport.com), connected to Florence's Santa Maria Novella railroad station by bus or train services; travel time approximately 1 hour. The PisaMover automatic service connects the airport with Pisa Centrale railroad station. Florence Airport (Amerigo Vespucci Airport) is at Peretola (☎ 055 306 1830; www.aeroporto.firenze.it), 4 miles outside the city.

Climate – average highs and lows for the month

Jan.	Feb.	Mar.	Apr.	May	Jun.	Jul.	Aug.	Sep.	Oct.	Nov.	Dec.
10°C	12°C	15°C	18°C	23°C	27°C	31°C	30°C	26°C	21°C	14°C	10°C
50°F	54°F	59°F	64°F	73°F	81°F	88°F	86°F	79°F	70°F	57°F	50°F
1°C	2°C	5°C	7°C	11°C	14°C	17°C	17°C	14°C	10°C	5°C	2°C
34°F	36°F	41°F	45°F	52°F	57°F	63°F	63°F	57°F	50°F	41°F	36°F

Florence Sights

Key to symbols

➕ map coordinates refer to the Florence map on pages 302–303 💷 admission charge:
$$$ more than €10, $$ €5–€10, $ less than €5
See page 5 for complete key to symbols

Cappelle Medicee

The beautiful Cappelle Medicee (Medici Chapels) were built as the mausoleum for Florence's most powerful family.

The Sagrestia Nuova, built by Michelangelo between 1520 and 1534, contains some of his most powerful sculptures. Carvings of reclining figures representing *Night* and *Day* and *Dawn* and *Dusk* decorate the tombs of Lorenzo, duke of Urbino, and Guiliano, duke of Nemours. The fluid lines are a perfect foil for the austerity of the architecture.
➕ C3 ⊠ Piazza Madonna degli Aldobrandini 6
☎ 055 2388 602; www.cappellemedicee.it ⊙ Daily 8:15–6, Apr.–Oct.; 8:15–5, rest of year. Closed first, third and fifth Mon., and second and fourth Sun. of the month 🚌 14, 22, 31, 23, 71, C1 💷 $$

Duomo, Battistero e Campanile di Giotto

The Gothic Duomo (Cathedral) of Santa Maria del Fiore, the first domed structure erected in Europe since Roman times, was built between 1296 and 1436. Its austere interior, with a Paolo Uccello fresco, leads to the 463 steps to the top of Brunelleschi's Cupola (Dome).

The chief draw of the 11th-century marble Battistero (Baptistery) is the three sets of bronze doors, with their Old Testament scenes. Andrea Pisano cast the south pair in 1326, and they inspired Lorenzo Ghiberti to design the doors at the north and east in the 1400s.

The Campanile (Bell Tower), designed by Giotto, was built between 1334 and 1359. Its marble walls are decorated with superb relief sculptures. The 280-foot, 414-step climb offers lovely, if vertiginous, views over Florence.
➕ C3 ⊠ Piazza del Duomo ☎ Duomo and Campanile: 055 230 2885; www.ilgrande museodelduomo.it ⊙ Duomo: Mon.–Fri. 10–5, Sat. 10–4:45, Sun. 1:30–4:45 (closes Thu. at 4:30 p.m., Jan.–Apr. and Nov.–Dec.; 4 p.m. May and Oct.). Cupola: Mon.–Fri. 8:30–7, Sat. 8:30–5:40. Battistero: Mon.–Sat. 11:15–7 (first Sat. of the month 8:30–2), Sun. 8:30–2. Campanile: daily 8:30–7:30. Check website for daily updated information 🚌 23, 71, C1, C2 💷 Duomo free; Cupola, Campanile, Battistero $$

Galleria dell'Accademia

Founded as an art school in 1784, the Galleria dell'Accademia (Academy Gallery) today houses the world's most important collection of Michelangelo sculptures including *David*, a huge and technically perfect nude male figure and possibly the most famous in the history of sculpture. However, more moving by far are the other sculptures by the artist, particularly the four *Prisoners*, the figures struggling to break free from their block of marble.
➕ D4 ⊠ Via Ricasoli 58–60 ☎ 055 238 8609; www.galleriaaccademiafirenze.beniculturali.it. Advance online booking is advised ⊙ Tue.–Sun. 8:15–6:50 🚌 1, 7, 10, 20, C1 💷 $$

The frescoes decorating the Cupola of the Duomo were created by Giorgio Vasari and Federico Zuccari

Galleria degli Uffizi

Arguably the world's greatest collection of Renaissance paintings, the Galleria degli Uffizi (Gallery of the Offices) is housed in an elegant arcaded building that was designed initially by Vasari to house administrative offices – hence the name.

Here, in chronological order, are paintings representing the greatest names in art, among them Giotto, Paolo Uccello, Botticelli, Piero della Francesca, Leonardo da Vinci, Michelangelo, Raphael and Caravaggio. Many of the stunning artworks date from the 12th to 17th centuries.

Come early or late to avoid waiting in the longest lines, though the surprisingly small rooms are likely to be thronged with visitors.

🞧 C2 ✉ Loggiato degli Uffizi 6 ☎ 055 294 883; www.uffizi.it. Advance booking via this website is advisable 🕔 Tue.–Sun. 8:15–6:50 (occasionally stays open later in summer) 🚌 C1, C2 🍴 Café inside gallery 💲 $$$

Museo Nazionale del Bargello

Surrounding a lovely courtyard, in a building dating from 1255, the Museo Nazionale del Bargello (National Bargello Museum) houses Italy's finest collection of Renaissance sculpture. On the first floor there are displays of works by Michelangelo, Benvenuto Cellini, the flamboyant Giambologna and other late Renaissance artists, but the vaulted second-floor hall contains the museum's masterpieces. Here are Donatello's bronze of a vulnerable, and much revered, *David*, his exquisite *St. George*, and the superb Baptistery door reliefs showing *The Sacrifice of Isaac* by Lorenzo Ghiberti and Brunelleschi, made for a competition in 1401.

Upstairs you will find a collection of bright enameled terra-cottas created by the della Robbia family.

🞧 D2 ✉ Via del Proconsolo 4 ☎ 055 238 8606; www.bargellomusei.beniculturali.it 🕔 Daily 8:15–5; closed 2nd and 4th Sun. of the month, 1st, 3rd, and 5th Mon. of the month 🚌 23, 71, C1, C2 💲 $$

Museo di San Marco

Rebuilt in 1437, the convent attached to the church of San Marco, and beautifully decorated by Fra Angelico, is one of Florence's loveliest treasures. It's a peaceful religious house, where each monk's cell is adorned with a tiny fresco to aid prayer. The pilgrim's hall contains many paintings by Fra Angelico and his school, and additional works can be seen in the cloisters and also on the stairs. Here is, notably, the radiant *Annunciation*.

🞧 D4 ✉ Piazza San Marco 3 ☎ 055 238 8608; www.polomusealetoscana.beniculturali.it 🕔 Mon.–Fri. 8:15–1:50, Sat.–Sun. 8:15–4:50. Closed first, third and fifth Sun., and second and fourth Mon. of the month. Closed Jan. 6, Easter, Apr. 25, Jun. 2, Aug. 15, Nov. 1 and Dec. 8 and 26 🚌 7, 10, 11, 25, 32, C1 💲 $

Ponte Vecchio

This most photographed Florentine bridge, the Ponte Vecchio (Old Bridge), was built in 1345 to replace an earlier one. It has been lined with exclusive goldsmiths and jewelers' shops since 1593. Above it runs a corridor used by members of the Medici family to travel from the Pitti Palace to the Uffizi. The sole bridge across the Arno river in Florence not destroyed by the Germans in World War II, the Ponte Vecchio also survived the floods in 1966.

🞧 C2 ✉ Ponte Vecchio 🚌 C3, D

Santa Croce

This huge Franciscan church was built in 1294, but was badly damaged by the 1966 floods. Today it contains superb early frescoes telling the story of the Santa Croce (Holy Cross). Michelangelo is buried here, along with Ghiberti, Machiavelli and Galileo Galilei.

In the serene cloisters is a museum featuring Cimabue's famous *Crucifix*, and the Cappella dei Pazzi (Pazzi Chapel) by Brunelleschi.

🞧 E2 ✉ Piazza Santa Croce 16 ☎ 055 246 6105; www.santacroceopera.it 🕔 Mon.–Sat. 9:30–5, Sun. 2–5 🚌 14, 23, 71, C3 💲 $$ (includes entry to adjoining Museo dell'Opera di Santa Croce)

A Day in Florence

Many Florentines start working by 8 a.m., when food stores also open. Since many people live in centrally located apartments, visitors have the chance to see the neighborhoods waking up. Housewives go to market early, children walk to school and people pause for a quick bar breakfast on their way to work.

For the tourist in Florence an early start makes sense. Head straight for major sights such as the Galleria degli Uffizi, Galleria dell'Accademia, Duomo or Palazzo Pitti (Pitti Palace) while you're still fresh and before the big tour groups arrive. Most of the museums open at 8:30 a.m. and the churches earlier, so it's feasible to pop into a specially noted church first thing.

Pause mid-morning for a drink and a rest, but bear in mind that some attractions shut for several hours in the middle of the day, as do stores. It's a good idea to follow the siesta habit – a leisurely lunch and a quiet hour or so digesting all you've seen will leave you fresh for more touring in the late afternoon. Early evening is a popular time for Florentines to shop, and a good opportunity for you to track down that must-have leather bag, beautiful fabric, silk tie or marbled paper souvenir.

Florentines are back at work and out on the streets again some time after 4:30, looking rested, relaxed and ready for the rest of the day and evening. By 6:30 the town is thronged with well-dressed crowds, strolling, meeting friends and wholeheartedly enjoying the evening *passeggiata* through the streets of their beautiful city. Crowds thin out and shops close around 8:30, when people head home or to a restaurant for dinner, and there's a break before the evening's activities.

Florence has plenty of nightlife to choose from, with a wealth of cultural offerings such as theater, opera and classical music, movies, and numerous discos and bars with live music. The streets are busy well into the early hours – especially in the height of summer – with locals and foreigners alike enjoying the balmy night air.

Detail from *Madonna with Child and Angels* c.1455, by Fra Filippo Lippi, in the Uffizi Gallery

Naples

Vibrant, noisy, crumbling Naples (Napoli), the capital of southern Italy and one of Europe's most beautifully located cities, is light years removed in atmosphere from the prosperous north. The city epitomizes southern Italy: confusing, passionate, dirty and charming, redolent with a rich and complicated history that has physically shaped it and emotionally shaped its residents. Naples can feel alien and intimidating, but also inspires fierce loyalty as visitors are quickly won over by its exuberance, way of life, attractions and, above all, its people.

Old Town, Naples is a maze of narrow streets

The people of southern Italy are generally charming, warm and enthusiastic, and Neapolitans are no exception. They live at what appears to be a fever pitch of excitement and noise, which you'll notice on the street. You'll find people eager to help, and anxious for you to enjoy Naples. Authorities have encouraged citizens to welcome tourists, and have succeeded admirably.

Getting Around

Central Naples is best tackled on foot, as the traffic is so horrendous that any form of transportation can be excruciatingly slow. Much of what you'll want to see is walkable, and sights are grouped together in different areas, so take a bus or cable car to your general destination and then walk. Wandering around is an essential and fascinating part of the Naples experience, as the street life is lively and beguiling – but stick to well-frequented areas.

You'll want to travel down the coast to Pompeii and the Sorrento peninsula; both can be reached by train.

The best way to appreciate the beauty of Naples' spectacular setting on the bay is from the sea; you could combine a visit to the Sorrento peninsula with a boat trip to Sorrento or to the ravishing islands of Capri and Ischia.

Safety in Naples

The city authorities have done much to clean up Naples in every way, making it a much safer and more attractive city to visit. However, it is still wise to avoid the labyrinthine back streets, the docks and, at night, the railroad station. Avoid carrying a lot of cash, and be aware of pickpockets, particularly in crowded tourist areas.

Be careful when crossing the street: Neapolitan drivers often ignore pedestrian crossings, and unless you step off the sidewalk you could be stranded for what seems like hours. Scooters appear to come out of nowhere, and they frequently use the sidewalks or go against the direction of traffic.

Mediterranean Flavors

Neapolitan cooking ranks among the best in Italy, with a strong emphasis on the freshest fish and seafood, and local fruit and vegetables from the fertile volcanic soil of the hinterland. Flavors are intense, and the combination of ingredients unusual and interesting. There are pasta dishes with shellfish, grilled fish of all varieties, mozzarella cheese dripping with freshness, and numerous salamis, as well as some excellent local prosciutto.

Naples is the home of thin, tasty and crisp pizzas; they are always baked in wood-fired ovens, and can be eaten as a snack or light meal. Neapolitan cakes and pastries are famous and best enjoyed from a *pasticceria* (a specialist pastry and cake shop). Try honeyed *stuffoli*, iced chocolate *mustaccioli, zeppola* (doughnuts) and *sfogliatelle* filled with ricotta cheese. Don't miss out on the fantastic ice cream. Local wines to try are Lacrima Christi and Greco di Tufo. Be sure to sample Limoncello, a lemon-flavored liqueur, or delicious *mirtillo* (bilberry) and *finocchietto* (fennel) liqueurs.

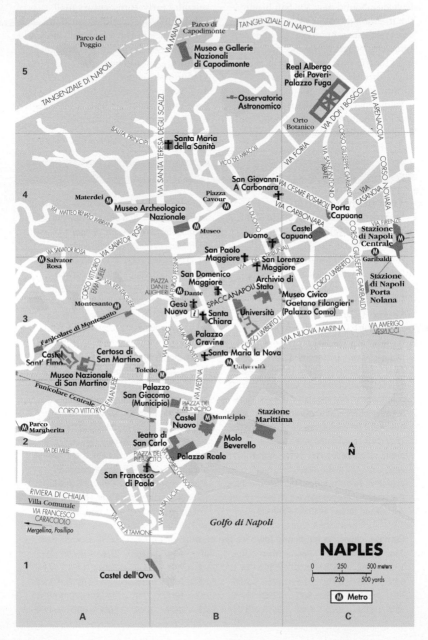

NAPLES

| 0 | 250 | 500 meters |
| 0 | 250 | 500 yards |

Ⓜ Metro

Shopping and Nightlife

Naples' upscale stores are clustered along the Via Toledo and the Via Chiaia, where you'll find outlets for Italy's top designers, as well as local stores selling fine leather goods, fashion and knitwear. Jewelers abound near Via San Biagio; the traditional best buys in Naples are coral necklaces, bracelets, earrings and cameo brooches. If you like antiques, head for Via Domenico Morelli, where stores specialize in 18th-century furniture and paintings.

Traditional nativity figurines are still made in the historic area around San Biagio, along with decorated masks and elaborately dressed dolls. Galleria Vanvitelli, in the Vomero district, is a useful shopping center, while downtown, you'll find a branch of the department store La Rinascente, and the Galleria Umberto I, an architecturally splendid early 20th-century mall.

If you like opera and classical music, a performance in the wonderful San Carlo opera house, the oldest working theater in Europe, should be high on your list. Traditional Neapolitan music is easy to find, and even the least tourist-oriented restaurants generally have musicians ambling through their premises serenading diners.

Essential Information

Tourist Information

Piazza del Gesù Nuovo 7 ☎ 081 551 2701; Via San Carlo 9 ☎ 081 402 394; Via Marino Turchi 16 ☎ 081 2400 911. Toll free information line (English) 800 134 034; www.infoturismonapoli.it

Urban Transportation

Neapolitan traffic makes any form of transportation slow, so it's best to walk if it's feasible. Longer distances can be covered by metro (subway), bus and *funiculari* (cable cars), all of which are slow. There are two types of *Giranapoli* tickets, valid for either 90 minutes or all day; they are interchangeable between buses, cable cars and the metro, and obtainable from tobacconists or newsstands. They must be validated in the special machines onboard buses; before boarding cable cars; and at the entrance to metro platforms. To travel around the bay, use the Circumvesuviana railroad, which leaves from the railroad station on Corso Garibaldi every half-hour and takes an hour to reach Sorrento, its farthest point. You also can travel to Sorrento by ferry or hydrofoil from the Mergellina or Molo Beverello docks; the same companies also serve Capri, Ischia and the other islands (www.caremar.it, www.alilauro.it, www.snav.it). There are taxi stands throughout the city, or you can call a cab (☎ 081 88 88 or book online at www.taxinapoli.it).

Airport Information

Naples' Capodichino Airport ☎ 081 789 6259 (for flight information see carriers' websites or go online to www.aeroportodinapoli.it, the main airport website), with internal and European flights, is northwest of the city center. The airport "Alibus" (☎ 0800 639 525, toll-free within Italy; www.anm.it) buses run at 20-minute intervals to the Stazione Marittima (port area) via Piazza Garibaldi (central station), daily 6 a.m.–11:30 p.m. Tickets cost €5.

Climate – average highs and lows for the month

Jan.	Feb.	Mar.	Apr.	May	Jun.	Jul.	Aug.	Sep.	Oct.	Nov.	Dec.
12°C	13°C	15°C	18°C	22°C	26°C	29°C	29°C	26°C	22°C	17°C	13°C
54°F	55°F	59°F	64°F	72°F	79°F	84°F	84°F	79°F	72°F	63°F	55°F
4°C	5°C	7°C	9°C	13°C	17°C	19°C	19°C	17°C	13°C	8°C	5°C
39°F	41°F	45°F	48°F	55°F	63°F	66°F	66°F	63°F	55°F	46°F	41°F

Naples Sights

Castel Nuovo

The five massive towers of the 15th-century Castel Nuovo (New Castle) dominate the Naples waterfront. A magnificent Renaissance gateway accesses the central courtyard, which is surrounded by buildings housing the Museo Civico (Civic Museum), the Gothic Sala dei Baroni (Barons' Hall) and the Cappella Palatina (Palatine Chapel), the only surviving part of a 13th-century building.

Nearby is the 17th-century Palazzo Reale (Royal Palace) and the San Carlo opera house.

B2 Piazza Municipio 081 795 7708; www.infoturismonapoli.it Mon.–Sat. 8:30–7 151, 154, C25 $$

Castel dell'Ovo

Encircled by the sea, the Castel dell'Ovo (Egg Castle), Naples' oldest castle, was built between the 9th and 16th centuries. Once run down, it is now restored and used for cultural events.

B1 Borgo Marinaro 081 795 4592 Mon.–Sat. 9–7:30, Sun. 9–2, Apr.–Oct.; Mon.–Sat. 9–6:30, Sun. 9–2, rest of year 140, R3; tram 1 Free

Certosa di San Martino

Visible from all over Naples is the hilltop complex of the Certosa di San Martino (St. Martin's Charterhouse), constructed mainly between the 16th and 18th centuries.

Highlights include the sumptuous baroque church, the arcaded Chiostro Grande (Main Cloister) and the lavish Quarto del Priore (Prior's Quarters).

Don't miss the exhibition of *presepi* (crib figures), a charming collection of figures and everyday objects fashioned for Christmas cribs in the 19th century, in the Museo Nazionale di San Martino (San Martino National Museum).

Pompeii

The 20,000 inhabitants of Roman Pompeii enjoyed a civilized lifestyle in their prosperous city, with fine civic amenities, temples, public baths, and housing suitable for every taste and pocket. The one drawback was Pompeii's location on the slopes of Vesuvius, an active volcano. In AD 79 its worst eruption occurred, engulfing the city and many of its inhabitants in a thick layer of pumice and volcanic ash. For nearly 1,700 years Pompeii remained buried, perfectly preserved beneath a hard layer of volcanic debris. About 1750 it was rediscovered, excavations started, and gradually the ruins emerged. It's a complete small city that can be explored like any other, wandering the streets and visiting the sites that appeal. It has the main features of every Roman city – the forum, two theaters, an amphitheater, a sports stadium and symmetrical streets laid out in a grid pattern.

Start at the forum and walk through the paved streets, looking into houses and shops. Track down the covered market, the bakery, the laundry and the taverns, some advertising bargain prices on the outside walls. The House of the Vetii, with its lovely garden and frescoed dining room, is a highlight, as is the House of the Tragic Poet, whose owners had a portrait mosaic of their dog displayed by the front door with "cave canem" (beware of the dog) carefully inscribed at the entry.

See page 285, D2 Pompeii 081 857 5347; www.pompeiturismo.it, www.pompeiisites.org. Note: Advance booking online only Daily 9–7:30, Apr.–Oct.; 9–5, rest of year Circumvesuviana or Trenitalia train to Pompeii Scavi station. Trenitalia–Pompeii (stop at Villa dei Misteri) SITA Napoli–Salerno (stop at Piazza Esedra); CSTP No. 4 Salerno Self-service restaurant and bar outside forum $$$ Last admission 90 minutes before closing

Naples' waterfront gem, Mergellina, lies at the foot of Posillipo Hill

➕ A3 ✉ Largo San Martino 5 ☎ 081 229 4502; www.polomusealecampania.beniculturali.it
🕐 Thu.–Tue. 8:30–7:30 🚇 Montesanto; funicular Petraio 🚌 V1 💷 $$ (price may differ due to temporary exhibitions)

Mergellina

This picturesque waterfront area, traditionally the fishermen's quarter, is a delightful place to stroll. Fishing boats and island ferries still operate here.
➕ Off map at A1 ✉ Mergellina 🚇 Mergellina
🚌 140, C12, C18, R7

Museo Archeologico Nazionale

This National Archeological Museum houses one of the world's most important collections of Classical sculpture, as well as mosaics, gems, glass, silver and Egyptian antiquities.

Finds from Pompeii are here; don't miss the graceful fresco portrayal of Flora. The *Farnese Hercules* and *Farnese Bull* are equally impressive; the *Bull* is the largest Classical sculptural group to have survived, dating from 200 BC.
➕ B4 ✉ Piazza Museo Nazionale 19 ☎ No phone; www.museoarcheologiconapoli.it 🕐 Wed.–Mon. 9–7:30 🚇 Museo, Piazza Cavour 🚌 168, 178, C53, C63, R4 💷 $$; $$$ during exhibitions

Museo e Gallerie Nazionali di Capodimonte

Built in the 18th century as a palace and museum, and surrounded by a wooded park, Capodimonte has been restored and rearranged. Don't miss Masaccio's *Crucifixion*, which is the star of the Renaissance painting collection, and the majolica and porcelain exhibits, much of it made by the Capodimonte factory.
➕ B5 ✉ Parco di Capodimonte, Via Miano 2
☎ 081 749 9111; www.museocapodimonte.beniculturali.it 🕐 Museum: Thu.–Tue. 8:30–7. Baroque rooms: 10 a.m., noon, 3 and 5 p.m. Park: daily 7:15 a.m.–7:30 p.m., Apr.–Sep.; 7:15–6, Oct., Feb.–Mar.; 7:15–5, Nov.–Jan. 🚌 168, 178, C63, R4
💷 Museum $$$; park free 🚌 Shuttle Bus, hourly from Piazza Trieste via Piazza Municipio, Piazza Dante and Museo Archeologico $$$ (includes museum entrance)

Spaccanapoli

Spaccanapoli is the name of the string of atmospheric, traffic-free streets slicing through Naples' historic core. Its length is lined with monuments from many different eras that help to piece together the city's story – medieval, Renaissance and baroque *palazzi*, churches and civic buildings.
➕ B3 ✉ Via Benedetto Croce, Via San Biagio dei Librai

Excursion to Capri

A favorite with the Roman emperors, Capri has been a tourist hot spot for many years. This tiny island, with its lovely scenery and crystal-clear waters, now welcomes more than 2 million visitors annually.

You can travel from Naples' Mergellina or Molo Beverello docks by ferry or hydrofoil, a trip that takes between 50 and 90 minutes. Spectacular views open up back to the city and across to Mount Vesuvius as you approach the hills of the Sorrento peninsula, with the island of Capri lying off its tip. Boats dock at Marina Grande, the island's main harbor.

The charm of Capri lies in the combination of lovely scenery, picturesque villages and a holiday atmosphere. The two main settlements are Anacapri and Capri; their whitewashed houses and narrow, winding streets are crammed with boutiques, outdoor cafés and lively fish restaurants. There are boat trips to Capri's most famous sight, the Grotta Azzurra (Blue Grotto), a spectacular sea cave filled with glorious refracted turquoise light. Another highlight is the beautiful Villa San Michele in Anacapri. Built in the late 19th century by Swedish physician Axel Munthe, this dreamlike villa is filled with Classical statues. There also is a peaceful green garden, and from its shady pergola you can enjoy some of the island's loveliest views.

Walk to the ruins of Villa Jovis, Emperor Tiberius' clifftop villa, from which he allegedly threw his enemies into the sea. Or stroll to a lookout above the Faraglioni, a cluster of offshore rocks, for beautiful sea views.

Capri ✚ See page 285, C2 🖉 Tourist offices: Banchina del Porto, Marina Grande ☎ 081 837 0634; Piazza Umberto I, Capri ☎ 081 837 0686, Via G. Orlandi 59, Anacapri ☎ 081 837 1524; www.capritourism.com 🚌 From Marina Grande to Marina Piccola, Capri and Anacapri 🚢 Ferry operator: Caremar from Molo Beverello, Naples. www.caremar.it (ticket sales and information online and by calling 001 1000 0000). Hydrofoil operators: Caremar, from Molo Beverello: www.caremar.it (ticket sales and information online and by calling 081 1896 6690); SNAV, from Mergellina (☎ 081 428 5555; www.snav.it) and Alilauro (☎ 081 497 2222; www.alilauro.it) also operate services to the islands and points in the Bay of Naples
Blue Grotto ☎ 081 837 7714; www.motoscafisticapri.com 🕓 Daily 9–1 hour before dusk 🚢 From Marina Grande 💲 $$$ (tickets available online via the website)
Villa San Michele, Anacapri ☎ 081 837 1401; www.villasanmichele.eu 🕓 Daily 9–6, May–Sep.; 9:30–5 Apr. and Oct.; 9–4:30 Mar.; 9–3:30, rest of year 🚌 From Capri 💲 $$
Villa Jovis ☎ 081 837 0381; www.polomusealecampania.beniculturali.it 🕓 Daily 10–4, Mar.–Dec. 🚌 From Capri 💲 $$

Large boats and sailing craft at Marina Grande, Capri, on the Bay of Naples

Venice

No matter how many pictures or films you've seen, nothing can prepare you for the impact of the real Venice (Venezia), one of the world's most captivating cities. Whether it's sparkling in late spring sunshine or shrouded in winter mist, it will enchant you in every way.

Tackling Venice

When you first arrive in Venice, don't head straight for the main sights (which will invariably be packed); take time to get a feel for the city, either from the vantage point of a ferry or by strolling the streets and squares.

As for accommodations, luxury hotels lining the Grand Canal (Canal Grande) are clearly the optimum choice, but

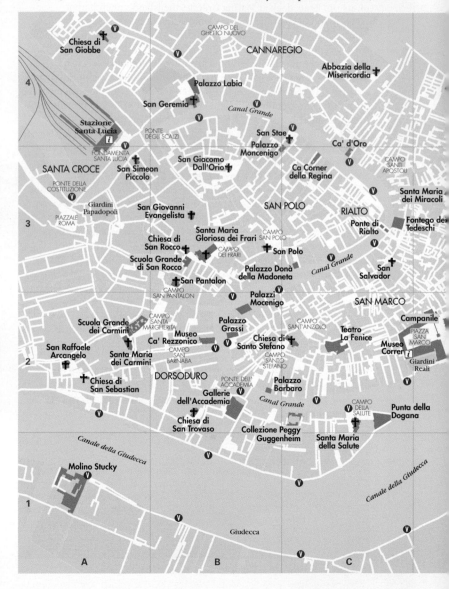

there are many with great charm elsewhere. The *sestieri* (city areas) of Dorsoduro, San Marco, Castello and San Polo are among the nicest parts of the city to stay. Avoid the area around the train station, which is noisy and less attractive and under no circumstances should you stay in Mestre, which is an industrial sprawl across the causeway on the mainland.

Accept that you will do a great deal of tiring walking around the city, and come prepared with comfortable shoes. Make a point of working out your daily itinerary; shortcuts across the city save valuable time. Main routes are clearly marked along the streets by yellow signs.

There are numerous tour options; if time is short these can be helpful, and you'll have the benefit of English-speaking guides.

Venetian Glass, Velvet Slippers

The city's main fashion and leather stores cluster along the Calle dei Fabbri, the Frezzeria and the so-called Mercerie, a district made up of the streets connecting Piazza San Marco with the Rialto area.

Glass is a true Venetian specialty, made for centuries on the island of Murano. Marbled paper, made here for centuries, is another good buy, and Venetian masks make wonderful souvenirs. Other typical products are velvet slippers in jewel-bright colors or a real gondolier's hat; you'll find one at Emilio Ceccato, near the Rialto.

Festivals

Carnival lasts for the 10 days before *martedì grasso* (Shrove Tuesday), the start of Lent, when thousands of people wearing costumes parade the city streets.

The summer sees several ancient festivals, most notably the feast of *La Sensa*, when the mayor and his entourage sail out into the lagoon in the state barge and enact a symbolic

Gondolas

The shiny black gondola – symbol of Venice – is a shallow-draft vessel propelled by a single oarsman, the gondolier, who stands at the back of the boat. A ride in a gondola is a great Venetian experience for many visitors, but it is expensive and normally follows a set route. Be sure to ascertain what you're getting before you set out.

marriage to the waters. This is followed in July by the *Festa del Redentore*, a thanksgiving festival for deliverence from the plague.

During the *Regata Storica* in September, there are races of spectacular decorated craft, manned by crews in period dress down the Grand Canal.

Essential Information

Tourist Information

Call center ☎ 041 2424 (for all information) San Marco 71f; Aeroporto Marco Polo; Stazione Santa Lucia; Piazzale Roma inside Autorimessa Comunale (municipal garage) www.veneziaunica.it
The Venezia Unica App is a free, downloadable interactive App that is constantly updated and packed with information.

Urban Transportation

If you arrive by car, you must leave the vehicle in one of the parking lots on the outskirts of the city. The parking at Piazzale Roma is the nearest to the city center. Venice's public transportation system is operated by ACTV (office at Piazzale Roma, ☎ 041 2424; actv.avmspa.it) and uses two types of boats – *vaporetti* (big and slow) and *motoscafi* (small and fast). All are numbered on the front of the boat and follow set routes. *Vaporetti* boats leave from *pontile* (floating docks), which are clearly marked with service numbers and a route map. As the same numbers head in two directions, check that you are going the right way before you board. Tickets (€7.50), valid for 100 minutes, can be bought at the *pontile* or at shops showing the ACTV sticker. Save money by buying 24-, 48-, 72-hour and 7-day tickets (€20, €30, €40 and €60 respectively). All tickets must be scanned by the iMob reader before boarding. There is a limited night service on most routes. *Vaporetti* stops are marked on the Venice city map with a "V." *Taxi motoscafi* (water taxis) are fast and expensive; they can be hailed on various canals, or Motoscafi ☎ 041 2406712 (Mon.– Fri. 9–6), 041 2406746 (Sat., Sun. 9–6), 041 522 2303 (Sat., Sun. 6 p.m.–9 a.m.); www.motoscafivenezia.it. Gondolas can penetrate even the narrowest canals, but are very expensive. The seven *traghetti* (ferries) crossing the Grand Canal at various points are useful. These ferries are old gondolas and are marked with green signs. Pay as you board, and be aware that it is customary to stand.

Airport Information

Venice's Marco Polo airport (☎ 041 260 9260; www.veniceairport.it) is 5 miles from the city center on the northern edge of the lagoon, and handles both domestic and international flights. For city connections take an ATVO shuttle bus (www.atvo.it) or ACTV bus No. 5 from the terminal to the Piazzale Roma at the edge of the city, where the road ends, and then connect with your hotel by *vaporetto* (water bus). The transfer takes 20 minutes by ATVO bus and 25 minutes by ACTV bus; ACTV tickets (€3) must be purchased from the office inside the airport arrivals terminal before boarding; buy ATVO tickets (€8) either inside the terminal or from the machines at the bus stop. An *Alilaguna* (boat) leaves from the dock outside the terminal for San Marco and the Lido; transfer time is around 50 minutes (www.alilaguna.it). The fastest way to reach the city is by water taxi; they leave from the dock outside the terminal and take 20 minutes to reach the center, but are expensive.

Climate – average highs and lows for the month

Jan.	Feb.	Mar.	Apr.	May	Jun.	Jul.	Aug.	Sep.	Oct.	Nov.	Dec.
5°C	8°C	12°C	17°C	21°C	24°C	27°C	26°C	23°C	18°C	12°C	8°C
41°F	46°F	54°F	63°F	70°F	75°F	81°F	79°F	73°F	64°F	54°F	46°F
0°C	2°C	5°C	9°C	13°C	17°C	19°C	18°C	16°C	12°C	7°C	3°C
32°F	36°F	41°F	48°F	55°F	63°F	66°F	64°F	61°F	54°F	45°F	37°F

Venice Sights

Venice

Key to symbols

➕ map coordinates refer to the Venice map on pages 314–315 💳 admission charge: $$$ more than €10, $$ €5–€10, $ less than €5

See page 5 for complete key to symbols

gilded, is a perfect example of the finest Venetian-Byzantine architecture.

Behind the facade is a beguiling small museum with an impressive *St. Sebastian* by Andrea Mantegna and a lovely *Madonna* by Giovanni Bellini, as well as sculptural fragments, bronzes and tapestries. All pieces are arranged in rooms around the *palazzo's* central *portego*, or inner courtyard.

➕ C4 ✉ Calle di Ca' d'Oro 3932, off Strada Nova ☎ 041 520 0345; www.cadoro.org; www.polomusealeveneto.beniculturali.it ⏰ Tue.–Sun. 8:15–7:15, Mon. 8:15–2 🚢 1 💳 $$$

Basilica di San Marco

The Basilica di San Marco (St. Mark's Basilica) is a fusion of western and Byzantine styles and is connected to the Doge's Palace. Dating from 1094, it stands on the site of the ninth-century basilica built to house the body of St. Mark.

On entering, admire the facade carvings, then proceed inside to take in the glittering mosaics and ornate marble pavements; the gem-encrusted altar screen, the Pala d'Oro, a masterpiece of Gothic-Byzantine goldsmith art; and the third-century bronze horses, which once adorned the facade.

➕ D2 ✉ Piazza San Marco 1 ☎ 041 270 8311; www.basilicasanmarco.it ⏰ Mon.–Sat. 9.30–5, Sun. 2–4:30, mid-Apr. to Oct.; Mon.–Sat. 9.30–5, Sun. 2–5, Nov. to mid-Apr. 🚢 1, 2, 4.1, 4.2, 5.2, N 💳 Basilica free; Loggia $$; Pala d'Oro $

Ca' d'Oro

The facade of the Ca' d'Oro (House of Gold), so called because it was once

Campanile

The graceful Campanile, Venice's tallest building, is just over 100 years old. The original bell tower, reputedly built in AD 912, collapsed in 1902, killing no one and leaving St. Mark's unscathed. A cry of *"Dov'era e com'era"* ("where it was and how it was") went up, and 10 years later a replica was completed. Take the elevator up for superb views – on a clear day you can see as far as the Alps.

➕ D2 ✉ Piazza San Marco ☎ 041 522 4064 ⏰ Daily 8:30 a.m.–9 p.m., late Apr.–Oct 15; 9–5:30, early April; 9:30–5:30, Nov.–Mar. Closed 3 weeks in Jan. 🚢 1, 2, 4.1, 4.2, 5.1, 5.2, N 💳 $$$

Canal Grande

The allure of the Canal Grande (Grand Canal), Venice's magical highway, never

The beautiful loggia of the Ca' d'Oro (House of Gold) overlooks the Grand Canal

seems to fade. Almost 4 miles long, with an average depth of 16 feet, it divides Venice in two and is crossed by four bridges. The canal is lined with palaces and churches, built over the course of 500 years.

By day many boats chug up and down the canal; at night it epitomizes romance, with reflected lights twinkling on the water. Take a No. 1 or No. 2 water bus *(vaporetto)* from stops on the Grand Canal.

➕ B2, B4, C2, C3, C4 🚉 1, 2, N

Collezione Peggy Guggenheim

American heiress Peggy Guggenheim's modern art collection (on public view since 1951) is installed in her 18th-century *palazzo* on the Grand Canal. Here you'll find works by Pablo Picasso and Salvador Dalí and fine examples of paintings by Jackson Pollock and Mark Rothko. The garden makes a wonderful background for some Henry Moore sculptures and Marino Marini's *Angel of the Citadel*.

➕ C2 ✉ Palazzo Venier dei Leoni, Dorsoduro 701 ☎ 041 240 5411; www.guggenheim-venice.it
🕐 Wed.–Mon. 10–6 🚉 1, 2 🚶 $$$

Gallerie dell'Accademia

Allow plenty of time to admire the masterpieces in the Gallerie dell'Accademia (Academy Galleries), the finest collection of Venetian painting in the world. Arranged chronologically, the gallery's 24 rooms contain masterpieces such as Giorgio Giorgione's enigmatic *Tempest*, Giovanni Bellini's luminous *Virgins*, and superb works by Mantegna. Don't miss the dramatic *Translation of the Body of St. Mark* by Jacopo Tintoretto and Paolo Veronese's sumptuous *Feast in the House of Levi*.

Among other highlights not to miss are two cycles of paintings; *The Miracle of the True Cross,* which had several contributors, while the *Life of St. Ursula* is by Vittore Carpaccio.

➕ B2 ✉ Campo della Carità 1050 ☎ 041 522 2247, reservations: 041 520 0345; www.gallerieaccademia.it

🕐 Tue.–Sun. 8:15–7:15, Mon. 8:15–2. Last admission 45 minutes before closing 🚉 1, 2 🚶 $$$

Palazzo Ducale

The huge Gothic complex of the Palazzo Ducale (Ducal Palace) was the seat of Venice's government, where the Council of Ten met, ambassadors were received and the Doge (Duke) held councils of state. The present building dates from the 15th century, with later alterations following two fires in the 1500s.

The marked route leads through rooms to the vast Sala del Maggior Consiglio (Great Council Chamber), dominated by Jacopo Tintoretto's *Paradiso*, the world's largest oil painting.

The famous Ponte dei Sospiri (Bridge of Sighs) spans a canal to the right of the *palazzo*'s waterfront facade.

➕ D2 ✉ Piazzetta San Marco ☎ 041 271 5911; www.visitmuve.it 🕐 Daily 8:30–7, Apr.–Oct. (last admission at 6 p.m.); 8:30–5:30, rest of year 🚉 1, 2, 4.1, 4.2, 5.1, 5.2 🚶 $$$. A Museum Pass giving access to all Musei Civici (Civic Museums) is the best value

Piazza San Marco

The only piazza in Venice (all the others are officially *campi*) is thronged around the clock with strolling and chattering crowds. Go early or late to avoid the worst crush, and marvel at the harmony of this wonderful open space.

Highlights here are the 15th-century Torre dell'Orologio (Clock Tower) and its zodiac clock, the graceful architecture of the Libreria Sansoviniana (Sansoviniana Library), and the two columns near the waterfront, topped by the lion of St. Mark and St.Theodore with his crocodile emblem.

➕ D2 ✉ Piazza San Marco 🚉 1, 2, 4.1, 4.2, 5.1, 5.2, N

Punta della Dogana

The Punta della Dogana (Custom's House Point) contains warehouses built between 1677 and 1682; customs officials once operated from the buildings. In 2007 François Pinhault, a wealthy collector, leased the neglected

The Sala del Maggior Consiglio (Great Council Chamber) in the Palazzo Ducale

buildings and spent €20 million on their restoration and conversion into a contemporary art space. The superb interior is a fitting backdrop to showcase cutting-edge 21st-century art, which reflects Pinhault's own taste.

🔳 C2 ⊠ Campo di Salute, Dorsoduro 2 ☎ 041 240 1308; www.palazzograssi.it ⏰ Wed.–Mon. 10–7 🚤 1, 2 💷 $$$

Rialto

Throughout the Middle Ages the Rialto was Europe's financial and banking center; the name had the same connotations as does Wall Street now. Today you can admire the bridge and browse in Venice's food markets, one of the city's great sights. Wander through the fruit and vegetable stalls, but leave time to enjoy the scents and sights of the fish market, full of the day's catch.

🔳 C3 ⊠ Rialto 🚤 1, 2

San Giorgio Maggiore

To visit the superb Palladian church of San Giorgio Maggiore (St. George the Great), whose serene bulk dominates the view of St. Mark's Basin, you must take a water bus across the canal of

St. Mark's to St. George's Island. Built by Andrea Palladio in 1559, the church embodies order, grace and harmony. Take the elevator up the campanile (bell tower) to enjoy extensive views across to the Doge's Palace and the Campanile of San Marco.

🔳 D1 ⊠ Campo San Giorgio, Isola di San Giorgio Maggiore ☎ 041 522 7827 ⏰ Mon.–Sat. 9–7, Sun. 9–10:30 and 12–7 p.m., Apr.–Oct.; Mon.–Sat. 8:30–6, Sun. 8:30–10:30 and 12–6, rest of year. Closed during services 🚤 2 💷 Free; $$ (elevator to campanile)

Santa Maria dei Miracoli

The jewel-like church of Santa Maria dei Miracoli (Our Lady of the Miracles) was built around 1480 to house an image of the Madonna credited with reviving a man who spent half-an-hour at the bottom of the Giudecca canal. Pietro Lombardo, who adorned the face of his church with colored marble and porphyry rock, created the harmonious interior as a frame for fine sculpture and beautiful carvings.

🔳 D3 ⊠ Campo dei Miracoli ☎ 041 275 0462 ⏰ Mon.–Sat. 10:30–4:30 🚤 1, 2 💷 $ or $$$ "Chorus Pass" for entry to Venice's minor churches (www.chorusvenezia.org)

The church of Santi Giovanni e Paolo

Santa Maria della Salute

During the 1630 plague the Senate promised to build a church in honor of the Virgin if she would save the city. The pestilence passed, an architect was commissioned and the great dome of Santa Maria della Salute (Our Lady of Health and Salvation) rose at the entrance to the Grand Canal. An outstanding skyline feature, the interior has fine sculptures and paintings.

✚ C2 ✉ Campo della Salute 1 ☎ 041 241 1018 🕐 Daily 9–12 and 3–5:30 🚋 1

Santa Maria Gloriosa dei Frari

Santa Maria Gloriosa dei Frari (Glorious Virgin Mary of the Brothers), a lofty Franciscan church, is the final resting place of Titian and the composer Claudio Monteverdi. Built about 1250, it contains Titian's great *Assumption*, hung over the high altar, and his *Madonna of Ca' Pesaro*. Best of all in the right transept of the church is Giovanni Bellini's *Madonna and Child with Saints* tryptych, considered to be one of the world's finest paintings.

✚ B3 ✉ Campo dei Frari ☎ 041 275 0462; www.chorusvenezia.org 🕐 Mon.–Sat. 9–6, Sun. 1–6 🚋 1, 2 🎫 $ (accepts multi-church "Chorus Pass" ticket $$$)

Santi Giovanni e Paolo

More than 20 of Venice's doges are buried in the Gothic church of Santi Giovanni e Paolo (St. John and St. Paul), rising majestically on one side of its *campo* (square). The square's focal point is the great equestrian statue of Bartolomeo Colleoni, a 15th-century Venetian army officer who left his wealth to the Republic in return for a monument. The 13th-century church contains many tombs, their monuments representing the best of Venetian medieval sculpture, and some lovely paintings, including Giovanni Bellini's *St. Vincent Ferrer*.

✚ D3 ✉ Campo SS Giovanni e Paolo ☎ 041 523 5913; www.basilicasantigiovanniepaolo.it 🕐 Mon.–Sat. 9–6, Sun. 12–6; closed during services 🚋 4.1, 4.2 🎫 $

Scuola di San Giorgio degli Schiavoni

Carpaccio painted one of the city's most delightful picture cycles between 1502 and 1508 for the headquarters of Venice's Dalmatian, or Slavic, community – the Scuola di San Giorgio degli Schiavoni (School of St. George of the Slavs). He used Dalmatia's patron saints, St. George, St. Tryphon and St. Jerome, as his inspiration. Highlights are *St. George Slaying the Dragon* and *St. Augustine in his Study*, with his dog.

✚ E3 ✉ Calle dei Furlani 3259/a ☎ 041 522 8828; www.scuoladalmatavenezia.com 🕐 Mon. 2:45–6, Tue.–Sat. 9:15–1 and 2:45–6, Sun. 9:15–1 🚋 1, 2, 5.2 🎫 $$

Scuola Grande di San Rocco

In 1564 the brotherhood of St. Roche ran a competition to choose an artist to decorate the walls of the Scuola Grande di San Rocco (Grand Meeting Halls of the Confraternity of St. Roche). Tintoretto (real name Jacopo Robusti) won, and spent 23 years working on a stupendous cycle of 54 paintings, including the wonderful *Crucifixion*. New Testament scenes line the walls of the ground floor's main hall. The many works on the staircase are by other artists.

✚ B3 ✉ Campo San Rocco ☎ 041 523 4864; www.scuolagrandesanrocco.it 🕐 Daily 9:30–5:30 🚋 1, 2 🎫 $$$

The Lagoon Islands

You can spend a delightful day exploring some of the islands in the lagoon. Most visitors opt for Murano, famous for its glass; Burano, with its lace-making; or Torcello, a virtually uninhabited island with an ancient cathedral and church. Guided excursions run to all three, but a more flexible option is to take the No. 12 boat, which leaves from the Fondamenta Nuove and takes around 40 to 50 minutes to reach Burano and (with a shuttle boat) Torcello.

Murano: Venetian glass has been made here since 1291, when the furnaces were moved away from the city to avoid the constant danger of fire. A visit to the fascinating Museo del Vetro (Glass Museum) will give you an idea of glassblowers' skills through the ages. Murano also has two exquisite churches: San Pietro Martire, which contains a glowing altarpiece by Giovanni Bellini; and Santi Maria e Donato, a beautiful 12th-century basilica with a colonnaded exterior apse and fine mosaics on its walls and floor.

Burano: Here, colorful canalside houses, narrow streets and sun-splashed squares are as picturesque as anything in Venice itself. This is still a fishing community, with a robust workaday atmosphere, and you'll see moored fishing boats and nets drying in the sun. Local women have always been skilled lace-makers, and you can admire the fragility of their exquisite work in the Lace Museum (Museo del Merletto).

Torcello: This is one of the most evocative and magical places in Venice. The sleepy island, with its overgrown canals and green fields, was the lagoon's first settled area, and once had fine buildings and palaces. A combination of the build up of silt and outbreaks of malaria caused its 12th-century decline. Today the only remaining signs of its past importance are the Cathedral of Santa Maria Assunta and the adjacent church, Santa Fosca. The cathedral's main glories are two 12th-century mosaics, which completely cover the apse and the opposite rear wall. High above the seventh-century altar is a lovely depiction of the Byzantine Madonna and Child, its poignant beauty highlighted by the simple gold background, while the graphic *Judgment* scenes make a telling contrast. The campanile (tower) is solid and square. The nearby church of Santa Fosca, with its arcaded porch, is lovely in its own way.

Modern glassware is still made on the island of Murano

Luxembourg

Introduction and Map 324

Timeline 326

Survival Guide 327

City of Luxembourg 328

Feature: Fortress Luxembourg 333

Hotels and Restaurants 483

Essential Information 542

Opposite: Medieval tranquility on the Alzette river in the district of Grund, City of Luxembourg

Luxembourg

Luxembourg

Luxembourg lies at the heart of the European landmass. It is a minuscule country, measuring 51 miles from north to south and a mere 35 miles from east to west. Belgium lies to the north and west, France to the south and Germany to the east. Because of its attractive financial laws and constitutional stability, it has become a center of European politics and finance.

And despite a rather turbulent history, Luxembourg retains its independence and sovereignty; it is a true survivor of the Continent's stormy past.

Luxembourg Landscapes

Luxembourg is a Grand Duchy, the only one in the world, with the city of Luxembourg as its main focus, although its rural areas are remarkably varied for such a small country.

They include part of the delightful Ardennes region, the hilly area that lies across the northern third of Luxembourg

The view from Château de Bourscheid

and extends into Belgium. The Ardennes have a distinctive landscape of forested plateaus sliced through by deep valleys that are drained by beautiful rivers, and fairy-tale castles crown heavily wooded bluffs. At Vianden, a medieval castle, one of the Grand Duchy's finest historic sites, dominates the landscape. The equally magnificent Bourscheid Castle stands guard high above the winding Sûre river. At Clervaux, the castle is matched in impact by the red-roofed Benedictine Clervaux Abbey, which stands amid the wooded heights above the beautiful town.

At the southern edge of the Ardennes, in the area where the hills meet the flatter, more fertile land known as Le Cour du Bon Pays, or "The Good Land," lies the picturesque little town of Diekirch. Only a short distance southwest is Ettelbrück, where there is a monument to General George S. Patton Jr. and the General Patton Memorial Museum containing many personal items from his life.

The most southerly part of Luxembourg is the country's economic powerhouse. Here in the "Good Land" are farms and orchards, forests and even more castles. In fact, the lovely valley of the Eisch river is known as the Vallée des Sept Châteaux (Valley of the Seven Castles).

Farther south from the city of Luxembourg is Les Terres Rouges, or

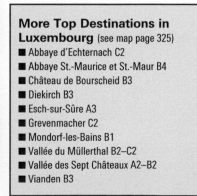

More Top Destinations in Luxembourg (see map page 325)
- Abbaye d'Echternach C2
- Abbaye St.-Maurice et St.-Maur B4
- Château de Bourscheid B3
- Diekirch B3
- Esch-sur-Sûre A3
- Grevenmacher C2
- Mondorf-les-Bains B1
- Vallée du Müllerthal B2–C2
- Vallée des Sept Châteaux A2–B2
- Vianden B3

"The Land of the Red Rocks" around the towns of Dudelange and Pétange, home to much of the country's industry.

East of here is Mondorf-les-Bains, a fashionable spa town on the edge of the famous Moselle region. This area, running north to south along the border with Germany, is Luxembourg's wine-growing district, which has a heritage of more than 2,000 years.

Exploring the Country

You will find Luxembourgers are very cosmopolitan and friendly, and a large percentage of them speak English. The Grand Duchy has an excellent road system and distances are short between the many towns and villages, making independent travel a good option. There also are numerous day trips organized from the city of Luxembourg.

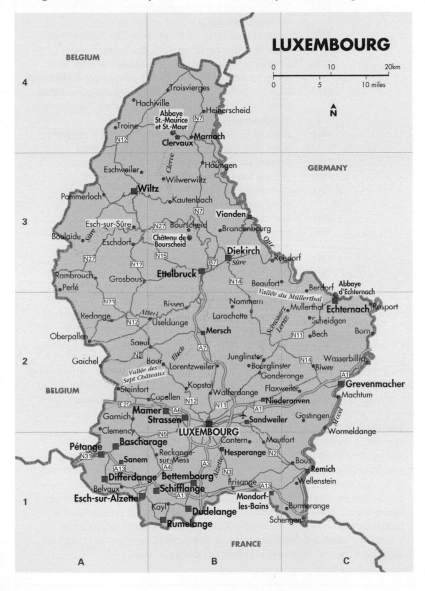

LUXEMBOURG

Timeline

AD 963	Count Siegfried of the Ardennes builds a castle called the Lützelburg ("Little Castle") on the Bock promontory.
1354	Luxembourg becomes a duchy.
1443	Philip the Good, Duke of Burgundy, conquers Luxembourg, which then becomes a province of The Netherlands.
1542	The city of Luxembourg is captured by the French.
1554	The Netherlands and Duchy of Luxembourg pass into the hands of the Spanish Habsburgs.
1684	Troops of Louis XIV take the Luxembourg City. French military engineer Vauban carries out fortification works.
1815	Congress of Vienna establishes Luxembourg as a Grand Duchy within The Netherlands under the rule of the German Confederation.
1839	Under the terms of the Treaty of London, the western part of the Grand Duchy is ceded to Belgium: The rest of the Duchy becomes an independent state.
1867	Under the terms of the Second Treaty of London, Luxembourg's status as an independent and neutral state is affirmed.
1914	Germany occupies Luxembourg in World War I.
1940	Germany invades Luxembourg again in World War II.
1944	American troops liberate Luxembourg; Germany launches its "Ardennes Offensive." The Battle of the Bulge follows.
1945	Luxembourg becomes a member of the United Nations.
1947	Luxembourg joins Belgium and the Netherlands in forming Benelux, a trading and economic union.
1949	Luxembourg abandons neutrality and joins NATO.
1957	Luxembourg becomes a founding member of the European Economic Community (now known as the European Union).
1984	Luxembourgish becomes the national language.
1994	City of Luxembourg declared a World Heritage Site by UNESCO.
2002	Luxembourg introduces the euro as the national currency.
2009	The Cabinet announces a relaxation of banking secrecy laws to help cut global tax evasion.
2015	A referendum in Luxembourg results in a "no" to voting rights being given to foreign nationals, who make up over half the population.
2017	Wide-reaching and popular social reforms are announced.

Luxembourg: the Great Survivor

Luxembourg, with its long history at the heart of Europe, has secured a major part in the working of the European Union. The country today is a constitutional monarchy ruled by HRH Grand Duke Henri, who heads a Cabinet of ministers appointed from an elected Chamber of Deputies. Consensus politics is used in Luxembourg's government, and coalitions of more than one party usually hold power. On the international front, Luxembourg is home to, among others, the General Secretariat of the European Parliament, the European Court of Justice, the Court of Auditors, the European Bank of Investment, the Plenary Hall of the European Parliament and several Directorates of the European Commision – all of which are based in the city of Luxembourg's Centre Européen (European Center).

Sidewalk cafés amid the downtown bustle of the city of Luxembourg

Survival Guide

■ The *Schueberfouer* (☎ 4796-4294; www.fouer.lu), one of Europe's largest city fairs, takes place from mid-August to early September.

■ Most shops in the city of Luxembourg are closed on Monday until noon and may close Tuesday through Friday between noon and 2 p.m., but often stay open until 8 p.m. on Thursdays.

■ The Luxembourg Card, available for 1, 2 or 3 days (€13/ €20/ €28 respectively), offers free public transportation and access to over 60 museums and attractions. Also family cards (2–5 persons) for 1, 2 or 3 days cost €28/€48/€68 respectively. Go to https://www.visitluxembourg.com/en/luxembourg-card.

■ Enjoy an evening in the Grund district. With its bars and restaurants, it has a different ambience from the city center, known as the Ville area.

■ Earthenware bird whistles (*peckvillerchers*) are a popular present given on Easter Monday, when their sound fills the air.

■ The city of Luxembourg has countless world-renowned designer shops along Grande-Rue and rue Philippe II. You'll find exquisite and tempting treats in Leonidas, the renowned Belgian chocolatiers.

■ Luxembourg City has some great markets. There's a huge flea market on the second and fourth Saturday of each month at Place d'Armes, while the Glacismart, Parking Hall Victor Hugo, is the place to buy local products. Glacismart is held every third Sunday of the month, March through July and also September through November.

■ If you travel in the Moselle wine-producing region, enjoy some of Luxembourg's dry white and sparkling vintages, such as the subtle Rivaner; Pinot Blanc to go with fish dishes; or the strong Pinot Gris to complement a meal of *judd mat gaardebounen* (roast, smoked pork).

■ Children will love the Jardin des Papillons (exotic butterfly garden; route de Trèves, Grevenmacher ☎ 75 85 39; www.papillons.lu ⓓ Daily 9:30–5, April to October. ⓦ $$$). Youngsters also will enjoy Parc Merveilleux (route de Mondorf, Bettembourg ☎ 51 10 48-1; www.parc-merveilleux.lu ⓓ Daily 9:30–6, early April to mid-October. ⓦ $$$), at the southern tip of Luxembourg, where there are attractions, animal enclosures and children's games of all types.

City of Luxembourg

The city of Luxembourg is known as the landlocked "Gibraltar of the North" because of its once-fortified location. It is set above the cliffs that flank the canyon-like valleys of the Alzette and Pétrusse rivers. Today, the city of Luxembourg is more fairy tale than fortress. The old city, especially, is a pleasing mix of the past and present. Its elegant towers, spires and turrets, and its walls of golden sandstone helped win Luxembourg the UNESCO designation of World Heritage Site in 1994.

The steep-sided plateau on which Luxembourg stands explains its origins. The Romans first set up camp here. They had one eye on military control and the other on the advantages of a strategic trading position at the crossroads of northern Europe. In AD 963, Count Siegfried of the Ardennes built a castle on the narrow Bock promontory above the Alzette river.

Over the next 900 years, Luxembourg evolved into one of the mightiest fortifications in Europe. In 1867, the terms of the 1839 Treaty of London were applied, and Luxembourg became a neutral state. The military fortress was dismantled and the encircling walls were replaced by wide outer boulevards.

Ville and Gare

The several distinct areas of the city of Luxembourg are the city center, known as Ville, perched on the high plateau above the Pétrusse and Alzette river valleys; and the more modern district, known as Gare, south of the river. The two are connected by bridges across the Pétrusse valley; the main ones are the pont Adolphe and the pont Viaduc, the latter known locally as Passerelle. Below the cliffs lies Grund, the main part of the city's valley settlements.

The area around the railroad station is emphatically modern. Buses leave regularly from outside the station and take you to place E.-Hamilius, on the western side of Ville. From here a short walk east along rue de la Poste leads to the central square of place d'Armes.

At the east end of place d'Armes is the handsome City Hall (Palais Municipal, or Cercle). Nearby in place Guillaume II is the Luxembourg City Tourist Office. Ask here for details on guided tours and the LuxembourgCard (available also as a free downloadable App), which is good for one, two or three days and costs €13, €20 and €28 respectively. The LuxembourgCard gives free entry to more than 60 museums and attractions, plus reductions to 10 other sites and free use of public transportation in the Grand Duchy (www.visitluxembourg.com/en/luxembourg-card).

The maze-like streets of the Old Town (Vieille Ville, see page 332) and the complex of steps and terraces that connect plateau and valley floor make Luxembourg a very walkable place.

Conversation and Music

The place d'Armes is a public space shaded by lime trees. In summer it is filled with the chairs and tables of the surrounding restaurants and cafés, where you can enjoy the hum of relaxed conversation and the music of regular concerts on the nearby bandstand.

All around the place d'Armes are the city's pedestrian-only shopping streets. To the north is Grande-Rue, known locally as Groussgaass, the city's main shopping street. Here, and in the

---

A Lift in Luxembourg

You can reach the riverside Grund district in the Alzette valley by public elevator from place du St.-Esprit, near the intersection with boulevard F. D.-Roosevelt. Look for the glass-fronted elevator shelter in the corner of the place du St.-Esprit. The elevator takes you to a tunnel that emerges at montée du Grund.

adjoining streets of rue Phillipe II and rue des Capucins, are fashion boutiques, as well as good restaurants and cafés. Stop for coffee at Namur, on the corner of Grande-Rue and rue des Capucins. At the east end of Grande-Rue look for the fountain known as Hämmelsmarsch, "The March of the Sheep."

Exploring Historic Luxembourg
To reach historic Luxembourg, leave the southeast corner of place d'Armes, where a covered passage leads between bookshops and into the large place Guillaume II. A colorful flower and vegetable market is held here on Wednesdays and Saturdays.

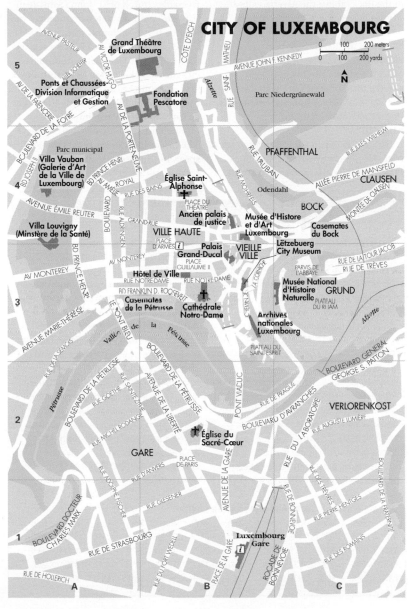

From here you can quickly reach the Palais Grand-Ducal (see page 332) on rue du Marché-aux-Herbes.

Behind the palace lies the Old Town. Look for rue de l'Eau, with its cluster of restaurants known as Îlot Gastronomique. Then head down rue Sigefroi to the stunning viewpoint of the Bock, above the Alzette valley.

From here you can see the famous pont Grande-Duchesse Charlotte, known as the Red Bridge because of its color. It connects the city center plateau with the Kirchberg plateau and the ultramodern European Center (Centre Européen), home of numerous European Union institutions (see page 326).

Visit the famous Bock Casemates (see page 331), the maze of underground tunnels in the cliffs, and then walk the Chemin de la Corniche, the terrace that leads south above the Alzette valley.

Discover the valley district of Grund, a riverside haven of well-preserved old houses, restaurants and taverns. From here you can turn left and wander along the paths and terraced lanes of the Alzette to reach the 17th-century riverside church of St. John (Saint-Jean Baptiste), with its rich baroque altar and famous Black Madonna statue.

The city center (Ville) is more relaxed than other European cities, although city life is sophisticated in its restrained way. Fine music can be enjoyed at the city's Grand Théâtre de la Ville de Luxembourg, Philharmonie Luxembourg and Music Conservatory. The top fashion stores of Grande-Rue speak for themselves, and Ville restaurants are excellent.

Essential Information

Tourist Information

Luxembourg National Tourist Office
6 rue Antoine de Saint-Exupéry
☎ 42 82 82 1; www.visitluxembourg.com
Luxembourg City Tourist Office
30 place Guillaume II, Luxembourg City
☎ 22 28 09; luxembourg-city.com

Urban Transportation

Buses are the main form of public transportation in the city of Luxembourg (a tram line is under construction). Visitors will probably require the service only between the airport or the railroad station and the city terminus at place E.-Hamilius as the city is largely pedestrian-only and most places are within walking distance. A flat fare of €2 is valid for 2 hours or you can buy a pack of 10 tickets for €16. Buses run daily from 5 a.m.–midnight. For information ☎ 24 65 24 65; www.autobus.lu. Taxis are expensive, but can be hired by calling City Taxis Centrale ☎ 48 00 58; www.citytaxis.lu.

Airport Information

Luxembourg's Findel Airport (☎ 2464-0; www.lux-airport.lu) is located 4 miles east of the city of Luxembourg. Public bus No. 16 runs every 10–15 minutes (30 minutes on Sundays) between the airport and the city center and railroad station (journey time is 25 minutes, fare €2, plus €2 for baggage, which can be refused during peak periods if too bulky). Taxis between the airport and city are expensive (around €30) ☎ 48 00 58; www.citytaxis.lu.

Climate – average highs and lows for the month

Jan.	Feb.	Mar.	Apr.	May	Jun.	Jul.	Aug.	Sep.	Oct.	Nov.	Dec.
3°C	4°C	9°C	14°C	18°C	21°C	23°C	22°C	19°C	13°C	7°C	4°C
37°F	39°F	48°F	57°F	64°F	70°F	73°F	72°F	66°F	55°F	45°F	39°F
-2°C	0°C	2°C	4°C	8°C	11°C	13°C	12°C	10°C	6°C	3°C	0°C
28°F	32°F	36°F	39°F	46°F	52°F	55°F	54°F	50°F	43°F	37°F	32°F

City of Luxembourg Sights

> **Key to symbols**
> ✚ map coordinates refer to the Luxembourg map on page 329 🎟 admission charge: $$$ more than €4, $$ €2–€4, $ less than €2
> See page 5 for complete key to symbols

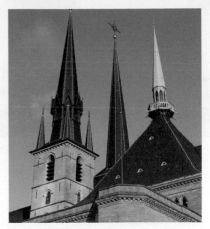

The steeples of Cathédrale Notre-Dame

Casemates de la Pétrusse

The great cliffs of the Pétrusse and Alzette valleys are honeycombed with tunnels, stairways and chambers called the Casemates, hollowed out of rock during the 17th and 18th centuries. Originally the network of Casemates measured over 14 miles and accommodated thousands of soldiers. There was room for the stabling of their horses, and for all the garrison supply services.

Today about 10 miles of the Casemates survive. Two sections, the Casemates du Bock (Bock Casemates) and the Casemates de la Pétrusse (Pétrusse Casemates), are open to the public in summer (see also Fortress Luxembourg, page 333).

Casemates de la Pétrusse ✚ A3 ✉ place de la Constitution ☎ 22 28 09 (4796-2709 for guided tours) 🕐 Daily 11–4, Jun.–early Sep.; Wed.–Sun. 11–4, Apr.–May 🚌 All city center buses 🎟 $$

Casemates du Bock ✚ C4 ✉ montée de Clausen ☎ 22 28 09 (4796-2709 for guided tours) 🕐 Temporarily closed 🚌 7, 9 🎟 $

Cathédrale Notre-Dame

The steeples of the 17th-century Cathédrale Notre-Dame (Cathedral of Our Lady) form a striking part of the city's skyline. Inside, the high altar is a shrine to Our Lady, "Comforter of the Afflicted." Stone steps lead to the crypt; at the rear, two bronze lions guard the barred entrance to the burial chamber of the grand-ducal family. A sarcophagus lies in a dark blue marble setting.

✚ B3 ✉ rue Notre-Dame ☎ 46 20 23 🕐 Mon.–Sat. 10–12 and 2–5:30, Sun. 2–5:30, except during services 🚌 No buses in city center 🎟 Free

Lëtzebuerg City Museum

The renamed (2017) Musée d'Histoire de la Ville de Luxembourg (Luxembourg City History Museum) is a superb must-see venue in the city of Luxembourg. Take care in some rooms where sunken channels containing hidden lighting run around the edges of the room. The museum is located in four old 17th-, 18th- and 19th-century, six-story town houses. This is a sophisticated, interactive museum; visitors are given a card to operate audiovisual displays and touch screens that explain the city's history from the 10th century to the present day. Follow the room numbers counterclockwise, and do not miss a trip in the glass elevator that transports you through many layers of Luxembourg's history as well as its architecture.

✚ B3 ✉ 14 rue du St.-Esprit ☎ 47 96 45 00; www.citymuseum.lu 🕐 Tue.–Sun. 10–6 (also Thu. 6–8 p.m.) 🚌 No buses in city center 🍴 Café 🎟 $$$

Musée National d'Histoire Naturelle

The Musée National d'Histoire Naturelle (National Museum of Natural History),

The magnificent Palace of the Grand Dukes is on a city street

or Natur Musée (Nature Museum), is in the Grund area, below the cliffs.

The museum is housed in the old Hospice of St. John, later a women's prison, and the building's splendid entrance survives. It features interactive activities of a geological and geographical nature, plus information on the local flora and fauna of the surrounding landscapes.

✚ C3 ✉ 24 rue Münster ☎ 46 22 33 1; www.mnhn.lu 🕐 Tue.–Sun. 10–6 (also Tue. 6–8 p.m. free) 🚌 14, 23 🍴 Café 💶 $$$

Palais Grand-Ducal

The Palais Grand-Ducal (Palace of the Grand Dukes), the official residence of Grand Duke Henri of Luxembourg, is on rue du Marché-aux-Herbes. The building is a much-renovated and extended replacement of a medieval town hall, which was destroyed in a fire in 1554. The 16th-century Spanish rulers of Luxembourg rebuilt it 20 years after the fire, and you can see the architectural influences of southern Spain in its Renaissance facade.

The interiors are exquisite, especially the Main Hall, the King's Room and the Banqueting Hall.

✚ B3 ✉ 17 rue du Marché-aux-Herbes 🕐 Guided tours run Tue.–Thu. 2:30–5, Sat. 10–11, mid-Jul. to Aug. English-language tours only Mon.–Fri. 4:30. Contact the Luxembourg City Tourist Office for details (☎ 22 28 09) 🚌 No buses in city center 💶 $$$

Vieille Ville

The city of Luxembourg Vieille Ville (Old Town) lies between the rear of the Palais Grand-Ducal and the Bock promontory. The Old Town comprises a small area, lying within narrow streets and squares such as rue de l'Eau, rue de la Loge, rue du Rost and the Marché aux Poissons (Fish Market).

The feeling of medieval Luxembourg is palpable here, although today's fine streets and buildings hardly reflect the widespread din and dirt of those days. Back then, the market was the heart of the community just outside the castle walls.

Down rue Sigefroi from the Marché aux Poissons is Église Saint-Michel (St. Michael's Church; open daily 10–5, except during religious functions; admission free). It is the oldest church in the city and is built on the site of the 10th-century castle church, but its oldest surviving parts date from the 17th century. The church's baroque altar is superb, and there is a wonderfully vivid carved oak pietà.

✚ B3

Villa Vauban (Galerie d'Art de la Ville de Luxembourg)

The elegant Villa Vauban (Luxembourg City Art Gallery) stands in City Park, on the foundation of the former Vauban Fort. The gallery has an excellent permanent collection of the works of Dutch and Flemish masters and of later European painters, and hosts many temporary exhibitions.

✚ A4 ✉ 18 avenue Emile Reuter ☎ 47 96 49 02; www.villavauban.lu 🕐 Mon., Wed.–Thu. and Sat.–Sun. 10–6, Fri. 10–9 🚌 21, 22, 29, 31 💶 $$$

Fortress Luxembourg

The history of the city of Luxembourg as a medieval fortress is fascinating. Ringed by impregnable cliffs on every side but the west, it was easy to secure the western approach by building a defensive wall. The narrow and rocky Bock promontory offered the first natural fortification.

It was here on this narrow shelf, 300 feet above the Alzette valley, that prehistoric settlers may have established a camp. The Romans built their own fortifications on the Bock and called it Castellum Lucilinburhuc. Then, in AD 963, Count Siegfried of the Ardennes built his castle and linked it to the main plateau by a drawbridge. This Lützelburg, the "Little Castle," gave the city and the country its present name.

By 1050 a defensive western wall nearly 30 feet high, with numerous towers and gateways, protected the castle and the community that was growing around it to the west. Soldiers and knights were billeted within Siegfried's fort, while traders and artists began to settle outside of its walls. This then gave the first impression of an upper and a lower city area, until the 12th century when stone ramparts were built to define the whole city.

In 1554 a massive explosion of stored gunpowder destroyed much of the settlement. New fortifications were built during a period of Spanish rule. They included excavation of the Pétrusse Casemates (Casemates de la Pétrusse, see page 331); the Bock Bastion; and the ramparts known today as the Corniche and dubbed the "Balcony of Europe" because of the spectacular views.

In the late 17th century Vauban, the French military engineer, reshaped and extended the ramparts. In the 18th century the Austrians extended them once more and excavated the Bock Casemates (Casemates du Bock, see page 331). Such was the strategic importance of Luxembourg as a fortification that all buildings on the Bourbon Plateau, where Gare (the modern town) now stands, were built of wood so that they could be quickly destroyed before an attack on the fortress, thus robbing the enemy of any cover.

On May 11, 1867, Luxembourg became an independent state. As part of the agreement, and after nearly a thousand years, the city's fortifications were dismantled or destroyed. At that time, the fortress walls enclosed an area to the west that was larger than the city.

What remains today are the Casemates, the retaining walls of the cliffs and ruins concentrated on the cliff edges, all adding to the city's already spectacular position. City boulevards and parkland lie where great walls and towers once protected the western approach.

The Bock Casemates above the Alzette river and alongside St. John's Church in the Grund

The Netherlands

Introduction and Map 336

Timeline 340

Survival Guide 341

Amsterdam 342

Feature: Amsterdam's Canals 348

The Hague 350

Feature: Delft 355

Hotels and Restaurants 484

Essential Information 546

Opposite: This historic windmill in Zaanse Schans outdoor museum is one of several on the site

The Netherlands

The Netherlands is a country where freedom has come with responsibility and hard work. It is a country where the word "land" means something special – a valuable resource won from the sea. For, in literal terms, when you walk on dry land in The Netherlands, your head is barely above sea level in some places, and well below it in others. Amsterdam itself is 10 feet below sea level.

Dutch Icons

To the outside world, the enduring image of The Netherlands is of a land unremittingly flat, crisscrossed by canals and dotted with windmills. Popular imagination conjures up pictures of clogs, cheese and swaths of brightly colored tulips. Then there is Amsterdam, the lively, lovely and evocative capital, seen by many as a slightly wicked city.

The Netherlands is, of course, a far more complex and fascinating entity than such assumptions imply. Although the country is often known as Holland, this name actually only relates to the country's heavily populated western

Buildings along Prinsengracht Canal, Amsterdam

provinces of Noord (North) and Zuid (South) Holland. These provinces contain the main cities, such as Amsterdam, Rotterdam and The Hague (Den Haag), known collectively as the Randstad, or "Ring Town."

Compared with this heavily urbanized area, The Netherlands' other provinces offer the visitor a remarkably diverse landscape and regional cultures that will correct any misconception that the country is homogeneous.

Land from the Sea

The Netherlands is a small country, around 16,500 square miles in area. Its eastern neighbor, Germany, is nine times larger. To the south lies Belgium, once part of the United Provinces of The Netherlands (see page 54) but an independent nation since 1830. To the north and west of The Netherlands lies the North Sea, and it is with this near neighbor that the Dutch have their most pressing relationship. You will not be too aware of the sea when you're in Amsterdam or The Hague. You will need to go north to Noord-Holland and Friesland, or south to Zeeland, to fully appreciate the astonishing control over their watery environment that the Dutch have engineered.

For the definitive story of land reclamation, visit the fascinating Zuiderzeemuseum in Enkhuizen or travel across the Afsluitdijk, a 20-mile dam that seals the great inland lake of IJsselmeer and connects Noord-Holland to Friesland.

You could go south to Zeeland, a glittering mosaic of water within a vast web of land. There you'll want to visit the Delta Expo at Neeltje Jans to learn about the Delta Plan, a massive engineering program. This system of huge dams and movable barriers was built after the storm-driven North Sea breached the existing dykes during a high spring tide in 1953, killed more than 1,800 people and devastated the countryside.

Exploring Inland

Beyond these water lands – and beyond
the great dunes and beaches of the
North Sea coast, and the neon-bright
lights of downtown Amsterdam – lie the
delights of the landlocked Netherlands.

In the south, Limburg is known as the
Dutch "hill country." In the province
of Noord-Brabant, the De Kempen
region's landscape of sandy heath and
woodland is a very different image from
that of the "flat" Holland most people
envision. You can explore Gelderland
meadows and orchards; the serene

**More Top Destinations in
The Netherlands**

- Arnhem B2
- De Hoge Veluwe B2
- Delta Expo A2
- Edam B3
- Enkhuizen B3
- Haarlem B3
- Het Loo B3
- Heusden B2
- Keukenhof B3
- Maastricht B1
- Orvelte C3
- Rotterdam A2
- Scheveningen A2
- Utrecht B2
- Zwolle C3

THE NETHERLANDS

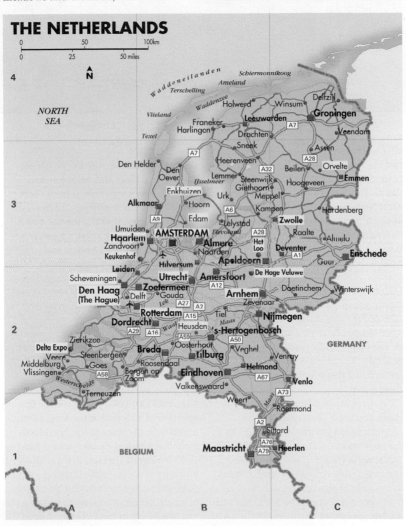

De Magere Brug (The Skinny Bridge) over the Amstel opens to allow a barge to pass through

villages and waterways of Overijssel; and the moorlands and flower-filled bogs of Drenthe, so beloved by Vincent van Gogh. They all add to the variety of rural Netherlands. In the north country in Groningen, the quintessential Dutch images of windmills, clogs and flat green landscapes reassert themselves. In neighboring Friesland you will find another country altogether, a province with its own language and distinctive cultural heritage.

Reaching these districts is not difficult since the public transportation system in The Netherlands is efficient and generally inexpensive. Most places are within a three-hour train ride of Amsterdam.

Excellent bus services run between cities, and there is an extensive bus network linking towns and villages in the provinces.

Driving in rural areas is convenient and reasonably straightforward, but in urban areas it can be stressful. Regular ferry services connect the mainland with the islands farther afield.

The Dutch

Generally speaking, the Dutch people are self-confident and accomplished, qualities that have evolved from their history and surroundings. Although they could easily boast of the way in which their environment has been mastered, they are refreshingly modest and restrained. Once the ice is broken, however, people are enthusiastic and friendly, and show tolerance and mutual respect for others.

Pancakes and Beer

Contemporary Dutch cuisine, especially fish dishes, is fast reversing the view that Dutch food is dull. In larger cities – especially in Amsterdam and The Hague – Holland's colonial past has left a fine tradition of Indonesian cooking. Most hotels have plentiful buffet breakfasts, including smoked meats, pickled herring and a variety of cheeses. For a traditional lunch try *erwtensoep*, a satisfying soup of peas and pork, accompanied by a hunk of crusty bread; or *uitsmijter*, an open sandwich of ham with cheese, topped

(molasses) or *poedersuiker* (powdered sugar). If you're on the move, street stalls also serve a smaller type of pancake, *poffertjes*.

Beer is the most popular drink. Dutch beers tend to be lighter, although you will know that you are drinking something substantial when you sample *Pils* in a Dutch "brown café" – a traditional bar. An excellent and popular light beer is Grolsch, often drunk with meals as a replacement for wine. Heavier Belgian beers also are available, as is *jenever*, a grain spirit. *Oude jenever* is the sweetest; *jonge* is for the stronger palate. These and vintage gins and liqueurs can be enjoyed in a *proeflokaal*, or "tasting house."

Porcelain and Jewelry

Some stores in Holland are closed all day Sunday and on Monday morning, but many open every day, and stores in the larger cities usually stay open late one night a week. Cities such as Amsterdam and The Hague have a variety of international clothing stores, but the real shopping experience is in the antiques and craft districts, looking for such Dutch specialties as jewelry and porcelain. In the provinces, look around and you will find some excellent regional buys.

with a fried egg. For dinner have a *hutspot* stew of vegetables, smoked bacon and meat; or *stampott*, mashed potatoes and vegetables with smoked sausage or bacon. For more exotic experiences, eat Indonesian specialties, especially *rijsttafel* ("rice table"), or any of several dozen other spiced, sauced, tangy, exquisite dishes. For sweets try *pannekoek*, pancakes with *stroop*

Blue-and-white Delft ceramics are known throughout the world

Timeline

AD 50	Iron Age Frisian and Batavi tribes settle in present-day Netherlands.
8th century	The Frankish Empire rules the Low Countries.
12th century	Herring fishermen settle at the mouth of the Amstel river, later site of Amsterdam.
1519	Charles V is crowned Holy Roman Emperor; the Low Countries come under Habsburg rule.
1566–67	Repression by Spain leads to lengthy struggle against Spanish control, known as the Dutch Revolt or Eighty Years War.
1579	Formation of Republic of the United Provinces of The Netherlands.
1602	Formation of United East India Company; "Golden Age" of Amsterdam as an affluent world trading center lasts for most of the 17th century.
1815	Northern and southern Netherlands become a united kingdom after fall of Napoleon.
1831	Southern Netherlands becomes independent as Belgium.
1914–18	The Netherlands remains neutral during World War I.
1940	Germany invades The Netherlands; Amsterdam liberated in 1945.
1947	Formation of Benelux Trade Treaty between Belgium, The Netherlands and Luxembourg.
1957	The Netherlands signs up as a founding member of the European Economic Community (now known as the European Union).
1980	Queen Beatrix is crowned.
2002	The Netherlands adopts the euro as its official currency.
2004	Queen Mother, Juliana, dies at the age of 94.
2010	Dissolution of the Netherlands Antilles. Caribbean islands of Bonaire, Sint Eustatius and Saba become special municipalities of the Netherlands.
2011	Range of new restrictions imposed on cannabis "coffee shops" in the Netherlands.
2013	Queen Beatrix abdicates on April 30, 2013. The successor to the throne is her son, crowned King Willem-Alexander of Orange.
2017	A parliamentary general election results in the VVD (Liberal) party winning most seats but not a majority. A coalition government must be formed with several political parties.
2019	Special events take place across the country to commemorate the 350th anniversary of artist Rembrandt's death.

Tulips

Tulips are a universal symbol of the country. They also are part of the Dutch flower trade, which accounts for 55 percent of the world market in exported flowers. In the 17th century the importation of tulip bulbs from Turkey led to "tulip mania;" during the 1630s, single bulbs sold for thousands of florins. The tulip has been a major focus of Dutch flower growing since, although carnations, roses and chrysanthemums outsell tulips today. The great floral explosion is in late April, when the fields just inland from the west coast are vibrant with color. Visit the 79-acre Keukenhof Gardens at Lisse, north of Leiden, for floral extravaganzas and about seven million spring-flowering bulbs from about mid-March to late May.

Tulips at Keukenhof Gardens; this 79-acre park is situated between The Hague and Amsterdam

Survival Guide

■ Large cities have regulated routes for pedestrians, cyclists, trams and automobiles. Next to the sidewalk there may be a bicycle lane. Always remember that bicycles approach silently, and always check to your left. Beyond the bicycle lane you may find a second sidewalk, then a tram track, then the main thoroughfare for buses and automobiles. This sequence is the same on both sides of the road. Remember that trams also approach quietly from the left.

■ There are few public restrooms, and those that exist are not known for their cleanliness. Railroad and bus stations, restaurants and the bigger cafés have public bathrooms with attendants. You are expected to pay about 50 cents to €1 to use them.

■ Eating out in The Netherlands is considered a fashion event as much as an eating experience. The Dutch tend to dress up a little when going out for a meal, although attitudes have become more relaxed.

■ You may tip for good restaurant service (restaurant bills include a service charge). Always tell the waiter that you're tipping them, and the amount; don't leave a cash tip on the table when you leave.

■ You may be tempted to sample raw herring. Follow local custom: Dip the herring in a bowl of diced onions, hold it by its tail, tip your head back, and savor.

■ For tasty snacks, try the always-available *patat* (french fries) with mayonnaise or spicy sauce dips; *kroketten*, small rolls of meat filling covered in bread crumbs and fried; and pickled herring or smoked eel. *Broodjes* are baguettes filled with smoked sausage, spicy meat and cheeses.

■ If you buy a present in a shop, especially chocolates, tell the assistant that it is a present and it will often be carefully wrapped in gift paper.

■ If you buy Delftware porcelain, make sure the trade name has a D, and buy from reputable outlets only.

Amsterdam

Amsterdam's past, canals and decorative buildings have all combined to make it one of the most exciting and seductive capitals in western Europe.

The city began life in the 12th century, when fishermen built a dam across the mouth of the Amstel river and settled nearby in wooden houses. Amsterdam developed on reclaimed land around a network of canals. By the end of the 17th century the city was the world's leading commercial port, its success based on entrepreneurial skills.

For most of the 18th century Amsterdam prospered – until its ships lost command of the seas to England. The city became the capital of The Netherlands in 1814. During World

War II, Amsterdam was occupied by the Germans. Since then its history has been characterized by consolidation, urban maturity and social liberalism – influences that have produced the vigorous and tolerant city of today.

First Impressions

Most visitors arrive by train at Amsterdam's Centraal Station, a smoothly run modern complex within a handsome 1880s neoclassic building. A helpful tourist information office (see Essential Information, page 344) is just outside the train station.

In front of the station is busy Stationsplein, a mix of tramline, bus track, bicycle lane and pedestrian concourse, with added passenger traffic heading to the subway station (45 feet underground). Straight ahead lies Damrak; watch out for traffic on this very busy street, and always wait patiently for the green light to show at pedestrian crossings.

A Cultural and Liberal City

Amsterdam's liberal traditions are apparent in the notorious Red Light District (De Wallen), located mainly between Warmoesstraat and Oudezijds Achterburgwal. Be advised – do not take photographs of prostitutes' booths. Be on the lookout for pickpockets.

The city also is notorious for its "coffee shops," where hashish and marijuana are sold for personal use to adults aged 18 and over. No alcohol is served but many offer a food menu. *Eetcafés*, on the other hand, are conventional cafés where coffee is served. "Brown cafés" (*bruine cafés*) are traditional bars where liquor is sold.

All this alternative culture is a minor aspect of the larger Amsterdam, a sophisticated city and a working community. There are peaceful canals and shaded, cobbled streets lined with narrow gabled houses. It's a flower-filled

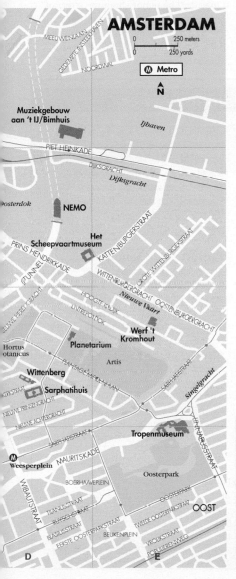

AMSTERDAM

0 — 250 meters
0 — 250 yards

Ⓜ Metro

N

Muziekgebouw aan 't IJ/Bimhuis

IJhaven

PIET HEINKADE

DIJKSGRACHT

Dijksgracht

Oosterdok   NEMO

Het Scheepvaartmuseum

PRINS HENDRIKKADE

(TUNNEL)

KATTENBURGERSTRAAT

WITTENBURGERGRACHT OOSTENBURGERGRACHT

HOOGTE KADIJK

ENTREPOTDOK

Nieuwe Vaart

Werf 't Kromhout

Hortus otanicus   Planetarium

Artis

Wittenberg

Sarphatihuis

Singelgracht

Tropenmuseum

Ⓜ Weesperplein   MAURITSKADE

Oosterpark

BOERHAAVEPLEIN

WIBAUTSTRAAT

OOST

BEUKENPLEIN

D   E

Supporting the City

Amsterdam is built on hundreds of thousands of pilings that have been driven through the surface layers of soft peat to rest soundly on hard sand. The 17th-century Royal Palace (Koninklijk Paleis, see page 346) on the Dam rests on 13,659 wooden pilings. Concrete pilings sunk to 65 feet have replaced the original ones.

city of exhilarating art museums, glorious civic buildings, medieval churches, quality stores, superb restaurants and entertaining street life.

Getting to Know Amsterdam

Purchase one of the "I Amsterdam City Cards" (valid for one, two, three or four days) for free or reduced admission to over 50 museums and attractions, unlimited use of the city's tram, bus and metro systems for the duration of the card, a free canal tour and various discounts, giveaways and offers. For a taste of the city's canal culture, take a trip on a Museum Line boat. You can do the whole 90-minute route or hop on and off at major museums along the way. Walking tours show you the city's architecture, history, art and special neighborhoods.

Amsterdam is a rewarding city to explore by foot. Enjoy street theater on Leidseplein, or walk in the footsteps of Rembrandt through the Jewish Quarter. The major shopping street of Kalverstraat leads to the busy open space of Spui, or try wandering down to the daily Bloemenmarkt (Flower Market) along the Singel canal.

Essential Information

Tourist Information

VVV (Vereniging Voor Vreemdelingenverkeer) Amsterdam Tourist Office
Stationsplein 10 (opposite Centraal Station entrance)

Holland Tourist Information (HTI), Amsterdam Airport Schiphol (arrival hall 2)
For general tourist information:
☎ 020 702 6000; www.holland.com, www.iamsterdam.com

Urban Transportation

Trains run from Centraal Station (central railroad station), Stationsplein. GVB Amsterdam is the public transportation authority. Amsterdam's metro (subway) mainly serves suburban areas, but also a few important points in the city center. Metro stations are marked with an "M" on the city map. There is a station and information desk at Centraal Station. For information on all public transportation within The Netherlands

☎ 0900 9292 (daily 7 a.m.–9 p.m.) or 0900 8011 (Mon.–Sat. 9–7); www.gvb.nl or www.9292.nl. Taxis are expensive, but can be picked up at the stands at Amsterdam Airport Schiphol, Centraal Station, Dam and Leidseplein. You also can call Taxicentrale (☎ 020 777 7777, 24-hour service; www.tcataxi.nl).

Airport Information

Amsterdam Airport Schiphol (☎ 0900 0141, or 020 794 0800 from outside The Netherlands; www.schiphol.nl) is 11 miles southwest of the city. Fast trains run from a station at the airport to Amsterdam's Centraal Station; the trip takes 15 to 20 minutes. The daily 24-hour service has trains departing every 15 to 30 minutes; hourly between 1 and 5 a.m. Check times at www.ns.nl. Buses run regularly to Amsterdam from Schiphol Plaza. Arrival hall 2 has post offices, banks, shops and a Holland Tourist Information office.

Climate – average highs and lows for the month

Jan.	Feb.	Mar.	Apr.	May	Jun.	Jul.	Aug.	Sep.	Oct.	Nov.	Dec.
5°C	5°C	9°C	11°C	15°C	18°C	20°C	21°C	18°C	13°C	9°C	7°C
41°F	41°F	48°F	52°F	59°F	64°F	68°F	70°F	64°F	55°F	48°F	45°F
1°C	0°C	3°C	5°C	8°C	11°C	13°C	13°C	10°C	8°C	4°C	2°C
34°F	32°F	37°F	41°F	46°F	52°F	55°F	55°F	50°F	46°F	39°F	36°F

Amsterdam Sights

Key to symbols
🔹 map coordinates refer to the Amsterdam map
on pages 342–343 🅖 admission charge:
$$$ more than €10, $$ €3–€10, $ less than €3
See page 5 for complete key to symbols

Amsterdam Museum

Once a monastery then a city orphanage
for four centuries, the Amsterdam
Museum is an elegant complex of bright
and airy rooms. Highlights include the
interactive Amsterdam DNA exhibition
with its images and sounds, and the
Little Orphanage adventure for children
aged 4 to 12 years.

To the right of the entrance is the glass
doorway into Schuttersgalerij. This was
once an open street and is now the
Amsterdam Gallery, with group portraits
painted between 1530 and 2007.
🔹 B3 ✉ Entrances: Kalverstraat 92 or Sint
Luciënsteeg 27 ☎ 020 523 1822;
www.amsterdammuseum.nl 🕙 Daily 10–5
🚃 Tram 1, 2, 4, 5, 9, 14, 16 🍴 Museum café 🅖 $$$

Anne Frank Huis

No matter how often you have heard
the Anne Frank story, a visit to Het
Achterhuis, "The Secret Annex," is
unforgettable. Here, in the Anne Frank
Huis (Anne Frank House), the Frank
family and their friends lived secretly in
Nazi-occupied Amsterdam until their
arrest just months before the Liberation.
The only one to survive the horrors of
the concentration camps was Anne's
father, Otto. The lively, passionate diary
kept by Anne during her years in hiding
was later published to worldwide
acclaim. The museum has absorbing
displays and multimedia installations,
but the Secret Annex is the heart of it
all. The stark emptiness intensifies the
experience. From every corner Anne
Frank bears witness on behalf of
millions of Nazi victims. After your visit,

a walk through the peaceful, reflective
Jordaan district is recommended.
🔹 B3 ✉ Prinsengracht 267 ☎ 020 556 7105;
www.annefrank.org 🕙 Daily 9 a.m.–10 p.m., Apr.–
Oct.; daily 9–7 (also Sat.7–10 p.m.), rest of year.
Admission by online prebooked time slot only 9–3.30.
After 3:30 p.m. you can buy tickets at museum door.
Last admission 30 minutes before closing. Closed Yom
Kippur 🚌 21, 170, 172, 174; tram 13, 14, 17
🚊 Museum Line stop 🍴 Museum café 🅖 $$

Begijnhof

Amsterdam's secluded Begijnhof
(Béguinage) is an outstanding example
of a medieval almshouse community.
It was built in the 14th century to
accommodate Béguines, a group of
pious single women of the Catholic
faith, who chose to live a religious and
charitable life but without the stricture
of holy vows.

The Béguines were later ostracized
because of their faith, and today the
discreet facade of the Béguinage's once

Traditional Dutch house, Begijnhof

The tomb of Michiel de Ruyter, a renowned 17th-century admiral, in the Nieuwe Kerk

clandestine Catholic church masks a haunting little Italianate chapel. Opposite is the original church that was transferred to the city's Protestant community in the late 16th century.

In the south corner of the Begijnhof is the 15th-century Houten Huys, one of Amsterdam's oldest houses, wooden-fronted and steeply gabled. Today's Begijnhof still accommodates single women of modest means.

✚ B2 ✉ Access via a gateway at Gedempte Begijnensloot (9–5) and then via the gate at Spui (after 5 p.m.) ☎ 020 622 1918 ⊕ Chapel: Tue.–Fri. 9–6:30, Sat.–Sun. 9–6, Mon. 1–6:30 ⊟ Tram 1, 2, 5 ⦿ Free

Nieuwe Kerk

The 17th-century Nieuwe Kerk (New Church) was new only in its original form, as compared with the more venerable Oude Kerk (Old Church). The New Church is a fine counterpoint to Dam square's Koninklijk Paleis (Royal Palace), with its vast, beautifully decorated rooms.

Today the church is used for major art exhibitions. There are a dozen or more side chapels and a magnificent vaulted roof. The fine organ and the pulpit are permanent features. The investiture of the new monarch, King Willem-Alexander of Orange, was held here in 2013.

✚ B3 ✉ Dam 34–38 ☎ 020 626 8168; www.nieuwekerk.nl ⊕ Daily 10–6 ⊟ Tram 1, 2, 4, 5, 9, 14, 16, 24, 25 🍴 Café ⦿ $$$

Oude Kerk

The Oude Kerk (Old Church) is the oldest building in Amsterdam. The church stands on the banks of the Oudezijds Voorburgwal canal in the heart of the Red Light District. Its glorious stained-glass windows, featuring Lambert van Noorts' *Annunciation* and *The Visit of Mary to Elizabeth*, look down on prostitutes' booths in the narrow Enge Kerksteeg, much as they might have done in medieval times. A triple nave and high-vaulted roof give a sense of added spaciousness to the bare interior of the Old Church. A poignant feature is the gravestone of Rembrandt's wife Saskia van Uylenburgh, below the choir organ.

✚ C3 ✉ Oudekerksplein 23 ☎ 020 625 8284; www.oudekerk.nl ⊕ Mon.–Sat. 10–6, Sun. 1–5:30 ⦿ Centraal Station or Nieuwmarkt ⊟ Tram 4, 9, 14,

16, 24, 25 🚊 $$ (may be more expensive for concerts and exhibitions; payment by credit or debit card only) ℹ️ Art exhibitions and music recitals at various times

Rijksmuseum

The Rijksmuseum (National Museum) contains some of the world's greatest works of Dutch art. The building dates from 1885 and was designed by Pierre Cuypers. Its neo-Gothic facade is something of a mirror image to Cuypers' Centraal Station.

The museum recently underwent a massive €375 million, 10-year-long renovation program, which has resulted in a lovely airy new reception and admissions area as well as brighter and more spacious galleries. The highlight of the collection is still Rembrandt's *The Nightwatch*, stunningly displayed to convey the magnificence of the canvas. The other Rembrandts in the collection, works by Van Gogh, and Johannes Vermeer's *The Kitchenmaid*, are all must-sees, but the scope of the entire collection is breathtaking. There are about 8,000 objects on display, from the core collection of over a million items. Also, don't miss the new restaurant, which has become one of the best dining spots in the city, but you will have to reserve ahead.

➕ B1 ✉️ Museumstraat 1 ☎️ 020 674 7000; www.rijksmuseum.nl 🕐 Daily 9–5 🚃 Tram 2, 5, 16 🚢 Museum Line stop 🍴 Café Cobra, Museumplein, RIJKS restaurant, Philips Wing 🚊 $$$ ℹ️ Audio tour available

Van Gogh Museum

To view the finest and largest collection of Vincent van Gogh's paintings, visit the Van Gogh Museum, where the artist's works (200 paintings and nearly 500 drawings) chart his intense and ultimately tragic life. The collection takes you through his early period, when he was a missionary in the Belgian coal fields; pieces include such dark social commentary as the Dutch peasants of *The Potato Eaters*. His later Parisian work reflects the influence of the Impressionists, but it is the paintings inspired by his life at Arles, in sunny Provence (France), that exhilarate with their fiery yellows and oranges. The most famous works are the iconic *Sunflowers* series. Conversely, *The Garden of St. Paul's Hospital*, painted at St.-Rémy mental asylum the year before Van Gogh's death, is a heartrending evocation of a dejected figure. But the sum of the Van Gogh Museum, the painter's legacy of outstanding work, is uplifting. There are other works on display by such contemporaries of Van Gogh as Toulouse-Lautrec, Gauguin and Redon.

➕ B1 ✉️ Museumplein 6 ☎️ 020 570 5200; www.vangoghmuseum.nl 🕐 Fri. 9–9, Sun.–Thu. 9–7, Sat. 9–6 🚃 Tram 2, 3, 5, 12 🚢 Museum Line stop 🍴 Museum restaurant 🚊 $$$ (tickets are timed and available to buy online only) ℹ️ Audio tour ($)

Vondelpark

Vondelpark, Amsterdam's principal park, is named for 17th-century playwright Joost van den Vondel. The park starts as a green avenue that leads southwest from a busy corner on Stadhouderskade, just south of Leidseplein. Soon it opens into a broad green space peppered with trees and interspersed with ornamental lakes and linked waterways. There are children's playgrounds, a sweetly scented rose garden, teahouses and a bandstand.

➕ A1 ✉️ Stadhouderskade 🕐 Daily dawn–dusk 🚃 Tram 1, 2, 3, 5, 12 🚢 Museum Line stop 🍴 t' Blauwe Theehuis ("The Blue Teahouse"), by the lake ℹ️ Open-air theater and concerts during summer

Wheatfield with Crows in the Van Gogh Museum

Amsterdam's Canals

So many northern European capitals claim the title "Venice of the North" that the sobriquet has become devalued. Some say there is no substitute for the real thing, but perhaps Amsterdam has the strongest claim to the title. While the city lacks Venice's romantic splendor, there is a restrained beauty about Amsterdam's canals (*grachten*) and their attendant buildings.

The finest canals are west of the city center, beyond the bustling main streets of Damrak and Nieuwezijds Voorburgwal, both of which once were canals. A stroll along side streets from Nieuwezijds Voorburgwal and across Spuistraat brings you to the great waterways of Singel, Herengracht, Keizersgracht and Prinsengracht.

Herengracht

Herengracht is the finest canal of the *grachtengordel*, the ring or girdle of canals that were built in the early 17th century to defend the city. The name Herengracht translates into English as "Gentlemen's Canal," a sign of contemporary male ascendancy. This was the district where the wealthiest Amsterdam merchant families built themselves handsome canalside mansions notable for their superb ornate gables. The houses were designed to be tall and narrow because of limited space.

Take a stroll down Herengracht to appreciate it all. You can start from the canal's northern end at its intersection with Brouwersgracht. The Brouwersgracht (Brewery Canal) is the short stretch of canal that links Herengracht to Singel canal at Haarlemmer Sluis, one of the 40 or so sluices that are opened each night to flush clean water through the canal system. Haarlemmer Sluis can be reached from Centraal Station by walking northwest along Prins Hendrikkade for about 300 yards and then turning left. Cross the wide sluice bridge. (There is a superb cheese shop, Kaasland de Roompot, on the opposite corner.) Go left, then turn right along Brouwersgracht to reach the tree-shaded bridges at the intersection with Herengracht.

Walk south, then east for a mile of scenic history to where Herengracht meets the Amstel river. You can stroll down either side of the great canal and cross over bridges to get the best views of the handsome canalside

houses. Herengracht 168, formerly the Theatermuseum, and the exquisite Bartolotti House next door are particularly impressive. The latter is a 17th-century Renaissance mansion built by the head of the Bartolotti Bank. Enjoy the *Gouden Bocht*, which translates as "Golden Bay" or "Bend," between Leidsestraat and Vijzelstraat – note the decorative double-fronted houses along the elegant curve of the canal.

The curve is an engaging motif amid Amsterdam's general flatness – in the decorativeness of house gables, the elegant bridges, the sweep of railings, even in the curved handlebars of the wonderful old upright bicycles still favored by Amsterdammers. There are said to be 700,000 bicycles in the city, and it seems that everybody cycles in Amsterdam. Elderly *dames* and *heren* (ladies and gentlemen) cruise past to the tinkling of bells. And stylishly dressed young people skim along with a wary eye on the tourists' uncertain bid to run across the street in front of them.

Connections

Explore Prinsengracht (Princes' Canal) and Keizersgracht (Emperors' Canal), as well as the main canals, and don't neglect the connecting waterways. There's Leidsegracht on the Golden Bend, or the peaceful, leafy Egelantiersgracht near the Anne Frank House (Anne Frank Huis, see page 345) that takes you into the quiet heart of the Jordaan district. Sidestep between Herengracht and Singel into enchanting streets such as Gasthuismolensteeg or Oude Spiegelstraat, where craft and antiques shops and boutiques rub shoulders with delightful little cafés and restaurants. And try a nighttime walk along the great canals, when many of the finest houses are floodlit and the numerous bridges twinkle with lights.

In summer the canals become venues for concerts by the water, rowing regattas, Chinese dragon boat races and various other events. Amsterdam is many things to many people, but the city's fascinating network of canals will always be the enduring motif of this very special city. For the walking route, see the city map on pages 342–343.

Above left to right: A tour in an open-topped pleasure craft along Amsterdam's canals; Blauwburgwal is a canal in the peaceful Jordaan district

The Hague

The Hague (Den Haag), third-largest city in The Netherlands, is justly proud of its status as the political and royal capital of this beautiful country and as a focus of international affairs. Although it lacks the fast pace and excitement of Amsterdam, a sense of well-being and security underpins the rich cultural and political heritage.

The city's name derives from Gravenhage, which means "the Count's hedge", and the city's official name is still 's-Gravenhage. In the 13th century the Count of Holland built a hunting lodge among sand dunes – this is where The Hague's historic center, the Binnenhof (Inner Court), now stands. The settlement that developed around the lodge was the Count's "hedge," sheltering him against the outside world.

In the 16th century the States General of the United Netherlands met at The Hague, and since then the city has been the seat of Dutch government. The Hague Convention of 1907, which formulated laws governing warfare worldwide, gave this city international status. The 1913 opening of the Peace Palace (Vredespaleis, see page 354) further enhanced The Hague's standing, and it is today considered a center of international diplomacy and business.

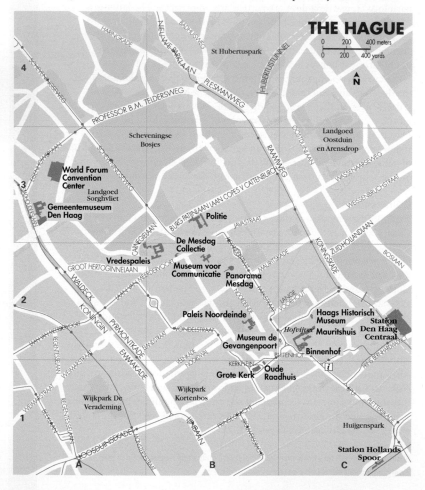

THE HAGUE

The Permanent Court of Arbitration and the International Court of Justice are located at the Peace Palace; numerous embassies, ministries and headquarters of international organizations also have their offices here.

In 1980 the royal residency was relocated from Utrecht to The Hague, and is home to King Willem-Alexander, Queen Maxima and their children.

Arrival

The Hague's main railroad station, Den Haag Centraal Station, is primarily used by trains for which the city is the final destination. Most through trains stop also at the Hollands Spoor station south of the city center. A short walk southwest from Centraal Station leads to the heart of The Hague, where the Binnenhof and several museums cluster around a graceful little lake, Hofvijver.

Guided bus, cycling and walking tours of the city are offered during summer, as well as self-guiding itineraries. Among these tours, available from the tourist information center between Centraal Station and the Binnenhof, are a walk discovering the city's lost Jewish Quarter; an introduction to the "Royal Miles" in and around the city; and coast-to-city cycling routes.

On Your Own

Exploring The Hague on your own on foot can be a very satisfying experience. The oldest section centers on the Hofvijver, the "Court Pond." On its south side the Hofvijver laps against the walls of the Binnenhof (see page 353) and the Mauritshuis (see page 354), which houses The Hague's outstanding art collection. Its northern side is lined with trees and is backed by the elegant 18th-century street Lange Vijverberg.

From the Hofvijver you can stroll north beneath the lime trees on the wide avenue Lange Voorhout. A colorful arts and antiques market is held here in August, one of the many annual events and festivals held in the city.

Continue past the grand facade of the Hotel des Indes to reach Denneweg, a charming street with a Parisian flavor and a host of interesting antiques and craft galleries, delicatessens, popular restaurants and cafés, and distinctive fashion boutiques.

Quickening Pace

West of the Hofvijver and the Binnenhof lies the bustling open area of the Buitenhof, where the pace quickens to that of a busy city.

Beyond the Buitenhof is The Hague's commercial and shopping district and the pedestrian-only streets that lead to the Kerkplein (Church Square) and the hexagonal-towered Grote Kerk

The Binnenhof (Inner Court) in The Hague

(Great Church), one of the city's oldest buildings and, for 380 years, the setting for royal weddings and baptisms.

North of the church is the Hofkwartier, one of the oldest areas of The Hague. There are quite a few specialty shops, restaurants and cafés here. Be sure to stroll along onto Hoogstraat (Palace Promenade) and on into Noordeinde, one of The Hague's most attractive streets. Along here you will find a marvelous selection of art galleries, antiques shops and fashion boutiques, restaurants and the Paleis Noordeinde (Royal Palace).

Enjoy this fine city by filling your day with activities involving the arts and history and then seek out the numerous musical and cultural events that take place in the summer.

A short ride on tram 1, 9 or 11, or bus 22 or 23 will take you to the coast and the popular resort of Scheveningen (proper pronunciation of the name Scheveningen is the sign of a true local; try "Shravin-eeng-e" and you might get by). You can break the journey halfway at the miniature "town" of Madurodam, a favorite with children.

In addition to Scheveningen's superb beach and promenade, the numerous attractions include the Holland Casino, the Muzee Scheveningen and a pier.

Hooigracht

Several ring canals were built around The Hague during the 17th century. Although many of them have been filled in, you can walk east from Denneweg to reach the serene little stretch of surviving canal, Hooigracht, its leafy banks lined with elegant and attractive old buildings.

Essential Information

Tourist Information

Tourist information centers are known as VVV (Vereniging Voor Vreemdelingenverkeer)

VVV, in the Central Library, Spui 68 ☎ 070 361 8860; www.denhaag.com Ⓖ Mon. noon–8, Tue.–Fri. 10–8, Sat.–Sun. and public holidays 10–5 VVV, Informatiepunt Scheveningen, Gevers Deynootweg 990–58 ☎ 0900 340 3505; www.denhaag.com

Urban Transportation

Den Haag has an excellent transportation system, HTM (www.htm.net), with tramlines serving The Hague, Scheveningen, Kijkduin and neighboring Voorburg, Rijswijk,

Wassenaar, Wateringen, Leidschendam, Delft and Nootdorp. For information and tickets for buses and trams inquire at the tourist information centers, or ☎ 0900 486436; www.journeyplanner.9292.nl. Taxi stands are located at the railroad stations and throughout the city. To call a taxi try HTMC ☎ 070 390 7722 or book online at www.htmc.nl.

Airport Information

Amsterdam Airport Schiphol (see page 344) serves The Hague. Trains for The Hague leave the airport at regular intervals (travel time 30 minutes). Trains from the airport stop first at Station Hollands Spoor, south of the city center. If you are going to the city center, stay on the train until Centraal Station.

Climate – average highs and lows for the month

Jan.	Feb.	Mar.	Apr.	May	Jun.	Jul.	Aug.	Sep.	Oct.	Nov.	Dec.
5°C	5°C	9°C	11°C	15°C	18°C	20°C	21°C	18°C	14°C	9°C	7°C
41°F	41°F	48°F	52°F	59°F	64°F	68°F	70°F	64°F	57°F	48°F	45°F
1°C	0°C	3°C	5°C	8°C	12°C	14°C	13°C	11°C	9°C	4°C	3°C
34°F	32°F	37°F	41°F	46°F	54°F	57°F	55°F	52°F	48°F	39°F	37°F

The Hague Sights

Key to symbols

⊞ map coordinates refer to The Hague map on
page 350 ▨ admission charge: $$$ more
than €10, $$ €3–€10, $ less than €3
See page 5 for complete key to symbols

Binnenhof

The Binnenhof (Inner Court) of the
original lodge of the Counts of Holland
is the oldest part of The Hague and is
where all matters political have taken
place for centuries – and still do today.

The turreted Ridderzaal (Knights'
Hall), where medieval guests were
received, stands at the heart of a
central square; behind it is the Dutch
parliament building.

The main room is the Knights' Hall,
restored in 1900 to its medieval glory,
with coats of arms, Dutch provincial
flags, stained glass and artifacts.
Ceremonies, including *Prinsjesdag*, the
day of the reigning monarch's speech to
the Dutch parliament, are held here.

There are guided tours of the Knights'
Hall and the two chambers of parliament
when they are not in use. Tours are in
Dutch (with an English-language audio
guide) or English.

⊞ C2 ✉ Binnenhof 8a ☎ 070 757 0200 ◷ Tours
Mon.–Sat. 10–4 ▤ 4, 5, 22; tram 10, 16, 17 ▨ $$$
(exhibition free) ⬛ Last tour at 3:45 p.m. (subject to
demand). Reservations recommended. Bookings can
also be made at www.prodemos.nl

Gemeentemuseum Den Haag

The Gemeentemuseum Den Haag
(The Hague Municipal Museum) has
collections of musical instruments and
ceramics, including Delftware and
The Hague silverware. The art collection
includes works by Pablo Picasso, Claude
Monet, and pieces by the 20th-century
Dutch painter Piet Mondrian. The
fashion department features exhibitions
of Dutch and international fashion,
including an exhibition showcasing
the opulent and fantastic "Romantic
Fashions."

Major visiting exhibitions can include
dramatic works by Damien Hirst and
large canvases by Mark Rothko.

⊞ A3 ✉ Stadhouderslaan 41 ☎ 070 338 1111;
www.gemeentemuseum.nl ◷ Tue.–Sun. 10–5
▤ 24; tram 16 ⏹ Museum café ▨ $$$

Haags Historisch Museum

Housed in a 17th-century guild house,
the Haags Historisch Museum (The
Hague Historical Museum) tells the
story of the city and its inhabitants in a
diverse collection that includes a vast
painting by Jan van Goyen, *View of The
Hague*, and a beautifully furnished doll's
house. A digital, chronological map
reveals the city's development while
townscapes tell of life in the
Netherlands' political and administrative
center through the ages.

⊞ C2 ✉ Korte Vijverberg 7 ☎ 070 364 6940;
www.haagshistorischmuseum.nl ◷ Tue.–Fri. 10–5,
Sat.–Sun. noon–5 ▤ 22, 24; tram 1, 9, 16, 17 ▨ $$

The Binnenhof is the complex where The Hague had its beginnings

Mauritshuis

The original Mauritshuis (Maurits' House) was built as a private home in the 17th century by Johan Maurits van Nassau-Siegen and was carefully reconstructed after a disastrous fire in 1704. It is home to the Royal Cabinet of Paintings, an outstanding collection of Dutch art which includes Johannes Vermeer's *Girl with a Pearl Earring* and the crowning glory, Rembrandt van Rijn's famous *The Anatomy Lesson of Doctor Nicolaes Tulp*.

➕ C2 ✉ Plein 29 ☎ 070 302 3456; www.mauritshuis.nl ⏰ Tue.–Wed. and Fri.–Sun. 10–6, Thu. 10–8, Mon. 1–6 🚌 4, 5, 22; tram 1, 16, 17 🍴 Café 💲 $$$

De Mesdag Collectie

Hendrik Willem Mesdag was a leading figure in the art world of The Hague during the 19th century.

Famous for his *Panorama Mesdag* (a cylinder-shaped painting of coastal resort Scheveningen in 1881), Mesdag was himself a painter and an avid collector of other artists' works. He was especially interested in compositions by the Barbizon School of French painters, including Jean-François Millet, Jean-Baptiste Camille Corot and Gustave Courbet. Their works – along with some by Mesdag himself as well as other members of The Hague School – grace the museum, built as an annex to Mesdag's house.

➕ B2 ✉ Laan van Meerdervoort 7f ☎ 070 362 1434; www.demesdagcollectie.nl ⏰ Wed.–Sun. noon–5 🚌 24; tram 1 🍴 Café 💲 $$

Museum de Gevangenpoort

A guided tour of the Museum de Gevangenpoort (Prisoner's Gate Museum) is great fun, but is not for the fainthearted. The Prisoner's Gate Museum was The Hague's notorious incarceration place for offenders for hundreds of years. Stark interrogation rooms, a debtors' chamber and a torture room give a gruesome picture of medieval justice. The Dutch treat the whole thing with humor.

The tour commentary is mostly in Dutch, but information sheets in other languages are available and the guides here will answer questions in English.

➕ B2 ✉ Buitenhof 33 ☎ 070 346 0861; www.gevangenpoort.nl ⏰ Tue.–Fri. 10–5, Sat.–Sun. noon–5 🚌 4, 5, 22; tram 1, 9, 16, 17 💲 $$ ℹ Tours daily 10:45–3:45 (extra tours Jul.–Aug.); English-language tour Sat.–Sun. at 2:15 p.m.; daily during school vacations

Vredespaleis

The Vredespaleis (Peace Palace) is an awe-inspiring building symbolizing the power of statehood. Scottish philanthropist Andrew Carnegie, who made his fortune in America, paid for its Gothic splendor in the early 20th century. The Vredespaleis' exquisite furnishings and artifacts were donated by nations around the world.

At the visitor center, a free film and exhibition offer an introduction to the Peace Palace and the institutions based there.

➕ B2 ✉ Carnegieplein 2 ☎ 070 302 4242; www.vredespaleis.nl ⏰ Visit by guided tour only by advance ticket purchase online 🚌 24; tram 1 💲 Tours $$

Mauritshuis (left) and the Peace Palace

Delft

Fine ceramics and architecture are the main features of Delft. The ceramics have been exported worldwide, but Delft's buildings remain much as they were when immortalized on canvas by Johannes Vermeer, a native of the city. The Vermeer Centrum, Voldersgracht 21, takes you into the painter's 17th-century world.

There are organized motorcoach trips to Delft from The Hague, and seats can be reserved through tourist information centers (see page 352). The town is only 20 minutes from The Hague via tram 1, and takes even less time by train. Tram and train both arrive at a two-lane highway, but a few steps along cobbled lanes transport you into a delightful medieval world enclosed by tranquil canals. Delft centers on an imposing main square, the Markt, where there are numerous stores, cafés and restaurants.

Delft is a popular tourist destination, and in summer the Markt can be especially crowded. Explore farther afield; follow the canalside street of Oosteinde from behind the New Church (Nieuwe Kerk) to reach the medieval city gate of Oostport. Visit the splendid Gothic Old Church (Oude Kerk), at the head of the lovely street of Oude Delft. View it from the Peperstraat Bridge, three bridges to the south on Oude Delft, to fully appreciate its remarkable leaning tower. Close to the Old Church is the Prinsenhof Museum (Museum Het Prinsenhof). This former convent became the palace of William of Orange during the Dutch war of liberation from Spain. William did not live to enjoy the fruits of victory; he was assassinated here in 1584. The museum has exhibits from that revolutionary struggle, along with tapestries, pottery, silver and paintings.

Many stores on the Markt sell Delft china. The Koninklijke Porceleyne Fles, a factory involved in producing Delftware since the 17th century, is at Rotterdamsweg 196 (☎ 015 760 0800; www.royaldelft.com) and has tours.
✉ Kerkstraat 3 ☎ 015 215 4051; www.delft.com

Canals thread through the pretty streets of Delft just as they did in medieval times

Norway

Introduction and Map 358

Timeline 362

Survival Guide 363

Oslo 364

Feature: Fjord and Mountain Line 369

Hotels and Restaurants 485

Essential Information 550

Opposite: The Geirangerfjord on Norway's west coast is a UNESCO World Heritage Site

Norway

Norway forms the edge of Europe's most northerly landmass, with land borders to Finland, Sweden and Russia, and where sea and mountains have merged to produce one of the world's most breathtaking and dramatic landscapes.

This is a country whose forebears, the Vikings, helped shape the history of northern Europe. The Vikings once controlled half of Britain, and sent mariners as far

west as Newfoundland and as far south as the Strait of Gibraltar, as well as establishing some cities in the Republic of Ireland.

It is this vigorous and resourceful national character, reflected in Viking tradition, that still exemplifies modern Norway. This is a nation that has mastered an inhospitable, though beautiful landscape, without despoiling it, becoming a leading oil and gas producer in the hostile environment of the North Sea.

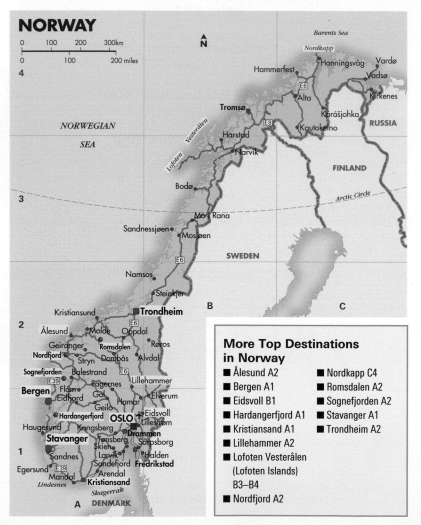

More Top Destinations in Norway

- Ålesund A2
- Bergen A1
- Eidsvoll B1
- Hardangerfjord A1
- Kristiansand A1
- Lillehammer A2
- Lofoten Vesterålen (Lofoten Islands) B3–B4
- Nordfjord A2
- Nordkapp C4
- Romsdalen A2
- Sognefjorden A2
- Stavanger A1
- Trondheim A2

Landscape

Norway's spectacular landscape is dominated by intervening seas – the Barents Sea to the north, the Norwegian Sea to the west, the North Sea to the southwest and the Skagerrak inlet farther south. The corrugated coastline measures nearly 13,600 miles, including fjords and the country's 150,000 offshore islands. This scattered mosaic of islands – the "Skerry Guard" – is Norway's natural sea defense. The islands break the onslaught of the ocean, creating the country's sheltered seaways to the north and south and protecting the gateways to the fjords.

Norway is shaped like a Viking club, narrowing in the north and with a broad base in the south. The country's mountain system runs from northeast to southwest and reaches its greatest height at Galdhøppigen, at 8,100 feet, in the Jotunheimen National Park.

The mountains separate the rugged western seaboard, known as the Vestlandet, from the gentler eastern region, the Øslandet.

The broad southwestern half of the country is known as Sørlandet, the South Country. Here, on the coastal fringe and around Oslo, is lowland Norway, where the sheltered coast is a favorite vacation destination for Norwegian families – a landscape of mellow woods and fields and tranquil blue waters. On the southern tip of Sørlandet is the sunny town of Kristiansand, with its flock of offshore islands. Southwest along the coast is Mandal, where attractive beaches catch the best of the summer sun; nearby is the promontory of Lindesnes, where a *fyr* (lighthouse) marks Norway's southernmost point.

Then the coast turns to the northwest, twisting through a rugged landscape of rocky headlands and deeply indented fjords, past the pleasant town of Egersund and finally through rich farming country to Stavanger and the open west.

Fjordland

Norway's famous Fjordland begins at Stavanger. Stretching for more than 375 miles is one of the most spectacular landscapes and seascapes in the world. In the Ryfylke area, east of Stavanger, lies the stunning Lysefjord, with its flat-topped and sheer-sided Pulpit Rock. Farther north is the mighty Hardangerfjord, with its massive cliffs, and the silver-white waterfalls of Skykkjedalsfoss and Vøringfoss, set off by snowcapped mountains.

Even farther north into Hordaland lies fascinating Bergen, against a setting of islands and mountains. Bergen is the starting point for boat journeys to the north along the coastal islands and into the 127-mile-long and 4,291-foot-deep Sognefjord, the deepest and longest fjord in Norway and second longest in the world. Its side fjords twist between towering cliffs and penetrate as far as Flåm and Gudvangen, at the head of Nærøyfjord (the narrowest fjord in Europe), and to Fjærland, below the southernmost edge of the great Jostedalsbreen glacier (the largest glacier in continental Europe, covering an area of 188 square miles).

Along Sognefjord are lovely villages such as Balestrand. Throughout the area, ancient pagoda-like stave churches survive at settlements such as Vik, Kaupanger and Urnes. Inland to the east lies the mountain range of Jotunheimen, known as the "Land of the Giants."

The Northern Fjords

Beyond the Sognefjord lies Nordfjord and then the county, or *fylke*, of Møre og Romsdal. The coastal town of Ålesund is renowned for its art nouveau architecture of turrets, towers and medieval motifs. Inland is the Geirangerfjord and its magnificent waterfalls. From Ålesund, spectacular roads lead over the mountains to the town of Åndalsnes and the Romsdalsfjord. Along the coast farther north is the Atlantic Road, a highway

A group of bronze bears by Norway's favorite sculptor, Skule Waksvik

narrow and twisting and where they pass through long tunnels.

Norway's public transportation system is excellent. This is a country that copes with some of the most difficult winter conditions in Europe. Only in severe conditions are train services to the northwest likely to be curtailed. Buses serve more remote villages throughout the north and west.

Travel by boat is a way of life in Norway, especially on the western seaboard. There is no finer way of touring Fjordland than by boat.

Most of Norway has a comparatively mild, wet, maritime climate, as it is influenced by the Gulf Stream. The west coast and mountains have high rainfall even in midsummer. But there can be long spells of fair weather, when Fjordland is glorious. In eastern and southeastern Norway, summers can be warm and dry. Winter in the higher elevations is cold and extremely snowy, creating excellent skiing conditions at Norway's winter resorts. In the far north the weather conditions border on the subarctic. The Norwegians are philosophical about their weather, preferring to think of it as invigorating.

linking a chain of islands. Northeast from here lies Trollheimen, the mountainous "Home of the Trolls," and then comes the great expanse of Trondheimsfjorden and Trondheim itself – once called Nidaros – the ancient capital of Norway.

Beyond Trondheim is the narrowing edge of Norway's northwestern seaboard, fertile coastal lands backed by barren mountains that reach into Nordland and to the Arctic Circle. At Narvik, you look out across the waters of Vestfjorden to the spectacular Lofoten Islands – including Austvågøy, Gimsøy, Vestvågøy and Flakstadøy – before continuing north to Tromsø, known as "The Paris of the North." You then go on through Finnmark, the land of the Sami people and of the midnight sun, to the Arctic island of Honningsvåg and Nordkapp (North Cape), the symbolic northern end of Europe.

Traveling in Norway
Norway is a rewarding country to explore, but to enjoy this magnificent land you should be selective about how and where you travel. Roads are well maintained throughout. Good driving skills are required, where roads are

The Norwegians
Norway, as a constitutional monarchy, is extremely well run. The moderate Labor Party dominated government from the 1930s to 1981 when coalition governments began to be the norm, with its ministers elected through a system of proportional representation. The Norwegians are a level-headed, open, courteous and generous people. Only in busy Oslo does an occasional impatience with visitors emerge.

The people share the Scandinavian tendency toward self-effacement, but they are understandably proud of their success at shaping a modern nation out of such a wild landscape.

Wooden houses on the small island of Omaholmen, amid Hardangerfjord's striking scenery

Timeline

2000–1000 BC	Early neolithic and Bronze Age people leave numerous rock carvings throughout Scandinavia.
AD 787	Viking expansion begins with increased expeditions to Britain and northern Europe.
870	Vikings settle in Iceland.
1000	Christianity is introduced to Norway; Lief Eriksson reaches the coast of Labrador.
1070	Bergen is founded on the southwest coast of Norway.
1262	Iceland finally accepts rule of Norwegian kingdom after long and bloody conflict.
circa 1300	Oslo becomes capital of Norway.
1350	The Black Death kills over half of Norway's population.
1397	Union of the Three Crowns of Denmark, Sweden and Norway signed at Kalmar.
1536	Norway is reduced to a "province" of Denmark and remains so for nearly 300 years.
1814	The country is forced into union with Sweden.
1905	Norway breaks the union with Sweden and Prince Carl of Denmark is invited to become king of the independent nation.
1911	Norwegian Roald Amundsen reaches the South Pole.
1914–18	Norway remains neutral during World War I.
1925	City of Christiana reverts to its original name of Oslo.
1940	Invasion of Norway by Germany, in spite of Norway's declaration of neutrality.
1945	German troops surrender; Norway becomes one of the founders of the United Nations.
1949	Norway becomes a founding member of NATO.
1970s	Oil and gas extraction from Norwegian sector of North Sea boosts Norway's economy.
1994	Norwegians vote to reject membership of the European Union.
2005	Norway celebrates 100 years of independence.
2011	Two sequential acts of terrorism are carried out by a Norwegian right-wing extremist leaving 77 people dead.
2014	Work begins on a new National Museum in Oslo
2017	A right-wing coalition narrowly defeats the center-left opposition in national elections.

The Viking Settlers

History has painted the Vikings as aggressive, anarchic sea raiders, but this view has changed somewhat in recent times. The restless voyaging that took the Vikings around the coast of Britain and into the deep estuaries of northern France led to bloody conflict. There seems no question that the Vikings plundered and destroyed. But modern theory argues that a desire for new territory made them settlers in foreign lands more often than just violent raiders. In later, more stable times, the Vikings' commercial success was just as powerful as their military ferocity had been.

Sunset among the cliffs of Nordkapp (North Cape), Magerøya Island

Survival Guide

■ Mid-June to mid-August is the national vacation period, and many Norwegians escape the cities and towns and head for the fjords, mountains and countryside. This summer period can be a good time to visit Oslo.

■ During the peak summer vacation season, North Cape (Nordkapp), Europe's northernmost viewpoint, and its approaches are very busy with traffic and visitors.

■ When driving in Norway, dimmed headlights must be kept on at all times, even during daylight hours.

■ Because of Norway's strict control on the sale of alcohol, you will have difficulty buying wines and spirits outside of larger towns. You cannot buy alcohol (except beer) from supermarkets. Special state-controlled Vinmonopolet outlets are the only liquor stores, and they are very expensive. You must be at least 18 to buy wine and beer and 20 to buy spirits. Most restaurants are licensed; you may be able to buy beer in some grocery stores.

■ Norwegians are catching up with international fashion and trends, but there is more interest in good-quality outdoor clothing. For something to wear that's thoroughly Norwegian try the Oslo Sweater Shop at the Radisson Blu Scandinavia Hotel (✉ Tullinsgate 5, ☎ 22 11 29 22; www.sweater.no) or the Clarion Royal Christiania Hotel (✉ Skippergaten/Biskop Gunnerus' gate 3, ☎ 22 12 12 25). Other souvenirs include ceramics, pewter, glass, wooden troll figures, enamel jewelry and woven wall hangings.

■ You can eat very well in Norway, especially in Oslo and the larger towns. Norwegians are experts at buffets, the ideal lunch experience, often with elaborate fish specialties. Smoked salmon and trout, and lamb dishes such as *fenalår* (smoked leg of lamb) are delicious, or try reindeer or elk for a taste of mountain Norway.

■ Overall, prices are higher here than elsewhere in Europe, with some things about 30 percent more expensive. Several passes and discount schemes offer reduced prices at hotels (contact your local travel agent for information). If you're self-catering and on a budget, watch for Lavpris (low-price) food stores.

Oslo

Oslo is a small, modern city of great character, but without the grandeur of many larger European capitals. Its spacious suburbs, forests and parks, all within sight and sound of the sea, give the city great vistas. It has outstanding art galleries and maritime museums, music venues, cafés, restaurants and fashionable boutiques. Yet there is always that inescapable feeling that wide-open spaces are not too far away.

Oslo Through History

Oslo was founded in 1000, but its progress to capital city was checkered. It was significant only as a fjord settlement during the Viking age. In the 11th century, the Norwegian King Harald Hardråde chose to make Oslo a rival to the northern capital of Trondheim. Oslo's fortunes rose and fell thereafter.

It was devastated by plague, and in the 17th century, following a disastrous fire and while under Danish rule, the settlement was rebuilt to the west of its original site and renamed Christiana, after the Danish King Christian IV.

Christiana became the capital of Norway in 1814. Throughout the 19th century the profitable timber trade and the economic advantages of union with Sweden increased its prosperity. By

1905, when Norway broke with the union, Christiana was a mature city economically and politically, and by 1925 the country was confident enough to reinstate the traditional name of Oslo.

The story of Oslo in the final decades of the 20th century was one of rapid modernization, in cultural, social, political and economic spheres. Wealth from the oil industry, the international-ization of Norwegian culture and a growing Norwegian self-confidence transformed the city into the vibrant capital that it is today.

The City's Stage

The most impressive way to arrive in Oslo is by sea. Viewed from the narrow neck of the Oslofjorden, the city's buildings are set against a backdrop of serene peninsulas and wooded hills. The hills are dotted with houses and accented by the Holmenkollen ski jump.

Arrival by train, however, brings you to Jernbanetorget, the big open space in front of Oslo's central railroad station. This is not the most attractive part of the city, but a short walk along Karl Johans Gate (the main street) takes you to Oslo

Vigeland Park, Oslo, has 227 sculptures

Nobel Peace Prize

The Nobel Peace Prize has been awarded in Oslo Rådhuset (Oslo City Hall) since 1990. The award was founded at the end of the 19th century by Swedish inventor and industrialist Alfred Bernhard Nobel (1833–96). The Peace Prize winner is decided on criteria in Nobel's will citing "the person(s) who shall have done the most or the best work for brotherhood between nations…" The ceremony takes place each year on December 10, the anniversary of Nobel's death. Famous recipients include Marie Curie (1911), Martin Luther King (1964), Mother Teresa (1979), Nelson Mandela (1993), Jimmy Carter (2002), Barack Obama (2009), Lin Xiaobo (2010) and the International Campaign to Abolish Nuclear Weapons (2017).

Cathedral (Oslo Domkirke) and the busy open space of Stortorget, with its colorful flower market.

A few steps farther on is the Parliament (Stortinget). Before it lies the open space of Eidsvollsplass, the busy city center, alive with action in summer. Its pond becomes a skating rink in winter.

To the northwest of Eidsvollsplass is the neoclassic Nationaltheatret (National Theater), where statues of Norwegian dramatists Bjørnstjerne Bjørnson and Henrik Ibsen stand guard. Farther northwest is tree-lined Slottsparken, which encompasses the unfenced and accessible Slottsparken (Royal Park) and the Kongelige Slott (Royal Palace) within its bounds.

To the south of the National Theater, down Olav V's Gate or Roald Amundsen Gate, lies Oslo Rådhus (Oslo City Hall) and the open space of Rådhusplassen. Adjoining this square is Rådhusbrygge (City Hall Pier) and the local ferryboat dock on Pipervika inlet. The ferry to the Bygdøy peninsula operates at this dock from April through September. From

here, you can take a pleasant waterfront walk to fashionable Tjuvholmen ("Thief Island"), good for contemporary art (the Astrup Fearnley Museet), fjord views and alfresco dining.

Exploring Oslo

Central Oslo is easily explored on foot, but public transportation is very efficient and easily understood. Visit the outlying Bygdøy peninsula, with its clutch of outstanding museums (see page 367 and page 368), or Frognerparken (Frogner Park) and Vigelandsparken (Vigeland Park), Norway's most visited attraction (see page 368).

Oslo's main street, Karl Johans Gate, is full of stores of all kinds. The stylish Paléet shopping mall (Nos. 37–43) has a mix of fashion boutiques and restaurants. Stop for coffee at the Grand Café, one of Henrik Ibsen's haunts, at the Grand Hotel (see page 485), Karl Johans Gate 31. For the best in Norwegian design, take a walk across the park to Norway Designs (Stortingsgata 28; www.norwaydesigns.no/).

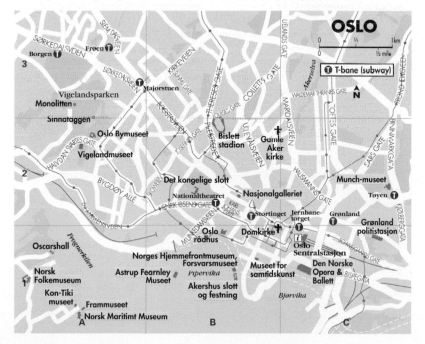

A short distance north of the Royal Palace is the busy shopping street of Hegdehaugsveien and its continuation, Bogstadveien. Down at the harbor, on the western side of Pipervika inlet in the converted shipyard buildings, is Aker Brygge, a modern complex with numerous stores, restaurants, cafés and entertainment venues. The area's attractive waterside setting adds to the character.

Eating out in Oslo offers a variety of local and international cuisine. Try traditional restaurants such as the excellent Engebret Café (see page 486) on Bankplassen, where you can enjoy Norwegian specialties. Feast on excellent music too, in the Oslo Konserthus on Munkedamsveien (tel 23 11 31 11; www.oslokonserthus. no), a little to the north of Aker Brygge, or the striking new Den Norske Opera & Ballett on the waterfront (see page 368).

The Oslo experience is a relaxed one because of the compactness of the city center. Its openness is reflected in the Norwegian people, who are brisk but friendly. English is a second language, especially for younger Norwegians, and you are never far away from advice and guidance to help you make the most of your stay.

Essential Information

Oslo Visitor Centre

VisitOSLO
In Ø (Østbanehallen) by Oslo Central Station (entrance on Jernbanetorget)
☎ 81 53 05 55;
www.visitoslo.com

Urban Transportation

Oslo's main railroad station is Sentralstasjon (Central Station), known as Oslo S. Oslo has an efficient bus and tram network. The bus terminal is next to Oslo Sentralstasjon. Six tramlines run east to west. The city also has a subway system, called the T-bane, with five lines running east to west identified by a "T" sign. Its main intersection is at Stortinget Station. For further information contact Ruter at Jernbanetorget 1, by Oslo S (Mon.–Fri. 7 a.m.–8 p.m., Sat. 9–6, Sun. 10–4); for travel outside Oslo go online at www.ruter.no). Taxis are available from Oslo Taxi (☎ 02323; www.oslotaxi.no).

Airport Information

Oslo Airport (☎ 67 03 00 00 within Norway; www.avinor.no), recently expanded to twice its previous size, is located at Gardermoen, 31 miles north of the city. An Airport Express Train (FlyToget; www.flytoget.no) runs between the airport and Oslo S (Central Station) every 10–20 minutes; the trip takes 19 to 22 minutes, however there are no services between 12:50 a.m. and 5:30 a.m. (from the airport) and midnight and 4:40 a.m. (to the airport). Regular train services stop at the airport and take less than 30 minutes to reach the main railroad station, Oslo S. The SAS Airport Express buses (☎ 40 00 11 66 within Norway; www.flybussen.no/oslo) run every 20 minutes between the airport and the Radisson Blu Scandinavia Hotel (journey time 50 minutes) via the Oslo Bussterminalen (Oslo Bus Station; travel time 40 minutes).

Climate – average highs and lows for the month

Jan.	Feb.	Mar.	Apr.	May	Jun.	Jul.	Aug.	Sep.	Oct.	Nov.	Dec.
0°C	0°C	4°C	9°C	16°C	19°C	22°C	20°C	16°C	9°C	4°C	0°C
32°F	32°F	39°F	48°F	61°F	66°F	72°F	68°F	61°F	48°F	39°F	32°F
-7°C	-7°C	-3°C	1°C	7°C	10°C	12°C	12°C	7°C	3°C	-2°C	-5°C
19°F	19°F	27°F	34°F	45°F	50°F	54°F	54°F	45°F	37°F	28°F	23°F

Oslo Sights

> **Key to symbols**
> ✚ map coordinates refer to the Oslo map on
> page 365 💷 admission charge: $$$ more than
> Kr80, $$ Kr50–Kr80, $ less than Kr50
> See page 5 for complete key to symbols

Akershus slott og festning

Akershus slott (Akershus castle) stands
on a rocky height on the harbor inlet of
Pipervika. It was founded in 1299 as a
royal residence, but by the end of the
17th century it had been transformed
into the powerful *festning* (fortress).

The Norges Hjemmefrontmuseum
(Norwegian Resistance Museum) here
is a compelling record of Norway's
experiences in World War II, when the
Nazi occupation headquarters were at
Akershus. Also here is the Forsvarsmuseet
(Armed Forces Museum), which follows
Norway's military history from Viking
times to the present day.

Slott, Festning ✚ B1 ✉ Oslo mil/Akershus ☎ 23 09
39 17; www.forsvarsbygg.no ⊕ Mon.–Fri. 10–4,
Sat.–Sun. 11–5, Jul.–Aug.; Sat.–Sun. noon–5, rest of
year. Grounds daily 6 a.m –9.pm, (or dusk if sooner).
Cloood during official engagements ⊖ Stortinget
🚊 Tram 12 🍴 Engebret Café, see page 486 💷 $$$;
Grounds free
Norges Hjemmefrontmuseum ✉ Oslo mil/Akershus
☎ 23 09 31 38 ⊕ Mon.–Sat. 10–5, Sun. 11–5,
Jun.–Aug ; Mon.–Fri. 10–4, Sat.–Sun. 11–4, rest of year
💷 $$
Forsvarsmuseet ☎ 23 09 35 82 ⊕ Daily 10–5,
May–Aug.; Sun. 10–4, rest of year. Closed Easter and
Whitsun Sat.–Sun. 💷 Free

Astrup Fearnley Museet

The sail-like glass roofs of this museum
on the waterfront of Tjuvholmen ("Thief
Island") embrace the contemporary art
collection of the Astrup Fearnley
shipping company. It stages exhibitions
by major international artists.

✚ B1 ✉ Strandpromenaden 2, Tjuvholmen ☎ 22 93
60 60; www.afmuseet.no ⊕ Tue.–Fri. 12–5 (Thu. also
5–7 p.m.), Sat.–Sun. 11–5 🚊 21, 32, 33, 54, 122, 129,
132; tram 12, 16 🍴 Café 💷 $$$

Frammuseet

The centerpiece of the Frammuseet
(Fram Museum) is the preserved Arctic
exploration vessel *Fram*, with a bow like
a battering ram and a hull as solid as a
castle wall. The *Fram* was launched in
1892 and was used by Norwegian
explorers Fridtjof Nansen, Otto
Sverdrup and Roald Amundsen in polar
expeditions. Go aboard the vessel to
appreciate its sturdiness and get a sense
of the tough life led by its crew.

✚ A1 ✉ Bygdøynesveien 36, Bygdøynes ☎ 23 28
29 50; www.frammuseum.no ⊕ Daily 9–6, Jun.–Aug.;
10–6 May and Sep.; 10–5, rest of year 🚊 30
🚢 Bygdøynes Boat 91, from Rådhusbrygge 3 (Apr.–Sep.)
🍴 Café 💷 $$$; combined ticket available with Kon-Tiki
Museum and the Norwegian Maritime Museum

Kon-Tiki museet

The Kon-Tiki museet (Kon-Tiki
Museum) is a colorful celebration of
Norwegian adventurer Thor Heyerdahl's
amazing voyages. It complements the
general maritime themes of the adjacent
Fram Museum and the Norwegian
Maritime Museum (seee page 368).

Heyerdahl's ethos of adventure, linked
to environmentalism and international
cooperation, is vividly expressed. The
Kon-Tiki balsa wood raft of his 1947
Pacific crossing and the papyrus vessel
Ra II of his 1970 Atlantic crossing both
reflect the Norwegian genius for
maritime exploration.

✚ A1 ✉ Bygdøynesveien 36, Bygdøynes ☎ 23 08
67 67; www.kon-tiki.no ⊕ Daily 9:30–6, Jun.–Aug.;
10–5, Mar.–May and Sep.–Oct.; 10–4, rest of year
🚊 30 🚢 Bygdøynes Boat 91, from Rådhusbrygge 3
(Apr.–Sep.) 💷 $$$; combined ticket available with
Fram Museum and the Norwegian Maritime Museum

Munch-museet

A celebration of Norway's famous artist,
Edvard Munch, the Munch-museet
displays his best-known painting – *The
Scream*. The world-famous cultural icon
is one of two versions; the other is in the
National Gallery (see page 368).

The Munch Museum holds nearly
28,000 pieces including paintings and

sculptures, tools and sketch books. All of the items provide an insight into Munch's complex personality.

➕ C2 ✉ Tøyengata 53 ☎ 23 49 35 00; www. munchmuseet.no ⏰ Daily 10–5 🚇 Tøyen 🚌 20 🍴 Café 💰 $$$ ℹ Guided tours (free) in English Sun. at 2 p.m. Jul.–Aug.

Nasjonalgalleriet

Oslo's Nasjonalgalleriet (National Gallery) has works by painters such as Georges Braque and Pablo Picasso, but its main collection is of work from 1800 up to 1950 by Norwegian masters such as Christian Krohg, Thomas Fearnley and Edvard Munch. Highlights include Krohg's lively portrait *Oda Krohg, the Painter* and the Romantic Fjordland paintings of Johan Christian Dahl. Look on the top floor for Ernst Josephson's *The Spanish Blacksmiths*. The room devoted to Munch shows masterpieces including a version of *The Scream*, the powerful *Dance of Life*, the sensual *Day After* and the most ravishing *Madonna*. The museum will close in early 2019 in preparation for a move to a new National Museum for Art, Architecture and Design which is being built on the waterfront.

➕ B2 ✉ Universitetsgata 13 ☎ 21 98 20 00; www.nasjonalmuseet.no/en ⏰ Tue.–Fri. 10–6 (also Thu. 6–7 p.m.), Sat.–Sun. 11–5 🚇 Nationaltheatret 🚌 33; tram 11, 13, 17, 18, 19 🍴 Café 💰 $$

Norsk Folkemuseum

The Norsk Folkemuseum (Norwegian Folk Museum) includes a parklike area with traditional buildings from different regions of Norway and some reconstructed 19th-century village streets.

The main buildings display crafts, folk costumes and examples of rural interiors. There also is an exhibition on the culture of the Sami, the indigenous people of northern Scandinavia.

➕ A1 ✉ Museumsveien 10, Bygdøynes ☎ 22 12 37 00; www.norskfolkemuseum.no ⏰ Daily 10–6, mid-May to mid-Sep.; Mon.–Fri. 11–3, Sat.–Sun. 11–4, rest of year 🚌 30 ⛴ Bygdøynes Boat 91, from Rådhusbrygge 3 (Apr.–Sep.) 🍴 Café 💰 $$$

Norsk Maritimt Museum

The Norwegian Maritime Museum is located on the tip of the Bygdøy peninsula and overlooks the calm waters of the Oslofjorden. In the main hall Norwegian artist Christian Krogh's great marine painting, *Leiv Eriksson's Discovery of America*, sets the scene for exhibits on all things to do with shipping and the sea. The basement theater shows a video on Norway's great maritime history. On the main floor is an escape boat, secretly (and daringly) made from rough planking by Norwegian sailors while imprisoned aboard German ships in West Africa during World War II.

➕ A1 ✉ Bygdøynesveien 37, Bygdøynes ☎ 22 12 37 00; www.marmuseum.no ⏰ Daily 10–5, May–Sep.; 10–4, rest of year 🚌 30 ⛴ Bygdøynes Boat 91, from Rådhusbrygge 3 (Apr.–Sep.) 🍴 Cafés 💰 $$$; combined ticket available with Fram Museum and Kon-Tiki Museum ℹ Audio tours

Den Norske Opera & Ballett

The massive, white building, designed by the Norwegian company Snøhetta, has captured several awards for its architecture and is a "must see."

➕ C1 ✉ Kirsten Flagstad plass 1 ☎ 21 42 21 21 (tickets); www.operaen.no ⏰ By guided tours only outside performances. Tours in English Mon.–Fri. and Sun. at 1 p.m., Sat. at noon 🚇 Oslo-S 🍴 Restaurant 💰 $$$

Vigelandsparken

One of Norway's most visited attractions, Vigelandsparken (Vigeland Park) represents the work of the Norwegian sculptor Gustav Vigeland (1869–1943) and is the world's largest sculpture park dedicated to a single artist. Concerts are held here in summer, and at the southern end of the park the interesting Vigeland-museet (Vigeland Museum) displays more of the sculptor's work.

➕ A3 ✉ Off Kirkeveien. Museum: Nobels gate 32 ☎ 23 49 37 00; www.vigeland.museum.no ⏰ Daily 24 hours. Museum: Tue.–Sun. 10–5, May–Aug.; 12–4, rest of year 🚇 Majorstuen 🚌 20; tram 12 🍴 Café 💰 Park: free; Museum: $$

Fjord and Mountain Line

Most visitors to Norway go to the western fjords during their stay. Even if your time is limited you can still make the famous "Norway in a nutshell" journey by train, bus and boat through some of the most magnificent scenery in western Norway. The trip can be completed in one to three days, depending on how much time you have available. It starts from Oslo, Bergen or Voss aboard the scenic Bergen Railway, the 292-mile rail link between Oslo and Bergen, northern Europe's highest railroad, rising at one point to 4,009 feet.

At Myrdal you'll transfer to the famous Flåmsbana (Flåm Railway), one of the high points of the tour. The stylish train, with its comfortable accommodations, takes 55 minutes to travel 12.5 miles down the wild Flåm valley, affording views of some of the most magnificent mountain scenery in Norway.

At Flåm (pronounced Flum) there is time to eat and to wander around before continuing the trip by boat on the Aurlandsfjord and into the Nærøyfjord, the narrowest fjord in Europe and on the UNESCO World Heritage List. Surrounded by mountains up to 5,900 feet high, the boat glides past small traditional farms clinging to the mountainsides. You will see goats grazing along the edge of the fjord and, if you're lucky, seals lying on rocks before the boat docks at Gudvangen.

The next stage of the trip is the bus ride up Stalheimskleiva (the steepest road in northern Europe – not passable October through April). Through 13 dramatic hairpin bends, offering views of the spectacular waterfalls Stalheimfossen and Sivlefossen, you'll arrive at the Stalheim Hotel, where there is a short stop before the trip carries on to Voss. From Voss you can continue your exploration by train to Bergen or Oslo for the last leg of one of the world's great round trips.

The "Norway in a nutshell" tour can be booked through Fjord Tours, Møllendalsveien 1A, 5009 Bergen (☎ 55 55 76 60; www.fjordtours.com) or Rail Europe (☎ Reservations 1-800-622-8600 (USA), 1-800-361-RAIL (Canada); www.raileurope.com/us).

Tumbling in several steep cascades, a waterfall crashes into Sognefjord in fjord country

Portugal

Introduction and Map 372

Timeline 376

Survival Guide 377

Lisbon 378

Feature: Lisbon Life 383

Feature: Sintra 385

Porto 386

Feature: Port Wine 391

Hotels and Restaurants 486

Essential Information 554

Opposite: Colorful boats in the fishing village of Sesimbra, south of Lisbon

Portugal

Portugal, lying on the western edge of the Continent and overshadowed by Spain, its larger neighbor to the east, was for many years considered the poor relation of southwestern Europe.

Political turmoil and poverty have long hindered development, but after joining the European Union in 1986, billions of dollars have poured into the country, helping to modernize its economy.

The Land

For travelers who knew Portugal a few decades ago, some things have changed beyond recognition; others remain stubbornly the same. In rural areas Portugal is still old-fashioned and underdeveloped, a real bonus for visitors seeking something a little different from mainstream European travel.

The country is small, geographically diverse and beautiful. Stretching 350 miles from north to south, it is packed with mountains, river valleys, flat dry plains, rolling forested hills and a truly beautiful coastline. Portugal borders the Atlantic, and weather conditions can range from hot and sunny to stormy and wet. In the northern Trás-os-Montes region, winter temperatures drop well below freezing; in summer, it is not uncommon for the thermometer to top 100 degrees Fahrenheit.

The Algarve, a popular vacation area on the southern coast that's often visited by northern Europeans, enjoys a Mediterranean climate, and the vegetation is subtropical. On the whole, summers are warm and dry, winters mild and wet, although it can be cold in the mountains. Mainland Portugal's highest mountain is the imposing, granite Torre, in the wilds of the Serra da Estrela, which rises above 6,500 feet. The Tagus (Tejo) river divides the country roughly in half. The Tagus and two other important rivers, the Douro and the Guadiana, rise in Spain, and Portugal must share their waters with its bigger neighbor, a factor which sometimes leads to difficulties in supply and environmental problems.

Portuguese Empire

It's easy to forget that Portugal was once at the head of a powerful empire. Beginning in the early 15th century, Portuguese explorers pushed far into the unknown, challenging the traditional view that the world ended somewhere west of Gibraltar. Madeira and the Azores were the first to be discovered, and these islands remain part of Portugal. Portuguese ships rounded the

More Top Destinations in Portugal (see map page 373)

- Alcobaça B3
- Batalha B3
- Braga B4
- Bragança C4
- Castelo de Vide B2
- Chaves B4
- Coimbra B3
- Douro B4
- Évora B2
- Fátima B3
- Guimarães B4
- Monsanto C3
- Óbidos A2
- Parque Nacional da Peneda-Gerês B4
- Sagres B1
- Serra de Monchique B1
- Silves B1
- Tomar B3
- Torres Vedras A2

View over Lisbon from Esplanada da Igreja da Graça

Cape of Good Hope in 1488, and in 1497 Vasco da Gama reached Calicut, India. By 1560, Portugal had claimed Brazil and had an empire stretching east as far as Japan, with missionary and trading posts in Africa, India, Malaysia, Macau and Timor.

Despite strong rivalry between Portugal and Spain over discoveries in the Americas, the 16th century was a Golden Age, with spices, slaves and gold making Portugal hugely rich. But the voyages and maintenance of an overseas empire were extremely costly, and the

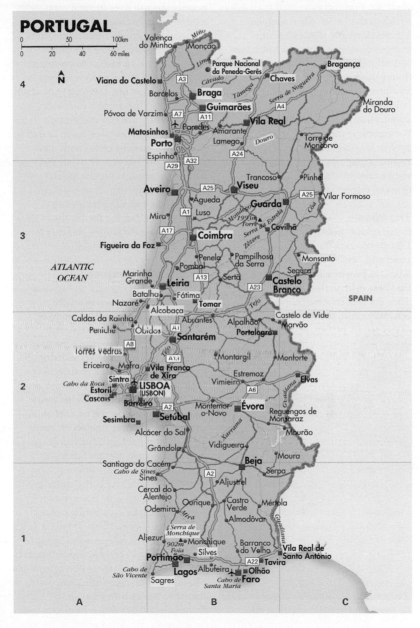

PORTUGAL

ATLANTIC OCEAN

SPAIN

home economy was worsening. By 1580, Philip II of Spain had claimed the throne, becoming Philip I of Portugal the following year. Within 100 years, many of the overseas possessions had fallen to the English and Dutch.

The legacy of the empire still exists, however. Portugal extricated itself from Africa in the 1970s, when Angola, Mozambique and Guinea became independent; East Timor in Indonesia was relinquished at the same time. Today there are buildings, churches and monuments wherever the Portuguese held power, but language became the country's most important legacy. Portuguese is the seventh most widely spoken language in the world. Brazil retains strong ties with Portugal and, unlike many former colonies, there is genuine respect between the countries.

The People
Geographical isolation from most of Europe has kept Portuguese bloodlines pure, and you'll notice a definite racial type – in provincial areas, most people are short, with dark eyes, skin and hair. They are conservative people who are generally courteous and respectful.

The Elevador da Bica climbs up a Lisbon street

Northerners, with a harsher climate and historically poorer living conditions, tend to be less easygoing than people in the south, and more religious. Even so, the Catholic church continues to hold great sway everywhere.

Approximately 40 percent of the population still lives in rural areas, with a large urban increase occurring in the 1970s, when people came home from former African colonies following independence. In Lisbon in particular, many Afro-Portuguese have integrated into Portuguese life; there's a good level of interracial harmony.

The country has one of Europe's highest emigration rates, more so due to the recent financial crisis, with more than four million people living and working abroad. With few natural resources, many people in northern Portugal are forced to seek work overseas; you can see the results of their labors in the new houses and cars found in even the poorest villages.

Society and Language
Being polite and friendly will smooth your path as you travel through Portugal. The Portuguese tend to be welcoming and unhurried, so be prepared for things to take a long time. There are traditional ideas and attitudes toward women, and the farther away from major towns you travel the more obvious this becomes. It's sometimes considered disrespectful to wear skimpy clothing, and it is customary to speak formally and politely until you get to know the people you are talking to.

One of the major hurdles in getting to know the Portuguese is the language barrier. Don't try your Spanish in Portugal. Despite – or because of – proximity to Spain, the Portuguese don't appreciate being addressed in Spanish. However, if you can read Spanish you'll have no problem reading Portuguese. It's a Romance language with Latin roots, similar to Spanish and Italian. Pronunciation is a different matter

A detail of the elaborate carving at the Mosteiro dos Jerónimos in the Belém district of Lisbon

altogether, however, and spoken Portuguese, with its sibilants, nasal vowels and guttural consonants, can sound like Russian and Slavic languages.

The Portuguese are excellent linguists; you'll find English spoken in major tourist areas, and in the countryside among the younger generation. Do try to tackle one or two words; your efforts will be appreciated and faces will light up when you try to communicate.

Changing Portugal

Since Portugal joined the European Union in 1986, huge changes have occurred. Once one of the poorest countries in Western Europe, Portugal had one of the highest economic growth rates in the 1990s. While unemployment plummeted, the cost was a widening gap between rich and poor, noticeable wherever you travel.

The enlargement of the EU since 2004, however, poses several challenges. As countries farther east in Europe have swelled the ranks, Portugal lost its advange of relatively cheap labor costs, and a high proportion of national earnings comes from overseas – a global

market that becomes ever more challenging. Agriculture in Portugal is still relatively unproductive due to lack of investment and the difficulty of using modern methods and large equipment on much of the terrain. Education levels are low by European standards, with a surprising percentage of the population having literacy problems.

As the world financial crisis broke in 2008, economic growth stalled at zero percent and the Portuguese government requested a financial bail-out package from the European Union. The economy is now growing, albeit very slowly, but it is still a cause for concern.

Portugal does export large amounts of certain products including cork, tomato paste and wine. It also earns through foreign tourism, an industry that continues to develop. Portugal has become a much-loved holiday destination for many Europeans. For visitors, the blend of old and new is alluring. Investment in infrastructure through the early 2000s has improved the visitor experience, while the rustic way of life is still evident away from the major cities and towns.

Timeline

1000 BC to AD 400	Occupation by Phoenicians, Carthaginians, Iberians, Celts, Romans and Visigoths.
AD 713	Moors control most of the country and remain in power for 400 years.
1179	Pope recognizes Kingdom of Portugal.
1255	Afonso III makes Lisbon the capital of Portugal.
1480–1500s	Age of Discovery.
1488	Bartolomeu Dias rounds Cape of Good Hope.
1580	End of Golden Age with invasion by Philip II of Spain, who declares himself Philip I of Portugal.
1668	Treaty of Lisbon recognizes Portuguese independence.
1755	Lisbon earthquake.
1910	Portuguese monarchy overthrown and replaced by republic.
1916–18	Portugal joins Allies in World War I.
1933	Estado Novo (New State) established. Falls in 1974.
1939–45	Portugal neutral throughout World War II.
1960s	Portuguese colony of Goa occupied by India; local nationalist uprisings in Angola, Guinea and Mozambique.
1976	New constitution drawn up after the fall of the Estado Novo.
1986	Portugal admitted to European Union; start of period of huge economic growth and social reform.
2001	Porto is named European Capital of Culture for 2001.
2004	Portuguese Prime Minister José Manuel Barroso is appointed President of the European Union.
2005–2006	Portugal's driest summer on record brings drought and forest fires.
2008–2011	The Portuguese economy struggles on the verge of collapse as EU enlargement and the world credit crisis take their toll.
2012	Portugal receives EU/IMF bailout package as economy in crisis.
2014	Portugal continues to meet its repayment schedule and exits the European Adjustment Program imposed by EU.
May 2017	Pope Francis canonizes Jacinta and Francisco Marta, two shepherd children who are said to have been visited by the Virgin Mary in 1917, at Fátima.
2017	Despite critics' fears, two years after elections, the economy shows strong signs of revival under a Socialist minority government.

Prince Henry the Navigator

The impetus for the great Portuguese "Age of Discovery" of the late 15th century came from the son of João I, Prince Henry, who was born in 1394. He can be credited with transforming Portugal into a great maritime power whose success was based on a scientific approach to exploration, navigation and cartography. At his base in the Algarve, Henry gathered together accomplished shipbuilders, sailors, navigators, instrument makers and astronomers, encouraging them to prepare for long voyages into the unknown. A new type of ship, the highly successful caravel, was designed: a speedy vessel that made the great voyages possible. Motivated by religion as well as commerce, Henry's ships sailed ever farther south, rounding Cape Bojador in West Africa, then thought to be the end of the world, in 1434. By Henry's death in 1460, the Portuguese had reached Sierra Leone, and the known world had become a far bigger place.

Survival Guide

- The Portuguese are committed wine drinkers. When you order house wine in restaurants it is generally very drinkable and is sometimes served in an earthenware jug.

- Water available everywhere is safe to drink, although sometimes it may taste less than delicious. Avoid tap water in the Algarve during the summer and drink bottled water instead, to be on the safe side.

- When visiting Lisbon or Porto make use of a tourist card which offers a range of free or discounted entrances and other advantages. The Lisboa Card (see www.lisboacard.org) is valid for 24 hours (€19), 48 hours (€32) or 72 hours (€40). The Porto Card (www.visitporto.travel), can be purchased with or without public transportation and is valid for 1, 2, 3 or 4 days with prices starting at €6 (1-day pass without public transportation) to €33 (4-day pass with transportation).

- In more rural areas, the modest Portuguese are often shocked by scanty clothes, especially men without shirts, except at the beach. If you are wearing a sleeveless top, take along a scarf to cover your shoulders as needed, particularly if you visit churches. Do not enter while a service is in progress.

- Take care when driving in Portugal. The accident rate here happens to be one of the highest in Western Europe.

- Telephone calls from your hotel room are expensive, but Portugal's telephone system is state of the art. The on-street Portugal Telecom (PT) phones which accept coins, credit cards and plastic phone cards, offer an easy way to connect. You can buy the phone cards from street kiosks.

- In cafés and restaurants, meals often start with a selection of appetizers, which arrive automatically to your table and are added to your bill if you eat them. Simply send them back if you do not wish to enjoy them.

- It is increasingly easy to find luxury accommodations and excellent service away from major tourist centers, with the opening of a large number of spas, fine country hotels and boutique-style bed-and-breakfast places.

- Portuguese food is traditionally rustic and served in hearty portions. Some dishes require an adventurous spirit, alternatively you can enjoy roasted meats, grilled fish and chicken in most restaurants.

- Leave small change in a bar; tipping is not expected, but 5–10 percent is an adequate tip for good service.

- Pousadas offer many interesting accommodations options in Portugal. These are state-owned but privately run, deluxe establishments located in historic or beautiful places such as former monasteries, palaces and castles. Advance reservations are highly recommended.

Shoppers and diners at the café terraces in Rua Augusta in La Baixa district, Lisbon

Portugal

Lisbon

Lisbon (Lisboa) is a beguiling city. It has a great past and, economic woes aside, a promising future. Its backstreets may easily strike the visitor as old-fashioned and crumbling, but these elements add to its charm. Look for the positive: the port city's vigor and life; its great colonial past; the atmospheric old trams; and the evocative sights, sounds and scents – laundry flapping in the wind, shoeshine men hawking their trade, the melancholy strains of *fado* music, the aroma of roasting coffee and chestnuts.

Most sights of interest are within walking distance of downtown, with the exception of the glorious attractions of suburban Belém (see page 384), to the west of the old city, a train, bus or tram ride away.

Lisbon Flavors and *Bacalhau*

Lisbon has restaurants at every price level, with the emphasis on traditional Portuguese cooking, although fast-food outlets are easy to find too. Breakfast consists of cakes and pastries, and hotels may offer a Continental-style breakfast buffet. Lunch is more substantial than in other European cities.

Heavy soups are popular, and salads, although sometimes limited in their ingredients, are readily available, as is freshly squeezed orange juice. Lisbon inhabitants eat a lot of fish and seafood, including *bacalhau* (dried, salted codfish), and the warming winter stews are excellent.

The Lisbon Earthquake

On All Saints' Day (November 1), 1755, the Lisbon earthquake struck. Churches were packed for this major feast day, and thousands of lighted candles toppled during the tremors, starting fires that were as destructive as the quake. A massive tidal wave followed, swallowing Lisbon's fleet and flooding the already-destroyed lower city. During the aftermath hospitals opened, prices were fixed and a tax levied to cover rebuilding costs, including the lower city, today known as the Baixa district. Although Lisbon largely recovered, 1755 marked the end of its role as Europe's leading port city.

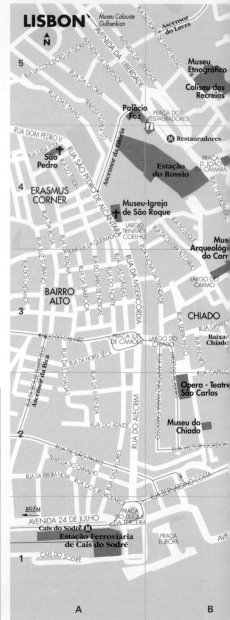

You may be surprised at the number of pastry and cake shops; the Portuguese are notoriously sweet-toothed, and Lisbon has many tempting, old-fashioned shops selling traditional specialties like the delicious *pastéis de* *Belém* (pastries filled with custard). Portugal makes very good red and white wine, national and foreign beers are everywhere, and all the usual spirits and aperitifs are available. It is known for the fortified wine, port.

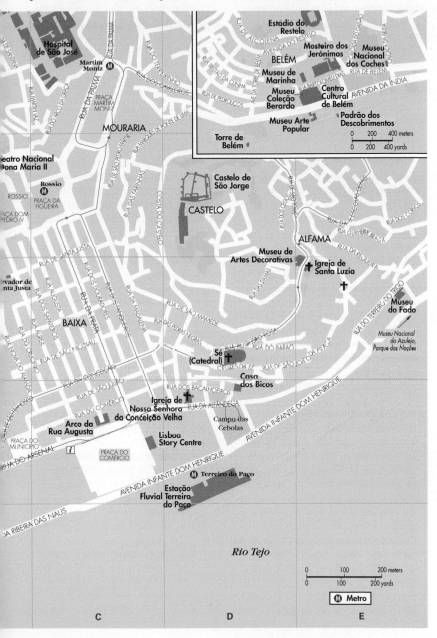

Souvenirs from Lisbon

Shopping is great fun in Lisbon and Portuguese crafts can be found. The area known as the Chiado, in downtown Lisbon, is the most fashionable shopping district, with streets lined with many classy clothing and jewelry boutiques.

Carpets from Arraiolos or the porcelain made by Vista Alegre (www.myvista alegre.com), linen and cotton sheets and tablecloths are all Portuguese specialties, as are the lovely glazed tiles, *azulejos*, which are made to order.

Film, Music and *Fado*

Lisbon offers a variety of music, theater, ballet and movies. Films are all shown in their original language with subtitles. *Fado*, a unique style of Portuguese music, is heard at its best in Lisbon and should be experienced. Its origins lie in history, a mix of Moorish and African elements, and can be described as a kind of soul music. The best place to hear it is at a *fado* house in the Upper Town of Lisbon (Bairro Alto, see page 381), or in the Alfama district.

Essential Information

Tourist Information

Turismo de Lisboa (Lisbon Tourist Office)
Welcome Center, Praça do Comércio
☎ 210 312 810
Santa Apolónia (railway station)
☎ 218 821 606
Lisbon International Airport (arrivals)
☎ 218 450 660
Jerónimos Monastery Quiosque ☎ 213 658 435
Palácio Foz, Praça dos Restauradores
☎ 213 463 314
Youth Tourist Office, Rua Jardim do Regedor 50 ☎ 213 472 134
Praça D. Pedro IV, Rossio ☎ 0910 517 914
Alameda dos Oceanos, Parque das Nações
☎ 910 518 028
www.visitlisboa.com or www.golisbon.com

Urban Transportation

Lisbon has a metro (subway) system, buses, trams, funiculars and ferries. Metro stations are marked with an "M" on the city map. A one-day travel card is available for the whole network. For visitors, the Lisboa Card, valid for 24, 48 or 72 hours, gives unlimited travel and free entry into 26 attractions. Zapping is a replenishable electronic card, valid on buses, metro and ferries, or you can buy bus and tram tickets when boarding, and metro tickets from a machine or office at the metro station. For information consult www.carris.pt for bus and tram services, and www.metrolisboa.pt for metro services. Ferry tickets are available from offices at the ferry stations; a ferry trip is recommended as part of your sightseeing. Prepaid taxi vouchers to various zones and destinations are available online and at three tourist information centers – the airport, Lisboa Welcome Center and Palácio Foz. There are taxi stands on the Rossio and the Praça da Figueira, or call a cab (☎ 217 932 756).

Airport Information

Lisbon Airport (☎ 218 413 700/500 for flight information, or online at www.ana.pt) is about 4 miles (a 20-minute drive, longer at peak times) north of the downtown area. The metro links the airport with downtown 6:30 a.m.–1 a.m. The Aero-Bus shuttle service (www.aerobus.pt) leaves every 20 minutes daily 8 a.m.–11 p.m. from outside the terminal to downtown Lisbon.

Climate – average highs and lows for the month

Jan.	Feb.	Mar.	Apr.	May	Jun.	Jul.	Aug.	Sep.	Oct.	Nov.	Dec.
13°C	15°C	17°C	19°C	21°C	25°C	28°C	29°C	27°C	21°C	18°C	14°C
55°F	59°F	63°F	66°F	70°F	77°F	82°F	84°F	81°F	70°F	64°F	57°F
8°C	9°C	10°C	12°C	12°C	15°C	18°C	18°C	17°C	14°C	10°C	9°C
46°F	48°F	50°F	54°F	54°F	59°F	64°F	64°F	63°F	57°F	50°F	48°F

Lisbon Sights

Bairro Alto

The Bairro Alto (Upper Town) is one of the five areas that constitute Lisbon's historic center and the atmospheric streets and squares tumble down slopes to the Baixa (the Lower Town) below. At night it's one of the city's liveliest quarters, where in *fado* houses you can hear melancholic Portuguese songs.

The Elevador de Santa Justa, a wonderfully clunky elevator built in 1902, takes people from the Baixa up to the Chiado and Bairro Alto.

➕ A3 ✉ Area on slopes to west of Baixa
🚇 Restauradores, Baixa-Chiado 🚌 758, 773; tram 28E
Elevador de Santa Justa ✉ Rua do Ouro 65
☎ 214 138 679 🕐 Daily 7:30 a.m.–11 p.m.,
May–Oct.; 7:30 a.m.–9 p.m., rest of year 🎫 $$

Baixa and Rossio

Rossio Square, properly known as Praça Dom Pedro IV, and the grid of streets forming the Baixa district will repeatedly draw you back. The Teatro Nacional (National Theater) and a soaring column topped by a statue of Dom Pedro IV dominate the spacious Rossio, which is lined with stores and cafés. The square has an ancient history and was the scene of brutal Inquisition burnings in the 16th century.

Between Rossio and the waterfront lies the Baixa, erected at the Marquês de Pombal's instigation after the 1755 earthquake (see panel, page 378). The orderly streets are lined with lovely old stores, modern chain stores, gracious buildings and tiled facades.

➕ C3, B4 ✉ Praça Dom Pedro IV and streets between it and Praça do Comércio 🚇 Baixa-Chiado, Rossio
🚌 All services to Rossio and Praça do Comércio

Castelo de São Jorge

Visible from many parts of Lisbon, the Castelo de São Jorge (St. George's Castle) stands on the site of the earliest settlement. Fortified sucessively by the Romans, Visigoths and Moors, it was besieged in 1147 by Afonso Henriques and his Christian army and finally fell after 17 weeks – a turning point in the struggle to evict the Moors from Portugal. The Moorish battlements still stand and offer superb views over the rooftops to the river.

Take in the small museum and the archeological site and, if time allows, the Alfama district around the palace is also worth exploring.

➕ D4 ✉ Rua Santa Cruz do Castelo ☎ 218 800 620;
www.castelodesaojorge.pt 🏰 Castle: daily 9–9,
Mar.–Oct.; 9–6, rest of year. Last admission 30 minutes before closing. Periscópio: daily 10–5 🚌 737; tram 12E, 28E 🎫 $$$ ℹ Free guided tours daily at 1 and 4 p.m.

You can see the Tagus river beyond Lisbon's rooftops from the Castelo de São Jorge

Mosteiro dos Jerónimos

The stunning architectural ensemble of the Mosteiro dos Jerónimos (Jerónimos Monastery), a UNESCO World Heritage Site, stands on the site of an earlier chapel, visited by Portuguese explorers before their great voyages.

Building began on the present church in 1501 to celebrate Vasco da Gama's successful voyage to the Indies. It took almost 100 years to complete and, as a result, the church and adjoining cloisters are a glorious mix of Gothic, Renaissance and Manueline styles.

Pause first at the magnificent south door. Its intricate carving includes the figure of Henry the Navigator; the west door, equally splendid, features Manuel I, who started the construction. The soaring interior contains the simple tomb of Vasco da Gama, a contrast to the surrounding riot of stonework. The cloisters are elaborately carved, a combination of delicacy and strength.

➕ See map inset ⊠ Praça do Império ☎ 213 620 034; www.mosteirojeronimos.pt ⊙ Tue.–Sun. 10–6:30, May–Sep.; 10–5:30, rest of year. Last admission 30 minutes before closing 🚆 Train: Belém 🚌 28, 714, 727, 729, 751; tram 15E 🚊 Belém 🚇 $$$; free first Sun. of the month

Museu Calouste Gulbenkian

Portugal's greatest museum, the Calouste Gulbenkian Museum was financed by a bequest from the Armenian magnate, whose private collection makes up the bulk of the exhibits. It consists of two sections: European art and artifacts, and Oriental and ancient pieces. The Lalique jewelry and glass, distinctive art deco pieces are displayed in a darkened room.

➕ Off map at A5 ⊠ Avenida de Berna 45A ☎ 217 823 000; www.gulbenkian.pt ⊙ Wed.–Mon. 10–6 (last entry at 5:30) 🚇 S. Sebastião or Praça de Espanha 🚌 713, 716, 726, 742, 746, 756 🍴 Restaurant and café 🚇 $$$; free to all Sun. 🎧 Audio guide ($$)

Museu Coleção Berardo

The city's modern, contemporary art museum has a wealth of works by well-known artists from across the globe and across artistic genres, including Pablo Picasso, Marc Chagall, Yves Klein, Joan Míro and Andy Warhol.

➕ See map inset ⊠ Praça do Império ☎ 213 612 878; www.museuberardo.pt ⊙ Daily 10–7 🚌 714, 727, 728, 729, 751; tram 15E 🚇 $$

Museu de Marinha

The Museu de Marinha (Maritime Museum) is one of the best of its kind in Europe. It's a huge collection, with full-size boats, royal barges, paintings, uniforms and archaic navigational instruments. Most evocative, perhaps, is the attractive wooden statue of the Archangel Raphael, said to have accompanied Vasco da Gama on his epic voyage to the Indies in 1497.

➕ See map inset ⊠ Praça do Império ☎ 210 977 388; ccm.marinha.pt ⊙ Tue.–Sun. 10–6, May–Sep.; 10–5, rest of year 🚆 Train: Belém 🚌 714, 727, 729, 751; tram 15E 🚇 $$; free first Sun. of the month

Museu Nacional do Azulejo

Throughout Lisbon and Portugal you'll notice the exquisite tiles, or *azulejos*, adorning the walls of buildings. The Museu Nacional do Azulejo (National Tile Museum) traces the history of the painted glazed tile, which has been used in Portugal since the 15th century. Blue and white has predominated since Chinese porcelain arrived in Europe; the wonderful tiled view of Lisbon, made in 1738, is a fine example.

➕ Off map at E3 ⊠ Rua da Madre de Deus 4 ☎ 218 100 340; www.museudoazulejo.pt ⊙ Tue.–Sun. 10–6. Last entry 30 minutes before closing 🚌 718, 742, 794 🍴 Café 🚇 $$; free first Sun. of the month 🎧 Audio guide (free)

Padrão dos Descobrimentos

The eye-catching white mass of the Padrão dos Descobrimentos (Monument to the Discoveries) soars up from the water's edge at Belém, serving as a reminder of Portugal's great maritime past. It was erected in 1960 to mark the 500th anniversary of the death of Henry the Navigator, and has an angular front

Lisbon Life

Everyday life in Lisbon, a relatively small and atmospheric city, is far more relaxed than in other European capital cities. The day starts around 7:30 a.m., when commuters are on the move and children make their way to school. Trams, the subway and buses are all crowded. Some people travel to town on the ferries that crisscross the Tagus. Many grab breakfast in a bar before work. Breakfast is usually coffee, with one of the cloyingly sweet pastries so loved by the Portuguese.

Lunch in Lisbon is taken seriously, and many people eat a full meal rather than a snack, although they eat it fast, often standing at a bar counter. Workers also use the lunch hour to shop for food or browse in stores. At the end of the afternoon, commuters head home but will often reemerge later to meet friends for a drink or more tea or coffee and cakes. Midweek evenings are often spent at home, although in the summertime the streets will be thronged for a few hours as people stroll around and chat outside.

Weekends are a different matter; people head for the Upper Town to eat and drink before going to concerts, movies or the theater, while young Portuguese enjoy the old district's waterfront clubs.

Saturday and Sunday are popular shopping days when crowds flock to huge malls on the outskirts of the city, which stay open late. Sundays, too, are high points for soccer fans, with the big matches attracting large crowds. Lisbon is blessed by its proximity to a beautiful coastline, and it's easy in summer to drive or catch a train to the coast for a day at the beach and dinner in an excellent fish restaurant. In midsummer, an outing to the cool green countryside around Sintra (see page 385), some 20 miles away, is another pleasant weekend option.

The exterior of the Teatro São Carlos in Lisbon's Chiado district

and curving form that represents a ship's prow and sails. Figures crowd the prow, led by Henry, who holds a ship. An elevator rises more than 435 feet to the top, offering panoramic views. Below, a mosaic map traces the important Portuguese voyages of exploration.

➕ See map inset ✉ Avenida de Brasília ☎ 213 031 950; www.padraodosdescobrimentos.pt ⏰ Daily 10–7, Apr.–Sep.; Tue.–Sun. 10–7, Mar.; Tue.–Sun. 10–6, rest of year. Last admission 30 minutes before closing 🚆 Train: Belém 🚌 714, 727, 729, 751; tram 15E 💲 $$ (temporary exhibitions free)

Parque das Nações

The Parque das Nações (Park of the Nations), constructed for the Expo '98, is used for trade fairs and exhibitions. Striking buildings, moorings, landscaped gardens, street cafés and restaurants front the Tagus river. From the water rises the Oceanário (Oceanarium), one of Europe's largest.

➕ Off map at E3 ✉ Parque das Nações ☎ 218 917 000 (Oceanarium); www.portaldasnacoes.pt or www.oceanario.pt ⏰ Oceanarium: daily 10–8, Apr.–Oct.; 10–7, rest of year. Last admission 1 hour before closing 🚆 Oriente 🚌 5, 25, 28, 44, 708, 759, 782, 794 💲 Park free; Oceanarium $$$

Praça do Comércio

One side of the spacious Praça do Comércio (Commercial Square) opens on the water, emphasizing its original purpose as an imposing gateway to the city from the sea. On another side is the state-of-the-art, multimedia Lisboa Story Centre, a great starting place to get a handle on the city's history, or you could take the elevator up the Arco da Rua Augusta (Rua Augusta Arch) for superb views.

To experience the square's original perspective, take the short ferry trip from the Terreiro do Paço (Palace Square) river station across the Tagus to the suburb of Barreiro. The vista gives a flavor of the city's past.

➕ C2 ✉ Praça do Comércio 🚆 Terreiro do Paço 🚌 All buses to Praça do Comércio; tram 15E 🚢 Terreiro do Paço for ferries to Cacilhas **Lisboa Story Centre** ✉ Terreiro do Paço 78–81 ☎ 211 194 099; www.lisboastorycentre.pt ⏰ Daily 10–8 💲 $$

Sé

Construction of the Sé (Cathedral) started in 1150, and was the city's first church, a solid and harmonious Romanesque edifice. Its two massive towers are a prominent city landmark. It escaped damage in the 1755 earthquake, making it a symbol of Lisbon's history. Inside, be sure to see the font where St. Anthony of Padua was baptized.

➕ D3 ✉ Largo da Sé ☎ 218 866 752 ⏰ Church: Tue.–Sat. 9–7, Sun.–Mon. 9–5. Cloister: Mon.–Sat. 10–6:30, Apr.–Oct.; Mon.–Sat. 10–5, rest of year. Museum: Mon.–Sat. 10–5 🚆 Terreiro do Paço or Baixa-Chiado 🚌 737; tram 12E, 28E 💲 Museum and cloister $

Torre de Belém

In the nearby suburb of Belém, the Torre de Belém (Belém Tower), a symbol of Portugal's maritime past, rises beside the Tagus river. Built between 1515 and 1520, it was designed by Francisco de Arruda, a Portuguese architect whose Moroccan travels influenced his style. His work shows delightful Moorish elements – corner towers, and arcaded windows and loggias. Built as a bastion against pirate attack, it later served as a prison. It is now a World Heritage Site.

➕ See map inset ✉ Avenida de Brasília ☎ 213 620 034; www.torrebelem.pt ⏰ Tue.–Sun. 10–6:30, May–Sep.; 10–5:30, rest of year. Last admission 30 minutes before closing 🚆 Train: Belém 🚌 714, 727, 729, 751; tram 15E 💲 $$; free first Sun. of the month

Visitors enjoy the views from the shady loggia of the Torre de Belém

Sintra

By far the most popular day trip from Lisbon is to beautiful Sintra, a small town packed with delights, set in lush and mountainous country some 20 miles northwest of Lisbon. Once there, the attractions are scattered over a wide area, so it makes sense to take a tour or rent a car and drive from the city. Alternatively, take the train from Lisbon and make use of the efficient Sintra buses which cover the main sites. Most tour operators include a detour to Cabo da Roca, the Continent's westernmost point.

For more than 500 years Sintra was the summer resort of Portuguese kings – a legacy that is apparent in the town's two astounding palaces (www.parquesdesintra.pt). The National Palace (Palácio Nacional) was first built by João I in the 15th century and remained in use until the end of the 19th century.

Architecturally imposing, it's nevertheless a muddle of mainly Gothic and Manueline styles. The interior is worth exploring. Note the superb ceramic tiles, as well as the elaborately decorated ceilings: one is painted with gold-collared swans and another with magpies.

The other main palace is the Pena National Palace (Palácio Nacional da Pena), built in the 1840s by Ferdinand of Saxe-Coburg-Gotha, husband of Queen Maria II. It's a creation of towers and battlements, and the inside is a riot of flamboyant furniture, wall hangings and paintings. Nearby is the eighth-century Castelo dos Mouros, a ruined Moorish stronghold.

The other outstanding attractions in Sintra are its gardens and parks. The warm, damp climate is ideal for a profusion of exotic trees, shrubs and roses, and you'll see everything from rhododendrons and camellias to tree ferns and palms. The Pena Gardens, below the Pena National Palace, are lovely, with lakes and mock temples. But the highlight is the Monserrate Gardens, west of Sintra. Two Englishmen laid out the gardens between 1790 and 1860, and they ramble over 74 acres.

Around Sintra lies the rugged and far-reaching Parque Natural Sintra-Cascais (www.cm-cascais.pt), stretching from the mountains of Sintra down to the dramatic Atlantic coastline at Guincho.

➕ See map page 373, A2

Tour Operators

Cityrama-Grayline ✉ Avenida João XXI 7BE ☎ 213 191 090 (within Portugal), 800 472 9546 (US/CA toll free); www.grayline.com/lisbon or www.cityrama.pt

Lisboasightseeing ✉ Rua Pascoal de Melo 3 ☎ 967 086 536; www.lisboasightseeing.com

Inside Lisbon ✉ Avenida Forças Armadas 95 ☎ 211 914 545 (within Portugal), 1 646 257 4042 (from US); www.insidelisbon.com

Diana Tours ✉ Campo Grande 30B ☎ 217 799 8540; www.dianatours.pt

The Palácio Nacional da Pena is a storybook castle with turrets and towers

Porto

Porto, Portugal's second-largest city with about 200,000 residents and about 1.7 million in the greater Porto area, lies on the steep north bank of the Douro river, a few miles from its outlet on the Atlantic. The city suburbs sprawl down to the coast. Many visitors encounter Porto on their way up the beautiful Douro valley. The city also is known for its association with port wine, which has been shipped from the suburb of Vila Nova de Gaia since the 17th century. It has long been referred to as "Oporto," a name never used by the Portuguese and now declining in use elsewhere.

Development of Porto

Founded in pre-Roman times, the city of Porto gave its name to the country, and was the birthplace of Prince Henry the Navigator, son of João I of Portugal and Philippa of Lancaster, granddaughter of Edward III of England, in 1394. Traditionally liberal, its residents have always had a strong rebellious streak, which goes well with the city's industrious and down-to-earth image.

Porto is a refreshing antidote to the faded elegance of Lisbon – a bustling, no-nonsense city lying at the center of Portugal's most important economic area, its layout inextricably entwined with the history of the port trade. Grandiose buildings testify to its 18th- and 19th-century wealth, but the true spirit of the city lies in the maze of narrow streets below the cathedral, the old docks and the waterfront houses. Areas throughout the city are decorated with blue-and-white *azulejos* (glazed ceramic tiles).

Suggested Itineraries

Two or three days should be sufficient to see the main sights of Porto. Nearly everything of interest is within a short walk or bus ride from the city center. The streets are steep and hilly, so wear comfortable shoes.

If you're on your way up the Douro valley, make time to visit the port lodges in Vila Nova de Gaia (see page 390), Porto's main tourist attraction. If you've got more time, the city can be neatly divided into cultural itineraries, focusing on medieval, baroque and neoclassic monuments and churches. And for a state-of-the-art attraction, Porto now boasts a world-class arts center, the Casa da Música (www.casadamusica.com).

The heart of modern Porto centers around Avenida dos Aliados, a broad avenue with the monumental town hall at one end and the Praça da Liberdade, a transportation hub, at the other. This stretch is a good place to people-watch. The main shopping areas are east and north of this avenue. You can use the river to help orient yourself to the city.

Porto Flavors

The people of Porto have traditionally been known as *tripeiros*, or "tripe-eaters," allegedly because they sacrificed all their meat except the tripe to their army during a legendary battle – an historic indicator that, until recent years, refined cooking wasn't a priority. That said, hearty food still dominates. Expect plenty of fish, with the much-beloved *bacalhau* (dried, salted codfish) and super-sweet desserts on every menu at any time of the day. On the other hand, a glass of smooth, silky and subtle port – drunk on its native soil – may convert even the most inveterate port-hater.

An especially atmospheric place to dine is beside the river at Ribeira (see page 389), in the heart of the oldest part of Porto. The area is filled with dozens of good, lively restaurants, cafés and bars under the medieval arches, with tremendous tourist appeal.

Crafts and Shopping

Porto is the place to track down northern handicraft specialties, fine port, locally made shoes and traditional gold filigree jewelry from the villages of the Minho.

The city's wonderfully old-fashioned stores, many of which still retain their early 20th-century facades and details, are worth a visit even if you're not buying. Highlights include the Lello and Irmão bookstore (www.livrarialello.pt) on Rua das Carmelitas, with its superb double staircase, now a magnet for *Harry Potter* fans, and Cardoso Cabeleireiro on Rua do Bonjardim, a shop specializing in wigs and toupees. Similar stores cluster together in Porto, so you'll find streets packed with hardware stores, seed merchants, jewelers and linen stores. Marques Soares (www.marquessoares.pt), a chic department store on Rua das Carmelitas, carries exquisite leather goods.

Excursions and Entertainment
There are several marine operators that run cruises on the Douro river, varying in price and ranging from a week-long trip up the river on a luxury cruiser

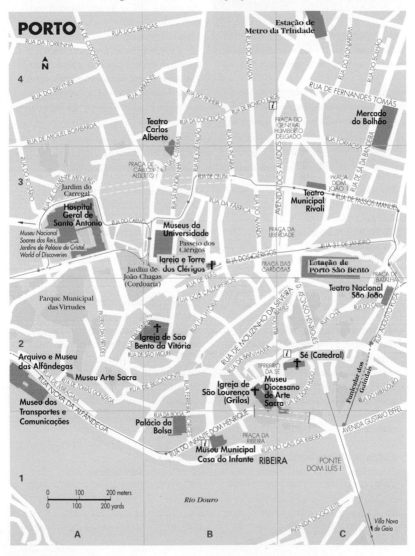

PORTO

Portugal

The Igreja and Torre dos Clérigos tower over Porto

reproduction of a *rabelo*, the glorious old boats once used to carry barrels of port downstream from the vineyards. Sections of the 19th-century narrow-gauge railway still operate in the Douro valley – this is a fun way to do a little exploring. Tour operators also run bus trips in, around and out of Porto; Porto Tours (☎ 300 501 920; www.portotours.com) is a reliable operator with English-speaking guides. Alternatively, tickets may be bought at the tourist office. Be sure to visit the port lodges in Vila Nova de Gaia, an essential stop on any Porto visit.

For evening entertainment, locals attend theaters, concerts and the movies, although many people prefer to while away the hours of warm, balmy evenings at a terrace café or simply strolling along the riverbank.

taking in the sights along the riverbank, to shorter trips of a couple of hours puttering around the lower reaches in a

Essential Information

Tourist Information
Turismo do Porto (Porto Tourism)
Casa da Camâra, Terreiro da Sé
☎ 300 501 920 (all offices);
www.visitporto.travel
Rua Clube dos Fenianos 25
Also informaton kiosks at: Campanhã Railway Station (all year); Porto airport (all year); Praça da Ribeira (May–Oct.)

Urban Transportation
The Sociedade de Transportes Colectivos do Porto (STCP) issues a Mapa de Transportes showing both day and nighttime bus, tram and metro routes (available from tourist offices). Pay as you get on the bus or the tram. A 1- or 3-day "Andante" card is valid on the city's tram and metro system (www.metrodoporto.pt). Porto

Tourism issues a Porto Card, valid for 1, 2 or 3 days, which offers unlimited use of public transportation as well as free entrance to many attractions. Taxis are inexpensive; there is an additional charge to cross the river to Gaia. For bus information ☎ 226 158 158 or 808 200 166 (within Portugal, toll free); www.stcp.pt.

Airport Information
Francisco Sá Carneiro International Airport (☎ 229 432 400; www.ana.pt) is 12 miles northwest of central Porto. Porto metro line E (☎ 808 20 50 60; www.metrodoporto.pt) links the airport with Trinidade station in the city; trains run from 6 a.m.–12:30 a.m. every 20 or 30 minutes; travel time is 35 minutes. Bus services 601 and 602 (daytime), 3M (night bus) also serve the airport.

Climate – average highs and lows for the month

Jan.	Feb.	Mar.	Apr.	May	Jun.	Jul.	Aug.	Sep.	Oct.	Nov.	Dec.
13°C	13°C	15°C	17°C	18°C	22°C	23°C	23°C	23°C	19°C	17°C	14°C
55°F	55°F	59°F	63°F	64°F	72°F	73°F	73°F	73°F	66°F	63°F	57°F
6°C	7°C	7°C	9°C	10°C	13°C	14°C	14°C	14°C	12°C	8°C	7°C
43°F	45°F	45°F	48°F	50°F	55°F	57°F	57°F	57°F	54°F	46°F	45°F

Porto Sights

Key to symbols

➕ map coordinates refer to the Porto map
on page 387 📋 admission charge:
$$$ more than €7:50, $$ €4–€7:50, $ less than €4
See page 5 for complete key to symbols

Igreja e Torre dos Clérigos

The soaring Torre dos Clérigos (Tower
of Clérigos), attached to an 18th-century
granite church (Igreja dos Clérigos),
affords fine city views. Nicolau Nasoni
designed the oval church, with its
elaborately festooned facade of swags
and garlands, in the 1730s.

➕ B3 ✉ Rua São Felipe de Nery ☎ 220 145 489;
www.torredosclerigos.pt 🕐 Church and tower: daily
9–7. Last admission 30 minutes before closing
🚇 D line: São Bento 🚌 All Praça da Liberdade
services 📋 Church free; Tower $$

Jardins do Palácio de Cristal

At the Jardins do Palácio de Cristal
(Crystal Palace Gardens), a lime
tree-lined avenue leads from pools and
fountains past magnolias, camellias and
rhododendrons to rose gardens and
terraces high above the river, and offers
one of the best vantage points in Porto.

➕ Off map at A3 ✉ Rua de Dom Manuel II ☎ 225
320 000 📋 Daily 8 a.m.–9 p.m., Apr.–Sep.; 8–7, rest
of year 🚌 200, 201, 207, 302,303, 501 🍴 Café

Museu Nacional Soares dos Reis

The Soares dos Reis National Museum,
named after the 19th-century sculptor, is
Porto's most important museum. Housed
in an impressive 1795 neoclassical
edifice, it was occupied in the 1800s
during the Peninsular War by first the
French and then the English. The
museum features works by dos Reis,
with exhibits of glass and porcelain; look
for pieces from the Vista Alegre factory.

➕ Off map at A3 ✉ Rua Dom Manuel II 44 ☎ 223
393 770; www.museusoaresdosreis.pt 🕐 Tue.–Sun.
10–6. Last admission 30 minutes before closing
🚌 200, 201, 207, 208, 302, 303, 501, 507, 601 🍴 Café
📋 $$; free first Sun. of the month

Palácio da Bolsa

Dominating one side of Praça Infante
D. Henrique, this neoclassical palace was
built in the 19th century to house the
Porto Stock Exchange. The magnificent
interior rooms were decorated by several
architects between 1842 and 1910. The
Arab room, featuring Moorish style and
designed by Gustavo Adolfo Gonçalves
de Sousa, is considered the highlight,
and is still used for civic banquets and
other public events.

➕ B1 ✉ Rua Ferreira Borges ☎ 223 399 000;
www.palaciodabolsa.com 🕐 Tue.–Sun. 9–6,
Apr.–Oct.; Tue.–Sun. 9–12:30 and 2–5:30, rest of year
🚌 500, 900, 901, 906 📋 $$

Ponte Dom Luís I

Five bridges span the Douro river, all
built high above the water over the river
gorge. The most impressive of these is
the Ponte Dom Luís I (Luis I Bridge),
a striking bi-level iron construction
designed by Théophile Seyring (one
of Gustave Eiffel's collaborators) and
dating from 1886.

➕ C1 ✉ Ponte Dom Luís I 🚇 D line: São Bento
🚌 900, 901, 906

Praça da Ribeira

The waterfront Ribeira Square is the
focal point of the Ribeira district, by far
the most atmospheric area of Porto and
designated a UNESCO World Heritage
Site. Many of the buildings were erected
between 1776 and 1782.

The Casa do Infante (House of the
Prince), Prince Henry the Navigator's
reputed birthplace, was originally built
in the 1350s as a customs house for the
poor. It was altered many times, the
interior courtyard being the oldest part
of the structure. The building sits on the
foundations of a Roman original, proving
the longevity of a settlement and a
community on this part of the river.

Casa do Infante ➕ B1 ✉ Rua da Alfândega 10,
Ribeira ☎ 222 060 435 🕐 Museum: Tue.–Sun. 10–1
and 2–5:30. Last admission 30 minutes before closing
🚇 D line: São Bento 🚌 500, 900, 901, 906 📋 $;
free Sat.–Sun.

Sé

Porto's magnificent Sé (Cathedral) stands high above the slopes leading to the river. Built in the 12th century as a fortress church, it was extensively altered in the 1700s in the baroque style, although the vast silver altarpiece in the north transept dates from the mid-16th century.

The two-story cloisters have solid granite lines enlivened with beautiful tiles, and there are fine views over the town. A museum in the treasury houses archeological finds from pre-Roman to Gothic times, plus liturgical objects from the 15th to 19th centuries.

➕ C2 ✉ Terreiro da Sé ☎ 222 059 028
🕐 Church: daily 9–7
Cloisters and Museum: daily 9–6:30, Apr.–Oct.; 9–5:30, rest of year 🚇 D line: São Bento 🚌 207, 303, 400, 500, 900, 901, 904, 905, 906, ZH 🎟 Church free; Cloisters $$

Vila Nova de Gaia

A separate municipality, Vila Nova de Gaia lies across the Douro river from Porto itself. Its name is synonymous with port, for until 1987 all Portuguese port had to be matured here to be so named. The riverside slopes are dominated by the the port warehouses, or lodges. There are many opportunities for free tours and to buy port; the white aperitif variety is hard to find abroad.

High above the river is the old monastery of Serra do Pilar, now the "House of the Northern Patrimony." Visit the circular cloister and take a guided tour of the dome. A cable car links the quayside to a station, Jardim do Morro, offering access to Serra do Pilar and fine views of the Porto skyline.

➕ Off map at C1 ✉ Largo de Aviz, Vila Nova de Gaia
🕐 Most lodges open Mon.–Fri. 10–12 and 2–6 (also Sat. in summer) 🚇 D line: Jardim do Morro 🚌 900, 901, 904, 905, 906

Serra do Pilar ✉ 4430 Vila Nova de Gaia ☎ 220 142 425 🕐 Tue.–Sun. 10–6:30, Apr.–Oct.; Tue.–Sun. 10–5:30, rest of year 🎟 $

Cable car ☎ 223 741 440; www.gaiacablecar.com
🕐 Daily 10–8, late Apr.–late Sep.; 10–7, late Mar.–late Apr. and late Sep.–late Oct.; 10–6, rest of year
🎟 Single journey $$, return trip $$$

World of Discoveries

This interactive theme park brings the Portuguese exploration of the New World to life. Different areas cover both the challenging sea voyages and the discovered territories in Africa, India, the Far East and South America. Costumed staff help put you in the mood to visit the time of Henry the Navigator and explain the inventions that made it all possible.

➕ Off map at A3 ✉ Rua de Miragaia 106 ☎ 220 439 770; www.worldofdiscoveries.com 🕐 Mon.–Fri. 10–6, Sat.–Sun. 10–7 🚌 1, 500 🎟 $$$

The cathedral cloisters are lined with blue-and-white *azulejos* (glazed ceramic tiles)

Port Wine

Port, one of Portugal's glories, is drunk all over the world, as an aperitif and a digestive aid. In the 18th century, its production area was the world's first demarcated wine zone, helping to make port one of the few wines with a flavor that has remained untouched for centuries. Be sure to try it in Porto, a city more associated with port than any other.

Port is a fortified wine, which means that brandy is added to the grapes during the production process. This both "fortifies" the wine, making it stronger, and halts the fermentation process, leaving half the natural grape sugar in the wine. These two factors give port its strength, sweetness and smoothness; its complex flavors come from the soil and climate where the grapes are grown.

To people accustomed to the lush vineyards of other countries, those in the upper Douro valley, which produce port, are a revelation. It's a stony, barren area, a microclimatic zone where temperatures reach extremes of heat and cold. The soil is a thin layer on top of schist, and the vine roots must force their way through the rock, sometimes as much as 20 feet, to find water. The Portuguese insist, probably rightly, that these conditions are what gives port its unique character.

The vineyards grow on steep terraces, so much of the harvesting is done by hand, and until recently the grapes were still even trodden by foot. (Treading the grapes by foot enables the flavor to be released without crushing the grape seed, which would add a bitter taste to the port.) Today more than 90 percent are crushed and fermented at a controlled temperature, sometime between mid-September and mid-October. The new wine is stored upriver in a lodge or *armazém*, to clear until the following spring. In March it's ready for transportation. Following strict tradition, until as recently as 1987 it could not be called port unless the maturation had taken place in Vila Nova de Gaia, across the Douro from Porto. Increasingly, as is now allowed, it is matured on site due to space consideration and transportation costs.

Port comes in several varieties: white, a semi-sweet light wine; ruby, a clear, intense red, tawny, which is older and more complex; and vintage and late bottled vintage port. Vintage port is aged in the bottle and comes from grapes from a single year; late bottled is matured for up to four years before further maturing after bottling.

Barrels of port are stored at Solar do Vinho do Porto (Port Wine Rooms) in the Romantic Museum

Spain

Introduction and Map 394

Timeline 400

Survival Guide 401

Madrid 402

Feature: Monasterio de El Escorial 409

Barcelona 410

Feature: Modernista Highlights 417

Santiago de Compostela 418

Feature: St. James and Santiago 422

Feature: A Day in Santiago 423

Seville 424

Feature: Active Spain 429

Hotels and Restaurants 487

Essential Information 558

Opposite: Casa Batlló designed by Gaudí is in the L'Eixample district of Barcelona

Spain

Spain is a country of diverse landscapes, climates, peoples and cultures, forged over the centuries into a political unity. Physically separated from the rest of Europe by the Pyrenees mountain chain, Spain also found itself isolated internationally during General Francisco Franco's dictatorship (1939–75). Since Franco's death, however, and with the restoration of its parliamentary monarchy (currently King Felipe VI and Queen Letizia), Spain has regained its place politically, economically and culturally within Europe.

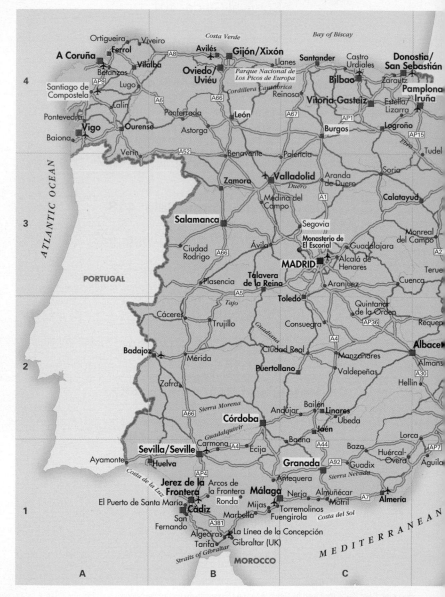

But despite the rate of progress, many aspects of Spanish life remain untouched, and Spain retains much of its traditional character.

Spain Today

Spain's long and checkered history peaked in the Golden Age of the 16th century, when it was one of the most influential nations of the world. It had immense power across Europe and possessed many overseas colonies. The following centuries saw a gradual decline and increasing isolation from the rest of Europe, culminating in the bitter Civil War (1936–39) and Franco's long dictatorship.

In Spain today, political, cultural, artistic and sporting life flourishes, along with national confidence. Several Spanish cities have been appointed Cultural Capitals of Europe, Valencia has twice hosted the Americas Cup sailing competition, and Spain's leading soccer teams, Real Madrid and F.C. Barcelona, are among the most successful in Europe.

However, after emerging from a severe financial crisis in 2015, Spain has been hit by an ongoing constitutional crisis triggered by Catalan demands for independence.

From Pyrenees to Portugal

One of Europe's most mountainous countries, Spain occupies much of the Iberian peninsula, stretching southwest from the Pyrenees. Much of the land area is covered by the mighty Meseta, a little-populated agricultural plateau surrounded by long mountain ranges. These ranges stretch from the Sierra Nevada in the south to the Cordillera

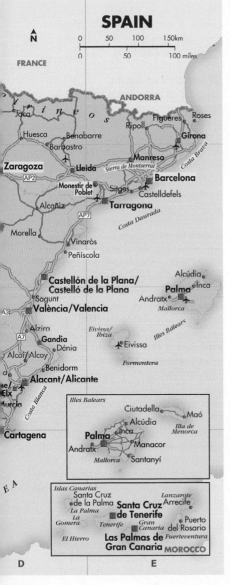

More Top Destinations in Spain

- Burgos C4
- Córdoba B2
- Costa Blanca D2
- Costa Brava E3
- Costa de la Luz A1
- Costa del Sol C1
- Costa Verde B4
- Granada C1
- León B4
- Monestir de Poblet E3
- Pamplona/Iruña D4
- Parque Nacional de Picos de Europa B4
- Peñíscola D3
- Ronda B1
- Salamanca B3
- Segovia C3
- Sierra de Montserrat E3
- Zaragoza D3

A passionate flamenco display in Madrid

Gibraltar, only 9 miles from Africa. Such diversity is echoed in Spain's climate, which varies from the mild, wet weather of the northern Atlantic coast to the typical Mediterranean hot, dry summers and mild, wet winters in the south. Winter inland can be very cold.

The island groups of the Balearics (Mallorca, Menorca, Ibiza and small Formentera) and the Canaries (including Gran Canaria, Tenerife, Lanzarote and the tiny La Gomera) have their own geographical and climatic characteristics.

Diversities of Spain

Regional differences are reflected in the Spanish people, their looks, their character, their attitudes and, above all, their cuisine. The 800 years of Moorish occupation, the eventual unification of a number of small kingdoms, and the power and wealth of 16th-century colonial Spain have aided the evolution of diverse provincial characteristics.

The concept of centralized power is alien to many Spaniards, and regionalism is very strong in Spain. It has its base in the peninsula's linguistic groups: Galician, spoken in the northwest; Basque, another northern language; Castilian, also known as Spanish; and Catalan, based in the northeast, with Valencian and Mallorcan variations of this. These are all co-official languages in Spain.

In 1977, when the present constitution was established, various regional groups were provided for through the establishment of 17 autonomous governments. The Basque Country and Catalonia are the two regions in Spain having the most autonomy – they are also two of the most prosperous regions, with a higher GDP per capita than most of the rest of the country.

Spanish Characters

There are physical differences between Spaniards from different parts of the peninsula. With a population of 47

Cantábrica in the north, and give Spain an average altitude of 2,100 feet. The highest mainland peak is the 11,414-foot Mulhacén in the Sierra Nevada, although Mount Teide on the Canary island of Tenerife is nearly 1,000 feet higher.

The mild, moist Atlantic coast of the Costa Verde in the north contrasts with the sun-baked Mediterranean beaches of the southern Costa del Sol. The grandeur of the Pyrenees is more than rivaled by the dramatic peaks of the Asturian mountains on Spain's northern coast, which some consider the most beautiful region in Spain. East of Asturias the Ebro valley slashes southeast toward the Mediterranean, where it bisects the coastal plain southwest of Barcelona.

The fertile gardens of Murcia and the agricultural flatlands of the Guadalquivir yield harvests rivaled only by the tourist crop drawn from the golden sands of the Mediterranean beaches.

The Mediterranean coast ends on the northern shore of the Straits of

million, there's room for diversity; contrary to popular belief, not all Spaniards are dark-eyed and olive-skinned. The Moorish genetic legacy is strongest in Andalucia, where many are delicate-featured and dark, personifying the Spanish stereotype.

Spaniards are sometimes thought of as an exuberant, passionate and light-hearted people, but nothing could be further from the truth. They are certainly passionate, but there's a strong streak of self-control in the national character. History has given them loyalty and tolerance. Kindness to children and respect for the elderly are the norm.

Young Spaniards enjoy a freedom and lifestyle their grandparents could never have imagined, yet society is still in a state of flux, and there are huge contrasts between different regions, towns and rural areas. But wherever you go you'll find the same hospitality and friendliness, particularly if you speak a little Spanish. English is widely spoken along the Mediterranean coast and by hotel staff in cities, but rarely elsewhere.

Cities, Towns and Villages

For visitors the three great cities are Madrid, Barcelona and Seville, but in Spanish eyes the industrial centers of Valencia and Bilbao are of equal importance, and the inhabitants of each region claim their capital as the most beautiful in Spain.

Andalucia, with the architectural treasures of Granada and Córdoba, is rich in Moorish history.

The region of Castille has Christian castles built during the struggle to oust the Moors.

A view along the seafront to Cádiz's cathedral, bathed in the golden light of the setting sun

The Mediterranean coast has many remains from centuries of Roman occupation, while the Atlantic port of Cádiz boasts 2,000 years of maritime history. Rural Spain continues largely unchanged; agriculture is more mechanized with the inevitable introduction of some modern harvesting equipment, but the way and pace of life are still deeply rooted in the past.

As in other European countries, however, the young are abandoning rural villages in favor of city life, and now almost 80 percent of Spain's population lives in urban areas.

Spanish Lifestyle

Daily life in Spain differs in one major way from other southern European countries; mealtimes are very late. Breakfast in hotels is served from around 7:30 until 9:30 or 10. Most Spaniards rise early and eat little first thing, so they are ready for a snack around 11. This delays lunch until at least 2 p.m., and dinner is often around 9:30 p.m. or later.

An early start means you can take advantage of the cool mornings, vital in a country where air-conditioning is not universal. Virtually everything – stores, offices, churches and museums – closes from 1:30 or 2 p.m. until 4 or 5, and most people sleep or take a break after lunch for an hour on the weekends, during the fabled siesta.

This break in the day bypasses the worst heat and leaves people ready to stay up late and enjoy the cooler evening air. It's a pleasure to sit at a café or restaurant table until 1 or 2 a.m. as the nightlife continues all around.

You'll find that most entertainment begins very late, around 10 p.m., and clubs don't get going until the early hours of the morning. Along the Mediterranean coast things are more geared toward visitors, and you may be able to have dinner soon after 8:30 p.m.

Spain is traditionally a Catholic country. When you visit churches, cover the tops of your arms and shoulders and avoid wearing shorts. The local fiestas held in towns and villages are always in honor of the Virgin or some favorite local saint, and if you get the chance to watch one, you will see how religion plays an integral part in everyday life.

Traveling in Spain

The economic boom of the last few decades may have stalled but the country's infrastructure is excellent. Spain has a very good network of well-marked toll roads and highways. Spaniards drive fast but safely, and you should have no problems if you rent a car. Public transportation is good, with a choice of internal flights, fast and punctual trains, and long-distance buses going to even the most remote corners.

Hotels are graded and inspected by the government, so you are guaranteed a clean and adequate room no matter how little you pay. Try to spend at least a few nights at one of the *paradores*. These are state-owned hotels in historic buildings such as castles and monasteries, often furnished with antiques and offering a high standard of comfort and service.

Spanish Passions

Spaniards throw themselves whole-heartedly into leisure pursuits and sporting events. Their most famous and controversial spectator event is bullfighting, although support for this has dwindled considerably in recent years and it is now illegal in Catalonia. Soccer is a national passion; huge crowds follow the fortunes of teams such as Real Madrid and F.C. Barcelona.

Spain has some of Europe's finest golf courses, chiefly along the Mediterranean coast, where you'll also find excellent marinas and water sports facilities, as well as untouched wilderness areas. Young people travel from all over Europe to experience Spain's club scene, at its most frenetic on the island of Ibiza.

Moorish-style decoration on a house in Alicante

Timeline

15,000–12,000 BC	Caves at Altamira painted; earliest sign of habitation.
218–210 BC	Rome begins conquest of Iberian peninsula.
AD 411	Visigoths invade and establish powerful kingdom at Toledo.
711	Moors defeat Visigoths and begin period of occupation.
1478–79	Spanish Inquisition against Jews, Moors and Protestants.
1492	Christopher Columbus discovers the New World.
1519	Spanish conquistadors move across America.
1588	Spanish Armada is sent against Protestant England; fleet destroyed and maritime preeminence lost.
1704	British capture Gibraltar.
1808–14	Peninsular War (War of Independence) sees expulsion of French and defeat of Napoleon.
1898	Philippines and Cuba rebel against Spanish rule; the United States occupies Puerto Rico; end of Spanish Empire.
1914–18	Spain remains neutral in World War I.
1936–39	Spanish Civil War; General Francisco Franco leads Nationalist troops from Morocco against Republicans.
1939	Franco becomes head of state; Spain enters period of isolation and remains neutral throughout World War II.
1955	Spain joins United Nations.
1975	Death of Franco; Juan Carlos becomes king.
1986	Spain joins the European Economic Commmunity (later known as the European Union).
1992	Barcelona hosts Olympic Games.
2004	Madrid suffers horrifying terrorist attack resulting in 191 deaths.
2010	Catalonia becomes the first Spanish region to ban bullfighting.
2014	King Juan Carlos abdicates. In June 2014, at parliamentary chambers, Crown Prince Felipe is proclaimed the new king.
2015	The Partido Popular party narrowly wins the general election, but fails to gain a majority. A second general election in 2016 results in a hung parliament, but a coalition government is formed.
2017	The city suffers horrific terrorist attacks. Catalonia votes to become independent from the rest of Spain, in a referendum deemed illegal by the Spanish government.

The Moorish Occupation

In AD 711 a faction of the ruling Visigoth tribe in Spain went to Islamic Africa to seek help with some domestic political problems. They returned with an army of 7,000; after victory at Cádiz, the Moors encountered little resistance in taking over all but a small strip of northern Spain over the next 30 years. Their tactics were a blend of intelligent strategy and diplomacy; they never demanded religious subordination, as long as Christians paid taxes. Beginning in AD 744, however, resistance against the invaders spread south from the small, unoccupied northern territory, fueled by the legend of St. James the Moorslayer. El Cid succeeded in capturing Toledo from the Moors in 1085, and despite some setbacks, a coalition of Christian armies was finally victorious at the Battle of Navas de Tolosa in 1212, the last great battle between Moors and Christians. The Moorish occupation left important legacies, however – they brought mathematics, papermaking, oranges, spices and rice to Spain.

The seafront promenade at L'Estartit on the Costa Brava

Survival Guide

- English is not widely spoken, even in large cities. Keep in mind that the Spanish you may have learned in high school differs in accent, pronunciation and some vocabulary from that spoken in Spain. In Barcelona, Catalan is widely spoken alongside Castilian.

- It's best not to discuss politics, since Spaniards are very proud and the subject could be sensitive.

- Public restrooms are few except in museums, but it's acceptable to use the facilities in a bar; leave a small tip on the counter or stop and have a cup of coffee while you're there.

- Inebriation is frowned on in Spain; the Spanish drink alcohol regularly, but in moderation.

- The Spanish are formal and polite; it is best to ask, in Spanish, if the person you're addressing speaks English before you start to speak, and shake hands with the person at the end of your conversation.

- Water is a precious commodity in many parts of Spain; you may find that hotel bathrooms have a shower rather than a tub. Shower pressure is generally low.

- You can safely drink the water throughout Spain. Bottled mineral water is widely available also and is inexpensive and served chilled. Ice is not generally served in drinks unless you ask.

- Throughout Spain, and especially along the Mediterranean coast, bars specialize in *tapas*, delicious selections of hot or cold savory mouthfuls served with drinks. Be sure to try some of the dozens available: fish, cured ham, grilled peppers, salads, *tortilla* (a thick, Spanish omelet), anchovies, local almonds, olives. A few little dishes will make a delicious lunch.

- All large cities have shopping malls, usually located away from the town center; downtown department stores; and a range of antiques stores, designer boutiques, local craft and souvenir shops, gourmet food stores, and clothing and bric-a-brac markets.

- Prices in Spain are comparable to those found in the rest of Europe; meals can be a little cheaper than in other parts of Europe.

- Try to arrange your trip so that it coincides with one of the major local festivals. Spain has some of the most colorful and exotic celebrations in Europe.

Madrid

Unlike most European capital cities, Madrid did not evolve as the nation's capital. It was chosen. In 1561, Philip II settled the court permanently in Madrid, as much for its position in the center of Spain as for political reasons. Today Madrid is fascinating, noisy, vibrant and chaotic – a city of great wealth and grueling poverty, but still the country's financial capital.

Like so much of Spain, Madrid's spirit is elusive and diffused, and will surprise you repeatedly. Plan to stay in the city center, so you can easily reach your hotel in the middle of the day, when many museums and monuments are closed for the siesta. The best way to tackle sightseeing is to concentrate on

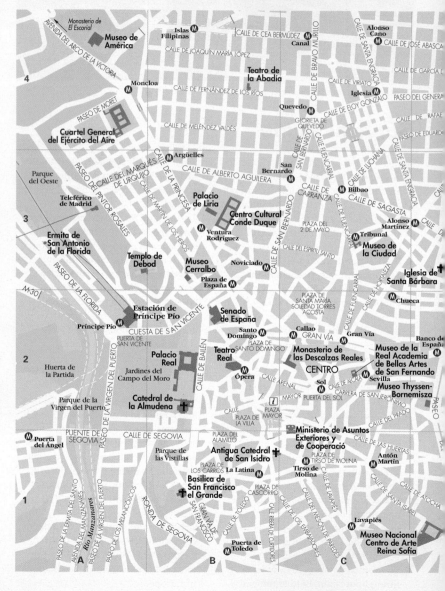

one section at a time. There are three historical areas of interest in the vicinity of the city's main plaza, Puerta del Sol (see page 408): Old Madrid (Viejo Madrid), centering on the Plaza Mayor (see page 408); the Western Quarter (Madrid de los Asturias), by the Palacio Real (see pages 407–408); and Bourbon Madrid, the heart of which is the sweeping avenues and sparkling

fountains around the Prado Museum (Museo Nacional del Prado, see page 406). A tourist bus (bus turístico; madrid.city-tour.com) links all three, allowing passengers to get on and off at will. Tickets are valid for one or two days, and there's English commentary. Turismo de Madrid organizes walking and bicycling tours in the city. Bookings should be made at the tourist office in Plaza Mayor 27 (☎ 91 578 7810; www.esmadrid.com). There are always English-speaking staff at the tourist office. The city also benefits from an efficient subway system.

Dining Out

Local specialties include tripe, but many regional restaurants feature traditional dishes from all over Spain. The cuisine of the Basque country and Galicia, with its emphasis on seafood, is very good, or you could try a Latin-American restaurant, where even the meat is imported from Argentina. Fast-food outlets abound and offer hamburgers, tortillas or even paella to go.

Most restaurants have a good value, fixed-price lunch menu Monday through Friday which will include a first and second course, a dessert and a drink. Madrid has many bars where you'll find everything from tea and coffee to beer, champagne and exotic cocktails. In summer, bar life moves onto the sidewalks, with hundreds of outdoor venues (terrazas) crowded until dawn.

Malls and Markets

The central department stores, such as El Corte Inglés, are clustered in the commercial area around the Puerta del Sol and the Gran Vía. If you're looking for malls, the large Príncipe Pío occupies an attractive 19th-century station near the Royal Palace; the ABC Serrano, between Serrano and Castellana in the city center, is smaller and more upscale.

The most fashionable shopping area is the Salamanca district around the streets of Calle de Serrano and Goya, where you'll find expensive stores. Madrid is a good place for Spanish souvenirs, and there are many antiques stores – the Salamanca district alone has more than 50. Visit the Rastro flea market on Sunday morning and public holidays or try the Mercado San Miguel for gourmet produce.

Evening Entertainment

Classical music, opera and theater thrive in Madrid, and the tourist office publishes an excellent monthly listings guide, *es Madrid*. It is available from tourist offices and hotels, or online at www.esmadrid.com. You might enjoy a *zarzuela* performance, a traditional form of musical, combining elements of opera, vaudeville and melodrama. Jazz is very popular, or, if you're looking for flamenco, there are several clubs (*tablaos*) where it is staged. Madrid has an exceptional nightclub scene and a number of movie theaters.

Essential Information

Tourist Information

**Oficinas de Información Turística
(Tourist Information Offices)**
Plaza Mayor 27, Aeropuerto de Madrid-Barájas (airport), Terminals 2 and 4;
Plaza de Colón (underground passage); information points on Paseo del Prado and by the Atocha railroad station; for all offices contact ☎ 91 578 7810
www.esmadrid.com
http://turismomadrid.es
SATE (Foreign Tourist Assistance Service)
The tourist police have translators available to help visitors in trouble and to report a crime
Calle Leganitos 19 (near Plaza de España)
☎ 90 210 2112 (24-hours)
🕙 9 a.m.–midnight

Urban Transportation

Getting around Madrid is simple on the metro (subway) and bus systems. Metro stations are marked on the Madrid city map by the letter "M" on a blue background inside a red diamond. The metro has 13 lines and runs daily 6 a.m.–1:30 a.m. Purchase tickets from machines or ticket offices in the stations. Go online at www.metromadrid.es for timetable and fare prices information only. The Metrobús ticket, valid for 10 trips on the metro and bus systems, is available from metro stations, tobacconists *(estancos)* and Municipal Transport Company (EMT) booths at some bus stops. Buses run daily 6 a.m.–midnight, with a limited, infrequent, all-night service. Pay the driver or stamp your pass in the machine when you board. Taxis are plentiful and can be hailed on the street. To call a taxi dial Tele-Taxi (☎ 91 371 2131).

Airport Information

Adolfo Suárez Madrid Barájas Airport (☎ 90 240 4704 or 91 321 1000) is 8 miles northeast of the city center, about a 30-minute drive. Express buses run every 20 minutes between the airport and Atocha railroad station – timetables are available online at www. emtmadrid.es. There is a metro (subway) line from the airport (with two stops, one for Terminals 1, 2, and 3, and another for Terminal 4) to Nuevos Ministerios (metro station of the same name). A train service links Terminal 4 with Chamartín, Atocha and other central city stations.

Climate – average highs and lows for the month

Jan.	Feb.	Mar.	Apr.	May	Jun.	Jul.	Aug.	Sep.	Oct.	Nov.	Dec.
9°C	12°C	15°C	18°C	21°C	27°C	32°C	31°C	26°C	19°C	13°C	10°C
48°F	54°F	59°F	64°F	70°F	81°F	90°F	88°F	79°F	66°F	55°F	50°F
1°C	2°C	4°C	6°C	9°C	14°C	17°C	17°C	13°C	9°C	4°C	2°C
34°F	36°F	39°F	43°F	48°F	57°F	63°F	63°F	55°F	48°F	39°F	36°F

Madrid Sights

Key to symbols

➕ map coordinates refer to the Madrid map on pages 402–403 ▓ admission charge: $$$ more than €6, $$ €3–€6, $ less than €3

See page 5 for complete key to symbols

Estadio Santiago Bernabéu

Home to the hugely successful soccer team Real Madrid, this vast stadium is a mecca for fans of Spanish soccer. Visitors can see the club's proudly displayed prestigious cups and trophies, and also can enjoy a stadium tour which includes a visit to the changing rooms and a special panoramic viewing terrace.

➕ Off map at D4 ✉ Avenida Concha Espina 1 ☎ 93 398 4370 ◷ Museum and Stadium tour (self-guiding): Mon.–Sat. 10–7, Sun. 10:30–6 (or 5 hours before kick-off on match days) Ⓜ Santiago Bernabéu 🚌 14, 27, 40, 43, 120, 126, 147, 150 ▓ $$$

Monasterio de las Descalzas Reales

The oddly named Convent of the Royal Barefoot Nuns was founded in 1557 as a convent for aristocratic ladies seeking the religious life. They and their families funded the decoration of 33 chapels with treasures by mainly Spanish artists.

➕ C2 ✉ Plaza de las Descalzas Reales 3 ☎ 91 454 8800 ◷ Tue.–Sat. 10–2 and 4–6:30, Sun. 10–3 Ⓜ Sol, Callao or Ópera 🚌 3, 25, 39, 148 ▓ $$ ℹ Guided visits only

Museo Arqueológico Nacional (MAN)

Spain's National Archaeology Museum contains more than 1,300,000 archeological artifacts from Spain and around the world. Highlights include the *Dama de Elche*, an Iberian female bust which dates from the 4th or 5th centuries BC, and Greek and Roman treasures and Visigothic votive crowns.

➕ D3 ✉ Calle de Serrano 13 ☎ 91 577 7912; www.man.es ◷ Tue.–Sat. 9:30–8, Sun and public holidays, 9:30–3 Ⓜ Serrano or Retiro 🚌 1, 9, 19, 51, 74 🍴 Café ▓ $$ ℹ Guided visits available

Eye-catching glass elevators scale the exterior of the Queen Sofía National Art Center

Museo Cerralbo

The 18th-century Marquis of Cerralbo donated his lavish home to the Spanish state on his death in 1922, along with most of his collection of artworks and antiquities. Now magnificently restored, the palace's sumptuous salons provide a fine setting for the art collection, as well as offering a glimpse into the intimate lives of this aristocratic family around the turn of the 20th century.

➕ B3 ✉ Calle Ventura de Rodríguez 17 ☎ 915 47 36 46; www.mecd.gob.es/mcerralbo ◷ Tue.–Sat. 9:30–3 (also Thu. 5–8 p.m.), Sun. 10–3 Ⓜ Ventura 🚌 74, 138 ▓ $$ ℹ Guided visits available

Museo Nacional Centro de Arte Reina Sofía

The spectacular Museo Nacional Centro de Arte Reina Sofía (Queen Sofía National Art Center) is housed in the former Hospital de San Carlos. Exterior

The Museo del Prado displays its collection of Spanish art to great effect in its large, well-lit rooms

glass elevators whisk you up to the permanent exhibitions.

Visitors flock to Pablo Picasso's *Guernica.* When it was commissioned, his only instruction was to paint a big picture; this black-and-white composition has long become a renowned symbol of antiwar sentiment. Other highlights include paintings by Salvador Dalí and Joan Miró.

➕ D1 ✉ Calle Santa Isabel 52 ☎ 91 774 1000; www.museoreinasofia.es ⊕ Mon. and Wed.–Sat. 10–9, Sun. 10–7 (ticket office closes at 2 p.m.). 🚇 Atocha 🚌 6, 59, 85 🍴 Café and restaurant 💲 $$$; senior citizens and under 18s free (free to all Mon. and Wed.–Sat. 7 p.m.–9 p.m., Sun. 1:30–7 p.m. Note: only part of the permanent exhibition and the temporary exhibits are accessible when free)

Museo Nacional del Prado

The Prado Museum has an unrivaled collection of Spanish paintings. Once the royal collection, the Prado represents the personal taste of the Spanish monarchs, with a noticeable emphasis on religious and courtly paintings. Space limitations allow only about 1,300 of the 22,000 works to be displayed. Some works, particularly those by Diego Velázquez attract huge crowds.

Highlights include Velázquez's *Las Meninas,* often described as "the finest painting in the world." Also, look for Goya's *Majas,* two paintings thought to be of the Duchess of Alba, one demure and clothed, the other sensuously naked. His *pinturas negras,* the black paintings, stand in stark contrast; they represent the apocalyptic vision of a man on the edge of madness. The Spanish monarchs were fascinated by the surreal work of Hiëronymous Bosch; his *Garden of Earthly Delights,* with its wealth of weird detail, is one of his finest works.

➕ D1 ✉ Paseo del Prado ☎ 90 210 7077; www.museodelprado.es ⊕ Mon.–Sat. 10–8, Sun. 10–7 🚇 Banco de España or Atocha 🚌 10, 14, 24, 34, 37, 45 🍴 Café 💲 $$$ (free Mon.–Sat. 6–8 p.m., Sun. 5–7 p.m and all day on certain national holidays. Under 18s free)

Museo de la Real Academia de Bellas Artes de San Fernando

Art lovers will enjoy this, the Royal Academy of Fine Arts, founded in the 18th century to emulate art venues in Paris and London. The academy has some fine paintings by Francisco Goya and a good Diego Velázquez portrait of Philip IV. The highlight is *Spring* by

The majestic Palacio Real (Royal Palace) was built in the 18th century

Italian artist Giuseppe Arcimboldo, a portrait in which the sitter's features are entirely composed of pieces of fruit and vegetables.

✚ C2 ✉ Calle Alcalá 13 ☎ 91 524 0864;
www.realacademiabellasartessanfernando.com
⦿ Tue.–Sun. 10–3. Closed Aug. ⓜ Sol or Sevilla
🚌 9, 15, 20 💲 $$$; senior citizens $$. Under 18s free.
Free to all on Wed.

Museo Thyssen-Bornemisza

Acquired in 1993 for about $350 million, the art collection of the Museo Thyssen-Bornemisza (Thyssen-Bornemisza Museum) includes much of the best of Western art produced in the last 800 years. It contains around 2,000 works, all acquired since the 1920s by Baron Heinrich and his son, Baron Hans-Heinrich Thyssen-Bornemisza. The Carmen Thyssen-Bornemisza Collection was incorporated in 2004.

Western paintings from the 13th to 20th centuries are arranged chronologically, so start on the top floor and work down. Early portraits and Renaissance works are grouped together, followed by Dutch interiors. Nineteenth-century American paintings feature a portrait of George Washington's cook by Gilbert Stuart and a sea scene by Winslow Homer. The 20th century is well represented by Joan Miró, Salvador Dalí and Mark Rothko. Expressionist artists include German Otto Kirchner and Norwegian Edvard Munch.

✚ D2 ✉ Paseo del Prado 8 ☎ 91 791 1370;
www.museothyssen.org ⦿ Mon. noon–4, Tue.–Sun.
10–7. Temporary exhibitions until 9 p.m. on Sat.
ⓜ Banco de España 🚌 10, 14, 24, 34, 37, 45
🍴 Café and restaurant 💲 $$$; free Mon. noon–4.
Fee for all temporary exhibitions

Palacio Real

The vast white bulk of the Palacio Real (Royal Palace) looks striking from the Campo del Moro, a peaceful garden behind the palace. After a fire destroyed the Moorish original, the palace was planned to be three times its existing size. In the 18th century, architect Francisco Sabatini began to rebuild and extend the palace. Funds ran out, and the present structure was completed in 1764. The palace was in full use until 1931, and is now occasionally used for state receptions. The entrance fee includes the Armory and the Royal Pharmacy.

The 1993 Cathedral of the Almudena nearby offers panoramic views from its

Relaxing under the shady parasols of a café in the stunning Plaza Mayor

vast dome; the Plaza de Oriente is a grand, café-lined square across the road, home to the Teatro Real (Opera Theater). 🚇 B2 ✉ Calle Bailén ☎ 91 454 8700; www. patrimonionacional.es 🕐 Daily 10–8, Apr.–Sep.; 10–6, rest of year. Closed during official events 🚇 Ópera 🚌 3, 148 💶 $$$ (free to E.U. citizens Mon.–Thu. 4–6 p.m., Oct.–Mar.; Wed. and Thu. 6–8 p.m., rest of year)

Parque del Retiro

The Parque del Retiro was laid out in the 1630s as part of the French-style pleasure gardens surrounding the Buen Retiro Palace. The building itself was destroyed during the Napoleonic Wars. Today the park is bright with flowers. Many people head for the lake, with its statue of Alfonso XII; other attractions include the Palacio de Cristal (Crystal Palace), a 19th-century glass palace.

A wood, the Bosque de Recuerdo, was laid out in memory of victims of the 2004 bomb attack on Madrid. 🚇 E1 ✉ Main entrance: Plaza de la Independencia 🕐 Daily dawn–dusk 🚇 Retiro or Ibiza 🚌 1, 2, 9, 15, 19, 20, 51, 52, 74, 146 💶 Free

Plaza Mayor

One of Europe's most dazzling squares, the present Plaza Mayor (Main Square) stands on the site of the medieval market, the Plaza del Arrabal (Outskirts Square), so called because it was outside the city walls. When Madrid became Spain's capital, Philip III ordered it to be rebuilt as the focal point. Completed in 1620, it took on its current form in the 18th century to designs by the celebrated architect Juan de Villanueva.

The plaza was used for fiestas, bullfights and proclamations, and was also the scene of executions during the later days of the Inquisition. 🚇 B2 ✉ Plaza Mayor 🚇 Sol 🚌 3, 17

Plaza de la Villa

The three different, main stone buildings around this plaza (Town Square) coexist harmoniously. The Gothic Torre de los Lujanes (Lujanes Tower), a 15th-century structure, is balanced by the Casa de Cisneros, a restored 1537 Plateresque-style palace. The Casa de la Villa was the meeting place for the town council from 1640 until 2008. 🚇 B2 ✉ Plaza de la Villa 🚇 Sol or Ópera 🚌 3

Puerta del Sol

Puerta del Sol has been a plaza since 1570, when the original gate was demolished. The headquarters of the regional government are housed on the south side, where a stone in the sidewalk marks Kilometer Zero, from which all distances in Spain are measured. Many Madrileños celebrate New Year here. 🚇 C2 ✉ Puerta del Sol 🚇 Sol 🚌 3, 5

Real Jardín Botánico de Madrid

Established in 1755, these beautiful botanic gardens display a wealth of exotic plants in elegantly manicured beds and handsome 18th- and 19th-century greenhouses. 🚇 D1 ✉ Plaza de Murillo 2 ☎ 91 420 3017; www.rjb.csic.es 🕐 Daily 10 a.m.–dusk 🚇 Atocha 🚌 10, 14, 27, 34, 37, 45 💶 $$ (under 10s free) ℹ Guided visits available also

Monasterio de El Escorial

Twenty-five miles northwest of Madrid, on the southern slopes of the Sierra da Guadarrama mountain range, stands the massive religious complex known as El Escorial, which can be visited on a day trip by train or tour bus. One of the most impressive monuments in Spain, the complex is easily accessible from Madrid and gives true insight into the extraordinary wealth and power of the 16th-century Spanish monarchy.

In 1557 the Spanish forces of Philip II defeated the French at St. Quentin. To give thanks to God, Philip conceived the idea of building a monastery dedicated to St. Lawrence (San Lorenzo), which would also serve as a royal palace and burial place. The vast complex was principally designed in 1584 by the architect Juan de Herrera, and it took 1,500 laborers to complete the work. It has more than 1,200 doors, 2,600 windows and 16 courtyards, and is nearly 670 feet long. The granite stone accentuates the severe lines of the building, which is built on a grid plan. The clear air has kept the stone and tiles pristine. Later Bourbon monarchs left their stamp on the palace through decoration, furnishings and pictures.

El Escorial Today

Philip II's modest private apartments contrast with his throne room. He lived in a suite of small rooms with direct access to the chapel.

Later Bourbon monarchs extended these impressive royal Habsburg apartments near the church to the third floor. You will find sumptuously painted ceilings, frescoes and a wonderful tapestry collection. A frescoed courtyard gives access to the marbled staircase leading down to the Royal Pantheon (Pantéon de los Reyes), where virtually all of the Spanish kings and queens from the time of Charles V onward are buried.

The church itself is on a monumental scale. Its 100-foot-high altarpiece with onyx, marble and jasper columns is punctuated by bronze sculptures. Move on to the equally opulent library, with its shelves made from rare types of wood, and with marble tables and ornate ceiling.

Perhaps the most famous artwork in the monastery is Rogier van der Weyden's luminous *Calvary*, which has been beautifully restored and is displayed in the Sala de los Honores.

🚩 See map page 394, C3 ✉ El Escorial ☎ 91 890 5903 🕐 Tue.–Sun. 10–8, Apr.–Sep.; 10–6, rest of year. Closes for official events 🚇 Train line C8 from Atocha and Chamartín (☎ 91 232 0320) 🚌 Autobuses Herranz (☎ 91 896 9028); buses 661 and 664 leave from the terminus at Madrid's Moncloa subway station 💰 $$$

The harmonious facade of El Escorial stretches for almost 670 feet

Barcelona

Barcelona, the capital of the autonomous Spanish region of Catalonia (Catalunya), is one of the Mediterranean's most vibrant cities. Catalonia is the most innovative and prosperous area of Spain, with a proud history, an independent spirit and a strong sense of identity.

In 1975, the then King Juan Carlos restored Catalonia's status as an autonomous region, which marked the beginning of Barcelona's renaissance. The pride and self-confidence engendered by a thriving economy and urban renewal culminated in the Barcelona Olympic Games of 1992. Since then, the city has continued to forge ahead. With its 2,000-year-old history, exhilarating atmosphere and superb architecture, it can't fail to please.

The City and Its People

Wherever you stay, the excellent public transportation system gives easy access to the entire city. For atmosphere, stay somewhere near the avenue La Rambla (see page 416) or in the old town, and thus within easy walking distance of many sights and the waterfront. The architecturally interesting L'Eixample area is more spacious, with excellent shopping and restaurants, and there are plenty of hotels close to the beaches. Barcelonins are helpful and polite, with an ability to combine efficiency with a relaxed Mediterranean attitude.

English is not widely spoken, although most hotel staff speak it adequately. There are two official languages in Catalonia: Spanish and Catalan, which are both Romance languages with Latin roots. Catalan is widely spoken, and street signs are exclusively in Catalan.

Barcelonan Themes

Since there's so much to see in Barcelona, concentrate on specific areas and themes. Spend a day on the waterfront taking in the Old Port (Port Vell, see page 416) district,

La Barceloneta (see page 413) and the ultra-modern Olympic Port (Port Olímpic). There's a choice of boat tours around the harbor and up the coast, which is the best way to admire the port.

Head for l'Eixample (see pages 413–414), the Passeig de Gràcia and the Sagrada Família (see page 416) to enjoy the fabulous Modernista architecture for which the city is renowned. Barcelona is blessed with two hills, Montjuïc and Tibidabo; each offers a refuge from the summer noise and heat and has magnificent views over the city.

Barcelona has more than 50 museums and galleries. The Maritime Museum, Museu Nacional d'Art de Catalunya (MNAC), the Pedralbes Monastery, the F.C. Barça Museum (Museu F.C. Barcelona, see page 415), the Barcelona City History Museum (Museu d'Història de Barcelona, see page 415), the Picasso Museum (Museu Picasso, see page 415) and Joan Miró Foundation (Fundació Joan Miró, see page 414) cater to a wide range of interests, and are all fascinating.

If time is short, there are plenty of English-language guided tours and excursions that take in the main city sights by day and night, and also offer a chance to explore some of the other parts of Catalonia.

Gaudí

Antoni Gaudí was born in Barcelona in 1852, and lived and worked in the city throughout his life. His architectural vision was unique and flamboyant and, guided by the premise that there are no straight lines in nature, he designed some of Barcelona's most outstanding Modernist buildings. Curved lines, organically inspired stone and towers are his trademarks, seen at their best in the remarkable Holy Family Temple (Temple Expiatori de la Sagrada Família, see page 416). He was run over by a tram in 1926, and was taken to a pauper's hospital where he was recognized and died. The people of Barcelona lined the streets for his funeral.

Parks and Pools

Barcelona is rich in relaxing parks. The Parc de la Ciutadella, near the Old Town and waterfront, is a haven of tranquility with shady trees, a lake and Spain's best zoo and is a great place for a picnic.

Other parks in the city include Park Güell (see page 416), with its ceramic sculpture, and several green, flower-filled gardens on the slopes of Montjuïc. Good beaches are within easy reach, as are the city's excellent public swimming pools.

Where to Shop

Prosperous Barcelona is a great shopping center. You'll find serious shopping along the Passeig de Gràcia and on its surrounding streets, which have all the big fashion names, expensive antiques stores and enticing interior design outlets. The wide avenue of Diagonal is lined with upscale stores, while the Plaça de Catalunya has a large branch of the department store El Corte Inglés.

For Spanish souvenirs, try the stores in Portal de l'Àngel and La Rambla. For the latest fashions and interior design head to the Born area. Mercat dels Encants is an interesting secondhand market located on the Plaça de les Glòries (open Mon., Wed., Fri. and Sat. 9–8).

Nightlife

Classical music, jazz, rock, dance, theater and movies are popular forms of entertainment; there are comprehensive listings in the *enBarcelona* (in Spanish) and *Time Out* (in Catalan), available

The Three Graces fountain on Plaça Reial

from newsstands; the online version, www.timeout.cat, is also available in English. Dancing is very popular, and the club scene is one of the best in Spain, ranging from the elegant to the avant-garde. Nightlife reaches its peak around 2 a.m. and continues until dawn.

Barcelona has some superb festivals throughout the year, often featuring decorated floats, fireworks and processions of dragon and demon figures known as *capgrossos*, or "big heads." The biggest and best festival is La Mercè at the end of September.

Essential Information

Tourist Information

Barcelona Turisme (Barcelona Tourism)
Plaça de Catalunya 17-S; Plaça Sant Jaume; Estació Barcelona-Sants (railroad station); Barcelona Airport (terminals 1 and 2B)
☎ For all inquiries: 93 285 3834
www.barcelonaturisme.com (also online shop)

Urban Transportation

Getting around is easy on the metro (subway) and bus systems. Metro stations are marked on the Barcelona city map by the letter "M" in a red circle. There are 12 lines on the metro (four are run by FGC); trains run Mon.–Thu. 5 a.m.–midnight, Fri. 5 a.m.–2 a.m., Sat. 24 hrs, Sun. 6 a.m.–midnight. The T10 ticket offers 10 rides on metro, trains and buses. Combination tourist tickets valid for 2, 3, 4 or 5 days give unlimited use of the bus, tram, metro and urban trains; tickets and maps are available from metro stations. Validate tickets before boarding trains, or on the bus or tram. Bus Turístic operates daily 9–8 (in summer), 9–7 (in winter) and has three routes that take you close to the city's main attractions. A cable car

links La Barceloneta and Montjuïc. Two funiculars serve Montjuïc and Tibidabo; the latter also is served by antique tram. Pick up a black-and-yellow taxi at a stand, hail one on the street, or call Radio Taxi (☎ 93 303 3033).

Airport Information

Barcelona International Airport (☎ 902 404 704) connects to most major European cities and is 11 miles southwest of the city center, about a 20- to 30-minute drive. A train connects to Estació Barcelona-Sants and Passeig de Gràcia station, daily 5:13 a.m.–11.14 p.m. (5:42 a.m.–11:38 p.m. from the airport); journey time 20 minutes. The Aerobús bus service departs from the Plaça de Catalunya (5:35 a.m.–1:05 a.m. A1 service for Terminal 1; 5:35 a.m.–1 a.m. A2 service for Terminal 2). Return services depart from Terminal 1 for the Plaça de Catalunya from 5:35 a.m.–1:05 a.m. (A1) and from Terminal 2 from 5 a.m.–12:30 a.m. (A2). Shuttle buses link the two airport terminals. A metro line runs from the airport to Zona Universitària metro station in 35 minutes (extra charge applies).

Climate – average highs and lows for the month

Jan.	Feb.	Mar.	Apr.	May	Jun.	Jul.	Aug.	Sep.	Oct.	Nov.	Dec.
13°C	14°C	15°C	17°C	21°C	24°C	28°C	28°C	25°C	21°C	17°C	14°C
55°F	57°F	59°F	63°F	70°F	75°F	82°F	82°F	77°F	70°F	63°F	57°F
5°C	6°C	8°C	10°C	12°C	17°C	20°C	20°C	19°C	13°C	9°C	8°C
41°F	43°F	46°F	50°F	54°F	63°F	68°F	68°F	66°F	55°F	48°F	46°F

Barcelona Sights

The Passion Facade of the Sagrada Família

La Barceloneta

The district of La Barceloneta (Little
Barcelona) occupies a triangle of
reclaimed land between the harbor and
the sea. Developed in the 18th century
to house seamen, fishermen and
dockworkers, this delightful
neighborhood retains its maritime
atmosphere. This is a great place to eat
at the many seafood restaurants.
⊞ C1 ✉ La Barceloneta 🚇 Barceloneta
🚌 39, 45, 59, 64, D20, V15

Barri Gòtic

A maze of narrow streets and squares
make up this area, built within the old
Roman walls when Barcelona was one
of the richest and most important
Mediterranean trading cities. At its heart
the Barri Gòtic (Gothic Quarter) is
centered around the Catedral and Plaça
Sant Jaume. This plaza, once the power
center of Catalonia's kings, is still the
site of the city hall and buildings of the
government of Catalonia. The Plaça del
Rei, formerly the medieval marketplace,
is said to be where King Ferdinand and
Queen Isabella welcomed Christopher
Columbus home from America in 1493.
Nearby is the Plaça Reial, an arcaded
square built in 1848. Gothic mansions
line the streets alongside museums,
churches, bars and restaurants.
⊞ B2 ✉ Bounded by Rambla, Universitat, Laietana
and Ferran 🚇 Jaume I 🚌 45, 59, 120, V13, V15, V17
🍴 Rasoterra, see page 489

Catedral

Nothing more strongly represents
Barcelona's historic past than the great
Catedral (Cathedral). It was built
between the 13th and 15th centuries
(with a 19th-century neo-Gothic facade),
and the soaring space beneath the
Catalan Gothic arches and numerous
side chapels houses a wealth of treasures.
The tranquil 14th-century cloister is
home to 13 geese, in honor of the
13-year-old martyr Saint Eulàlia.
⊞ B2 ✉ Plaça de la Seu ☎ 93 342 8262;
www.catedralbcn.org 🕐 Church: daily 8–12:45 and
5:45–7:30. Cloister 8:30–12:30 and 5:45–7
Museum: 10–12:30 and 5:45–7 🚇 Jaume I 🚌 59,
V13 💧 Cathedral cultural visit $$ (Mon.–Fri.
12:30–7:45, Sat. 12:30–5:30, Sun 2–5:30; includes
chapel, museum, and roof terrace). Cathedral worship
free (donation welcome). Access to roof terrace and
chapel $

Eixample

Between 1860 and 1920 Barcelona
expanded into a grid of uniform streets
parallel to the sea, an area known as
l'Eixample (the Extension). This is now a
residential and business district, divided
by the Diagonal, a grand avenue that cuts
through the grid at a 45-degree angle.

An interesting example of innovative
town planning, it contains Barcelona's
finest Modernist buildings (see page
417). Some of the best are in the Passeig

Ventilation chimneys on the roof of Casa Milà, also known as La Pedrera and designed by Antoni Gaudí

de Gràcia; look for No. 43, Gaudí's Casa Batlló, with a mosaic facade and wavy roofline that represent St. George's dragon. The block at No. 92 is Casa Milà, known as La Pedrera, Gaudí's last secular work, built without one straight line or sharp corner (see page 417).

✚ C3 🚇 Diagonal, Catalunya or Passeig de Gràcia

Fundació Joan Miró

More than 10,000 vibrantly colored paintings, along with sculptures, tapestries and drawings, are gathered in the white, bright space of the Fundació Joan Miró (Joan Miró Foundation).

Born in Barcelona in 1893, Miró spent most of his life in the city before retiring to Mallorca in 1956. In 1971 he established the foundation to house the largest collection of his works and to promote contemporary art.

✚ A1 ✉ Avenida Miramar, Parc de Montjuïc
☎ 93 443 9470; www.fmirobcn.org 🕐 Tue.–Sat. 10–8 (also Thu. 8–9 p.m.), Sun. 10–2:30, Jul.–Sep.; Tue.–Sat. 10–6 (also Thu. 7–9 p.m.), Sun. 10–2:30, rest of year 🚇 Espanya 🚌 55, 150; Montjuïc funicular from metro station Paral.lel 🍴 Café in museum ✋ $$$

Mercat de la Boqueria

Make time to visit the glorious Mercat de la Boqueria (Boqueria Market), housed since the 1830s in a covered hall just off La Rambla. Memories of the scents and colors of the fish, hams, freshly picked fruit and vegetables, and the babble of noise from the area will stay with you forever. At lunchtime, take advantage of the many snack bars.

✚ B2 ✉ Plaça de la Boqueria ☎ 93 318 2584
🕐 Mon.–Sat. 8 a.m.–8:30 p.m. Note: stalls may close earlier; fish stalls closed on Mon. 🚇 Liceu 🚌 59, V13

Montjuïc

The green hill of Montjuïc, 698 feet high, dominates Barcelona's southern suburbs. It is a pleasant recreational area, dotted with gardens, museums and various sports facilities. The most impressive approach is through the monumental Plaça d'Espanya and the Font Màgica (Magic Fountain). The fountain stands below the pavilions, built for the 1929 International Exhibition on the avenue linking it to Plaça d'Espanya.

Also here is the 1992 Olympic complex, the Anella Olímpica.

✚ A1 ✉ Montjuïc 🕐 Font Màgica displays: Wed.–Sun. 9:30 p.m. and 10 p.m., Jun.–Sep; Thu.–Sun. 9 p.m. and 9:30 p.m., Apr.–May and Oct.; Thu.–Sun. 8 p.m. and 8:30 p.m., Nov.–Jan. 6 and Mar. Closed Jan. 7–Feb. 🚇 Subway to Paral.lel station, then funicular to Parc de Montjuïc and the *telefèric* cable car to Mirador and Castell; subway to Espanya for fountains 🚌 55, 150; all buses to Plaça d'Espanya for Font Màgica

Museu F.C. Barcelona (Camp Nou Experience)

F.C. Barcelona is one of the most popular and successful soccer teams in the world, with a massive international following. This museum celebrates the club's achievements with video footage of match highlights, displays of trophies and a visitor's book inscribed with the names of illustrious fans. A visit includes a tour of the Camp Nou stadium.

Off map at A4 ✉ Camp Nou, Avenida Aristides Maillol s/n ☎ No phone; www.fcbarcelona.com ⊙ Daily 9:30–7:30, Apr. to mid-Oct.; Mon.–Sat. 10:30–6:30, Sun. 10–2:30, rest of year. Hours reduced on match days 🚇 Les Corts 🚌 75, 113, H8, L12 💲 $$$

Museu d'Història de Barcelona

Barcelona's fascinating City History Museum covers more than two millennia of history. It is built above the subterranean ruins of Roman Barcino, where you can still walk along ancient roads rutted by cart wheels, and admire the faded remnants of original mosaics. Above ground, the visit continues in the magnificent Saló del Tinell, a Gothic throne room spanned by vast stone arches. This is where Isabella and Ferdinand received Columbus after his second transatlantic voyage. Adjoining the throne room is the Capella de Santa Àgata, a dainty Gothic chapel built in 1302, which is dedicated to St. Agatha.

B2 ✉ Plaça del Rei s/n ☎ 93 256 21 00; http://.museuhistoria.bcn.cat ⊙ Tue.–Sat. 10–7, Sun. 10–8 🚇 Jaume I or Liceu 🚌 45, V15, V17 💲 $$$ (free Sun. 3–8 p.m.)

Museu Nacional d'Art de Catalunya (MNAC)

The National Museum of Catalonian Art contains a vast collection, spanning more than a millennium. The highlight is the medieval art collection, one of the finest in the world. Catalan Romanesque art, with its solid rounded forms and stunning simplicity, is represented by sculpture and carving, gold, enamel and textiles. The outstanding treasures are the 11th- and 12th-century murals, from isolated country churches. The superb Gothic collection features ornately gilded paintings and altarpieces, while the Modernista section displays furnishings by Gaudí, as well as artwork. These collections are complemented by the Thyssen-Bornemisza bequest of about 100 masterworks by Fra Angelico, Raphael and Titian, among others.

The rooftop terrace offers spectacular city views ($).

A2 ✉ Palau Nacional, Parc de Montjuïc ☎ 93 622 0376; www.museunacional.cat ⊙ Tue.–Sat. 10–8, Sun. 10–3, May–Sep.; Tue.–Sat. 10–6, Sun. 10–3, rest of year 🚇 Espanya 🚌 13, 55, 150 🍴 Museum café and restaurant 💲 $$$ (free for seniors and under 16s, Sat. after 3.p.m. and first Sun. of the month); guided tours by appointment

Museu Picasso

Pablo Picasso, born in Andalucia in 1881, lived in Barcelona from 1895 until 1904, and he held his first exhibition in the city in 1900. The Picasso Museum is the most important collection of his early works in Spain. Set in five splendid palaces, it also hosts temporary exhibitions.

C1 ✉ Calle Montcada 15–23 ☎ 93 256 3000; www.museupicasso.bcn.cat ⊙ Tue.–Sun. 9–7 🚇 Jaume I 🚌 17, 40, 45, 120, V17 🍴 Café 💲 $$$ (free Sat. after 3 p.m., first Sun. of the month) 🎫 Guided tours Sun. 11 a.m. by reservation, $$ (no tours in Aug.)

A series of unique tiles in Parc Güell by Jujol, one of Gaudí's main collaborators

Park Güell

Güell Park has architectural elements by Antoni Gaudí scattered across its 50 acres. Planned as a residential landscaped area by Gaudí's main patrons, the Güell family, only the grand entrance, the plaza, the paths and the steps were completed. These are interspersed with sculptures, fountains and columns, many decorated with pieces of colorful broken ceramics (trencadís). Inside the park is the Casa Museu Gaudí (tel: 93 219 3811 www.casamuseugaudi.org; open daily 9–8, Apr.–Sep.; 10–8, rest of year; $$).

⊞ C4 ✉ Calle Olot s/n ☎ 93 409 18 31; www.parkguell.cat 🕒 Daily 8 a.m.–9:30 p.m. (last admission 8:30 p.m.), May–Aug.; 8 a.m.–8:30 p.m. (last admission 7:30 p.m.), Apr. and Sep.–Oct.; 8:30–6:15, (last admission 5:30 p.m.), rest of year 🚇 Vallcarca, Lesseps 🚌 24, 32, 92, H6 💲 $$$ (admission fee is for the Monumental Area; timed ticket only); rest of park free

Poble Espanyol

The streets and squares of the Spanish Village, built for the 1929 World Exhibition, give a glimpse of the country's many architectural styles. Buildings range from the white houses of Andalucia to the flat granite facades of Galicia, and house workshops where you'll find crafts and artifacts from all over Spain. In summer, stores stay open into the evening when there is also live music and flamenco.

⊞ A2 ✉ Avenida Francesc Ferrer i Guàrdia 13 ☎ 93 508 6300; www.poble-espanyol.com 🕒 Daily 9–8. Bars and clubs are open late 🚇 Espanya 🚌 13, 23, 150 💲 $$$

Port Vell

The Port Vell (Old Port) district, once run-down, was transformed for the 1992 Olympics. An integral part of the city again, it is a busy recreation area, with a modern marina and elegant bridges and walkways connecting its attractions. The centerpiece is Maremagnum, a shopping and leisure center, with an aquarium with a glass-walled "walk through" tunnel.

⊞ B1 ✉ Port Vell 🚇 Drassanes or Barceloneta 🚌 14, 59, 64, D20, H14, V17

La Rambla

La Rambla, Barcelona's most famous street, runs from Plaça de Catalunya to the waterfront. It's a vibrant tree-lined promenade joining the old and new parts of the city. The name Rambla is Arabic, from ramla, "a torrent," – the street follows an old watercourse. Here is the Liceu opera house, and near the waterfront is the statue of Christopher Columbus on a 164-foot iron plinth; take the elevator to an observation deck.

⊞ B1–B2 ✉ La Rambla 🚇 Catalunya, Drassanes or Liceu 🚌 59, 91, V13

Santa Maria del Mar

Built between 1329 and 1384, the beautiful Gothic church of Santa Maria del Mar (Our Lady of the Sea) is tucked away in the Ribera district. Its stark, serene interior allows the elegant architecture to speak for itself.

⊞ C1 ✉ Plaça de Santa Maria ☎ 93 310 2390; www.santamariadelmarbarcelona.org 🕒 Mon.–Sat. 9–1 and 5–8:30, Sun. 10–2 and 5–8 🚇 Jaume I 🚌 17, 19, 40, 45 🎫 Tours $$ (includes the towers) Mon.–Sat. 1–5, Sun. 2–5

Temple Expiatori de la Sagrada Família

The famous Catalan Modernist architect Antoni Gaudí worked on the Temple Expiatori de la Sagrada Família (known now as the Basílica de la Sagrada Família) for over 40 years. He envisioned a vast church, with facades to show the birth, death and resurrection of Christ, and 18 towers to represent the Twelve Apostles, the Four Evangelists, the Virgin and Christ. At his death in 1926 only the Nativity Facade, the crypt and one of the towers was complete. In 2010 Pope Benedict XVI consecrated the as-yet-unfinished temple. The plan is to finish this magnificent building by 2026.

⊞ C3 ✉ Plaça de la Sagrada Família ☎ 93 208 0414; www.sagradafamilia.cat 🕒 Daily 9–8, Apr.–Sep.; 9–7, Oct. and Mar.; 9–6, Nov.–Feb. 🚇 Sagrada Família 🚌 19, 33, 34, 43, 44, 50, 51, B20, B24 💲 $$$ (includes audio guide); guided tours $$$ 🎫 Reserve online for cheaper admission fee and to avoid lines

Modernista Highlights

At the turn of the 20th century, Barcelona's streets bloomed with extraordinary buildings created in the newly fashionable Modernista style. Chief among the style's proponents was Antoni Gaudí, but fellow architect, Domènech i Montaner, also created some iconic buildings.

Casa Vicens (1878–1888)
Gaudí was inspired by Mudéjar art and architecture in his designs for this residence, which features lavish tiling and ornamental red-brick turrets.

➕ B4 ✉ Carrer Carolines 18–24 ☎ 93 547 5980; http://casavicens.org

Palau Güell (1900–1914)
This mansion was Gaudí's first important commission for Eusebi Güell, who became the architect's most committed patron. Less playful than Gaudí's later designs, it displays his ingenuity with light and curves.

➕ B1 ✉ Carrer Nou de la Rambla 88 ☎ 93 472 5775; http://palauguell.cat

Hospital de Sant Pau (1901–1930)
A masterpiece by Montaner, this renovated former hospital complex now has extravagantly decorated and graceful pavilions set in fine gardens.

➕ Off map at C3 ✉ Carrer Sant Antoni Maria Claret ☎ 93 553 7154; www.santpaubarcelona.org

Casa Batlló (1904–1906)
The Casa Batlló is a fairy-tale mansion with a shimmering tiled facade and wrought-iron balconies of intricate delicacy. Inside, the staircase culminates in a curving, tiled roof which is said to resemble a dragon's scaly back. In summer there are concerts and cocktails on the terrace.

➕ B2 ✉ Passeig de Gràcia 43 ☎ 93 216 0306; www.casabatllo.es

Palau de la Música Catalana (1905–1908)
This sumptuous concert hall is by Domènech i Montaner. The main concert hall (pictured below) is lit by a vast stained-glass ceiling with an inverted dome, and dominated by a stage in which Valkyries erupt from the arch.

➕ C2 ✉ Carrer Palau de la Música 4–6 ☎ 93 295 7200; www.palaumusica.cat

Casa Milà – "La Pedrera" (1906–1910)
Gaudí's Casa Milà apartment building was quickly nicknamed "La Pedrera" (the stone quarry) for its apparently unfinished facade, unlike anything seen before. In summer, jazz concerts are held on the rippling rooftop terrace.

➕ B3 ✉ Carrer Provença 261–265 ☎ No phone; www.lapedrera.com

Santiago de Compostela

Tucked away in the green fringes of Galicia, in northwest Spain, is the beautiful granite city of Santiago de Compostela – one of the great shrines of medieval Christendom. Millions of pilgrims braved hazardous journeys to worship at the shrine of St. James, the patron saint of Spain. People still come here on pilgrimages, especially during holy years, which occur when St. James' Day (July 25) falls on a Sunday.

Santiago is a perfect medieval city – a mix of religious and secular buildings, with an ancient and thriving university and a unique spiritual atmosphere. It is also home to the parliament of Galicia, which is an autonomous region, and there is a lively and prosperous modern town surrounding the central core.

Old Santiago

The historic heart is pedestrian-only and can be traversed on foot in less than a half-hour; everything you'll want to see lies within this small area. Santiago offers quality, not quantity, so most visitors find a stay of a few days ample.

The two main streets, Rúa do Franco and Rúa do Vilar, lead south from the cathedral square and are lined with bustling stores, bars and restaurants. Pick up a map at the tourist office; it's easy to lose your bearings.

Santiago Flavors

Galician cooking is delicious and relies on the excellent quality of local ingredients. Seafood and shellfish are extensively farmed in the *rias*, deeply indented coastal inlets, and are of superb quality. Regional specialties include *pulpo* (octopus) cooked in various ways; blood puddings and sausages; and *empanadas*, flat pies with a meat or fish filling. Local lamb and beef are particularly good. Santiago has many pastry shops, where you'll find wonderful cakes and cookies.

Galicia produces excellent wines, including the *albariños* from the

D.O. Baixas, and the lesser known, but much praised reds from the D.O. Ribeira Sacrá. If the weather's cold, try a cup of hot chocolate; thick enough to eat, it's some of the best in Spain.

Souvenirs and Entertainment

Santiago's streets are lined with stores selling all types of pilgrim souvenirs – medals, rosaries, key rings, holy pictures and statues, many decorated with the image of St. James and his scallop shell emblem. The traditional material for pilgrimage souvenirs is jet, polished and cut, or fashioned into the *figa*, a clenched-fist amulet. The guild of silversmiths, hugely important in the past, is still active and makes fine pieces.

This is a university town with a thriving cultural life, and there are year-round classical concerts, as well as the clubs frequented by students. You'll often hear bagpipes, Galicia's national instrument, played on the streets; this is a favorite way for students to make extra cash to pay their way through university.

Santiago Festivals

Santiago's biggest festival is on July 25, the Fiesta de Santiago (feast of St. James), when the city is packed with pilgrims, tourists and local people. The night before sees the Fuego del Apóstol (Apostle's Fire), a spectacular fireworks display in front of the cathedral (detail picture opposite). The feast itself represents a solemn Mass, with music, choirs and Galician bagpipes. The huge incense burner, the *botafumeiro*, is swung in the cathedral. The feast falls in the middle of Santiago's folklore festival, a two-week celebration of Galician culture, with street music, parades, concerts and markets. An international music festival is held in July and draws crowds from across Europe.

Essential Information

Tourist Information

Turismo de Santiago
Rúa do Vilar 63 ☎ 98 155 5129;
Airport ☎ 98 189 7194;
Pilgrim information office, Rúa Carretas 33,
☎ 98 156 8846
www.santiagoturismo.com

Urban Transportation

Santiago's historic center is pedestrian-only; vehicular access is for taxis and delivery vehicles. It takes 15 to 20 minutes to walk from one end of the center to the other, and most sights and hotels are within this area. If you are staying outside the historic center, take a taxi to the edge of the old town and then walk. Taxis can be found at stands outside the old city, or call Radio Taxi (24 hours) ☎ 98 156 9292). Maxitaxi (☎ 98 111 9080) operate wheelchair-adapted taxis.

Airport Information

Santiago de Compostela Airport (☎ 902 404 704), with services to many European cities, is 7 miles east of the city, about a 15- to 30-minute drive. Buses into Santiago run every 30 minutes from the terminal, daily 7 a.m.–1 a.m. (travel time 30 minutes). Buses run from the bus station and several other central stops to the airport from 6 a.m.–midnight. Taxis also leave from the terminal.

Climate – average highs and lows for the month

Jan.	Feb.	Mar.	Apr.	May	Jun.	Jul.	Aug.	Sep.	Oct.	Nov.	Dec.
13°C	14°C	15°C	17°C	19°C	22°C	25°C	25°C	24°C	20°C	17°C	14°C
55°F	57°F	59°F	63°F	66°F	72°F	77°F	77°F	75°F	68°F	63°F	57°F
5°C	6°C	7°C	8°C	10°C	14°C	16°C	16°C	14°C	12°C	9°C	7°C
41°F	43°F	45°F	46°F	50°F	57°F	61°F	61°F	57°F	54°F	48°F	45°F

Santiago de Compostela Sights

Key to symbols

⊞ map coordinates refer to the Santiago map on page 418 📖 admission charge: $$$ more than €6, $$ €3–€6, $ less than €3

See page 5 for complete key to symbols

Barrio Antiguo

The Barrio Antiguo (Old Quarter) of Santiago is packed with beautiful, historic buildings. The main streets are lined with arcaded old granite houses in the traditional Galician style.

East of the cathedral, the spacious Praza da Quintana is surrounded by notable buildings, including the arcaded Casa da Conga (Canon's Residence). This faces a gracious flight of steps leading up to the 17th-century Casa da Parra (House of the Bunch of Grapes). On the third side is the austere facade of San Paio de Antealtares Monastery, founded in the ninth century. Opposite, the Puerta del Perdón (Door of Pardon) opens onto the east end of the cathedral. On the cathedral's north side stands the huge complex of the Monasterio de San Martín Pinario, with its church and three cloisters. Behind the monastery lies the 17th-century Convento de San Francisco, commemorating a pilgrimage by St. Francis of Assisi in 1213. It is now a museum devoted to the Holy Land and incorporates a hotel.

⊞ A2–B2 ⊠ Barrio Antiguo

Catedral

The present Catedral (Cathedral) dates from the 11th to 13th centuries. The simple Romanesque lines of the interior provide a superb contrast to the ornate facade, added in 1750, at the cathedral's main entrance. Here stands the 12th-century triple doorway known as the Pórtico da Glória (Doorway of

Glory), one of the sculptural marvels of Spain. Prophets and Apostles surround Christ the Savior and the Four Evangelists, all carved with exceptional imagination and fluidity. Behind the worn entrance pillar and the statue of St. James is a figure said to be Maestro Mateo, the cathedral's designer.

The Tribune is a second-floor gallery that runs above the aisles. It features exquisite carvings and provides a good vantage point of the cathedral's interior.

The pulley system, high above the transept, operates the *botafumeiro*, a monster incense burner used during major feasts, which requires eight men to swing it through a huge arc above the transept. The silverwork and gilded figures of the High Altar glitter under the lights of the candelabra.

⊞ A2 ⊠ Praza do Obradoiro ☎ 98 156 9327; http://catedraldesantiago.es/en/ 🕐 Daily 7 a.m.–8:30 p.m.; hours sometimes vary 📖 Roof visit by guided tour $$$ (includes access to museum). Catedral tribune $$$ (includes access to museum)

Museo das Peregrinacións e de Santiago

The Pilgrimage Museum tells the story of pilgrimage in general, and the Santiago pilgrimage in particular. Exhibits show how the cathedral and town grew around the apostle's tomb, how the routes west across Europe developed, what the pilgrims wore and how they traveled. There's a facsimile of the fascinating *Codex Calixtinus*, a 13th-century guide to the route, full of tips about travel and information about Santiago (the original is in the cathedral, but not on display). Look for the souvenirs of 14th-century pilgrims.

⊞ A2 ⊠ Praza das Praterías 2 ☎ 88 186 7315; http://museos.xunta.gal/es/peregrinacions 🕐 Tue.–Fri. 9:30–8:30, Sat. 11–7:30, Sun 10:15–2:45 📖 $

Museo do Pobo Galego

Santiago is more than a noted shrine, it's also one of the main towns in Galicia. The Museo do Pobo Galego (Museum of the Galician People), set in the old convent of San Domingo, explains Galicia and the traditional way of life here. There are displays of pottery, tools, costumes, handicrafts and musical instruments, as well as exhibits on Galicia's dolmens, stone circles and hill forts. The galleries encircle the 17th-century cloister; in one corner a superb staircase, with three intertwining flights of steps, rises through the building.

➕ B2 ✉ Rúa de San Domingo de Bonaval
☎ 981 583 620; www.museodopobo.gal
🕐 Tue.–Sat. 10:30–2 and 4–7:30, Sun. 11–2 ✋ $$

Museo y Tesoro de la Catedral

The Museo y Tesoro de la Catedral (Cathedral Museum and Treasury) is housed around the magnificent cloisters adjoining the cathedral, as well as in the Palacio del Gelmírez, the former Bishop's Palace, which dates from the 12th century. It also includes the Romanesque Old Cathedral (a crypt beneath the Pórtico da Glória) and the Chapel of San Fernando, which opens off the interior of the cathedral. In the latter you can see gem-encrusted gold crucifixes and statues still used for important feasts. The museum includes a fine collection of tapestries from the most prestigious workshops. The cloisters, a lovely blend of Castilian-Gothic and Renaissance architecture, are some of the largest in Spain. Stairs lead up to the gallery, completed in 1590, which offers a good viewing point over the cathedral square.

➕ A2 ✉ Praza do Obradoiro ☎ 98 156 9327;
www.catedraldesantiago.es 🕐 Daily 9–8, Apr.–Oct.;
10–8, rest of year ✋ $$$

Praza do Obradoiro

The sweeping expanse of Praza do Obradoiro (Obradoiro Square), in front of the cathedral, is surrounded on its other sides by the Hostal Reyes Católicos (Hostel of the Catholic Monarchs), the Colegio de San Jerónimo (College of St. Jerome) and the Pazo de Raxoi, or Ayuntamiento (City Hall). The oldest building fronting the square is the luxurious Hostal Reis Católicos, a *parador*, originally founded by Ferdinand and Isabella as a pilgrims' lodging house. It has an elegantly plain facade centered by a superb Plateresque doorway. Inside, the building is laid out around four patios.

Across from the hostel is the college and its charming balcony, which dates mainly from the 17th century – although its doorway is 200 years younger. Facing the cathedral, the 18th-century City Hall seems to unite the whole ensemble.

➕ A2 ✉ Praza do Obradoiro

The baroque facade of La Catedral

St. James and Santiago

To medieval Europeans, a pilgrimage (*peregrinación*) was a means of
earning extra grace and thus attaining entry to heaven more quickly.
Pilgrimages were made to many holy places, but the great goals were
Jerusalem, Rome and Santiago de Compostela. The apostle St. James is
known as "Sant Iago" in Spanish. The city which bears his name also
is the site of his shrine and burial place. According to legend, he had
preached in Spain before returning to martyrdom in Judea in AD 44. His
disciples brought his body back to Spain, where it lay hidden until AD 844.

Legend tells that he appeared in a vision to Christian leaders and led
them to victory against the Muslim invaders, earning him the title of
Matamoros, the Moorslayer. His body and relics were rediscovered at
Compostela, which became the center of devotion for Spain's new patron
saint. By the 11th century, pilgrims arrived from all over Europe.

The *Camino de Santiago*

Pilgrims traveled from France, Britain, Germany, Italy and Scandinavia, as
well as Spain and Portugal, many taking years to complete their journey.
By the mid-12th century, between 500,000 and 2 million people were on
the move annually, a vast number in relation to the total population.

Roads to Spain threaded their way across Europe, but once over the
Pyrenees they converged into a well-organized network of routes across
northern Spain. This became known as the *Camino de Santiago*, the Way
of St. James. Administered by a religious military order, the *camino* was
policed and marked along its length with hostels, inns and churches
offering practical and spiritual sustenance to travelers. Towns grew up at
the stopping points, with their own churches, hospitals and hospices.

Dressed in sandals and heavy capes and armed with stout staffs, pilgrims
also wore the scallop shell emblem of the saint on their broad-brimmed
hats. On arrival in Santiago, the custom was to enter the cathedral and
embrace the golden effigy of the saint placed above his tomb, while giving
alms and thanks in gratitude for the safe completion of the pilgrimage.

The *Camino* Today

Interest in walking the *camino* has varied over the centuries, but today
thousands of people, locals and visitors alike, make the journey to
Santiago on foot, as well as by car, train and plane. Those who complete
the journey on foot, or by bicycle or horseback, and have fulfilled certain
requirements, can receive a certificate called "La Compostela."

The Cathedral of St. James with its soaring towers dominates the city skyline

A Day in Santiago

A Spiritual Morning

Your first stop should be a visit to the excellent Pilgrimage Museum (Museo das Peregrinacións e de Santiago, see page 420), where you can learn about the history of pilgrimage. It provides a sense of perspective and will pave the way for a visit to the cathedral (Catedral, see page 420), which should be next on the list. The worn stones of the entrance pillar show where pilgrims once touched them as a gesture on their arrival, but the stones are now protected and touching is no longer allowed.

Spend time admiring the architecture and artistic treasures, then join the line and mount the steps behind the altar to embrace the effigy of St. James, as pilgrims have done for more than 1,000 years. You could time your visit to coincide with the daily Pilgrims' Mass at noon.

A Secular Afternoon

Head up Rúa do Franco or Rúa do Vilar, Santiago's main streets, and choose one of the many restaurants for lunch – shellfish or octopus are both traditional Galician specialties. After lunch, you could head back toward the cathedral and visit the Museo y Tesoro de la Catedral (Cathedral Museum and Treasury, see page 421) before walking back across town to the Museo do Pobo Galego (Museum of the Galician People, see pages 420–421). At about 6 p.m. the streets begin to fill with shoppers and university students, and the bars become busy.

A Peaceful Evening

There's no problem finding an excellent restaurant for dinner; try some fish, such as bass, hake or turbot, or one of the flavorful Galician meat dishes, often pork-based, with potatoes and turnip tops. Be sure to order some of the local dome-shaped cheese, and finish with a slice of *tarta de Santiago*, a special almond pastry originally made only here. As you wander through the ancient streets after dinner, you'll probably hear the strains of bagpipes (*gaita* in Galician) echoing through some hidden courtyard. For the walking route, see the city map on page 418.

Restaurant terraces in Rúa San Clemente in Santiago de Compostela

Spain

Seville

Some of Spain's quintessential images are of whitewashed streets, Moorish architecture, flamenco dresses, orange trees and proud horsemen.

This mental picture actually reflects Andalucia and its capital, Seville (Sevilla). It is the fourth-largest city in Spain, the seat of a university founded in the early 16th century, an important industrial city and the center of a rich agricultural region.

The Exposition building in Plaza de España

Renowned for architectural treasures, great festivals and a relaxed lifestyle, Seville has attracted visitors for many years, and cares for them far better than many other Spanish cities.

Seville on Foot

In Seville, every building, garden and street is designed as an escape from the sun. If you're visiting in summer, take lengthy siestas during the hottest hours. The central old core is relatively small, and you'll be able to walk to many of the main sights. The narrow, twisting streets can be confusing, so always take a city map with you; maps are free and available at the tourist office and many hotels. Blue-and-white signs direct visitors to the main sights. There's plenty of information in English, and helpful multilingual guides – often university students – offer assistance at all of the main attractions.

There's plenty to see in Seville besides the main attractions. The range of museums, fine churches and civic buildings attracts many visitors: the Casa de Pilatos, an elegant private palace, is a favorite. Look for the Tobacco Factory (Fábrica de Tabacos), now part of the university but also where Carmen (of opera fame) worked.

Walking is only one option. Visitors can take an open-carriage drive from outside the cathedral that takes in many of the sights. Alternatively, 30-minute cruises run from the Torre del Oro on the Guadalquivir river, one of Spain's greatest waterways, and this is a relaxing way to admire Seville.

Festivals in Seville

Seville has two major festivals: the *Semana Santa* (Holy Week), the last week of Lent, and the *Feria de Abril* (April Festival), held the last week in April. If you plan to visit the city during either of these events, reserve a room months in advance as the city will be packed. Holy Week is a deeply religious time, celebrated by processions of *pasos* held by rival brotherhoods in Seville's different districts. *Pasos* are huge carriers supporting religious statues, richly decorated and carried by up to 60 men.

The April Festival is secular, a week-long celebration of Andalucia's love affair with horses, music and beautiful women. Carriages filled with girls in ruffled dresses, accompanied by horseback riders in traditional dress, parade the streets, and the graceful *sevillanas* is danced all night.

Eating Southern Style

Eating is a pleasure in Seville, with a wide range of restaurants and tapas bars. More than almost anywhere else in Spain, tapas has a special place here. There's a fabulous choice of dishes, traditionally eaten with a glass of *fino*, or white sherry, a fortified wine from nearby Jerez de la Fontera.

Mealtimes are late, particularly in summer, with lunch often finishing around 4 or 5 and dinner starting at

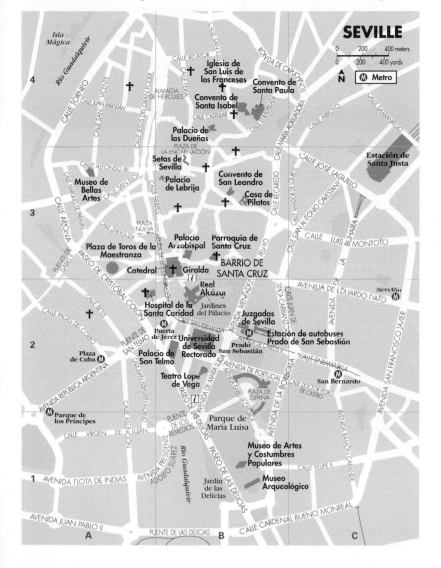

11 p.m. or midnight. The more touristy restaurants are geared to foreigners' dining habits. Andalucian coffee is very strong, so it's best to ask for a *café Americano* if you like it weaker.

Mantillas and Castanets

Shoppers throng Calle Sierpes – "the Serpent" – the winding pedestrian-only street running north from near the cathedral. It's a good place to shop for Sevillian fans, mantillas, shawls, flamenco dresses, castanets and gourmet candies. You'll find attractive pottery at tiny stores in Santa Cruz or across the river in the Triana district, where they also make fine wrought-iron goods, saddles and guitars.

Flamenco

Flamenco is a synthesis of dance and music, ideally performed spontaneously to express joy and sorrow about everyday life, religion and work. Its heartland lies in Andalucia, but its origins stretch as far afield as Egypt and India. It reaches its zenith in the soulful songs known as *cante jondo* (deep song), expressions of deep feelings. The profound meaning of flamenco is hard for foreigners to grasp, but the music, played on guitars *(toque)*, the dance, the distinctive costume, the rhythmic hand-clapping *(palmas)* and the click of castanets can be enjoyed by all. In 2010 UNESCO added flamenco to its list of Masterpieces of the Oral and Intangible Heritage of the World.

Essential Information

Tourist Information

Oficinas Municipales de Turismo (Municipal Tourist Offices)
Costurero de la Reina, Avenida de las Delicias 9 ☎ 95 423 4465
Castillo de San Jorge, Plaza de Altozano s/n, ☎ 95 433 2240
Paseo Marqués de Contadero ☎ 95 547 1232; www.visitasevilla.es
The Servicio de Atención al Turistico Extranjero (SATE) office (police station for visitors) is at the Alcázar ☎ 95 547 4029 🕔 Daily 9–2

Urban Transportation

Seville's MetroCentro is a tram which runs from Plaza Nueva to Prado. There is one metro line which runs from San Bernardo railroad station to the outskirts of the city. There is an efficient bus system; some routes run past the cathedral to the Plaza Nueva, and other lines terminate at Plaza de la Encarnación. Buy single tickets when you board, or show your 1- or 3-day tourist pass, available at newsstands or the Tussam bus office. A rechargeable multitrip card also is available. A tourist bus *(bus turístico)* (☎ 95 456 0693; https://sevilla.busturistico.com) is a hop-on-and-off service covering the main sights; tickets valid all day. For summer sightseeing cruises on the Guadalquivir river, as well as trips to Sanlúca de Barrameda, go to http://crucerosensevilla.com. White-and-yellow taxis can be hailed on the street or at a stand, or call Radio Taxi Giralda (☎ 95 467 5555).

Airport Information

Seville International Airport (☎ 902 404 704), with connections to major European cities, is 6 miles northeast of the city. An airport bus (line EA) runs every 20–30 minutes from the terminal to Prado de San Sebastián, Mon.–Fri. 4:30 a.m.–12:30 a.m.; less often on weekends.

Climate – average highs and lows for the month

Jan.	Feb.	Mar.	Apr.	May	Jun.	Jul.	Aug.	Sep.	Oct.	Nov.	Dec.
15°C	16°C	18°C	22°C	27°C	32°C	35°C	35°C	32°C	25°C	20°C	16°C
59°F	61°F	64°F	72°F	81°F	90°F	95°F	95°F	90°F	77°F	68°F	61°F
5°C	7°C	8°C	10°C	13°C	17°C	18°C	19°C	18°C	14°C	10°C	4°C
41°F	45°F	46°F	50°F	55°F	63°F	64°F	66°F	64°F	57°F	50°F	39°F

Seville Sights

Key to symbols
🔲 map coordinates refer to the Seville map on page 425 💷 admission charge: $$$ more than €6, $$ €3–€6, $ less than €3
See page 5 for complete key to symbols

Barrio de Santa Cruz
The whitewashed Barrio de Santa Cruz (Santa Cruz Quarter), with its narrow streets, ironwork grilles and sunny squares shaded by orange trees, typifies Seville. Originally the Jewish quarter, until the Jews were expelled from Spain in 1492, it was popular with 17th-century nobility.
🔲 B3 ✉ Santa Cruz 🚌 1, 5, 21, C5; tram T1

Catedral
Seville's Catedral (Cathedral), built on the site of the Moorish mosque, is the third largest in Europe. It was built between 1401 and 1507, a magnificent blend of Gothic austerity and Spanish flamboyance. The interior is dominated by the chancel, the Capilla Mayor, its splendidly carved Flemish altarpiece glistening with gold leaf behind immense grilles. Opposite lie the choir stalls. Stand between the two and look up at the transept roof, 184 feet above your head; this riot of stone filigree is supported by massive arches and columns, but even these are dwarfed by the scale of the cathedral.

Other highlights include Christopher Columbus' tomb in the south transept; the treasury and sacristy, packed with paintings and precious altar vessels; and the domed Royal Chapel, the burial place of Alfonso X of Castile.
🔲 B3 ✉ Avenida de la Constitución s/n 🕿 95 456 5743; www.catedraldesevilla.es 🕐 Mon. 11–3:30, Tue.–Sat. 11–5, Sun. 2:30–6, Jul.–Aug.; Mon. 9:30–2:30, Tue.–Sat. 9:30–4, Sun. 2:30–6, rest of year 🚌 C5; tram T1 💷 $$$ (combined ticket for Cathedral and Giralda). Free Mon. 4:30–6:30 p.m. Book online well in advance ➕ Admission with audio guide by prior reservation on Mon. afternoon year-round

Giralda
When Christians destroyed the mosque to build the cathedral, they kept the minaret and transformed it into the new cathedral's bell tower. Nicknamed the Giralda, the "weather vane," the 322-foot-tall tower was built in the 12th century. Instead of stairs, you climb a series of interior ramps; 17 levels lead to the top and views over Seville.

Below the tower lies the lovely Patio de los Naranjos (Courtyard of the Orange Trees), once part of the mosque.
🔲 B3 ✉ Plaza Virgen de los Reyes 🕿 95 456 5743 🕐 Open same days and hours as the Catedral, via the same entrance and with the same ticket 🚌 C5; tram T1 💷 $$$ (combined ticket for Cathedral and Giralda). Free Mon. 4:30–6 p.m., email in advance to reservas@catedraldesevilla.es

Isla Mágica
The Isla de la Cartuja, an island between two branches of the Guadalquivir river, is now the site of Isla Mágica, a theme park devoted to the Spanish discovery of the New World in the 15th and 16th centuries. Roller coasters, a 4D cinema and an enormous virtual-reality theater are among the attractions.
🔲 A4 ✉ Avenida Camino de los Descubrimientos 🕿 902 16 17 16; www.islamagica.es 🕐 Daily 11–11 (till midnight on Sat.), Jul. to mid-Sep.; days and times vary, mid-Apr. to Jun. and mid-Sep. to Oct. Closed Nov. to mid-Apr. 🚌 C1, C2 💷 $$$ (reduction for half-day)

Museo de Bellas Artes
Seville's Fine Arts Museum, housed in an 18th-century convent, concentrates on the Golden Age of Spanish painting. The former church is devoted to the Spanish religious painter Bartolomé Murillo, and the highlight here is his painting, *Immaculate Conception*. Francisco de Zurbarán also is represented with stunning artistic creations such as *La Virgen de las Cuevas* and *San Hugo en el Refectorio*.
🔲 A3 ✉ Plaza del Museo 9 🕿 95 554 2942; http://www.museosdeandalucia.es/cultura/museos/MBASE/ 🕐 Tue.–Sat. 9–8, Sun. 9–3 🚌 40, 41, 43, C5 💷 $

Spain

Plaza de España and Parque de María Luisa

Built as the centerpiece for the 1929 International Exhibition, the Plaza de España overlooks María Luisa Park. Traditionally styled and lavishly decorated with thousands of colored tiles, the 650-foot-wide plaza is framed by a semicircular range of buildings and encircled by a canal. The park is a tranquil area but it plays a central part in Seville's Spring Festival, when hundreds of horsemen accompany carriages of silk-robed girls around the park.

B1–B2 Plaza de España 34, C2

Plaza de Toros de la Maestranza

Seville's Plaza de Toros (Bullring) is one of the oldest and most prestigious in Spain. Once built of wood, the present 14,000-seat ring was designed around the Prince's Balcony and is actually oval in shape. Tours include the Museo Taurino, the stables and the chapel.

A3 Paseo Colón 12 95 421 0315; www.realmaestranza.com Museum and Plaza: daily 9:30–9, Apr.–Oct.; 9:30–7, rest of year 3, 21, 40, 41 $$$

Real Alcázar

The unforgettable Real Alcázar (Royal Palace) epitomizes the elegance of Mudéjar secular architecture. Little remains of the original Moorish Alcaza. Most of the palace you see today was built by Pedro the Cruel in the 1360s, long after the Moors left Spain, but the builders were Christianized Moors, the inventors of Mudéjar style, and this "Arabian Nights" complex is one of the purest examples of their art remaining today. It's a labyrinth of courtyards, delicate stucco and tile rooms, terraces and coffered chambers, fountains and arched patios. From here you pass into the 16th-century Palace of Charles V, with its tapestries and lavish rooms. Outside are gardens with terraces, pools and shady magnolia and orange trees.

B2 Patio de Banderas 95 450 2324; www.alcazarsevilla.org Tue.–Sun. 9:30–7, Apr.–

The spectacular Setas de Sevilla

Sep.; 9:30–5, rest of year 21, 23, 25, 26, 30, 31, 32, 34, 40, 41, 42, C3, C4 $$$ (students and senior citizens $) Night visits also are available

Setas de Sevilla (Metropol Parasol)

This striking building is formed by six huge, wooden parasols, which resemble mushrooms (*setas*). Designed by German architect Jürgen Mayer, it is the largest wooden structure in the world. The interconnected parasols form a gigantic canopy and cover for a cultural and entertainment complex, which contains the Antiquarium, a high-tech museum set around subterranean Roman and Andalucian ruins, a market, a restaurant and a viewing platform (*mirador*), which snakes along the top of the parasols.

B3 Plaza de la Encarnación 954 561 512 Mirador: Fri.–Sat. 10 a.m.–11:30 p.m., Sun.–Thu. 10 a.m.–11 p.m. Antiquarium: Tue.–Sat. 10–8, Sun. 10–2 Plaza Nueva (T1) 27, 32 Mirador $$; Antiquarium $

Active Spain

Spain is a superb destination for active visitors – whether you want to ski in the Pyrenees, hike through the hills of Mallorca or sail around pristine Galician islands, Spain has it all. Useful websites include www.spain.info and www.magrama.gob.es/es/red-parques-nacionales/nuestros-parques/.

Skiing and Winter Sports

Spain boasts Europe's most southerly ski resort in the glorious Sierra Nevada, near Granada in Andalucía. There are more ski stations in the Sierra de Guadarrama near Madrid, and in the Picos de Europa. However, the finest skiing can be had in the lofty peaks of the Catalan Pyrenees, particularly the smart resort of Baqueira-Beret, which is where the Spanish royal family spend their winter vacations. The ski season is relatively short, and is best between mid-December and late February.

Hiking

The European network of long-distance paths, called GR (*Gran Recorrido* in Spanish), provide some of the most spectacular treks in Spain. Particularly striking are the GR11, which traverses the Pyrenees from coast to coast, and the GR7, which runs the entire length of the Mediterranean coastline. Spain's 15 national parks are superb destinations for hiking. Spring and autumn are usually the best times, as summer can be overpoweringly hot, unless hiking in the cooler mountainous areas – but access may be restricted during the winter.

Sailing and Water Sports

Spain's extensive coastline is dotted with marinas, while sailing, water-skiing, jet-skiing, snorkeling and diving are just some of the sports commonly offered at the main resorts along the Costa Brava, Costa Blanca, Costa del Sol and the islands of Mallorca, Menorca and Ibiza. There are more marinas along the Atlantic coast to the north, which also is a mecca for surfers. The marine reserves at Illes Medes (Costa Brava), the Islas Cies (Galicia) and the Cap de Creus (Catalunya) are ideal for sailing, snorkeling and diving.

Other Activities

Golf is popular throughout Spain, with numerous world-class courses. Facilities for horseback-riding, fishing and tennis are found throughout the country.

The clear waters off Las Salinas beach in Ibiza are popular with water sports enthusiasts

Sweden

Introduction and Map 432

Timeline 434

Survival Guide 435

Stockholm 436

Feature: A Stroll Around Gamla Stan 442

Hotels and Restaurants 490

Essential Information 562

Opposite: Kornhamnstorg Square, in the Gamla Stan area of Stockholm, with the spire of Tyska Kyrkan behind

Sweden

Sweden is the largest of the Scandinavian countries, famed for the perceived efficiency of its people and the pragmatism of its government. This is a land of wide-open spaces, where even a large city like Stockholm seems to merge urban and rural elements in a way that benefits the people.

Swedish Landscapes

Southern Sweden is an area of forests and farmland punctuated by a vast number of lakes, of which two – Vänern and Vättern – dominate the landscape. The south also is the center of Sweden's industrial powerhouse. The main cities are Gothenburg (Göteborg) and Malmö on the southwest coast.

The southernmost province, Skåne, is a rich farming area where you will find a hint of Danish features in the people, architecture and landscape; the area was long occupied by the Danes. This is Sweden's vacation land. Off the east coast, the islands of Gotland and Öland in the Baltic Sea have superb beaches that benefit from calm waters and warm summer sunshine.

Stockholm lies on the east coast of Sweden, within a beautiful mosaic of inland lakes and offshore islands. In the surrounding provinces there is a richly varied countryside centered on mighty Lake Mälaren. North of Stockholm is Sweden's ancient capital, the university town of Uppsala. This area is accessible by ferries and cruise boats that ply a network of waterways and lakes.

Northern Sweden is known as Norrland, with similarities to northern Finland, and it enjoys the same "Land of the Midnight Sun" tag. It is a country of vast forests and tumbling rivers that are fed by icy, crystal waters from the mountains. Lapland, or Sápme (see page 434), is a vast and magnificent wilderness of mountains, moorland, birch forest and tundra.

Travel and Climate

Sweden has an extensive road network, but public transportation throughout the country also is a very efficient and convenient way to get around. Trains are modern and comfortable, and buses serve even the most remote northern parts of the country.

Sweden's climate is similar to that of its neighbors, but the country is generally much drier than Norway's western regions. Summers can be as warm and sunny as anywhere else in northern Europe, and along the southern coast you may even find yourself enjoying a Scandinavian heat wave. Conversely, visitors need to be prepared for wet weather in Sweden's maritime climate.

A remarkable number of Swedes are fluent in English, and most people in the cities have at least some command of English. The people are generally very helpful, and have a great awareness of the world in general; they are politely curious about visitors and are lively conversationalists, once their initial reserve is overcome.

Swedes are conservative by nature, and may seem overly serious about life. They are very aware that their society operates on the basis of willingness and cooperation and accepting the norm.

You may mistake Swedish directness for impatience, especially in Stockholm, but this simply reflects a national confidence about how things work.

Old merchants' houses in Gamla Stan

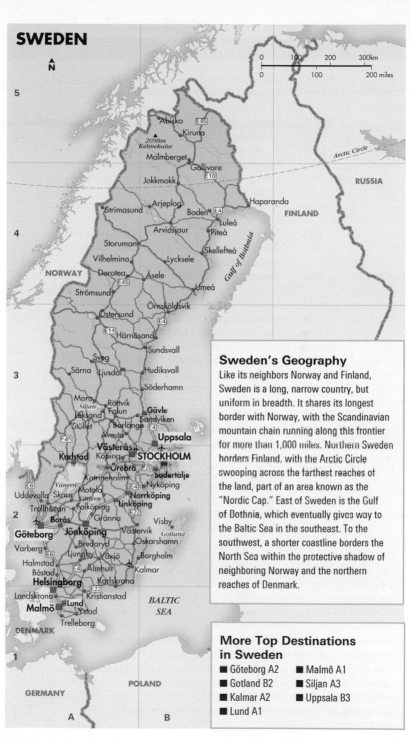

SWEDEN

N

| 0 | 100 | 200 | 300km |
| 0 | | 100 | 200 miles |

Abisko E45
Kiruna
2098m
Kebnekaise
Malmberget
Gällivare E10
Jokkmokk
Arctic Circle
RUSSIA
Strimasund
Arjeplog
Boden E4
Haparanda
FINLAND
Arvidsjaur
Luleå
Piteå
Storuman
Vilhelmina
Lycksele
Skellefteå
Dorotea
Åsele
E45
Strömsund
Umeå
Örnsköldsvik
Östersund
E14
Härnösand
Sundsvall
Sveg
Särna
Ljusdal
Hudiksvall
Söderhamn
Mora
Siljan
Rättvik
Falun
Gävle
Leksand
Borlänge
Sandviken
Slöttet
Avesta
E4
Västerås
Uppsala
Karlstad
Köping
STOCKHOLM
Örebro
E20
Söbertälje
Katrineholm
Nyköping
Vänern
Motala
E4
Uddevalla
Skara
Vättern
Norrköping
Trollhättan
Falköping
Linköping
Borås
Gränna
E22
Göteborg
Jönköping
Västervik
Visby
Gotland
Varberg
Bredaryd
Oskarshamn
E6
Ljungby
Växjö
Halmstad
Borgholm
Båstad
E4
Almhult
Kalmar
Helsingborg
Karlskrona
Landskrona
Kristianstad
BALTIC
SEA
Malmö
Lund
Ystad
Trelleborg
DENMARK
POLAND
GERMANY
A
B

Sweden's Geography

Like its neighbors Norway and Finland, Sweden is a long, narrow country, but uniform in breadth. It shares its longest border with Norway, with the Scandinavian mountain chain running along this frontier for more than 1,000 miles. Northern Sweden borders Finland, with the Arctic Circle swooping across the farthest reaches of the land, part of an area known as the "Nordic Cap." East of Sweden is the Gulf of Bothnia, which eventually gives way to the Baltic Sea in the southeast. To the southwest, a shorter coastline borders the North Sea within the protective shadow of neighboring Norway and the northern reaches of Denmark.

More Top Destinations in Sweden

- Göteborg A2
- Gotland B2
- Kalmar A2
- Lund A1
- Malmö A1
- Siljan A3
- Uppsala B3

Timeline

8000 BC	Hunter-gatherers move throughout Scandinavia in the wake of retreating ice sheets; the Sami (Lapp) people are thought to descend from these early settlers.
1500 BC	Germanic tribes in southern Sweden develop trading links with the European lands to the south, from which they came.
AD 750	The legendary Battle of Bråvalla; the Svear emerge as the dominant tribe and give their name to the country Sverige.
800–1000	Swedish "Vikings" travel east via the great rivers of eastern Europe, as far as Constantinople.
1397	Union of Kalmar unites Denmark, Sweden and Norway under Queen Margaret of Denmark.
1523	Gustav Vasa establishes Sweden's independence; becomes King Gustav I; Lutheran Protestantism becomes the country's main religion.
1658	Treaty of Roskilde secures all of southern Swedish mainland from Danish control.
1814	Sweden wins control of Norway from Denmark.
1905	Norway achieves independence from Sweden.
1914–18	Sweden remains neutral during World War I.
1939–45	Sweden again remains neutral during World War II.
1946	Sweden maintains neutrality and joins the United Nations.
1973	Carl XVI Gustaf becomes king.
1989	The Sami people are granted their own parliament, known as the Sametinget.
1995	Sweden joins the European Union.
2000	The 10-mile Øresund tunnel and bridge linking Malmö and Copenhagen opens.
2003	In a referendum, the majority of Swedes reject the euro.
2011	Swedish surgeons carry out the first synthetic organ transplant.
April 2017	A terrorist drives a truck through central Stockholm, killing four people and wounding many others.
2018	Sweden builds the first road that enables electric vehicles to recharge as they are driven.

The Sami

The Sami are the indigenous people of Sápme, the area popularly called Lapland. They are known historically as Lapps, but this is not a native name and is one that the Sami themselves feel is derogatory. The ancient name Sápme, a form of Sami which is said to mean "the people of the interior," is now considered accepted usage. Sápme covers the Scandinavian Arctic region from the Russian Kola peninsula to the northwest coast of Norway, and extends down either side of the Norwegian-Swedish border to the central area of both countries. There are an estimated 70,000 Sami people today, of which some 20,000 live in Sweden. A minority of Sami are reindeer herders, but the Sami also are developing alternative livelihoods while strengthening their self-awareness and political position within Scandinavia. Tourism is increasing in Scandinavian Lapland, but some Sami people are concerned about what they believe is too much intrusion on their fragile environment and culture.

Survival Guide

■ For lunch you must experience *smörgåsbord*, a Scandinavian institution, although less common these days. The name translates as *smörgås* for "bread," *bord* for "table." The reality of a true *smörgåsbord* means much more than this simple image implies. There may be more than 100 different dishes in a true *smörgåsbord*, with items ranging from *gravad lax* (salmon slices in herbs) to *köttbullar* (tasty meatballs), *sillbullar* (herring rissoles) or *kåldolmar* (stuffed cabbage rolls).

■ Like Norway and Finland, Sweden exercises tight control over alcohol sales and alcohol is expensive. The government-controlled liquor monopoly, Systembolaget, has branches throughout the country, (open Mon.–Fri. 9–6, Sat. 10–3). They sell spirits, wines and strong beers; the minimum age to purchase at Systembolaget is 20. Light beers can be bought at grocery stores and supermarkets by anyone 18 or over. Try some aquavit with your food. The beverage is distilled from grain or potatoes and flavored with spices or herbs. Gulp down small quantities.

■ July is a popular month to travel in Sweden and the countryside and coast are very busy.

■ Swedish design is world famous; the Småland area in southeast Sweden is particularly noted for its fine glassware. Stores such as NK in Stockholm's Hamngatan have good selections of glassware, or, for an education in Swedish home decor (though prices are high) check out r.o.o.m. (room.se) at Täby Centrum, Stora Marknadsvägen 15, a large mall in Täby, a 15-minute hop on the train from Östra Station (East Station).

■ Home furnishings are a Swedish specialty. Visit the world's second-largest IKEA store at Kungens Kurva, southwest of Stockholm. A free bus

Lake Kallston in the north of the country

leaves Mon.–Fri. every hour between 10 and 7:15 (90 minutes later in the day), from Vasagatan 10, just outside Central Station. The return bus leaves every hour on the half hour from Kungens Kurva between 10.30 and 7:45 and takes 20 minutes, stopping at Hornstul, Fridhemsplan and Kungshelmstorg. Or try stylish Nordiska Galleriet, at Nybrogatan 11 (www.nordiskagalleriet.se).

■ Don't miss the lively Stockholm Jazz Festival (www.stockholmjazz.com), in October. Venues across Stockholm host world-famous Swedish and international artists and groups playing jazz, blues, soul and Latin American music.

■ In big cities there are public restrooms along some main streets, in main subway stations and department stores. Signs are *Damer* for ladies and *Herrar* for men. The charge is usually 10SKr, but many self-cleaning restrooms in Stockholm are free.

Stockholm

Stockholm is one of the world's most beautiful capitals, probably the only city in the world where you can catch a salmon at a busy road intersection under the walls of a royal palace, and where the city's subway stations double as eye-catching art galleries. The salmon thrive in Stockholm's clean waters at the very heart of the city, and local anglers fish from the Strömbron bridge. The artwork that enlivens subway stations is just one expression of the vigorous cultural life that makes Stockholm one of the world's most civilized cities.

City of Islands

Modern Stockholm is a large, exhilarating city. The scale of its public buildings is monumental, the bustle of its streets all-embracing, yet the city is given a uniquely open character by the 24,000 islands in its archipelago and by the mirror images of lakes that pepper its hinterland. Stockholm stands on 14 interlocking islands; the city is a mosaic of land, lake and waterway stitched together by 50 bridges, making it a vibrant urban environment.

Gamla Stan (Old Town, see pages 442–443) lies at the heart of old Stockholm, a dramatic and fascinating expression of heritage and tradition. It stands on an island in the middle of the narrow bottleneck channel between the salty Baltic Sea and the freshwater lake of Mälaren, the third-largest lake in Sweden, after Vänern and Vättern. To the south is the hilly island of Södermalm, a suburban area with generous expanses of grass and trees. North of Gamla Stan and the buildings of state (the Royal Palace and the Parliament House) is Norrmalm, the business and commercial district. This is the heart of the modern city – glass, steel, concrete and good Swedish design – a cityscape of towering buildings, stylish shopping malls, busy streets and traffic-free concourses that satisfy the demands of both vehicles and pedestrians. East of Norrmalm is the residential district of Östermalm and the city's island park, Djurgården, the world's first National City Park. To the west is Kungsholmen, one of the many islands that inhabit the expanse of Lake Mälaren, Stockholm's "inland" sea.

Compass Bearings

Most visitors arrive at the city's central railroad station in Norrmalm, and the experience can be disorienting at first. The Tourist Center is opposite the station. Just east, along Klarabergsgatan is the big sunken square of Sergels Torg, with its landmark Kristall tower of glass and steel and a huge glass facade on the south side. This is Stockholm's contemporary hub. You can orient yourself here and relax in spite of the surrounding traffic and noise. Running north and south of Sergels Torg are busy shopping streets, such as the pedestrian-only Drottninggatan. The northern section of Drottninggatan has many more stores.

Continuing east from Sergels Torg into the street of Hamngatan takes you past elegant NK, the best name in Swedish shopping. This huge department store

---

Subway Art

When the Stockolm *Tunnelbana* was built in the late 1940s (68 miles long) a decision was made to decorate the stations with individual artworks. Ninety of the network's 100 stations now have artworks. T-Centralen has the most, with examples ranging from installations to mosaics, paintings and wrought-ironwork. Visit the Blue Line's amazing Kungsträdgården station; it has many sculptures, some modern and some that were unearthed during the redevelopment of the city center in the 1960s. In summer, free guided art walks are available in English; you will need only a valid metro ticket to join a tour. For information go to Customer Services online at www.sl.se.

has floor after floor of luxury goods and such fashionable restaurants as Bobergs Matsal. Also in Hamngatan (No. 37) is Gallerian, a big shopping mall. Farther along is the great open swath of the Old Royal Gardens (Kungsträdgården). The park sweeps south to the waters of Strömmen, the magnificent Kungliga Slottet (Royal Palace, see pages 439–440) and enchanting Gamla Stan.

Seeing Stockholm

For all its size, Stockholm is a city that can be enjoyed on a human scale. You can see it by tour bus, sightseeing boat or with an organized tour accompanied by a knowledgeable guide. Try a boat trip for the wider view of Stockholm's islands, and visit some attractions, such as Djurgården (see pages 440–441) and Drottningholms Slott (Drottningholm Palace, see page 439), by ferry boat.

Ask at the tourist center about the Stockholm Pass which offers admission for one, two, three or five days (645SKr, 845SKr, 1,045SKr and 1,345SKr respectively), to around 60 museums and the hop-on-hop-off buses and boats (boats run from the end of April to beginning of September only). For an extra fee, you can include a Travelcard (see page 438, Essential Information) for use on all public transportation in Stockholm and the surrounding area.

Stockholm is neatly packaged into separate entities because of its island

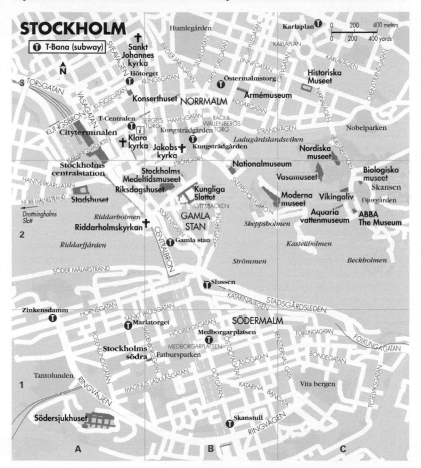

nature, making it easy to plan your visit one day at a time. At night the city becomes even more majestic when it is lit up and vibrant with music and lively entertainment.

Stockholmers

Stockholm's confidence is infectious. Listen closely to advice and don't be afraid to ask for clarification or guidance. Then let the magic of the city take over and relax. Stockholmers have created one of the most endearing and enchanting cities in the world, and know how to enjoy it.

The setting sun casts a glow on Stockholm

Essential Information

Tourist Information

Stockholm Visitor Center
Kulturhuset, Sergels Torg 5 ☎ 08 508 285 08;
www.visitstockholm.com

Urban Transportation

Stockholms Centralstation (Central Station ✉ Vasagatan ☎ (0) 771 757 575; www.sj.se) is the main railroad station. The Tunnelbana (subway) or T-Bana; has three lines: green, red and blue. T-Bana stations are indicated by signs bearing a blue "T" on a white background (city map shows T-Bana stations as a letter "T" in a red circle). There is an efficient bus system. Public transportation in Stockholm has a unified ticket system, allowing transfer between systems. Cash cannot be used on any public transportation. Buy a single-use Travelcard or load money onto an SL Access Card (electronic smart card), bought from subway and train stations or from the SL information center in the T-Centralen T-Bana station (☎ 08 600 1000; www.sl.se). For taxis contact: Taxi Kurir

☎ 08 30 00 00, or Taxi 020 ☎ 020 20 20 20 (or ☎ 46 8 850400 from overseas).

Airport Information

Stockholm-Arlanda Airport (☎ 0 10 109 10 00; www.swedavia.se/arlanda/) is 28 miles north of the city. The Arlanda Express train (☎ (0) 771 720 200; www.arlandaexpress.com) links the airport and Central Station at 10- or 15-minute intervals daily 4:20 a.m.–12:35 a.m. from Stockholm and 4:50 a.m.–1:05 a.m. from Arlanda. The trip takes 20 minutes. The Flygbussarna airport buses (☎ (0) 771 515 252; www.flygbussarna.se) run at 10-minute intervals at peak times (less at night) and take 45 minutes to reach the Cityterminalen (City Terminal) at Klarabergsviadukten 72. Bromma Airport (☎ 0 10 109 40 00; www.swedavia. com/bromma/) is 5 miles west of Stockholm and handles domestic and some international flights. Flygbussarna buses run between Bromma Airport and the City Terminal; travel time 20 minutes. For information ☎ (0) 771 515 252; www.flygbussarna.se.

Climate – average highs and lows for the month

Jan.	Feb.	Mar.	Apr.	May	Jun.	Jul.	Aug.	Sep.	Oct.	Nov.	Dec.
-1°C	-1°C	3°C	8°C	15°C	19°C	21°C	20°C	15°C	9°C	4°C	0°C
30°F	30°F	37°F	46°F	59°F	66°F	70°F	68°F	59°F	48°F	39°F	32°F
-5°C	-6°C	-3°C	0°C	5°C	11°C	13°C	13°C	9°C	4°C	1°C	-2°C
23°F	21°F	27°F	32°F	41°F	52°F	55°F	55°F	48°F	39°F	34°F	28°F

Stockholm Sights

Key to symbols
🔲 map coordinates refer to the Stockholm map on page 437 🔲 admission charge: $$$ more than 100SKr, $$ 50SKr–100SKr, $ less than 50SKr
See page 5 for complete key to symbols

ABBA The Museum
The aim of this museum is to make each visitor feel like a fifth member of the iconic band. You will see the gold discs, scrapbooks and other memorabilia, but you also can touch the band's mixing desk in the Polar Studio, squeeze into replica stage costumes, and be a full-on dancing queen on The Dance Floor alongside 3D holograms of the members of the band. A self-playing piano springs into action when the real Benny Andersson plays the piano in his studio (away from the museum).

🔲 C2 🔲 Djurgårdsvägen 68 🔲 08 121 328 60; www. abbathemuseum.com 🔲 Daily 9–7, May–Aug.; Fri.–Tue. 10–6, Wed.–Thu. 10–7, rest of year 🔲 44; tram 7 🔲 Slussen 🔲 Restaurant 🔲 $$$ 🔲 Guided tours $$

Drottningholms Slott
Drottningholms Slott (Drottningholm Palace) is on Lovön island. The palace, home of Sweden's royal family since 1981, is set amid its own gardens, a mix of French and English styles, and overlooks Lake Mälaren. On the grounds is the 18th-century Kina Slott (Chinese Pavilion), where Asian meets rococo.

Nearby is the 18th-century baroque Slottsteater (Palace Theater), which is a venue for opera from late May to mid-August. A museum showcases the work of Dutch sculptor Adriaen de Vries (1556–1626).

Drottningholms Slott 🔲 Off map at A2 🔲 Drottningholm 🔲 08 402 62 80; www.kungahuset.se 🔲 Daily 10–5:30, May–Sep.; Tue.–Sun.10–4 Apr. and Oct; Sat.–Sun. 10–4, Nov. to mid-Dec. and Jan.–Mar. Closed mid- to end Dec.

Kina Slott 🔲 Drottningholm 🔲 08 402 62 80; www.kungahuset.se 🔲 Daily 11–5, May–Sep.

Slottsteater 🔲 Drottningholm 🔲 0771 707 070 (box office); www.dtm.se 🔲 By guided tours only daily 11–4 , on the hour (in English)

Drottningholms Slott, Kina Slott and Slottsteater 🔲 T-Brommaplan; then bus 301 or 323 🔲 176, 177 🔲 Stadshuskajen (in summer) 🔲 $$$ for each part (includes guided tour); a combined ticket also is available in summer

Kungliga Slottet
The monumental Kungliga Slottet (Royal Palace), the official residence of the king and queen, is a stunning mix of classical styles developed throughout the 18th century on the site of the original Castle of Three Crowns. The Representationsvåningarna (Royal Apartments) within the palace are a mix of French baroque, rococo and imperial styles. There are several museums within the palace, including the Tre Kronor Museum, with remnants of the Tre Kronor Castle; the Skattkammaren (Treasury), where state regalia are on

Drottningholm Palace is a superb 17th-century baroque building in the style of Versailles

display; Gustav III's Antikmuseum
(Gustav III's Museum of Antiquities),
with an extensive collection of classical
sculptures; and the Livrustkammaren
(Royal Armory), which depicts Sweden's
military history.

**Representationsvåningarna, Tre Kronor Museum,
Skattkammaren and Gustav III's Antikmuseum**
B2 Slottsbacken 3 08 402 61 30;
www.kungahuset.se Tue.–Sun. 10–5, May–Sep.,
10–4, rest of year, depending on official royal
receptions; check before you visit Gamla Stan
2, 3, 43, 53, 55, 71, 76 $$$ (includes guided
tours). The ticket includes all three attractions and is
valid for 2 days ($$$)
Livrustkammaren Slottsbacken 3 08 402 3030;
www.livrustkammaren.se Daily 10–6, Jul.–Aug.;
11–5, May–Jun.; Tue.–Sun. 11–5 (also Thu. 5–8 p.m.),
rest of year Gamla Stan 3, 43, 46, 53, 55, 59,
62, 65 $$$ Guided tours

Moderna museet

Stockholm's Modern Museum includes
works by Andy Warhol, Willem de
Kooning, René Magritte and Pablo
Picasso. Look out for Salvador Dalí's
startling *The Enigma of William Tell* and
Marcel Duchamp's *Fountain*. There also
are works by Swedish artists Vera
Nilsson and Siri Derkert.

B2–C2 Skeppsholmen, Exercisplan 4 08
5202 3500; www.modernamuseet.se Tue. and Fri.
10–8, Wed.–Thu. 10–6, Sat.–Sun. 11–6
Kungsträdgården 65 Slussen Café and
restaurant Free. Special exhibitions $$$

The 14 islands of Stockholm are superb for sailors

Nationalmuseum

The National Museum is a dignified
Italianate building on little Blasieholmen
peninsula, across the water east of
Gamla Stan and facing the Royal Palace.
Reopened in October 2018, after a
five-year renovation and space
expansion, the National Museum's
collections include paintings and
drawings as well as sculpture from the
Renaissance period to 1900.

B2 Södra Blasieholmshamnen 08 5195 4300
and 08 5195 4410; www.nationalmuseum.se
Kulturhuset Stadsteatern Sergels Torg 08 5062
0200 Galleries: Mon. 4–7, Tue.–Fri. 1–7, Sat.–Sun.
11–5 T-Centralen 54, 57, 69 Restaurant
and café Exhibitions $–$$

Nordiska museet

Standing at the entrance to Djurgården,
the superb building housing the
Nordiska museet (Northern Museum)
has a gabled facade of brick and stone
with elegant turrets and a handsome
central steeple. Exhibits within illustrate
Swedish and general Nordic cultural life
from the medieval period onward. There
is a section depicting the life of the Sami
(Lapp) people (see page 434) and
exhibits of traditional Swedish dress.

C3 Djurgårdsvägen 6–16, Djurgården
08 519 546 00; www.nordiskamuseet.se/en
Wed. 10–8, Thu.–Tue. 10–5 Karlaplan
67, 69, 76; tram 7 from Nybroplan Slussen
Restaurant $$$ (free Tue. 1–5 p.m.)
Audio tours (free)

Skansen

The Skansen open-air museum is on
Djurgården, Stockholm's island park,
which was once the hunting domain of
Swedish royalty. At the heart of
Djurgården, Skansen features more than
150 traditional buildings from the 18th
to 20th centuries, and in summer it is a
lively working environment for artisans.
You can sample traditional Swedish
delicacies, such as *smörgåsbord* and
waffles with cream and cloudberries.
Here also is the zoo and aquarium.
Scattered around Djurgården are other

museums and art galleries including the Vasamuseet (Vasa Museum, see below) and the Nordiska museet (Northern Museum, see page 440), the Gröna Lunds Tivoli amusement park, and the zoo and aquarium.

🔳 C2 ✉ Djurgårdsslätten 49–51, Djurgården
☎ 08 442 82 00; www.skansen.se ⏱ Daily 10–6
🚋 44; tram 7 from Norrmalmstorg or Nybroplan
🛳 Slussen (year-round); Nybroplan (early Aug.–early Oct.) 🍴 Restaurants and cafés 💰 $$$ (varies during the year)

Stadshuset

Stockholm's City Hall is perhaps the city's finest example of early 20th-century Scandinavian Romantic Nationalistic style. Built of red brick and with a magnificent Italianate tower, it stands on the shore of Lake Mälaren. The City Hall Tower (Stadshustornet) tapers to an upper platform that supports the gleaming Tre Kroner, the three crowns symbol of the city. Interiors are no less striking; the highlight is the Golden Hall with its marble floor. Admission to City Hall is by guided tour only (45 minutes) on a first come, first served basis. From April to September you can climb the 348-foot tower – or take the elevator halfway – for fine views over the city.

🔳 A2 ✉ Hantverkargartan 1 ☎ 08 508 290 58 (for tours) or 08 508 29349 (Tower, May–Sep.); www.stockholm.se/stadshuset ⏱ Guided tours in English daily at 10, 11, 12, 1, 2 and 3, though subject to change; additional tours Jun.–Aug. Tower: daily 9:10–5:10, Jun.–Aug.; 9:10–3.50, May and Sep.
🚇 Rådhuset 🚌 3, 50 🍴 Restaurant 💰 City Hall $$$ ($$ Nov.–Dec.); Tower $$

Stockholms Medeltidsmuseet

Stockholms Medeltidsmuseet (Museum of Medieval Stockholm) is located below the Riksdagshuset (Parliament House) on the tiny island of Helgeandsholmen, in the Gamla Stan area of the city. In the late 1970s, whilst excavations were being carried out for a planned parking lot, archeologists uncovered several layers of medieval remains.

Depicting the history of Stockholm from the 1250s to the 1520s, the museum is entered via steps leading down from Norrbro, the bridge between Gustav Adolfs Torg and Gamla Stan.

🔳 B2 ✉ Strömparterren 3 ☎ 08 508 316 20; www.medeltidsmuseet.stockholm.se ⏱ Tue.–Sun. noon–5 (also Wed. 5–8 p.m.) 🚇 Gamla Stan, T-Centralen or Kungsträdgården 🚌 2, 54, 55, 57, 65, 69 💰 Free 🛈 Guided tours in English daily at 2, Jul.–Aug.

Vasamuseet

The focus of the Vasamuseet (Vasa Museum) is the sailing ship *Vasa*, which sank spectacularly in Stockholm harbor within minutes of starting its maiden voyage in 1628. At 230-feet long and fully restored and rigged, the *Vasa* is the only intact 17th-century ship in the world. Its finest features were well-preserved in the muddy Baltic waters for more than 330 years. The museum tells the story of the people who salvaged the *Vasa* in 1961, and exhibits 12,000 recovered artifacts.

🔳 C2 ✉ Galärvarvsvägen 14, Djurgården ☎ 08 519 548 00 or 08 519 558 10; www.vasamuseet.se ⏱ Daily 8.30–6, Jun.–Aug.; 10–5 (also Wed. 5–8 p.m.), rest of year 🚇 Karlaplan 🚌 67, 69, 76 (to Djurgårdsbron); tram 7 from Sergels Tor 🛳 Slussen (all year); Nybroplan (early Aug.–early Oct.) 🍴 Restaurant 💰 $$$; free for under 18s 🛈 Guided tours in English (included in admission fee) daily 9:30–4:30 (every 30 minutes), Jun.–Aug.; Mon.–Fri. 11:30, 1:30 and 3:30, Sat.–Sun., 10:30, 11:30, 12:30, 1:30, 2:30 and 3:30, rest of year

Vikingaliv

Instructive but fun, and aiming to dispel the stereotypical image of marauding Vikings, Stockholm's new museum on the waterfront mixes imaginative displays, the world's biggest collection of Viking artifacts and interactive experiences. Ragnfrid's Saga, an 11-minute journey through the places visited by the Vikings, is a highlight.

🔳 C2 ✉ Djurgårdsvägen 48 ☎ 08 400 22990; www.vikingaliv.se ⏱ Daily 10–6, Jun. to mid-Aug.; 10–5, rest of the year 🚌 67; tram 7 🛳 Djurgårdsfärjan ferry 🍴 Restaurant 💰 $$$

A Stroll Around Gamla Stan

Stockholm's Gamla Stan (Old Town) – or *staden mellan broarna*, "the city between the bridges," as it is more lyrically known to Swedes – is not a perfectly preserved medieval townscape by any means. Disastrous fires in 1407 and 1640 destroyed the original wooden buildings of medieval Gamla Stan. But the island nature of the settlement, its small area and its crowded layout have spared Gamla Stan from too much modernization. What remains today is a superb enclave of attractive old stone buildings dating from the 15th to the 18th centuries.

You can wander through the Old Town without getting lost – on this tiny island you are never far from the waterside or a bridge to reorient yourself. It is best experienced on foot, so pick up a large-scale Gamla Stan map, widely available in stores, restaurants and tourist venues, to help you find specific places.

There are many easily missed treasures hidden away from the main streets of Västerlånggatan and Österlånggatan. Pay a visit to the Cathedral of Stockholm (Storkyrkan). Dating from the 13th century, it is the city's oldest building and is just south of the courtyard of the Royal Palace. The church's finest artifact is the oak- and elkhorn-gilded sculpture of *St. George and the Dragon*, a 15th-century Gothic masterpiece of thorny carving by sculptor Bernt Notke. You may catch a lunchtime organ recital or musical performance in the church. The Riddarholmskyrkan is the memorial place and royal burial ground for past Swedish kings.

From the church, walk along the narrow street of Trångsund and then turn left past a charming old phone booth to reach Stortorget (Great Square). This was the scene in 1520 of the notorious Stockholm "Blood Bath," when Christian II of Denmark slaughtered 82 Swedish nobles and citizens in a bid to seal with blood his overlordship of Sweden. This brutal act inspired Gustav Vasa, son of a murdered nobleman, to rebel successfully against Denmark and to secure Sweden's independence. On the west side of Stortorget is a row of gabled houses. The 18th-century Bourse, or Stock Exchange, commands the north side of the square and contains the Nobelmuseet (Nobel Museum, open daily 9–8, Jun.–Aug.; Tue.–Thu. 11–5, Fri. 11–8, Sat.–Sun.10–6,rest of year; www.nobelmuseum.se). The Swedish Academy, the body that selects Nobel prize winners, meets at the Bourse.

Leave the square via the east side and walk down Köpmangatan, "Street of the Merchants," the oldest street in the Old Town and home to several fine antiques stores with attractively painted ceilings. At the end of

Köpmangatan, in the little square of Köpmantorget, is a dramatic reprise of the Great Church's statue of *St. George and the Dragon*, this time in bronze but just as powerful. Farther east is Österlånggatan, a long, winding street that was once the Old Town's shoreline. Here you'll find many stores selling authentic Gustavian furniture.

Bear right, down the short slope of Köpmanbrinken street, and then keep right along Österlånggatan, past stylish restaurants, antiques and craft stores, and fashion salons. There are lots of gift possibilities here, especially for children, in stores such as Kalikå at Osterlånggaten 18, and Tomtar & Troll at Södra Benickebrinken 4 (www.tomtar.se), which has a wonderful array of painted wooden handicrafts. The narrow streets running east to the sea, such as Drakens Gränd, Ferkens Gränd and Packhusgränd, mark the old piers of the early medieval era. Near the end of Österlånggatan is the well-known restaurant Den Gyldene Freden (see page 491).

Soon you reach Järntorget (Iron Square), a name probably derived from the days when the Old Town's fortunes were built on its status as the main outlet for the Swedish iron and copper trade. Here, against the wall of the old Central Bank, is the remarkably lifelike statue of Swedish poet and songwriter Evert Taube, a popular performer who died in 1976. Built in the late 17th century, the Riksbank is thought to be one of the oldest bank buildings in Europe. Take a break at the nearby Sundbergs Konditori, established in 1785, making it the oldest bakery in the city.

From Järntorget, turn right onto Västerlånggatan, the busiest street in the Old Town, especially in the summer, crammed with stores and tempting restaurants and cafés. On the right, just past the Mårten Trotzig restaurant, you'll pass the narrow entrance to Mårten Trotzigs Gränd, reputed to be the narrowest alleyway in Stockholm and named after a German medieval copper trader who had a business here. In fact, German architectural influence can be easily identified in many of the winding streets and buildings of the Old Town.

All the way along Västerlånggatan you will be tempted by souvenir stores and Swedish craft stores, such as Handkraft Svea Rike at No. 24. Note the glass-paneled ceilings of many of the stores.

To end your excursion, stroll to where the bridge over the canal Stallkanalen leads through the arched passage to the gate at Riksgatan. Follow this back into Stockholm via Drottninggatan.

Above left to right: Skeppsbron waterfront glows in the early morning sun; café terraces are popular meeting places in summer

Switzerland

Introduction and Map 446

Timeline 448

Survival Guide 449

Geneva 450

Feature: The Red Cross 455

Zurich 456

Feature: Swiss Flavors 460

Hotels and Restaurants 491

Essential Information 566

Opposite: The Lauterbrunnen Valley in the Bernese Oberland

Switzerland

With stunning Alpine scenery, lush meadows, a medley of beautiful lakes, attractive and neat cities and towns, Switzerland has a wonderful variety of natural and man-made attractions.

Neutral Territory

The Swiss Constitution, modeled on that of the United States, was drawn up in 1848 and revised in 1874, and then again in 1999; it is still in force today. Modern Switzerland is a federation of districts (cantons), and neutrality has traditionally been the cornerstone of state policy. Switzerland has interfered in no foreign conflicts and has made no alliances, although it became a member of the United Nations in 2002.

Remaining neutral through both world wars, Switzerland emerged in 1945 as a powerful commercial player. Banking has long thrived here due to the political stability of the country and because of Swiss financial acumen. The superb infrastructure of railroads, tunnels and roads has overcome the daunting mountainous terrain and allows the country to exploit a trading position at the center of Europe.

The Swiss Landscape

Europe's continental watershed runs through Switzerland, a landlocked country, with a central lowland sandwiched between the tree-clad slopes of the Jura mountains to the north and the mighty Alps to the south. The mountain glaciers and peaks of the Swiss Alps occupy around 60 percent of the country. Dense forests cover another quarter of the land and the rest is a delightful picture-postcard mix of lakes, winding rivers and green meadow pasture.

Switzerland has a varied climate with snow on the high peaks year-round, and warm, wet summers in the valleys. On some days the *Föhn* – a warm, dry wind – blows from the northern slopes of the Alps, sparking avalanches.

More Top Destinations in Switzerland

- Ascona D1
- Baden C3
- Basel B3
- Bern B2
- Brienz C2
- Château de Chillon B1
- Engelberg C2
- Fribourg B2
- Grindelwald C2
- Gstaad B2
- Interlaken C2
- Lausanne B2
- Montreux B2
- St.-Moritz E2
- Schaffhausen C3
- Villars B1
- Wilderswil C2
- Zermatt C1

SWITZERLAND

| 0 | 20 | 40 | 60 | 80km |
| 0 | 10 | 20 | 30 | 40 | 50 miles |

N

FRANCE

Porrentruy A1

La Chaux-de-Fonds Biel Bienne

Neuchâtel A5

Lac de Neuchâtel

Yverdon-les-Bains A1 Fribour

A12

Bulle

Morges Lausanne Gsta

Lac Léman Montreux

Nyon A1 Château de Chillon Aigle Villars

Genève (Geneva) Champery

Martigny Le Rh

FRANCE

A B

Language and Manners

Reflecting Switzerland's location in central Europe, the Swiss speak four different languages: Schwyzerdütsch, a number of Swiss-German dialects (although German is used for reading and writing); French; Italian; and Romansch (Rhaeto-Romanic), an ancient Latin tongue. This linguistic diversity results in very different types of people; you'll notice this as you travel.

On the whole, the Swiss are extremely law-abiding, and consider punctuality very important. They have a reputation for being aloof, but this is a misunderstanding. Manners are formal, with hand-shaking and serious toasts in all social circumstances. Efficient, civic-minded and polite, they make Switzerland a very well-run country.

Vacationing in Switzerland

The fabled Swiss efficiency has many positive benefits for visitors: trains run punctually, hotels are clean and comfortable, opening times for attractions are reliable, and everyone connected with tourism speaks English.

You will discover also that Switzerland is very expensive, so if you're watching your budget, don't plan on staying here too long.

There's something to enjoy throughout the year – skiing in the mountains during the winter, walking, sailing and other outdoor pursuits all summer. Late spring sees the countryside at its best, with carpets of mountain and meadow wildflowers; fall, when the leaves turn and the first snow whitens the lower peaks, also is magnificent.

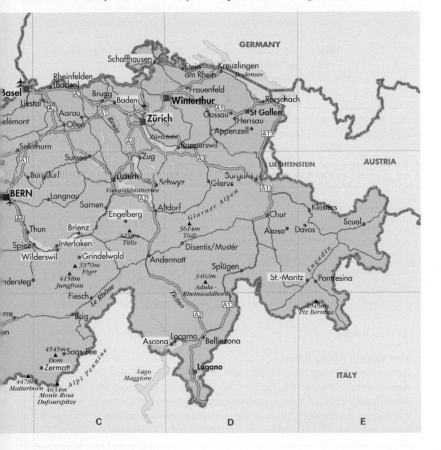

Switzerland

Timeline

3,000 BC	Evidence of earliest neolithic settlers by Lake Neuchâtel.
circa 100 BC	Romans invade from the south, incorporating Helvetic tribes.
circa AD 400	Romans expelled southward; Burgundians occupy western areas (modern French-speaking Switzerland) and Alemans the north and east (German-speaking Switzerland).
1032	Existing country incorporated into Holy Roman Empire, followed by gradual emergence of powerful independent nobles.
1506	Formation of the Papal Swiss Guard, a force that still serves the Pope and the Vatican.
1515	Defeat at Battle of Marignano inaugurates neutrality.
1526	Zwingli's Reformation takes hold in Zurich, continued by John Calvin in Geneva beginning in 1536.
1648	Treaty of Westphalia recognizes Swiss neutrality and independence of 13 cantons.
1798	French invasion and rule under Napoleon, who establishes Helvetic Republic.
1815	Congress of Vienna guarantees Swiss independence.
1848	Adoption of Swiss Constitution, which defines political organization of the country.
1864	First Convention of Geneva is accepted and signed by 16 nations; the Red Cross is founded.
1914–18	Switzerland remains neutral during World War I.
1919	President Woodrow Wilson chooses Geneva as headquarters of the League of Nations.
1939–45	Switzerland remains neutral during World War II, but image is tarnished by pro-Nazi activities.
1946	United Nations takes over role of League of Nations; Geneva retained as European headquarters.
1990	Population votes to freeze nuclear power development.
1999	Ruth Dreifuss becomes Switzerland's first woman president.
2002	Switzerland becomes the 190th member of the United Nations.
2009	The Large Hadron Collider at CERN (the European Center for Nuclear Research) near Geneva is switched on. In 2012 the LHC uncovers evidence for the existence of the Higgs boson particle.
2015	Plans are announced to build Europe's tallest skyscraper at Vals.
February 2017	Swiss people vote to allow changes to citizenship rules making it easier for third-generation immigrants to become Swiss citizens.
2019	Switzerland begins to phase out nuclear power in favor of renewable energy.

The Swiss Army Knife

The Swiss Army knife was first manufactured in 1897 as an accessory for soldiers in the Swiss army. More than 200 models of this versatile, world-renowned penknife now exist, each with a distinctive white cross in a shield on a red background. Its blades and attachments, ranging from tweezers and magnifying glasses to tiny hacksaws, scissors and nail files, are designed to perform a wide range of tasks. It has justifiably been called the "smallest toolbox in the world."

The tranquil tourquoise waters of Oeschinnensee, Berner Oberland

Survival Guide

■ Keep more money available than you think you will need; cash seems to be spent alarmingly fast in Switzerland. Credit cards are widely accepted throughout the country.

■ Although most Swiss are excellent linguists, it's polite to ask if they speak English before starting a conversation or asking a question.

■ Be polite to everyone – *bitte*, *prego* or *je vous en prie* is the equivalent of "you're welcome," and it's important to use one of these expressions when you're thanked. When you use public transportation, it's customary to give up your seat for elderly people, pregnant women and people with disabilities.

■ Be punctual; if you're likely to be checking in to your hotel later than planned, let them know you've been held up.

■ In cities other than Zurich, Basel and Bern it is considered rude to eat or drink on the street. If you purchase food to go, find somewhere to sit down and eat it.

■ Don't drop litter; it is a finable offense. When getting rid of trash, make sure you put it in the compartment designated for that particular type of waste.

■ Although informality is the norm in active, health-conscious Switzerland, very casual clothing – like beachwear – isn't usually seen in cities.

■ There is no state medical health service in Switzerland; treatment must be paid for on the spot. Therefore, it is very important to carry medical travel insurance valid in Switzerland. Many drugs can be bought over the counter. If you require a prescription drug, the prescription must be written by a Swiss doctor.

■ In smaller towns, stores are often closed on Monday mornings. Museums are generally closed on Mondays.

■ Always cross the street at designated crossings where possible, and wait for the green man symbol.

■ Each canton (district) and community is responsible for its own laws and law enforcement. The police uniform differs widely from place to place, as do local bylaws. Respect authority at all times, even if you see no point in what you are being requested to do.

■ Use the superbly efficient public transportation system rather than the inordinately expensive taxis.

■ You'll save money by eating and drinking in smaller establishments away from the more upscale areas.

■ There is no need to tip in Switzerland; a service charge is automatically added to all bills.

Geneva

Sparkling Geneva (Genève), beautifully situated by the shores of the crescent-shaped Lake Geneva (Lac Léman) and backed by the Jura mountains and the Alps, is indeed an elegant city. With its key role as an important international meeting place, many visitors are in the city on business, but others come to enjoy the scenic location, excellent museums, stores and restaurants, and the lively cultural life.

The Modern City

Strategically positioned at the head of the Rhône river, Geneva joined the Swiss Confederation in 1815, after Napoleon's downfall. Since then the city has grown, prospered and become increasingly cosmopolitan.

Today Geneva hosts meetings, exhibitions, conventions and many organizations involved with humanitarian and social causes. It plays a major part in Swiss industry, finance and commerce, but has succeeded in retaining much of its French style and attitude, resulting in a pleasing blend of charm and efficiency.

An important university and scientific center, Geneva also is home to CERN, the European Organisation for Nuclear Research. The city is ringed with attractive countryside – the ski slopes of the French Alps are less than an hour away, and Lake Geneva offers superb water sports facilities.

Old Town and Beyond

Geneva is used to foreign visitors, and it's an easy city with which to become familiar. Getting around by public transportation is simple, and the center of the city is small enough to cover on foot, with much of the Old Town pedestrian-only. It's worth spending a couple of hours getting your bearings by walking around the town center, which lies on either side of the Rhône river.

Much of what you'll want to see is in or around the Old Town and is well marked, although with more than 30 museums to choose from, you are likely to take a bus at some point. A tourist mini-train trundles through the Old

A pleasure boat on Lake Geneva (Lac Léman), with mountains rising up behind the city

Town, leaving from place du Rhône, and is a relaxing way to enjoy the city. Alternatively, guided walking tours are available.

Tour buses travel to Lausanne and Château de Chillon, and into the Alps to Mont Blanc and Gstaad. Many lake cruises are offered, most lasting from one to three hours and many with commentary in English.

Gourmet Geneva

Like all Swiss cities, Geneva has a wide range of restaurants offering cuisine from around the world. It also has its own specialties, many of which have more in common with France than the rest of Switzerland. Eating out can be expensive, although away from the city center you'll find friendly neighborhood restaurants, where prices are much lower and the food is just as good.

Many places serve Swiss specialties such as fondue, sausage and *rösti* (potato cake), but you can choose from French, Italian, Thai, Japanese, Korean, Chinese,

Festivals and Fun

Geneva's biggest traditional festival is the *Escalade*, a December commemoration of a 1602 battle. A wonderful parade in 17th-century costumes marches through the Old Town, and the whole city is out in the streets to celebrate. The *Bol d'Or* annual sailing regatta, the biggest lake sailing race in Europe, is held in June, when more than 500 boats and their crews take over the lakeshore, and early in August the city is lit up by musical fireworks displays during the renowned *Fêtes de Genève* when hundreds of concerts are performed along the banks of the lake.

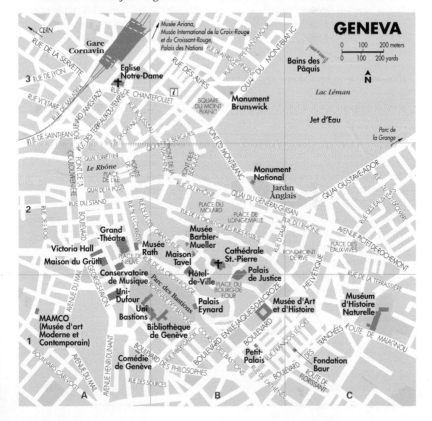

GENEVA

Russian, Spanish, Australian, Moroccan and many other types of cuisine.

You'll find all the usual fast-food outlets in the city center, and it's fun to shop for a picnic to enjoy in one of the lakeside parks.

There's a plethora of bars throughout the city; the nicest are in the Old Town and also along the lakeside.

Designer Style and Souvenirs

Geneva stores do not usually close at lunchtime and are open until 8 or 9 p.m. on Thursday evening. There are vast malls on the city outskirts, but it's likely you'll be shopping in the downtown city area, where the most attractive and elegant stores are all located. You will find many of them along rue du Rhône, rue du Mont Blanc and other fashionable neighboring streets.

Don't miss Globus, on rue du Rhône, a large department store that's a Geneva institution. You'll find watches, expensive jewelry, high fashion and superb leather goods from stylish outlets such as Dolce & Gabbana, Christian Dior, Giorgio Armani, Gucci, Hermès and Chanel.

If you're looking for interesting gifts or souvenirs to take home, try the tourist boutique in Globus, Swiss Corner on rue des Alpes, or Montblanc Boutique on place du Port.

Essential Information

Tourist Information

Genève Tourisme (Geneva Tourism)
Rue du Mont-Blanc 18 ⊙ Mon.–Sat. 9–6,
Thu. 10–6, Sun. 10–4 ☎ 022 909 7000;
www.geneve.com

Urban Transportation

Geneva is efficiently served by trams, trolley buses and buses; Zone 10 covers the city center. Buy and validate your ticket from the machines at each bus stop, which also have route maps and instructions about using the system. A simple ticket is the Saut de Puce (Short Hop), valid for 3 stops on land, or a single boat ride. For more flexibility, the Tout Genève (All Geneva) ticket is valid for 60 minutes. The best ticket is the Geneva Transport Card, which is given free to visitors when they check in at their hotel, hostel or campsite and allows use of all public transportation during their stay. To board or leave the vehicle, press the red button near the door; doors will open and close automatically. For information contact the Transports Publics Genevois (TPG) at offices at Geneva Cornavin Station and Rond-Point de Rive or call the Mobility Call Center (☎ 00800 022 02120 free info line; www.tpg.ch). Taxis are at stands in the city center, can be hailed on the street or called: Taxi-Phone SA Genève (☎ 022 331 4133; www.taxi-phone.ch).

Airport Information

Genève Aéroport (Geneva Airport, ☎ 022 717 7111; www.gva.ch) is 3 miles north of the city center. It is linked to the central railroad station by trains departing every 12 minutes (peak times), daily 5:30 a.m.–12:30 a.m., with a 6-minute journey time. Bus No. 10 runs every 10–15 minutes between the airport and the city and takes 20–25 minutes. Taxis wait at the airport terminal. Fares from the airport to the city are SFr35–SFr45. Get a free ticket for public transportation from the machine in the arrivals baggage collection area.

Climate – average highs and lows for the month

Jan.	Feb.	Mar.	Apr.	May	Jun.	Jul.	Aug.	Sep.	Oct.	Nov.	Dec.
4°C	5°C	10°C	13°C	18°C	22°C	25°C	25°C	20°C	13°C	8°C	4°C
39°F	41°F	50°F	55°F	64°F	72°F	77°F	77°F	68°F	55°F	46°F	39°F
-2°C	0°C	2°C	3°C	7°C	12°C	14°C	14°C	11°C	6°C	2°C	0°C
28°F	32°F	36°F	37°F	45°F	54°F	57°F	57°F	52°F	43°F	36°F	32°F

Geneva Sights

Key to symbols
⊞ map coordinates refer to the Geneva map on page 451 💵 admission charge: \$\$\$ more than SFr10, \$\$ SFr7–SFr10, \$ less than SFr7
See page 5 for complete key to symbols

Cathédrale St.-Pierre

The vast and austere Cathédrale St.-Pierre (St. Peter's Cathedral) has been a Protestant church since 1536. It was constructed in the 12th and 13th centuries, and its current neoclassic facade was added in the 18th century. This is where John Calvin preached; his seat is still in the north aisle. Climb the 157 steps up the tower for views over Geneva and the lake or take a tour of the archeological site below the cathedral, telling the story of the medieval building and city.

The cathedral has a long-standing musical tradition; the original Clémence, the largest bell in the tower, weighed more than 6 tons and was placed in the carillon there in 1407.

⊞ B2 ⊠ Cour Saint-Pierre ☎ 022 311 7574; tours 022 310 2929; www.cathedrale-geneve.ch ⏰ Cathédrale: Mon.–Fri. 9:30–6:30, Sat 9:30–5, Sun. 12–6:30, Jun.–Sep.; Mon.–Sat. 10–5:30, Sun. 12–5:30, rest of year. Site archéologique: daily 10–5 🚌 2, 3, 5, 7, 12, 16, 17, 20, 36; tram 12 💵 Cathédrale free; tower \$; Site archéologique \$\$\$

Fondation Baur

An elegant 20th-century mansion houses the Fondation Baur (Baur Foundation), the extensive Far Eastern art collection of connoisseur Alfred Baur (1865–1951). Among the many exhibits you'll find exquisite Chinese ceramics and samples of jade, snuff bottles from the 10th to the 19th centuries, prints and *netsuke* (Japanese carved toggles), and intricate Japanese and Chinese lacquerwork. Don't miss the Japanese Garden (*kare sansui* or "dry garden") with raked gravel, which symbolizes water, and 20 symbolic stones.

⊞ C1 ⊠ rue Munier-Romilly 8 ☎ 022 704 3282; www.fondation-baur.ch ⏰ Tue.–Sun. 2–6 (Wed. also 6–8 p.m. for guided tours during temporary exhibitions) 🚌 1, 5, 8, 36 💵 \$\$

Jardin Anglais

Statues, trees and a riot of colorful flowers help make the lakeside Jardin Anglais (English Garden) and its mountain views the perfect place to escape the city's bustle. Admire the 1862 fountain, with numerous reclining nymphs, before spending a few minutes at the Floral Clock. This huge timepiece, made entirely of 6,500 flowers and plants, was installed in 1955 as a symbol of the Geneva watch industry. From the garden, the Jet d'Eau can be seen, a towering spray of water over the lake. A short walk along the lake will bring you to Parc de la Grange, a lovely rose garden seen at its best in mid-June.

⊞ B2–C2 ⊠ promenade du Lac ⏰ Daily 24 hours 🚌 2, 8, 25 🍴 Cafés and restaurants

Musée Ariana

The Musée Ariana is Switzerland's only public museum dedicated entirely to ceramics and glass. With some 25,000 objects, this collection is one of Europe's largest, covering centuries of European, Middle Eastern and Asian ceramic and glass manufacture. The main techniques represented are ceramics, stoneware, faïence and porcelain.

⊞ Off map at B3 ⊠ avenue de la Paix 10 ☎ 022 418 5450; www.geneve.com/en/attractions/musee-ariana ⏰ Tue.–Sun. 10–6 🚌 5, 8, 11, 18, 22, F, V, Z; tram 15 💵 Free; exhibitions \$\$\$

Musée d'Art et d'Histoire

Behind the grandiose facade of Geneva's Musée d'Art et d'Histoire (Museum of Art and History) lies a dauntingly large collection of paintings, archeological finds and objets d'art. Ancient history fans will enjoy the Egyptian, Greek, Roman and Etruscan rooms. With more than 6,000 paintings, the galleries cover the full range of European painting, but concentrate on Swiss specialties, such as

Ferdinand Hodler's *Geneva Bay and Mont Blanc at Dawn* or Konrad Witz's 1444 altarpiece; its background is one of Europe's first accurate landscape representations. Other rooms contain applied arts collections, examples of fine furniture, silver and armory.

✚ B1 ✉ rue Charles-Galland 2 ☎ 022 418 2600; www.geneve.com/en/attractions/musee-d'art-et-d'histoire ◷ Tue.–Sun. 11–6 🚌 1, 3, 5, 7, 8, 36; tram 12 🍴 Restaurant 🎟 Free; some exhibitions $–$$$

MAMCO (Musée d'Art Moderne et Contemporain)

The Museum of Modern and Contemporary Art, known as MAMCO, is the largest museum of contemporary art in Swtizerland and showcases artistic innovation from the 1960s to the present day. Works by Swiss artists are featured, but artists from around the world are represented also.

✚ A1 ✉ rue des Vieux-Grenadiers 10 ☎ 022 320 6122; www.mamco.ch ◷ Tue.–Fri. noon–6, Sat.–Sun. 11–6 🚌 1; tram 12, 15 🎟 $$$ free first Sun. of the month

Musée Barbier-Mueller

Situated in the heart of the Old Town, the Barbier-Mueller Museum was founded in 1977 to conserve, restore and exhibit an extensive collection of works of art begun by Josef Mueller in 1907. The collection consists of more than 7,000 pieces of tribal and classical art and ornaments from "primitive" civilizations, and includes pieces collected by Mueller's son-in-law, Jean Paul Barbier. The museum has earned an international reputation for its traveling exhibitions, loans to museums and the publication of catalogs and art books.

✚ B2 ✉ rue Jean-Calvin 10 ☎ 022 312 0270; www.barbier-mueller.ch ◷ Daily 11–5 🚌 2, 3, 6, 7, 10, 36; tram 12 🎟 $$

Musée International de la Croix-Rouge et du Croissant-Rouge

The Musée International de la Croix-Rouge et du Croissant-Rouge (International Red Cross and Red Crescent Museum), explains the principles and history of the organization during some of the world's most serious humanitarian crises.

✚ Off map at B3 ✉ avenue de la Paix 17 ☎ 022 748 9511; www.redcrossmuseum.ch ◷ Tue.–Sun. 10–6, Apr.–Oct.; Tue.–Sun. 10–5, rest of year 🚌 8, 28 🍴 Restaurant 🎟 $$$

Muséum d'Histoire Naturelle

The splendid Natural History Museum has exhibits that cover everything from the history of the Earth through the dinosaur age to displays of animals, birds, reptiles and fish from all over the world, complete with realistic sound effects. Make sure you see Janus, the museum's popular two-headed turtle.

✚ C1 ✉ route de Malagnou 1 ☎ 022 418 6300; http://institutions.ville-geneve.ch/fr/mhn ◷ Tue.–Sun. 10–5 🚌 1, 5, 8, 25; tram 12 🍴 Café 🎟 Free

Palais des Nations

Built between 1929 and 1936 to house the League of Nations, the Palais des Nations (Palace of Nations) is now the European seat of the United Nations. The vast marble and travertine-stone complex is situated on the slopes above the lake, with views of Mont Blanc. You can tour the 1,800-seat Salle des Assemblées, one of the world's most active conference centers.

✚ Off map at B3 ✉ avenue de la Paix 14 ☎ 022 917 4896; www.unog.ch ◷ Mon.–Fri. 10 a.m.–12 (tours at 10:30 a.m. and 12), 2–4 (tours at 2:30 and 4) 🚌 5, 8, 11, 28, F, V, Z; tram 15 🍴 Café 🎟 $$$ ℹ Passport or identity card required for entry

Place du Bourg-de-Four

Bourg-de-Four square is the heart of Old Geneva, historically the site of the Roman market, medieval trade fairs, and political and religious meetings. Many of the fine buildings date from the 16th century; note their extra floors, added later to accommodate the flood of Protestant religious exiles. Today it is a lovely place to enjoy a drink.

✚ B1 ✉ place du Bourg-de-Four 🚌 3, 7, 36 🍴 Cafés and restaurants nearby

The Red Cross

In 1859, Jean Henri Dunant (1828–1910), son of a prominent Genevan family, set off to appeal to Napoleon III of France on a personal matter. Dunant caught up with Napoleon the day after the Battle of Solferino, where he saw more than 40,000 wounded men desperately in need of care and attention.

Dunant returned to Geneva and wrote a moving book, *Souvenir of Solferino*, in which he proposed the establishment of a body of volunteer male nurses to impartially care for the wounded in wartime. He further suggested that these men be recognized through an international agreement. Three friends added their support, the book was published and the International Committee of Help for the Wounded in Case of War (Comité Internationale de Secours aux Blessées en Cas de Guerre) was set up.

In 1864, the First Convention of Geneva was accepted and signed by 16 nations; a revised version of its standards of treatment for prisoners of war is still in effect today. An easily recognizable logo for the new movement was needed, and a reverse version of the colors of the Swiss flag was used; a red cross on a white background, rather than a white cross on a red background – a symbol now known the world over.

The Red Cross, present in more than 190 countries throughout the world, works hand in hand with the Red Crescent, an identical body functioning in Muslim and other non-Christian countries. Jean Henri Dunant was awarded the first Nobel Peace Prize in 1901, along with Frédéric Passy.

The Red Cross functions at both international and national levels. The international headquarters are in Geneva, and it is from here that major humanitarian relief work is coordinated. Each participating country has its own national committee that deals with day-to-day work in that particular country. The Red Cross is still manned largely by volunteers, who cover everything from terrorist attacks and natural disasters to organizing collections for war victims and refugees, as well as training the public in emergency aid procedures.

The headquarters of the International Red Cross in Geneva

Zurich

Primarily a business center, with an emphasis on international finance and banking, this prosperous and clean city has plenty for visitors to enjoy. It is dotted with fine buildings, museums, historic churches and green spaces, the perfect background for affluent stores, elegant cafés and well-dressed citizens.

Lakeside City

Zurich surrounds the northern end of Zürichsee (Lake Zurich), from which the Limmat river flows to bisect the city. The oldest part lies on either side of the river, with the 19th-century grandeur of the Bahnhofstrasse area on the west. East of the river, hills rise to the university complex, while boulevards, parks and gardens run along the lake.

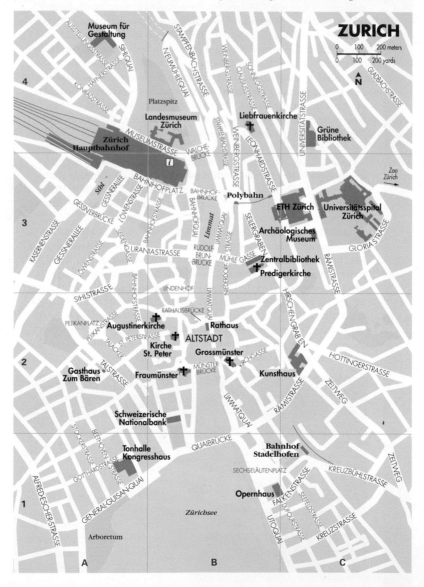

ZURICH

A tram ride is an essential experience; these vehicles ensure that city streets are virtually traffic-free. You can borrow a free bike from several places in the city, including the main railroad station (daily 8 a.m.–9:30 p.m., ID and deposit of SFr20 required); www.zuerirollt.ch.

Evenings Out
There's a range of excellent restaurants in Zurich, most of them expensive. You can eat well and relatively cheaply on the east side of the river. You'll find fast-food outlets, cafés and tearooms, and cozy taverns and wine cellars.

Notice boards all over the city list movie theaters (often showing American films in English), concerts, theater and opera. For a relaxed evening with the locals, you'll find plenty of packed bars, open late, on and around Limmatquai; on summer nights there is an array of street performers. Zurich also has a number of cabarets and discos.

Chocolates and Watches
Bahnhofstrasse is one of Europe's great shopping streets, lined with upscale stores filled with luxury items. Schweizer Heimatwerk in Bahnhofstraße specializes in Swiss handicraft. Don't miss Sprüngli, a mouthwatering chocolate store. The narrow old streets on each side of the river are packed with antiques stores.

Essential Information

Tourist Information
Zürich Tourismus (Tourist Service)
Hauptbahnhof (Central Station)
☎ 044 215 4000; www.zuerich.com
🕐 Mon.–Sat. 8:30–7, Sun. 9–6

Urban Transportation
Zurich's extremely efficient tram and bus system runs daily 4:30 a.m.–12:30 a.m. Tickets must be purchased and validated before boarding; all bus stops have ticket machines with transportation maps and instructions for buying and validating your ticket. Blue ticket machines accept cash or credit cards. You can buy a ZürichCARD for unlimited travel in the city for 1–3 days. These are valid for trams, buses, local trains and some boats, and offer discounts to some museums, shops and restaurants. Numbers and stops (which are named) are displayed on the front of the vehicles and inside. Press the red button on the door to open it before getting off; it will close automatically. For information about public transportation ☎ 0848 988 988; www.zvv.ch. Taxis are an expensive option; call Taxi 7X7 (☎ 044 777 7777) or Taxi 444 (☎ 044 444 4444). Boats run on Lake Zurich April through October. Timetables are listed at departure points.

Airport Information
Zurich Airport (☎ 043 816 2211, or for flight information ☎ 0900 300 313 toll call; www.zurich-airport.com) is about 6 miles north of the city center. Trains run every 5–10 minutes from the Hauptbahnhof, daily 5:30 a.m.–12:30 a.m., with a ride time of around 10 minutes. There are two arrivals terminals, 1 and 2, which are interconnected. Taxis are available from outside the terminals; the journey from the airport to downtown costs SFr70, or telephone Airport Taxi (☎ 0848 850 852).

Climate – average highs and lows for the month
	Jan.	Feb.	Mar.	Apr.	May	Jun.	Jul.	Aug.	Sep.	Oct.	Nov.	Dec.
	2°C	3°C	8°C	12°C	16°C	19°C	22°C	22°C	18°C	12°C	6°C	3°C
	36°F	37°F	46°F	54°F	61°F	66°F	72°F	72°F	64°F	54°F	43°F	37°F
	-2°C	-2°C	2°C	4°C	8°C	11°C	14°C	14°C	11°C	7°C	2°C	0°C
	28°F	28°F	36°F	39°F	46°F	52°F	57°F	57°F	52°F	45°F	36°F	32°F

Zurich Sights

Switzerland

Altstadt

The narrow streets and peaceful squares on either side of the Limmat river make up the Altstadt (Old Town) with its well-preserved old buildings. Take in Lindenhof, a square planted with lime trees on the site of the original Roman settlement, then cross the river to amble down the east side's lively Niederdorfstrasse and Hirschengasse.

➕ B2 ✉ Altstadt ☎ 044 215 4000 for information on guided tours 🚊 Tram 3, 6, 7, 11, 13 🖐 Tours $$$

Fraumünster

The graceful spire of the Fraumünster (Our Lady's Minster Church), founded in the ninth century by two German princesses, rises near the west riverbank in the Old Town. The interior dates from 1250 and earlier; against its gray stone serenity, Marc Chagall's stained-glass choir windows vibrate with green, blue and yellow. Augusto Giacometti designed the transept glass.

➕ B2 ✉ Münsterhof ☎ 044 221 2063; www.fraumuenster.ch 🕐 Daily 10–6, Mar.–Oct.; 10–5, Jan.–Feb.; 10–4, rest of year. Check website for services 🚊 Trams 2, 13 🖐 Free ℹ Interactive, touch-screen audio guides are available at the west entrance ($). For guided tours ☎ 044 221 2063

Grossmünster

The Grossmünster (Great Cathedral) played a major part in Zurich's Reformation (a 16th-century movement which aimed at reforming the Roman Catholic Church and resulted in the establishment of Protestant churches). It was here that Ulrich Zwingli, the father of Swiss Protestantism, preached and taught. He transformed this Catholic foundation into a theological college that became the focal point of the University of Zurich. The church, galleries and three naves were built between 1100 and 1260, a superb Romanesque basilica with fine sculpture on the capitals of its columns.

Be sure to visit the tranquil cloister, where exhibits tell the story of the Reformation. From the cloister climb the tower for views over Zurich and the lake.

➕ B2 ✉ Grossmünsterplatz ☎ 044 252 5949; 🕐 Mon.–Sat. 10–6, Sun. noon–6, Mar.–Oct.; daily 10–5, rest of year. Open Sun. when services over 🚊 Tram 6, 16 🖐 Church free; tower $

Kirche St. Peter

The oldest church foundation in Zurich, Kirche St. Peter (St. Peter's Church) stands in a quiet square at the heart of the Old Town, its restrained baroque interior typifying the city's God-fearing prosperity.

Four churches predate the existing one, which preserves the late Romanesque choir and 13th-century tower. All is harmony and balance, from the richly carved choir stalls to the superb plasterwork. The clock in the tower is Europe's largest clockface, measuring some 28.5 feet across.

➕ B2 ✉ St. Peterhofstatt ☎ 044 221 0674; www.zuerich.com 🕐 Mon.–Fri. 8–6, Sat. 10–4, Sun. 11–5 🚊 Tram 4, 15 🖐 Free

Kunsthaus

Zurich's Kunsthaus (Art Gallery), a lively museum that often mounts important temporary exhibitions, is mainly devoted to 19th- and 20th-century paintings and artworks. Earlier times are represented by a clutch of Venetian paintings, as well as some splendid Dutch works.

The diverse exhibits of modern art are housed in the newer wing. Here you'll find the largest collection of works by Edvard Munch outside Scandinavia, some striking paintings by Marc Chagall, and many pieces by the Dadaists, the antiwar art movement

A street dominated by the clock tower of St. Peter's Church

which was born at the Cabaret Voltaire in Zurich in 1916.

🏛 C2 ✉ Hoimplatz 1 ☎ 044 263 8484; www.kunsthaus.ch 🕐 Tue. and Fri.–Sun. 10–6, Wed.–Thu. 10–8 🚌 31, tram 3, 5, 8, 9 🍴 Restaurant 💷 $$$

Landesmuseum Zürich

Housed in a bizarre-looking castle complete with towers and turrets, the Landesmuseum Zürich (Swiss National Museum) should not be missed. This is the place to learn about Switzerland's history and development, and it is one of Europe's best organized museums.

The permanent History of Switzerland exhibition covers migration, politics and religion and includes the 19th-century Dufour map of the country, which served as Switzerland's national map until 1939. The homes and furnishings collection is fascinating with its staged period rooms showing how Swiss homes have changed over the centuries.

➕ B4 ✉ Museumstrasse 2 ☎ 044 218 6511; www.nationalmuseum.ch 🕐 Tue.–Sun. 10–5 (also Thu. 6–7) 🚌 3, 4, 6, 10, 11, 13, 14, 17, 31, 46 🍴 Café and restaurant 💷 $$

Zoo Zürich

A regular list of new arrivals testifies to the success of the zoo breeding program.

Part of the zoo's conservation program is dedicated to The Masoala Rainforest. This important rain forest is home to many animals whose natural habitat is being seriously eroded.

The Kaeng Krachan Elephant Park, a highlight of the zoo, even allows visitors to observe elephants swimming from an underwater viewpoint. In the winter don't miss the opportunity to join the penguins for a walk around the zoo.

➕ Off map at C3 ✉ Zürichbergstrasse 221 ☎ 044 254 2500; www.zoo.ch 🕐 Daily 9–6, Mar.–Oct.; 9–5, rest of year 🚌 39, 751; tram 6 🍴 Cafés and restaurant on zoo grounds 💷 $$$

Swiss Flavors

Switzerland has a range of regional dishes – German, French and Italian – rather than a national cuisine. With many foreigners working in the country, there's plenty of choice, and in the cities you'll find everything from Japanese to Tex-Mex.

Swiss Cheese Specials

The country's best-known specialty, fondue, is made by melting a selection of Swiss hard cheeses, such as Gruyère, Emmentaler and Vacherin, in white wine spiked with garlic and then adding spices and kirsch. The bubbling pot sits in the middle of the table on a little brazier, and you help yourself by dipping forkfuls of bread into the thick mixture. Be careful not to drop the bread in the pot – traditionally the culprit has to buy the next bottle of wine. Fondues also are made by cooking cubed beef in either hot oil (*fondue bourguignonne*) or beef stock (*fondue chinoise);* these are served with a variety of tasty dipping sauces. The traditionally French *raclette* is undergoing a revival and is popular throughout Switzerland, particularly with large groups. A whole block of cheese is cut into slices and melted under a grill and then draped over boiled potatoes to be eaten with gherkins, smoked ham and sausage. It's delicious!

Main Dishes

Bündnerfleisch – raw, dried smoked beef – is well worth sampling, as are the many kinds of *Wurst*, sausages eaten cold, grilled or boiled. The traditional accompaniment is *Rösti*, a crisp potato cake studded with onions and bacon. Hungry diners might enjoy the *Berner Platte*, a groaning plate of sausage, beef and ham served with potatoes and sauerkraut. The Swiss also are fond of liver, pork and veal. Traditional fish recipes in this landlocked country involve lake trout, carp and perch.

A Little Something Sweet

Chocolate and cream feature heavily in Swiss desserts; in addition to the ubiquitous Nestlé and Cailler, Lindt, Sprüngli, Teuscher and Tobler are varieties of chocolate worth sampling. There are some splendid local cakes; try *Leckerli* (spiced bread with honey), meringues and delicious kirsch-flavored cakes and fruit breads. Start the day with a breakfast bowl of muesli, a tasty mixture of grains, fruit and nuts.

Skiers build up a hearty appetite on the mountains for the delicious local fare

Hotels and Restaurants

- Austria 463
- Belgium 465
- Britain 467
- Czech Republic 470
- Denmark 471
- Finland 473
- France 473
- Germany 476
- Greece 478
- Hungary 479
- Ireland 479
- Italy 480
- Luxembourg 483
- The Netherlands 484
- Norway 485
- Portugal 486
- Spain 487
- Sweden 490
- Switzerland 491

Hotels and Restaurants

The hotels and restaurants in this book were selected by on-site contributing authors. Since price is often the best indication of the level of facilities and quality of service guests can expect, a three-tiered price guide appears at the beginning of the listings for each city. Prices vary widely depending on the country. Because variable rates will affect the amount of foreign currency that can be exchanged for dollars, price ranges are given in the local currency.

Although price ranges and any given days/times restaurants are closed were accurate at press time, this information is always subject to change. If you are interested in an establishment, it is advisable to call ahead or go online to check the hours of operation. Smaller places may not have a phone or website.

Facilities suitable for travelers with disabilities vary greatly and you are strongly advised to contact an establishment directly. Buildings in the old areas of city centers may not be suitable for visitors with limited or impaired mobility.

Accommodations

Accommodations have been selected with two considerations in mind: a particularly attractive character or sense of local flavor, or a central location. Establishments in different price ranges are included for each city.

Map Coordinates

Map coordinates given in each listing relate to the city maps and give an idea of the approximate area in which each establishment is located. Although you may be able to find some of the street locations on these maps, it is always a good idea to pick up a more detailed city map from the local tourist office to help you find places.

City-center hotels fill up quickly, especially during summer; make reservations well in advance. In-room bathrooms (referred to as "en suite facilities") sometimes may not be available in smaller budget hotels.

European hotels normally provide a light breakfast of rolls or croissants and coffee (if not, the listing description is "room only"). Breakfast in British and Irish hotels, however, can be a filling meal of bacon, sausages, eggs, fried potatoes and toast.

Some hotels offer a price for their overnight accommodations that includes an evening meal (known as "half-board" in Britain and Ireland and *demi-pension* in French-speaking countries).

Eating Out

Listed restaurants range from upscale places to small cafés. Some are close to attractions; where this is the case, there is a cross-reference under the attraction listing. Other possibilities are the cafeterias and restaurants on the premises of museums and galleries.

Be sure to sample the amazing variety of indigenous European fast food: *crêpes* (filled pancakes) in France; tasty hot *Wurst* (sausages) in Germany and Austria; fish and chips (fish fillets and french fries) in Britain; savory tapas appetizers served in Spanish bars; and pizzas in Italy – served crusty and piping hot from charcoal ovens or *al taglio* (sliced to go) on street corners.

Many European hotels, especially the larger ones in big cities, are not only options for an overnight stay but also for a meal. Their lounges and bars often are comfortable, quiet places to relax.

Alcoholic beverages have a rich European heritage. France, Germany and Spain produce memorable wines; beers in the Czech Republic, Belgium and Britain are justly famed; and Guinness, of course, is an Irish institution. The nonalcoholic fruit juices (*portokalada freska*) served in Greece are wonderfully refreshing.

Cities are shown in the order that they appear in the book.

VIENNA HOTELS

Price guide: (double room with breakfast for two people)
$ €60–€80
$$ €80–€160
$$$ over €160

25 Hours Hotel Vienna $$

A stylish, modern boutique hotel where the design theme is the theater and the circus. The rooms have been given a playful makeover that recalls the 1950s and 1960s.
⊞ 27 C2 ✉ Lerchenfelder Strasse 1–3 ☎ 0521 51-0; www.25hours-hotels.com/wien 🚇 U2 to Volkstheater 🚌 3A AX, DC, MC, VI

Grand Hotel Wien $$$

Here you'll find the ultimate in luxury and style, with the personal service of a majestic old European hotel with modern comforts. Ask about the packages which typically include a champagne buffet breakfast, dinner for two in the hotel's restaurant, Le Ciel, and tickets to concerts, exhibitions or museums.
⊞ 27 D2 ✉ Kärntner Ring 9 ☎ 01 515-800; www.grandhotelwien.com 🚇 Karlsplatz 🚌 2A; tram 1, 2, D AX, DC, MC, VI

Hollmann Beletage Design & Boutique Hotel $$$

The outside of this small hotel in a 19th-century Old Town house with a small garden oozes wall-to-wall Vienna tradition. However, inside, you'll experience contemporary style and comforts, a touch of design humor and innovative features like its own mini movie theater.
⊞ 27 D2 ✉ Köllnerhofgasse 6 ☎ 01 96 11 960; www.hollmann-beletage.at 🚇 Schwedenplatz, Stephansplatz 🚌 3A; tram 1, 2 AX, DC, MC, VI

Hotel Kugel $$

In the trendy Spittelberg district, this family-run hotel in an historic building has 25 individually designed rooms. The generous buffet breakfast is included in the room rate and features hot and cold regional specialties and Viennese pastries.
⊞ 27 B2 ✉ Siebensterngasse 43 ☎ 01 523 3355; www.hotelkugel.at 🚇 Neubaugasse 🚌 13A; tram 1, 1A, 1B, 49 MC, VI

VIENNA RESTAURANTS

Price guide: (dinner per person, excluding drinks)
$ €10–€15
$$ €15–€30
$$$ over €30

Augustinerkeller $$

Delicious Austrian- and Viennese-style dishes are complemented by locally produced wines. It's popular with visitors.
⊞ 27 C2 ✉ Augustinerstrasse 1 ☎ 01 533 1026; www.bitzinger.at 🚇 Karlsplatz 🚌 2A; tram 1, 2, D AX, DC, MC, VI

Café Bräunerhof $$

This centrally located coffeehouse draws far more locals than tourists, who come here for the well-done Austrian dishes and the timeless charm and ambience.
⊞ 27 C2 ✉ Stallburggasse 2 ☎ 0512 38 93; www.braeunerhof.at 🕐 Mon.–Fri. 8 a.m.–8:30 p.m., Sat. 8–6:30, Sun. 10–6:30 🚇 Stephansplatz, Karlsplatz 🚌 1A, 2A AX, DC, MC, VI

Café Drechsler $–$$

This traditional coffeehouse is close to the Naschmarkt. Hot food from the classically Viennese menu is served throughout the day and international newspapers and magazines are available. On several evenings a month, DJs spin the decks.
⊞ 27 C2 ✉ Linke Wienzeile 22 ☎ 01 581 2044; www.cafedrechsler.at 🕐 Sun.–Thu. 8 a.m.–midnight, Fri.–Sat. 8 a.m.–2 a.m. 🚇 Karlsplatz, Kettenbrückengasse 🚌 59A No credit cards

Plachutta $$–$$$

This is one of the best restaurants for original Viennese dishes in the Old Town. Typical items include *Wiener Tafelspitz* (boiled rump of beef with apple and horseradish sauce) or perch with garlic butter, and pork with dumplings and cabbage. Reservations are advisable.
⊞ 27 D2 ✉ Wollzeile 38 ☎ 01 512 1577; www.plachutta.at 🕐 Daily 11:30 a.m.–midnight 🚇 Stubentor 🚌 3A; tram 2 AX, DC, MC, VI

Restaurant Wiener $$

Come to this welcoming *beisl* (tavern) for classic Austrian dishes and wonderful, traditional desserts. Book in advance.
⊞ 27 B2 ✉ Hermanngasse 27a ☎ 0524 52 52; www.restaurant-wiener.at 🕐 Mon.–Sat. 5 p.m.–2 a.m., Sun. 5 p.m.–midnight 🚇 Neubaugasse 🚌 13A; tram 49 MC, VI

INNSBRUCK HOTELS

Price guide: (double room with breakfast for two people)
$ €50–€70
$$ €70–€150
$$$ over €150

Best Western Plus Hotel Goldener Adler $$–$$$

At this charming hotel in the heart of old Innsbruck, modern comfort combines with Tyrolean character. Past guests have included Mozart, Wagner and several emperors.
⊞ 35 A2 ✉ Herzog-Friedrich-Strasse 6 ☎ 0512 571111 0; www.goldeneradler.com 🚌 A, C, J, O, TS, W; tram 1, 3 AX, DC, MC, VI

Grand Hotel Europa $$$

Innsbruck's top hotel has a wide range of rooms at varying prices, some elegant public areas, and friendly and welcoming staff.
⊞ 35 C1 ✉ Südtiroler Platz 2 ☎ 0512 5931; www.grandhoteleuropa.at 🚌 F; tram 3 AX, DC, MC, VI

Hotel Maximilian $$–$$$

The comfortable rooms at this welcoming hotel on the edge of the Old Town are stylish, light and modern. A good breakfast buffet is included.
⊞ 35 A2 ✉ Marktgraben 7–9 ☎ 0512 599 67; www.hotel-maximilian.com 🚌 A, C, J, O, TS, W AX, DC, MC, VI

Weisses Kreuz $–$$

Mozart and his father once stayed at this 15th-century Old Town hotel, which combines Tyrolean charm with modern comfort. Rooms at the lower prices can be small. There are restaurants on the premises.
⊞ 35 A2 ✉ Herzog-Friedrich-Strasse 31 ☎ 0512 594790; www.weisseskreuz.at 🚌 A, C, J, O, TS, W; tram 1, 3 AX, MC, VI

INNSBRUCK RESTAURANTS

Price guide: (dinner per person, excluding drinks)
$ €10–€15
$$ €15–€30
$$$ over €30

KEY TO SYMBOLS

✚	map page number and coordinates
✉	address
☎	telephone number
◷	days/times closed
Ⓜ	nearest subway station
🚌	nearest bus/trolley bus/ tram/funicular route
⛴	ferry
$$$	expensive
$$	moderate
$	inexpensive
AX	American Express
DC	Diners Club
MC	MasterCard
VI	VISA

Eating in Innsbruck

Most of Innsbruck's best – and most expensive – restaurants are located in a tiny area of Old Town, along with some excellent cafés and coffeehouses. Many of these places serve meals all day, so you can eat when you feel like it, a bonus if you've been skiing or hiking. Maria-Theresien-Strasse has a number of self-service and fast-food restaurants if you're looking for a quick lunchtime snack. For lunch with a view, take the Hungerburgbahn to Hoch-Innsbruck, where there are several restaurants with pretty terraces, or ride the cable car up to Seegrube mountain and eat on the terrace while enjoying a superb mountain panorama. The daily market, held in the Markthalle building beside the river, is an excellent place to buy provisions for a picnic.

Dengg $$

Known for its international cooking, Dengg offers contemporary fare that includes vegetarian dishes, lunch specials and a degustation menu.
✚ 35 B2 ✉ Riesengasse 11–13 ☎ 0512 582347; www.dengg.co.at ◷ Mon.–Fri. 8:30 a.m.–midnight, Sat. 10 a.m.–midnight 🚌 A, C, J, O, TS, W; tram 1, 3 AX, DC, MC, VI

Lichtblick/360° $$$

Lichtblick is a stylish wine bar and restaurant located above the Rathausgalerien shopping mall. Diners can enjoy stunning panoramas of the city and the mountains beyond.
✚ 35 B1 ✉ Rathaus Galerien, Maria-Theresien-Strasse 18, 7th Floor ☎ 0512 566550; www.360-grad.at ◷ Mon.–Sat. 10 a.m.–1 a.m. 🚌 D, E, F, H, R, TS; tram 3 AX, DC, MC, VI

Ottoburg $–$$

This historic restaurant was established around 1745 in a former watchtower that some say is the oldest in Innsbruck. Dishes take in standard classics with fish, meat and noodles, but there are some innovative additions to the menu.
✚ 35 A2 ✉ Herzog-Friedrich-Strasse 1 ☎ 0512 584338; www.ottoburg.at ◷ Daily noon–2:30 and 6–midnight 🚌 A, C, J, O, TS, W; tram 1, 3 AX, DC, MC, VI

Stiftskeller $$

In the heart of the Old Town, this brewery-restaurant with several dining rooms and a beer garden offers a menu of filling Tyrolean and Austrian specialties.
✚ 35 B2 ✉ Stiftgasse 1 ☎ 0512 570706; www.stiftskeller.eu 🚌 A, C, J, O, TS, W; tram 1, 3 AX, DC, MC, VI

Die Wilderin $–$$

A popular bar and restaurant in the center of town. Owner Claudia Kogler and her team source their menu of modern Austrian dishes from local farms and markets.
✚ 35 A2 ✉ Seilergasse 5 ☎ 0512 562728; www.diewilderin.at ◷ Closed Mon. 🚌 A, C, J, O, TS, W; tram 1, 3 AX, DC, MC, VI

SALZBURG HOTELS

Price guide: (double room with breakfast for two people)

$	€50–€70
$$	€70–€150
$$$	over €150

Boutiquehotel Am Dom $$–$$$

Reserve ahead to ensure one of just 15 rooms at this restored 14th-century building in the heart of Salzburg's historic center.
✚ 40 B3 ✉ Goldgasse 17 ☎ 0662 842 765; www.hotelamdom.at 🚌 3, 5, 6, 10, 20, 25, 28 AX, DC, MC, VI

Goldener Hirsch $$$

This luxurious, baronial-style hotel is one of Salzburg's oldest and most famous accommodations, and provides service to match. Rooms and suites are finished in vibrant colors and the restaurant is renowned throughout Austria.
✚ 40 B3 ✉ Getreidegasse 37 ☎ 0662 80 84-0; www.goldener hirsch.com 🚌 1, 4, 8, 22 AX, DC, MC, VI

Schloss Mönchstein $$$

This luxury-class hotel is beautifully situated in thickly wooded grounds high above the old center of Salzburg. Sumptuous rooms are complemented by gleaming marble bathrooms. There is a spa and a choice of dining venues, including an intimate four-seater dining room.
✚ 40 A3 ✉ Mönchsberg Park 26 ☎ 0662 848 555-0; www.monchstein. at 🚌 1, 4, 7, 8, 10, 22 AX, DC, MC, VI

Wolf-Dietrich $$–$$$

This family-run hotel near the city's historic center has a good restaurant, an indoor swimming pool, and a spa and sauna. Rooms include family suites for up to five people.
✚ 40 C4 ✉ Wolf-Dietrich-Strasse 7 ☎ 0662 871 275; www.wolf-dietrich. at 🚌 2, 4, 21, 22 AX, DC, MC, VI

SALZBURG RESTAURANTS

Price guide: (dinner per person, excluding drinks)

$	€10–€15
$$	€15–€30
$$$	over €30

Augustiner Bräu $–$$

This restaurant serves beer, *Wurst* and simple Austrian fare in wood-paneled halls. The beer garden is extremely popular and can get very crowded. Brewery tours available.
✚ 40 A4 ✉ Lindhofstrasse 7 ☎ 0662 431 246; www. augustinerbier.at ◷ Daily 3–11 p.m. 🚌 7, 8, 20, 21, 24, 27, 28 No credit cards

Restaurant Zur Festung Hohensalzburg $$

Located in the Hohensalzburg Fortress (see page 43), this restaurant has panoramic views of the Salzburg area and serves good Austrian cooking (reservations required for dinner Jul.–Aug.).
➕ 40 C2 ✉ Hohensalzburg, Mönchsberg 34 ☎ 0662 841 780; www.salzburg-burgen.at ⏱ Closed late Jan.–early Feb. 🚋 Festungbahn funicular AX, DC, MC, VI

St. Peter Stiftskeller $$

Said to be Central Europe's oldest restaurant, this is a popular beer cellar serving stylish seasonal food and vegetarian choices.
➕ 40 B2 ✉ St. Peter Bezirk 1–4 ☎ 0662 841 268; www.stpeter-stifts keller.at ⏱ Daily 11:30 a.m.–11 p.m. 🚋 1, 4, 5, 22 AX, MC, VI

Zirkelwirt $–$$

A small, atmospheric restaurant in a traditional building with an attractive garden terrace, the Zirkelwirt is popular for its homestyle Austrian cooking. Prices are surprisingly good given its location in the heart of the Old Town. The goulash with dumplings comes highly recommended.
➕ 40 C2 ✉ Pfeifergasse 14 ☎ 0662 842 796; www.zumzirkelwirt. at ⏱ Daily 11:30 a.m.–midnight 🚋 3, 5, 6, 7, 8 MC, VI

BRUSSELS HOTELS

Price guide: (double room with breakfast for two people)
$ under €100
$$ €100–€200
$$$ over €200

A La Grande Cloche $–$$

Excellent value for central Brussels, A La Grande Cloche is an older style hotel but rooms are pleasant and spacious. There's free WiFi in the rooms.
➕ 56 A2 ✉ 10 place Rouppe, 1000 ☎ 02 512 6140; www.hotel grandecloche.com ⏱ Anneessens 🚋 Tram 3, 4, 32 AX, MC, VI

Amigo $$$

This charming hotel near the Grand' Place, part of the Rocco Forte group, is luxurious, offers perfect service, and is both lively and relaxed. It has a fine dining Italian restaurant. Rooms have lovely central views.
➕ 56 B2 ✉ rue de l'Amigo 1–3, 1000 ☎ 02 547 4747; www. roccofortehotels.com ⏱ Gare Centrale 🚋 All bus and tram routes to Gare Centrale AX, DC, MC, VI

Le Dixseptième $$–$$$

This luxurious and stylish boutique hotel, in a grand 17th-century house in a great location behind the Grand' Place, was once the residence of the Spanish Ambassador. The old part of the hotel houses the breakfast room and several beautifully decorated suites, while the modern addition has 12 comfortable rooms.
➕ 56 B2 ✉ rue de la Madeleine 25, 1000 ☎ 02 517 1717; www. ledixseptieme.be ⏱ Gare Centrale 🚋 Tram: all routes to Gare Centrale AX, DC, MC, VI

Métropole $$

Built in 1895, the Métropole's glorious and flamboyant facade and ground floor are now a protected monument. Although the interiors have been updated and renovated, they retain a period touch.
➕ 56 B3 ✉ place De Brouckère 31, 1000 ☎ 02 217 2300; www.metro polehotel.com ⏱ De Brouckère 🚋 126, 127, 128; tram 3, 4, 32 AX, DC, MC, VI

Welcome Hotel $$

The decor in the individually designed rooms at this small, downtown, family-owned hotel was inspired by exotic destinations from around the world resulting in a distinctive look all of its own. This is a good value choice.
➕ 56 B3 ✉ 23 Quai du Bois à Brûler, 1000 ☎ 02 219 9546; www.hotelwelcome.com ⏱ St. Catherine AX, MC, VI

BRUSSELS RESTAURANTS

Price guide: (dinner per person, excluding drinks)
$ under €35
$$ €35–€60
$$$ over €60

Belga Queen $$–$$$

The superb Hôtel de la Poste, with its grand entrance hall and beautiful, stained-glass windows, is now a trendy dining complex with fine dining, oyster bar and beer bar.
➕ 56 B3 ✉ rue fossé aux Loups 32, 1000 ☎ 02 217 2187; www.belgaqueen.be ⏱ De Brouckère 🚋 29, 66, 71, 81; tram 3, 4, 32 AX, DC, MC, VI

Le Chou de Bruxelles $–$$

This small bistro is *the* place for *moules* and *frites* (mussels and fries). You can choose from 30 different sauces to accompany your shellfish. There also is a lovely terrace for summer dining.
➕ 56 off B1 ✉ rue de Florence 26, 1050 ☎ 02 537 6995; www.lechoude bruxelles.be ⏱ Closed Sun. and Mon. 🚋 Tram 93, 94 MC, VI

Comme Chez Soi $$$

Try Brussels' top gastronomic experience at the celebrated Comme Chez Soi. New Belgian cuisine with more traditional specialties is featured. Reserve well in advance.
➕ 56 A2 ✉ place Rouppe 23, 1000 ☎ 02 512 2921; www.commechezsoi. be ⏱ Closed Sun. and Mon., and Tue.–Wed. lunch, mid-Jul. to mid-Aug. ⏱ Anneessens 🚋 Tram 3, 4, 32 AX, DC, MC, VI

Fin de Siecle $$

Generous portions of Belgian cuisine, including Flemish beef stew and ham hock form the staple of the menu at this informal restaurant. There are also always a number of vegetarian dishes on the menu.
➕ A3 ✉ 9 rue de Chartreaux, 1000 ☎ 02 512 5123; no website ⏱ Closed lunch Mon.–Fri., dinner Sat.–Sun. 🚋 51, 86 MC, VI

Vincent $$–$$$

At this traditional Bruxellois restaurant, skilled waiters prepare specialties like *steak flambée* or *steak tartare* with a flourish at your table. Entrance to the atmospheric, old-fashioned tiled dining room is through the kitchen.
➕ 56 B3 ✉ 8–10 rue des Dominicains, off rue des Bouchers, 1000 ☎ 02 511 2607; www. restaurantvincent.com ⏱ Closed Tue., Jan. 1–12 and Aug. 1–15 ⏱ De Brouckère, Gare Centrale AX, DC, MC, VI

Wine Bar Les Caves du Sablon $$

This is an excellent wine bar with a cozy dining room in the cellar. The menu is compact, concentrating on continental fare. Wines are available by the glass.
➕ 56 B2 ✉ rue des Pigeons, 1000 ☎ 02 513 1220; www.cavesdusablon. be ⏱ Closed Sun., daily lunch, and mid-Jul. to mid-Aug. ⏱ Grand Sablon 🚋 27, 95 DC, MC, VI

KEY TO SYMBOLS

⊕ map page number and coordinates
✉ address
☎ telephone number
🚫 days/times closed
Ⓜ nearest subway station
🚌 nearest bus/trolley bus/ tram/funicular route
⛴ ferry
$$$ expensive
$$ moderate
$ inexpensive
AX American Express
DC Diners Club
MC MasterCard
VI VISA

Chocolates Galore

By far the best chocolate shop in Bruges is the family-run Spegelaere at Ezelstraat 92. The house specialty is bunches of chocolate grapes filled with marzipan or *pralinée*. Here you can see the daily production of fresh chocolate in a workshop where traditional methods are used – from the preparation of the chocolate in melting cauldrons to the hand-making process. Choco-Story is a fascinating chocolate museum at St. Jansplein (Wijnzakstraat 2; ☎ 050 612 237; www.choco-story-brugge. be, daily 10–6, Jul.–Aug., 10–5, rest of year. Last entry 45 minutes before closing). It explains the history of chocolate and the process of making chocolates. Finish your visit with a taste of freshly made chocolates by one of Belgium's master *chocolatiers*. The Museum of Cocoa and Chocolate in Brussels is at rue de la Tête d'Or 9–11, off Grand' Place (☎ 02 514 2048; www. choco-story-brussels.be, daily 10–5. Last admission 4:30 p.m.).

Price guide: (double room with breakfast for two people)
$ under €100
$$ €100–€200
$$$ over €200

Eco Hotel Fevery $–$$

This small family-owned eco-label hotel is centrally located and also offers gluten-free breakfast options, WiFi and private parking.
⊕ 62 B3 ✉ Collaert Mansionstraat 3, 8000 ☎ 050 331 269; www.hotel fevery.be 🚌 4, 14, 43, 90 MC, VI

Hotel Patritius $–$$

The family-owned Patritius is set in a 17th-century building with large bedrooms, courtyard garden and private parking (extra charge).
⊕ 62 B3 ✉ Riddersstraat 11, 8000 ☎ 050 338 454; www.hotelpatritius. be 🚌 6, 12, 16, 88 AX, MC, VI

Hotel Van Cleef $$$

The historic home of the van Cleef family (notable Counts of the region), this boutique hotel offers luxury on the banks of a delightful Bruges canal. The interior is beautifully updated with sumptuous furnishings and fabrics, and the service is good.
⊕ 62 C3 ✉ Molenmeers 11, 8000 ☎ 050 346 414; www.hotelvancleef. be 🚌 6, 16, 88, then a short walk AX, MC, VI

The Pand Hotel $$–$$$

This hotel is hidden away on a backwater close to the Markt. Rooms are luxurious and tastefully decorated. The proprietors also own an antiques and objets d'art shop, Kasimir's Antique Studio.
⊕ 62 B2 ✉ Pandreitje 16, 8000 ☎ 050 340 666; www.pandhotel.com 🚌 6, 12, 16, 88, 91 AX, DC, MC

Price guide: (dinner per person, excluding drinks)
$ under €35
$$ €35–€60
$$$ over €60

Bistro Pro Deo $–$$

This city town house has been transformed into a cozy period bistro. Gluten-free and vegetarian options are available.
⊕ 62 C3 ✉ 161 Langestraat, 8000 ☎ 050 337 355; www.bistroprodeo. be 🚫 Closed Sun. and Mon., late Apr. to mid-May 🚌 6, 16, 88 MC, VI

De Garre $–$$

Come to this historic downtown bar for a typical traditional cozy Belgian atmosphere to enjoy a huge range of local beers accompanied by plates of salami, cheese and pickles.
⊕ 62 B2 ✉ De Garre 1, 8000 ☎ 050 341 029; www.degarre.be 🚌 No public transportation MC, VI

Park $$–$$$

Classic Belgian cuisine is served in this elegant setting, including excellent seafood. There also is a very good choice of wines.
⊕ 62 B2 ✉ Minderbroedersstraat 1, 8000 ☎ 497 801 872; www. parkrestaurant.be 🚫 Closed lunch, and Mon. and Thu. dinner ⓘ No public transportation AX, DC, MC, VI

Réliva $$

This modern, bistro-style, organic restaurant brings traditional dishes from around Europe to the table. It also offers vegetarian and some vegan dishes.
⊕ 62 B2 ✉ Goezeputstraat 6, 8000 ☎ 050 331 307; www.reliva.be 🚫 Closed Mon.–Thu. lunch, Tue.–Wed. dinner ⓘ No public transportation MC, VI

Sanseveria $–$$

If you just want a quick bite or light lunch while touring the city, this casual eatery serves excellent bagels, quiches and salads that will keep your energy levels high.
⊕ 62 B2 ✉ Predikherenstraat 11, 8000 ☎ 050 348 143; www. sanseveria.be 🚫 Closed dinner 🚌 6, 16, 88 MC, VI

Price guide: (double room with breakfast for two people)
$ under €100
$$ €100–€200
$$$ over €200

Boutique Hotel Onderbergen $–$$

This is a delightful hotel just outside the traffic-free zone. On site here is Patrick Foley's, a popular Irish restaurant and bar.
⊕ 70 A2 ✉ Onderbergen 65, 9000 ☎ 09 223 6200; www.hotel onderbergen.be 🚌 Tram 1, 22 AX, MC, VI

Ghent Marriott Hotel $$$

Housed behind a facade of historical waterside mansions, this hotel is

renowned for its excellent service.
➕ 70 A1 ✉ Korenlei 10, 9000
☎ 09 233 9393; www.marriott.com
🚋 Tram All services for Korenmarkt
AX, DC, MC, VI

Hotel Erasmus $–$$

This charming family-run hotel is in
an impressive town house in the
center of town, yet it is very quiet.
The 10 bedrooms are furnished in
Flemish style. Friendly service.
➕ 70 A3 ✉ Poel 25, 9000 ☎ 09
224 2195; www.erasmushotel.be
🚋 1, 3, 17, 18, 22, 24, 38, 39 AX, DC,
MC, VI

Hotel Harmony $$

A modern interior wrapped in two
canalside town houses, the Harmony
combines history with modern
facilities, including a swimming pool.
The lovely courtyard garden is an
added bonus.
➕ 70 B4 ✉ Kraanlei 37, 9000
☎ 09 324 2680; www.hotel-harmony.
be 🚋 Tram 1, 4 AX, MC, VI

NH Gent Belfort $$

This is a contemporary hotel in the
historic heart of the city, opposite the
Town Hall. Its many amenities,
including a restaurant and fitness
room, make it a decent value.
➕ 70 B3 ✉ Hoogpoort 63 ☎ 09
233 3331; www.nh-hotels.com 🚫 No
public transportation AX, MC, VI

GHENT RESTAURANTS

Price guide: (dinner per person,
excluding drinks)
$ under €35
$$ €35–€60
$$$ over €60

Avalon $

Avalon is one of a new generation of
vegetarian restaurants that sources
local and organic ingredients to
produce contemporary dishes.
➕ 70 B4 ✉ Geldmunt 32, 9000
☎ 09 224 3724; www.restaurant
avalon.be 🕐 Closed Mon., Tue.–Sun.
dinner 🚋 Tram 4 AX, MC, VI

Brasserie Pakhuis $$–$$$

Set in a large and spectacular
warehouse (pakhuis in Flemish) is
this wonderful restaurant. The
mouthwatering French-Italian
cuisine here is popular with locals.
➕ 70 A3 ✉ Schuurkenstraat 4, 9000
☎ 09 223 5555; www.pakhuis.be
🕐 Closed Sun. 🚋 Tram All services
for Korenmarkt AX, MC, VI

Oak $$$

Here you'll find contemporary,
innovative cuisine which is artfully
delivered. Oak is certainly creating a
buzz in the city. With only 30 covers,
tables are in high demand.
➕ Off map at 70 A4 ✉ Hoogstraat
167, 9000 ☎ 09 353 9050;
www.oakgent.be 🕐 Closed Sun.
and Mon., and Sat. dinner 🚋 3, 17,
18, 38, 39; tram 4 AX, MC, VI

De Rechters $–$$

This centrally located bistro and bar
serves a great range of seasonal
Belgian dishes along with Belgian
beer. It's a great option for lunch
or dinner.
➕ 70 B2–C2 ✉ Sint-Baatsplein 23,
9000 ☎ 09 224 3109; www.
derechters.be 🕐 Closed Mon.–Tue.
🚋 Tram 1, 4, 21, 22 MC, VI

LONDON HOTELS

Price guide: (double room with
breakfast for two people)
$ £75–£150
$$ £150–£225
$$$ over £225

The Berkeley $$$

Savor luxurious comfort in a chic
setting here, along with great views
from the rooftop pool. Marcus
Wareing's restaurant offers some of
the best dining in London. Book the
chef's table for a special experience.
➕ 86 A3 ✉ Wilton Place,
Knightsbridge ☎ 020 7235 6000;
www.the-berkeley.co.uk 🚇 Hyde
Park Corner AX, DC, MC, VI

Dukes London $$$

This gem of a hotel is one of Britain's
most desirable boutique hotels. Don't
miss the martinis or the afternoon teas.
➕ 86 C2 ✉ 35 St. James's Place
☎ 020 7491 4840; www.dukeshotel.
com 🚇 Green Park AX, DC, MC, VI

The Goring $$$

The Goring offers spacious comfort
within easy reach of Buckingham
Palace – the now Duchess of
Cambridge stayed here the night
before the royal wedding in 2011.
➕ 86 C2 ✉ Beeston Place ☎ 020
7396 9000; www.thegoring.com
🚇 Victoria AX, DC, MC, VI

Lancaster Gate Hotel
$$–$$$

This is a grand town house hotel
where the styling is modern and
functional and there's a restaurant

on site. Paddington railway station
and Hyde Park are both close by.
➕ 86 A3 ✉ 66 Lancaster Gate
☎ 020 7262 5090; www.lancaster
gatehotelhydepark.co.uk
🚇 Lancaster Gate or Paddington
AX, DC, MC, VI

Shangri-La Hotel at
The Shard $$$

Stay here and enjoy The Shard's
stupendous views 24/7. The hotel
occupies floor 35 (with Ting
Restaurant) up to floor 52, where you
can enjoy the infinity pool and have
a drink in the cocktail bar.
➕ 87 F2 ✉ 31 St. Thomas Street
☎ 020 7234 8000; www.shangri-
la.com/london 🚇 London Bridge
AX, DC, MC, VI

LONDON RESTAURANTS

Price guide: (dinner per person,
excluding drinks)
$ under £30
$$ £30–£50
$$$ over £50

Bread Street Kitchen
$$–$$$

Expect high-octane, all-day dining in
this warehouse-style restaurant,
close to St. Paul's Cathedral. The
menu includes grills and stone-baked
dishes. Sunday brunch is a highlight.
➕ 87 E3 ✉ 10 Bread Street ☎ 020
3030 4050; www.gordonramsay
restaurants.com 🚇 Mansion House,
St. Paul's or Bank AX, MC, VI

Café Murano $$–$$$

Angela Hartnett's relaxed eatery is a
sophisticated take on a pop-in-every-
day Italian. The flavors are inspired
and the fixed-price lunch and dinner
options offer good value. There's
another branch in Covent Garden.
➕ 86 C2 ✉ 33 St. James's Street
☎ 020 3371 5559; www.cafemurano.
co.uk 🕐 Closed Tue., Sun. dinner
🚇 Green Park AX, MC, VI

Dinner by Heston
Blumenthal $$$

The innovative British chef pushes fine
dining to new levels, and his exciting
modern twists bring the wow-factor to
many classic recipes dating from 1390
to 1940. The restaurant setting is
stylish and the dining experience here
is memorable.
➕ 86 B2 ✉ Mandarin Oriental Hyde
Park, Knightsbridge ☎ 020 7201
3833; www.dinnerbyheston.com
🚇 Knightsbridge AX, DC, MC, VI

KEY TO SYMBOLS

✚	map page number and coordinates
⊠	address
☎	telephone number
Ⓒ	days/times closed
Ⓢ	nearest subway station
🚌	nearest bus/trolley bus/ tram/funicular route
⛴	ferry
$$$	expensive
$$	moderate
$	inexpensive
AX	American Express
DC	Diners Club
MC	MasterCard
VI	VISA

English Pubs

The traditional English pub, from the term "public house," is another of those treasured institutions by which an entire culture is measured. The great thing about traditional pubs is their spirit of easygoing informality. Pubs were always the focus of local life, places where people exchanged views and took their hard-earned leisure. It is no coincidence that village pub and village church often stand cheek by jowl. In medieval times, churches and monasteries often owned the local pub, or "hostelry." In and around Oxford you will find traditional pubs that have not compromised with modern fashion, while still maintaining the highest standards of comfort and service. Try the Chequers, off High Street; the King's Arms, on Holywell Street; the Turf Tavern, in Bath Place; the Isis Farmhouse on the towpath at Iffley Lock; or The Rose and Crown on North Parade Avenue.

Pizzaro $–$$

Top-notch authentic, modern Spanish cuisine is the order here in this south of the River Thames, trendy Bermondsey bistro. The open kitchen sets the buzz, and look out for the daily specials.

✚ 87 F2 ⊠ 194 Bermondsey Street ☎ 020 7378 9455; www.josepizarro.com Ⓢ Bermondsey, Borough, London Bridge AX, MC, VI

Raison d'Etre $

A café serving hearty breakfasts and delicious light lunches and offering a friendly welcome is just what you want during a long day of sightseeing in the English capital. You'll find all of the above in this West London eatery.

✚ 86 A1 ⊠ 18 Bute Street, South Kensington ☎ 020 7584 5008; www.raisondetrecafe.com Ⓒ Closed dinner, all day Sun Ⓢ South Kensington MC, VI

EDINBURGH HOTELS

Price guide: (double room with breakfast for two people)

$	under £125
$$	£125–£200
$$$	over £200

The Balmoral Hotel $$$

This classic Edwardian building dominates the east end of Princes Street with superb views over the city. All rooms are elegantly furnished and air-conditioned.

✚ 99 D3 ⊠ 1 Princes Street ☎ 0131 556 2414; www.roccoforte hotels.com 🚌 City-center buses AX, DC, MC, VI

Mercure Edinburgh City $$

This is a great mid-price option, in an enviable location on Princes Street. Rooms have private balconies with panoramic views, especially those from the seventh floor.

✚ 99 C2 ⊠ Princes Street ☎ 0131 226 8400; www.mercure edinburgh.co.uk 🚌 City-center buses AX, MC, VI

Radisson Collection Royal Mile Hotel $$$

Luxurious and funky, this stylish hotel is a great choice in the heart of the Old Town, with a cocktail bar and Italian restaurant on site.

✚ 99 D2 ⊠ 1 George IV Bridge ☎ 0131 220 1666; www.radissoncollection.com 🚌 City-center buses AX, MC, VI

Sheraton Grand Hotel & Spa $$$

This modern hotel close to the famous castle boasts one of the best spas in Scotland – check out the top-floor hydro pool and the relaxing thermal suite.

✚ 98 B1 ⊠ 1 Festival Square ☎ 0131 229 9131; www. starwoodhotels.com 🚌 City-center buses to Lothian Road AX, MC, VI

Waldorf Astoria Edinburgh $$$

A Waldorf Astoria Hotel, the "Caley," (formerly the Caledonian Hotel) is a haven of luxury and style. Request a bedroom with a castle view.

✚ 98 B2 ⊠ Princes Street ☎ 0131 222 8888; www.waldorfastoria edinburgh.com 🚌 City-center buses AX, DC, MC, VI

EDINBURGH RESTAURANTS

Price guide: (dinner per person, excluding drinks)

$	under £30
$$	£30–£50
$$$	over £50

21212 $$$

Talented chef Paul Kitching serves French cuisine in this Georgian town house near Calton Hill. The set three-course lunch is a good value.

✚ 99 E3 ⊠ 3 Royal Terrace ☎ 0131 523 1030; www.21212 restaurant.co.uk Ⓒ Closed Sun. and Mon.; 2 weeks in Jan. 🚌 City-center buses AX, MC, VI

The Kitchin $$$

A former whisky warehouse in Leith's dockside is home to one of Scotland's most dynamic chefs, Tom Kitchin. Expect passionate attention to the flavors of the finest local and seasonal ingredients. The set lunch is a good option.

✚ 99 off map at E3 ⊠ 78 Commercial Quay, Leith ☎ 0131 555 1755; www.thekitchin.com Ⓒ Closed Sun.–Mon., first 2 weeks in Jan. 🚌 16, 22 AX, MC, VI

Number One, The Balmoral $$$

Located in the grand baronial-style Balmoral Hotel near Waverley Station, this smart modern dining room offers dynamic Scottish cooking.

✚ 99 D3 ⊠ 1 Princes Street ☎ 0131 557 6727; www.roccoforte hotels.com Ⓒ Closed 2 weeks in Jan. 🚌 City-center buses AX, DC, MC, VI

The Scran & Scallie $–$$

Hearty traditional and modern Scottish cuisine meet in perfect harmony at this fashionable dining pub, located near the Botanic Gardens. The menu is seasonal.
☩ 99 off map at C3 ✉ 1 Comely Bank Road, Stockbridge ☎ 0131 332 6281; www.scranandscallie.com ⊟ 8, 23, 27 MC, VI

Timberyard $$$

Enjoy creative modern cooking in the cool setting of this former warehouse, with its leafy courtyard. Food is locally supplied and foraged.
☩ 99 C1 ✉ 10 Lady Lawson Street ☎ 0131 221 1222; www.timberyard. co ⊙ Closed Sun., Mon., 1 week in Apr., and Oct. MC, VI

OXFORD HOTELS

Price guide: (double room with breakfast for two people)
$ £75–£150
$$ £150–£225
$$$ over £225

Belmond Le Manoir aux Quat'Saisons $$$

This is one of the UK's most delightful and intimate hotels, set in a pretty Oxfordshire village. Guests here can enjoy beautifully designed rooms, lovely English gardens and a fabulous restaurant.
☩ 107 off map at C1 ✉ Church Road, Great Milton ☎ 0184 427 8881; www.belmond.com ☎ No public transportation AX, MC, VI

Macdonald Randolph Hotel $$$

This landmark hotel, with neo-Gothic architectural features and elegant interiors, has very comfortable rooms and luxury service. Visit the spa for treatments or its sauna and Jacuzzi. It is near to the Ashmolean Museum.
☩ 107 A2 ✉ Beaumont Street ☎ 01865 256400; www.macdonaldhotels.co.uk ⊟ City-center buses AX, MC, VI

Malmaison Oxford $$–$$$

The city's medieval castle is now a luxury boutique hotel offering comfortable beds with luxurious bathrooms – a far cry from the days when the building served as the town's jail. There also is a brasserie.
☩ 107 off map at A2 ✉ Oxford Castle, 3 New Road ☎ 01865 268400; www.malmaison.com ⊟ City-center buses AX, MC, VI

Manor House Hotel $$

This small, family-run hotel in a Victorian-era building, a mile from the center, has a comfortable lounge, bar and breakfast facilities.
☩ 107 off map at C1 ✉ 250 Iffley Road ☎ 01865 727627; www.manorhousoxford.com ⊟ 3 MC, VI

Mercure Oxford Eastgate Hotel $$–$$$

The scholars J. R. R. Tolkein and C. S. Lewis once favored this historic hotel, now stylishly refurbished and equipped to a high standard of comfort, with a good New York Italian restaurant. It's an easy stroll from the city center, and close to the Botanic Garden.
☩ 107 C1 ✉ 73 High Street ☎ 01865 248332; www.mercure.com ⊟ City-center buses AX, MC, VI

OXFORD RESTAURANTS

Price guide: (dinner per person, excluding drinks)
$ under £30
$$ £30–£50
$$$ over £50

Brasserie Blanc $–$$$

A popular and stylish yet friendly brasserie owned by the renowned French chef Raymond Blanc. The restaurant serves seasonal ingredients of the finest quality.
☩ 107 off map at C3 ✉ 71–72 Walton Street ☎ 01865 510999; www.brasserieblanc.com ⊙ Closed Dec. 25 ⊟ 2, 6 AX, MC, VI

Kazbar $–$$

Kazbar is a popular and inexpensive tapas restaurant with a souk-inspired setting and great wine list. Sip a glass of Rioja while nibbling on chili prawns or oven-roasted pork ribs.
☩ 107 off map at C1 ✉ 25–27 Cowley Road ☎ 01865 202920; www.kazbar.co.uk ⊙ Closed lunch Mon.–Fri. ⊟ 5, 10, 12 MC, VI

The Oxford Kitchen $$–$$$

Rubbing shoulders with high-end boutiques and stylish delis to the north of downtown, this modern British restaurant is becoming a foodie landmark in the city. The fixed price lunch offers great value.
☩ 107 off map at A3 ✉ 215 Banbury Road, Summertown ☎ 01865 511149; www.theoxfordkitchen.co.uk ⊙ Closed Mon., first 2 weeks Jan. ⊟ City-center buses MC, VI

The Punter $–$$

This pub is a gastronomic treat found on Osney Island, in the River Thames. Sample The Punter's own ale, and relax in the eclectic setting, to enjoy some tasty homestyle fare.
☩ 107 off map at A1 ✉ 7 South Street ☎ 01865 248832; www.thepunteroxford.co.uk ⊟ City-center buses MC, VI

BATH HOTELS

Price guide: (double room with breakfast for two people)
$ £75–£150
$$ £150–£225
$$$ over £225

No. 15 Great Pulteney $$

This small and luxurious boutique hotel has rooms of different styles and sizes, but all are elegant and beautifully furnished. There's a small spa and a gourmet café on site.
☩ 113 C2 ✉ 15 Great Pulteney Street ☎ 01225 807767; www no15greatpulteney.co.uk ⊟ 265 AX, MC, VI

The Gainsborough Bath Spa $$$

The sumptuous Gainsborough Bath Spa is well known for delightful and comfortable rooms and excellent service. Enjoy treatments at the luxury spa and fine dining at the restaurant on site.
☩ 113 B2 ✉ Beau Street ☎ 01225 358888; www.thegainsboroughbathspa.co.uk ⊟ No direct public transportation AX, MC, VI

Henrietta House $–$$

The 19 en-suite, calm and restful rooms of the Henrietta House are furnished with art and antiques. There is a garden to enjoy and parking is available (fee payable).
☩ 113 C3 ✉ 33 Henrietta Street ☎ 01225 632632; www.henriettahouse.co.uk ⊟ No direct public transportation MC, VI

The Royal Crescent $$$

Housed behind the facades of the famous Royal Crescent, this five-star hotel is arguably the grandest place to stay downtown, but it's still an intimate place to stay. The luxury spa and fine dining restaurant add to the allure.
☩ 113 A3 ✉ 16 Royal Crescent ☎ 01225 823333; www.royalcrescent.co.uk ⊟ No direct public transportation AX, MC, VI

KEY TO SYMBOLS

✚   map page number and coordinates
✉   address
☎   telephone number
◷   days/times closed
Ⓜ   nearest subway station
🚌   nearest bus/trolley bus/ tram/funicular route
⛴   ferry
$$$ expensive
$$ moderate
$ inexpensive
AX   American Express
DC   Diners Club
MC   MasterCard
VI   VISA

Danish Smørrebrød

Like their fellow Scandinavians, Danes are great believers in hearty lunches, and nothing is more mouthwatering or filling than *smørrebrød*, which translates simply as "buttered bread." If it sounds like "smothering," then that's exactly what happens to the large slice of rye bread that is the basis of *smørrebrød* when it is piled high with a tasty mix of salads and garnishes, shrimp and chunks of fish, beef or pork. You can accompany this mini-banquet with a Danish lager or a small glass of chilled *akvavit* (aquavit). You also can enjoy the Danish *kolt bord*, or cold table, an array of meat and fish dishes, salads and savory dips, hot dishes, and a selection of bread and rolls.

Price guide: (dinner per person, excluding drinks)
$ under £30
$$ £30–£50
$$$ over £50

The Marlborough Tavern $–$$

Hearty English dishes are raised to a new standard at this popular and friendly pub. There's a large terrace at the back for summer dining.
✚ 113 A3 ✉ 35 Marlborough Buildings ☎ 01225 423731; www.marlborough-tavern.com
🚌 7, 31 MC, VI

Menu Gordon Jones $$$

This Scottish chef is a rising culinary talent and offers an exciting and innovative set menu. This is not just food, it's art on a plate and eating here is an event. It's worth taking the short taxi ride from downtown.
✚ 113 A1 ✉ 2 Wellsway ☎ 01225 480871; http://menugordonjones.co. uk ◷ Closed Sun. and Mon. 🚌 No direct public transportation AX, MC, V

Pump Room $$–$$$

Open for breakfast, lunch and afternoon tea, the Pump Room is steeped in Roman splendor – you can even taste the spa water here.
✚ 113 B2 ✉ Church Street ☎ 01225 444477; www.roman baths. co.uk/pump-room-restaurant
◷ Closed dinner 🚌 3, 4 MC, VI

Same Same but Different $–$$

This casual eatery has a short menu, written on the chalkboard daily, and serves dishes using ingredients only sourced in Bath and the local area.
✚ 113 B3 ✉ 7a Princes Building, Bartlett Street ☎ 01225 466856; www.same-same.co.uk ◷ Closed Sun. and Mon. dinner 🚌 6, 6a, 7 MC, VI

The Scallop Shell $–$$

Come here for some of the finest fish and chips in Britain. However, the Scallop Shell is so much more than a simple British fish and chip restaurant. Here you'll find a menu full of different fish, as well as shellfish such as razor clams and also oysters when in season.
✚ 113 A2 ✉ 22 Monmouth Place ☎ 01225 420928; www.thescallop shell.co.uk ◷ Closed Sun. 🚌 19, 19a, 37, 39 MC, VI

Woods $–$$

A part of Bath's culinary scene for almost 40 years, Woods is a casual brasserie with Gallic flair. It's been family owned and run since being opened by David Price and his French wife Claude in 1979. The menu is contemporary and Mediterranean. Lunch is a good value.
✚ 113 B3 ✉ 9–3 Alfred Street ☎ 01225 314812; www.woods restaurant.com ◷ Closed Sun. and Mon.; Open first Mon. of the month
🚌 6, 6a, 7 MC, VI

Price guide: (double room with breakfast for two people)
$ 1,000Kč–2,500Kč
$$ 2,500Kč–4,500Kč
$$$ over 4,500Kč

Hotel Savoy $$$

A relaxed atmosphere prevails at this stunning, five-star top Prague hotel, located behind Prague Castle. Rooms are well designed and modernized.
✚ 124 off map at A4 ✉ Keplerova 6 ☎ 224 302 430; www.hotelsavoy prague.com 🚌 Tram 22, 23 AX, DC, MC, VI

NYX Hotel Prague $$

This trendy hotel offers a good-value accommodation, just a short walk from Wenceslas Square (Václavské náměstí) and within easy strolling distance of the Old Town.
✚ 125 D3 ✉ Panská 9 ☎ 226 222 800; www.leonardo-hotels.com
Ⓜ Mustek 🚌 Tram 3, 5, 6, 9, 14, 24 MC, VI

Penzion U Medvídků $$

The name of this tavern means "The Little Bear." There are 33 rooms in two categories: all have bathrooms, but the "historic rooms" cost more. There's a breakfast buffet.
✚ 125 C3 ✉ Na Perštýně 7 ☎ 224 211 916; www.umedvidku.cz
Ⓜ Narodní třída 🚌 Tram 2, 9, 18, 22, 23 AX, DC, MC, VI

U Zlaté Studně $$$

This luxury boutique hotel, perched on a hill overlooking Malá Strana, is always in high demand, so book well in advance. It is worth it, though, for the 17th-century period charm, and the chance to dine on the terrace.
✚ 124 B4 ✉ U Zlaté Studně 4 ☎ 257 011 213; www.goldenwell.cz
Ⓜ Malostranská 🚌 Tram 12, 15, 20, 22, 23 AX, DC, MC, VI

PRAGUE RESTAURANTS

Price guide: (dinner per person, excluding drinks)

$ 100Kč–200Kč
$$ 200Kč–600Kč
$$$ over 600Kč

Francouzská Restaurace $$$

This stylish art nouveau, Czech-style pub, on the ground floor of the landmark Obecní dům (Municipal House), offers traditional specialties served amid grand, end-of-the-20th-century splendor.

⊞ 125 E4 ✉ Náměstí Republiky 5 ☎ 222 002 770; www.francouzska restaurace.cz ⦿ Náměstí Republiky 5 🚋 Tram 6, 8, 15, 26 AX, DC, MC, VI

Lokál $$

Solid Czech pub fare, including good roasted pork and *Wiener Schnitzel*, plus, arguably, the best beer in Prague make this a tough tub to get during meal times. Book in advance or try off-peak times (before 11:30 a.m. for lunch, before 6 p.m. for dinner). The restaurant's great location is a short walk from Old Town Square.

⊞ 125 D4 ✉ Dlouhá 33 ☎ 734 283 874; http://lokal-dlouha.ambi.cz ⦿ Staroměstská No credit cards

Mistral $–$$

The Mistral serves great value, traditional Czech cuisine as well as some select international dishes, and is just a few stops away from the Old Town Square. Discounted two- and three-course daily lunch specials make this the perfect mid-sightseeing stopover, though the dining room has an upscale feel that works for a nice dinner as well.

⊞ 124 C4 ✉ Valentinská 11 ☎ 222 317 737; www.mistralcafe.cz ⦿ Staroměstská 🚋 22; tram 17, 18 AX, DC, MC, VI

Sansho $$–$$$

The world-class Asian fusion cooking at Sansho is a welcome change from the ubiquitous roast pork and *sauerkraut*. The creative menu features the likes of soft-shell crab sliders and pork belly in hoisin sauce. Reserve ahead.

⊞ 125 E4 ✉ Petrská 25 ☎ 222 317 425; www.sansho.cz ⊗ Closed Sun.–Mon., Sat. lunch ⦿ Náměstí Republiky 🚋 Tram 6, 8, 15, 26 AX, DC, MC, VI

U modré kachničky $$$

This traditional Czech inn comes highly recommended for its excellent Czech cooking. Request a table upstairs near the piano for an extra-special evening.

⊞ 124 B3 ✉ Nebovidská 6 ☎ 257 320 308; www.umodrekachnicky.cz ⦿ Malostranská 🚋 Tram 12, 15, 20, 22, 23 AX, DC, MC, VI

COPENHAGEN HOTELS

Price guide: (double room for two people)

$ DKr600–DKr1,000
$$ DKr1,000–DKr2,000
$$$ over DKr2,000

71 Havn $$$

Two 19th-century warehouses on the waterfront have been transformed into a luxury hotel featuring crisp modern design and exposed beams. The rooms are comfortable and some suites have two floors.

⊞ 141 D3 ✉ Nyhavn 71 ☎ 33 43 62 00; www.71nyhavnhotel.com ⦿ Kongens Nytorv 🚌 1A, 26 AX, DC, MC, VI

Axel Hotel Guldsmeden $$–$$$

The Axel is very close to the central railroad station and has individually decorated rooms with four-poster beds. Guests can enjoy delicious breakfasts, a luxurious spa and a garden bar, all with eco credentials.

⊞ 140 A1 ✉ Colbjørnsensgade 14 ☎ 33 31 32 66; www.guldsmeden hotels.com ⦿ S-train København H 🚌 6A, 10, 14, 26 AX, MC, VI

Hotel Alexandra $$–$$$

If you love 20th-century Danish design, you will like this hotel. The light and airy rooms are well-equipped and furnished, and the staff are very helpful.

⊞ 140 B2 ✉ H. C. Andersen Boulevard 8 ☎ 33 74 44 44; www. hotelalexandra.dk ⦿ Vesterport 🚌 5A, 6A, 14 AX, DC, MC, VI

Hotel Bethel Sømandshjem $–$$

For a very central location at a reasonable price it's hard to beat this hotel. Its rooms are full of character with comfortable beds, and staff are friendly.

⊞ 140 D3 ✉ Nyhavn 22 ☎ 33 13 03 70; www.hotel-bethel.dk ⦿ Kongens Nytorv 🚌 1A, 26, 66, 350S AX, DC, MC, VI

Hotel Sanders $$$

Attention to detail is paramount in this boutique hotel (52 rooms), which opened near the Royal Danish Theater in 2017. The rooms are sumptuous yet classy.

⊞ 140 D2 ✉ Tordenskjoldsgade 15 ☎ 45 46 40 00 40; www.hotelsanders.com ⦿ Kongens Nytorv AX, MC, VI

COPENHAGEN RESTAURANTS

Price guide: (dinner per person, excluding drinks)

$ DKr100–DKr250
$$ DKr250–DKr500
$$$ over DKr500

Christianshavn Ferry Café $

This is a lively and convivial waterside spot for open sandwiches, herring dishes and salads, washed down with homemade schnapps and finished with Danish apple cake. The evening menu includes daily specials such as pork belly.

⊞ 141 D2 ✉ Strandegade 50 ☎ 32 54 46 24; www.faergecafeen.dk ⦿ Christianshavn 🚌 2A, 9A AX, MC, VI

Nyhavns Færgekro $$

This is one of the best restaurants on canalside Nyhavn, with a nautical theme reflecting the area's maritime history, which includes model boats hanging from the ceiling. Superb lunchtime buffets featuring a variety of herring dishes are a great deal ($); the Danish and French dinner menu is more expensive.

⊞ 140–141 D2 ✉ Nyhavn 5 ☎ 33 15 15 88; www.nf.dk ⦿ Kongens Nytorv 🚌 1A, 26, 66, 350S MC, VI

Restaurant Els $$–$$$

Original 1850s wall panels adorn this traditional Nyhavn restaurant. There are good-value three-course seasonal menus in addition to à la carte items, and lunch plates and sandwiches also are available to 5 p.m. Reservations are advised.

⊞ 140 D2–D3 ✉ Store Strandstræde 3 ☎ 33 14 13 41; www.restaurant-els.dk ⦿ Kongens Nytorv 🚌 1A, 26, 66, 350S AX, DC, MC, VI

RizRaz $–$$

RizRaz takes its inspiration from world cuisine and offers delicious low-fat, healthy options. There's plenty of choice, but especially

KEY TO SYMBOLS

✚	map page number and coordinates
✉	address
☎	telephone number
🕐	days/times closed
Ⓜ	nearest subway station
🚌	nearest bus/trolley bus/ tram/funicular route
🛳	ferry
$$$	expensive
$$	moderate
$	inexpensive
AX	American Express
DC	Diners Club
MC	MasterCard
VI	VISA

popular is its all-you-can-eat fresh, seasonal salad buffet, to which you can add prime steak, salmon or kebabs cooked over an open-flame grill. There are two restaurants – the other one at Kannikestræde 19 has an attractive large courtyard which is very popular in summer.

✚ 140 C2 ✉ Kompagnistræde 20
☎ 33 15 05 75; www.rizraz.dk
Ⓜ Nørreport 🚌 14 DC, MC, VI

Salt $$

In a great position on the harbor promenade, Salt offers a choice of two-, three- and four-course menus in an architecturally stunning space. Expect Danish classics. In summer (mid-Apr. to mid-Sep.), Salt Café opens on the terrace.

✚ 141 D3 ✉ Tolbodgade 24–28
☎ 33 74 14 44; www.saltrestaurant. dk Ⓜ Kongens Nytorv 🚌 1A, 66 AX, DI, MC, VI

ODENSE HOTELS

Price guide: (double room with breakfast for two people)

$	DKr400–DKr700
$$	DKr700–DKr1,200
$$$	over DKr1,200

City Hotel Odense $$

This comfortable, older-style hotel is in the heart of the Old Town. The cozy lounge has a log fire in cooler months, and there is a quiet rooftop terrace. Apartments also are available to rent.

✚ 146 C2 ✉ Hans Mulesgade 5
☎ 66 12 12 58; www.city-hotel-odense.dk AX, DC, MC, VI

First Hotel Grand $$

One of Odense's most illustrious hotels, the Grand, is situated in a handsome old building across from the art gallery, Brandts 13. There is a brasserie-style restaurant, a cocktail bar and a modern gym. Rooms are spacious with hardwood floors and comfortable beds.

✚ 146 B2 ✉ Jernbanegade 18
☎ 66 11 71 71; www.firsthotels.com AX, DC, MC, VI

Hotel Domir $–$$

The medium-size Hotel Domir has simple but comfortable rooms and a café-bar and restaurant. Spotlessly clean and bright, it is a good budget option that is close to the railroad.

✚ 146 A3 ✉ Hans Tausens Gade 19
☎ 66 12 14 27; www.domir.dk AX, DC, MC, VI

Pjentehus $

Located just outside the city center, this is a small, comfortable bed-and-breakfast housed in a pleasant villa.

✚ 146 C3 ✉ Pjentedamsgade 14
☎ 66 12 15 55; www.pjentehus.dk No credit cards

Radisson Blu H. C. Andersen Hotel $$–$$$

This luxurious, modern hotel is close to the Concert Hall. It has spacious rooms (a standard room can accommodate up to four adults), and its own restaurant. Amenities include sauna, solarium and casino.

✚ 146 C2 ✉ Claus Bergsgade 7
☎ 66 14 78 00; www.radissonblu. com AX, DC, MC, VI

ODENSE RESTAURANTS

Price guide: (dinner per person, excluding drinks)

$	DKr100–DKr250
$$	DKr250–DKr300
$$$	over DKr300

Den Gamle Kro $$$

This restaurant occupies a magnificent 1683 building. Meals are served in several rooms, including the brick-vaulted cellar. Expect excellent Danish cuisine.

✚ 146 B2–C2 ✉ Overgade 23
☎ 66 12 14 33; www.dengamlekro.eu AX, DC, MC, VI

Den Grimme Ælling $

"The Ugly Duckling" is a charming little restaurant on a cobbled lane and is known in the city for its extravagant buffets.

✚ 146 B2 ✉ Hans Jensens Stræde 1 ☎ 65 91 70 30; www. grimme-aelling.dk AX, MC, VI

Nordatlanten $$–$$$

This sleek restaurant in the Nordatlantisk cultural center in the Harbor, Odense's newly developed canal basin, specializes in pan-Nordic cuisine. Come on the weekend for a great brunch on the terrace (reserve ahead), with waterside views.

✚ 146 off map at B3
✉ Nordatlantisk Promenade 1
☎ 22 39 76 00; www.restaurant-nordatlanten.com AX, MC, VI

Restaurant Air Pub $–$$

This pub and restaurant has a lively atmosphere, hearty Danish cooking and a good selection of beers. Lighter dishes also are served, and there is

---

Russian Restaurants

You can sample authentic Russian cuisine in Helsinki at one of the city's several Russian restaurants. Russian food is not noted for its lightness of touch, but it can be innovative. You can even start with caviar and sour cream if you want, before plunging into hearty meat dishes with cakes, fruit pies and ice cream for dessert. Two notable places to try are Troikka at Caloniuksenkatu 3 (☎ 09 445 229; www.troikka.fi) and Bellevue at Rahapajankatu 3 (☎ 09 179 560; www. restaurantbellevue.com).

live music from 10 p.m. Fri. and Sat.
➕ 146 A2 ✉ Kongensgade 41
☎ 66 14 66 08; www.air-pub.dk
🌐 Closed Sun. AX, MC, VI

Restaurant Under Lindetræet $$$

Close to the Hans Christian Andersen Museum, this elegant restaurant serves inventive Scandinavian, Alsatian and Tuscan dishes. On summer weekends, the terrace here is a great choice for brunch.
➕ 146 B2 ✉ Ramsherred 2 ☎ 66 12 92 86; www.underlindetraet.dk
🌐 Closed Sun. and Mon. dinner AX, MC, VI

Price guide: (double room with breakfast for two people)
$ €50–€100
$$ €100–€150
$$$ over €150

F6 Hotel $$

This stylish, family-run hotel just off the Esplanade has many homely touches, wonderful beds and a small gym. Bicycles are available for guests to use.
➕ 159 C2 ✉ Fabianinkatu 6
☎ 09 6899 9666; www.hotelf6.fi
🚋 Tram 4, 5, 7 AX, DC, MC, VI

GLO Hotel Art $$–$$$

Once the elegant home of the Helsinki Students Union, this Jugend-style hotel in the Design District has thick granite walls and cool modern furnishings. Breakfast is served in the cozy cellar.
➕ 159 C4 ✉ Lönnrotinkatu 29
☎ 01 03 44 41 00; www.glohotels.fi
🚌 20, 20N; tram 6 AX, DC, MC, VI

Hotel Fabian $$$

This traditional town house in the heart of Helsinki has been converted into a boutique hotel with stylish rooms, a cozy bar and a leafy courtyard. A stylish choice, Hotel Fabian is at the lower end of the upper price bracket.
➕ 159 C2 ✉ Fabianinkatu 7
☎ 09 6128 2000; www.hotelfabian.fi
🚋 24; tram 1, 2, 10 AX, DC, MC, VI

Scandic Grand Marina Hotel $–$$$

You can step from ferry to foyer, if you travel to Helsinki by Viking Line, and stay in this large hotel on the western side of the harbor. Rooms are elegant and there are several

bars and a restaurant. Children under 12 stay free.
➕ 159 C2 ✉ Katajanokanlaituri 7
☎ 09 16661; www.scandichotels.fi
🚋 4T AX, DC, MC, VI

Price guide: (dinner per person, excluding drinks)
$ €10–€25
$$ €25–€50
$$$ over €50

Ask $$$

The neighborhood feel of Ask belies its seriously good Nordic cooking (one Michelin star) created from impeccably sourced ingredients.
➕ 159 C3 ✉ Vironkatu 8 ☎ 040 581 8100; www.restaurantask.com
🌐 Closed Sun., Mon., and lunch Tue.–Thu. 🚋 Tram 1A, 7 AX, DC, MC, VI

Juuri $$

This bright, unpretentious restaurant creates exciting twists on traditional Finnish dishes and ingredients as well as a choice of *sapas* – tasty morsels similar to *tapas*.
➕ 159 B2 ✉ Korkeavuorenkatu 27
☎ 09 635 732; www.juuri.fi
🌐 Closed Sun. lunch 🚋 24; tram 10 AX, DC, MC, VI

Kappeli $$–$$$

This restaurant and café, in a pavilion of cast iron and glass that dates from 1867, serves Scandinavian cuisine. In summer, music concerts take place at the bandstand.
➕ 159 B2 ✉ Etelaesplanadi 1
☎ 010 766 3880; www.kappeli.fi
🚋 13, 64S, 77S; tram 1, 1A AX, MC, VI

Kellohalli $–$$

All things foodie have found a home in Helsinki's old abattoir. Among them is Kellohalli, whose lunch menus tour the world's cuisines.
➕ 159 C4 ✉ Työpajankatu 2 rakennus 1e ☎ 050 339 5400; www.kellohalli.fi 🌐 Closed Mon.–Fri. dinner 🚋 Kalasatama
🚋 68 AX, MC, VI

Sea Horse $$–$$$

This historic restaurant in a Jugend mansion serves truly Finnish specialties – meatballs, fillet of reindeer and crispy fried herrings.
➕ 159 B1 ✉ Kapteeninkatu 11
☎ 09 628 169; www.seahorse.fi
🚋 24; tram 3 AX, MC, VI

Price guide: (double room with breakfast for two people)
$ under €150
$$ €150–€225
$$$ over €225

Bristol Paris $$$

The Louis XV-style rooms affirm the elegance of this hotel, which boasts a rooftop indoor swimming pool, pampering spa and restaurant.
➕ 174 B3 ✉ 112 rue du Faubourg-St.-Honoré, 75008
☎ 01 53 43 43 00; www.lebristolparis.com 🚇 Miromesnil AX, DC, MC, VI

Hôtel Crayon $-$$

A quirky and contemporary boutique hotel that is owned – and was decorated by – French artist Julie Gauthron. It is great value for the central location.
➕ 175 C3 ✉ 25 rue du Bouloi, 75001 ☎ 01 42 36 54 19; www.hotel crayon.com 🚇 Louvre Rivoli or Les Halles AX, MC, VI

Hôtel des Grandes Écoles $–$$

This typically French hotel has pretty bedrooms and is set in a garden on a narrow street in the Latin Quarter.
➕ 175 D1 ✉ 75 rue Cardinal-Lemoine, 75005 ☎ 01 43 26 79 23; www.hotel-grandes-ecoles.com
🚇 Cardinal-Lemoine MC, VI

Hôtel New Orient $–$$

Pleasantly decorated, small and personal, this is a little gem for the room prices and is located 10 minutes on foot from the Opéra.
➕ 174 B4 ✉ 16 rue de Constantinople, 75008 ☎ 01 45 22 21 64; www.hotelneworient.com
🚇 Villiers AX, MC, VI

Pavillon de la Reine $$$

This is a romantic and luxurious hotel, complete with four-poster beds in some rooms and suites. The spa offers a range of treatments and massages.
➕ 175 E2 ✉ 28 place des Vosges, 75003 ☎ 01 40 29 19 19; www.pavillon-de-la-reine.com
🚇 Saint-Paul AX, DC, MC, VI

Price guide: (dinner per person, excluding drinks)
$ under €35
$$ €35–€60
$$$ over €60

KEY TO SYMBOLS

- ⊞ map page number and coordinates
- ✉ address
- ☎ telephone number
- ⊘ days/times closed
- Ⓜ nearest subway station
- 🚌 nearest bus/trolley bus/ tram/funicular route
- ⛴ ferry
- $$$ expensive
- $$ moderate
- $ inexpensive
- AX American Express
- DC Diners Club
- MC MasterCard
- VI VISA

The *Belle Époque* in Nice

The *belle époque*, or "beautiful era," was the name the French gave to the early 20th century. During this period Nice's fame soared with the influx of up to 150,000 wealthy English and Russians who came here to while away northern winters in elegance. They expected luxury, and it was for them that sumptuous and grandiose hotels and villas were built. Some buildings survive along the promenade des Anglais. The Négresco is the most famous; enjoy a drink there in Edwardian style.

L'Ange 20 $$

This is a cozy, old-style bistro in the heart of the Marais area of the city. There is an excellent fixed-price daily French menu.

⊞ 175 D2 ✉ 44 rue des Tournelles, 75004 ☎ 01 85 15 23 92; www. lange20.com ⊘ Closed Mon.–Tue. Ⓜ Chemin Vert AX, MC, VI

Chez Paul $–$$

Chez Paul is a traditional Paris bistro with decor and a menu that has little changed since the 1950s. Soak in the atmosphere over generous portions of simple French food.

⊞ 175 E2 ✉ 13 rue de Charonne, 75011 ☎ 01 47 00 34 57; www. chezpaul.com Ⓜ Bastille AX, VI

Le Cinq $$$

The three Michelin stars awarded to chef Christian Le Squer are testament to the quality and attention to detail at this French restaurant. The dining room is elegant and there's a garden for summer dining.

⊞ 175 B3 ✉ Hotel Four Seasons Georges V, 31 avenue Georges V, 75008 ☎ 01 49 52 71 54; www. restaurant-lecinq.com Ⓜ Georges V AX, DC, MC, VI

La Coupole $$–$$$

This sprawling art deco brasserie, renowned in the 1920s, serves seafood, fish and steaks. Sole *meunière* and *Châteaubriand* are among the specialties.

⊞ 175 C1 ✉ 102 boulevard du Montparnasse, 75014 ☎ 01 43 20 14 20; www.lacoupole-paris.com Ⓜ Vavin AX, DC, MC, VI

La Poule au Pot $$

The sumptuous 1930s decor at La Poule au Pot hints at the age of this classic bistro that serves almost till dawn. The menu hasn't changed either and the signature *poule au pot*, a type of chicken stew, is a great choice.

⊞ 175 D3 ✉ 9 rue Vauvilliers, 75001 ☎ 01 42 36 32 96; www.lapouleau pot.com ⊘ Closed daily lunch, Mon. dinner Ⓜ Châtelet-Les-Halles, Rivoli MC, VI

LYON HOTELS

Price guide: (double room with breakfast for two people)
$ under €125
$$ €125–€200
$$$ over €200

Collège Hôtel $$

Styled around the theme of an old college dorm, this hotel is delightfully quirky. Rooms are brilliant white and have terraces with lovely views of the city.

⊞ 186 A4 ✉ 5 place St.-Paul, 69005 ☎ 04 72 10 05 05; www.college-hotel.com Ⓜ St.-Paul or Vieux Lyon (St.-Jean) AX, MC, VI

Hotel Sofitel Lyon Bellecour $$–$$$

This deluxe hotel, centrally located on the Rhône river, is a good choice. There are two restaurants on site.

⊞ 186 B1 ✉ 20 quai Gailleton, 69002 ☎ 04 72 41 20 20; www.sofitel.com Ⓜ Bellecour AX, DC, MC, VI

Mercure Lyon Centre Beaux-Arts $$–$$$

An early 20th-century building houses this comfortable hotel in the center of the Presqu'Île.

⊞ 186 B3 ✉ 75 rue Président Édouard-Hérriot, 69002 ☎ 04 78 38 09 50; www.mercure.com Ⓜ Cordeliers or Bellecour AX, DC, MC, VI

St.-Paul $

Consider staying at this excellent budget choice in the Old Town. It has simple, clean and airy rooms.

⊞ 186 B3 ✉ 6 rue Lainerie, 69005 ☎ 04 78 28 13 29; www.hotelsaint paul.eu AX, DC, MC, VI

La Villa Florentine $$$

A former convent, this deluxe hotel with many amenities – including a pretty garden – stands above the Old Town, on the slopes of Fourvière.

⊞ 186 A3 ✉ 25–27 montée St.-Barthélémy, 69005 ☎ 04 72 56 56 56; www.villaflorentine.com Ⓜ Vieux Lyon AX, DC, MC, VI

LYON RESTAURANTS

Price guide: (dinner per person, excluding drinks)
$ under €35
$$ €35–€60
$$$ over €60

L'Archange $

L'Archange is a traditional *bouchon* (tavern) with a fixed menu and an excellent price range. Its chef offers a classy and contemporary twist on French classics.

⊞ 186 B4 ✉ 6 rue Hippolyte, Flandrin ☎ 04 78 28 32 26;

www.archangecafe.com 🄒 Closed lunch daily and Mon. dinner; May 🚇 Hotel de Ville MC, VI

L'Instant Fromage $

A small, simple eatery serving platters of French cheese, local salami and ham, matched with French wines, plus a good range of salads and delicious desserts. ➕ 186 B1 ✉ 31 rue St-Hélène, 69002 ☎ 04 78 92 93 54; www. instant-fromage.fr 🄒 Closed Sun. and Mon. 🚇 Ampère 🚌 11, 14, 15, 88 MC, VI

Jérémy Galvan $$–$$$

This young chef has worked with the best chefs in Lyon and now serves his own upscale contemporary dishes in the Old Town. ➕ 186 A3 ✉ 29 rue de Boeuf, 69005 ☎ 04 72 40 91 47; www.jeremy galvanrestaurant.com 🄒 Closed Sun.–Mon., and Sat. lunch 🚇 Vieux Ville AX, MC, VI

Le Musée $

One of Lyon's most popular *bouchons* (taverns), this tiny restaurant serves a range of classic local dishes. ➕ 186 C3 ✉ 2 rue des Forces, 69002 ☎ 04 78 37 71 54 🄒 Closed Sun. and Mon. 🚇 Cordeliers AX, MC, VI

Le Neuvieme Art $$$

The art of gastronomy is well represented at this contemporary Michelin-starred restaurant. Chef Christophe Roure trained under the legendary French chef Paul Bocuse ➕ 186 off map at B4 ✉ 173 rue Cuvier, 69006 ☎ 04 72 74 12 74; www.leneuviemeart.com 🄒 Closed Sun. and Mon. 🚇 Massena MC, VI

NICE HOTELS

Price guide: (double room with breakfast for two people)
$ under €125
$$ €125–€200
$$$ over €200

Gounod $–$$

This moderately priced *belle époque* choice is in a quiet location just a short, 10-minute walk from the sea. 🏨 194 B1 ✉ 3 rue Gounod, 06000 ☎ 04 93 16 42 00; www.gounod-nice. fr 🚌 3, 7, 9, 10, 22, 27, 38 AX, MC, VI

Hotel La Perouse $$$

Overlooking the Baie des Anges and at the foot of the Vielle Ville, this

well-placed, refurbished hotel offers opulence with a personal touch. ➕ 195 D1 ✉ 11 quai Rauba Capeu ☎ 04 93 62 34 63; www.leshotels duroy.com 🚌 T32 AX, DC, MC, VI

Négresco $$$

This is one of the world's great hotels in the flamboyant *belle époque* style; superb comfort, service and facilities. ➕ 194 B1 ✉ 37 Promenade des Anglais, 06000 ☎ 04 93 16 64 00; www.hotel-negresco-nice.com 🚌 8, 11, 52, 59, 62, 70, 94 AX, DC, MC, VI

WindsoR $–$$

This famous hotel is centrally located and has a garden pool and beautifully frescoed rooms, each with soundproofing. ➕ 194 B1 ✉ 11 rue Dalpozzo, 06000 ☎ 04 93 88 59 35; www.hotelwindsor nice.com 🚌 3, 7, 9, 10, 22, 27, 38, 59 AX, DC, MC, VI

NICE RESTAURANTS

Price guide: (dinner per person, excluding drinks)
$ under €35
$$ €35–€60
$$$ over €60

Illia Pasta $

A cozy bistro in the Old Town specializing in tasty pasta dishes – the pasta is made fresh on the premises. It's a great place to stop for a cup of coffee too. ➕ 194–195 D2 ✉ 74 rue Droite, 06300 ☎ 06 52 82 95 52; www. illiapasta.com 🄒 Closed Tue. and Wed. Sep.–Jun. 🚌 8, 11, 52, T61, 62, 70; tram Masséna VI

Oliviera $$

This compact bistro serves Provençal dishes with the freshest ingredients accompanied by excellent value local wines. They also stock and sell their own top-class olive oil on site. ➕ 195 D1 ✉ 8b rue de Collet, 06300 ☎ 04 93 13 06 45; www.oliveira.com 🄒 Closed Sun. and Mon. 🚇 Cathédrale 🚌 3, 8, 11, 14, 17, 27, 35, 38, 52, 59, 70, 98, 217 No credit cards

Restaurant Le Panier $$$

With an ever changing menu, Le Panier is an excellent bistro overseen by a young team and headed up by local chef Gaël Passigli. ➕ 195 D1 ✉ 5, rue Barillerie, 06300 ☎ 04 89 97 14 37;

www.restaurantlepanier.com 🄒 Closed Tue.–Wed. 🚌 3, 8, 11, 14, 17, 27, 35, 38, 52, 59, 70, 98, 217; tram Cathedrale MC, VI

Le Sejour Café $$–$$$

A small, family team has brought a bright and lively seasonal menu to this contemporary bistro, which has a lovely relaxed atmosphere. ➕ 195 C2 ✉ 711 rue Grimaldi ☎ 04 93 27 37 84; www. lesejourcafe.fr 🄒 Closed Sun. 🚌 3, 7, 9, 10, 22, 27, 38, 59 MC, VI

STRASBOURG HOTELS

Price guide: (double room with breakfast for two people)
$ under €125
$$ €125–€200
$$$ over €200

Cathédrale $$–$$$

This excellent hotel is close to Strasbourg's main sights and some of the city's best restaurants. Rooms are air-conditioned and soundproofed and there is a small bar. ➕ 200 B2 ✉ 12–13 place de la Cathédrale, 67000 ☎ 03 88 22 12 12; www.hotel-cathedrale.fr 🚋 Tram A, B, C, D, F AX, DC, MC, VI

Dragon $–$$

This cozy, renovated 17th-century town house lies just outside the canal zone but within a five-minute walk from quite a few of the downtown sights. ➕ 200 B1 ✉ 12 rue du Dragon, 67000 ☎ 03 88 35 79 80; www. dragon.fr 🚋 10 AX, DC, MC, VI

Hotel Cour du Corbeau $$$

You'll find contemporary, cool interiors set in a 16th-century historic shell at this attractive hotel, just a stone's throw away from the main sites. A beautifully situated oasis of luxury. ➕ 200 C1 ✉ 6 rue des Couples, 67000 ☎ 03 90 00 26 26; www.cour-corbeau.com 🚋 10; tram A, D AX, DC, MC, VI

Hotel Rohan $$$

This pretty hotel, on a picturesque and historic street close to the cathedral, is an easy stroll from the main sights and a choice of some good restaurants. ➕ 200 B1 ✉ 17–19 rue du Maroquin, 67000 ☎ 03 88 32 85 11; www.hotel-rohan.com 🚋 Tram A, B, C, D, F AX, DC, VI

KEY TO SYMBOLS

⊞	map page number and coordinates
⊠	address
☎	telephone number
⊘	days/times closed
Ⓜ	nearest subway station
🚍	nearest bus/trolley bus/ tram/funicular route
⛴	ferry
$$$	expensive
$$	moderate
$	inexpensive
AX	American Express
DC	Diners Club
MC	MasterCard
VI	VISA

Strasbourg Specials

Visualize French flair and imagination combined with high-quality ingredients and German influences, and you'll begin to understand the gastronomic delights that await you in Strasbourg. This is the home of *foie gras*, fatted goose liver eaten whole or made into pâté; *choucroute* (sauerkraut), assorted meats and spicy sausages served with mounds of pickled cabbage; and *kougelhupf*, yeast cake traditionally eaten for breakfast. There are other, less well-known regional dishes; look for *bæckeoffe*, a slow-cooked casserole featuring three different meats, and *tarte flambée*, a rich hot onion tart. The smooth, pungently aromatic Munster is Strasbourg's local cheese.

STRASBOURG RESTAURANTS

Price guide: (dinner per person, excluding drinks)

$	under €35
$$	€35–€50
$$$	over €50

L'Epicerie $

A perfect rest stop while exploring the Old Town. The cakes, tarts and light meals can be enjoyed amid the delightful rustic decor.

⊞ 200 A1 ⊠ 6 rue du Vieux Siegle 6, 67000 ☎ 03 88 32 52 41; www.lepicerie-strasbourg.com 🚍 Tram A, D MC, VI

La Gavroche $$$

For classy French dining, this restaurant is one of the best in the city. Chef Benoit Fuchs and his son, Alexy, are masters of the art of haute cuisine and the service is excellent. The menu is dictated by the seasonal produce of the area.

⊞ 200 C1 ⊠ 4 rue Klein, 67000 ☎ 03 88 36 82 89; www.restaurant gavroche.com ⊘ Closed Sat.–Sun. 🚍 Tram A, D AX, MC, VI

Au Petit Tonnelier $$

Dine in either the contemporary interior or on the summer terrace and enjoy stylishly presented regional and seasonal dishes.

⊞ 200 B1 ⊠ 16 rue des Tonneliers, 67000 ☎ 03 88 32 53 54; www. aupetittonnelier.com ⊘ Closed Sun. 🚍 Tram A, D AX, MC, VI

La Table du Gayot $–$$

In a picturesque square in the Old Town, this bistro-style eatery serves typical French dishes and salads. The lovely shaded terrace in the summer is perfect for alfresco dining.

⊞ 200 C2 ⊠ 8 place du Marché Gayot, 67000 ☎ 03 88 36 30 27 ⊘ Closed Tue. and Wed. 🚍 Tram B, C, F MC, VI

BERLIN HOTELS

Price guide: (double room with breakfast for two people)

$	under €75
$$	€75–€150
$$$	over €150

Ackselhaus Hotel $$$

Located in the tranquil streets of Prenzlauer Berg, this boutique hotel, in a restored 19th-century building, offers spacious, individually themed rooms, a small urban garden and an on-site café.

⊞ 217 E4 ⊠ Belforter Strasse 21 ☎ 030 44337633; www.ackselhaus. de Ⓜ U-Bahn Senefelderplatz 🚍 Tram M2 No credit cards

Hotel Adlon Kempinski $$$

Opposite the Brandenburg Gate, this is a luxurious and modern hotel. The facilities include restaurants, swimming pool and wellness center. Check the website for special offers and packages.

⊞ 217 D3 ⊠ Unter den Linden 77 ☎ 030 22610; www.kempinski.com/ en/berlin/hotel-adlon Ⓜ U-Bahn to to Brandenburger Tor 🚍 100 AX, DC, MC, VI

Hotel Vivaldi $–$$

This small hotel in a converted 19th-century town house is on a quiet shopping street close to Kurfürstendamm and the Savignyplatz restaurants and is also conveniently located for public transportation.

⊞ 216 B2 ⊠ Knesebeckstrasse 29 ☎ 030 887 02260; www.hotel-vivaldi-berlin.de Ⓜ U-Bahn Uhlandstrasse 🚍 109, 110, 204, 209, M19, M29, X9 AX, DC, MC, VI

Transit $

The Transit has small, comfortable rooms and is located above the lively bars and restaurants of the Kreuzberg quarter. A good value choice in this city.

⊞ 217 D1 ⊠ Hagelberger Strasse 53–54 ☎ 030 789 0470; www.hotel-transit.de Ⓜ U-Bahn Mehringdamm 🚍 119, 219 MC, VI

BERLIN RESTAURANTS

Price guide: (dinner per person, excluding drinks)

$	under €15
$$	€15–€30
$$$	over €30

Alt Luxemburg $$$

This is one of the city's best restaurants. Chef Karl Wannemacher combines traditional German and French dishes with the creative use of Asian spices.

⊞ 216 A2 ⊠ Windscheidstrasse 31 ☎ 030 323 8730; www.alt-luxemburg.de ⊘ Mon.–Sat. from 5 p.m. Ⓜ U-Bahn Sophie-Charlotte-Platz 🚍 309 AX, DC, MC, VI

Borchardt $$$

Stylish Berliners and politicians love this large 1920s-style bistro, where the daily changing menu features "new-German" seasonal and regional dishes.

🔢 217 D2 ✉ Französische Strasse 47 ☎ 030 8188 6262; www.borchardt-restaurant.de Ⓤ U-Bahn Französische Strasse 🚌 47 AX, MC, VI

Cookies Cream $$$

This stylish vegetarian restaurant is artfully concealed in an alleyway behind Unter den Linden. Chef Stephan Hentschel creates healthy alternatives to the mainly meat-based cuisine of Germany.

🔢 217 D3 ✉ Behrenstrasse 55 ☎ 030 2749 2940; www. cookiescream.com Ⓧ Closed lunch Ⓤ U-Bahn Französische Strasse 🚌 100 AX, DC, MC, VI

Peter-Paul $–$$

If you want to sample a variety of German foods in one meal, the tapas-sized portions here fit the bill. The many choices include meatballs, rutabaga, cured pork and a typically local dish called *Sauerbraten* (braised beef in vinegar).

🔢 217 E3 ✉ Torstrasse 99 ☎ 030 4377 3043; www.peterpaul.berlin Ⓧ Closed lunch Ⓤ U-Bahn Rosenthaler Platz 🚌 142 MC, VI

Zum Nussbaum $

"The Nut Tree," a little gem of a tavern-cum-restaurant, in the partly restored medieval Nikolaiviertel area, serves up hearty helpings of traditional German fare.

🔢 217 E3 ✉ Am Nussbaum 3 ☎ 030 242 3095 Ⓤ U-Bahn Klosterstrasse 🚌 M48, 248 MC, VI

Price guide: (double room with breakfast for two people)
$ under €75
$$ €75–€150
$$$ over €150

Das Kleine Stapelhäuschen $–$$

This hotel comprises two adjacent town houses on a pretty cobbled plaza close to the Rhine. Rooms are basic and only standard rooms have en suite bathrooms. There is an on-site restaurant that serves regional cuisine.

🔢 225 C3 ✉ Fischmarkt 1–3 ☎ 0221 272 7777; www. kleines-stapelhaeuschen.de 🚌 Tram 1, 7, 9 MC, VI

Hotel im Kupferkessel $$

Just outside the city center, this family-run hotel in a town house from 1900, has neatly furnished rooms in a modern style. Room rates take it just out of budget level.

🔢 225 off map at A4 ✉ Probsteigasse 6 ☎ 0221 270 7960; www.im-kupferkessel.de Ⓤ U-Bahn to Christophstrasse, Mediapark 🚌 12, 15 MC, VI

Mondial am Dom $$–$$$

Situated between the cathedral and the river, this hotel is ideally placed for exploring the Old Town. There is a good restaurant on site.

🔢 225 B3 ✉ Kurt-Hackenberg-Platz 1 ☎ 0221 20630; www.accorhotels. com Ⓤ Dom/Hbf AX, DC, MC, VI

Viktoria $$

This early 20th-century Jugendstil building by the Rhine offers some rooms with river views and a generous breakfast buffet.

🔢 225 off map at C4 ✉ Worringer Strasse 23 ☎ 0221 973 1720; hotel viktoria.com Ⓤ Reichenspergerplatz AX, DC, MC, VI

Price guide: (dinner per person, excluding drinks)
$ under €15
$$ €15–€30
$$$ over €30

Bei Oma Kleinmann $$

Discover good old-fashioned German cooking at Granny Kleinmann's, well-known for its super-sized *schnitzel*. The restaurant is in a busy area and is popular with students.

🔢 225 off map at A1 ✉ Zülpicher Strasse 9 ☎ 0221 232 346; www. beiomakleinmann.de Ⓧ Closed Mon. 🚌 Tram 9 MC, VI

Brauhaus Sion $$–$$$

This busy side-street beer hall is popular for hearty German food and for strong *Kölsch* beer. Waiters sport traditional dress.

🔢 225 B3 ✉ Unter Taschenmacher 5–7 ☎ 0221 257 8540; www.brau haus-sion.de 🚌 Tram 1, 7, 9 MC, VI

Hase $$

Popular with locals and visitors alike, Hase is a central, bistro-style restaurant with a small, changing menu that utilizes fresh ingredients from local sources.

🔢 225 A3 ✉ Sankt-Apern-Strase

17 ☎ 0221 254375; www. hase-restaurant.de Ⓤ U-Bahn Appellhofplatz 🚌 Tram 3, 4, 5, 16, 18 MC, VI

Kintaro $$–$$$

Japanese dishes are served in this popular sushi restaurant, where entrées include seaweed *(hijiki)* and octopus, and cucumber and seaweed in vinegar *(tako su)*. Reserve ahead.

🔢 225 A3 ✉ Friesenstrasse 16 ☎ 0221 135 255; www.kintaro.de Ⓤ Friesenplatz AX, MC, VI

Price guide: (double room with breakfast for two people)
$ under €75
$$ €75–€150
$$$ over €150

Hotel Gästehaus Englischer Garten $$

This hotel, at the edge of the English Garden in Schwabing, is housed in a converted water mill. Breakfast is served in the garden in summer.

🔢 231 off map at D4 ✉ Liebergesellstrasse 8 ☎ 089 383 9410; www.hotelenglischergarten. de Ⓤ Münchner Freiheit AX, DC, MC, VI

Hotel am Viktualienmarkt $$

This small, family-owned hotel has a modern design and offers rooms with from one to four beds. It's a good value for its central location.

✉ 231 C2 ✉ Utzschneiderstrasse 14 ☎ 089 231 1090; www.hotel-am-viktualienmarkt.de 🚌 Tram 17, 18 AX, MC, VI

Mariandl $–$$

In a quiet zone between the city center and Theresienwiese, the Mariandl has elegantly furnished rooms, the Café am Beethovenplatz and its own gardens.

✉ 230 A1 ✉ Goethestrasse 51 ☎ 089 55 29 100; www.mariandl. com Ⓤ Sendlinger Tor 🚌 58 AX, DC, MC, VI

Torbräu $$$

There has been a hotel on this site by the old city gate since 1490. Today, its modern successor retains the hotel's reputation for traditional Bavarian hospitality.

✉ 231 C2 ✉ Tal 41 ☎ 089 24 23 40; www.torbraeu.de Ⓤ Marienplatz or Isartor AX, MC, VI

KEY TO SYMBOLS

✚	map page number and coordinates
⊠	address
☎	telephone number
⊘	days/times closed
Ⓜ	nearest subway station
🚌	nearest bus/trolley bus/tram/funicular route
⛴	ferry
$$$	expensive
$$	moderate
$	inexpensive
AX	American Express
DC	Diners Club
MC	MasterCard
VI	VISA

Water in Greece

It's important not to waste water in Greece, especially on the islands, where it often has to be shipped in by tankers. Although Athens' tap water is drinkable, bottled water is inexpensive and tastes better. Greeks are water connoisseurs, discussing the flavor and mineral properties of favorite spring varieties. Glasses of water are served alongside every drink you order in cafés: Drink it, or pour it in your ouzo and watch the clear spirit turn milky white. Since it's often hot in Greece and most places are not air-conditioned, it's important to drink plenty of water.

Price guide: (dinner per person, excluding drinks)

$	under €15
$$	€15–€30
$$$	over €30

Augustiner Grossgaststätten $–$$

Munich's oldest surviving brewery serves Bavarian dishes in the large beer hall, under the art nouveau glass dome of the Mussel Hall and in the arcaded courtyard.
⊠ 231 B2 ⊠ Neuhauser Strasse 27 ☎ 089 23 18 32 57; www.augustiner-restaurant.com Ⓜ Karlsplatz 🚌 Tram 16, 17, 18, 20, 27 AX, MC, VI

Halali $$$

Top quality regional cooking is offered here. Game dishes and mushrooms are seasonal specialties.
⊠ 231 C3 ⊠ Schönfeldstrasse 22 ☎ 089 28 59 09; www.restaurant-halali.de ⊘ Closed Sat. lunch, Sun. and holidays Ⓜ Odeonsplatz 🚌 100 AX, MC, VI

Ratskeller $$

Hearty local dishes are served in the Ratskeller tavern, situated in the New Town Hall's vaulted cellars.
⊠ 231 C2 ⊠ Marienplatz 8 ☎ 089 21 99 89-0; www.ratskeller.com Ⓜ Marienplatz AX, MC, VI

Spatenhaus an der Oper $$–$$$

The atmosphere is relaxed and the service good at this favored after-theater restaurant. The menu features Bavarian, regional and international dishes.
⊠ 231 C2 ⊠ Residenzstrasse 12 ☎ 089 290 7060; www.spatenhaus.de Ⓜ Marienplatz or Odeonsplatz; tram 19 AX, MC, VI

Price guide: (double room with breakfast for two people)

$	€50–€80
$$	€80–€140
$$$	over €140

Attalos Hotel $$

The Attalos is a comfortable hotel located halfway between Omónia and Monastiráki squares. The roof garden/bar has good views of the Acropolis, a 20-minute walk away.
✚ 244 B3 ⊠ 29 Athinas ☎ 210 321 2801-3; www.attaloshotel.com

Ⓜ Omónia or Monastiráki AX, DC, MC, VI

Grande Bretagne $$$

Athens' most historic, grandest and very traditional hotel offers a high level of service and amenities.
✚ 244 C2 ⊠ Syntagmatos ☎ 210 333 0000; www.grandebretagne.gr Ⓜ 1, 18, 15 AX, DC, MC, VI

Pallas Athena $$$

This fun boutique hotel oozes chic style and has several light and airy loft suites. Some rooms are decorated by local artists.
✚ 244 C3 ⊠ 65 Athinas ☎ 210 325 0900; www.grecotel pallasathena.com Ⓜ Omónia AX, DC, MC, VI

Phaedra $–$$

A location at the quieter end of Pláka makes up for one or two fairly small rooms at this pleasant hotel.
✚ 244 C2 ⊠ Cherefontos 16 & Adrianou ☎ 210 323 8461; www.hotelphaedra.com Ⓜ Akrópoli 🚌 9, 11, 15 AX, DC, VI

Saint George Lycabettus $$$

Beautifully situated on the quiet, shady slopes of Lycabettus Hill, this first-class hotel offers lovely views from its rooftop restaurant. Rooms have good, modern facilities.
✚ 244 D3 ⊠ 2 Kleomenous-Dexamini ☎ 210 729 0711; www.sglycabettus.gr 🚌 3, 8, 13 AX, DC, MC, VI

Price guide: (dinner per person, excluding drinks)

$	€10–€20
$$	€20–€40
$$$	over €40

O Platanos $

This friendly Pláka taverna serves simple and delicious food at both indoor and outdoor tables.
✚ 244 B2 ⊠ 4 Diogenous, Pláka ☎ 210 322 0666; http://eleinitsa.wixsite.com/platanos 🚌 1, 9, 11, 18 No credit cards

Psaras $$

Tucked below the Acropolis on one of Pláka's prettiest streets is its oldest taverna, serving home-cooked traditional dishes.
✚ 244 B2 ⊠ 16 Erekteos and Erotokritou Pláka ☎ 210 321 8733;

www.psaras-taverna.gr 🅖 Thission
🅔 1, 9, 11, 18 AX, DC, MC, VI

Saita $

This basement restaurant in the Pláka
has good food and friendly service.
(The sidewalk tables close to the door
belong to another restaurant.)
🚼 244 B2 ✉ 21 Kidathineon
☎ 210 322 6671 🅔 1, 5, 9, 18
No credit cards

Spondi $$$

To enjoy state-of-the-art Greek
cooking, eat at the 2-Michelin star
Spondi and sample their "Discovery"
tasting menu. Dining out gets no
better than this.
🚼 244 B3 ✉ 5 Pyrronos ☎ 210
756 4021; www.spondi.gr 🅖 Agios
Ioannis AX, DC, MC, VI

Tudor Hall $$$

With superb views across to the
Acropolis, Tudor Hall's location is
matched by the stellar food here.
🚼 244 D2 ✉ Hotel King George, 1
Vasileos Georgiou A ☎ 210 322 2210;
www.tudorhall.gr 🅖 Syntagma
AX, DC, MC, VI

BUDAPEST HOTELS

Price guide: (double room with
breakfast for two people)
$ under Ft25,000
$$ Ft25,000–Ft60,000
$$$ over Ft60,000

Four Seasons Hotel Gresham Palace $$$

Near the eastern end of Széchenyi
bridge, this majestic hotel offers
every comfort, including luxurious
suites and a spa and health center.
🚼 258 B2 ✉ Széchenyi István tér 5
☎ 1 7688 6000; www.fourseasons.
com/budapest/ 🅖 Vörösmarty tér
AX, DC, MC, VI

Hotel Palazzo Zichy $$$

Set in the trendy Palace Quarter, this
boutique hotel offers modern comfort
in a 19th-century setting within easy
walking distance of shops and the
National Museum. A good buffet
breakfast is included.
🚼 258 D2 ✉ Lőrinc pap tér 2
☎ 1 235 4000; www.hpz.hu
🅖 Rákóczi tér AX, MC, VI

Kempinski Hotel Corvinus Budapest $$$

Among its many sumptuous rooms,
this luxury hotel includes a lavish
royal suite. It's popular with business

travelers and has a good fitness
center and pool.
🚼 258 C2 ✉ Erzsébet tér 7–8
☎ 1 429 3777; www.kempinski.com
🅖 Deák tér AX, DC, MC, VI

St. George Residence $$

This characterful and historic
older-style hotel is immaculately
maintained and run by attentive
staff. The spacious rooms include
kitchenettes.
🚼 258 A3 ✉ Fortuna utca 4
☎ 393 5700; www.stgeorgehotel.hu
🅖 Szell Kálmán tér, then 🅔 16, 16A
No credit cards; cash only

BUDAPEST RESTAURANTS

Price guide: (dinner per person,
excluding drinks)
$ under Ft5,000
$$ Ft5,000–Ft10,000
$$$ over Ft10,000

Alabárdos $$$

This stylish, formal restaurant serves
Hungarian dishes in ancient vaulted
dining rooms. Presentations are
beautiful and the staff attentive.
There are only a few tables, so it's
always best to reserve in advance.
🚼 258 A3 ✉ Országház utca 2
☎ 1 356 0851; www.alabardos.hu
🅧 Closed Sun.; lunch Mon.–Fri.
🅖 Szell Kálmán tér, then Várbusz
(Castle Bus) AX, DC, MC, VI

Café Kor $–$$

Daily changing specials, including
authentic Hungarian dishes, and the
bustling atmosphere make it a good
place to stop. Its location near to St.
Stephen's Basilica adds to its appeal.
🚼 258 B3 ✉ Sas utcá 17 ☎ 1 311
0053; no website 🅧 Closed Sun.
🅗 Arany Janos utca AX, MC, VI

Costes $$$

Costes is consistently one of the top
venues for fine dining in Budapest,
with highest standards of attention
to detail paid at all levels. Its good
reputation means that advance
booking is essential. A sister
restaurant, Costes Downtown, is
located in the Prestige Hotel near
the Széchenyi bridge.
🚼 258 C1 ✉ Ráday utcá 4
☎ 1 219 0696; www.costes.hu
🅧 Closed Mon.–Tue. 🅖 Kálvin tér
AX, DC, MC, VI

Művész Kávéház $

This coffeehouse, standing opposite
the Opera House, has retained the

ambience of Budapest's golden
era of café society. The dark wood
interior and gilt candelabras evoke
the sense of grandeur and charm
that belonged to a bygone age.
🚼 258 C3 ✉ Andrássy út 29
☎ 1 343 3544; www.muveszkavehaz.
hu 🅖 Opera MC, VI

Panoráma $$

In the art nouveau Danubius Hotel
Gellért, this restaurant, sited over a
thermal spring, has fine river views.
Pike, perch and veal are specialties.
A band plays Hungarian music in the
evenings, and there's a brasserie for
less formal dining.
🚼 258 C1 ✉ Szent Gellért tér 2
☎ 1 889 5500; www.danubius
hotels.com 🅧 Closed Tue.–Sat.
lunch and Sun. dinner 🅖 Szent
Gellért tér AX, DC, MC, VI

DUBLIN HOTELS

Price guide: (double room with
breakfast for two people)
$ under €100
$$ €100–€180
$$$ over €180

Ashling Hotel $$$

Located on the banks of the River
Liffey, this stylish contemporary
hotel is west of the center, close
to Phoenix Park. There's a good
restaurant and spacious family
rooms, plus great transportation
links to the city center.
🚼 274 off map at A3 ✉ Parkgate
Street ☎ 01 677 2324; www.
ashlinghotel.ie 🅖 LUAS Museum or
Houston AX, MC, VI

The Clarence $$–$$$

This is a tasteful hotel in the heart of
the city overlooking the River Liffey,
and it has a great restaurant, Cleaver
East. The two-bedroom penthouse
is especially chic, and even has a
grand piano.
🚼 274 B3 ✉ 6–8 Wellington Quay
☎ 01 407 0800; www.theclarence.ie
AX, DC, MC, VI

Camden Court Hotel $$

This inexpensive, modern hotel in
the city center has contemporary
features, plus attractive extras
including a small indoor pool, gym
and Jacuzzi. The Aircoach stops
outside the hotel.
🚼 274 B1 ✉ Camden St, Dublin 2
☎ 01 475 9666; www.
camdencourthotel.com 🅖 Harcourt
Street MC, VI

KEY TO SYMBOLS

- map page number and coordinates
- ✉ address
- ☎ telephone number
- ⊘ days/times closed
- Ⓜ nearest subway station
- 🚌 nearest bus/trolley bus/tram/funicular route
- ⛴ ferry
- $$$ expensive
- $$ moderate
- $ inexpensive
- AX American Express
- DC Diners Club
- MC MasterCard
- VI VISA

Bread, Cakes and Cookies

In Italy, bread comes from a *panificio* or *forno*, cakes and cookies from a *pasticceria*. In Tuscany there is no salt in bread, a legacy of an age when baking was done once a week and saltless bread didn't get moldy. Once you're accustomed to it, it goes well with the strong, salty flavors of prosciutto or salami. Italian cakes are outstanding: luscious creations piled with fruit, filled with cream, oozing chocolate and soaked with liqueur. Italians often buy a large cake or selection of smaller ones to eat for Sunday dessert, or a piece of *panforte*, a traditional spiced fruit confection from Siena. It's acceptable to buy a single pastry or cake and eat it on the spot in the shop.

The Schoolhouse Hotel
$$–$$$

A former schoolhouse has been converted into this comfortable boutique hotel with spacious rooms in a leafy neighborhood, close to the Aviva Stadium. There's also a restaurant and a pub on-site.

 274 off map at C2 ✉ 2–8 Northumberland Road ☎ 01 667 5014; www.schoolhousehotel.com Ⓜ DART Pearse Station. The Aircoach 702 stops outside AX, DC, MC, VI

The Shelbourne $$$

A Dublin institution, this elegant hotel offers the highest standard of comfort. Bedrooms are first-class, some with views over St. Stephen's Green, and facilities include a spa, leisure suite and fine dining. The afternoon tea here is legendary.

 274 C2 ✉ 27 St. Stephen's Green ☎ 01 663 4500; www.marriot.com Ⓜ DART Pearse Station; LUAS St. Stephen's Green AX, MC, VI

Price guide: (dinner per person, excluding drinks)

$ €15–€30
$$ €30–€45
$$$ over €45

Chapter One $$$

This chic restaurant located in the basement of the Dublin Writers Museum serves fine Irish cuisine with an international influence. The pretheater menu is a good value.

 274 B4 ✉ 18–19 Parnell Square ☎ 01 873 2266; www.chapterone restaurant.com ⊘ Closed Sun.–Mon. and Sat. lunch Ⓜ Parnell AX, MC, VI

Gallagher's Boxty House $–$$

This is a great place to sample authentic Irish cuisine. Choose from a selection of mains that include traditional Irish potato boxty pancake and beef stew, and finish with a dessert such as Baileys cheesecake.

 274 B3 ✉ 20–21 Temple Bar ☎ 01 677 2762; www.boxtyhouse.ie 🚌 All city-center buses MC, VI

Restaurant Patrick Guilbaud $$$

French cuisine of the highest standard makes this Ireland's premier fine-dining venue. The styling and the menu are modern. Advance booking is recommended.

 274 C2 ✉ 21 Upper Merrion Street ☎ 01 676 4192; www.restaurantpatrickguilbaud.ie ⊘ Closed Sun.–Mon. Ⓜ DART Pearse Station; LUAS St. Stephen's Green AX, DC, MC, VI

The Winding Stair $–$$

Top-quality Irish fare is the promise in this simple restaurant above the bookshop of the same name, overlooking the River Liffey and the Ha'penny Bridge. Menus include local seafood options, charcuterie and cheeses. Its sister restaurant, The Woollen Mills, is next door.

 274 B3 ✉ 40 Ormond Quay Lower ☎ 01 872 7320; www.winding-stair.com 🚌 37, 39, 39A, 70 MC, VI

Price guide: (double room with breakfast for two people)

$ under €125
$$ €125–€250
$$$ over €250

Campo de Fiori $–$$

You'll find comfortable rooms and a pleasant roof garden at this pretty and moderately priced hotel. It is near one of Rome's liveliest squares.

 292 C2 ✉ Via del Biscione 6 ☎ 06 687 4886; www.hotelcampo defiori.com 🚌 40, 46, 62, 64, 116, 190, 571, 916 AX, DC, VI

Hotel Indigo Rome St. George $$–$$$

Bang in the upscale heart of the *centro storico*, this boutique hotel combines style and comfort with more than a nod to its Renaissance surroundings. Great rooms, buffet breakfasts, library, bar, roof terrace, spa and one of the area's best restaurants all combine to make this a wonderful place to stay.

 292 B2 ✉ Via Giulia 62 ☎ 06 686 611; www.hotelindigorome.com 🚌 30, 56, 60 AX, DC, MC, VI

Hotel NH Vittorio Veneto $$$

Sleek modern comfort is the hallmark of this big hotel, situated near the Borghese gardens. Some rooms are bigger than others; specify when you book. Breakfast is buffet style and there is a good restaurant.

 293 D4 ✉ Corso d'Italia 1 ☎ 06 84591 (within Italy); www.nh-hotels.com/hotel/nh-collection-roma-vittorio-veneto Ⓜ Barberini 🚌 52, 53, 116 AX, DC, MC, VI

Hotel Panda $–$$

Close to upscale Piazza di Spagna, the Panda offers excellent value accommodations. Rooms may be oddly shaped in some cases, but they're clean and bright. Breakfast is not included in the price.

🎯 294 C3 ✉ Via della Croce 35 ☎ 06 678 0179; www.hotelpanda.it 🚇 Spagna 🚌 116, 117, 119, 590 AX, DC, MC

Piazza di Spagna $$

Just a few minutes' stroll from the Spanish Steps, the rooms here are light and airy with good bathrooms, and the staff are exceptionally helpful. There's also a small terrace.

🎯 292 C3 ✉ Via Mario de' Fiori 61 ☎ 06 679 3061; www. hotelpiazzadispagnarome.com 🚇 Spagna 🚌 117 AX, DC, MC, VI

ROME RESTAURANTS

Price guide: (dinner per person, excluding drinks)

$	under €30
$$	€30–€55
$$$	over €55

L'Arcangelo 1887 $$$

Wood paneling, old photographs and leather banquettes all add to the charm of this restaurant. The excellent menu features dishes that display a new twist on old favorites.

🎯 292 C3 ✉ Via Giuseppe Gioacchino Belli 59 ☎ 06 321 0992; www.larcangelo.com 🚇 Lepanto 🚌 30, 49, 70, 87, 130, 224, 990 AX, DC, MC, VI

De Armando al Pantheon $$

Come here to sample traditional Roman cooking. The menu features classics such as *zuppa di farro* (spelt soup) and *saltimbocca* (veal with bacon and sage). Vegetarian dishes also are available.

🎯 292 C2–C3 ✉ Salita de' Crescenzi 31 ☎ 06 6880 3034; www. armandoalpantheon.it 🕐 Closed Sat. p.m. and Sun. 🚇 Vittorio Emanuele 🚌 64, 70, 81, 119 and all services to city center AX, MC, V

Da Baffetto $$

For the best pizza in town, stand in line to get a table at this tiny pizzeria. It stays open until 1 a.m.

🎯 292 B3–C3 ✉ Via del Governo Vecchio 114 ☎ 06 686 1617; www. pizzeriabaffetto.it 🚌 30, 70, 81, 87, 116, 130, 186, 492, 628 No credit cards

Fa-Bìo $

This is the perfect place to grab a healthy and delicious lunch on the go. Organic ingredients are used in the seasonal sandwiches, wraps, soups, salads and juices.

🎯 292 B3 ✉ Via Germanico 43 ☎ 06 6452 5810; www.fa-bio.com 🚇 Ottaviano-San Pietro 🚌 232, 32, 49, 492, 990 No credit cards

FLORENCE HOTELS

Price guide: (double room with breakfast for two people)

$	under €125
$$	€125–€250
$$$	over €250

Antica Dimora Firenze $–$$

Just 10 minutes' walk from San Marco, this upscale *residenza* (bed-and-breakfast) is wonderfully comfortable with individually styled rooms. Breakfasts are delicious, and there's free tea and coffee on offer all day, and an honesty bar.

🎯 302 off map at D4 ✉ Via San Gallo 72 ☎ 055 462 7296; www. antichedimorefiorentine.it 🚌 7, 10, 11, 25, 32 AX, DC, MC

Brunelleschi $$–$$$

Reserve in advance to stay in this hotel, with tastefully decorated rooms situated around a medieval tower in the heart of Florence.

🎯 302 C3 ✉ Piazza Santa Elisabetta 3 ☎ 055 27370; www.hotelbrunel leschi.it 🚶 In the pedestrian zone. C2, C3 AX, DC, MC, VI

Casci $

This excellent mid-range hotel is just two minutes from the Duomo. The charming owners keep clean, well-appointed rooms.

🎯 302 B4 ✉ Via Cavour 13 ☎ 055 211686; www.hotelcasci.com 🕐 Closed 2 weeks in Jan. 🚌 10,11, 25, 31, 82, C1 AX, DC, MC, VI

Hotel La Scaletta $$–$$$

A 15th-century palazzo is home to this stylish hotel in the Oltrarno area of Florence. Modern design and light colors contrast with many beautiful and classic architectural details, and there are excellent bathrooms. A real bonus is the fabulous roof terrace, with its superb views of the peaceful Boboli gardens.

🎯 303 B1 ✉ Via Guicciardini 13 ☎ 055 283 028; www.hotellascaletta. it 🚌 B, C, D, 11 AX, DC, MC, VI

Loggiato dei Serviti $$–$$$

This beautiful hotel, housed in a 16th-century building, is set on one of Florence's loveliest squares a short stroll from the Duomo. Inside, corridors and public areas have kept the original architectural features and are furnished with Tuscan antiques; bedrooms are traditionally styled, with every modern comfort. There's a lovely vaulted breakfast room and the cozy bar is a great place for a drink.

🎯 303 D4 ✉ Piazza della Santissima Annunziata 3 ☎ 055 289592; www.loggiatodeiservitihotel. it 🚌 1, 7, 20, C1 AX, DC, MC, VI

FLORENCE RESTAURANTS

Price guide: (dinner per person, excluding drinks)

$	under €30
$$	€30–€55
$$$	over €55

Buca Mario $$

Founded in 1886, this is a truly traditional *buca*, the word used in Florence to describe restaurants tucked away in low-ceilinged ground-floor rooms. Desserts are all homemade and the wine list includes a good choice of reds.

🎯 302 B3 ✉ Piazza degli Ottaviani 16r ☎ 055 214179; www.bucamario. com 🚌 4, 22, 36, 37, C2 MC, VI

'Ino $

Open from morning to late afternoon, this is a fun and buzzing gourmet *paninoteca* (sandwich bar). It offers imaginative *panini* and an ever-changing wine list.

🎯 302 C2 ✉ Via Accademia dei Georgofili 3r/7r ☎ 055 214 154; www.inofirenze.com 🚌 A, B No credit cards

La Martinicca $–$$

Locals and tourists alike love this restaurant near Santa Maria Novella. Classic Tuscan dishes head up the menu including *bruschetta* (toasted country bread with different toppings) or ravioli stuffed with ricotta and spinach.

🎯 302 B3 ✉ Via del Sole 27/r ☎ 055 218928; www.ristorante-lamartinicca.com 🕐 Closed Sun. 🚌 6, 11, 22, C2 No credit cards

Rosticceria La Spada $

This is an old-style Florentine *rosticceria* where you can eat in or take out. Everything is freshly prepared, with the accent on grilled

KEY TO SYMBOLS

🔢 map page number and
coordinates
✉ address
☎ telephone number
⊘ days/times closed
Ⓜ nearest subway station
🚌 nearest bus/trolley bus/
tram/funicular route
⛴ ferry
$$$ expensive
$$ moderate
$ inexpensive
AX American Express
DC Diners Club
MC MasterCard
VI VISA

---

meat, fresh pasta dishes, grilled
vegetables and tasty *crostini*.
🔢 302 B3 ✉ Via della Spada 62r
☎ 055 218757; www.laspadaitalia.
com 🚌 C1, C2 No credit cards

Trattoria da Ruggero $–$$

Food and old-fashioned ambience
don't come more Tuscan than here,
where you can sample specialties
such as *pappa al pomodoro* (tomato
and bread soup), *ribollito* (twice
cooked vegetable soup), *bollito misto*
(mixed boiled meat with green sauce)
and fantastic steaks and grills.
🔢 302 off map at A1 ✉ Via Senese
89r ☎ 055 220 542 ⊘ Closed
Tue.–Wed. 🚌 36, 37 No credit cards

Trattoria del Carmine $$

This local favorite serves authentic,
good-value food. Tuscan specialties
are offered, and dishes change with
the seasons. There's a good wine
list to choose from as well as
straightforward house wines by
the glass or carafe.
🔢 302 A2 ✉ Piazza del Carmine 18r
☎ 055 218 601; no website 🚌 C3,
11, 6 AX, MC, VI

NAPLES HOTELS

Price guide: (double room with
breakfast for two people)
$ under €125
$$ €125–€250
$$$ over €250

Hotel Cimarosa $–$$

Located in central Vomero, Naples'
most stylish area, Hotel Cimarosa
has elegant rooms and bathrooms.
Public areas are spacious and there's
a good breakfast.
🔢 309 off map at A3 ✉ Via
Domenico Cimarosa 29 ☎ 081 556
7044; www.hotelcimarosa.it
Ⓜ Vanvitelli; funiculars Montesanto
to via Morghen, Centrale to piazzetta
Fuga, Chiaia to via Cimarosa 🚌 C28,
C31, C32 AX, DC, MC, VI

Hotel Piazza Bellini $$

A 16th-century building with a lovely
courtyard has had a 21st-century
update, resulting in a hotel that's
both individual and modern. Helpful
staff, quiet rooms and a great
location add to its appeal. Free WiFi
and excellent buffet breakfast.
🔢 309 B3 ✉ Via Santa Maria di
Constantinopoli 101 ☎ 081 451732;
www.hotelpiazzabellini.com
Ⓜ Dante 🚌 1, 4, 151, 154, C25
AX, MC, VI

Micalò $–$$

Wood, glass and travertine marble
are the key design notes at this calm
oasis in classy Chiaia, a 10-minute
walk from both sights and beaches.
Expect understated elegance, linen
sheets and delicious breakfasts.
🔢 309 A2 ✉ Riviera di Chiaia 88
☎ 081 7617 131; www.micalo.it
🚌 R3 and all buses to Mergellina
AX, DC, MC, VI

Miramare $$$

Housed in an art nouveau building
near the Castel dell'Ovo, the
Miramare offers beautifully furnished
rooms and elegant public areas.
However, the chief draw here is the
terrace, where you can eat breakfast
while gazing over the Bay of Naples.
🔢 309 B1–B2 ✉ Via Nazario
Sauro 24 ☎ 081 764 7589;
www.hotelmiramare.com 🚌 128,
154, C25, E6 AX, DC, MC, VI

NAPLES RESTAURANTS

Price guide: (dinner per person,
excluding drinks)
$ under €30
$$ €30–€55
$$$ over €55

Al 53 $$

Naples' oldest restaurant, complete
with 17th-century furnishings and
original mosaic floor, serves great
appetizers, seafood pasta and
delicious Neapolitan desserts.
🔢 309 B3 ✉ Piazza Dante
Alighieri 53 ☎ 081 549 9372
Ⓜ Dante 🚌 139, 168, 201, E1, R4,
DC, MC, VI

Cantina del Gallo $–$$

This classic Neapolitan *osteria-
pizzeria* has been pleasing the locals
since 1898, serving classic southern
dishes made with first-rate local
ingredients and thin, crispy *pizze*.
🔢 309 A4 ✉ Via Alessandro
Telesina 21 ☎ 09081 544 1521;
www.cantinadelgallo.com
Ⓜ Materdei 🚌 C53, C63, R4
AX, MC

Da Michele $

The fifth generation of the Condurro
family craft, and what many consider
to be Naples' finest *pizze*. Choose
only between a *margherita* with
cheese and *marinara* without, cooked
in a traditional wood-fired oven.
🔢 309 C3 ✉ Via Cesare Sersale 1/3
☎ 081 553 9204; www.damichele.net
🚌 202, E2, R2 No credit cards

Plan Ahead for Venice

To enjoy a stress-free visit
in Venice it is absolutely
necessary to make hotel
reservations ahead of time.
Reservations for June to
September should be made
during the previous fall, as
should those for the two
weeks in February in which
Carnival falls (although you
may be able to get
something closer to the
time of your visit if you hunt
around). Three months
ahead should be enough
time for other months. If
you would like to eat at a
specific restaurant it's also
advisable to make
reservations; your hotel
concierge will be happy to
call and set them up.

Osteria da Tonino $–$$

Usually full of Italians, this buzzing restaurant has been crowd pleasing since 1880. Food is classic Neapolitan, so expect wonderful specialties such as lentils with pasta, and local fish, fresh off the boats.
⊞ 309 A2 ⊠ Via Santa Teresa e Chiaia 47 ☎ 081 421533; no website ⊚ Amadeo ▤ C24, C25, C26, C27 No credit cards

VENICE HOTELS

Price guide: (double room with breakfast for two people)
$ under €150
$$ €150–€250
$$$ over €250

Hotel Canada $

This excellent budget choice is a comfortable place to stay, with friendly staff and free WiFi throughout. Breakfast is served in an airy upstairs room. Some of the bedrooms have canal views.
⊞ 314 D3 ⊠ Campo San Lio, Castello 5659 ☎ 041 522 9912; www.canadavenice.com ▤ Vaporetto Rialto   AX, MC, VI

Locanda ai Santi Apostoli $–$$

Two of the 12 rooms in this good-value palazzo-hotel overlook the Grand Canal. There's a spacious bar area and a private landing stage.
⊞ 314 C3 ⊠ Campo Santi Apostoli, Cannaregio 4391/A ☎ 041 241 1652; www.locandasantiapostoli.com ▤ Vaporetto Ca d'Oro   DC, MC, VI

Oltre il Giardino $$

This small hotel combines tranquility and elegance. Rooms are a good size and decorated with light tones. The welcome here is warm and there are little extra comforts at every turn.
⊞ 314 B3 ⊠ Fondamenta Contarini, San Polo 2542 ☎ 041 275 0015; www.oltreilgiardino-venezia. com ▤ Vaporetto San Tomà   AX, DC, MC, VI

Palazzo Stern $$–$$$

Palazzo Stern is one of the prettiest Grand Canal *palazzi* in Venice. Outside, the breakfast terrace is set right on the water. Rooms are furnished in Venetian style, and there's a fun rooftop Jacuzzi.
⊞ 314 B2 ⊠ Calle del Traghetto, Dorsoduro 2792/A ☎ 041 277 0869; www.palazzostern.it ▤ Vaporetto 1 to Ca' Rezzonico   AX, DC, MC, VI

VENICE RESTAURANTS

Price guide: (dinner per person, excluding drinks)
$ under €30
$$ €30–€55
$$$ over €55

All'Anfora $

Tucked away behind the Grand Canal, this friendly pizzeria offers a huge range of super sized, imaginative and good value *pizze*. Service is efficient and the décor is clean and basic. There's always a lively atmosphere, and tables spill onto the street and into the pretty courtyard in summer.
⊞ 314 B4 ⊠ Lista Vecchia de Bari, San Polo 1223 ☎ 041 524 0325; www.pizzeriaallanfora.com ▤ Vaporetto San Biagio DC, MC

Alla Palanca $–$$

Across the wide Giudecca canal lies the Palanca, a neighborhood bar and restaurant, run by friendly staff who are passionate about food, drink and their restaurant. Prices are a steal considering the quality.
⊞ 314 B1 ⊠ Fondamenta Ponte Piccolo, Giudecca 428 ☎ 041 528 7719 ▤ Vaporetto Palanca AX, MC, VI

Antiche Carampane $$$

This off-the-beaten-track restaurant specializes in elegantly cooked and served seafood and fish. The style is a modern take on tradition, with dishes such as *spaghetti alla granseola* (pasta with spider crab) or *branzino in salsa di peperoni* (sea bass in a sweet pepper sauce).
⊞ 314 C3 ⊠ Ponte delle Tette, San Polo 1911 ☎ 041 524 0165; www.antichecarampane.com ⊙ Closed Sun. and Mon. lunch ▤ 1, 2   AX, DC, MC, VI

Bancogiro $–$$

Housed in a 16th-century building by the Rialto market, the Bancogiro is a well-run restaurant that doubles as a bar serving *ciccheti*, typical Venetian snacks. The brick-vaulted interior is understated and elegant, while the outside tables make it one of Venice's best alfresco dining spots.
⊞ 314 C3 ⊠ Campo San Giacometto, San Polo 122 ☎ 041 523 2061; www.osteriabancogiro.it ⊙ Closed Mon. ▤ 1, 2   AX, DC, MC, VI

LUXEMBOURG HOTELS

Price guide: (double room with breakfast for two people)
$ under €120
$$ €120–€180
$$$ over €180

Français $$

Ideal for strolling to the Old Town, this hotel is at the heart of the city and has its own restaurant, with a terrace on the central square.
⊞ 329 B3 ⊠ 14 place d'Armes ☎ 47 45 34; www.hotelfrancais.lu ▤ All city-center buses   AX, DC, MC, VI

Grand Hotel Cravat $$$

Aimed at both tourists and business travelers, this 60-room, family-run hotel has good-size bedrooms and excellent public rooms. It's within an easy walk of the top sights and there is a bar and restaurant.
⊞ 329 B3 ⊠ 29 boulevard Roosevelt ☎ 22 19 75; www.hotelcravat.lu ▤ All city-center buses   AX, DC, MC, VI

Hotel Vauban $$

Location is a big selling point for this hotel, right in the heart of town. Rooms are simple and modern; some overlook the central square. Staff are helpful and friendly. Excellent value for money though some rooms are small and there can be late-evening noise from outside. Free WiFi.
⊞ 329 B3 ⊠ 10 place Guillaume II ☎ 22 04 93; www.hotelvauban.lu ▤ All city-center buses   AX, DC, MC, VI

Le Place d'Armes $$$

Beautifully set on one of the old city's most iconic squares, this hotel marries traditional comfort with 21st-century style. It also has a choice of bars and restaurants.
⊞ 329 B3–B4 ⊠ 18 Place d'Armes ☎ 27 47 37; www.hotel-leplace darmes.com ▤ All city-center buses AX, MC, VI

LUXEMBOURG RESTAURANTS

Price guide: (dinner per person, excluding drinks)
$ under €35
$$ €35–€50
$$$ over €50

Am Tiirmschen $$$

Luxembourg specialties and classics feature on the menu here, such as boiled meats served with mustard

KEY TO SYMBOLS

⊞	map page number and coordinates
⊠	address
☎	telephone number
⊙	days/times closed
Ⓜ	nearest subway station
▤	nearest bus/trolley bus/ tram/funicular route
⛴	ferry
$$$	expensive
$$	moderate
$	inexpensive
AX	American Express
DC	Diners Club
MC	MasterCard
VI	VISA

---

sauce. The charming restaurant has open stonework and flagged flooring.
⊞ 329 B3 ⊠ 32 rue de l'Eau ☎ 26 27 07 33; www.amtiirmschen.lu ⊙ Closed Sun. and public holidays, Mon. and Sat. lunch ▤ All city-center buses AX, DC, MC, VI

Clairefontaine $$$

Come here for high-end dining in the heart of the government district. There's a five-course gourmet menu – dishes might include black truffle ice-cream. Dress smartly.
⊞ 329 B3 ⊠ 19 place Clairefontaine ☎ 46 22 11 30; www.restaurantclairefontaine.lu ⊙ Closed Sat., Sun. ▤ All city-center buses MC, VI

La Cristallerie $$$

This Michelin-starred restaurant offers dishes such as Japanese Kobé beef. There are various set menus, some of which can be served vegan.
⊞ 329 B3–B4 ⊠ 18 Place d'Armes ☎ 27 47 37 421; www.la-cristallerie.com ⊙ Closed Sun., Mon. and Sat. lunch ▤ City-center buses AX, MC, VI

La Lorraine $$$

Located on place d'Armes, this bright, attractive restaurant offers French cuisine with excellent fish dishes. You can choose your lobster from a tank by the door.
⊞ 329 B3 ⊠ 7 place d'Armes ☎ 47 14 36 ▤ All city-center buses AX, MC, VI

AMSTERDAM HOTELS

Price guide: (double room with breakfast for two people)

$	€75–€150
$$	€150–€300
$$$	over €300

Ambassade Hotel $$

On the splendid Herengracht, the city's most elegant canal, this beautifully furnished hotel offers comfortable rooms and a very good breakfast.
⊞ 342 B2 ⊠ Herengracht 341 ☎ 020 555 0222; www.ambassade-hotel.nl ▤ Tram 1, 2, 5 AX, DC, MC, VI

Amstel Botel $$

Moored in Amsterdam's redeveloped waterfront, this floating hotel has interesting rooms with harbor views.
⊞ 342 off map at B4 ⊠ NDSM Pier 3 ☎ 020 626 4247; www.amstel

botel.nl ⛴ NDSM ferry from Centraal Station AX, DC, MC, VI

Hotel de L'Europe $$$

The private boat landing at this expensive luxury hotel on the Amstel river says it all. It has a fine Victorian exterior, and inside it has been renovated to offer every modern amenity. The finest *haute cuisine* and wine list can be found at the hotel's Bord'Eau restaurant.
⊞ 342 C2 ⊠ Nieuwe Doelenstraat 2–4 ☎ 020 531 1777; www.leurope.nl ▤ Tram 4, 9, 14, 16, 24, 25 AX, MC, VI

Nova Hotel $$

This family-run hotel has a central location but is sheltered from street noise. The en-suite rooms are spotless and the service is friendly.
⊞ 342 C3 ⊠ Nieuwezijds Voorburgwal 276 ☎ 020 623 0066; www.novahotel.nl ▤ Tram 1, 2, 5 AX, DC, MC, VI

Singel Hotel $$

A short walk from Centraal Station along the Singel canal, this 32-room hotel occupies three converted canalside houses. It has an historic feel but modern amenities.
⊞ 342 C2 ⊠ Singel 13–17 ☎ 020 626 3108; www.singelhotel.nl Ⓜ Amsterdam Centraal ▤ Tram 1, 2, 5, 13, 17 AX, DC, MC, VI

AMSTERDAM RESTAURANTS

Price guide: (dinner per person, excluding drinks)

$	€10–€20
$$	€20–€30
$$$	over €30

t'Blauwe Theehuis $

If you're in the Vondelpark then a visit to this 1937 café in a circular building is a must. Drinks and meals are served as well as simple sandwiches and snacks.
⊞ 342 A1 ⊠ Vondelpark ☎ 020 662 0254; www.blauwetheehuis.nl ▤ Tram 1, 2, 3, 5, 12 MC, VI

In de Waag $–$$

Come to this friendly restaurant for late-night Continental cuisine, when it is atmospherically lit by hundreds of candles. The generous three-course lunch and early evening menu offer good value.
⊞ 342 C3 ⊠ Nieuwmarkt 4 ☎ 020 422 7772; www.indewaag.nl Ⓜ Nieuwmarkt AX, DC, MC, VI

De Silveren Spiegel $$$

This chic restaurant offers fine dining in a restored 17th-century redbrick building. A highlight is the five- to seven-course tasting menu.
342 C4 Kattengat 4–6 020 624 6589; www.desilverenspiegel.com Closed lunch and Sun. Centraal Station Tram 1, 2, 5, 13, 17 AX, DC, MC, VI

Toscanini $$–$$$

This stylish Jordaan district restaurant with an open kitchen features excellent Italian food and wines.
342 B4 Lindengracht 75 020 623 2813; www.restauranttoscanini.nl Closed lunch and Sun. Tram 3, 10 AX, DC, MC, VI

d'Vijff Vlieghen $$$

The name translates as The Five Flies, for the five canalside houses that contain nine dining rooms serving traditional Dutch fare but with contemporary flair.
342 B2 Spuistraat 294–302 020 530 4060; www.vijffvlieghen.nl Closed lunch Tram 1, 2, 5 AX, MC, VI

THE HAGUE HOTELS

Price guide: (double room with breakfast for two people)

$	€75–€150
$$	€150–€300
$$$	over €300

Best Western Delft Museumhotel $$

While in Delft, spend at least one night in this tastefully furnished hotel overlooking a tranquil canal.
350 off map at B2 Oude Delft 189 015 215 3070; www.museumhotels.nl Delft Centraal Station Tram 1 AX, DC, MC, VI

Carlton Ambassador Hotel $$–$$$

This luxury hotel in a tree-lined and elegant neighborhood is within easy walking distance of the city center, shops and restaurants.
350 B2 Sophialaan 2 070 363 0363; www.carlton.nl 4, 5, 22, 24; tram 1, 17 AX, DC, MC, VI

Grand Hotel Amrath Kurhaus $$$

If you are in Scheveningen and want a hotel with a sun lounge and terrace overlooking the beach, consider this Old European-style hotel, built in the 1880s. Some of the comfortable rooms have a balcony.
350 off map at B4 Gevers Deynootplein 30, Scheveningen 070 416 2636; www.amrathkurhaus.com 21, 22, 23; tram 1, 9 AX, DC, MC, VI

't Goude Hooft $$–$$$

Dating back to 1423, The Hague's oldest inn has 21st-century comforts and good food.
350 B1 Dagelijkse Groenmarkt 13 070 744 8830; www.tgoudehooft.nl 25, tram 2, 3, 4, 6 AX, MC, VI

Hotel Mozaic $$$

Near the Peace Palace and the historic center, each contemporary-styled room in this hotel is different.
350 B2 Laan Copes van Cattenburch 38 070 352 2335; www.mozaic.nl Tram 9 AX, DC, MC, VI

Mercure Hotel Den Haag Central $–$$

Near to the railroad station and convenient for the city center, this modern hotel also has a bar and restaurant.
350 C1 Spui 180 070 203 9002; www.mercure.com 18, 22, 24; tram 1, 15, 16 AX, DC, MC, VI

THE HAGUE RESTAURANTS

Price guide: (dinner per person, excluding drinks)

$	€10–€20
$$	€20–€30
$$$	over €30

Bodega De Posthoorn $$

Dutch classics and Indonesian favorites are on the menu at this popular meeting place with a heated outdoor terrace.
350 C2 Lange Voorhout 39a 070 360 4906; www.bodegadeposthoorn.nl Tram 9 MC, VI

ETXEA $$$

Off the attractive, historic Denneweg, this Basque restaurant serves good seafood dishes and has a lovely terrace for summer dining.
350 C2 Hooistraat 4a 070 365 8789; www.etxea.nl Closed Sat. lunch, Sun. and Mon. 18, 22, 29; tram 9 MC, VI

Restaurant Basaal $$$

Featuring contemporary European food and using local and regional produce, this canalside restaurant also opens a terrace for dining with a view in summer.
350 off map at C1 Dunne Bierkade 3 070 427 6888; www.restaurantbasaal.nl Closed Mon. and lunch 18; tram 1, 9, 15, 16 MC, VI

OSLO HOTELS

Price guide: (double room with breakfast for two people)

$	Kr800–Kr1,000
$$	Kr1,000–Kr1,400
$$$	over Kr1,400

Grand Hotel $$$

The Grand is one of Oslo's most prestigious places to stay with well-appointed rooms, a sauna and pool. The Grand Café here is a destination restaurant.
365 B1 Karl Johans Gate 31 23 21 20 00; www.grand.no Stortinget 37; tram 11, 13, 17, 18 AX, DC, MC, VI

Hotel Continental $$$

Located between the Royal Palace and City Hall, this is a member of "The Leading Hotels of the World." It has four good restaurants and cafés, including the atmospheric Theatercaféen and the sumptuous Restaurant Eik Annen Etage.
365 B1 Stortingsgaten 24–26 22 82 40 00; www.hotelcontinental.no Nationaltheatret 33; tram 13, 19 AX, DC, MC, VI

Saga Hotel Oslo Central $$

The contemporary feel, comfortable rooms and attractive public areas make this a popular mid-price accommodation choice. There is a family room that sleeps four.
365 B1 Address Kongens Gate 7 23 10 08 00; www.sagahoteloslo.com Stortinget Tram 12, 13, 19 AX, MC, VI

The Thief $$$

A distinctive and elegant hotel at Tjuvholmen with direct access to the Oslo Fjord. The hotel has a bar, restaurant, rooftop terrace and spa.
365 B1 Tjuvholmen 24 00 40 00; www.thethief.com Nationaltheatret 21, 54, N54; tram 12 AX, DC, MC, VI

Thon Hotel Opera $–$$

Near the main train station and with views of the opera house, this large

KEY TO SYMBOLS

⊞	map page number and coordinates
✉	address
☎	telephone number
⊘	days/times closed
Ⓜ	nearest subway station
🚌	nearest bus/trolley bus/tram/funicular route
⛴	ferry
$$$	expensive
$$	moderate
$	inexpensive
AX	American Express
DC	Diners Club
MC	MasterCard
VI	VISA

hotel has bright and stylish rooms.
⊞ 365 C1 ✉ Dronning Eufemias Gate 4 ☎ 24 10 30 00; www.thonhotels.com Ⓜ Jernbanetorget 🚌 Tram 12, 13,19 AX, DC, MC, VI

OSLO RESTAURANTS

Price guide: (dinner per person, excluding drinks)

$	Kr100–Kr250
$$	Kr250–Kr400
$$$	over Kr400

Café Christiania $$$

Traditional Norwegian food is served in museumlike surroundings here. In summer you can dine on the terrace overlooking the Parliament building.
⊞ 365 B1 ✉ Nedre Vollgate 19 ☎ 22 01 05 10; www.cafe christiania.no ⊘ Closed Sun. year-round, Mon. in Jul. Ⓜ Stortinget 🚌 Tram 11, 18, 19 AX, DC, MC, VI

Engebret Café $$

Founded in 1857, this restaurant offers Norwegian (reindeer is a specialty) and international cuisine, including traditional fish dishes, in a cozy dining room.
⊞ 365 B1 ✉ Bankplassen 1 ☎ 22 82 25 25; www.engebret-cafe. no ⊘ Closed Sat. lunch and Sun. Ⓜ Stortinget 🚌 Tram 12 AX, DC, MC, VI

Gamle Rådhus $$$

In a 17th-century building next to Akershus Castle, this restaurant is billed as Oslo's oldest eating establishment. International cuisine and fish specialties are served. Reservations are strongly advised.
⊞ 365 B1 ✉ Nedre Slottsgate 1 ☎ 22 42 01 07; www.gamleraadhus. no ⊘ Closed Sun. and 3 weeks in Jul., and Sat. lunch Ⓜ Stortinget 🚌 Tram 12 AX, DC, MC, VI

Sentralen Restaurant $–$$

This informal restaurant in a converted bank serves small bites and substantial platters to share. There are good pizzas too.
⊞ 365 B1 ✉ Øvre Slottsgate 3 AS ☎ 22 33 33 22; www.sentralen.no ⊘ Closed Sun. Ⓜ Stortinget 🚌 54; tram 12, 13, 19 AX, MC, VI

LISBON HOTELS

Price guide: (double room with breakfast for two people)

$	under €125
$$	€125–€200
$$$	over €200

Britânia $$$

This friendly, art deco-style hotel, just east of Avenida da Liberdade, was refurbished in the 1990s.
⊞ 378 off map at A5 ✉ Rua Rodrigues Sampaio 17 ☎ 213 155 016; www.hotel-britania.com Ⓜ Avenida 🚌 All buses for Avenida da Liberdade AX, DC, MC, VI

International Design Hotel $$–$$$

Situated on the Rossio and easily recognized by its striking violet-colored exterior, this hotel offers design-oriented rooms.
⊞ 379 B4 ✉ Rua Betesga 30 ☎ 213 240 990; www.idesighotel. com Ⓜ Rossio 🚌 All buses for Rossio AX, MC, VI

Palacete Chafariz del Rei $$$

This beautiful, light-filled hotel in the historic Alfama area dates from 1909. The decor, inside and out, combines art nouveau with classic elegance; many of the rooms have river views.
⊞ 379 E2 ✉ Tv Chafariz del Rei 6 ☎ 218 886 150; www.chafarizdelrei. com Ⓜ Terreiro do Paço 🚌 206, 210, 728,735; tram 25 AX, MC, VI

Pensão Portuense $–$$

All rooms in this family-run guesthouse are simple and spacious. While it's a no frills stay, it is an excellent value with a friendly staff.
⊞ 379 B5 ✉ Rua das Portas de Santo Antão 149–157 ☎ 213 464 197; www.pensaoportuense.com Ⓜ Restauradores AX, MC, VI

Sete Colinas Hotel $

Well serviced by the metro system, the Sete Colinas is a small, modern hotel in the heart of the city, making it a popular budget option.
⊞ 379 off map at C5 ✉ Avenida Almirante Reis 67 ☎ 213 510 720; www.setecolinas.com.pt Ⓜ Anjos 🚌 208, 708, 712, 726, 730, 736 AX, MC, VI

LISBON RESTAURANTS

Price guide: (dinner per person, excluding drinks)

$	under €30
$$	€30–€40
$$$	over €40

100 Maneiras $$$

Book in advance to savor 100 Maneiras' innovative 10-course tasting menu with ingredients

sourced from the Ribeira market.
🏠 378 A4 ✉ Rua do Teixeira 35
☎ 910 918 181; http://100maneiras.
com 🕲 Closed daily lunch
🚇 Restauradores and Gloria elevator
AX, DC, MC, VI

As Salgadeiras $$–$$$

Excellent Portuguese cuisine with a
contemporary twist is served in the
cozy surroundings of this converted
old bakery in the Barrio Alto District.
🏠 378 A3 ✉ Rua das
Salgadeiras 18 ☎ 213 421 157;
www.as-salgadeiras.com 🕲 Closed
lunch 🚋 Tram 28E MC, VI

Bonjardim $

This Lisbon institution offers great
chicken *piri-piri* and fries – it is
known as the *Rei dos Frangos*
(King of Chickens).
🏠 379 B5 ✉ Tv de Santo Antão 11
☎ 213 424 389; no website
🚇 Restauradores 🚌 and tram: all
services to Restauradores MC, VI

Cantinho Lusitano $

This tiny, eatery serves *petiscos*,
small taster-sized portions of
traditional Portuguese favorites.
There is a good choice of local wines.
🏠 378 off map at A4 ✉ Rua dos
Prezares 52 ☎ 218 065 185; www.
cantinholusitano.com 🕲 Closed
lunch and Sun. 🚇 Marquês de
Pombal 🚌 727, 707 MC, VI

Pap' Açôrda $$–$$$

Founded in the 1980s, this iconic
restaurant, now in the cutting edge
riverside Cais do Sodré area, serves
classic Portuguese dishes.
🏠 379 A1 ✉ Mercado da Ribeira,
Avenida 24 de Julho ☎ 213 951 274;
www.papacorda.com 🚇 Cais do
Sodré AX, MC, VI, DI

Price guide: (double room with
breakfast for two people)
$ under €100
$$ €100–€175
$$$ over €175

Hotel da Musica $–$$

Set in a refurbished market hall, this
hotel has contemporary, chic spaces
with light, bright rooms. The hotel's
restaurant serves kosher dishes.
🏠 387 off map at A4 ✉ Mercado
Bom Successo, Largo Ferreira Lapa
☎ 226 076 000; www.hoteldamusica.
com 🚌 402, 508, 704, 803, 907
🚇 Casa da Musica AX, DC, MC, VI

Hotel Moov Porto Central $

A spirited art deco building, once a
cinema, has been transformed into
a stylish contemporary hotel close
to the station.
🏠 387 C3 ✉ Praça da Batalha 32/34
☎ 220 407 001; www.hotelmoov.com
🚇 São Bento 🚌 701,702
AX, MC, VI

Hotel Peninsular $

This centrally situated hotel has both
en-suite rooms and some with
shared bathrooms. The excellent
value for money and friendly staff
make this a good budget choice.
🏠 387 C3 ✉ Rua Sá da Bandeira 21
☎ 222 003 012; https://
hotel-peninsular.pt 🚇 São Bento
🚌 701, 702 AX, MC, VI

Infante de Sagres $$–$$$

Porto's landmark hotel has a pretty
terrace and some lovely bedrooms.
Stylish design is used throughout.
🏠 387 B3 ✉ Praça Filipa de
Lencastre 62 ☎ 223 398 500; www.
hotelinfantesagres.pt 🚇 Aliados
🚌 All buses for Praça da Liberdade
AX, DC, MC, VI

Pestana Vintage Porto $$$

In the heart of the historic Ribeira
district, within a UNESCO heritage
site, this boutique hotel offers
comfortable rooms with river views
and friendly staff.
🏠 387 B1 ✉ Praça da Ribeira 1
☎ 223 402 300; www.pestana.com
🚌 500, 900, 901, 906 AX, MC, VI

Price guide: (dinner per person,
excluding drinks)
$ under €30
$$ €30–€40
$$$ over €40

Abadia $$

With huge portions of hearty
Portuguese food, Abadia has been a
favorite for many years. The food is
the real draw here, not the setting.
🏠 387 C3 ✉ Rua do Ateneu
Comercial do Porto 22 🕲 Closed
Sun., Mon. lunch ☎ 222 008 757;
www.abadiadoporto.com 🚇 Aliados
🚌 All buses for Praça da Liberdade
AX, MC, VI

Brick Clérigos $

Here, diners may sit round a huge
central table to enjoy the healthy,
platters. Plenty of vegetarian options
are a bonus.

Hotel Moov Porto Central $
🏠 387 B2 ✉ Rua Campo Mártires
da Pátria, 103 ☎ 223 234 4735; no
website 🕲 Closed Sun. 🚇 São
Bento 🚌 All services to Praça da
Liberdade AX, MC, VI

Casinha São João $–$$

The city's most authentic *tapas* bar,
with local wines and sangria, in
a simple vaulted dining room on
the waterfront.
🏠 387 C1 ✉ Cais da Ribeira 9
☎ 220 197 889 🕲 Closed Mon.
(also Sun. evening in winter)
🚌 900, 901, 906 MC, VI

ODE Porto Wine House $$$

You'll find an excellent modern twist
on traditional Portuguese dishes at
this atmospheric eatery in
a historic building close to the river.
🏠 387 C1 ✉ Largo do Terreiro 7
☎ 913 200 010 🕲 Closed lunch,
Sun. dinner 🚌 900, 901, 906
No credit cards

Tapabento $–$$

Fresh seafood *tapas* forms the heart
of the menu at this small and lively
restaurant. The peanut butter foam
dessert is a must.
🏠 387 C3 ✉ Rua da Madeira 222
☎ 912 881 272; www.tapabento.com
🕲 Closed Mon., Tue. lunch 🚇 São
Bento MC, VI

Price guide: (double room with
breakfast for two people)
$ €50–€100
$$ €100–€150
$$$ over €150

Hospedaje Romero $

This is an affordable, family-run
guesthouse with well-kept rooms.
🏠 402 B2 ✉ Gran Vía 64 ☎ 91 559
76 61; www.hospedajeromerogranvia.
com 🚇 Gran Vía MC, VI

Hotel Atlàntico $$–$$$

Occupying a splendid turn-of-the-
20th-century building, this hotel has
elegant and sound-proofed rooms.
Guests can enjoy panoramic views
from the hotel's roof terrace.
🏠 402 C2 ✉ Gran Vía 38 ☎ 91
522 64 80; www.hotelatlantico.es
🚇 Callao AX, MC, VI

Only You Hotel Atocha $$–$$$

Eclectic, contemporary design,
fantastic restaurants, and the slick

KEY TO SYMBOLS

✚	map page number and coordinates
✉	address
☎	telephone number
🕐	days/times closed
Ⓜ	nearest subway station
🚌	nearest bus/trolley bus/tram/funicular route
⛴	ferry
$$$	expensive
$$	moderate
$	inexpensive
AX	American Express
DC	Diners Club
MC	MasterCard
VI	VISA

Andalucian Cuisine

Simplicity is all in Andalucian cooking, in which the superb quality of the ingredients, combined with a Moorish legacy of spices, almonds and oranges, has created one of Spain's most enjoyable cuisines. *Tapas* originated here, as did *gazpacho*, the cold summer soup, and sherry, a fortified wine drunk as an aperitif and used in cooking. There are tasty stews and soups, thickened with lentils, potatoes or almonds, and every dish is redolent with olive oil, garlic and tomatoes. Excellent bread and rich Arab-inspired pastries and desserts complete the picture.

feel of a private club make this the perfect place for a city break.
✚ 402 D1 ✉ Paseo Infanta Isabel 13 ☎ 91 409 78 76; www.onlyyouhotels.com Ⓜ Atocha AX, MC, VI

The Principal $$$

One of Madrid's plushest luxury hotels, with a spa, rooftop terrace and restaurant. It enjoys a superb location overlooking the Gran Vía.
✚ 403 C2 ✉ Calle Marqués de Valdeiglesias 1 ☎ 91 521 87 43; www.theprincipalmadridhotel.com Ⓜ Banco de España AX, MC, VI

MADRID RESTAURANTS

Price guide: (dinner per person, excluding drinks)
$	€10–€25
$$	€25–€50
$$$	over €50

La Bola $$

This long-established tavern specializes in Madrid *cocido* – delicious stews cooked slowly in traditional clay pots.
✚ 402 B2 ✉ Calle Bola 5 ☎ 91 547 69 30; www.labola.es 🕐 Closed Sun. dinner Ⓜ Ópera MC, VI

Mercado de San Miguel $–$$

The century-old, wrought-iron Mercado (Market) de San Miguel has been transformed into the gastronomic hub of the old city. As well as the stalls selling the finest gourmet produce (including oils, hams, cheeses, seafood and conserves), it has several wonderful bars serving fine wines accompanied by all manner of delicious treats.
✚ 402 B2 ✉ Plaza de San Miguel ☎ 91 542 49 36; www.mercadodesanmiguel.es 🕐 Mon.–Thu. 10 a.m.–midnight, Fri.–Sun. 10 a.m.–1 a.m. Ⓜ Sol

Rayén Vegano $

A "slow food" temple, this colorful vegan lunch spot turns out delicious and imaginative cuisine to the boho local crowd.
✚ 402 C1 ✉ Carrer Lope de Vega 7. ☎ 675 382 072; www.reyanvegan.com 🕐 Closed dinner and Tue. Ⓜ Antón Martín MC, VI

La Terraza del Casino $$$

At this restaurant, chef Paco Roncero's stellar cuisine is paired with sumptuous decor and one of Madrid's

most beautiful terraces (in summer).
✚ 402 C2 ✉ Calle Alcalá 15 ☎ 91 521 87 00; www.casinodemadrid.es 🕐 Closed Sun. and Mon. Ⓜ Antón Martín AX, MC, VI.

BARCELONA HOTELS

Price guide: (double room with breakfast for two people)
$	€60–€120
$$	€120–€180
$$$	over €180

B-Hotel $$

Bright, modern rooms are complemented by the excellent service at this hotel near the Plaça Espanya. The B-Hotel also has a fantastic sun deck with plunge pool.
✚ 411 A1 ✉ Gran Vía de les Corts Catalanes 389–391 ☎ 93 552 95 00; www.b-hotel.com Ⓜ Jaume I MC, VI

Hotel Arts $$$

This 44-story, luxury waterfront hotel, with superb views across the city, is still the city's premier address.
✚ 411 A1 ✉ Carrer de la Marina 19–21 ☎ 93 221 10 00; www.hotelartsbarcelona.com Ⓜ Ciutadella/Vila Olímpica AX, DC, MC, VI

Hotel Neri $$$

Hotel Neri is one of the ciy's finest boutique hotels, hidden away in the Gothic heart of old Barcelona.
✚ 411 B1 ✉ Carrer Sant Sever 5 ☎ 93 304 06 55; www.hotelneri.com Ⓜ Liceu AX, MC, VI

The Praktik Bakery $$

This hotel has an in-house bakery. Pay extra to stay in one of the light-filled, exterior rooms.
✚ 411 B3 ✉ Carrer Provença 279 ☎ 93 488 00 61; www.hotelpraktikbakery.com Ⓜ Diagonal MC, VI

BARCELONA RESTAURANTS

Price guide: (dinner per person, excluding drinks)
$	€10–€25
$$	€25–€50
$$$	over €50

Café de l'Acadèmia $$

Perfect for a romantic dinner, particularly on the pretty terrace, this restaurant serves excellent Catalan fare. The cod dishes are tasty.
✚ 411 C2 ✉ Carrer Lledó 1, Plaça Sant Just ☎ 93 319 82 53 🕐 Closed Sat.–Sun. and 3 weeks in Aug. MC, VI

El Nacional $$

This stunning former warehouse is packed with bars offering a wide choice of dining options, from *tapas* to the freshest seafood.

✚ 411 B2 ✉ Passeig de Gràcia 24 bis ☎ 93 518 5053; www.elnacionalbcn.com 🚇 Jaume I or Barceloneta MC, VI

Kaiku $$

This is one of the best seafood restaurants in the city, although you'd never guess it from the plain exterior. It's most famous for the *arròs del xef*, a paella-style dish made with smoked rice, but this is complemented each day by a range of fabulously fresh seafood. Book a table on the terrace for sea views.

✚ 411 C1 ✉ Plaça del Mar 1 ☎ 93 221 90 82; www.restaurant kaiku.cat 🕐 Closed Mon., and dinner (in winter) 🚇 Barceloneta MC, VI

Rasoterra $

High ceilings and big scrubbed tables make an inviting setting for delicious veggie and vegan cuisine, prepared, where possible, with local and organic ingredients. They offer a good set lunch, and a selection of organic wines and beers.

✚ 411 B1 ✉ Carrer de Palau 5 ☎ 93 318 6926; www.rasoterra.cat 🕐 Closed Mon. 🚇 Jaume I MC, VI

Set Portes $$–$$$

One of Barcelona's best and most historic restaurants serves a wide range of excellent Catalan food and fine wines. It is famous for the quality of its paella.

✚ 411 C1 ✉ Passeig de Isabel II 14 ☎ 93 319 30 33; https://7portes.com 🚇 Barceloneta AX, DC, MC, VI

Price guide: (double room with breakfast for two people)
$ €60–€120
$$ €120–€180
$$$ over €180

Hostal Alfonso $

For location, comfort and price, it's hard to beat this friendly little *hostal*. The rooms are simple, but immaculately kept, and some have views across the square to the cathedral. Book well in advance – with just six rooms, this hotel fills up very quickly.

✚ 418 off map at A1 ✉ Rúa do

Pombal 40 ☎ 981 585 685; www.hostalalfonso.com MC, VI

Hotel Costa Vella $

This enchanting hotel overlooks a beautiful garden on the edge of Santiago de Compostela's old quarter. Bedrooms are comfortable.

✚ 418 B3 ✉ Rúa da Porta da Pena 17 ☎ 981 56 95 30; www.costavella.com MC, VI

A Quinta da Agua $$$

A charming 18th-century villa set in its own gardens, this ultra-chic retreat boasts plush rooms, a spa and outstanding service.

✚ 418 off map at A3 ✉ Paseo da Amaia 23B ☎ 98 153 46 36, www.aquintadaauga.com AX, MC, VI

San Miguel $$

A beautiful hotel in an historic building near the cathedral, this has light-filled, modern rooms set around a pretty garden courtyard. The excellent restaurant, with tables out on the terrace, is perfect for relaxing after a long day's sightseeing.

✚ 418 B2 ✉ Praza de San Miguel dos Agros 8 ☎ 981 555 779; www.sanmiguelsantiago.com MC, VI

Price guide: (dinner per person, excluding drinks)
$ €10–€25
$$ €25–€50
$$$ over €50

Casa Marcelo $$

This chic gastro-tavern has three bar areas and serves an interesting menu of *platillos* (small plates), including many contemporary Gallego dishes.

✚ 418 A2 ✉ Rúa das Hortas 1 ☎ 981 558 580; www.casamarcelo.net 🕐 Closed Sun. and Mon. MC, VI

A Horta d'Obradoiro $$

Two talented and enthusiastic young chefs are behind this charming and stylish little spot, which serves a short but creative menu that focuses on the freshest seasonal produce.

✚ 418 A2 ✉ Rua Hortas 16 ☎ 881 031 375; http://ahortadoobradoiro.com 🕐 Closed Mon. and Sun. dinner No credit cards

Pedro Roca $$–$$$

Come to Pedro Roca to sample great Spanish cooking in a cooly elegant and tranquil environment.

✚ 418 off map at A3 ✉ Domingo

García Sabell 1 ☎ 981 585 776; www.pedroroca.es 🕐 Closed Sun. dinner MC, VI

Price guide: (double room with breakfast for two people)
$ €50–€100
$$ €100–€150
$$$ over €150

Alfonso XIII $$$

Seville's top hotel, set in an attractive palm-shaded garden, offers every comfort in its elegant, luxurious rooms. The staff here provide exceptional service.

✚ 425 B2 ✉ Calle San Fernando 2 ☎ 95 491 70 00, www.hotel-alfonso xiii-seville.com 🚇 21, 37, C3, C4; tram T1 AX, DC, MC, VI

Hostal Callejón del Agua $

Definitely one of the best budget choices in town, this charming *hostal* is located in a 19th-century town house in the old quarter. The elegantly furnished bedrooms are set around a tranquil, plant-filled patio. There are good views from the roof terrace.

✚ 425 B3 ✉ Calle Corral del Rey 23 ☎ 95 421 20 98; www.callejondel agua.com 🚇 21, 37, C3, C4; tram T1 MC, VI

Hotel Alminar $–$$

This modest hotel has a dozen simple but tastefully decorated rooms in an ideal location near the cathedral. The personalized service ensures you will want to return again and again.

✚ 425 A3 ✉ Calle Álvarez Quintero 52 ☎ 95 429 39 13; www.hotelalminar.com 🚇 C5; tram T1 MC, VI

Hotel Casa 1800 $$–$$$

This 19th-century *palacete* (small palace) has been converted into a smart boutique hotel. Rooms are sumptuously decorated, and touches include free afternoon tea on the patio. The roof terrace has a plunge pool. To reach the hotel you will need to take a taxi and then walk the final 55 yards.

✚ 425 B3 ✉ Calle Rodrigo Caro 6 ☎ 95 456 18 00; www.hotelcasa 1800sevilla.com 🚇 1 AX, DC, MC, VI

Hotel Mercer $$$

There are just a dozen contemporary rooms at this enchanting luxury hotel, which is set in a splendid

KEY TO SYMBOLS

🗺 map page number and coordinates
✉ address
☎ telephone number
🕐 days/times closed
Ⓜ nearest subway station
🚌 nearest bus/trolley bus/ tram/funicular route
⛴ ferry
$$$ expensive
$$ moderate
$ inexpensive
AX American Express
DC Diners Club
MC MasterCard
VI VISA

Swiss Food and Wine Festivals

From summer through fall, there are food and wine festivals held in every region of Switzerland. The grape harvests during August prompt wonderful festivities in Anzère, the Lake Geneva region and eastern Switzerland, while Locarno, Ascona and the Ticino area also celebrate the chestnut harvest. In Charmey, Jaun and Fribourg *la Bénichon* culinary feast features a special mustard, and at the Basel Herbstmesse (Autumn Fair), the delicious confectionary *mässmogge* is a must-try.

19th-century mansion. The restaurant is excellent and the rooftop terrace has a plunge pool.
🗺 425 A3 ✉ Calle Castelar 26
☎ 95 422 30 04; www.mercersevilla. com 🕐 03, 21, 40, 41, A2, C5
AX, MC, VI

Ítaca Sevilla $$

A great value hotel set in a traditional town house close to the Setas. Rooms (including family rooms) are arranged around a charming central patio, and there's a sun deck and plunge pool on the roof terrace.
🗺 425 B3 ✉ Calle Santillana 5–7
☎ 954 22 81 56; www.itchoteles. com/hotel-itaca-sevilla-en-sevilla/
🚌 27, 32; tram T1 MC, VI

Price guide: (dinner per person, excluding drinks)
$ €10–€25
$$ €25–€50
$$$ over €50

Becerrita $$

This long-established restaurant serves traditional Andalucian food and prides itself on its desserts.
🗺 425 B3 ✉ Calle Recaredo 9
☎ 95 441 20 57; www.becerrita.com
🕐 Closed Sun. dinner and 2 weeks in Aug. 🚌 1, 24, 27, A1, A2, C3 MC, VI

conTenedor $–$$

This popular, stylish and relaxed local restaurant is part of the "slow food" movement. There is a delicious seasonal menu of mostly organic and local produce.
🗺 425 B4 ✉ Calle San Luis 50
☎ 95 491 63 33; https://restaurante contenedor.com 🚌 C5 MC, VI

La Flor de Toranza $

Known to locals as "Trifón," this much-loved, friendly haunt is a great spot for breakfast, a quick lunch or some *tapas*.
🗺 425 A3 ✉ Calle Jimios 1
☎ 95 422 95 15 🚌 C5; tram T1
No credit cards

Petit Comité $$

This miniature *tapas* bar serves delicious dishes, each lovingly prepared with the finest seasonal produce. It's a popular place, so get there early to bag a good spot.
🗺 425 A3 ✉ Carrer Dos de Mayo 30
☎ 95 422 95 95; http:// petitcomitesevilla.com.es 🚌 03, 21, 40, 41, A2, C5 MC, VI

Price guide: (double room with breakfast for two people)
$ 800SKr–1,500SKr
$$ 1,500SKr–2,200SKr
$$$ over 2,200SKr

Diplomat $$–$$$

This comfortable hotel in a handsome early 20th-century building overlooks the waterfront on the road to Djurgården. The on-site T/BAR is a delightful place to stop for tea.
🗺 437 C3 ✉ Strandvägen 7C
☎ 08 459 68 00; www.diplomathotel. com 🕐 Östermalmstorg 🚌 69, 76; tram 7 AX, DC, MC, VI

Grand Hôtel Stockholm $$$

At this hotel across from the Royal Palace, facilities are luxurious. The Mathias Dahlgren restaurant is one of the finest in the city, and the Veranda restaurant is famous for its *smörgåsbord*.
🗺 437 B2 ✉ Södra Blasieholmshamnen 8 ☎ 08 679 35 00; www.grandhotel.se
🕐 Kungsträdgården 🚌 2, 55, 65, 76; tram 7 AX, DC, MC, VI

Haymarket by Scandic $$

Close to the Concert Hall, this large, bright and characterful hotel with a popular bar (think art deco rather than Nordic minimalism) often has good deals. Rooms come in several sizes, so choose carefully.
🗺 437 A3 ✉ Hötorget 13–15 ☎ 08 5172 6700; www.scandichotels.com
🕐 Skanstull 🚌 3, 53 AX, DC, MC, VI

Hotel Skepps Holmen $$

With a country-in-the-city feel, this hotel on Skeppsholmen, near the Modern Art Museum, offers waterfront views and spacious rooms filled with sleek Scandinavian furniture, as well as the free use of bicycles.
🗺 437 B2 ✉ Gröna gången
☎ 08 407 23 00; www.hotel skeppsholmen.se 🚌 65 ⛴ From Slussen AX, DC, MC, VI

Story Hotel $$

Converted from an old apartment building, this arty hotel combines modern comforts with vintage details. It is ideally placed for Stockholm's best shops and nightlife.
🗺 437 B3 ✉ Riddargatan 6 ☎ 08 5450 3940; www.storyhotels.com

Ⓢ Östermalmstorg 🚌 54;
tram 13, 14 AX, DC, MC, VI

Price guide: (dinner per person,
excluding drinks)
$ 50SKr–200SKr
$$ 200SKr–400SKr
$$$ over 400SKr

Den Gyldene Freden $$$

Established in 1722, this famous Old Town restaurant attracts the rich and famous, including Nobel Prize selection committee members. Even the restroom has 18th-century poetry on the wall. The cuisine is excellent. Reservations are required.
🔲 437 B2 ✉ Österlånggatan 51 ☎ 08 24 97 60; www.gyldene freden.se 🕐 Closed Sun. Ⓢ Gamla Stan, Slussen 🚌 2, 3, 53, 55, 57, 59, 76 AX, DC, MC, VI

Hermans $

This vegetarian restaurant has a glassed-in terrace and open garden overlooking Stockholm Harbor and Djurgården island. Its buffet includes dishes from Asia, Mexico, India, the Mediterranean and the Middle East.
🔲 437 C1 ✉ Fjällgatan 23B ☎ 08 643 94 80; www.hermans.se Ⓢ Gamla Stan 🚌 71 MC, VI

Hjerta $$

On the waterfront, Hjerta serves flavorful Scandinavian dishes such as black pudding with potato pancakes or cod with beetroot and capers.
🔲 437 B3 ✉ Slupskjulsvägen 28b, Skeppsholmen ☎ 08 520 238 70. www.restauranghjerta.se Ⓢ Kungsträdgården 🚌 65 Slussen AX, DC, MC, VI

Meatballs for the People $$

Join the locals in this friendly restaurant in Södermalm for tasty classic and innovative versions of the famous Swedish comfort food.
🔲 437 B1 ✉ Nytorgsgatan 30 ☎ 08 466 6099; www.meatball.se Ⓢ Medborgarplatsen 🚌 2, 3, 53, 76 AX, MC, VI

Oaxen Slip $$$

Combine a trip to Abba The Museum with lunch or dinner at this bustling Nordic bistro right on the waterfront. It shares premises with its more sophisticated (and pricier) sister, Oaxen Krog.
🔲 437 C2 ✉ Beckholmsvägen 26

☎ 08 55 15 31 05; www.oaxen.com 🚌 67; tram 7 Slussen, Skeppsholmen AX, DC, MC, VI

Price guide: (double room with breakfast for two people)
$ SF100–SF250
$$ SF250–SF400
$$$ over SF400

Beau Rivage $$$

Founded in 1865 on the shore of Lac Léman (Lake Geneva), the Beau Rivage is one of the most famous and luxurious hotels in the world. Its refined elegance and perfect service embody the dream and the qualities of "Old Europe."
🔲 451 B3 ✉ quai du Mont-Blanc 13 ☎ 022 716 6666; www.beau-rivage.ch 🚌 1 AX, DC, MC, VI

Edelweiss $–$$

A popular choice with tourists, this chalet-style hotel near the lakeside has 42 attractive rooms and stages folklore evenings in its restaurant.
🔲 451 B3 ✉ place de la Navigation 2 ☎ 022 544 5151, www.hoteledelweissgeneva.com 🚌 1 AX, DC, MC, VI

Hotel Central $–$$

Well-situated in the heart of the city, this budget, family-run hotel is a good option in expensive Geneva. Room possibilities range from self-catering mini-apartments, through double, single and family rooms to suites; all are clean and comfortable. Bathrooms can be small; breakfast is included in the rate and served in your room.
🔲 451 B2 ✉ rue de la Rotisserie 2 ☎ 022 818 81 00, www.hotelcentral. ch 🚌 2, 3, 6, 7, 10, 36 AX, MC, VI

Hotel Kipling $–$$

Blending the style and colors of the Orient with European standards, this hotel is extremely good value. Rooms are a good size, with well-equipped bathrooms. There's free WiFi, two restaurants and a breakfast buffet.
🔲 451 B3 ✉ rue de la Navigation 27 ☎ 022 544 4040; www.hotelkipling geneva.com 🚌 1 AX, DC, MC, VI

Tor Hotel $

The Tor is a centrally located hotel with a range of simply decorated rooms including family rooms. There is no restaurant, and breakfast is served in your room.

🔲 451 A3 ✉ rue Ami-Levriér 3 ☎ 022 909 8820; www.torhotel.com 🚌 1, 5, 8, 25 AX, MC, VI

Warwick Geneva $$–$$$

This sleek hotel is ideally situated opposite the station, with easy access to city sights. Penthouse terrace rooms have great views.
🔲 451 A3 ✉ rue de Lausanne 14 ☎ 022 716 8000; www.warwick hotels.com/geneva 🚌 1, 5, 8, 25 AX, DC, MC, VI

Price guide: (dinner per person, excluding drinks)
$ SF25–SF45
$$ SF45 SF60
$$$ over SF60

Auberge de Savièse $

Enjoy a selection of Swiss specialties at this friendly restaurant, which features different types of fondue.
🔲 451 B3 ✉ rue des Pâquis 20 ☎ 022 732 8330; www.aubergede saviese.com 🚌 1, 25; tram 15 AX, DC, MC, VI

Brasserie Lipp $$$

Diners are transported to Paris at this late-opening French restaurant in the Confédération Centre shopping mall.
🔲 451 B2 ✉ rue de la Confédération 8 ☎ 022 318 8030; www.brasserie-lipp.com 🚌 2, 5, 7, 10, 29; tram 12 AX, DC, MC, VI

Café du Bourg-de-Four $$

Part café, part wine bar, part bistro, this is a charming and cozy place for a pause if you're sightseeing in the old city center.
🔲 451 B2 ✉ place du Bourg de Four 13 ☎ 022 311 9076, www. cafedubourgdefour.ch 🚌 2, 7, 9, 12; tram 12 AX, MC

Café du Centre $$–$$$

This classic brasserie specializes in oysters and seafood, and prides itself on its seasonal ingredients. There's a changing daily special; on Sundays the brunch menu is very popular.
🔲 451 B2 ✉ place du Molard 2 ☎ 22 311 85 86; www.cafeducentre. ch 🚌 2, 3, 6, 7, 10 AX, DC, MC, VI

Le Patara $$$

This is the best Thai restaurant in Geneva. Expect impeccable service in tasteful surroundings.
🔲 451 B3 ✉ Hôtel Beau Rivage, quai du Mont-Blanc 13 ☎ 022 731

KEY TO SYMBOLS

✚	map page number and coordinates
✉	address
☎	telephone number
⊘	days/times closed
Ⓜ	nearest subway station
🚍	nearest bus/trolley bus/ tram/funicular route
⛴	ferry
$$$	expensive
$$	moderate
$	inexpensive
AX	American Express
DC	Diners Club
MC	MasterCard
VI	VISA

5566; www.patara-geneva.ch
🚍 1 AX, DC, MC, VI

Saveurs du Liban $–$$

Head here to sample the fresh flavors of genuine Lebanese food. A favorite with diners are the *mezzes*, featuring a selection of traditional dishes served in bowls to be shared by all.
✚ 451 B3 ✉ place de la Navigation 8 ☎ 022 731 0928; www.lessaveurs duliban.ch 🚍 1 MC, VI

Price guide: (double room with breakfast for two people)

$	SF150–SF250
$$	SF250–SF400
$$$	over SF400

Altstadt $$

In the heart of old Zurich, this comfortable hotel has 25 stylish rooms. The bar serves breakfast, lunch or a late nightcap.
✚ 456 B2 ✉ Kirchgasse 4 ☎ 044 250 5353; www.hotel-altstadt. ch 🚍 Tram 4, 15 AX, DC, MC, VI

Eden au Lac $$$

This elegant lakeside hotel, built in 1909 and renovated in 2018, offers the ultimate in comfort, luxury and service.
✚ 456 B1 ✉ Utoquai 45 ☎ 044 266 2525; www.edenaulac.ch 🚍 Tram 1, 4 AX, DC, MC, VI

Hotel Marta $

Pick this hotel for its location – it is within walking distance of the lake, old town and the station, and is close to the city's bars and restaurants.
✚ 456 B3 ✉ Zahringerstrasse 36 ☎ 044 269 9595; www.hotelmarta.ch 🚍 Tram 6, 7, 17 AX, MC, VI

Marktgasse $$

In the heart of the old city, this charming boutique hotel features sleek design within an old building. There's a restaurant and buzzy café, a great terrace and a library stocked with books and board games.
✚ 456 B2 ✉ Marktgasse 17 ☎ 044 266 1010; www.marktgasse hotel.ch 🚍 31; tram 4, 15 AX, MC, VI

Storchen $$$

The "Stork" enjoys a beautiful waterside setting. Guests can dine at the Rotisserie or on the riverside terrace with its lovely views, and enjoy drinks in the Barchetta Bar.
✚ 456 B2 ✉ Storchengasse 16/ Weinplatz 2 ☎ 044 227 2727; www.storchen.ch 🚍 Tram 2, 8 AX, DC, MC, VI

Price guide: (dinner per person, excluding drinks)

$	SF25–SF45
$$	SF45–SF60
$$$	over SF60

Au-Gust $–$$

Au-Gust offers nose-to-tail eating, with the accent very firmly on the pig – try one of the specialty sausages. Surroundings are spacious, and many products are for sale to go.
✚ 456 B3 ✉ Rennweg 1 ☎ 044 224 2828; www.au-gust.ch 🚍 Tram 6, 7, 11, 13, 17 AX, DC, MC, VI

Haus Hiltl $–$$

The world's oldest vegetarian and vegan restaurant is a revelation. There are several city branches.
✚ 456 A2 ✉ Haus Hiltl, Sihlstrasse 28 ☎ 044 227 7000; www.hiltl.ch 🚍 Tram 4, 15 AX, DC, MC, VI

Haus zum Rüden $$$

Overlooking the Limmat river, this historic restaurant serves the best of Swiss specialties.
✚ 456 B2 ✉ Limmatquai 42 ☎ 044 261 9566; www. haus-zum-rueden.ch ⊘ Closed Sun.–Mon. and Sat. lunch 🚍 Tram 4, 15 AX, DC, MC, VI

Kronenhalle $$$

This long-established restaurant offers traditional dishes beneath artworks by Chagall and Matisse.
✚ 456 B2 ✉ Rämistrasse 4 ☎ 044 262 9900; www.kronen halle.ch 🚍 912, 916; tram 4, 8, 9, 11, 13, 15 AX, DC, MC, VI

Restaurant Reithalle $$

An atmospheric restaurant serving Swiss and fusion food, with tables set up in former stables. There is a buzzing beer garden in the summer.
✚ 456 A3 ✉ Gessner-Allee 8 ☎ 044 212 0766; www.restaurant-reithalle.ch 🚍 Tram 3, 4 MC, VI

Zum Kropf $–$$

This popular restaurant has been serving generous portions of local dishes since 1888.
✚ 456 A2 ✉ In Gassen 16 ☎ 044 221 1805; www.zumkropf.ch ⊘ Closed Sun. 🚍 Tram 11 AX, MC, VI

Essential Information

■ Austria 494
■ Belgium 498
■ Britain 502
■ Czech Republic 506
■ Denmark 510
■ Finland 514
■ France 518
■ Germany 522
■ Greece 526
■ Hungary 530
■ Ireland 534
■ Italy 538
■ Luxembourg 542
■ The Netherlands 546
■ Norway 550
■ Portugal 554
■ Spain 558
■ Sweden 562
■ Switzerland 566

U.S. CITIZENS

The information in this guide has been compiled for U.S. citizens traveling as tourists.

AAA recommends travelers consult online U.S. State Department travel advisories when planning travel abroad. Find this information at http://travel.state.gov/content/passports/english/alertswarnings.html.

Travelers who are not U.S. citizens, or who are traveling on business, should check with their embassies and tourist offices for information on the countries they wish to visit.

Entry requirements are subject to change at short notice, and travelers are advised to check the current situation before they travel.

National Flag

Essential for Travelers*

● **Required** ● **Recommended** ● **Not required**

Passport	●
Visa (check regulations before you travel)	●
Travel, medical insurance	●
Round-trip or onward airline ticket	●
Local currency	●
Traveler's checks	●
Credit cards	●
First-aid kit and medicines	●
Inoculations*	●

*see also *Health* section

Essential for Drivers*

Driver's license	●
International Driving Permit	●
Car insurance (for nonrental cars)	●
Car registration (for nonrental cars)	●

*see also *Driving* section

Important Addresses

Austrian National Tourist Office
61 Broadway 1701
New York, NY 10006
☎ (212) 575 7723
www.austria.info (email: info@austria.info)

**Österreich Werbung
(Austrian National Tourist Office)**
Albertinaplatz/Maysedergasse
1010 Vienna, Austria
☎ 0800 400 20000
Fax 0810 101819
www.austria.info/at

American Citizen Services
Boltzmanngasse 16
1090 Vienna, Austria
☎ 01 31 339-0
http://at.usembassy.gov
Mon.–Fri. 8:30–4:30
(outside these hours ☎ 01 31 339-0)

Customs

✔ **Duty-free limits on goods brought in from non-European Union countries:**
200 cigarettes or 100 cigarillos or 50 cigars or 250 g. tobacco; 1 L. alcohol over 22% volume; or 2 L. alcohol under 22% volume and 4 L. nonsparkling wine, and 16 L. beer; plus any other duty-free goods (including gifts) to the value of €430 for travelers arriving by air, and €300 for all other travelers. This information applies to visitors age 17 and over.

Currency worth €10,000 or more must be declared. There is no limit on the importation of tax-paid goods purchased within the European Union, provided they are for your own personal use.

✘ No unlicensed drugs, weapons, ammunition, obscene material, pets or other animals, counterfeit money or copied goods, meat or poultry.

For customs limits for returning U.S. citizens see page 16.

Money

Euro (€)
Austria's currency is the euro (€), a currency shared by 18 other European Union countries.

The euro is divided into 100 cents (¢).
The denominations of euro bills are 5, 10, 20, 50, 100, 200 and 500.
There are coins of 1, 2, 5, 10, 20 and 50¢ and €1 and €2.

ATMs are located in most towns and cities and can be used to withdraw local currency. Credit, debit and prepaid cards are widely accepted. It is a good idea to carry a mix of large and small euro denominations.

Tips and Gratuities

Tips *(Trinkgeld)* are welcomed and expected in restaurants and cafés.

Restaurants (even when service is included)	10%
Cafés/bars	10%
Taxis	10%
Porters	at your discretion
Chambermaids	at your discretion
Hairdressers (and change to shampooer)	5%

Communications

Post Offices

Buy stamps *(Briefmarken)* at a post office *(Postamt)*, or newsstand/tobacconist *(Tabak Trafik)* or from a hotel. Post offices can be recognized by a golden trumpet symbol and can often be found close to the main square or railroad station. Hours for out-of-town post offices may vary. Mail-boxes are yellow or orange.

Telephones

Use cash or prepaid phone cards *(Callingcards)* to make a call. Telephones have direct dialing for national and international calls. Buy phone cards from gas stations, newsstands, post offices and hotels. Some booths take credit cards. Check overseas cellphone usage with your provider.

Phoning inside Austria
All Austrian telephone numbers in this book include an area code: dial the number that is listed. To call the operator dial 11 88 77.

Phoning Austria from abroad
The country code for Austria is 43. Note that Austrian numbers in this book do not include the country code; you will need to prefix this number if you are phoning from another country. To phone Austria from the United States or Canada, omit the first zero from the Austrian number, and add the prefix 011 43. (Note that the number of digits in Austrian area codes varies.) Example: 01 12 23 34-4 becomes 011 43 1 12 23 34-4.

Phoning from Austria
To phone the United States or Canada from Austria, prefix the area code and number with 00 1. Example: (111) 222-3333 becomes 00 1 111 222-3333. To call national and international information dial 11 88 77.

Emergency Telephone Numbers

Police *(Polizei)* **133**   Fire service *(Feuerwehr)* **122**
Ambulance *(Krankenwagen)* **144**
Mountain rescue service *(Bergrettung)* **140**
Emergency calls are free from phone booths.
General emergency number within the E.U. **112**

Time Zones

Vienna: 12 noon
New York: 6 a.m. (-6 hours)
Chicago: 5 a.m. (-7 hours)
Denver: 4 a.m. (-8 hours)
Los Angeles: 3 a.m. (-9 hours)

Hours of Operation

Stores are open Monday to Friday 8:30–6. Saturday is early closing day; shops close between noon and 5 p.m. Thursday or Friday is late-night shopping (until 7 or 8).

Banks are open Monday to Friday 8 a.m.–12:30 p.m. and 1:30–3. Some open until 5:30 p.m. on Thursday.

Post offices operate Monday to Friday 8–noon and 2–6. Some may also open 8–10 a.m. on Saturday. Main and station post offices in larger cities are open 24 hours, including weekends and public holidays.

Museums can usually be visited daily, 10–6.

Pharmacies usually follow store opening hours with a 2-hour lunch break. There is always one pharmacy open late in each city: details are displayed in pharmacy windows.

National Holidays

Banks, businesses and most stores close on these days. Also, some museums may be closed or have restricted hours.

Jan. 1	New Year's Day
Jan. 6	Epiphany
Mar./Apr.	Easter Monday
May 1	Labor Day
May	Ascension Day
May/Jun.	Pentecost Monday
May/Jun.	Corpus Christi
Aug. 15	Assumption of the Virgin
Oct. 26	National Day
Nov. 1	All Saints' Day
Dec. 8	Immaculate Conception
Dec. 25	Christmas Day
Dec. 26	St. Stephen's Day

Photography

Magnificent and varied subject matter awaits the photographer in Austria. Away from the city, the Alpine peaks give enormous scope for landscape photography, and the light is generally very good. Camera batteries are readily available and there are many places offering download and CD services for digital cameras. Most museums will not allow you to take pictures; check first.

Health

Medical Insurance

The cost of medical treatment in Austria is high, and private medical insurance is recommended. Ärztekammer für Wien (Vienna Doctors' Chamber) can suggest a doctor *(Arzt)* or hospital *(Krankenhaus)*: Weihburggasse 10–12, Vienna, ☎ 01 51 406 3000; www.aertztekammer. at. Other Austrian towns and regions have their own such chambers. The south and east of the country are home to *Zecken* – a kind of tick that can transmit encephalitis. This disease can be lethal, therefore it is essential to seek medical advice if you are bitten. An inoculation is available.

Dental Services

A dentist *(Zahnarzt)* will charge for any treatment given. Dental work is expensive, so check that it is covered by your medical insurance. Dentists are listed in the telephone directory, or ask for English-speaking dentists at your embassy, a tourist office or hotel.

Sun Advice

Austria has strong sun during the summer months so sun protection is needed. Wear a hat, cover shoulders, drink plenty of fluids and use sunscreen.

Drugs

Pharmacies *(Apotheken)* can dispense prescriptions. Many assistants speak English, and a schedule displayed on the door enables you to find a late-opening or 24-hour pharmacy in every town.

Safe Water

Tap water is safe to drink throughout Austria. Mineral water *(Mineralwasser)* is widely available.

Restrooms

Public restrooms *(Toiletten/WC)* are generally easy to find and immaculately clean. A small charge is levied.

Electricity

Austria has a 230-volt power supply. Electrical sockets take plugs with two round pins. American appliances will need a plug adapter and will require a transformer if they do not have a dual-voltage facility.

National Transportation

Train *(Zug)*

The Austrian Federal Railways (Österreichische Bundesbahnen or ÖBB; www.oebb.at) runs a comfortable and efficient service, with connections to all European countries. If you like a slower pace try a steam-train journey through valleys along lakesides or a cable-car trip; local tourist offices can give details. For rail information ☎ 05 1717.

Bus *(Bus)*

Austria has a good network of local, federal and private bus companies. Bus travel is slower but less expensive than the train; for information contact ÖBB ☎ 05 1717.

Ferry *(Fähre)*

Several companies offer boating services on Austria's rivers and lakes, including a daily ferry service along the Danube river between Vienna and Slovakia's capital, Bratislava. The Austrian National Tourist Office website (www.austria.info) has a good overview of domestic options. For information on trips to Bratislava, contact Twin City Liner (☎ 01 904 8880; www.twincityliner.com).

Driving

Drive on the right

Speed Limits

Police impose on-the-spot fines (for which receipts are issued), although a foreign motorist may refuse and instead be asked to make a surety payment.

 Limited-access highways *(Autobahnen)*
130 k.p.h. (80 m.p.h.)

 Main roads
100 k.p.h. (62 m.p.h.)

Urban areas
50 k.p.h. (31 m.p.h.)

Seat Belts

Must be worn in front and back seats at all times. Children under 14 are not allowed to use a front seat, unless in a child safety seat.

Blood Alcohol

The legal blood alcohol limit is 0.05%. The limit is 0.01% for drivers with under 3 years' driving experience. Random breath tests on drivers are carried out frequently. Penalties are severe.

Driving (continued)

Tolls

To use toll highways, purchase a windshield sticker *(Vignette)* at automobile clubs in Austria or abroad, or at a border crossing, gas station, post office or tobacconist. There are charges for some other major roads. Nonpayment of tolls results in a fine.

Car Rental

The leading car-rental firms have offices at airports and train stations. Hertz offers discounted rates for AAA members (see page 15). For reservations:

	United States	Austria
Alamo	(888) 233-8749	01 7007 32812
Avis	(800) 633-3469	0800 0800 8757
Budget	(800) 218-7992	01 7007-32711
Europcar	(877) 940-6900	01 431 866 1614
Hertz	(877 826-8782	01 512 8677

Fuel

Many gas stations *(Tankstelle)* are self-service, and 24-hour facilities are common. Unleaded gas *(Bleifrei)* is available at 95 and 98 octane. Diesel is available.

AAA Affiliated Motoring Club

Österreichischer Automobil-, Motorrad-und Touring Club (ÖAMTC) Schubertring 1-3, A-1010 Vienna
☎ 01 711 90; www.oeamtc.at. If you break down while driving, call ☎ 120 (ÖAMTC breakdown service). Not all automobile clubs offer full services to AAA members.

Breakdowns and Accidents

There are 24-hour emergency phones at regular intervals on highways. All accidents involving personal injury must be reported to the police (☎ 133). Most car-rental firms provide their own free rescue service; if your car is rented, follow the instructions given in the documentation. Use of a car-repair service other than those listed by your rental company may violate your rental agreement. By law, you must carry a first-aid kit, a warning triangle and a fluorescent vest (one for each person in the vehicle) in case of a breakdown or accident. Failure to comply could result in a heavy fine.

Other Information

The minimum age for driving a car is 18 (may be higher for some car-rental firms). An International Driving Permit (IDP) is required. A Green Card (international motor insurance certificate) is recommended if driving a private car (see page 15). Only hands-free phone use is permitted while driving. In winter, snow tires or chains are essential, and are legal Nov. 1–Apr. 15. Rent chains at automobile clubs and border crossings.

Useful Words and Phrases

The official language in Austria is German, although Austrians are very proud of their brand of the language *(Österreichisch)*, and are offended if it is treated as a mere dialect of "standard" German *(Hochdeutsch)*. On paper, the differences between the two varieties are not obvious, but the Austrian accent is distinctive, and especially strong in rural regions.

There are numerous words that are peculiar to Austria and the south of Germany. The Austrian diminutive is *-el* or *-lein* compared with the German *-chen*, so *Mädchen* (girl) in German becomes *Mädel* in Austrian. A small number of Austrian words, such as *Fauteil* (armchair) and *Plafond* (ceiling), are in fact of French origin.

See page 525 for a pronunciation and basic vocabulary guide to the German language; the following list is an eclectic sample of words peculiar to Austrian German.

Everyday life

friend, guy	*Haberer*
funny	*hetzig*
goodbye	*pfiat di*
guitar	*Klampfe*
hello	*Grüss Gott*
legs	*Laxen*
policeman	*Gendarm*
work	*Hockn*

Food and drink

blood sausage	*Blunzn*
carrot	*Karotte*
corn	*Kukuruz*
croissant	*Kipferl*
doughnut	*Krapfen*
green beans	*Fisole*
green salad	*Häuplsalat*
lemonade	*Kracherl*
milky coffee	*Melange*
mushroom	*Schwammerl*
potato	*Erdäpfel*

Common words and phrases

breakfast	*Frühstück*
closed	*geschlossen*
excuse me	*Entschuldigen*
how much?	*Wieviel kostet es?*
I don't understand	*Ich verstehe nicht*
I'd like	*Ich möchte*
key	*Schlüssel*
no smoking	*nicht rauchen*
open	*geöffnet*
please	*bitte*
room	*Zimmer*
shower	*Dusche*
thank you	*danke*
where is…?	*Wo ist…?*

National Flag

Essential for Travelers

● Required ● Recommended ● Not required

Passport	●
Visa (check regulations before you travel)	●
Travel, medical insurance	●
Round-trip or onward airline ticket	●
Local currency	●
Traveler's checks	●
Credit cards	●
First-aid kit and medicines	●
Inoculations	●

Essential for Drivers*

Driver's license	●
International Driving Permit	●
Car insurance (for nonrental cars)	●
Car registration (for nonrental cars)	●

*see also *Driving* section

Important Addresses

**Belgian Tourist Office/Information Office
Flanders Belgium** (Flemish-speaking areas)
620 Eighth Avenue, 44th Floor, New York,
NY 10018
☎ 212 584 2336; www.visitflanders.com
Wallonie Bruxelles (French-speaking areas)
Avenue Comte de Smet de Nayer 14,
5000 Namur, Belgium ☎ 02 899 0478;
www.walloniebelgiquetourisme.be
Also at du Marche aux Herbes 25, 1000,
Brussels, Belgium

American Embassy
Boulevard du Régent 27/Regentlaan 27,
1000 Brussels, Belgium
☎ 02 811 4000 Fax 02 811 4500
https://be.usembassy.gov. Open Mon.–Fri. 9–6

American Embassy Consular Service
☎ 02 811 43000. Open Mon.–Thu. 1:30–3:30 p.m.,
Fri. 10 a.m.–noon.

Customs

✔ **Duty-free limits on goods brought in from
non-European Union countries:**
200 cigarettes or 100 cigarillos or 50 cigars or
250 g. tobacco; 1 L. alcohol over 22% volume or
2 L. alcohol under 22% volume; 4 L. wine, 16 L.
beer; plus any other duty-free goods (including
gifts) to the value of €430 for visitors entering
the E.U. (and Belgium) by air or by sea or €300 if
arriving by other means.

There is no limit on the importation of tax-paid
goods, for personal use, purchased within the E.U.

Visitors must declare cash over the value of
€10,000 (or equivalent).

✘ No unlicensed drugs, weapons, ammunition,
obscene material, pets or other animals,
counterfeit money or copied goods, meat or
poultry.

**For customs limits for returning U.S. citizens
see page 16.**

Money

Euro (€)
Belgium's currency is the euro (€), a currency
shared by 18 other European Union countries.

The euro is divided into 100 cents (¢).
The denominations of euro bills are 5, 10, 20, 50,
100, 200 and 500.
There are coins of 1, 2, 5, 10, 20 and 50¢ and
€1 and €2.

ATMs are located in most towns and cities and
can be used to withdraw local currency. Credit,
debit and prepaid cards are widely accepted. It
is a good idea to carry a mix of large and small
euro denominations.

Tips and Gratuities

Tips are not obligatory; a service charge is usually
included for restaurants, cafés and taxis.

Restaurants (where service is not included)	10%
Cafés/bars	change
Taxis	change
Porters	€1 per item
Chambermaids	€1 per day
Cloakroom attendants	€1–€2

Communications

Post Offices

Buy stamps *(timbres/postzegels)* at a post office *(bureau de poste/postkantoor)*, a tobacconist or newsstand *(tabac/ tabaksverkoper)*, or from a vending machine. Allow a week for mail to reach the United States. Mailboxes are painted red. Hours for out-of-town post offices may vary.

Telephones

The Belgian Government repealed a law which called for phone companies to install public pay phones on the basis of need (such as for emergency use). Subsequently, due to lack of revenue, all public phones have been taken out of service by telephone companies. If you need to make calls, use the phone system at your accommodations or your mobile. Before you travel, check overseas cell phone usage with your mobile phone provider. Call costs may be high.

Phoning in Belgium
All Belgian phone numbers in this book include an area code: dial the entire number. To call the English-speaking operator dial 1404 for domestic numbers and 1304 for international numbers (French language).

Phoning Belgium from abroad
The country code for Belgium is 32. Belgian numbers in this book do not include the country code; you will need to prefix this number if you are phoning from another country. To phone Belgium from the United States or Canada, dial 011 32 then omit the first zero from the Belgian number. (Note that Belgian area codes have two or three digits.) Example: 01 122 3344 becomes 011 32 1 122 3344.

Phoning from Belgium
To phone the United States or Canada from Belgium, prefix the area code and number with 00 1. Example: (111) 222-3333 becomes 00 1 111 222-3333. To call international directory assistance, dial 13 04.

Emergency Telephone Numbers

Police *(Police)* **101**
Fire service *(Pompiers)* **100**
Ambulance *(Ambulance)* **100**
Red Cross ambulance **105**
General emergency number within the E.U. **112**

Time Zones

Brussels: 12 noon
New York: 6 a.m. (-6 hours)
Chicago: 5 a.m. (-7 hours)
Denver: 4 a.m. (-8 hours)
Los Angeles: 3 a.m. (-9 hours)

Hours of Operation

Stores are open Monday to Saturday 9–6. While Sunday is the official closing day, souvenir shops in many towns stay open, usually 10–4.

Many **bakeries and patisseries** open at 7:30 or 8 a.m. and also open on Sunday morning.

Department and major stores often stay open until 7 p.m. on weekdays and 8 or 9 p.m. on Friday. Smaller stores may close for lunch.

Banks operate Monday to Friday 8–4.

Post offices are open Monday to Friday 8–5, although some city post offices and banks are open on Saturday morning. Post offices and banks outside cities and large towns may close for lunch.

Museums open 10–5. It is common for museums to close on Monday (except for some small museums) and open later one evening a week. Some close for 2 hours at lunchtime.

National Holidays

Banks, businesses and most stores close on these days. Each region has its own feast day. Most cities, towns and villages celebrate their patron saint's day, but most places stay open.

Jan. 1	New Year's Day
Mar./Apr.	Easter Monday
May 1	Labor Day
May	Ascension Day
May/Jun.	Pentecost Monday
Jul. 21	National Day
Aug. 15	Assumption of the Virgin
Nov. 1	All Saints' Day
Nov. 11	Armistice Day
Dec. 25	Christmas Day

Photography

Camera batteries are readily available and there are many places offering digital equipment, download services for digital cameras and rapid developing services. Most museums will not allow you to take pictures; check first.

Health

Medical Insurance

Private medical insurance is recommended. Visitors from non-European Union countries can receive treatment in a hospital emergency room but are charged if admitted to a hospital *(hôpital/ziekenhuis)*. Doctors *(médecin/dokter)* may also charge for a consultation.

Dental Services

Dental treatment is not available free of charge; all dentists practice privately. A list of dentists *(dentiste/tandarts)* can be found in the *Yellow Pages (Pages Jaunes/Gouden Gids)*. Check that dental treatment is covered by your private medical insurance.

Sun Advice

The warmest months are July and August, with average daytime temperatures of 60 degrees Fahrenheit. Belgian weather can be unpredictable and although the sun is not often very fierce, protection is still required.

Drugs

Prescription and nonprescription medicines are available from a pharmacy *(pharmacie/apotheek)*. If you need a medicine outside regular hours, the addresses of 24-hour facilities are posted on the door of all pharmacies.

Safe Water

Tap water is safe to drink and mineral water *(eau minérale/mineraalwater)* is widely available. The origin of the English word "spa" is in fact the Belgian town of Spa, especially popular during the 19th century for its mineral springs.

Restrooms

Public restrooms *(toilettes/toiletten)* are not always easy to find but are usually clean. If you need to use the facilities at a restaurant or café purchase a drink first. Restrooms in the larger restaurants and cafés sometimes have attendants; you should tip them €1–€2, which goes toward their wages.

Electricity

Belgium has a 220-volt power supply. Electrical sockets take plugs with two round pins. American appliances will need a plug adapter and will require a transformer if they do not have a dual-voltage facility.

National Transportation

Train *(Train/Trein)*

The national rail network is the SNCB/NMBS (Societé Nationale des Chemins de Fer Belges in French, and Nationale Maatschappij der Belgische Spoorwegen in Flemish). Check online at www.belgianrail.be or by phone ☎ 02 528 28 28 for information or for reservations. The Eurostar trains from London arrive in the Gare du Midi (☎ 02 400 67 31; www.eurostar.com). Brussels has good connections with the Thalys network that operates high-speed trains to Paris, Amsterdam, Cologne and Geneva. For information go to www.raileurope.com or www.thalys.com).

Bus *(Bus/Bus)*

Local bus service timetables are available from local tourist offices. Low-cost international buses to most European capitals are operated by Eurolines (☎ 02 274 13 50; www.eurolines.com).

Driving

Drive on the right

Speed Limits

Police impose on-the-spot fines (receipts are issued), although a foreign motorist may refuse and instead be asked to make a surety payment.

 Limited-access highways *(autoroutes/autoweg)* **120 k.p.h. (74 m.p.h.)** Minimum speed on straight, level stretches **70 k.p.h. (43 m.p.h.)**

Main roads **90 k.p.h. (56 m.p.h.)** In Flanders some main roads **70 k.p.h (43 m.p.h.)**

Urban areas **50 k.p.h. (31 m.p.h.); 30 k.p.h. (18 m.p.h.)** on roads in central Brussels (the Pentagon), cycle streets and school zones; **20 k.p.h. (12 m.p.h.)** on residential streets.

Seat Belts

Must be worn in front and back seats; children under 18 years and shorter than 135cm (4ft 5in) must have a seat belt/restraint suitable for their height and weight. If a child seat is unavailable, they must travel in the rear, restrained by the factory-fitted seat belt.

Blood Alcohol

The legal blood alcohol limit is 0.05% (0.02% for drivers with less than 3 years' driving experience). Random breath tests on drivers are carried out often. Penalties for offenders are severe.

Driving (continued)

Tolls

There are no tolls on Belgian highways, but there is a toll on the Liefkenshock Tunnel to the north of Antwerp.

Car Rental

The leading car-rental firms have offices at airports, train stations and ferry terminals. Hertz offers discounted rates for AAA members (see page 15). For reservations:

	United States	Belgium
Alamo	(884) 345 6962	30 692 1399
Avis	(800) 633 3469	070 223 001
Budget	(800) 472-3325	02 789 8664
Hertz	(800) 654-3001	02 717 3201

Fuel

Gasoline *(essence/benzine)* and diesel are priced in liters and are expensive. There are two grades of unleaded gas *(sans plomb/loodvrij)*: normal (95 octane) and super (98 octane). Most gas stations are self-service, and 24-hour facilities are common.

AAA Affiliated Motoring Club

Touring Club Belgium (TCB) 44 rue de la Loi, 1040 Brussels ☎ 02 233 2211; www.touring.be. If you break down while driving, phone TCB breakdown service ☎ 070 344 777 or, on a limited-access highway, use one of the emergency telephones located every 1.2 miles. Ask for *"Touring-Secours."* Not all automobile clubs offer full services to AAA members.

Breakdowns and Accidents

Most car-rental firms have their own free rescue service; if your car is rented, follow the instructions given in the documentation. Use of a car-repair service other than those authorized by your rental company may violate your rental agreement. If you are involved in an accident phone for police assistance ☎ 101. You must carry a warning triangle and a fluorescent vest in your car.

Other Information

The minimum age for driving a car is 18 (may be 21 for some car-rental firms). An International Driving Permit (IDP) is recommended; some car-rental firms require it, and it can speed up formalities if you are involved in an accident. A Green Card (international motor insurance certificate) is recommended if you are driving a private car; see page 15 for more information. Drivers must yield the right of way to vehicles approaching from the right (except on major roads) and to vehicles on rails, public transport buses, and cycles on designated cycle streets. Beware of cobbled roads, which can be slippery in wet weather.

Useful Words and Phrases

A linguistic battle has existed in Belgium for many centuries; settlers have long entered from neighboring countries, and as a result there are three distinct language communities: French, Dutch and German.

The two dominant languages are Walloon (a form of French, spoken in the south) and Flemish (related to Dutch, spoken in the north). Passions run deep between the two groups; prosperity has moved back and forth between them over the centuries, and their relationship is still difficult to this day. The Flemish fear their language is being diminished, aware of the strength that French has as a world language. In addition, German is spoken in the east.

Both Walloon and Flemish hold equal status as official languages, and although the bilingual signs can be confusing to the visitor, English is widely spoken.

In Brussels, where Flemish and French are both spoken, the street signs also are in both languages. Place-names are not usually a problem, since the Flemish and French proper names have similarities, but there can be differences.

Following is a selection of locations:

English	Flemish	French
Aalst	Aalst	Alost
Antwerp	Antwerpen	Anvers
Bruges	Brugge	Bruges
Brussels	Brussel	Bruxelles
Ghent	Gent	Gand
Jodoigne	Geldenaken	Jodoigne
Kortrijk	Kortrijk	Courtrai
Liège	Luik	Liège
Louvain	Leuven	Louvain
Mechelen	Mechelen	Malines
Mons	Bergen	Mons
Mouscron	Moeskroen	Mouscron
Nivelles	Nijvel	Nivelles
Ostend	Oostende	Ostende
Roeselare	Roeselare	Roulers
Ronse	Ronse	Renaix
Scheldt	Schelde	Escaut
Tongeren	Tongeren	Tongres
Tournai	Doornik	Tournai
Veurne	Veurne	Furnes
Ypres	Ieper	Ypres

For useful phrases in French, see page 521; for phrases in German, see page 525; for phrases in Dutch, see page 549.

National Flag

Essential for Travelers

● **Required** ● **Recommended** ● **Not required**

Passport	●
Visa (check regulations before you travel)	●
Travel, medical insurance	●
Round-trip or onward airline ticket	●
Local currency	●
Traveler's checks	●
Credit or debit cards	●
First-aid kit and medicines	●
Inoculations	●

Essential for Drivers*

Driver's license	●
International Driving Permit	●
Car insurance (for nonrental cars)	●
Car registration (for nonrental cars)	●

*see also *Driving* section

Important Addresses

VisitBritain
www.visitbritain.com

City of London Information Centre
St. Paul's Churchyard
London EC4M 8BX, U.K.
☎ 020 7332 3456
Mon.–Sat. 9:30–5:30, Sun. 10–4

American Embassy
33 Nine Elms Lane,
London, SW11 7US, U.K.
☎ 020 7499 9000 (24hrs)
https://uk.usembassy.gov
Mon.–Fri. 9:30–5:30

U.S. Consulate General
3 Regent Terrace
Edinburgh EH7 5BW, U.K.
☎ 0131 556 8315
https://uk.usembassy.gov/embassy-consulates
Mon.–Fri. 8:30–5

Customs

✔ **Duty-free limits on goods brought in from non-European Union countries:**
200 cigarettes or 100 cigarillos or 50 cigars or 250 g. tobacco; 4 L. wine; 16 L. beer; 1 L. alcohol over 22% volume or 2 L. alcohol under 22% volume; 60 ml. perfume; 250 ml. toilet water; plus any other duty-free goods (including gifts) to the value of £390.

There is no limit on the importation of any currency or of tax-paid goods purchased within the European Union, provided the goods are for your own personal use. Currency in amounts over €10,000 or equivalent must be declared on entry if you arrive from outside the E.U.

✘ No unlicensed drugs, weapons, self-defense sprays, obscene material, counterfeit and copied goods, meat, poultry or dairy products.

For customs limits for returning U.S. citizens see page 16.

Money

Pound sterling (£)
Britain's currency is the pound sterling (£), which is divided into 100 pence (p).
The denominations of pound bills are 1 (Scotland only), 5, 10, 20, 50 and 100 (Scotland only).
There are coins of 1, 2, 5, 10, 20 and 50p and £1 and £2.

You can exchange dollars or traveler's checks at banks, main post offices, exchange offices and some travel agencies.

Credit, debit and prepaid cards are widely accepted throughout Britain, and ATMs are plentiful in towns and cities. When sightseeing, it is a good idea to carry a mix of large and small value coin denominations.

Tips and Gratuities

Tips are welcomed in restaurants and cafés, although service is often included.

Restaurants (where service is not included)	10–15%
Cafés/bars	change
Taxis	10%
Porters	£2–£5
Hairdressers	10%
Tour guides	£2–£5
Chambermaids	£2–£5
Cloakroom attendants (where no charges)	30p–50p

Communications

Post Offices

Buy stamps at post offices, gas stations, some tourist attractions and supermarkets. Out-of-town post offices often close from 1–2. Mailboxes ("pillar-boxes") are red, and are usually free-standing, though some may be set into walls. Pillar-boxes show who was monarch at the time of their installation (ER II, for instance, stands for Elizabeth Regina II).

Telephones

Public telephones can be hard to find, and the traditional red booths are rare in towns and cities. Use cash, or a credit or debit card. Most public telephones accept 10p, 20p, 50p, £1 and £2 coins, but only unused coins are returned. There is a minimum charge of 60p (includes 40p connection charge). If using a credit card there is a £1.20 minimum fee (includes £1 connection charge). Check overseas cell phone usage with your provider.

Phoning in Britain
All British numbers in this book have an area code: dial the number listed. For the operator dial 100.

Phoning Britain from abroad
The country code for Britain is 44. British numbers in this book do not include the country code; you need to prefix it if you are phoning from another country. To phone Britain from the United States or Canada, omit the first zero from the British number, and add the prefix 011 44. Example: 011 2233 4455 becomes 011 44 11 2233 4455.

Phoning from Britain
To phone the United States or Canada from Britain, prefix the area code and number with 00 1. Example: (111) 222-3333 becomes 00 1 111 222-3333. To call the international operator dial 155.

Emergency Telephone Numbers

Police **999** or **112**
Fire service **999** or **112**
Ambulance **999** or **112**
Emergency calls are free from phone booths

Time Zones

London: 12 noon
New York: 7 a.m. (-5 hours)
Chicago: 6 a.m. (-6 hours)
Denver: 5 a.m. (-7 hours)
Los Angeles: 4 a.m. (-8 hours)

Hours of Operation

Stores are generally open Monday to Saturday 9–5:30. Many **malls** and city-center **stores** open for longer hours (late-night hours one day a week, usually Wednesday or Thursday) and also open on Sunday (11–5). Convenience grocery stores stay open until late in the evening.

Banks and **post offices** operate Monday to Friday 9–5. Main town banks and post offices open on Saturday mornings.

Museums generally open 10–6 but times can vary. Some major sights close on Monday and open later one evening a week; more modest sights of interest may close off season, so it is advisable to check with the local tourist office.

Note that many restaurants do not open for dinner until around 6 or 7 p.m. Before then, chain restaurants and fast-food outlets are usually the only places serving meals.

Pharmacies operate Monday to Saturday 9–5:30, but you can find pharmacies in some large food stores that are open also on Sundays 11–5.

National Holidays

Banks, businesses and smaller stores close on these days, although larger stores may remain open.

Jan. 1	New Year's Day
Jan. 2	Bank Holiday (Scotland only)
Mar./Apr.	Good Friday
Mar./Apr.	Easter Monday (not in Scotland)
First Mon. of May	May Day
Last Mon. of May	Spring Bank Holiday
First Mon. of Aug.	Summer Bank Holiday (Scotland only)
Last Mon. of Aug.	Summer Bank Holiday
Dec. 25	Christmas Day
Dec. 26	Boxing Day

When December 25 and 26 fall on a weekend, the following Monday and Tuesday are public holidays. If January 1 falls on a weekend, usually the first Monday in January is a public holiday.

Photography

Memory cards and camera batteries are readily available and there are many places offering download and CD services for digital cameras.

Health

Medical Insurance

Private insurance is recommended. Visitors can receive treatment in emergency rooms but are charged if admitted to a hospital. You can seek advice from a doctor at a surgery or health center; you must make an appointment, and will be charged. Doctors are listed in the *Yellow Pages*, or ask at your hotel or a tourist office.

Dental Services

Dentists charge for consultations or treatment. Emergency treatment is available after hours in towns and cities (see the *Yellow Pages*). Check if emergency dental treatment is covered by your medical insurance.

Sun Advice

Although not renowned for very warm weather, Britain does have its moments, and it is not unheard of for July and August to be as hot as the Mediterranean. Visiting historic sights can involve being outside for prolonged periods, so cover up, apply sunscreen and drink plenty of fluids.

Drugs

Prescription and nonprescription medicines are available from pharmacies (chemists). Pharmacists can advise on medication for common ailments. Notices in all pharmacy windows give details of emergency facilities open outside regular hours.

Safe Water

Tap water is safe to drink, even in remote areas. Mineral water is widely available in stores but can be quite expensive in restaurants.

Restrooms

Public restrooms (toilets, lavatories, WCs or, in everyday parlance, "loos") are generally easy to find and maintained to a high standard. Most are free, but there may be a charge for those at major rail stations (about 30p).

Electricity

Britain has a 240-volt power supply. Electrical sockets take plugs with three square pins, so an adapter is needed for American appliances. A transformer is also required for appliances operating on 110 or 120 volts.

National Transportation

Train

Rail services are good in Britain. First class is comfortable but considerably more expensive than standard. Intercity (high-speed) trains connect cities. A variety of discount railcards are available – check the National Rail Enquiries website in advance for eligibility and restrictions. Once you are in Britain, Rail Rover passes are good value for regional rail travel. There is online information at www.nationalrail.co.uk.

Bus

It is cheaper to travel by bus than by rail. The main operator for long-distance bus/coach travel in Britain is National Express. There is online information at www.nationalexpress.com. Euroline's buses operate from Britain to the rest of Europe. There is online information at www.eurolines.com.

Ferry

The busiest ferries run between southeast England and France (a high-speed train also shuttles passengers and cars through the Channel Tunnel). Service is frequent, especially in summer. Ferries also serve the smaller British islands, plus Ireland, Spain, Belgium and The Netherlands.

Driving

Drive on the left

Speed Limits

British speed limits are stringently enforced by police patrols and also by strategically positioned cameras that detect speeding motorists.

 Limited-access highways (motorways); divided highways (dual carriageways)
70 m.p.h.

 Main roads
50 or 60 m.p.h.

 Urban areas
20, 30 or 40 m.p.h.

Seat Belts

Must be worn in front and rear seats at all times.

Blood Alcohol

 The legal blood alcohol limit in England and Wales is 0.08%; in Scotland it is 0.05%. Random breath tests on drivers are carried out frequently. Penalties are severe.

Driving (continued)

Tolls

Limited-access highways are free except for the M6 Toll Road (junction 4 to 11a). Some bridges or tunnels levy a toll. In central London there is a weekday congestion charge (see page 16) ☎ 0343 2222 1234 or visit www.tfl.gov.uk for payment information.

Car Rental

The leading car-rental firms have offices at airports, train stations and ferry terminals. Hertz offers discounted rates for AAA members (see page 15). For reservations:

	United States	Britain
Avis	(800) 633 3469	0808 284 0014
Budget	(800) 472-3325	0808 284 4444
Hertz	(800) 654-3001	020 7026 0077

Fuel

Gasoline (petrol) and diesel are priced in liters and are expensive. There are two grades of unleaded gas: super (98 octane) and premium (95 octane). Most gas stations are self-service, and 24-hour facilities are common.

AAA Affiliated Motoring Club

The Automobile Association (AA) Ltd., Fanum House, Basing View Basingstoke, Hampshire RG21 4EA; www.theaa.com.
AAA members staying in the U.K. for up to 3 months get free AA Breakdown Service. If you break down while driving a privately owned car in the U.K., ☎ 0800 887766 (AA Breakdown Service). If you're driving a rental car, contact the rental company's assistance partner. If you're staying for longer than 3 months, call the AA on 0800 085 2721 when you arrive in the U.K. to obtain AA Breakdown Service. You also can purchase the service online: www.theaa.com.

Breakdowns and Accidents

There are emergency telephones at intervals on limited-access and divided highways. If you have an accident ☎ 999 or 112 for police, fire and ambulance. Most car-rental firms provide a rescue service; if your car is rented, follow the rental instructions. Use of an unauthorized car-repair service may violate your rental agreement.

Other Information

The minimum age for driving a car is 17. An International Driving Permit (IDP) is recommended. A Green Card (international motor insurance certificate) is recommended if you are driving a private car; see page 15 for more information.

Useful Words and Phrases

Spotting the differences between American and British English is fun, especially as some regional accents are almost incomprehensible to the untrained ear! Britons have become familiar with Americanisms through American television shows, but it is still possible to make a blunder. Below are some illustrations of the "Atlantic divide."

American	British
ATM	*cashpoint*
to call collect	*to reverse the charges*
check	*cheque*
check (in a restaurant)	*bill*
elevator	*lift*
first/second floor (etc.)	*ground/first floor (etc.)*
movie theater	*cinema*
phone booth	*phone box*
reserve (reservation)	*book (reservation)*
restroom	*toilet/loo (colloquial)*
Scotch™ tape	*sticky tape/Sellotape™*
trash or garbage can	*dustbin or rubbish bin*
Food and drink	
arugula	*rocket salad leaf*
beer	*bitter (dark)*
lager	*(light)*
bun	*bap*
candy	*sweets*
(potato) chips	*crisps*
cookies	*biscuits*
corn	*sweetcorn*
cotton candy	*candyfloss*
eggplant	*aubergine*
french fries	*chips*
grocery store	*supermarket*
Jell-O™	*jelly*
jelly	*jam*
liquor store	*off-licence*
oatmeal	*porridge*
Saranwrap™	*cling film*
zucchini	*courgette*
Fashion	
bangs	*fringe*
pants	*trousers*
pantyhose	*tights*
suspenders	*braces*
undershirt	*vest*
vest	*waistcoat*
Getting around	
hood (of a car)	*bonnet*
one-way trip	*single*
parking lot	*car park*
paved shoulder	*lay-by*
rotary/traffic circle	*roundabout*
round trip	*return ticket*
sidewalk	*pavement*
stick shift	*manual*
subway	*tube/underground*
truck	*lorry*
trunk (of a car)	*boot*

National Flag

Essential for Travelers

● Required ● Recommended ● Not required

Passport	●
Visa* (check regulations before you travel)	●
Travel, medical insurance	●
Round-trip or onward airline ticket	●
Local currency	●
Credit cards	●
First-aid kit and medicines	●
Inoculations	●

*U.S. citizens can stay in the Czech Republic for up to 90 days without a visa. For stays of longer than 90 days, visas must be obtained from an embassy outside the Czech Republic.

Essential for Drivers*

Driver's license	●
International Driving Permit	●
Car insurance (for nonrental cars)	●
Car registration (for nonrental cars)	●

*see also *Driving* section

Important Addresses

Czech Tourist Authority CzechTourism
1109 Madison Avenue
New York, NY 10028
☎ (212) 288-0830
www.czechtourism.com

CzechTourism
Information Center
Staroměstské náměstí 5, Prague 1
☎ 221 580 611
www.czechtourism.com

American Embassy
Tržiště 15
118 01 Praha 1, Czech Republic
☎ 257 022 000
http://cz.usembassy.gov

Customs

✔ **Duty-free limits on goods brought in from non-European Union countries:**
200 cigarettes or 100 cigarillos or 50 cigars or 250 g. tobacco; 1 L. alcohol more than 22% volume or 2 L. less than 22% volume; 2 L. nonsparkling wine; 50 ml. perfume or 250 ml. toilet water; plus any other duty-free goods (including gifts) to the value of 7,500Kč. Persons importing alcohol must be 18 and over, for cigarettes and tobacco products 17 and over.

There is no restriction on the import or export of Czech or foreign currencies, but amounts in excess of 250,000Kč must be declared.

✘ No unlicensed drugs, firearms, ammunition, offensive weapons, obscene material, unlicensed animals, counterfeit or copied goods, meat and poultry.

For customs limits for returning U.S. citizens see page 16.

Money

Koruna česká (Kč)
The Czech Republic's currency is the Koruna česká (Kč) – or Czech crown – which is divided into 100 haléřů (h) – or hellers – although these tiny coins no longer circulate.

The denominations of Kč bills are 100, 200, 500, 1,000, 2,000 and 5,000.
There are coins of 1, 2, 5, 10, 20 and 50Kč.

Credit, debit and prepaid cards are widely accepted, and ATMs are plentiful in the Czech Republic for withdrawing local currency.

Tips and Gratuities

Tips are welcomed in restaurants and cafés, although service is normally included.

Restaurants (even when service is included)	5–10%
Cafés/bars	5–10%
Taxis	5–10%
Porters	40Kč
Hairdressers	10%
Tour guides	20–50Kč

Communications

Post Offices

✉ Buy stamps *(známky)* at a post office *(pošta)*, a newsstand/kiosk *(trafika/tabák)* or from a hotel. The postal service is generally reliable and not expensive.

Mailboxes are orange. Hours for out-of-town post offices may vary.

Telephones

☎ Pay phones either accept coins (less common, usually in more remote locations) or telephone cards *(telefonní karta* or *TRICK)*, which cost 200 or 300Kč. Phone cards can be bought from newsstands, tobacconists, post offices, shops, hotels and travel agencies. Most card phone booths have English instructions. Check overseas cell phone usage with your provider.

Phoning inside the Czech Republic

There are no area codes in the Czech Republic; all numbers are nine digits: dial the number that is listed. For national directory inquiries dial 1180.

Phoning the Czech Republic from abroad

The country code for the Czech Republic is 420. You will need to prefix this number to the numbers in this book if you are phoning from another country. To phone the Czech Republic from the United States or Canada dial the prefix 011 420. Example: 112 233 445 becomes 011 420 112 233 445.

Phoning from the Czech Republic

To phone the United States or Canada from the Czech Republic, prefix the number with 00 1. Example: (111) 222-3333 becomes 00 1 111 222-3333. To call international information dial 1181.

Emergency Telephone Numbers

All emergencies **112**
Police – national *(Policie Česká republiky)* **158**
City police *(Městská policie)* **156**
Fire service *(požár)* **150**
Ambulance *(ambulance)* **155**
Emergency calls are free from phone booths.

Time Zones

Prague: 12 noon
New York: 6 a.m. (-6 hours)
Chicago: 5 a.m. (-7 hours)
Denver: 4 a.m. (-8 hours)
Los Angeles: 3 a.m. (-9 hours)

Hours of Operation

Stores open Monday to Saturday 8–6. Some close early on Saturday; many close at noon or 1. Some stores may close for an hour for lunch, normally between noon and 1.

Food stores in the large cities open at 7 a.m., and large stores and shopping centers stay open until 8 or 10 p.m. (4 p.m. on Saturday). In Prague, most stores open all day Saturday and Sunday.

Banks are open Monday to Friday 9–5 or 6. Some may close earlier on Friday, and some are open Saturday morning.

Post offices open Monday to Friday 8–6:30, and some may open on Saturday morning. Tourist resorts may have special opening times.

Museums usually open 10–5 and often close on Monday and days following public holidays. Opening times may be reduced during the winter.

Pharmacies are open weekdays 8–6.

National Holidays

Banks, businesses and most stores close on these days. Monuments, museums and galleries usually open on public holidays (except Jan. 1, Easter, and Dec. 25 and 26) but are closed the following day.

Jan. 1	New Year's Day and Day of Restoration of Independent Czech State
Mar./Apr.	Good Friday and Easter Monday
May 1	Labor Day
May 8	Liberation Day
Jul. 5	SS Cyril and Methodius' Day
Jul. 6	Jan Hus Day
Sep. 28	Czech Statehood Day
Oct. 28	Independence Day
Nov. 17	Day of Fight for Freedom and Democracy
Dec. 24	Christmas Eve
Dec. 25	Christmas Day
Dec. 26	St. Stephen's Day

Photography

📷 Czechs are enthusiastic photographers and you will have no difficulty in finding spare equipment for your digital camera. Several shops in Prague will do on-the-spot digital printing. An excellent shop is Foto Škoda at Vodičkova 47.

Health

Medical Insurance

Private medical insurance is recommended. U.S. and Canadian visitors should go to a hospital *(nemocnice)* to seek treatment for an accident or emergency. You will be asked to show a passport. Bring cash or credit card, as payment will be levied on the spot. The following clinics in Prague have English-speaking doctors: Na Homolce Hospital, Roentgenova 2 ☎ 257 271 111; www.homolka.cz. Also Canadian Medical Care, Veleslavínská 1 ☎ 235 360 133; www.canadian.cz.

Dental Services

A dentist *(zubař)* will charge for any treatment given. Check if it is covered by your medical insurance. For an English-speaking dentist, ask at your hotel or embassy, at a tourist office or the Elite Dental Clinic, Na Příkopě 15 ☎ 222 510 888; http://elitedental.cz.

Sun Advice

June through August is the sunniest period, when adequate sun protection should be applied.

Drugs

A pharmacy *(lékárna)* is the only place you can buy over-the-counter medicines. Pharmacies also dispense many drugs normally available only by prescription in other Western countries. However, it is advisable to bring supplies of your own medicines with you. If you need a pharmacy after regular hours, information about the nearest all-night facility is posted at some pharmacies.

Safe Water

Tap water is safe to drink but may have an unpleasant taste. Bottled water is available everywhere.

Restrooms

Public restrooms *(WC)* are scarce and usually require a payment of 5–10Kč. Metro stations in Prague will have a reasonably clean restroom. The best bet is to use the facilities of a hotel or restaurant.

Electricity

The Czech Republic has a 230-volt power supply. Electrical sockets take plugs with two round pins. American appliances will need a plug adapter, and will require a transformer if they do not have a dual-voltage facility.

National Transportation

Train *(Vlak)*

Czech Railways (České dráhy, CD) is extensive and inexpensive, but often crowded. The fast trains stop at major cities; local trains stop everywhere but usually provide only second-class service. All long-distance trains have two classes; some have dining carriages and overnight services. Reserve seats on express trains. For information: ☎ 221 111 122 (24-hours); www.cd.cz.

Bus *(Autobus)*

Buses are inexpensive and popular with Czechs. Reserve for weekends, national holidays or early morning. Purchase tickets from the bus station kiosk or the driver. For information: ☎ 900 144 444 toll call (daily 6 a.m.–10 p.m.); www.florenc.cz. Large items of luggage will be stowed for a small charge. Euroline's buses connect to other countries: ☎ 731 222 111; www.elines.cz.

Ferry *(Prévos)*

From April to September boats cruise the Vltava river as far as Troja Château to the north of Prague and Slapy Dam to the south: ☎ 724 202 505; www.evd.cz.

Driving

Drive on the right

Speed Limits

Police can give on-the-spot fines. If this should happen to you, ask for a receipt.

 Limited-access highways *(dalnice)* **130 k.p.h. (80 m.p.h.)**. Minimum speed **80 k.p.h. (49 m.p.h)**

 Main roads **90 k.p.h. (56 m.p.h.)**

Urban areas **50 k.p.h. (31 m.p.h.)**

Seat Belts

Must be worn in front and back seats at all times. Children under 4 feet 11 inches or 79 pounds must not travel in the front.

Blood Alcohol

 The legal blood alcohol limit is zero. Random breath tests on drivers are carried out frequently, especially late at night, and the penalties for offenders are severe.

Driving (continued)

Tolls

A tax is levied for use of highways and express roads. A sticker *(vignette)* must be purchased and displayed; failure to do so will result in a fine. Stickers can be bought for one week, one month or one year at the Czech border, ÚAMK offices, gas stations or post offices.

Car Rental

The leading car-rental firms have offices at airports and train stations. Hertz offers discounted rates for AAA members (see page 15). For reservations:

	United States	Czech Republic
Avis	(800) 879-2847	221 851 225
Budget	(800) 218-7992	235 325 713
Enterprise	(855) 266-9289	220 113 454
Hertz	(800) 654-3131	225 345 021

Fuel

Gas, sold in liters, is unleaded *(natural)* sold as 95 and 98 octane, diesel *(nafta)* or LPG *(autoplyn* or *plyn)*. Some out-of-town stations *(benzinová pumpa)* close for lunch and after 6 p.m. There are 24-hour gas stations in cities and along highways.

AAA Affiliated Motoring Club

Ústřední automotoklub České republiky (ÚAMK; CR) Na Strži 9, CZ-140 02 Prague 4 ☎ 261 104 333; www.uamk.cz. If you break down while driving phone ☎ 1234 (24-hours; ÚAMK breakdown service). Not all automobile clubs offer full services to AAA members.

Breakdowns and Accidents

There are 24-hour emergency phones at regular intervals on highways or ☎ 158 for police assistance. Most car-rental firms provide their own free rescue service; if you have an accident, follow the rental documentation instructions supplied with the car. Use of an unauthorized repair company may violate your rental agreement. You must carry a first-aid kit and a warning triangle in the car.

Other Information

The minimum age for driving a car is 18 (may be higher for some car-rental firms). An International Driving Permit (IDP) is formally required, though police and car-rental companies will usually accept a U.S. state driver's license. A Green Card (international motor insurance certificate) is required for a private car; see page 15 for more information. You are required by law to use dimmed headlights at all times when driving.

Useful Words and Phrases

The official language of the Czech Republic is Czech *(česky)* – a highly complex Slavic tongue. Czech sounds and looks daunting, but apart from a few special letters, each letter and sound is pronounced as it is written – the key is to stress the first syllable of a word.

Any attempt to speak Czech will be heartily appreciated, although English is spoken by many involved in the tourist trade. Below are a few words that may be helpful.

Do you speak English?	*Mluvíte anglicky?*
What is your name?	*Jak se jmenujete?*
hello, goodbye (casual)	*ahoj*
good morning	*dobré ráno*
goodbye	*na shledanou*
good night	*dobrou noc*
How much?	*Kolik?*
excuse me	*promiňte*
I am American	*Jsem Američan(ka)*
I would like	*Chtěl(a) bych*
I don't understand	*Nerozumím*
no smoking	*kouření zakazano*
okay	*dobře*
open	*otevřeno*
closed	*zavřeno*
please	*prosím*
thank you	*děkuji*
ticket	*lístek*
(one-way/round trip)	*(jednosměrnou/ zpáteční)*
Where is...?	*Kde je...?*
yes/no	*ano/ne*
you're welcome	*prosím*
the hotel	***hotel***
breakfast	*snídaně*
key	*klíč*
reservation	*rezervaci*
room	*pokoj*
single/double room	*jednolůžkový dvoulůžkový pokoj*
Where is the toilet?	*Kde je toalet?*
bathroom	*koupelna*
shower	*sprcha*
the restaurant	***restaurace***
beef	*hovězí*
beer	*pivo*
bread	*chleb*
the check	*účet*
chicken	*kuře*
coffee	*káva*
dessert	*moučník*
dish of the day	*nabídka dne*
fish	*ryba*
lamb	*jehněčí*
meat	*maso*
pork	*vepřové maso*
seafood	*mořské ryby*
starter	*předkrm*
wine	*víno*

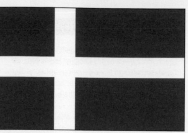

National Flag

Essential for Travelers*

● Required ● Recommended ● Not required

Passport	●
Visa (check regulations before you travel)	●
Travel, medical insurance	●
Round-trip or onward airline ticket	●
Local currency	●
Traveler's checks	●
Credit cards	●
First-aid kit and medicines*	●
Inoculations	●

*see also *Health* section

Essential for Drivers*

Driver's license	●
International Driving Permit	●
Car insurance (for nonrental cars)	●
Car registration (for nonrental cars)	●

*see also *Driving* section

Important Addresses

VisitDenmark
655 Third Avenue
Ste. 1810
New York, 10017
☎ (212) 885-9700
Email: usa@visitdenmark.com
www.visitdenmark.com

VisitDenmark
Islands Brygge 43, 3rd Floor
DK-2300 København S, Denmark
☎ 32 88 99 00
Fax 32 88 99 01
Email: contact@visitdenmark.com
www.visitdenmark.com

American Embassy
Dag Hammarskjölds Allé 24
DK-2100 København Ø, Denmark
☎ 33 41 71 00
Fax 35 43 02 23
https://dk.usembassy.gov

Customs

✔ Duty-free limits on goods brought in from non-European Union countries:
200 cigarettes or 100 cigarillos or 50 cigars or 250 g. tobacco; 4 L. wine, 1 L. alcohol over 22% volume or 2 L. alcohol under 22% volume; 16 L. beer; 50 ml. perfume; 250 ml. toilet water; plus any other duty-free goods (including gifts) to the value of DKr3,250 if you arrive by plane or ship, or DKr2,250 if you arrive by other transport.

There is no limit on the importation of tax-paid goods purchased within the European Union, provided they are for your own personal use. Limits for alcohol and tobacco products apply to visitors aged 17 or over.

There are no currency regulations.

✘ No unlicensed drugs, weapons, ammunition, fireworks, obscene material, pets or other animals, counterfeit money or copied goods, plants, meat or poultry.

For customs limits for returning U.S. citizens see page 16.

Money

Krone (DKr)
Denmark's currency is the krone (DKr), which is divided into 100 øre.

The denominations of krone bills are 50, 100, 200, 500 and 1,000.
There are coins of 50 øre and 1, 2, 5, 10 and 20DKr.

ATMs are plentiful and credit, debit and prepaid cards are accepted in hotels, large stores and upscale restaurants; check first in small or rural establishments.

Senior citizens and holders of International Student Identity Cards (ISIC) can often obtain discounts on travel and entrance fees.

Tips and Gratuities

Tips are not expected, but may be given for outstanding service.

Restaurants (service is always included)	change
Cafés/bars	change
Taxis (tips included in fare)	change
Porters	change
Chambermaids	change
Cloakroom attendants	change

Communications

Post Offices

Stamps *(frimerker)* can be bought at a post office *(postkontoret)*, newsstand *(aviskiosk)* or stationer *(papirhandel)*.

Mailboxes *(postkasse)* are red with a horn and crown detail. Hours for out-of-town post offices may vary. For postal service inquiries telephone Post Denmark ☎ 70 70 70 30; www.postnord.dk. You can buy postage for letters and parcels via the PostNord app.

Telephones

There are no public telephones in Denmark. Although you will be able to make calls from your hotel, this tends to be expensive, so it is advisable to bring your own cell phone. Check the cost of overseas cell phone usage with your provider before traveling. You can buy a pre-paid SIM card for use in your own cell providing your cell is compatible and isn't locked. These are available from newsstands and kiosks such as 7-Eleven. Again, check with your provider before you visit.

Phoning inside Denmark

All telephone numbers are 8 digits and include the regional code. Dial all digits when making a call. To call the operator dial 110; to call collect dial 115.

Phoning Denmark from abroad

The country code for Denmark is 45. Note that Danish numbers in this book do not include the country code. To phone Denmark from the United States or Canada add the prefix 011 45. Example: 11 22 33 44 becomes 011 45 11 22 33 44

Phoning from Denmark

To phone the United States or Canada from Denmark, prefix the area code and number with 00 1. Example: (111) 222-3333 becomes 00 1 111 222-3333. To call directory inquiries in Denmark dial 118. To call international information dial 113.

Emergency Telephone Numbers

Police *(politi)* **112** Fire service *(brandvæsen)* **112**
Ambulance *(sygevogn)* **112**
Emergency calls are free from phone booths.

Time Zones

Copenhagen: 12 noon
New York: 6 a.m. (-6 hours)
Chicago: 5 a.m. (-7 hours)
Denver: 4 a.m. (-8 hours)
Los Angeles: 3 a.m. (-9 hours)

Hours of Operation

Stores are open Monday to Saturday; some open on Sundays and many stay open later on Fridays. The exceptions to this are public holidays when they must close at 3 p.m.

Department stores and **supermarkets** often stay open later than 5:30/6 p.m. Bakeries, florists and souvenir stores are often open seven days a week.

Large **gas stations** sell convenience foods seven days a week.

Banks operate Monday to Friday 10–4, but in Copenhagen they are open until 5 p.m. On Thursday all banks are open until 6 p.m.

Post offices open at weekdays at 9 or 10 and close at 5 or 6; some post offices open on Saturday morning.

Museums tend to be open 10–5; check before you visit.

Pharmacies are open Monday to Friday 9–5:30.

National Holidays

Banks, businesses and most stores close on these days.

Jan. 1	New Year's Day
Mar./Apr.	Maundy Thursday
Mar./Apr.	Good Friday
Mar./Apr.	Easter Monday
Apr./May	Great Prayer Day
May/Jun.	Ascension Day
May/Jun.	Pentecost Monday
May/Jun.	Whit Sunday
May/Jun.	Whit Monday
Jun. 5	Constitution Day
Dec. 24	Christmas Eve
Dec. 25	Christmas Day
Dec. 26	St. Stephen's Day
Dec. 31	New Year's Eve

Photography

Denmark is not renowned for its sunshine and the winter months have short daylight hours. Some museums may not allow photography; check before taking photographs. Batteries are sold throughout the city and there are plenty of places to download and print digital images.

Denmark

Health

Medical Insurance

Private medical insurance is recommended. In an emergency, visitors from the U.S. and Canada can receive free temporary treatment in a hospital *(hospitalet)*. You will be charged for more extensive treatment. Health offices *(kommunes social og sundhedforvaltning)* have lists of hospitals and doctors, or ask at your hotel.

Dental Services

Dentists *(tandlægen)* will charge for any treatment given. They are listed in the telephone directory, and after-hours treatment is available in some clinics. Advice can be sought at tourist and health offices. Be sure that treatment is covered by your medical insurance.

Sun Advice

The warmest months are July and August. The sun in Denmark is not fierce, but sun protection is still advised, especially on boats or near the water.

Drugs

To obtain a prescription medicine at a pharmacy *(apotek)* it must be prescribed by a Scandinavian doctor, so make sure that your supply of prescribed medicines will last your stay. If you are bringing prescription drugs for personal use into Denmark, bring a copy of your prescription to prove that the drugs relate to you. Additionally, some preparations available over the counter in the U.S. may be obtained in Denmark only with a prescription. After regular hours, the nearest all-night facility is posted at all pharmacies.

Safe Water

Tap water is safe to drink, and mineral water *(mineralvand)* is widely available.

Restrooms

Public restrooms *(toiletterne)* are easy to find, clean, well equipped and usually free. They are often indicated by a symbol, or marked WC or *Damer* (women) and *Herrer* (men).

Electricity

Denmark has a 220-volt power supply. Electrical sockets take plugs with two round pins. American appliances will need a plug adapter and will require a transformer if they do not have a dual-voltage facility.

National Transportation

Train *(Tog)*

Copenhagen is an important meeting point for trains between Europe and the rest of Scandinavia. Danish State Railways, Danske Statsbaner (DSB), runs an efficient service with trains linking to Germany and, via the Øresund Link, to Sweden. Most domestic trains have refreshment facilities; seat reservations are recommended. Call for information (☎ 70 13 14 15 to book tickets in English. For international routes ☎ 70 13 14 18; www.dsb.dk).

Bus *(Bus)*

The domestic bus service is good; ask for details at local tourist offices. Abildskou runs a service between cities in Denmark, and destinations in Sweden and Norway (☎ 70 21 08 88; www.Abildskou.com).

Ferry *(Færge)*

There are numerous ferry services from Denmark, with year-round connections to many northern European countries. DFDS Seaways has an office in Denmark, ☎ 33 42 30 10 (Mon.–Fri. 9–4:30); www.dfdsseaways.com.

Driving

Drive on the right

Speed Limits

Police can impose on-the-spot fines.

Limited-access highways *(motorvej)* **130 k.p.h. (80 m.p.h.)** or **110 k.p.h. (68 m.p.h.)**

Main roads **80 k.p.h. (50 m.p.h.)** Minimum speed **40 k.p.h. (24 m.p.h.)**

Urban areas **50 k.p.h. (31 m.p.h.)** but **40 k.p.h. (24 m.p.h.)** in central Copenhagen

Seat Belts

Must be worn in front and back seats at all times. Children under 8 years must be fastened in a child's seat.

Blood Alcohol

The legal blood alcohol limit is 0.05%. Random breath tests on drivers are carried out frequently, especially late at night, and the penalties for offenders are severe.

Note: It is illegal to drive while using a hand-held cellphone.

Denmark

Driving (continued)

Tolls

There are no tolls on highways. However, the Storebælt (Great Belt) tunnel and bridge from Korsør to Nyborg, and the impressive 10-mile Øresund tunnel and bridge from Copenhagen to Malmö (Sweden) both levy a toll.

Car Rental

The leading car-rental companies have offices at airports, principal train stations and ferry terminals. Hertz offers discounted rates for AAA members (see page 15). For reservations:

	United States	Denmark
Alamo	(888) 233-8749	70 21 23 50
Avis	(800) 633-3469	33 26 80 80
Budget	(800) 218 7992	32 52 39 00
Hertz	(800) 654-3001	33 17 90 00

Fuel

Gas (benzin) is sold in liters; unleaded gas (blyfri) comes in 92 and 95 octane ratings. Self-service gas stations (tank selv or selvbetjening) are common, except on limited-access highways. Most gas stations take credit cards, and some have automatic pumps for DKr50, DKr100 and sometimes DKr200 bills.

AAA Affiliated Motoring Club

Forenede Danske Motorejere (FDM)
Firskovvej 32, 2800 Lyngby
70 13 30 40; www.fdm.dk. Not all automobile clubs offer full services to AAA members.

Breakdowns and Accidents

Report accidents to the Dansk Forening for International Motorkøretøjsforsikring (DFIM; www.dfim.dk), Philip Heymans Allé 1, DK-2900 Hellerup (41 91 90 69, 10 a.m.–3 p.m.). If you are involved in an accident 112 for police, fire or ambulance services.

Most car-rental firms provide their own free rescue service; if your car is rented, follow the instructions given in the documentation. Use of a car-repair service other than those authorized by your rental company may violate your agreement. You must carry a warning triangle in your car.

Other Information

The minimum legal age for driving a car is 18 (may be 20 to 25 for some car-rental firms).

An International Driving Permit (IDP) is recommended; some car-rental firms require it, and it can speed up formalities if you are involved in an accident. A Green Card (international motor insurance certificate) is recommended if you are driving a private car; see page 15 for more information. Use dimmed headlights at all times.

Useful Words and Phrases

Danish is a Germanic language, close to Swedish and Norwegian, but it is tricky to pronounce because some letters (d, g) are silent in the middle or at the end of words, h before a v becomes silent, and some specifically Scandinavian vowels (å, ø, and æ) are awkward to say correctly. But Danes are aware of this, and most of them speak very good English. In addition, menus are often in English or German.

In the Danish alphabet, the following letters come after z: å, ø and æ. (Århus, for example, comes at the end of the alphabet.) Å is used in place of aa, although the city of Aalborg prefers to write the two vowels out in full.

The following words and phrases should help you:

Do you speak English?	*Taler de Engelsk?*
excuse me	*undskyld*
hello/goodbye	*hej/farvel*
how much is…?	*hvor meget koster det?*
I am American	*jeg er Amerikaner*
I'd like…	*jeg vil gerne have…*
I don't understand	*jeg forstår det ikke*
open/closed	*åben/lukket*
please/thank you	*værså venlig/tak*
ticket (one-way/	*billet (enkeltbillet/*
round trip)	*en tur-retur)*
where is/are…?	*hvor er…?*
yes/no	*ja/nej*
the hotel	**hotel**
breakfast	*morgenmad*
key	*nøgle*
for one/two nights	*en nat/to nætter*
for one person/	*enkeltværelse/*
two people	*dobbeltværelse*
room	*værelse*
shower	*brusebad*
the restaurant	**restaurant**
beef	*bøf*
bread	*brød*
butter	*smør*
cheese	*ost*
the check	*regningen*
chicken	*kylling*
cod	*torsk*
coffee/tea	*kaffe/the*
Danish pastry	*Wienerbrød*
dessert	*dessert*
fish	*fisk*
fruit salad	*frugtsalat*
herring	*sild*
pork	*suinkød*
potatoes	*kartofler*
shellfish	*skaldyr*
shrimps	*rejer*
starter	*forret*
trout	*ørred*
vegetables	*grøntsager*
wine	*vin*

Finland

National Flag

Essential for Travelers

● **Required** ● **Recommended** ● **Not required**

Passport	●
Visa (check regulations before you travel)	●
Travel, medical insurance	●
Round-trip or onward airline ticket	●
Local currency	●
Traveler's checks	●
Credit cards	●
First-aid kit and medicines	●
Inoculations	●

Essential for Drivers*

Driver's license	●
International Driving Permit	●
Car insurance (for nonrental cars)	●
Car registration (for nonrental cars)	●

*see also *Driving* section

Important Addresses

Visit Finland
297 York Street
Jersey City
NJ 07302
☎ (917) 863-5484
www.visitfinland.com

Visit Finland
P.O. Box 358
Porkkalankatu 1
C/O Finpro
FIN-00181, Helsinki, Finland
☎ 09 3101 3300
www.visitfinland.com

American Embassy
Itäinen Puistotie 14B
FIN-00140 Helsinki, Finland
☎ 09 616 250 (embassy)
https://fi.usembassy.gov

Customs

✔ **Duty-free limits on goods brought in from non-European Union countries:**
200 cigarettes or 100 cigarillos or 50 cigars or 250 g. tobacco; 1 L. alcohol over 22% volume or 2 L. alcohol under 22% volume; 4 L. wine; 16 L. beer; 50 ml. perfume; 250 ml. toilet water; plus any other duty-free goods (including gifts) to the value of €430 for visitors entering the E.U. by air or by sea or €300 if arriving by other means.

Visitors must declare cash over the value of €10,000 (or equivalent).

✘ No unlicensed drugs, weapons, ammunition, obscene material, counterfeit money or copied goods.

For customs limits for returning U.S. citizens see page 16.

Money

Euro (€)
Finland's currency is the euro (€), a currency shared by 18 other European Union countries.

The euro is divided into 100 cents (¢).
The denominations of euro bills are 5, 10, 20, 50, 100, 200 and 500.
There are coins of 1, 2, 5, 10, 20 and 50¢ and €1 and €2.

Credit, debit and prepaid cards are widely accepted. ATMs for withdrawing local currency are plentiful in Finland.

Tips and Gratuities

Tips are welcomed, but not expected.

Restaurants	change
Cafés/bars	change
Taxis; hairdressers	none
Porters; restroom attendants	change
Chambermaids	change
Cloakroom attendants; hotel/restaurant doormen	€1

Communications

Post Offices

Helsinki's main post office at Elielinaukio 2F is open Monday to Friday 8–8, Saturday 10–4, Sunday noon–4. Stamps *(postimerkki)* can be bought at post offices, bookstores, newsstands (R-kiosks), train and bus stations. Mailboxes can be freestanding or set into a wall.

Telephones

Public phone boxes have been phased out in Finland. To use your own cell phone without incurring potentially high roaming charges, you can buy and insert a prepaid SIM card, providing your cell phone is compatible and it isn't locked. Check with your provider before leaving home. Alternatively, consider buying a very basic cellphone with a prepaid SIM when you arrive in Finland for use during your stay.

Phoning inside Finland
All Finnish telephone numbers in this book include an area code: dial the number listed. For directory assistance information dial 118.

Phoning Finland from abroad
The country code for Finland is 358; to phone Finland from the United States or Canada, omit the first zero from the Finnish number and prefix with 011 358. (Finnish area codes have two or three digits including the first zero.) Example: 01 122 3344 becomes 011 358 1 122 3344.

Phoning from Finland
To phone the United States or Canada from Finland, prefix the area code and number with 00 1. (There are other exit codes, depending on what telephone system you are using: 990, 991, 992, 994, 996, 998, or 999, followed by 1.) Example: (111) 222-3333 becomes 00 1 111 222-3333. For national information, dial 02 02 02; for international information, dial 02 02 08.

Emergency Telephone Numbers

Police *(poliisi)* **112**
Fire service *(palokunta)* **112**
Ambulance *(ambulanssi)* **112**

Time Zones

Helsinki: 12 noon
New York: 5 a.m. (-7 hours)
Chicago: 4 a.m. (-8 hours)
Denver: 3 a.m. (-9 hours)
Los Angeles: 2 a.m. (-10 hours)

Hours of Operation

Stores, department stores and **shopping malls** operate Monday to Saturday 9–6; some stores close at 2 or 3 on Saturday. During the week, large stores extend their hours to 8 or 9, and open on Sunday from June through August and during December. Grocery stores stay open until 8 or 9 p.m. Some supermarkets and convenience stores open on Sunday. The Design District organizes late-night shopping six times a year, with special events.

Some **gas stations** close on Sunday.
Banks generally operate Monday to Friday 9:30–4:30.
Post offices are open Monday to Friday 9–6, but out-of-town post offices may have shorter hours. Some city post offices and banks stay open into the evening.
Museum opening times vary according to the season. Check with the local tourist office.
Pharmacies *(apteekki)* open Monday to Friday 8–7, but some may open for a few hours on Saturday. In Helsinki, the Apteekki Yliopiston, Mannerheimintie 5, ☎ 0300 20200, is open daily 7 a.m.–midnight.

National Holidays

Banks, businesses and most stores close on these days.

Jan. 1	New Year's Day
Jan. 6	Epiphany
Mar./Apr.	Good Friday
Mar./Apr.	Easter Monday
May	Ascension
Jun. 21–22	Midsummer's Day Eve and Midsummer's Day
Nov. 1	All Saints' Day
Dec. 6	Independence Day
Dec. 24	Christmas Eve
Dec. 25	Christmas Day
Dec. 26	St. Stephen's Day

Photography

Camera batteries and memory cards are readily available and there are many places offering digital equipment and download services for digital cameras. Bring a tripod if you hope to photograph the northern lights *(aurora borealis)*. Check whether or not photography is permitted in museums.

Finland

Health

Medical Insurance

Private medical insurance is recommended. All treatment in a hospital *(sairaala)* has to be paid for. Foreign visitors can receive good service at a private hospital or health center *(lääkäriasema);* for 24-hour medical advice ☎ 09 310 10023. For private medical care contact Mehiläinen, Töölö, Pohjoinen Hesperiankatu 17, Helsinki ☎ 010 414 0200 (24 hours).

Dental Services

Dentists *(hammaslääkäri)* charge for treatment and can be expensive, so find out if treatment is covered by your medical insurance. City hospitals have 24-hour clinics.

Sun Advice

Southeast Finland has the highest summer temperature in Scandinavia, so precautions are necessary. Use a suitable sunscreen and cover up sensitive skin.

Drugs

Prescription and nonprescription medicines are available from pharmacies *(apteekki)*. If you need a pharmacy outside regular hours, information about the nearest all-night facility is posted at all pharmacies.

Safe Water

Tap water is safe to drink, and mineral water *(kivennäisvesi)* is widely available.

Restrooms

Public restrooms are easy to find, immaculately clean and modern, and are designated by *Miehille/Miehet* (men) and *Naisille/Naiset* (women). There may be a small charge, but many are free. Attendants welcome loose change as a tip.

Electricity

Finland has a 230-volt power supply. Electrical sockets take plugs with two round pins. American appliances will need a plug adapter and will require a transformer if they do not have a dual-voltage facility.

National Transportation

Train *(Juna)*

The Finnish Railway (Valtion Rautatiet, or VR) extends north to southern Lapland. For timetable information *(Suomen kulkuneuvot)* ☎ 0600 41 900 (toll call); www.vr.fi. If you are planning extensive rail travel, buy a Eurail Finland pass before you arrive in Finland. For information go online at www.raileurope.com or www.eurail.com.

Bus *(Bussi)*

Bus lines run to even the most remote corners of Finland. Bus passes (discount cards) are available for those traveling long distances; valid 7 days (€149) or 14 days (€249). For information contact the inner-city bus service Matkahuolto, ☎ 0200 4000; www.matkahuolto.fi/en.

Ferry *(Laiva)*

There are many excursions exploring Finland's eastern lake system and the country's canal network. Trips into Russia, Estonia, Latvia and Lithuania are possible; check with the tour operator whether a short-term visa is required. These can be obtained through the country's embassy or a travel agent. Contact Tallink Silja ☎ 0600 15700; www.tallinksilja.com, and Viking Line ☎ 0600 41577; www.vikingline.fi.

Driving

Drive on the right

Speed Limits

Minor fines can be imposed on the spot, but not collected. Payment can be made at banks.

 Limited-access highways *(moottoritie)* **120 k.p.h. (74 m.p.h.)** in summer **100 k.p.h. (62 m.p.h.)** in winter Divided highways **100 k.p.h. (62 m.p.h.)**

 Main roads **80 k.p.h. (49 m.p.h.)**

 Urban areas **50 k.p.h. (31 m.p.h.)**

Seat Belts

Must be worn in front and back seats at all times.

Blood Alcohol

 The legal blood alcohol limit is 0.05%. Random breath tests on drivers are carried out frequently, especially late at night, and the penalties for offenders are severe.

Driving (continued)

Tolls

There are no highway tolls in Finland.

Car Rental

The leading car-rental firms have offices at airports and train stations. Hertz offers discounted rates for AAA members (see page 15). For reservations:

	United States	Finland
Avis	(800) 633-3469	09 822 833
Budget	(800) 527-0700	010 4362 300
Europcar	(888) 233-8749	04 0306 2800
Hertz	(800) 654-3131	0205 552 100

Fuel

There is no leaded gas in Finland. There are two grades of unleaded gas, 95 and 98 octane. Diesel is available. Gas stations are open Monday to Saturday 7 a.m.–9 p.m., shorter hours on Sunday. Credit cards are acccepted at most filling stations.

AAA Affiliated Motoring Club

Autoliitto (AL) P.O. Box 35, Hämeentie 105A, FI-00551 Helsinki 09 7258 4400; www.autoliitto.fi. If you break down while driving, 02 00 80 80 (24 hours) for the AL breakdown service. Not all automobile clubs offer full services to AAA members.

Breakdowns and Accidents

There are 24-hour emergency phones at regular intervals on highways. If you are involved in an accident, 112 for police, fire or ambulance. Accidents should be reported to Finnish Motor Insurers' Center (Liikenne-vakuutuskeskus), Itämerenkatu 11–13, 00180, Helsinki, 040 450 4520 (claims); www.lvk.fi.

Most car-rental firms provide their own free rescue service. Use of a car-repair service other than those authorized by your rental company may violate your agreement. You must carry a warning triangle and a fluorescent vest in your car.

Other Information

The minimum age for driving a car is 18 (19–25 for car-rental firms). An International Driving Permit (IDP) is recommended; some car-rental firms require it, and it can speed up formalities if you are involved in an accident. A Green Card (international motor insurance certificate) is recommended if you are driving a private car; see page 15 for more information. Dimmed headlights must be used at all times. In winter, snow tires or chains are essential. From December through February, winter tires (with or without studs) or tires intended for year-round use are compulsory.

Driving (continued)

You can buy or rent winter driving equipment from Autoliitto. Watch out for signs warning of elk and reindeer crossing roads, indicating the approximate length of danger zones – these animals are more active at dusk.

Useful Words and Phrases

Finnish is a complex and difficult language to learn, and bears little or no resemblance to neighboring languages. However, Swedish is Finland's second, more accessible language, and most people speak some English.

Finnish uses compound words, which are pronounced exactly as they are written. The first syllable of a word is always stressed, and each letter is pronounced individually.

Do you speak English?	*Puhutteko englantia?*
excuse me	*anteeksi*
hello	*terve*
goodbye	*näkemiin*
how much?	*kuinka paljon?*
how are you?	*kuinka voitte?*
Is it near?	*Onko se lähellä?*
I'd like...	*Haluaisin...*
I don't understand	*en ymmärrä*
no smoking	*tupakointi kielletty*
okay	*ja lyh*
open/closed	*avoinna/suljettu*
please/thank you	*olkaa hyvä/kiitos*
ticket (one-way/ round trip)	*menolippu meno-paluulippu*
where is...?	*missä on...?*
yes/no	*kyllä or joo/ei*
the hotel	***hotelli***
breakfast	*aamiainen*
key	*avain*
room	*huone*
shower	*suihku*
it's too expensive	*se on liian kallis*
the restaurant	***ravintola***
beef	*nauta*
bread	*leipä*
chicken	*kana*
coffee	*kahvi*
dessert	*jälkiruoka*
fish	*kala*
lamb	*karitsa*
main course	*pääruoka*
milk	*maito*
pork	*sianliha*
seafood	*äyriäisiä*
soup	*keitto*
steak	*pihvi*
wine	*vini*

National Flag

Essential for Travelers

● Required ● Recommended ● Not required

Passport	●
Visa (check regulations before you travel)	●
Travel, medical insurance	●
Round-trip or onward airline ticket	●
Local currency	●
Traveler's checks	●
Credit cards	●
First-aid kit and medicines	●
Inoculations	●

Essential for Drivers*

Driver's license	●
International Driving Permit	●
Car insurance (for nonrental cars)	●
Car registration (for nonrental cars)	●

*see also *Driving* section

Important Addresses

French Embassy USA
4101 Reservoir Road, N.W.
Washington, D.C., 20007
☎ (202) 944-6000; www.franceintheus.org

Atout France
(French Government Tourist Office)
79–81 rue de Clichy, 75009 Paris, France
(not open to the public)
☎ 01 42 96 70 00; us.france.fr
To receive information in the USA by post, write to:
Maison de la France at: 825 Third Avenue, 29th
Floor, New York, NY 10022 ☎ (212) 838 7800 or
9454 Wilshire Boulevard, Suite 210, Beverley Hills,
CA 90212, ☎ (310) 271 2693

American Embassy
2 avenue Gabriel, 75008 Paris, France
☎ 01 43 12 22 22; Fax 01 42 66 97 83
http://fr.usembassy.gov

American Consulate for American Citizen Affairs
4 avenue Gabriel, 75008 Paris, France
☎ 01 43 12 22 22
Open by appointment only

Customs

✔ **Duty-free limits on goods brought in from non-European Union countries:**
200 cigarettes or 100 cigarillos or 50 cigars or
250 g. tobacco; 1 L. alcohol over 22% volume or
2 L. alcohol under 22% volume or sparkling wine
and 4 L. still wine, 16 L. beer; plus any other
goods/gifts to the value of €430 if arriving by air
or sea, €300 if arriving overland (€150 for travelers
under 15). See http://ec.europa.eu/taxation_
customs/common/travellers/enter_eu/index_en.
htm.

There is no limit on the importation of tax-paid
goods bought within the E.U. if they are for your
own use.

Visitors must declare cash over the value of
€10,000 (or equivalent).

✗ No unlicensed drugs, weapons, ammunition,
obscene material, pets or other animals,
counterfeit money or copied goods, meat or poultry.

**For customs limits for returning U.S. citizens
see page 16.**

Money

Euro (€)
France's currency is the euro (€), a currency shared
by 18 other European Union countries.

The euro is divided into 100 cents (¢).
The denominations of euro bills are 5, 10, 20, 50,
100, 200 and 500.
There are coins of 1, 2, 5, 10, 20 and 50¢ and
€1 and €2.

Credit, debit and prepaid cards are widely
accepted. ATMs are plentiful throughout most
of France. It is a good idea to carry a mix of
large and small euro denominations.

Tips and Gratuities

Tips *(pourboires)* are welcomed, but not expected.

Restaurants (service is almost always included)	change
Cafés/bars (service is almost always included)	change
Taxis	€1–€2
Porters	€1–€2
Chambermaids	€2–€10
Hairdressers	€1–€2
Cloakroom attendants	50¢–€1

Communications

Post Offices

Buy stamps *(timbres-poste)* at a post office *(la poste)*, newsstand *(marchand de journaux)* or tobacconist *(tabac)*.

Hours of out-of-town post offices may vary. Mailboxes are yellow and wall-mounted or free-standing; there may be separate compartments for local mail *(départemental)*, for elsewhere in France, and abroad *(autres départements/destinations)*.

Telephones

The telephone system in France is efficient, and phone booths with instructions in English are easy to find. Most phones are operated solely with a phone card *(télécarte)*, which can be bought in 50 or 120 units from post offices, France Telecom offices, newsstands, tobacconists *(tabacs)* and SNCF (railway) counters. Most booths accept credit cards. Check overseas cell phone usage with your provider.

Phoning inside France

All telephone numbers are 10 digits, and include the regional code. Paris and Île de France numbers begin with 01; the rest of France is divided into four zones (02, 03, 04 and 05). Dial all digits when making a call.

Phoning France from abroad

The country code for France is 33. Note that French numbers in this book do not include the country code; you need to prefix this number if you are phoning from another country. To phone France from the United States or Canada, omit the first zero from the French number, and add the prefix 011 33. Example: 01 22 33 44 55 becomes 011 33 1 22 33 44 55.

Phoning from France

To phone the United States or Canada from France, prefix the area code and number with 00 1. Example: (111) 222-3333 becomes 00 1 111 222-3333. For directory inquiries dial 118 700.

Emergency Telephone Numbers

Police *(police)* 17; Fire service *(pompiers)* 18 Ambulance *(ambulance)* 15
112 (pan-European general emergency number)
Emergency calls are free from phone booths.

Time Zones

Paris: 12 noon
New York: 6 a.m. (-6 hours)
Chicago: 5 a.m. (-7 hours)
Denver: 4 a.m. (-8 hours)
Los Angeles: 3 a.m. (-9 hours)

Hours of Operation

Most **stores** open Monday to Saturday 8:30–6, and some close a half-day Monday, although some food establishments, especially bakeries, open Sunday mornings. **Hypermarkets** (large all-purpose stores) are open Monday to Saturday 9–9 or 10 p.m. Opening hours are longer in resort areas and major towns and cities.

Banks operate Monday to Friday 8–12:30 and 1:30–3. Out-of-town banks may stay closed on Monday, while city banks may open on Saturday morning.

Post offices are open Monday to Friday 8–noon and 2–6, and 8–noon on Saturday.

Museum times vary considerably, and it is best to check before a visit. Municipal museums close on Monday, while national museums close on Tuesday (except Versailles and Trianon Palace which close on Monday). Many museums close on national holidays.

Pharmacies are open Monday to Friday 8–noon and 2–6.

National Holidays

Banks, businesses and most stores close on these days.

Jan. 1	New Year's Day
Mar./Apr.	Easter Monday
May 1	May Day
May 8	VE Day
May	Ascension Day
May/Jun.	Pentecost Monday
Jul. 14	Bastille Day
Aug. 15	Assumption of the Virgin
Nov. 1	All Saints' Day
Nov. 11	Armistice Day
Dec. 25	Christmas Day

Photography

The range of subjects to photograph in France is enormous. All sizeable towns will have a camera store with digital equipment and photo developing facilities, though development may not be the same day and will be expensive.

Some museums and churches will allow you to photograph inside, but permission for flash photography is usually required.

France

Health

Medical Insurance

Private medical insurance is recommended. Visitors from non-E.U. countries have to pay for all medical treatment; keep all receipts and medicine labels to claim on your travel insurance. If you wish to see an English-speaking doctor *(médecin)* ask at your consulate or hotel.

Dental Services

A dentist *(dentiste)* charges for treatment. Emergency help is available from dentists listed in the *Yellow Pages (pages jaunes)*. Make sure that your private medical insurance covers dental treatment.

Sun Advice

The yearly average for sunshine is high: 2,500 hours (3,000 hours along the coast). Summers, particularly July and August, can be dry and hot, especially in the south. When outside wear a hat and drink plenty of fluids. On the beach a high-SPF sunscreen is essential.

Drugs

Prescription medicines and medical advice can be obtained from a pharmacy *(pharmacie)*, designated by a green cross sign. If you need medicines after regular hours, information about the nearest 24-hour facility is posted on the door of all pharmacies.

Safe Water

It is safe to drink tap water, but never drink from a fountain marked *"eau non potable"* ("not drinking water"). Many French people prefer the taste of bottled mineral water *(l'eau minérale en bouteille)*, which is widely available. A less expensive alternative is *l'eau de source*, which is spring water.

Restrooms

It is not difficult to find a restroom *(toilettes* or *WC*, pronounced *vay-say* in French), although you may still find the old-fashioned "squat" variety. Hygiene is usually of a reasonable standard. There is a small fee to use facilities in train stations. If you need to use the restroom in a café or bar, buy a drink first.

Electricity

France has a 220-volt power supply. Electrical sockets take plugs with two round pins (occasionally with three round pins). American appliances will need a plug adapter and will require a transformer if they do not have a dual-voltage facility.

National Transportation

Train *(Train)*

The state rail company is the Société Nationale des Chemins de Fer Français (SNCF; ☎ 3635; www.sncf.com. Trains are fast, reliable and comfortable, with numerous discounts available. A round-the-clock car-carrying rail service from Calais (Le Shuttle) to Folkestone, England, and a Paris–London passenger train, Eurostar (☎ 01 70 70 60 88, toll call; www.eurostar.com) both run through the tunnel under the English Channel. International train services from Paris to cities in Belgium, The Netherlands and Germany are operated by Thalys ☎ 08 25 84 25 97; www.thalys.com.

Bus *(Autobus)*

Bus services in cities are excellent, but rural areas may be less well served. Long-distance bus stations are usually close to train stations, and major train and bus services usually coordinate (a long-distance bus is called a *car)*. Bus services shown on train timetables are run by the SNCF, and rail tickets are often valid for them. The Eurolines international bus network operates in France (☎ 08 92 89 90 91, toll call; www.eurolines.com).

Ferry *(Ferry)*

There are frequent ferry sailings to Britain from ports along the English Channel. Some Mediterranean ferries operate in summer only and may need reservations in advance.

Driving

Drive on the right

Speed Limits

Traffic police can impose severe on-the-spot fines.

Limited-access toll highways *(autoroutes à péage)* **130 k.p.h. (80 m.p.h.)**
Outer lane minimum **80 k.p.h. (49 m.p.h.)**
On wet roads **110 k.p.h. (68 m.p.h.)**
In fog with visibility less than 50m (55 yards) **50 k.p.h. (31 m.p.h.)**
Toll-free highways *(autoroutes)* and divided highways **110 k.p.h. (68 m.p.h.)**

Main roads **90 k.p.h. (56 m.p.h.)**
On wet roads **80 k.p.h. (49 m.p.h.)**

Urban areas. **50 k.p.h. (31 m.p.h.)**, sometimes reduced to **30 k.p.h. (18 m.p.h.)**

Driving (continued)

Seat Belts
Must be worn in front and back seats at all times.

Blood Alcohol
The legal blood alcohol limit is 0.05% (0.02% for drivers with less than 3 years' driving experience). Random breath tests on drivers are carried out frequently, and the penalties for drivers in excess of the legal limit are severe.

Tolls
There are tolls on many limited-access highways *(autoroutes à péage)*. Collect a ticket on entry and keep it in a safe place: you must show the ticket and pay when exiting. Cash and credit cards are accepted.

Car Rental
The leading car-rental firms have offices at airports and train stations. Hertz offers discounted rates for AAA members (see page 15). For reservations:

	United States	France
Alamo	(884) 345 6962	08 05 54 25 10
Avis	(800) 633 3469	08 21 23 07 60
Budget	(800) 472-3325	08 25 00 35 64
Hertz	(800) 654-3001	09 69 39 40 49

Fuel
Gas stations are generally easy to find, and highway service areas are open 24 hours. Gas *(essence)* is unleaded *(sans plomb)* and sold in liters. Credit cards are accepted at most filling stations; many pumps read cards directly, so the customer does not have to pay at the counter; check with your card issuer for usage in France.

AAA Affiliated Motoring Club

Automobile Club de L'Ile de France (FFAC)
9 rue d'Artois, Paris 75008
01 40 55 43 00; 01 43 80 90 51;
www.automobile-club.org. Not all automobile clubs offer full services to AAA members.

Breakdowns and Accidents
If you are involved in an accident, 17 or 112 for police assistance. There are orange emergency telephones every 2 km (1.2 miles) on highways. Most car-rental firms provide their own free rescue service; follow the instructions given in the rental documentation. Use of a car-repair service other than those authorized by your rental company may violate your agreement. Vehicles must carry an emergency pack containing a high visibility vest and luminous warning triangle in case of breakdown. In the event of a breakdown the vest must be worn when you are outside your vehicle.

Driving (continued)

Other Information
The minimum age for driving a car is 18 (between 21 and 25, for some car-rental firms). An IDP (International Driving Permit) is recommended; some car-rental firms require it. A Green Card (international motor insurance certificate) is recommended if driving a private car (see page 15). In built-up areas you must yield the right-of-way to vehicles coming from a side street on the right. All vehicles must carry a breath alcohol analyzer.

Useful Words and Phrases

You'll be well received if you try to pronounce words correctly. Final consonants are seldom pronounced. For instance, the masculine adjective *ouvert* (open) is pronounced [oo-ver]; the feminine *ouverte* [oo-vert]. The final consonant in a word like *vin*, *bon* or *grand* alters the last vowel, making it nasal.

h is silent	*hôtel* [o-tel]
th is *t* (but *ch* is *sh*)	*thé* [tay]; *chaud* [show]
ou is full	*tout* [too]
u is tight, as in cupola	*tu* [tu], *menu* [meuh-nu]
c and *g* hard before *a, o, u,*	*car* [car], *guide* [geed]
c and *g* soft before *i* or *e*	*cigarette, age* [arzh]
ç is soft (before an a)	*français* [frahn-say]
gn as in union	*agneau* [an-yo]

Do you speak English?	*Parlez-vous anglais?*
excuse me	*excusez-moi*
hello/goodbye	*bonjour/au revoir*
How much is this?	*C'est combien?*
I am American	*Je suis Américain/e*
I'd like...	*je voudrais...*
I don't understand	*Je ne comprends pas*
open/closed	*ouvert/fermé*
please/thank you	*s'il vous plaît/merci*
ticket	*billet*
(one-way/round trip)	*(simple/aller-retour)*
where is…?	*où est…?*
yes/no	*oui/non*
you're welcome	*de rien*
the hotel	***l'hôtel***
breakfast	*petit déjeuner*
I have a reservation	*j'ai réservé*
for one/two nights	*pour une/deux nuit(s)*
one/two people	*une/deux personne(s)*
room	*une chambre*
shower	*une douche*
with en-suite bathroom	*avec salle de bains*
the restaurant	***le restaurant***
beef	*boeuf*
bread	*pain*
the check	*l'addition*
dish of the day	*plât du jour*

Germany

National Flag

Essential for Travelers*

● **Required** ● **Recommended** ● **Not required**

Passport	●
Visa (check regulations before you travel)	●
Travel, medical insurance	●
Round-trip or onward airline ticket	●
Local currency	●
Traveler's checks	●
Credit cards	●
First-aid kit and medicines	●
Inoculations	●

*see also *Health* section

Essential for Drivers*

Driver's license	●
International Driving Permit	●
Car insurance (for nonrental cars)	●
Car registration (for nonrental cars)	●

*see also *Driving* section

Important Addresses

German National Tourist Office (Administration)
122 East 42nd Street, 52nd Floor
New York, NY 10168-0072
☎ (212) 661-7175
www.germany.travel

**Deutsche Zentrale für Tourismus e.V
(German National Tourist Office)**
Beethovenstrasse 69
60325 Frankfurt am Main, Germany
☎ 069 974 64-0
Fax 069 97464-233
www.germany.travel

American Embassy Consular Section
Clayallee 170
14191 Berlin, Germany
☎ 030 8305-0
American Citizen Services
Mon.–Fri. 8–noon, by appointment only
https://de.usembassy.gov

Customs

✓ **Duty-free limits on goods brought in from
non-European Union countries:**
200 cigarettes or 100 cigarillos or 50 cigars or
250 g. tobacco; 1 L. alcohol over 22% volume and
2 L. alcohol under 22% or 2 L. sparkling or fortified
wine and 4 L. still wine; 16 L. beer; 50 ml. perfume;
250 ml. toilet water; plus any other duty-free goods
(including gifts) to the value of €430 if arriving by
air or sea, and €300 for all other travelers (€150
for travelers under 15).

There is no limit on the importation of tax-paid
goods purchased within the E.U., provided they are
for personal use.

Visitors must declare cash amounting to €10,000
(or equivalent).

✗ No unlicensed drugs, weapons, ammunition,
obscene material, pets or other animals,
counterfeit money or copied goods, meat or poultry.

**For customs limits for returning U.S. citizens
see page 16.**

Money

Euro (€)
Germany's currency is the euro (€), a currency
shared by 18 other European Union countries.

The euro is divided into 100 cents (¢).
The denominations of euro bills are 5, 10, 20, 50,
100, 200 and 500.
There are coins of 1, 2, 5, 10, 20 and 50¢ and
€1 and €2.

Credit, debit and prepaid cards are accepted at
most larger merchants and upscale restaurants,
however, cash is still more widely accepted
throughout most of Germany.

Tips and Gratuities

Restaurants (where service is not included)	10%
Cafés/bars (where service is not included)	10%
Taxis	10%
Porters	change
Chambermaids	change
Hairdressers	change
Restroom attendants	change
Cloakroom attendants	change

Communications

Post Offices

Buy stamps *(Briefmarken)* at a post office *(Postamt)*. Hours for out-of-town post offices may vary. Mailboxes are bright yellow.

Telephones

Cell phone use has drastically reduced the availability of public phones, but they can still be found at main post offices, railway stations and airports. Look for the pink and white telephone stands. Telephone cards *(Telefonkarten)* can be bought at any post office. Free WiFi hotspots can be found extensively in Berlin, Cologne and Munich. Check overseas cell phone usage with your provider.

Phoning inside Germany
German telephone numbers in this book include an area code: dial the number listed.
To call the operator dial 11833 (extra cost).

Phoning Germany from abroad
The country code for Germany is 49. Note that German numbers in this book do not include the country code; you will need to prefix this number if you are phoning from another country. To phone Germany from the United States or Canada, omit the first zero from the German number, and add the prefix 011 49. (Note that the number of digits in German area codes varies.) Example: 011 22 33 44 becomes 011 49 11 22 33 44.

Phoning from Germany
To phone the United States or Canada from Germany, prefix the area code and number with 00 1. Example: 111 222-3333 becomes 00 1 111 222-3333. For national and international information in English, ☎ 11837.

Emergency Telephone Numbers

Police *(Polizei)* **110**
Fire service *(Feuerwehr)* **112**
Ambulance *(Krankenwagen)* **112**
112 (pan-European general emergency number)
Emergency calls are free from phone booths.

Time Zones

Berlin: 12 noon
New York: 6 a.m. (-6 hours)
Chicago: 5 a.m. (-7 hours)
Denver: 4 a.m. (-8 hours)
Los Angeles: 3 a.m. (-9 hours)

Hours of Operation

Store opening hours vary considerably, but are generally open Monday to Saturday. In larger cities, some stores stay open until 8–10 p.m. Many **banks** are open Monday to Friday 8:30–4 but close between 1–2 p.m. ATMs are accessible outside banking hours.

Post offices open Monday to Friday 8–6, and 8–noon on Saturday. Post offices at airports and train stations sometimes operate longer hours.

Museums often close on Monday and open late on Thursday; some outside cities close for lunch.

Pharmacies are open Monday to Friday 9–6:30, and tend to close earlier on Saturday.

National Holidays

Banks, businesses and most stores close on the following days.

Jan. 1	New Year's Day
Jan. 6	Epiphany (Bavaria, Baden-Württemberg and Saxony only)
Mar./Apr.	Good Friday
Mar./Apr.	Easter Monday
May 1	Labor Day
May	Ascension Day
May/Jun.	Pentecost Monday
Aug. 15	Assumption of the Virgin (Bavaria and Saarland only)
Oct. 3	Day of German Unity
Nov. 1	All Saints' Day (Baden-Württemberg, Bavaria, North Rhine-Westphalia, Rhineland-Palatinate and Saarland only)
Dec. 25	Christmas Day
Dec. 26	St. Stephen's Day

Photography

Memory cards, quality brand-name batteries and other accessories are easy to find. There are stores for digital equipment and facilities for downloading and printing. Some museums and churches allow photography (without flash). Check at each location.

Health

Medical Insurance
U.S. and Canadian visitors must pay for medical treatment from a doctor or at a hospital *(Krankenhaus)*. Keep all receipts to claim on your travel insurance. For details on emergency, weekend or English-speaking doctors, ask your hotel or consulate.
Note: Large parts of the countryside, particularly but not exclusively in the south, are home to *Zecken* – a kind of tick that can transmit a disease. It is essential to seek medical advice if you are bitten. An inoculation is available; go online at www.zecken.de.

Dental Services
A dentist *(Zahnarzt)* always charges for treatment. Emergency help is available from dentists listed in the local telephone directory. Find out if your private medical insurance covers dental treatment.

Sun Advice
Germany's continental climate brings cold, clear winters and warm summers, when sun protection is needed. Use sunscreen; children and those with fair skin should be vigilant.

Drugs
Prescription medicines and advice can be obtained from a pharmacy *(Apotheke)*; cosmetics and toiletries at a *Drogerie*. If you need medicine outside regular hours, information about the nearest 24-hour facility is posted on the door of all pharmacies.

Safe Water
Water is safe to drink in Germany, but you may prefer to drink bottled mineral water *(Mineralwasser)*, which is widely available.

Restrooms

Finding a restroom *(Toilette)* is not difficult; they are usually identified by symbols, or are designated *Herren* (men) and *Damen* or *Frauen* (women). Most toilets in restaurants, bars and coffee shops are free. Public toilets, however, are not free and often are operated by a 50¢ coin. If there is an attendant, small change is appreciated as a tip (50¢ usual amount).

Electricity

Germany has a 230-volt power supply. Electrical sockets take plugs with two round pins or sometimes three pins in a vertical row. American appliances will need a plug adapter and will require a transformer if they do not have a dual-voltage facility.

National Transportation

Train *(Zug)*
Germany's rail network is operated by Deutsche Bahn (DB), and local companies. ICE is a fast service of long-distance, high-speed trains. IC and EC trains operate between major towns and cities. Regional (RE, Regio) trains are modern and comfortable, and connect with long-distance services. Local services are called S-Bahn or U-Bahn. For fare reductions and information call ☎ 01806 996633 (24hrs; toll call).

Bus *(Bus)*
Towns and villages not served by the rail network usually have bus links, with timetables and routes coordinating with trains. German towns have their own buses, and one ticket is often good for other types of city transportation. The Eurolines (Deutsche Touring GmbH) international bus service operates in Germany: ☎ 069 9719 44833.

Ferry *(Fähre)*
Ferries from the ports of Lübeck, Kiel and Rostock in the north connect to Denmark, Norway, Sweden, Finland and the Baltic countries. Boats also offer a service to German islands and on many German lakes, rivers and canals. Ask for details at your travel agency or a local tourist office, where reservations can often be made.

Driving

Drive on the right

Speed Limits
Traffic police can impose severe on-the-spot fines.

 Limited-access highways *(Autobahn)*: unless signposted there is no speed limit but the suggested limit is **130 k.p.h. (80 m.p.h.)**

 Main roads **100 k.p.h. (62 m.p.h.)**

Urban areas **50 k.p.h. (31 m.p.h.)** or **30 k.p.h. (18 m.p.h.)** or as otherwise posted

Seat Belts
Seat belts must be worn at all times. Children must use a suitable restraint or seat.

Blood Alcohol
The legal blood alcohol limit is 0.05% (zero for novice drivers). Random breath tests on drivers are carried out frequently, especially late at night, and the penalties for offenders are severe.

Driving (continued)

Tolls

 Autobahn (highway) tolls may come into force by 2019.

Car Rental

The leading car-rental firms have offices at airports and train stations. Hertz offers discounted rates for AAA members (see page 15). For reservations:

	United States	Germany
Alamo	(877) 222-9075	0800 723 9253
Avis	(0800) 633 3469	069 5007 0020
Budget	(800) 472-3325	069 7104 45596
Hertz	(800) 654-3001	01806 333535

Fuel

Gas *(Benzin)* and diesel fuel are sold in liters. Gas stations are easy to find, and most highway services are open 24 hours. Self-service stations are called *Selbstbedienung* or *SB-Tanken,* and credit cards are widely accepted.

AAA Affiliated Motoring Club

Allgemeiner Deutscher Automobil-Club E.V. (ADAC) Hansastrasse 19, 80686 Munich; www.adac.de. If you break down while driving, 01802 22 22 22 (ADAC breakdown service). Not all automobile clubs offer full services to AAA members.

Breakdowns and Accidents

Most car-rental firms provide their own free rescue service; if your car is rented, follow the instructions given in the documentation. Use of a car-repair service other than those authorized by your rental company may violate your agreement. If you are involved in an accident, 110 or 112 for police.

Other Information

The minimum age for driving a car if you are a foreign license holder is 18 (it may be higher for some car-rental firms). You must keep an official translation with your driver's license; your embassy or a tourist office can help. An International Driving Permit (IDP) is highly recommended; some car-rental firms require it, and it can speed up formalities if you are involved in an accident. A Green Card (international motor insurance certificate) is recommended if you are driving a private car; see page 15 for more information. On-the-spot fines can be imposed if you run out of gas on a highway. Using a cell phone while driving is not permitted.

Useful Words and Phrases

German has many dialects. Language in the north is descended from Old Saxon, and in the south from Old High German. Their differences were resolved by Standard German *(Schriftdeutsch),* created by Martin Luther when he translated the Bible in the 16th century.

Germans are helpful to visitors who attempt to communicate in German, although English is widely spoken.

ü is like the u in cupola	*über* (over)
ie sounds like heat	*Sie* (you)
ei sounds like height	*Eingang* (entrance)
ch is a harsh rasp…	*J. S. Bach*
j is like the English y	*ja* (yes)
r is a guttural sound	*Fräulein* (Miss)
w sounds like English v	*wo* (where)
z is like English ts	*Zeit* (time)
Do you speak English?	*Sprechen Sie Englisch?*
excuse me	*Verzeihung*
hello	*Guten Tag*
goodbye	*Auf Wiedersehen*
How much is…?	*Wieviel kostet…?*
I am American	*Ich bin Amerikaner (in)*
I'd like…	*Ich hätte gerne*
I don't understand	*Ich verstehe nicht*
nonsmoking	*Nichtraucher*
open/closed	*offen/geschlossen*
please/thank you	*bitte/danke*
one-way ticket	*einfache Fahrkarte*
round-trip ticket	*Rückfahrkarte*
where is…?	*wo ist…?*
yes/no	*ja/nein*
you're welcome	*bitte*
the hotel	**das Hotel**
breakfast	*Frühstück*
reservation	*Reservieren/ Reservierung*
key	*Schlüssel*
for one/two nights	*für eine Nacht/ zwei Nächte*
for one person/ two people	*für eine Person/ zwei Personen*
room	*Zimmer*
shower	*Dusche*
the restaurant	**das Restaurant**
beefsteak	*Steak*
bread	*Brot*
the check	*Rechnung*
chicken	*Hähnchen*
coffee	*Kaffee*
dessert	*Dessert*
dish of the day	*Tagesgericht*
entree	*Hauptgericht*
first courses	*Vorspeisen*
fish	*Fisch*
lamb	*Lamm*
pork	*Schweinefleisch*
seafood	*Meeresfrüchte*
wine	*Wein*

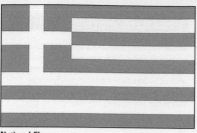

National Flag

Essential for Travelers*

● **Required** ● **Recommended** ● **Not required**

Passport	●
Visa (check regulations before you travel)	●
Travel, medical insurance	●
Round-trip or onward airline ticket	●
Local currency	●
Traveler's checks	●
Credit cards	●
First-aid kit and medicines*	●
Inoculations	●

*see also *Health* section

Essential for Drivers*

Driver's license	●
International Driving Permit	●
Car insurance (for nonrental cars)	●
Car registration (for nonrental cars)	●

*see also *Driving* section

Important Addresses

Greek National Tourism Organization
800 3rd Avenue, 23rd Floor,
New York, NY 10022
☎ (212) 421-5777
Fax (212) 826-6940
www.visitgreece.gr

**Hellenic Tourism Organization
(Greek National Tourism Organization)**
Tsoha 24
11521 Athens, Greece
☎ 210 870 7000
www.visitgreece.gr

American Embassy
91 Vassilissis Sophias Avenue
10160 Athens, Greece
☎ 210 721 2951
Mon.–Fri. 8:30–5
https://gr.usembassy.gov/

Customs

✔ **Duty-free limits on goods brought in from non-European Union countries:**
200 cigarettes or 100 cigarillos or 50 cigars or 250 g. tobacco; 4 L. wine, 16 L. beer; 1 L. alcohol over 22% volume; 2 L. alcohol under 22% volume; 50 ml. perfume; 250 ml. toilet water; plus any other duty-free goods (including gifts) to the value of €430 if arriving by sea or air, otherwise €300.

There is no importation limit for tax-paid goods purchased within the European Union for personal use.

Visitors must declare cash of €10,000 (or equivalent). Up to $1,000 in foreign currency may be exported by visitors.

✘ No unlicensed drugs, weapons, ammunition, obscene material, pets or other animals, counterfeit money or copied goods, meat or poultry.

For customs limits for returning U.S. citizens see page 16.

Money

Euro (€)
The Greek currency is the euro (€), a currency shared by 18 other European Union countries.

The euro is divided into 100 cents (¢).
The denominations of euro bills are 5, 10, 20, 50, 100, 200 and 500.
There are coins of 1, 2, 5, 10, 20 and 50¢ and €1 and €2.

Credit, debit and prepaid cards are widely accepted. ATMs for withdrawing euros are plentiful throughout most of Greece.

Tips and Gratuities

Tips are welcomed, but not expected or obligatory.

Restaurants (where service is not included)	10–15%
Cafés/bars	change
Taxis	change
Porters	€2
Chambermaids	€2 per day
Cloakroom attendants	change

Communications

Post Offices

Buy stamps *(ghramatósima)* at a post office *(takhithromio)*, distinguished by a yellow "OTE" sign. Lines can be long at post office counters; if you simply need stamps, check whether there's a window that sells only stamps. A corner kiosk *(periptero)* will sell stamps if you are buying postcards. Hours for out-of-town post offices may vary.

Telephones

Most public telephones take phone cards available from kiosks, local stores and OTE *(Organismos Tilepikoinonion Ellados,* pronounced *O-tay)* offices. If your calls are short and local, use a street kiosk *(periptero)* where you pay after the call. Coin-operated phones are hard to find in the more urban and resort areas of Greece. Check overseas cell phone usage with your provider.

Phoning inside Greece
All Greek telephone numbers in this book include an area code: dial the number that is listed. To call the operator dial 132 (or 131 in Athens).

Phoning Greece from abroad
The country code for Greece is 30. Note that Greek numbers in this book do not include the country code; you will need to prefix this number if you are phoning from another country. To call a Greek number from the United States or Canada, add the prefix 011 30. Example: 210 122 3344 becomes 011 30 210 122 3344.

Phoning from Greece
To phone the United States or Canada from Greece, prefix the area code and number with 00 1. Example: (111) 222-3333 becomes 00 1 111 222-3333. To call international information dial 00 162.

Emergency Telephone Numbers

General emergencies **112**
Police *(astínomia)* **100**
Tourist police (Athens only) **171**
Fire service *(fotyá)* **199**
Ambulance *(asthenoforo)* **166**
Emergency calls are free from phone booths.

Time Zones

Athens: 12 noon
New York: 6 a.m. (-6 hours)
Chicago: 5 a.m. (-7 hours)
Denver: 4 a.m. (-8 hours)
Los Angeles: 3 a.m. (-9 hours)

Hours of Operation

Stores are open Monday to Saturday 9–3:30 and again at 5:30–7. In tourist areas stores open at 8 a.m. and close late; they have shorter hours off-season, and some close completely in winter.

Banks operate Monday to Friday 8–2 and close at 2.30 on Fridays. They may stay open longer hours at peak season in resort areas. *At time of press the opening hours of banks in Greece are uncertain – please check before leaving the U.S.*

Post offices open Monday to Friday 8–1 and close at noon on Saturday.

Archeological sites usually close in the afternoon; some reopen in the evening in the summer, but all sites vary their hours depending on the time of year. It is best to check locally. Many archeological sites, museums and monuments close completely or partly on Monday.

Pharmacies are open Monday to Friday 8–1 and 5–7.

National Holidays

Banks, businesses and most stores and museums close on these days, but restaurants and some stores in tourist areas may stay open.

Jan. 1	New Year's Day
Jan. 6	Epiphany
Feb./Mar.	Shrove Monday
Mar. 25	Independence Day
*Apr./May	Good Friday
*Apr./May	Easter Monday
May 1	Labor Day
May/Jun.	Pentecost Monday
Aug. 15	Assumption of the Virgin
Oct. 28	Óchi Day
Dec. 25	Christmas Day
Dec. 26	St. Stephen's Day

* Greece observes the Orthodox calendar, and the date on which Easter falls may differ from that observed by other Western nations.

Photography

Camera batteries are widely available. Digital equipment and printing facilities are available in cities and large towns.
Never take photos near military bases or airports, and ask first in museums and churches.

Health

Medical Insurance

Private medical insurance is recommended. Visitors from non-E.U. countries can receive basic treatment at hospital emergency rooms. Admittance to a hospital *(nosokomío)* or consultation with a doctor *(iatrós)* will entail a fee. Ask your hotel, consulate or the tourist police for information on English-speaking doctors.

Dental Services

Dentists *(odhondoyatrós)* always charge for treatment, so find out if your medical insurance covers it; keep all receipts for insurance purposes. Treatment is available from English-speaking dentists listed in the telephone directory, or ask at your hotel.

Sun Advice

Summer, particularly July and August, can be oppressively hot and humid. Seek shelter inside a museum, or cover up, apply sunscreen and drink plenty of fluids. Be especially careful on boats or near the water.

Drugs

A pharmacy *(farmakío)*, distinguished by a green cross, has staff qualified to offer medical advice and provides a wide range of prescription medicines. Information about the nearest all-night facility is usually posted at pharmacies. Note that codeine is banned and you can be fined for carrying it.

Safe Water

Tap water is safe to drink but because of the high level of minerals it can cause upsets. Bottled water *(metaliko nero)* is available everywhere at a reasonable cost.

Restrooms

Finding a clean restroom *(toualéta)* away from tourist areas can be difficult. It is advisable to use facilities in cafés and restaurants after buying a drink. Restrooms are free. The Greek sewage system does not take toilet tissue, even in café and restaurant facilities; always use the wastebin provided.

Electricity

Greece has a 220-volt power supply. Electrical sockets take plugs with two round pins. American appliances will need a plug adapter and will require a transformer if they do not have a dual-voltage facility.

National Transportation

Train *(Tréno)*

Greek mainland trains are run by Organismos Sidirodromon Ellados (OSE; www.ose.gr). The network is limited. Reservations are essential on most express trains. For rail information in Athens: ☎ 145 (domestic services) or 147 (international services).

Bus *(Leoforío)*

Buses are popular and frequent; few villages or ferry ports are without a bus link. Buy city-to-city tickets from the bus station; in rural areas tickets *(isitirio)* are issued by a conductor on the bus. For bus information in Athens: ☎ 185.

Ferry *(Féribot)*

Ferries serve all of the Greek islands, and boat excursions run from May to October. You can take a boat from the port of Piréas to most islands. You can usually buy a ticket on the day of travel unless you are reserving a cabin or taking a car. You may need to reserve in advance in mid-August and over the Easter period; ask at a travel agency or tourist office.

Note: frequent transit strikes take place in Greece; check travel details with transportation company.

Driving

Drive on the right

Speed Limits

Police can impose on-the-spot fines but they cannot collect them.

Limited-access highways
130 k.p.h. (80 m.p.h.)

Main roads
90 k.p.h. (56 m.p.h.) or
110 k.p.h. (68 m.p.h.)

Urban areas
50 k.p.h. (31 m.p.h.)

Seat Belts

Must be worn in the front seat at all times and in the rear seat where fitted. Children over three years and under 1.5m (just under 5 feet) tall are not allowed to travel in the front seat.

Blood Alcohol

The legal blood alcohol limit is 0.05% (0.02% for novice drivers). Random breath tests on drivers are carried out frequently, especially late at night. Penalties are severe.

Driving (continued)

Tolls

 There are some, but not many, highway tolls in Greece.

Car Rental

The leading car-rental firms have offices at airports, train stations and principal ferry terminals. Hertz offers discounted rates for AAA members (see page 15).

For reservations:

	United States	Greece
Alamo	(844) 354-6962	210 353 3325
Avis	(800) 230-4898	210 687-9800
Budget	(800) 218-7992	213 018 6300
Hertz	(800) 654-3001	210 921 4771

Fuel

Gas *(venzini)* is sold in liters and usually comes in five grades: super *(sooper)*, regular *(apli)*, unleaded *(amolyvdhi)*, super unleaded *(sooper amolyvdhi)* and diesel *(petrelaio)*. There are few stations in remote areas; they are less likely to be open on weekends and may not take credit cards.

AAA Affiliated Motoring Club

Automobile and Touring Club of Greece (ELPA) 395 Messoglon Street, 153 43 Agia Paraskevi, Athens ☎ 201 606 8800; fax 201 606 8800. If you break down while driving, phone ☎ 10400 (ELPA breakdown service).
Not all automobile clubs offer full services to AAA members.

Breakdowns and Accidents

There are emergency telephones at regular intervals on highways. If you are involved in an accident, ☎ 100 for police. Most car-rental firms provide their own free rescue service; if your car is rented, follow the instructions given in the documentation. Use of a car-repair service other than those authorized by your rental company may violate your agreement.

Other Information

The minimum age for driving a car is 18 (may be higher for some car-rental firms). An International Driving Permit (IDP) is recommended; some car-rental firms require it, and it can speed up formalities if you are involved in an accident. A Green Card (international motor insurance certificate) is recommended if you are driving a private car; see page 15 for more information. You can be fined for unnecessary use of the horn. You must carry a fire extinguisher, a first-aid kit and a warning triangle in your car.

Useful Words and Phrases

The Greek language can be daunting to the visitor; it uses a different alphabet and is spoken with staccato rapidity. The way words and place-names are converted into English varies considerably according to which transliteration system a translator happens to prefer.

With patience and a keen ear, you should be able to recognize what sounds these unfamiliar letters stand for. Learning the Greek alphabet may enable you to deduce the meaning of signs and notices. The easiest thing to do, however, is to learn a few basic courtesy phrases.

The Greeks realize how difficult their language appears to foreigners, and they appreciate visitors' attempts to speak it.

Do you speak English?	*milate angliká?*
excuse me	*signomi*
hello/goodbye	*yásou/chérete*
how much?	*póso?*
I'd like	*tha íthela*
I do not understand	*dhen katalavéno*
nonsmoking	*khoros ya mi kapnízondes*
okay	*endáysi*
open/closed	*aniktos/klistos*
please/you're welcome	*parakaló*
thank you	*efharistó*
ticket	*isitíro*
one-way/round trip	*apló/isitiro met epistrofis*
where is...?	*poo íne...?*
yes/no	*né/óhi*
the hotel	***xenodochia***
breakfast	*proino*
key	*klidhí*
for one/two nights	*ya mía/dýo vradhiés*
for one/two people	*yia éna/dyo átoma*
room	*éna dhomátio*
shower	*doos*
the restaurant	***estiatorio***
beans	*fasólia*
beer	*bira*
bread	*psomi*
the check	*logariasmós*
chicken	*kotópoulo*
coffee	*kafé*
dessert	*glíkisma*
food	*fagitó*
lamb	*arnáki*
lobster	*astakós*
meat balls	*kefthédes*
olives	*eliés*
pork	*hirino*
red mullet	*barboúnia*
squid	*kalamarákia*
starter	*proto piato*
stuffed vine leaves	*dolmadakia*
water	*neró*
wine	*krasí*

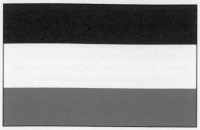

National Flag

Essential for Travelers

● Required   ● Recommended   ● Not required

Passport ●
Visa (check regulations before you travel) ●
Travel, medical insurance ●
Round-trip or onward airline ticket ●
Local currency ●
Traveler's checks ●
Credit cards ●
First-aid kit and medicines ●
Inoculations ●

Essential for Drivers*

Driver's license ●
International Driving Permit ●
Car insurance (for nonrental cars) ●
Car registration (for nonrental cars) ●
*see also *Driving* section

Important Addresses

Hungarian National Tourist Office
450 Fashion Avenue, #2601,
New York, NY 10123
☎ (212) 695-1221
www.hellohungary.com

Budapest Tourinform
Sütő utca 2
H-1052 Budapest
Hungary
☎ 1 438 8080 (daily 8–8)
www.budapest.com

American Embassy
Szabadság tér 12
H-1054 Budapest
Hungary
☎ 1 475 4400 (Mon.–Fri. 8–5)
U.S. citizens only out of hours
https://hu.usembassy.gov

Customs

✔ **Duty-free limits on goods brought in from non-European Union countries:**
200 cigarettes or 100 cigarillos or 50 cigars or 250 g. tobacco; 2 L. still wine; 1 L. spirits or strong liqueurs over 22% volume or 1 L. fortified wine, sparkling wine or other liqueurs; 50 ml. perfume; 250 ml. toilet water; plus any other duty-free goods (including gifts) up to a value of Ft55,000 ($193).

Tax-paid goods purchased in the E.U. and imported for personal use are not liable for duty. However, there are upper limits on these imports – check at www.vam.gov.hu.

If you bring in cash or traveler's checks to the value of $10,935, customs must be notified and proof of ownership will be required.

✘ No unlicensed drugs, weapons, ammunition, obscene material, pets or other animals, counterfeit money or copied goods, meat or poultry.

For customs limits for returning U.S. citizens see page 16.

Money

Forint (Ft or HUF)

Hungary's currency is the forint (Ft or HUF), which is divided into 100 fillérs, although fillérs are no longer legal tender.

The denominations of forint bills are 500, 1,000, 2,000, 5,000, 10,000 and 20,000.
There are coins of 5, 10, 20, 50, 100 and 200 forints.

ATMs can be found throughout Hungary.
You can exchange dollars or traveler's checks *(utazasi csekket)* at a bank *(bank)*, exchange office *(penzvalto)*, post office *(posta)* and some hotels. Credit card acceptance is limited. It is a good idea to carry a mix of large and small forint denominations. In tourist destinations you may find that euros also are accepted.

Tips and Gratuities

Tips *(borravaló)* are welcomed, but not expected, where service is not included.

Restaurants	10%
Cafés/bars	10%
Taxis	10%
Porters	to reflect quality of service
Chambermaids	to reflect quality of service
Hairdressers	10%
Cloakroom attendants	change

Communications

Post Offices

Buy stamps *(bélyeg)* at a post office *(posta)*, newsstand/tobacconist *(dohanyaruda)* or from a hotel. Mailboxes are wall-mounted and red with a calling-horn emblem.

Telephones

Public phone booths are disappearing, but you will still find a few scattered around the city. You can use cash and prepaid phone cards for calls in Hungary. For direct dialing for national and international calls, use Ft20, Ft50 and Ft100 coins (minimum Ft20). International calls can be made from red phone booths. Phone cards of 50 and 100 units can be bought from newsstands/tobacconists, gas stations, post offices and hotels. Check overseas cell phone usage with your provider.

Phoning inside Hungary
Hungarian telephone numbers include an area code of one or two digits (there is no initial zero). For long-distance calls within Hungary precede the number with 06. Numbers in Budapest are seven digits, not including the area code; the area code is 1. To call the national operator dial 191.

Phoning Hungary from abroad
The country code for Hungary is 36. Note that Hungarian numbers in this book do not include the Hungarian country code; prefix the country code if you are phoning from another country. To phone Hungary from the United States or Canada, add the prefix 011 36 before the area code and number. Example: 1 122 3344 becomes 011 36 1 122 3344.

Phoning from Hungary
To phone the United States or Canada from Hungary, prefix the area code and number with 00 1. Example: (111) 222-3333 becomes 00 1 111 222-3333. To call the international operator dial 190; for international directory inquiries dial 199.

Emergency Telephone Numbers

General emergencies **112**
Police *(rendörség)* **107** or **112**;
Tourist Police 06-1-438-8080 (24 hours);
Fire service *(tűzoltóóság)* **105** or **112**;
Ambulance *(mentők)* **104** or **112**
Dial 190 for the international operator

Time Zones

Budapest: 12 noon
New York: 6 a.m. (-6 hours)
Chicago: 5 a.m. (-7 hours)
Denver: 4 a.m. (-8 hours)
Los Angeles: 3 a.m. (-9 hours)

Hours of Operation

Stores are open Monday to Saturday 9–7.
Department stores open Monday to Friday 10–6, Saturday 9–1. Saturday afternoon they close early, and few stores remain open after 1 or 2. Thursday is late-night shopping until 7 or 8.

Grocery stores and other food stores have longer hours and may open on Sunday morning. In large cities, a few stores stay open 24 hours.

In smaller towns, stores close over lunchtime. Large shopping centers in cities are open Monday to Saturday 9–9, Sunday 10–7.

The **Central Bank of Hungary** is open Monday 10–6, Tuesday to Thursday 8–3, Friday 7 a.m.–noon. Most other banks close at 1 p.m. on Friday.

Post offices open Monday to Friday 8–6, and 8–1 on Saturday.

Many **museums** close on Monday.

Pharmacies are open Monday to Friday 9–5.

National Holidays

Banks, businesses and all stores are closed on these days. If a public holiday falls on a Tuesday or a Thursday, the day between it and the weekend also becomes a holiday.

Jan. 1	New Year's Day
Mar. 15	Day of the Nation (anniversary of 1848 revolution)
Mar./Apr.	Good Friday/Easter Monday
May 1	Labor Day
May/Jun.	Pentecost Monday
Aug. 20	Constitution Day
Oct. 23	Day of the Proclamation of the Republic
Nov. 1	All Saints' Day
Dec. 25–26	Christmas

Photography

Hungary has spectacular landscapes, including the Danube bend north of Budapest, one of the most beautiful stretches of this great river, and romantic Lake Balaton, framed by vineyards. Digital camera equipment and printing services are widely available in towns and cities.

Health

Medical Insurance

Private medical insurance is recommended. U.S. and Canadian visitors can receive free essential first-aid and emergency treatment. All further treatment and care has to be paid for. Fees for medical care are set by the individual hospital or practice. There is a 24-hour private medical care service with English-speaking doctors in Budapest: Falck SOS Hungary. It also has its own ambulance service ☎ 1 240 0475; www.soshungary.hu.

Dental Services

Dentists *(forgovos)* charge for any treatment, but quality dental work is relatively inexpensive. Check to be sure it is covered by your medical insurance. Dentists are listed in the *Yellow Pages*; ask for English-speaking dentists at your embassy or hotel, or at a tourist office. A good dental clinic in Budapest is SOS Dental Service ☎ 1 383 3333.

Sun Advice

Hungary has up to 2,500 hours of sun annually, one of the highest levels in Europe. In summer, 9 or 10 hours a day can be expected, so protection is essential.

Drugs

A pharmacy *(gyógyszetár* or *patica)* sells both prescription and nonprescription medicines (bring your own medication if you need a specific product). Most are cheaper than similar U.S. products. Information about the nearest 24-hour facility is posted at all pharmacies.

Safe Water

Although tap water is safe, you may find it causes mild upsets. Bottled mineral water *(ásvány víz)* and soda water *(szoda víz)* are widely available and advised.

Restrooms

Public restrooms *(mosdó)* are fairly easy to find, and are usually indicated by a symbol or marked WC, and designated by *férfi* for men and *női* for women. There may be a charge of between Ft100 and Ft200.

Electricity

Hungary has a 220/230-volt power supply. Electrical sockets take plugs with two round pins. American appliances will need a plug adapter and will require a transformer if they do not have a dual-voltage facility.

National Transportation

Train *(Vonat)*

The state railroad, MÁV-Start, serves most towns. Express trains link Budapest with provincial centers. Fares are low, and MÁV-Start offers many discounted fares and passes, including rail cards for unlimited travel; ☎ 1 349 4949; https://jegyvasarlas.mav-start.hu.

Bus *(Busz)*

Long-distance buses are expensive, but can be quicker than trains. The main Budapest terminal is at Erzsébet tér. The main operator, state-owned Volánbusz, serves all communities. Volánbusz is a member of Eurolines, who operate an international bus service; ☎ 1 382 0888 (domestic and international); www.volanbusz.hu.

Ferry *(Komp)*

Ferries run from spring to late fall on Lake Balaton, the Danube between Budapest and Esztergom, and the Tisza river (for Sárospatak, Tokaj, Szolnok, Csongrád and Szeged). A hydrofoil also links Budapest and Esztergom, and Budapest to Vienna. Information is available from Mahart at the Vigadó tér landing stage; ☎ 1 484 4000; www.mahartpassnave.hu.

Driving

Drive on the right

Speed Limits

Fines of up to Ft30,000 can be imposed by the police. These must be paid using a money transfer order *(készpénzáetutalási)*.

 Limited-access highways *(autópályára)*
130 k.p.h. (80 m.p.h.)
Divided highways **110 k.p.h. (68 m.p.h.)**

 Main roads
90 k.p.h. (56 m.p.h.)

Urban areas
50 k.p.h. (31 m.p.h.)
Some resorts and residential zones
30 k.p.h. (18 m.p.h.)

Seat Belts

Must be worn in front and rear seats at all times.

Blood Alcohol

 The legal blood alcohol limit is zero. Random breath tests on drivers are carried out frequently, especially at night.

Driving (continued)

Tolls

Driving on highways requires the pre-purchase of a *matrica e-vignette*, available at border crossings and gas stations (for information, see www.toll-charge.hu).

Car Rental

The leading car-rental firms have offices at airports and train stations. Hertz offers discounted rates for AAA members (see page 15). For reservations:

	United States	Hungary
Avis	(800) 633 3469	1 296 6421
Budget	(800) 472-3325	1 70 931 8001
Enterprise	(800) 261-7331	1 225 2174
Hertz	(800) 654-3001	1 296 0996

Fuel

Unleaded fuel *(ólommentes benzine)* is graded 95 octane. Diesel can be bought along major routes and in cities. Many gas stations *(benzinkút)* are self-service, although you may not be able to use a credit card in smaller stations. A map of rural gas stations is available from MAK (see below).

AAA Affiliated Motoring Club

Magyar Autóklub (MAK) H-1043 Budapest, Berda József útca 15 ☎ 1 345 1800. If you break down while driving, ☎ 188 or www.autoklub.hu (MAK breakdown service). Not all automobile clubs offer full services to AAA members.

Breakdowns and Accidents

If you have an accident, phone the police ☎ 107 and ask for an interpretor at the scene. You are legally required to report personal injury. Most car-rental firms provide their own free rescue service; if you break down follow the instructions given in the documentation. Use of an unauthorized car-repair service may violate your agreement. Vehicles with damaged bodywork may only leave the country with an official certificate.

Other Information

The minimum age for driving a car is 17 (21 for some car-rental firms). An International Driving Permit (IDP) is recommended; some car-rental firms require it, and it can speed up formalities if you are involved in an accident. A Green Card (international motor insurance certificate) is needed if you are driving a private car; see page 15 for more information. Dimmed headlights must be used by cars at all times outside built-up areas. You must have a first-aid kit, a warning triangle and a fluorescent vest in your car.

Useful Words and Phrases

Hungarian, called Magyar by its speakers, is a difficult language, related to Finnish and Estonian. German is traditionally the second language, but English is gradually replacing it, especially among the younger generation.

Apart from a few international words *(posta, telefon)*, Hungarian offers few clues as to its meaning. However, pronunciation is regular — letters consistently stand for the same sounds. By learning basic words, street signs, notices and labels will begin to make sense.

Do you speak English?	*Beszél angolul?*
What is your name?	*Hogy hívnak?*
excuse me	*elnézést*
hello	*jó napot kivanok*
goodbye	*viszontlátásra*
yes/no	*igen/nem*
how much?	*mennyibe kerul?*
I am American	*Amerikai vagyok*
I don't understand	*nem értem*
nonsmoking	*nem domanyzo*
open	*nyitva*
closed	*zárva*
please	*kérem*
thank you	*köszönöm*
ticket	*jegy*
(one-way/round trip)	*(egyiranyu/retur)*
where is...?	*hol van...?*
the hotel	***szálloda***
you're welcome	*szívesen*
Where is the restroom?	*Hol a mosdó?*
breakfast	*reggeli*
reservation	*foglalás*
key	*kulcs*
room	*szoba*
shower	*zuhany*
the restaurant	***étterem/vendeglo/ etkezde***
beef	*marha*
beer	*sör*
bread	*kenyer*
the check	*szamla*
coffee/tea	*kávé/tea*
dessert	*édesség*
fish	*hal*
fruit	*gyümölcs*
ice cream	*fagylalt*
meat	*hús*
pork	*sertés*
potato	*burgonya*
poultry	*csirke*
starter	*elöételek*
vegetable	*zöldség*
wine	*bor*

Ireland

National Flag

Essential for Travelers

● **Required** ● **Recommended** ● **Not required**

Passport	●
Visa (check regulations before you travel)	●
Travel, medical insurance	●
Round-trip or onward airline ticket	●
Local currency	●
Credit/debit/prepaid currency cards	●
First-aid kit and medicines	●
Inoculations	●

Essential for Drivers*

Driver's license	●
International Driving Permit	●
Car insurance (for nonrental cars)	●
Car registration (for nonrental cars)	●

*see also *Driving* section

Important Addresses

Tourism Ireland (Republic of Ireland and Northern Ireland)
345 Park Avenue, New York, NY 10154
☎ 1 212 418 0800
www.ireland.com; www.discovernorthernireland.com
Discover Ireland Information Office
14 Upper O'Connell Street, Dublin 1, Republic of Ireland ☎ 1850 230 330
www.visitireland.com
American Embassy (Republic of Ireland)
42 Elgin Road, Ballsbridge
Dublin 4, Republic of Ireland
☎ 01 668 8777
https://ie.usembassy.gov
American Citizens Services: by appointment; see details and make reservation via website
Visit Belfast Welcome Centre
9 Donegall Square North,
Belfast BT1 5GB, Northern Ireland
☎ 028 9024 6609
www.visitbelfast.com
US Consulate General (Northern Ireland)
Danesfort House, 223 Stranmills Road
Belfast BT9 5GR
☎ 028 9038 6100
https://uk.usembassy.gov

Customs

✓ **Duty-free limits on goods brought in from non-European Union countries**:
200 cigarettes or 100 cigarillos or 50 cigars or 250 g. tobacco; 4 L. still wine or 16 L. beer; 1 L. spirits or strong liqueurs over 22% volume or 2 L. fortified wine, sparkling wine or other liqueur; 50 ml. perfume; 250 ml. toilet water; plus any other duty-free goods (or gifts) to the value of €430.

There is no limit on the importation of tax-paid goods bought within the E.U., if they are for your own personal use.

There are no currency regulations.

✗ No unlicensed drugs, weapons, ammunition, obscene material, pets or other animals, counterfeit money or copied goods, meat, poultry or dairy products.

For customs limits for returning U.S. citizens see page 16.

Money

Euro (€)
The Republic of Ireland's currency is the euro (€), a currency shared by 18 other European Union countries.

The euro is divided into 100 cents (¢).
The denominations of euro bills are 5, 10, 20, 50, 100, 200 and 500.
There are coins of 1, 2, 5, 10, 20 and 50¢ and €1 and €2.

ATMs are available in the major cities. Credit, debit and prepaid cards are accepted in hotels, large stores and upscale restaurants; check first in small or rural establishments.
Exchange dollars at a bank, exchange office, post office or a hotel.

For information about currency in Northern Ireland, see page 502.

Tips and Gratuities

Restaurants (if service is not included)	10–15%
Cafés/bars (if service is not included)	10%
Taxis	€1 (IR) or round up to nearest £1 (NI)
Porters	€1 (IR) or £1 (NI) per bag
Hairdressers	€2 (IR) or £1 (NI)
Tour guides	€2 (IR) or £1 (NI)
Cloakroom attendants	€1 (IR) or £1 (NI)

Communications

Post Offices

Buy stamps at post offices, newsstands/tobacconists, large grocery stores and hotels. Out-of-town post office times vary. Mailboxes are green in the Republic of Ireland and red in Northern Ireland.

Telephones

Public phone booths are either blue and cream or the glass-booth style, although many are now glass and metal. They take cash or prepaid phone cards bought from newsstands, post offices and local stores. Some city phones take credit cards. For phone calls made to or from Northern Ireland, except calling Northern Ireland from the Republic (see below), follow the instructions for Britain on page 503. Check overseas cell phone usage with your provider.

Phoning inside Ireland
All Irish phone numbers in this book include the area code; dial the number listed. There is operator assistance in Northern Ireland only; dial 100.

Phoning the Republic of Ireland from abroad
The country code for the Republic of Ireland is 353. To phone the Republic from another country, prefix 353 to the number given. To phone the Republic from the United States or Canada, omit the first zero from the Irish number, and add the prefix 011 353. (The number of digits in Irish area codes varies.) Example: 01 122 3344 becomes 011 353 1 122 3344.

Phoning from Ireland
To phone the United States or Canada from Ireland, prefix the area code and number with 00 1. Example: (111) 222-3333 becomes 00 1 111 222-3333. To phone Northern Ireland from the Republic of Ireland, replace the code 028 with 048. Example: 028 1122 3344 becomes 048 1122 3344. To call international directory inquiries dial 11890 (Republic), 118118 (NI).

Emergency Telephone Numbers

General emergencies **112 or 999**
Police *(gardai)* **112 or 999**
Fire service **112 or 999**
Ambulance **112 or 999**
Emergency calls are free from phone booths.

Time Zones

Dublin: 12 noon
New York: 7 a.m. (-5 hours)
Chicago: 6 a.m. (-6 hours)
Denver: 5 a.m. (-7 hours)
Los Angeles: 4 a.m. (-8 hours)

Hours of Operation

Hours given below are for the Republic of Ireland; hours for Northern Ireland may differ slightly. Some **stores** open Monday to Saturday 9–6; some may stay open until 8 or 9 p.m. on Thursday or Friday. On Sunday some bigger stores and many supermarkets open from noon until 5 or 6. In rural areas stores close in the afternoon on one day of the week.

Banks operate Monday to Friday 10–4. Some banks in small towns close 12:30–1:30. Banks open until 5 p.m. one day a week (Thursdays in Dublin and Belfast). Nearly all banks are closed on Saturday and Sunday.

Post offices are open Monday to Friday 9–5:30. In larger cities and towns, post offices stay open during lunchtime and until 5 on Saturdays. In suburban and rural areas, they typically close for lunch (1–2:15) and are closed on Saturdays.

Hours for **museums** and tourist sights vary; always check with the local tourist office. Some places close from October to March, although most major sights are open all year.

Pharmacies usually open Monday to Friday 9–6. Some may open on Saturday morning.

National Holidays

Banks, businesses and most stores close on these days. Museums also may have restricted hours.

Jan. 1	New Year's Day
Mar. 17	St. Patrick's Day
Mar./Apr.	Good Friday
Mar./Apr.	Easter Monday (also day after in NI)
1st Mon. in May	May Bank Holiday
Last Mon. in May	Spring Bank Holiday (NI)
1st Mon. in Jun.	June Bank Holiday (ROI)
Jul. 12	Battle of the Boyne (NI)
1st Mon. in Aug.	August Bank Holiday (ROI)
Last Mon. in Aug.	Summer Bank Holiday (NI)
Last Mon. in Oct.	October Bank Holiday (ROI)
Dec. 25	Christmas Day
Dec. 26	St. Stephen's Day

Photography

The light is frequently poor. Bring a tripod for landscape work. Digital equipment and printing facilities are widely available. Camera batteries also are available countrywide.

Health

Medical Insurance

Private medical insurance is recommended. U.S. and Canadian visitors can receive treatment in emergency rooms, but are charged if admitted to a hospital bed. A doctor (general practitioner or GP) also will charge for services.

Dental Services

Dental work is expensive, so check to see if it is covered by your medical insurance. Dentists are listed in the *Golden Pages* (IR) or *Yellow Pages* (NI). Alternatively, ask at your hotel or embassy. For the Irish Dental Association, ☎ 01 295 0072; www.dentist.ie.

Sun Advice

The sunniest months are May and June, with 5–6.5 hours of sun a day (the extreme southwest is the sunniest). July and August are the warmest. During these months you should take sensible precautions against the sun.

Drugs

Pharmacies (also called chemists) sell a range of prescription and nonprescription medicines. If you need medicine outside regular hours, information about the nearest 24-hour facility should be posted on the door of all pharmacies.

Safe Water

Tap water is safe to drink throughout Ireland. If, however, you prefer mineral water you will find it widely available.

Restrooms

Identify restrooms by *Fir* (men) and *Mná* (women). A small charge is levied in restrooms at some train stations, but most other facilities are free. The standards of hygiene are moderate. You will be welcomed into any local pub if you need to use their facilities, but stop for a drink and a talk while you are there.

Electricity

The Republic of Ireland has a 230-volt and Northern Ireland a 240-volt power supply.

Electrical sockets either take plugs with two round pins or three square pins. American appliances will need a plug adapter and will require a transformer if they do not have a dual-voltage facility.

National Transportation

Train

The Republic of Ireland's rail company is Iarnród Éireann (IÉ or Irish Rail). Trains are generally reliable and comfortable, but the network is limited and one-way tickets can cost almost as much as round-trip tickets. There are many special offers on fares, and for extensive rail travel consider a Trekker Pass or Explorer ticket. For information: ☎ 01 836 6222; www.irishrail.ie. For Northern Ireland call Translink ☎ 028 9066 6630; www.translink.co.uk.

Bus

Bus Éireann (Irish Bus) operates a network of express bus routes serving most of the country (some run summer only). For information ☎ 1850 836 611 or check online at www.buseireann.ie. Translink is the integrated service operator for Northern Ireland ☎ 028 9066 6630; www.translink.co.uk for information.

Ferry

A car ferry runs between Ballyhack (County Wexford) and Passage East (County Waterford); ☎ 051 382 480; www.passageferry.ie, saving 60 miles on the road trip. Another serves Killimer (County Clare) and Tarbert (County Kerry); ☎ 065 905 3124; www.shannonferries.com. There also are ferries to several islands; ask for details at a local tourist office. There are regular ferries from Belfast, Larne, Dublin, Dun Laoghaire and Rosslare to ports on the mainland of Britain, and from Cork, Dublin and Rosslare to France. For information go to www.stenaline.co.uk or www.brittanyferries.ie.

Driving

Drive on the left

Speed Limits

Traffic police can impose on-the-spot fines.

 Limited-access highways (motorways/blue) **120 k.p.h. (74 m.p.h.)**

 Main roads (national/green) **100 k.p.h. (62 m.p.h.)**; in some areas **80 k.p.h. (49 m.p.h.)**. Regional/local/white **80 k.p.h. (49 m.p.h.)**

 Urban areas (RI) **50 k.p.h. (31 m.p.h.)** Northern Ireland: **50–60 k.p.h (31–37 m.p.h.)**

Seat Belts

 Must be worn in front and back seats at all times.

Driving (continued)

Blood Alcohol

The legal blood alcohol limit is 0.05% (0.02% for novice drivers). Random breath tests on drivers are carried out frequently, especially at night. Penalties for offenders are severe.

Tolls

Tolls are charged at some locations: Dublin Port Tunnel; Limerick Tunnel; M50 (radial route around Dublin); East Link Bridge and West Link Bridge (both Dublin); M1 (Drogheda Bypass); M3 (Navan–Kells); M4 (Kinnegad-Enfield-Kilcock); N6 (Galway–Ballinasloe); M7/M8 (Portlaoise); N8 (Rathcormac/Fermoy Bypass); N25 (Waterford Bypass). For details see www.tii.ie.

Car Rental

The leading car-rental firms have offices at airports, train stations and large ferry terminals. Hertz offers discounted rates for AAA members (see page 15). Advise the car-rental company if you plan on traveling between the Republic and Northern Ireland. For reservations:

	United States	Republic of Ireland
Alamo/	(844) 354 6962	01 844 5848
Enterprise		
Avis	(800) 633 3469	01 605 7500
Budget	(800) 472-3325	01 844 5150
Hertz	(800) 654-3001	01 844 5466

Fuel

Gas is unleaded and sold in liters; diesel also is easily purchased. Gas stations in villages stay open until 8 or 9 p.m. and usually open after Mass on Sunday.

AAA Affiliated Motoring Club

AA Ireland 61A South William Street, Dublin 2, ☎ 674 0447; www.theaa.ie. If you break down while driving, ☎ 01 649 7460 (AA Ireland breakdown service). Not all automobile clubs offer full services to AAA members. Northern Ireland: see Britain section (see page 505).

Breakdowns and Accidents

There are 24-hour emergency phones at regular intervals on major highways. ☎ 112 or 999 if involved in an accident. Most car-rental firms provide their own free rescue service; if your car is rented, follow the instructions given in the documentation. Use of a car-repair service other than those authorized by your rental company may violate your agreement.

Other Information

The minimum age for driving a car is 17 (may be higher for some car-rental firms). An International Driving Permit (IDP) is recommended; some car-rental firms require it, and it can speed up

Driving (continued)

formalities if you are involved in an accident. A Green Card (international motor insurance certificate) is recommended if you are driving a private car; see page 15 for more information.

In the Republic of Ireland road signs are marked in kilometers, but you may find old signs in miles. In Northern Ireland all road signs are in miles.

Useful Words and Phrases

Although the Republic of Ireland is officially bilingual, and the Irish language (Gaelic or Gaeilge) is learned by all schoolchildren, English is more commonly spoken. There are around 82,000 native speakers of Irish (data from 2011 census), making it Europe's least widespread official language.

Because it often reflects expressions in Gaelic, Irish English is famed for its picturesque turns of phrase, much more poetic than American or British English.

The Gaelic language is enjoying a revival: radio, television and the Internet all stir up interest in the old language. There are Gaelic-speaking clubs as far away as the U.S. West Coast.

Following are pronunciations of words you may come across:

Bord Fáilte (Irish Tourist Board)	bord falt-cha
Ceilidh (traditional dance night)	kaylee
Gaeilge (the Irish language)	gale-geh
Gaeltacht (Irish-speaking country)	gale-tackt
Garda (policeman)	gawrdah
Fleadh (traditional music evening)	flah
Taoiseach (prime minister)	teeshock

Numbers:

1	*a haon*	a hay-on
2	*a do*	a doe
3	*a trí*	a tree
4	*a ceathair*	a ca-hir
5	*a cuíg*	a koo-ig
6	*a sé*	a shay
7	*a seacht*	a shocked
8	*a hocht*	a huct
9	*a naoi*	a neigh
10	*a deich*	a de

Other words:

good day	*lá maith*	law mah
goodbye	*slán*	slawn
goodnight	*oíche mhaith*	ee-ha vah
How are you?	*Conas taio?*	co-nus tee?
please	*más é do thoil é*	maws eh duh hull eh
thanks	*gúsmaith agat*	gurrah mah a-gut
pub	*tábhairne*	taw-er nay
water	*uisce*	ishkek
whiskey	*fuisci*	fwishgee
yes	sea	shah

National Flag

Essential for Travelers

● **Required** ● **Recommended** ● **Not required**

Passport	●
Visa (check regulations before you travel)	●
Travel, medical insurance	●
Round-trip or onward airline ticket	●
Local currency	●
Traveler's checks	●
Credit cards	●
First-aid kit and medicines	●
Inoculations	●

Essential for Drivers*

Driver's license	●
International Driving Permit	●
Car insurance (for nonrental cars)	●
Car registration (for nonrental cars)	●

*see also *Driving* section

Important Addresses

Italian National Tourist Board
686 Park Avenue, 3rd Floor
New York, NY 10065
☎ (212) 245-5618
🕐 Mon.–Fri. 9–5
www.italiantourism.com

**Ente Nazionale Italiano per il Turismo
(Italian State Tourist Board)**
Via Marghera 2/6
00185 Rome, Italy
☎ 06 49711
www.enit.it

American Embassy
Via Vittorio Veneto 121
00187 Rome, Italy
☎ 06 46741
https://it.usembassy.gov
Nonemergency services are available through an
online appointment system.

Customs

✔ **Duty-free limits on goods brought in from
non-European Union countries:**
200 cigarettes or 100 cigarillos or 50 cigars or
250 g. tobacco; 2 L. wine; 1 L. alcohol over 22%
volume or 2 L. alcohol under 22% volume; 50 ml.
perfume; 250 ml. toilet water; plus any other
duty-free goods (including gifts) to the value of
€300 if arriving by land, €430 if arriving by sea
or air.

There is no limit on the importation of tax-paid
goods purchased within the European Union,
provided they are for your own personal use.

Foreign or local currency in excess of $10,000
must be declared on arrival.

✘ No unlicensed drugs, weapons, ammunition,
obscene material, pets or other animals,
counterfeit money or copied goods, meat
or poultry.

**For customs limits for returning U.S. citizens
see page 16.**

Money

Euro (€)
Italy's currency is the euro (€), a currency shared
by 18 other European Union countries.

The euro is divided into 100 cents (¢).
The denominations of euro bills are 5, 10, 20, 50,
100, 200 and 500.
There are coins of 1, 2, 5, 10, 20 and 50¢ and
€1 and €2.

Exchange dollars or traveler's checks *(assegni
turistici)* at a bank *(banca)* or exchange office
(ufficio di cambio). Hotels may exchange traveler's
checks but stores do not.

ATMs *(sportello automatico)* are plentiful and
credit, debit and prepaid cards are accepted in
hotels, large stores and upscale restaurants;
check first in small or rural establishments. It
is a good idea to carry a mix of large and small
euro denominations.

Tips and Gratuities

Restaurants (service usually included but add 50¢ per person)	
Cafés/bars	small change
Taxis	15%
Porters	€1
Chambermaids	€1 per day
Restrooms	minimum
Cloakroom attendants	50¢

Communications

Post Offices

Buy stamps *(francobolli)* at a post office *(ufficio postale)* or at a tobacconist *(tabaccaio)*. Mailboxes *(caselles di posta)*, red or blue, often have two slots, one for local mail *(per la città)*, the other for out-of-town mail *(tutte le altre destinazioni)*. Mail can take up to three weeks; to speed delivery send it priority *(posta prioritaria)* or recorded *(raccomandata)* post.

Telephones

Pay phones can be found in bars and other public places. Prepaid cards *(carta or scheda telefonica)* for card-operated phones are available from tobacconists, bars, post offices, newsstands, train stations and dispensers showing a Telecom Italia (TI) logo. Use a prepaid card for international calls; tear the corner off before using it. Check overseas cell phone usage with your provider.

Phoning inside Italy

All telephone numbers in Italy include an area code that must be dialed. To call the operator dial 170.

Phoning Italy from abroad

The country code for Italy is 39. Note that Italian numbers in this book do not include the country code; you will need to prefix this number if you are phoning from another country. To call Italy from the United States or Canada dial the prefix 011 39. Include the first zero of the regional code. There is no standard number of digits in Italian numbers. Example: 01 122 3344 becomes 011 39 01 122 3344.

Phoning from Italy

To phone the United States or Canada from Italy, prefix the area code and number with 00 1. Example: (111) 222-3333 becomes 00 1 111 222-3333. To call international information dial 4176.

Emergency Telephone Numbers

Police *(policia)* **113** (local) or **112** (national)
Fire service *(pompieri)* **115** or **112**
Ambulance *(ambulanza)* **118** or **112**
Emergency calls are free from phone booths.

Time Zones

Rome: 12 noon
New York: 6 a.m. (-6 hours)
Chicago: 5 a.m. (-7 hours)
Denver: 4 a.m. (-8 hours)
Los Angeles: 3 a.m. (-9 hours)

Hours of Operation

Stores are open Monday to Saturday 8–1 and 4–7. Department stores, some grocery stores and stores in major cities and tourist areas may not close at lunchtime and sometimes stay open until later in the evening. Some stores close on Monday morning and may close on Saturday afternoon in summer; most stores close on Sunday. Many stores, especially in Rome, Florence and Venice (less so in Naples) now stay open from 1 to 4.

Banks usually open Monday to Friday 8:30–1:30 and 2:30–3:30. Some close at 2 and do not reopen later in the afternoon.

Post offices open Monday to Friday 8:30–2 and 3–6:30. Times may vary slightly; some may be open Saturday 8:30–noon.

Many **museums** are open in the late afternoon (typically 4–7), others are open all day, and a few stay open late into the evening. Many museums close early on Sunday (around 1), and many are closed on Monday.

Pharmacies are open weekdays 9–1 and 3–5.

National Holidays

Banks, businesses and most stores and museums close on these days. Most cities, towns and villages celebrate their patron saint's day, but generally most establishments remain open.

Jan. 1	New Year's Day
Jan. 6	Epiphany
Mar./Apr.	Easter Monday
Apr. 25	Liberation Day 1945
May 1	Labor Day
Jun. 2	Anniversary of the Republic
Aug. 15	Assumption of the Virgin
Nov. 1	All Saints' Day
Dec. 8	Immaculate Conception
Dec. 25	Christmas Day
Dec. 26	St. Stephen's Day

Photography

Digital equipment is available in towns and cities. Photography may be banned in museums and churches.

Medical Insurance

Private medical insurance is strongly recommended. Visitors from non-European Union countries can receive treatment in a hospital accident and emergency room, but will be charged if admitted to a bed. A general practitioner *(medico)* can deal with less urgent cases, but also will charge for treatment.

Dental Services

Emergency dental treatment is available from English-speaking dentists listed in the *Yellow Pages (pagine gialle;* www.paginegialle.it). A fee will be charged, so check that you are adequately covered for treatment on your private medical insurance.

Sun Advice

In summer, especially July and August, it can be oppressively hot and humid in cities. On sunny days cover your head and shoulders and use a sunscreen. Cathedrals and other stone buildings can be refreshingly cool. Take frequent breaks in the shade and drink plenty of fluids.

Drugs

A pharmacy *(farmacia)* displays a green cross symbol and has staff who can provide prescription medicines and offer advice on minor ailments. Information about the address of the nearest 24-hour facility is normally posted at every pharmacy.

Safe Water

In isolated rural areas it is not advisable to drink tap water. However, across most of the country tap water is perfectly safe, although most Italians prefer to drink bottled mineral water *(acqua minerale)*, which is inexpensive and widely available.

Restrooms

Finding a restroom *(gabinetto/bagno)* can be difficult away from airports, train and bus stations, highway service areas and museums. Leave a tip (about 50¢) for the attendant. If using the facilities in a bar you will be expected to buy a drink. Some bars have separate restrooms for men *(signori)* and women *(signore)*.

Electricity

Italy has a 220-volt power supply (in some areas, 125 volts). Electrical sockets take plugs with two round pins or three pins in a vertical row. American appliances will need a plug adapter and will require a transformer if they do not have a dual-voltage facility.

National Transportation

Train *(Treno)*

Italian State Railways provides an efficient range of services (information available online only at www.trenitalia.com). *Regionale* and *Interregionali* trains are slow for long journeys; Intercity are faster, though tickets carry a supplement. The Frecce network, traveling at speeds of up to 300 k.p.h. (186 m.p.h.), are the fastest and most expensive.

Bus *(Autobus)*

There is no national bus company, but each major city has its own company for short-, medium- and some long-distance bus travel. International Eurolines buses run from the main Italian cities: ☎ 0861 199 1900; www.eurolines.it.

Ferry *(Traghetto)*

Genoa and Naples are the main Mediterranean ports, with regular services to Sicily and Sardinia. Naples also has services to Capri and other islands. Many services are reduced off-season, and some are cut altogether. Reserve well in advance for car ferries. *Note: frequent transit strikes take place in Italy; check travel details with transportation company.*

Driving

Drive on the right

Speed Limits

Police can demand up to a quarter of an imposed fine to be paid on the spot.

 Limited-access highways *(autostrade)* **130 k.p.h. (80 m.p.h.)** Some designated stretches of *autostrade* have a **150 k.p.h. (93 m.p.h.)** limit.

 Main roads **90–110 k.p.h. (56–68 m.p.h.)**

Urban areas **50 k.p.h. (31 m.p.h.)**

Note: keep your headlights on low beam at all times in built-up areas.

Seat Belts

Must be worn in front and back seats at all times.

Blood Alcohol

 The legal blood alcohol limit is 0.05% (zero for novice drivers). Random breath tests are carried out frequently, especially late at night.

Driving (continued)

Tolls

You will be issued a toll-card on entering nearly every limited-access highway *(autostrada)*: pay on leaving. You can buy a prepaid card *(viacard)* at tollbooths, service areas, tourist offices and tobacconists.

Car Rental

The leading car-rental firms have offices at airports, train stations and ferry terminals. Hertz offers discounted rates for AAA members (see page 15). For reservations:

	United States	Italy
Avis	1 800 633 3469	199 100 133
Budget	800-218-7992 (US number only)	
Europcar	Online only; go to www.europcar.com or www.europcar.it	
Hertz	Online only; go to www.hertz.com	

Fuel

Gas *(benzina)* is unleaded *(senza piombo)* 95 and 98 octane. Outside urban areas, stations are open daily 7–12:30 and 3–7:30. Highway services are open 24 hours. Credit cards are accepted at most filling stations.

AAA Affiliated Motoring Club

Automobile Club D'Italia (ACI) Via Marsala 8, 00185 Rome, ☎ 803116 in Italy (24 hours a day); or 06 491 115 or 800 000 116 (toll-free in Italy); www.aci.it. If you break down while driving, ☎ 803116. Not all automobile clubs offer full services to AAA members.

Breakdowns and Accidents

There are emergency phones at regular intervals on all highways. If you are involved in an accident, ☎ 112. Most car-rental firms provide their own free rescue service; if you have an accident, follow the rental documentation instructions. Use of an unauthorized repair company may violate your agreement. In the event of a breakdown, you must wear a fluorescent vest when outside your car. You must carry a warning triangle in your car.

Other Information

The minimum age for driving a car in Italy is 18 (may be higher for some car-rental firms). An International Driving Permit (IDP) is recommended; some car-rental firms require it, and it can speed up formalities if you are involved in an accident. A Green Card (international motor insurance certificate) is recommended if you are driving a private car (see page 15). Dimmed headlights are required by law at all times outside built-up areas and when visiblity is poor. Many historic downtown areas have a Zone a Traffico Limitato (ZTL) with automatic fines for non-approved vehicles.

Useful Words and Phrases

Italian pronunciation is consistent with spelling, and vowels are always pronounced. The letter h is always silent, but can modify the sound of letters c and g. As a general rule, accentuate the next-to-last syllable.

c is hard before a, o, u, h	*medico; Chianti*
c is soft before i or e	*ciao* [chow]
g is hard before a, o, u, h	*Gucci*, Lamborghini
g is soft before i or e	*gelati* [jel-ah-tee]
gl as in Amelia	*figlia* [fee-lyah]
gn as in union	*gnocchi* [nyee-ok-kee]
sc before i or e is soft	*prosciutto* [pro-shoot-toh]

Where two consonants appear together, each belongs to a different syllable.

Do you speak English?	*Parla inglese?*
excuse me	*mi scusi*
goodbye	*arrivederci*
hello	*buongiorno*
How much is…?	*Quanto costa…?*
I am American	*sono Americano/-a*
I'd like…	*vorrei…*
I don't understand	*non capisco*
nonsmoking	*per non fumatori*
okay	*va bene*
open/closed	*aperto/chiuso*
please/thank you	*per favore/grazie*
ticket (one-way/ round trip)	*biglietto (andata sola/andata ritorno)*
where is…?	*dov'è…?*
yes/no	*sì/no*
you're welcome	*prego*
the hotel	***l'albergo***
breakfast	*prima colazione*
I have a reservation	*ho una prenotazione*
key	*una chiave*
for one/two nights	*per una/due notte/-i*
one/two people	*una/due persona/-e*
room	*una camera*
shower	*una doccia*
with en-suite bathroom	*con bagno privato*
the restaurant	***il ristorante***
beef	*il manzo*
bread	*il pane*
the check	*il conto*
chicken	*il pollo*
coffee	*il caffè*
dessert	*il dolce*
dish of the day	*il piatto del giorno*
entrée	*il secondo*
fish	*il pesce*
lamb	*l'agnello*
pork	*il maiale*
seafood	*i frutti di mare*
starter	*l'antipasto*
wine	*il vino*

National Flag

Essential for Drivers

● Required ● Recommended ● Not required

Passport	●
Visa (check regulations before you travel)	●
Travel, medical insurance	●
Round-trip or onward airline ticket	●
Local currency	●
Traveler's checks	●
Credit cards	●
First-aid kit and medicines	●
Inoculations	●

Essential for Drivers*

Driver's license	●
International Driving Permit	●
Car insurance (for nonrental cars)	●
Car registration (for nonrental cars)	●

*see also *Driving* section

Important Addresses

Luxembourg National Tourist Office
17 Beekman Place
New York, NY 10022
☎ (212) 935-3589
www.visitluxembourg.com

**Office National du Tourisme
(Luxembourg National Tourist Office)**
P.O. Box 1001
L-1010 Luxembourg
☎ 42 82 82 11
www.visitluxembourg.com

Embassy of the United States
22 boulevard Emmanuel Servais
L-2535 Luxembourg
☎ 46 01 23 00
http://luxembourg.usembassy.gov
Mon.–Fri. 8:30–5:30

Customs

✔ **Duty-free limits on goods brought in from non-European Union countries:**
200 cigarettes or 100 cigarillos or 50 cigars or 250 g. tobacco; 2 L. wine; 1 L. alcohol over 22% volume or 2 L. alcohol under 22% volume; 50 ml. perfume; 250 ml. toilet water; plus any other duty-free goods (including gifts) to the value of €175 (€90 for children under 15).

There is no limit on the importation of tax-paid goods purchased within the European Union, provided they are for your own personal use.

There are no restrictions on the import or export of cash or traveler's checks in euros or other foreign currency.

✗ No unlicensed drugs, weapons, ammunition, obscene material, pets or other animals, counterfeit money or copied goods, meat or poultry.

For customs limits for returning U.S. citizens see page 16.

Money

Euro (€)
Luxembourg's currency is the euro (€), a currency shared by 18 other European Union countries.

The euro is divided into 100 cents (¢).
The denominations of euro bills are 5, 10, 20, 50, 100, 200 and 500.
There are coins of 1, 2, 5, 10, 20 and 50¢ and €1 and €2.

ATMs are plentiful and credit, debit and prepaid cards are accepted in hotels, large stores and upscale restaurants; check first in small or rural establishments. It is a good idea to carry a mix of large and small euro denominations.

Tips and Gratuities

Restaurants (service is usually included)	€1 or €2
Cafés/bars (service is usually included)	€1 or €2
Taxis	15%
Porters, chambermaids	€1–€2
Hairdressers	€2
Restroom attendants	50¢–€1
Cloakroom attendants	50¢ per coat

Communications

Post Offices

Buy stamps *(timbres-poste)* at a post office *(poste)*, newsstand/tobacconist *(tabac-journaux)* or at a bookstore. Mailboxes are yellow. Luxembourg City's main post office is ✉ 25 rue Aldringen ☎ 80 02-80 04 🕑 Monday to Friday 9–6, Saturday 8–5. Also at ✉ 20 rue de Reims ☎ 80 02 80 04 🕑 Monday to Friday 7–7, Saturday 9–6. Hours for out-of-town post offices may vary.

Telephones

Public telephones *(cabine téléphoniques)* are easy to find. Phone booths usually have pictorial instructions, with French and German text. You can use most denominations of coins, or buy a prepaid phone card *(télécarte)* from a post office or train station. International phone booths display a yellow sign showing a telephone dial with a receiver in the center. Check overseas cell phone usage with your provider.

Phoning inside Luxembourg

There are no area codes in Luxembourg; dial the number that is listed. For the operator dial 118 171.

Phoning Luxembourg from abroad

The country code for Luxembourg is 352. Note that Luxembourg numbers in this book do not include the country code; you will need to prefix this number if you are phoning from another country. To phone Luxembourg from the United States or Canada, add the prefix 011 352. Example: 11 22 33 becomes 011 352 11 22 33.

Phoning from Luxembourg

To phone the United States or Canada from Luxembourg, prefix the area code and number with 00 1. Example: (111) 222-3333 becomes 00 1 111 222-3333. To call the international operator dial 11816.

Emergency Telephone Numbers

Police *(police)* **112** or **113**
Fire service *(pompiers)* **112**
Ambulance *(ambulance)* **112**
Emergency calls are free from phone booths.

Time Zones

City of Luxembourg: 12 noon
New York: 6 a.m. (-6 hours)
Chicago: 5 a.m. (-7 hours)
Denver: 4 a.m. (-8 hours)
Los Angeles: 3 a.m. (-9 hours)

Hours of Operation

Most **stores** open 9–6, Monday to Saturday. Many do not open until noon on Monday, and most are closed on Sunday. Many establishments have long lunch breaks (typically noon–2).

Banks open Monday to Friday 9–noon and 2–4:30. Provincial banks may have shorter hours, but some stay open at lunchtime and open on Saturday morning.

Post offices are open weekdays 8–noon and 1:30–5. Some post offices open earlier and stay open in the evening.

Opening times for **museums** vary; they are frequently closed on Monday – check with the local tourist office.

Pharmacies are open Tuesday to Saturday 9–6.

National Holidays

Banks, businesses and most stores close on these days.

Jan. 1	New Year's Day
Mar./Apr.	Easter Monday
May 1	May Day
May/Jun.	Ascension Day
May/Jun.	Whit Monday
Jun. 23	National Day
Aug. 15	Assumption of the Virgin
First Mon. in Sep.	Luxembourg City Fete (City of Luxembourg only)
Nov. 1	All Saints' Day
Dec. 25	Christmas Day
Dec. 26	St. Stephen's Day

National holidays falling on a Sunday are normally observed on the following Monday.

Photography

Luxembourg enjoys a temperate climate, and the light is good. Make sure that photography is permitted before taking pictures in museums. Camera batteries can be bought from tourist stores. Digital equipment and printing facilities are available in major towns.

Health

Medical Insurance

Private medical insurance is recommended; U.S. and Canadian visitors can be treated in emergency rooms, but are charged if admitted to a hospital *(hôpital)*. For 24-hour information on hospitals and also for information on English-speaking doctors, ☎ 112.

Dental Services

A dentist *(dentiste)* will charge a fee for treatment, so check whether this is covered by your medical insurance. Emergency clinics are available in city hospitals. To find a dentist look in the *Yellow Pages (pages jaunes)* or ask at your hotel.

Sun Advice

You will not experience extremes of temperature in Luxembourg, but the sunshine during summer months can burn, so good sun protection is essential.

Drugs

Prescription medicines and advice can be obtained from a pharmacy *(pharmacie)*, identified by a green cross. Information about the nearest 24-hour facility is posted at all pharmacies.

Safe Water

Tap water in Luxembourg is safe to drink, and bottled mineral water *(eau minérale)* is widely available.

Restrooms

Restrooms *(toilettes)* are usually clean, modern and easy to find. They also may be called "WC" (pronounced *vay-say*). Coin-operated facilities exist; those with an attendant usually charge 50¢ or €1.

Electricity

Luxembourg has a 220-volt power supply. Electrical sockets take plugs with two round pins. American appliances will need a plug adapter and will require a transformer if they do not have a dual-voltage facility.

National Transportation

Train *(Train)*

The national rail company is the Societé Nationale des Chemins de Fer Luxembourgeois (CFL; www.cfl.lu). Most services run through the City of Luxembourg. Combined train and bus one-day travel cards (the "Billet Longue Durée") are good value at €4 and are valid until 8 a.m. the following day. "Short distance" train and bus tickets are available for €2 and are valid for 2 hours or 6 miles. At Luxembourg City train station there is an information office (🛈 (Mon.–Sat. 6 a.m.–8 p.m., Sun. 8–8). National information and tickets ☎ 2489-2489.

Bus *(Bus)*

Long-distance, CFL-operated buses complement the rail network (☎ 24 89 24 89; www.cfl.lu). The Eurolines European bus network serves Luxembourg, arriving at place de la Gare, in front of Gare Centrale.

River Boat *(Bateau-mouche)*

There are many excursions (mostly Easter to October) exploring Luxembourg's fine Moselle river. For details, contact Entente Touristique de la Moselle Luxembourgeoise, 115 route du Vin, L-5405 Bech-Kleinmacher ☎ 26 74 78 74; www.visitmoselle.lu.

Driving

Drive on the right

Speed Limits

Police impose minor on-the-spot fines.

 Limited access highways *(autoroutes)* **130 k.p.h. (80 m.p.h.), 110 k.p.h. (68 m.p.h.)** when wet or in snow conditions

 Main roads **90 k.p.h. (56 m.p.h.)**

 Urban areas **50 k.p.h. (31 m.p.h.)**

Seat Belts

Must be worn in front and back seats at all times. Children aged 3 to 18 years and/or under 4 feet 11 inches in height must use an appropriate child restraint system.

Blood Alcohol

The legal blood alcohol limit is 0.5% (0.2% for novice drivers). Random breath tests on drivers are carried out frequently, especially at night. Penalties for offenders are severe.

Driving (continued)

Tolls

 There are no highway tolls in Luxembourg.

Car Rental

The leading car-rental firms have offices at airports and train stations. Hertz offers discounted rates for AAA members (see page 15). For reservations:

	United States	Luxembourg
Alamo	0800 028 2390 (US number only)	
Avis	0800 633 3469	48 95 95
Budget	800 472 3325 (US number only)	
Hertz	800 654 3131	43 46 45

Fuel

Most gas stations *(stations de service)* are self-service, and 24-hour facilities are common. Stations on highways often have café services. The price of gas is fixed by the government, but self-service stations often offer discounts. Major credit cards are accepted.

AAA Affiliated Motoring Club

Automobile Club du Grand-Duché de Luxembourg (ACL) 54 route de Longwy, L-8007 Bertrange, 45 00 45-1 (Mon.–Fri. 8:30–6); www.acl.lu. If you break down while driving, 26000 (ACL 24-hour breakdown service). Not all automobile clubs offer full services to AAA members.

Breakdowns and Accidents

There are emergency phones at regular intervals on highways. If you are involved in an accident, phone for emergency assistance (112 or 113 for police or 112 for fire or ambulance). Most car-rental firms provide their own free rescue service; if your car is rented, follow the instructions given in the documentation. Use of a car-repair service other than those authorized by your rental company may violate your agreement. In the event of a breakdown, you must put on a fluorescent vest when you are outside your vehicle. You must carry a warning triangle in your vehicle.

Other Information

The minimum age for driving a car is 18 (may be higher for some car-rental firms). An International Driving Permit (IDP) is recommended; some car-rental firms require it, and it can speed up formalities if you are involved in an accident. A Green Card (international motor insurance certificate) is recommended if you are driving a private car; see page 15 for more information.

Useful Words and Phrases

Because the Grand Duchy of Luxembourg is tucked between Belgium, France and Germany, Luxembourgers often slip unconsciously between different languages.

The language of legislation (and, unofficially, the language of the elite) is French, but German is used for many situations. In addition to this, there is a third, everyday language: Lëtzebuergesch, a symbol of both national identity and Luxembourg's ability to assimilate other cultures.

The roots of Luxembourg's own language are Germanic, but it has evolved into a dialect that Germans no longer understand. The use of Lëtzebuergesch is primarily an oral tradition. It was only in 1984 that its spelling was decreed by law; up until then Luxembourgers spelled words more or less as they pleased.

French, German and Lëtzebuergesch are taught in schools, and English also is widely spoken, especially among the young and those working in the tourist trade. However, English is not widely spoken in rural areas of Luxembourg.

Lëtzebuergesch is resilient enough to exist side-by-side with such widely spoken languages as French and German, but as the patois of a tiny, landlocked duchy it's evidently not very exportable. So if you have the opportunity to speak a word or two of this country's uniting language you'll raise a smile and a welcome.

good morning/hello	*moien*
goodbye	*eddi*
thank you (very much)	*merci (villmols)*
sorry	*pardon*
excuse me	*entschellegt*
please	*wanneschglift*
I don't understand	*ech verstin net*
Food and drink	
apple cake	*Äppelkuch*
blood sausage	*Trèipen*
cheesecake	*Kéiskuch*
chicken in Riesling sauce	*Hong am Rèisleck*
coffee	*Kaffi*
crayfish	*Kriibsen*
green bean soup	*Bou'neschlupp*
nettle soup	*Brennesselszopp*
pike in green liquor	*Hiecht mat Kraïderzooss*
pork in aspic	*Jhelli*
potato dumplings	*Gromperekniddeln*
potato soup	*Gromperenzopp*
tripe	*Kuddelfleck*
trout in Riesling sauce	*F'rell am Rèisleck*

For useful phrases in French, see page 521; for phrases in German see page 525.

National Flag

Essential for Travelers

● **Required**   ● **Recommended**   ● **Not required**

Passport	●
Visa (check regulations before you travel)	●
Travel, medical insurance	●
Round-trip or onward airline ticket	●
Local currency	●
Traveler's checks	●
Credit cards	●
First-aid kit and medicines	●
Inoculations	●

Essential for Drivers*

Driver's license	●
International Driving Permit	●
Car insurance (for nonrental cars)	●
Car registration (for nonrental cars)	●

*see also *Driving* section

Important Addresses

The Netherlands Board of Tourism & Conventions
215 Park Avenue South
Suite 2005
New York, NY 10003
☎ (917) 720 1283
www.holland.com

**Nederlands Bureau voor Toerisme & Congressen
– NBTC (Netherlands Board of Tourism
& Conventions – NBTC)**
P.O. Box 63470
2502 JL The Hague,
The Netherlands
☎ 070 370 5705
www.holland.com

American Embassy
John Adams Park 1
2244 BZ Wassenaar,
The Netherlands
☎ 070 310 2209
https://nl.usembassy.gov

Customs

✔ **Duty-free limits on goods brought in from
non-European Union countries:**
200 cigarettes or 100 cigarillos or 50 cigars or
250 g. tobacco; 2 L. wine; 1 L. alcohol over 22%
volume or 2 L. alcohol under 22% volume or
sparkling wine and 4 L. still wine, 16 L. beer; plus
any other goods/gifts to the value of €430 if
arriving by air or sea, €300 if arriving overland (€150
for travelers under 15).

There is no limit on the importation of tax-paid
goods bought within the E.U. if they are for your
own use.

Currency worth more than €10,000 (or equivalent)
must be declared.

✘ No unlicensed drugs, weapons, ammunition,
obscene material, pets or other animals,
counterfeit money or copied goods, meat or poultry.

**For customs limits for returning U.S. citizens
see page 16.**

Money

Euro (€)
The Dutch currency is the euro (€), a currency
shared by 18 other European Union countries.

The euro is divided into 100 cents (¢).
The denominations of euro bills are 5, 10, 20, 50,
100, 200 and 500.
There are coins of 1, 2, 5, 10, 20 and 50¢ and
€1 and €2.

ATMs are plentiful and credit, debit and prepaid
cards are accepted in hotels, large stores and
upscale restaurants; check first in small or rural
establishments. It is a good idea to carry a mix
of large and small euro denominations.

Tips and Gratuities

Restaurants (service is always included)	change
Cafés/bars (service is always included)	change
Taxis (service is always included)	change
Porters	change
Hairdressers	change
Chambermaids	change
Restroom attendants	€1
Cloakroom attendants	none

Communications

Post Offices

Buy stamps *(postzegels)* at a post office *(postkantoor* or *Post NL)*, tobacco shop, newsstand or souvenir shop. If you are buying from a counter make sure you are in a line for stamps. Mailboxes have two slots; foreign mail should be dropped into the slot marked *Overige*. Hours for out-of-town post offices may vary.

Telephones

You can use cash (uncommon), credit cards and prepaid phone cards *(telefoonkaart)* to make calls. Phone cards can be bought from post offices, VVV tourist offices and shops displaying the phone-card symbol. Orange-and-gray-colored booths require a different phone card, available from Wizzl shops and railroad ticket offices. Calls also can be made from post offices and *KPN Telehouse* booths. Check overseas cell phone usage with your provider.

Phoning inside The Netherlands

All Dutch telephone numbers in this book include an area code; dial the number listed. To call the operator dial 0800 0410.

Phoning The Netherlands from abroad

The country code for The Netherlands is 31. Dutch numbers in this book do not include the country code; include the country code if you are phoning from another country. To phone The Netherlands from the United States or Canada, omit the first zero from the Dutch number and dial the prefix 011 31. Example: 011 223 3445 becomes 011 31 11 223 3445.

Phoning from The Netherlands

To phone the United States or Canada, prefix the area code and number with 00 1. Example: (111) 222-3333 becomes 00 1 111 222-3333. To call international information dial 0900 8418 (toll call). For national information dial 0900 8008 (toll call).

Emergency Telephone Numbers

General emergencies **112**
Police *(politie)* **112**
Fire service *(brandweer)* **112**
Ambulance *(ziekenwagen)* **112**
Emergency calls are free from phone booths.

Time Zones

The Hague: 12 noon
New York: 6 a.m. (-6 hours)
Chicago: 5 a.m. (-7 hours)
Denver: 4 a.m. (-8 hours)
Los Angeles: 3 a.m. (-9 hours)

Hours of Operation

Stores are open Monday 11–6, Tuesday to Saturday from 9 a.m. Some close at 5 p.m. on Saturday. In Amsterdam many stores open Sunday noon–7 and in The Hague and Rotterdam noon–5. In other Dutch cities stores open one Sunday a month. Larger city stores stay open until 9 p.m. on Thursday or Friday. In rural areas many stores close for lunch.

Banks open Monday to Friday 9–5; they generally open at 1 p.m. on Mondays.

Post offices also are open Monday to Friday 9–5 and on Saturday morning. Some city post offices stay open into the evening (Thursday or Friday).

Museums usually open Monday to Saturday 10–5. Some open on Sunday 1–5; some may close on Monday. In rural areas they may be closed October through March.

Pharmacies are open weekdays 8:30–6.

National Holidays

Banks, businesses and most stores close on these days, except for Good Friday, when most shops remain open.

Jan. 1	New Year's Day
Mar./Apr.	Good Friday
Mar./Apr.	Easter Monday
Apr. 27	King's Day. Celebration of the birthday of King Willem-Alexander
May 5	Liberation Day (occurs every 5 years; next in 2019)
May/Jun.	Ascension Day
May/Jun.	Pentecost Monday
Dec. 25	Christmas Day
Dec. 26	St. Stephen's Day

Photography

The Dutch climate is essentially maritime; conditions for outdoor photography are gentle but changeable. Some museums do not allow photography; check before taking pictures. Camera batteries are widely available. Digital equipment and printing services are available in towns and cities.

The Netherlands

Health

Medical Insurance

Private medical insurance is recommended. U.S. and Canadian visitors can receive emergency treatment, but are charged if admitted to a hospital *(ziekenhuis)*. For the name of a doctor *(dokter)* see the list of doctors at the beginning of the telephone directory; English is widely spoken throughout the medical profession in The Netherlands. Tourist Medical Service: doctor ☎ 020 592 3355.

Dental Services

Dentists charge for treatment and can be expensive; check if this is covered by your medical insurance. Look in the telephone directory, or ask about local English-speaking dentists at your hotel or embassy.

Sun Advice

The Netherlands' maritime climate is not one of extremes, but precautions against sunburn must be taken from June through August.

Drugs

For nonprescription medicines go to a pharmacy *(drogisterij)*. If you need prescription medicines you will have to go to an *apotheek*, where staff also are trained to treat minor ailments. If you need medicine after regular hours, information about all-night facilities is posted at all pharmacies.

Safe Water

Tap water is safe to drink throughout The Netherlands. However, mineral water also is widely available.

Restrooms

There are not many public restrooms, although you will usually find adequate and clean facilities in museums, department stores and roadside service areas. Cafés provide restrooms for the use of customers; buy a drink if you need to use them.

Electricity

The Netherlands has a 230-volt power supply. Electrical sockets take plugs with two round pins. American appliances will need a plug adapter and will require a transformer if they do not have a dual-voltage facility.

National Transportation

Train *(Trein)*

The Netherlands Railways, or *Nederlandse Spoorwegen (NS)*, network is fast, clean, modern, punctual and inexpensive. Information in English is widely available from stations; ☎ 0900 9296 (toll call) for international train service, ☎ 0900 9292 (toll call) for all domestic transportation services; www.ns.nl.

Bus *(Bus)*

Bus travel is well-organized, with many connections to trains (bus and railroad stations are usually next to each other). If you're planning several trips ask for the *Nationale Buswijzer*, which provides maps and full route details; ☎ 0900 9292 (toll call) for information. The Eurolines European bus network operates in The Netherlands ☎ 088 076 1700.

Ferry *(Veerboot)*

There are ferry services from the mainland across the Waddenzee to the Wadden islands (from Den Helder for Texel; Harlingen for Vlieland and Terschelling; Holwerd for Ameland; and Lauwersoog for Schiermonnikoog), and in summer services between the islands. For details about canal trips, contact VVV tourist information centers.

Driving

Drive on the right

Speed Limits

Police can impose on-the-spot fines.

 Expressways *(autowegen)* 100 k.p.h. (62 m.p.h.). Motorways *(autos- nelwegen)* 130 k.p.h. (81 m.p.h.). Minimum speed on motorways 60 k.p.h. (37 m.p.h.)

 Main roads 80 k.p.h. (49 m.p.h.)

Urban areas 50 k.p.h. (31 m.p.h.)

Seat Belts

 Must be worn in front and back seats at all times. Children must use a suitable restraint system for their height/weight.

Blood Alcohol

 The legal blood alcohol limit is 0.05% (0.02% for novice drivers). Random breath tests on drivers are carried out frequently, especially at night. Penalties for offenders are severe.

Driving (continued)

Tolls

There are no highway tolls in The Netherlands, but there are tolls for the Dordtse Kil tunnel near Dordrecht and the Westerschelde tunnel.

Car Rental

The leading car-rental firms have offices at airports and train stations. Hertz offers discounted rates for AAA members (see page 15). For reservations:

	United States	Netherlands
Alamo	(844) 354 6962	020 740 0950
Avis	(800) 331-1212	088 284 7020
Budget	(800) 218-7992	088 284 7620
Hertz	(800) 654-3001	020 502 0240

Fuel

Many gas stations are self-service and 24-hour facilities are common. Unleaded gas *(Super-Plus* and *Euro-Super)*, lead-replacement fuel and diesel are available, and credit cards are accepted at most gas stations.

AAA Affiliated Motoring Club

Koninklijke Nederlandse Toeristenbond (ANWB) Wassenaarseweg 220, 2596 The Hague ☎ 088 269 2222; www.anwb.nl. If you break down while driving, ☎ 088 269 2888 (ANWB breakdown service, toll free). Not all automobile clubs offer full services to AAA members.

Breakdowns and Accidents

There are yellow 24-hour emergency phones at regular intervals on highways. All accidents involving personal injury must be reported to the police; ☎ 112. Most car-rental firms provide their own free rescue service; if your car is rented, follow the instructions given in the documentation. Use of a car-repair service other than those authorized by your rental company may violate your agreement.

Other Information

The minimum age for driving a car is 18 (usually between 21 and 25 for car-rental firms). An International Driving Permit (IDP) is recommended; some car-rental firms require it, and it can speed up formalities if you are involved in an accident. A Green Card (international motor insurance certificate) is recommended if you are driving a private car; see page 15 for more information. Drivers should yield to vehicles approaching from the right. In built-up areas, trams and buses have the right of way when leaving bus stops. Beware of cyclists and skaters.

Useful Words and Phrases

It is not easy to reproduce the guttural sounds that make up the Dutch language. There are many similarities between German and Dutch, although the Dutch go to lengths to point out the differences. English is spoken fluently by a large proportion of the population, who learn foreign languages from an early age.

Dutch pronunciation is similar to English, with some variations:

j as in *y*ellow
v like an f as in *f*ar
w like a v as in *v*at
ng as in bri*ng*
nj as in o*ni*on

Double consonants keep their separate sounds: for instance, k and n together are never pronounced as in the English "know."

Some letters and diphthongs are tricky. If the letter is doubled, the vowel sound is lengthened. For example:

a as in s*a*p,	*aa* as in *a*rt
e as in l*e*t,	*ee* as in f*a*te
o as in m*o*p,	*oo* as in m*o*pe
oe as in f*oo*d	
au, ou and *ui* as in h*ow*	
ei and *ij* as in l*i*ne	
ch as in Ba*ch*	
tje as in *ch*urch	
tie as in *tee*	

Do you speak English?	*Spreekt u Engels?*
excuse me	*pardon*
hello	*hallo or dag*
goodbye	*tot ziens*
yes/no	*ja/nee*
how much is?	*wat kost?*
I want…	*ik wil…*
I don't understand	*Ik begrijp het niet*
open/closed	*open/gesloten*
please	*alstublieft*
thank you	*bedankt*
ticket (one-way/ round trip)	*enkele reis retour*
where's the…?	*waar is…?*
the airport	*de luchthoven*
the room	*de kamer*
the breakfast	*het ontbijt*
the dinner	*het diner*
May I order?	*Mag ik even bestellen?*
bread	*brood*
chicken	*kip*
coffee/tea	*koffie/thee*
dish of the day	*dagschotel*
lamb	*lamsvlees*
pork	*varkensvlees*
sandwich	*broodje*
steak	*biefstuk*
wine	*wijn*

National Flag

Essential for Travelers

● **Required** ● **Recommended** ● **Not required**

Passport	●
Visa (check regulations before you travel)	●
Travel, medical insurance	●
Round-trip or onward airline ticket	●
Local currency	●
Traveler's checks	●
Credit cards	●
First-aid kit and medicines	●
Inoculations	●

Essential for Drivers*

Driver's license	●
International Driving Permit	●
Car insurance (for nonrental cars)	●
Car registration (for nonrental cars)	●

*see also *Driving* section

Important Addresses

Innovation Norway
655 Third Avenue, Suite 1810
New York, NY 10017-9111
☎ (212) 885-9752
www.visitnorway.com

Innovation Norway
Akersgata 13
N-0158 Oslo, Norway
☎ 22 00 25 00
www.visitnorway.com

American Embassy
Morgedalsvegen 36
0378 Oslo, Norway
☎ 21 30 85 40 (emergencies 24 hours)
https://no.usembassy.gov/
🕐 Mon.–Fri. 8:30–5

Customs

✔ **Duty-free limits on goods brought in from non-European countries:**
200 cigarettes or 250g. tobacco and 200 cigarette papers; 1 L. alcohol 23–60%; 1.5 L. alcohol up to 22%; 2 L. beer. If you have no alcohol 23–60% you are allowed 1.5 L. extra alcohol up to 22%, or 5L. beer if no other alcohol. Alcohol limits are higher if you have no tobacco. See www.toll.no/en. Also goods to the value of Kr6,000, which must include your tobacco and alcohol allowances. You must be 20 or over to bring in spirits and 18 or over to bring in wine, beer and tobacco products.

You may import or export local or foreign currency to the value of Kr25,000. Larger amounts must be declared to the customs authorities. This does not apply to traveler's checks.

✘ No unlicensed drugs, weapons, ammunition, fireworks, obscene material, pets or other animals, counterfeit money or copied goods, alcohol over 60%, meat or poultry.

For customs limits for returning U.S. citizens see page 16.

Money

Krone (NOK or Kr)
Norway's currency is the krone (NOK or Kr), which is divided into 100 øre.
The denominations of krone bills are 50, 100, 200, 500 and 1,000.
There are coins of Kr1, Kr5, Kr10 and Kr20.

New banknotes featuring sea motifs are being introduced into circulation up to 2019. The old-style 100 Kr and 200 Kr bills featuring famous Norwegians have ceased to be legal currency but can still be exchanged at banks.

You can exchange dollars or traveler's checks *(reisesjekk)* at an exchange office *(vekslekontor)*, post office *(posten)* or hotel; you will need ID. Credit, debit and prepaid cards are widely accepted. ATMs are readily available for withdrawal of local currency.

Tips and Gratuities

Restaurants (service is included)	5–10%
Cafés/bars (service is included)	5–10%
Taxis (service is included)	10% (optional)
Porters	Kr10 per bag
Hairdressers	change
Chambermaids	Kr10
Restroom attendants	Kr5

Communications

Post Offices

Buy stamps *(frimerker)* at a post office *(posten)*, a newsstand/tobacconist such as Narvesen or from a hotel. Hours for out-of-town post offices may vary. Mailboxes are red.

Telephones

Most phone booths have direct dialing for international calls. Some still accept Kr1, Kr5, Kr10 and Kr20 coins (minimum charge Kr5), and euro coins, as well as phone cards and credit cards. NOTE: green kiosks do not accept cash. International phone calls are provided by BBG, call (toll-free) ☎ 800 33 200 and follow instructions. If you use your own cell phone, be sure to check the cost with your provider before leaving home; alternatively, consider buying a local SIM card (check that your phone is unlocked).

Phoning inside Norway
There are no area codes in Norway; all numbers are eight digits: dial the number that is listed. To call the operator dial 117; for directory inquiry information dial 1881.

Phoning Norway from abroad
The country code for Norway is 47. Note that Norwegian numbers in this book do not include the country code; you will need to prefix this number if you are phoning from another country. To phone Norway from the United States or Canada, simply add the prefix 011 47. Example: 11 22 33 44 becomes 011 47 11 22 33 44.

Phoning from Norway
To phone the United States or Canada from Norway, prefix the area code and number with 00 1. Example: (111) 222-3333 becomes 00 1 111 222-3333. To call international information dial 1882. For the international operator dial 115.

Emergency Telephone Numbers

Police *(politi)* 112
Fire service *(brannvesen)* 110
Ambulance *(ambulanse)* 113
Sea emergency 120
Emergency calls are free from phone booths.

Time Zones

Oslo: 12 noon
New York: 6 a.m. (-6 hours)
Chicago: 5 a.m. (-7 hours)
Denver: 4 a.m. (-8 hours)
Los Angeles: 3 a.m. (-9 hours)

Hours of Operation

Stores are open Monday to Saturday 10–6. On Thursday most stores open at 9 a.m. and remain open until between 6 and 8 p.m. On Saturday, some smaller stores close early (4 p.m.).

Supermarkets are generally open Monday to Friday 9–8 or 9, Saturday 9–4 or 6. Many shopping complexes are open until 8 p.m. (4 or 6 on Saturday). Kiosks are open daily and stay open until 10 or 11. Most stores are closed on Sunday. Stores around tourist attractions may have special hours.

Banks open weekdays 9–3:30 and generally close half an hour earlier from mid-May to mid-September, but stay open until 5 p.m. on Thursday all year.

Post offices are open Monday to Friday and Saturday. Some post offices may not open until 9 and close at 4. They are open 9–1 on Saturday.

Museums often close on Monday, and hours of operation may be reduced during the winter.

Pharmacies are open Monday to Friday 10–5.

National Holidays

Banks, businesses and most stores close on these days.

Jan. 1	New Year's Day
Mar./Apr.	Maundy Thursday
Mar./Apr.	Good Friday
Mar./Apr.	Easter Monday
May 1	Labor Day
May 17	Constitution Day
May	Ascension Day
May/Jun.	Pentecost Sunday and Monday
Dec. 25	Christmas Day
Dec. 26	St. Stephen's Day

Photography

Spectacular shots are possible in fjord country if the weather is right (bear in mind that Norway is susceptible to poor light, especially during the winter). Photography is not permitted in some museums and places of historic interest – check before taking pictures. Camera batteries are readily available in towns. Digital photography equipment and facilities for downloading and printing also are widely available.

Health

Medical Insurance

U.S. and Canadian visitors will be charged for medical assistance, including treatment in a hospital *(sykehus)* emergency room. For medical emergency service in Oslo contact Oslo kommune Legevakt, Storgata 40 ☎ 116 117 (24 hours). For general practitioners, look for *Lege* in the phone directory.

Dental Services

A dentist *(tannlege)* will charge you for treatment, so check your medical insurance coverage. Many dentists speak English; ask a tourist office or your hotel to find one for you. For after-hours emergency treatment *(tannlegevakten)* in Oslo contact Oslo kommunale Tannlegevakt, Schweigaardsgate 6 (☎ 23 43 01 00).

Sun Advice

Despite its northerly location, Norway has warm weather during the summer months. Use an appropriate sunscreen.

Drugs

A pharmacy *(apotek)* sells prescription medicines; many pharmacists speak English. Information about the nearest late-night or 24-hour facility is posted at all pharmacies. For a 24-hour pharmacy in Oslo go to Vitus Apotek, Jernbanetorget 4B, near Oslo Central Station (☎ 23 35 81 00).

Safe Water

Tap water is safe to drink throughout Norway. Mineral water *(mineralvann)* is widely available.

Restrooms

Public restrooms *(toaletter)* are easy to find. Facilities are separate for men *(herrer)* and women *(damer)*, and are identified by symbols or a "WC" sign. They are invariably clean and modern, and a small charge (usually Kr5) may be made.

Electricity

Norway has a 220-volt power supply. Electrical sockets take plugs with two round pins. American appliances will need a plug adapter and will require a transformer if they do not have a dual-voltage facility.

National Transportation

Train *(Tog)*

The Norges Statsbaner (NSB) network operates as far north as the Arctic Circle. Travel is comfortable but not cheap. Reservations are recommended on train trips and compulsory on long-distance and overnight trains; (☎ 81 50 08 88, press 9 for information in English; or go online at www.nsb.no).

Bus *(Buss)*

Buses are an inexpensive way to travel in Norway. NOR-WAY Bussekspress (☎ 21 31 31 50; www.nor-way.no) is the national operator. Buy your ticket on board; it is not necessary to book in advance.

Ferry *(Ferje)*

Norway relies heavily on ferries and express boats/catamarans, which connect with trains and buses. Car ferries operate on a first-come, first-served system; payment is made on board. Some waterways have ferry services. *Hurtigruten*, a grand coastal steamer, links Bergen with Kirkenes, in northern Norway, calling at 34 ports en route over an 11-day round trip (☎ 03 00 00; www.hurtigruten.com).

Driving

Drive on the right

Speed Limits

Speed controls are stringent. Police can impose on-the-spot fines.

 Limited-access highways *(motorvei)*
90 k.p.h. (56 m.p.h.) or
100 k.p.h. (62 m.p.h.)

 Main roads
80 k.p.h. (49 m.p.h.)

Urban areas **50 k.p.h. (31 m.p.h.)**; usually
30 k.p.h. (18 m.p.h.) in residential areas

Seat Belts

Must be worn in front and back seats at all times. Children under 4 feet 5 inches or 79 pounds must use child safety equipment.

Blood Alcohol

The legal blood alcohol limit is 0.02%. Random breath tests on drivers are carried out frequently, especially late at night, and the penalties for offenders are extremely severe.

Driving (continued)

Tolls

There are tolls to enter Bergen, Oslo, Stavanger and Trondheim, as well as some highways, bridges and tunnels.

Car Rental

The leading car-rental firms *(bilutleie)* have offices at airports and train stations. Hertz offers discounted rates for AAA members (see page 15). For reservations:

	United States	Norway
Avis	(800) 633 3469	81 53 30 44
Budget	(800) 218 7992	67 25 55 20
Europcar	(877) 940 6900	67 16 58 20
Hertz	(800) 654-3001	21 51 37 00

Fuel *(Olje)*

Unleaded gas is 95 and 98 octane; diesel is available. Gas stations *(bensinstasjon)* have varying opening hours and there are few in remote areas, so keep your eye on the gauge.

AAA Affiliated Motoring Club

Norges Automobil-forbund (NAF)
Østensjøveen 14, Postboks 6682, Etterstad, NO-0609 Oslo ☎ 23 21 31 00 (from abroad: 926 08505); www.naf.no. If you break down while driving, ☎ 08 505 (24-hour NAF breakdown service). A fee is charged for the service. Not all automobile clubs offer full services to AAA members.

Breakdowns and Accidents

NAF patrols main roads and mountain passes mid-June to mid-August. There are 24-hour emergency phones on all highways. All accidents involving personal injury must be reported to the police (☎ 112). Most car-rental firms provide their own free rescue service; if you break down follow the instructions given in the documentation. Use of an unauthorized car-repair service may violate your rental agreement. You must carry a warning triangle in your car.

Other Information

The minimum age for driving a car is 18 (may be higher for car-rental firms). An International Driving Permit (IDP) is recommended; some car-rental firms require it, and it can speed up formalities if you are involved in an accident. A Green Card (international motor insurance certificate) is highly recommended if you are driving a private car (see page 15 for more information). You are required by law to use dimmed headlights at all times when driving. Snow tires and chains are advised from November 1 until the first Sunday after Easter (mid-Oct. through Apr. 30 in northern Norway); rent tires and chains from NAF or at border crossings.

Useful Words and Phrases

There are two official, and similar forms of Norwegian. Riksmal, or Bokmal ("book language"), is an old form of Norwegian. Athough many bureaucrats speak in Bokmal, it is mostly used in its written form. Landsmål, or Nynorsk, has its roots in Old Norse dialects but developed out of the wave of Norwegian nationalism in the 19th century. You will encounter both during your stay; it is not uncommon for speakers to use a combination of both, but writing rarely mixes styles. The phrases below are translated into Bokmal:

Do you speak English?	*Snakker du engelsk?*
excuse me	*unnskyld meg*
hello	*god dag*
goodbye	*ha det bra*
how much?	*hvor mye?*
I would like	*Jeg vil gjerne*
I don't understand	*Jeg forstår ikke*
nonsmoking	*røyking forbudt*
open/closed	*åpen/stengt*
please	*vær så snill*
thank you	*takk*
ticket (one-way/	*enkeltbillett/*
round trip)	*tur-returbillett*
Where is…?	*Hvor er…?*
yes/no	*ja/nei*
early/late	*tidlig/sent*
hot/cold	*varm/kald*
big/small	*stor/liten*
good/bad	*god/dårlig*
airport	*flyplass*
you're welcome	*vær så god*
the restaurant	**restaurant**
beef	*oksekjøtt*
bread	*brød*
breakfast	*frokost*
the check	*regningen*
chicken	*kylling*
coffee/tea	*kaffe/te*
cookies	*kjeks*
cranberries	*tranebær*
dessert	*dessert*
entree	*hovedrett*
fish	*fisk*
herring	*sild*
hot-dog	*pølse*
ice cream	*is*
lamb	*lammekjøtt*
lobster	*hummer*
pork	*svinekjøtt*
salad	*salat*
sandwich	*smørbrød*
seafood	*sjømat*
starter	*forrett*
waffles	*vafler*
wine	*vin*

National Flag

Essential for Travelers

● Required ● Recommended ● Not required

Passport	●
Visa (check regulations before you travel)	●
Travel, medical insurance	●
Round-trip or onward airline ticket	●
Local currency	●
Traveler's checks	●
Credit cards	●
First-aid kit and medicines	●
Inoculations	●

Essential for Drivers*

Driver's license	●
International Driving Permit	●
Car insurance (for nonrental cars)	●
Car registration (for nonrental cars)	●

*see also *Driving* section

Important Addresses

Portuguese National Tourist Office
590 5th Avenue #4, New York. NY 10036
☎ 1 646-723-0200
www.visitportugal.com

Turismo de Portugal (Portugal Tourist Office)
Rua Ivone Silve, Lote 6, 1050-124 Lisboa
☎ 211 140 200
www.visitportugal.com

American Embassy
Avenida Forças Armadas
1600-081 Lisbon, Portugal
☎ 217 273 300
https://pt.usembassy.gov
🕓 Mon.–Fri. 8–noon and 1:30–5

Customs

✔ **Duty-free limits on goods brought in from non-European Union countries:**
200 cigarettes or 100 cigarillos or 50 cigars or 250 g. tobacco; 4 L. wine; 1 L. alcohol over 22% volume or 2 L. alcohol under 22% volume, 16 L. beer; 60 ml. perfume; 250 ml. toilet water; plus any other duty-free goods (including gifts) to the value of €430 (€300 if you enter by road, rail, private boat or plane).

Local or foreign currency (including coins, notes, traveler's checks or other monetary securities) exceeding €10,000 must be declared on entry and when leaving the country.

There is no limit on the importation of tax-paid goods purchased within the European Union if they are for personal use.

✗ No unlicensed drugs, weapons, ammunition, obscene material, pets or other animals, counterfeit money or copied goods, meat or poultry.

For customs limits for returning U.S. citizens see page 16.

Money

Euro (€)
Portugal's currency is the euro (€), a currency shared by 18 other European Union countries.

The euro is divided into 100 cents (¢).
The denominations of euro bills are 5, 10, 20, 50, 100, 200 and 500.
There are coins of 1, 2, 5, 10, 20 and 50¢ and €1 and €2.

Credit, debit and prepaid cards are widely accepted. ATMs are plentiful throughout Portugal. It is a good idea to carry more notes of smaller euro denominations.

Tips and Gratuities

Restaurants (where service is not included)	5–10%
Cafés/bars (where service is not included)	change
Taxis	10%
Porters	50¢–€1
Hairdressers	€3–€5
Chambermaids	€3–€5
Restroom attendants	50¢
Cloakroom attendants	50¢

Communications

Post Offices

Buy stamps *(selos)* at a post office *(correios)*, identified by a sign showing a white horse on a red background. You may also see the words "Correios." Hours for out-of-town post offices may vary.

Telephones

You can use coins or a phone card, available from post offices, in a phone booth *(cabine telefónico)*. Public phones are easily found on the street and in cafés, main post offices and at some newsstands and tourist offices. Contact Portugal Telecom (☎ 18 20) for information. Check overseas cellphone usage charges with your provider.

Phoning inside Portugal
All Portuguese telephone numbers in this book include an area code; dial the number listed from anywhere in the country. To call an international operator dial 117. To call information dial 118.

Phoning Portugal from abroad
The country code for Portugal is 351. Note that Portuguese numbers in this book do not include the country code; you will need to prefix this number if you are phoning from another country. To phone Portugal from the United States or Canada dial the prefix 011 351. Example: 111 223 344 becomes 011 351 111 223 344.

Phoning from Portugal
To phone the United States or Canada from Portugal, prefix the area code and number with 00 1. Example: (111) 222-3333 becomes 00 1 111 222-3333. For an international operator dial 117. To call international information dial 1820.

Emergency Telephone Numbers

Police *(polícia)* **112**
Fire service *(bombeiros)* **112**
Ambulance *(ambulância)* **112**
Emergency calls are free from phone booths.

Time Zones

Lisbon: 12 noon
New York: 7 a.m. (-5 hours)
Chicago: 6 a.m. (-6 hours)
Denver: 5 a.m. (-7 hours)
Los Angeles: 4 a.m. (-8 hours)

Hours of Operation

Stores are open Monday to Friday 10–1 and 3–7, Saturday 10–1. Stores in large malls are open Monday to Sunday 10 a.m.–midnight. Grocery stores are usually open until 9 p.m.
Banks operate on weekdays 8:30–3 and in rural areas often close for lunch. A few banks in Lisbon stay open until 6 p.m.
Post offices open Monday to Friday 9–6.
Museums are open 10–12:30 and 2–5 and generally close on Monday (others close on Wednesday). Smaller sights may have shorter hours of operation off-season.
Pharmacies open on weekdays 9–1:30 and 3–7.

National Holidays

Banks, businesses and most stores close on these days. There also are many local festivals when everything comes to a halt.

Jan. 1	New Year's Day
Feb./Mar.	Shrove Tuesday (unofficial holiday but widely observed)
Mar./Apr.	Good Friday
Apr. 25	Liberty Day
May 1	Labor Day
May/Jun.	Corpus Christi
Jun. 10	Portugal Day
Aug. 15	Assumption of the Virgin
Oct. 5	Republic Day
Nov. 1	All Saints' Day
Dec. 1	Independence Day
Dec. 8	Immaculate Conception
Dec. 25	Christmas Day

Photography

Finding adequate light is rarely a problem in Portugal; rise early for atmospheric shots of fishing ports, villages, castles and the mountains. You will not be permitted to photograph at airports or military areas, and ask permission before taking pictures in museums and churches. Digital peripherals and commercial digital printers are widely available, along with batteries.

Health

Medical Insurance

U.S. and Canadian visitors will be charged for emergency medical treatment, consultation with a doctor and/or admittance to a hospital *(hospital)*. Ask at a tourist office or your hotel to find an English-speaking doctor.

Dental Services

Dental treatment is charged for in Portugal. Ask at a tourist office or your hotel for a list of English-speaking dentists. Check whether dental treatment is covered by your medical insurance.

Sun Advice

The sun is strong during summer (and some days in winter), particularly in the south. Do not be deceived by the cooling breeze off the Atlantic. Avoid prolonged exposure and protect yourself with a sunscreen or cover up.

Drugs

Prescription medicines are available from a pharmacy *(farmácia)*, distinguished by a large green cross. Pharmacists can prescribe remedies for minor ailments, and many speak English. Information about the nearest late-night or 24-hour facility is posted at all pharmacies.

Safe Water

Tap water is generally safe, but does not always taste too pleasant. It is advisable to drink bottled water *(agua mineral)*, especially in rural areas; *sem gas* means noncarbonated, *com gas* means carbonated.

Restrooms

Public restrooms *(casa de banho* or *lavabos)* are easy to find. Ladies' *(senhoras)* restrooms may occasionally charge a small fee and are generally clean. Men's *(homens)* restrooms are usually free.

Electricity

Portugal has a 220-volt power supply. Electrical sockets take plugs with two round pins. American appliances will need a plug adapter and a transformer if they do not have a dual-voltage facility.

National Transportation

Train *(Comboios)*

The Caminhos de Ferro Portugueses (CP) operates three types of service: *regional* and *Intercidade* (which both stop at most stations) and *Alfa Pendular* (express between Braga in the north and Faro in the south). For information ☎ 707 210 220 from inside and outside Portugal; www.cp.pt.

Bus *(Autocarros)*

Rede Expressos operates a network to all major destinations with connections to smaller towns (☎ 707 22 33 44; www.rede-expressos.pt). Buses are modern and comfortable. Several companies also maintain an extensive network in the regions of the country.

Ferry *(Barcos)*

Ferries cross the Rio Tejo from Cais do Sodré to Cacilhas, Seixal and Montijo; Terreiro do Paço to Barreiro; Belém to Trafaira; and Porto to Brandão (☎ 808 20 30 50; www.transtejo.pt). From Setúbal ferries cross the Rio Sado to the Tróia peninsula. Tickets can be bought at the boat stations' ticket offices.

Driving

Drive on the right

Speed Limits

Police can impose on-the-spot fines.

Limited-access highways *(autoestrada)*
120 k.p.h. (74 m.p.h.).
Minimum speed **50 k.p.h. (31 m.p.h.)**
Divided highways **100 k.p.h. (62 m.p.h.)**

Main roads
90 k.p.h. (56 m.p.h.)

Urban areas
50 k.p.h. (31 m.p.h.). Some areas **20 k.p.h** **(12 m.p.h.)**

Seat Belts

Must be worn in front and back seats at all times.

Blood Alcohol

The legal blood alcohol limit is 0.05%. (0.02% for drivers with less than 3 years' driving experience). Random breath tests on drivers are carried out frequently, especially late at night, and the penalties for offenders are severe.

Portugal

Driving (continued)

Tolls

There are tolls on highways *(autoestrados)* in Portugal. Highway numbers are prefixed by the letter A. There are an increasing number of highways where tolls are calculated electronically and paid through pre-paid devices or by a credit card registered with the payment authorities. For information in English see www.portugaltolls.pt.

Car Rental

The leading car-rental firms have offices at airports and train stations. Hertz offers discounted rates for AAA members (see page 15). For reservations:

	United States	Portugal
Alamo	(884) 345 6962	21 848 6191 (Enterprise)
Avis	(800) 633 3469	800 201 002
Budget	(800) 218-7992	808 252 627
Hertz	(800) 654-3001	21 942 6300

Fuel *(Gasolina)*

Gas and diesel are sold in liters, and most stations *(posto de gasolina)* are self-service. Gas stations, generally open daily 7 a.m.–10 p.m. (some 24 hours), are not as common in the more remote northern areas of Portugal. Credit cards are mostly accepted.

AAA Affiliated Motoring Club

Automóvel Club de Portugal (ACP)
Rua Rosa Araújo 24–26, 1250–195 Lisbon
213 180 100 or 808 222 222 for 24-hour global assistance: www.acp.pt. Not all automobile clubs offer full services to AAA members.

Breakdowns and Accidents

There are 24-hour emergency phones at regular intervals on highways. If you are involved in an accident 112 for police assistance. Most car-rental firms provide their own free rescue service; if your car is rented, follow the instructions given in the documentation. Use of a car-repair service other than those authorized by your rental company may violate your agreement.

Other Information

The minimum age for car rental is 21 (some rental firms stipulate 23). An International Driving Permit (IDP) is a good idea; some car-rental firms require it, and it can speed up formalities if you are involved in an accident. A Green Card (international motor insurance certificate) is essential if you are driving a private car; see page 15 for more information. You are required by law to carry photographic ID at all times. Carrying a fluorescent jacket is advised for all drivers of non-Portuguese registered vehicles. It is compulsory for Portuguese registered vehicles.

Useful Words and Phrases

Portuguese is a Latin language, so an acquaintance with French, Spanish or Italian makes written Portuguese quite easy to understand. Understanding spoken Portuguese, however, is more difficult. Although on paper Portuguese words look similar to Spanish, they actually sound very different. English is widely spoken in tourist areas, but using a few Portuguese words will make your trip more rewarding.

Do you speak English?	*Fala Inglês?*
I'm sorry	*desculpe*
hello/goodbye	*olá/adeus*
yes/no	*sim/não*
how much?	*quanto?*
I am American	*sou Americano*
I would like a	*queria um/uma*
I don't understand	*não entendo*
nonsmoking	*não fumadores*
okay	*está bem*
today/tomorrow	*hoje/amanhã*
open/closed	*aberto/fechado*
right/left	*direita/esquerda*
near/far	*perto/longe*
big/little	*grande/pequeno*
cheap/expensive	*barato/caro*
please	*se faz favor*
thank you	*obrigado (m.)/ obrigada (f.)*
ticket	*bilhete*
one way/return	*ida/ida e volta*
where is…?	*onde é…?*
the hotel	***hotel***
breakfast	*pequeno almoço*
lunch	*almoço*
dinner	*jantar*
I have a reservation	*tenho uma marcação*
key	*chave*
for one night	*para uma noite*
room	*quarto*
shower	*duche*
with bathroom	*com casa de banho*
the restaurant	***restaurante***
beef	*bife*
bread	*pão*
cheese	*queijo*
the check	*a conta*
chicken	*frango*
coffee/tea	*café/chà*
dessert	*sobremesa*
dish of the day	*prato do dia*
fish	*peixe*
ham	*fiambre*
lamb	*carneiro*
pork	*porco*
starter	*entrada*
veal	*vitela*
wine	*vinho*
Is the service included?	*O serviço está incluido?*

Spain

National Flag

Essential for Travelers

● **Required** ● **Recommended** ● **Not required**

Passport	●
Visa (check regulations before you travel)	●
Travel, medical insurance	●
Round-trip or onward airline ticket	●
Local currency	●
Traveler's checks	●
Credit cards	●
First-aid kit and medicines	●
Inoculations	●

Essential for Drivers*

Driver's license	●
International Driving Permit	●
Car insurance (for nonrental cars)	●
Car registration (for nonrental cars)	●

*see also *Driving* section

Important Addresses

Tourist Office of Spain
60 East 42nd Street, Suite 5300
New York, NY 10165
☎ (212) 265-8822
www.spain.info
Visitors by appointment only

US Consulate Barcelona
Passeig Reina Elisenda de Montcada 23
08034 Barcelona, Spain
☎ 93 280 2227

American Embassy
Calle Serrano 75
28006 Madrid, Spain
☎ 91-587-2200. For visa queries: 91 123 8866
(from within Spain); 703 543 9306 (from the U.S.)
http://madrid.usembassy.gov
Personal inquiries: Mon.–Fri. 8:30–1
Emergencies: ☎ 91 587 2200

Customs

✓ **Duty-free limits on goods brought in from non-European Union countries:**
200 cigarettes or 100 cigarillos or 50 cigars or 250 g. tobacco; 2 L. wine; 1 L. alcohol over 22% volume; 2 L. alcohol under 22% volume; 50 ml. perfume; plus any goods (including perfume and electronic goods) up to a value of €430 for air or sea travelers; up to €300 for other travelers.

The import of currency of any denomination of €10,000 must be declared on arrival in Spain.

There is no limit on the importation of tax-paid goods purchased within the European Union if they are for personal use.

✗ No unlicensed drugs, weapons, ammunition, obscene material, pets or other animals, counterfeit money or copied goods, meat or poultry.

For customs limits for returning U.S. citizens see page 16.

Money

Euro (€)
Spain's currency is the euro (€), a currency shared by 18 other European Union countries.

The euro is divided into 100 cents (¢).
The denominations of euro bills are 5, 10, 20, 50, 100, 200 and 500.
There are coins of 1, 2, 5, 10, 20 and 50¢ and €1 and €2.

ATMs are plentiful and credit, debit and prepaid cards are accepted in hotels, large stores and upscale restaurants; check first in small or rural establishments. It is a good idea to carry a mix of large and small euro denominations.

Tips and Gratuities

Locals rarely tip, though they may add a few euros to a large bill. There are different expectations of visitors, however. If you receive good service, consider tipping as follows. Most hotel, restaurant and café checks will include a service charge.

Restaurants (service is normally included)	5–10%
Cafés/bars (service is normally included)	change
Taxis	5%
Porters, chambermaids	€1
Cloakroom attendants	change

Communications

Post Offices

Buy stamps *(sellos)* at a post office *(correos)*, a tobacconist *(estancos)* denoted by a "T" or at some hotels. Out-of-town post office hours may vary. Opening times for post offices are shorter in August.

Telephones

There are very few public telephones in Spain and most accept credit cards rather than coins. However, if you purchase an inexpensive mobile phone, Spanish SIM cards are readily available (most of the main Spanish mobile phone operators have outlets at El Corte Inglés department stores). You can top-up credit online, at ATMs or at stores.
If using your American mobile, check overseas cell phone usage charges with your provider.

Phoning inside Spain
All Spanish phone numbers in this book include an area code; dial the number that is listed. To call the operator dial 11818.

Phoning Spain from abroad
The country code for Spain is 34. Note that Spanish numbers in this book do not include the Spanish country code; you will need to prefix this number if you are phoning from another country. To phone Spain from the United States or Canada dial the prefix 011 34. (Note that the number of digits in Spanish area codes varies.) Example: 11 122 3344 becomes 011 34 11 122 3344.

Phoning from Spain
To phone the United States or Canada from Spain, prefix the area code and number with 00 1. Example: (111) 222-3333 becomes 00 1 111 222-3333. To call international information dial 11825.

Emergency Telephone Numbers

General emergencies **112**
Police *(policía)* **112**
Fire service *(bomberos)* **112**
Ambulance *(ambulancía)* **112**
Emergency calls are free.

Time Zones

Madrid: 12 noon
New York: 6 a.m. (-6 hours)
Chicago: 5 a.m. (-7 hours)
Denver: 4 a.m. (-8 hours)
Los Angeles: 3 a.m. (-9 hours)

Hours of Operation

Stores are open Minday to Saturday 9:30–1 and 4–7:30. Department stores are open Monday to Saturday 10–10. In Madrid, stores also open on the first Sunday of each month. In December stores in big towns also are open on Sundays.
Banks generally open weekdays 8–2 and are open Saturdays 9–1 in winter.
Post offices are open Monday to Friday 8–2:30.
Most **museums** open Tuesday to Saturday 10–7, but many are open 9–2 on Sunday.
Pharmacies are open weekdays 9:30–1 and 4–7.

National Holidays

Banks, businesses and most stores close on these days. Days marked (*) are not national holidays but are celebrated in Catalonia, when shops and offices may close.

Jan. 1	New Year's Day
Jan. 6	Epiphany
Mar. 19	St. Joseph's Day (not Catalonia)
Mar./Apr.	Good Friday
***Mar./Apr.**	Easter Monday
May 1	Labor Day
***May/Jun.**	Pentecost Monday
***Jun. 24**	St. John's Day
Aug. 15	Assumption of the Virgin
***Sep. 11**	National Day (Catalonia)
***Sep. 24**	Our Lady of Mercy Day
Oct. 12	National Day
Nov. 1	All Saints' Day
Dec. 6	Constitution Day
Dec. 8	Immaculate Conception
Dec. 25	Christmas Day
***Dec. 26**	St. Stephen's Day
Dec. 31	New Year's Eve (some businesses close in the afternoon)

Photography

Take your pictures early in the morning or late in the evening. Ask permission before taking pictures in museums and churches. Digital camera equipment and printing facilities are widely available.

Health

Medical Insurance

U.S. and Canadian visitors can receive treatment in a hospital emergency room, but are charged if admitted to a bed. There also are private clinics, such as Unidad Médica (Conde de Aranda, Madrid ☎ 91 435 1823; www.unidadmedica.com), where English is spoken.

Dental Services

You will be charged for dental treatment, so check whether it is covered by your medical insurance. Dentists *(dentistas)* are listed in the *(páginas amarillas) Yellow Pages*.

Sun Advice

The sun is strong during summer, particularly in the south. Dress sensibly, avoid prolonged exposure and protect yourself with a sunscreen.

Drugs

Prescription medicines are available from pharmacies *(farmacias)*, designated by a red or green cross. Information about the nearest late-night or 24-hour facility can be found posted at all pharmacies.

Safe Water

Tap water is generally safe, although it can be heavily chlorinated. Mineral water *(agua mineral)* is inexpensive and is sold *con gas* (carbonated) and *sin gas* (noncarbonated). Drink plenty of fluids during hot weather.

Restrooms

Public restrooms *(servicios)* can usually be found in large department stores, museums and other places of interest to visitors. Elsewhere, restrooms may not be easy to find, but there is no charge. If you use the facilities in a bar you will be expected to buy a drink. Spanish words are *señores* for men and *señoras* for women.

Electricity

Most of Spain has a 220-volt power supply. Electrical sockets take plugs with two round pins. American appliances will need a plug adapter, and either a dual voltage facility or a transformer.

National Transportation

Train *(Tren)*

The Red Nacional de los Ferrocarriles Españoles (RENFE) rail network is inexpensive to use. There are express services for long-distance travel: Alaris, Euromed, Talgo 200 and AVE (reservations required/advisable for all). For information and reservations ☎ 902 320 320 (24 hours); www.renfe.com.

Bus *(Autobus)*

Spain has a good bus system. Ask at a tourist office for details. The Eurolines international bus service operates in Spain: ☎ 902 405 040 (Barcelona); www.eurolines.es.

Ferry *(Transbordador)*

Barcelona is the Mediterranean's biggest port and offers a regular ferry service to the Balearic islands. One of the largest ferry operators is Acciona Trasmediterranea: ☎ 902 45 46 45. "Mini-cruises" of two or three days operate from northern Spain to and from Britain; obtain details from a travel agent.

Driving

Drive on the right

Speed Limits
Police can impose on-the-spot fines.

 Limited-access highways *(autopistas)*
120 k.p.h. (74 m.p.h.)
Divided highways **100 k.p.h. (62 m.p.h.)**

 Main roads
100 k.p.h. (62 m.p.h.)

 Urban areas
50 k.p.h. (31 m.p.h.)

Seat Belts

Must be worn in front and back seats at all times.

Blood Alcohol

The legal blood alcohol limit is 0.05% (0.03% for drivers with less than 2 years' driving experience). Random breath tests on drivers are carried out frequently, especially late at night, and the penalties for offenders are severe.

Driving (continued)

Tolls

A toll *(peage)* is levied on limited-access highways; a toll highway is signed *autopista de peaje* (AP). Take a ticket when you enter and pay when exiting.

Car Rental

The leading car-rental firms have offices at airports and train stations. Hertz offers discounted rates for AAA members (see page 15). For reservations:

	United States	Spain
Avis	1 800 352-7900	902 248 824
Budget	1 800 214 6094	902 112 585
Hertz	1 800 654 4173	902 027 659
Sixt	1 888 SIXT CAR	902 49 16 16
	(749 8227)	

Fuel

Gas *(gasolina)* and diesel are sold in liters. Many gas stations *(gasolineras)* in towns and cities and on highways are open 24 hours.

AAA Affiliated Motoring Club

Real Automóvil Club de España (RACE) Paseo de las Delicias 97 ☎ 900 100 992; www.race.es. If you break down while driving, ☎ 900 112 222 (RACE members' breakdown service). Not all automobile clubs offer full services to AAA members.

Breakdowns and Accidents

There are 24-hour emergency phones on highways. If you are involved in an accident, ☎ 112. Most car-rental firms provide their own free rescue service; if your car is rented, follow the instructions given in the documentation. Use of a car-repair service other than those authorized by your rental company may violate your agreement. In the event of a breakdown, you must put on a fluorescent vest when you are outside your vehicle. You must carry two warning triangles in your vehicle.

Other Information

The minimum age for driving a car is 18, however, most car-rental firms require a driver to be at least 21, and more often 25, to rent a vehicle. An International Driving Permit (IDP) is recommended; some car-rental firms require it, and it can speed up formalities if you are involved in an accident. A Green Card (international motor insurance certificate) is recommended if you are driving a private car; see page 15 for more information. All drivers are required to carry a driver's license, car permit and insurance papers (minimum third-party coverage).

Useful Words and Phrases

Castilian is the main language in Spain, with three important regional languages: Catalan, spoken in Catalonia, the Balearics and Valencia; Basque, the official language of the Basque north; and Galician, spoken in the northwest.

Catalan is closely related to Occitan (or Provençal), and Galician has noticeable links with Portuguese. The Basque tongue is unique, having no connection with any language in Europe.

The following words and phrases are in Castilian:

Do you speak English?	*¿Habla usted inglés?*
excuse me	*perdone*
hello	*hola*
goodbye	*adiós*
yes/no	*si/no*
how much?	*¿cuánto?*
I would like	*me gustaría*
I don't understand	*no entiendo*
no smoking	*prohibido fumar*
okay	*vale*
open/closed	*abierto/cerrado*
today/tomorrow	*hoy/mañana*
here/there	*aquí/allí*
more/less	*más/menos*
please	*por favor*
thank you	*gracias*
you're welcome	*de nada*
how/what	*cómo/qué*
left/right	*izquierda/derecha*
What time is it?	*¿Qué hora es?*
travel ticket	*el billete*
one way/return	*ida/ida y vuelta*
where is…?	*¿dónde está…*
the hotel	**el hotel**
breakfast	*el desayuno*
lunch	*la comida*
dinner	*la cena*
I have a reservation	*Tengo una reserva*
key	*la llave*
room	*la habitación*
shower	*la ducha*
the restaurant	**el restaurante**
beef	*la ternera*
bread	*el pan*
the check	*la cuenta*
cheese	*el queso*
chicken	*el pollo*
coffee	*el café*
dessert	*el postre*
dish of the day	*el plato del día*
fish	*el pescado*
fixed-price lunch menu	*el menú del día*
pork	*la carne de cerdo*
starter	*el primer plato*
wine, red/white	*el vino tinto/blanco*

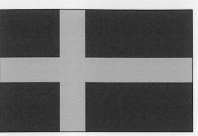

National Flag

Essential for Travelers

● **Required** ● **Recommended** ● **Not required**

Passport	●
Visa (check regulations before you travel)	●
Travel, medical insurance	●
Round-trip or onward airline ticket	●
Local currency	●
Traveler's checks	●
Credit cards	●
First-aid kit and medicines	●
Inoculations	●

Essential for Drivers*

Driver's license	●
International Driving Permit	●
Car insurance (for nonrental cars)	●
Car registration (for nonrental cars)	●

*see also *Driving* section

Important Addresses

Visit Sweden
There is no official Sweden Tourist Office in the U.S. For information go online at www.visitsweden.com.

Stockholm Visitor Center
Sergels Tor
10327 Stockholm
☎ 08 5082 8508
www.visitstockholm.com

Visit Sweden
Sveavägen 21
Stockholm
☎ 08 789 1000

American Embassy
Dag Hammarskjölds Väg 31
SE-115 89 Stockholm, Sweden
☎ 08 783 53 00
www.usemb.se

Customs

✔ **Duty-free limits on goods brought in from non-European Union countries:**
200 cigarettes or 100 cigarillos or 50 cigars or 250 g. tobacco; 1 L. alcohol over 22% volume or 2 L. fortified or sparkling wine; 4L. of wine; 16 L. beer; a reasonable quantity of perfume or toilet water; plus any other duty-free goods (including gifts) to the value of 4,300SKr.

There are no longer restrictions on the importation of tax-paid goods purchased within the European Union. You must be 18 years or over to import tobacco products and 20 or over to import alcohol.

There is no restriction on the import of Swedish or foreign currencies, but amounts in excess of $14,800 must be declared.

✘ No unlicensed drugs, weapons, ammunition, obscene material, pets or other animals, counterfeit money or copied goods, meat, poultry, fish or shellfish.

For customs limits for returning U.S. citizens see page 16.

Money

Krone (SEK, SKr or Kr)
Sweden's currency is the krona (SEK, SKr or Kr; plural kronor), which is divided into 100 öre. The denominations of krona bills are 20, 50, 100, 500 and 1,000.
There are coins of 1, 2, 5 and 10SKr.

Credit, debit and prepaid cards are widely accepted. ATMs for withdrawing local currency are plentiful throughout most of Sweden.

Tips and Gratuities

Tips are welcomed but not expected or obligatory. In restaurants it is usual to round off the check to the nearest 10SKr.

Restaurants, cafés/bars (service is included)	change
Taxis	10%
Hairdressers, chambermaids	none
Porters, restroom attendants	change
Cloakroom attendants	8SKr

Communications

Post Offices

PostNord Sverige, the Swedish postal service, has subcontracted most of its work to supermarkets, newsstands, grocery stores and gas stations. Such outlets display a sign with a yellow horn on a blue background, They sell stamps *(frimärken)*, and deal with other postal matters. Blue post boxes are for local mail; yellow boxes are for national and international mail.

Telephones

Public phone booths were removed in Sweden in 2015. To avoid high roaming fees on your own cell phone, you can buy a prepaid SIM card for use in your own phone, providing your cell is compatible (some U.S. cell phones are not) and isn't SIM locked. Check with your provider before leaving home. Alternatively, consider buying a very basic mobile phone with a prepaid SIM when you arrive in Sweden for use during your stay. Phone service operators in Sweden speak English.

Phoning inside Sweden
All Swedish numbers in this book include an area code; dial the number that is listed. To call the operator, ☎ 90130; for directory assistance, ☎ 118118.

Phoning Sweden from abroad
The country code for Sweden is 46. Note that Swedish numbers in this book do not include the Swedish country code; you will need to prefix this number if you are phoning from another country. To phone Sweden from the United States or Canada, omit the first zero from the Swedish number and add the prefix 011 46. For example: 01 122 33 44 becomes 011 46 1 122 33 44.

Phoning from Sweden
To phone the United States or Canada from Sweden, prefix the area code and number with 00 1. Example: (111) 222-3333 becomes 00 1 111 222-3333. For national operator assistance, ☎ 0018. For international operator assistance, ☎ 07977.

Emergency Telephone Numbers

Police *(polis)* **112**
Fire service *(brandkår)* **112**
Ambulance *(ambulans)* **112**

Time Zones

Stockholm: 12 noon
New York: 6 a.m. (-6 hours)
Chicago: 5 a.m. (-7 hours)
Denver: 4 a.m. (-8 hours)
Los Angeles: 3 a.m. (-9 hours)

Hours of Operation

Stores are open Monday to Saturday 8:30–6 but, in large towns, department stores stay open until 7 or 10 p.m., and some also are open Sunday from around noon to 4. Stores often close on Saturday afternoon between 2 and 4, and usually close early the day before a public holiday. Some smaller stores may close for lunch.

Banks are open Monday to Friday 8–12:30 and 1:30–3, also on Thursday until 4 or 5 and in some cities until 6.

Post offices open weekdays 8–6 and may stay open later in main cities. They also are open Saturday 9–1. The post office at Centralstationen (Central Station) in Stockholm is open Monday to Friday 7 a.m.–10 p.m., Saturday and Sunday 9–6.

Museums are open 10–6; some may close on Monday but stay open late one or two nights a week.

Pharmacies *(apotek)* are open Monday to Friday 8–noon and 2–6. In major cities some are open 24 hours.

National Holidays

Banks, businesses and most stores close on these days; they also may be closed or close earlier the day before a holiday.

Jan. 1	New Year's Day
Jan. 5–6	Epiphany
Mar./Apr.	Good Friday
Mar./Apr.	Easter Monday
May 1	Labor Day
May	Ascension Day
May/Jun.	Pentecost Monday
Jun. 6	Sweden's National Day
Jun.	Midsummer's Eve (Fri. before Jun. 21)
Jun.	Midsummer's Day (Sat. nearest Jun. 21)
Nov. 1	All Saints' Day
Dec. 24	Christmas Eve
Dec. 25	Christmas Day
Dec. 26	St. Stephen's Day
Dec. 31	New Year's Eve

Photography

Poor light conditions occur in winter. Taking photographs in museums may be forbidden; check first. Digital photography equipment and printing services are available.

Sweden

Health

Medical Insurance

Private medical insurance is recommended. There are no general practitioners; go straight to a hospital clinic *(Akutmottagning* or *Vårdcentral)*, taking your passport with you. You will be charged for treatment (free for under 16s). For information contact Stockholm Care AB, ☎ 08 672 24 00; www.stockholmcare.se.

Dental Services

Dentists *(tandläkeren)* always charge for treatment; check whether it is covered by your medical insurance. Emergency treatment is available after hours in major cities. Clinics are indicated by "*Tandläkare*" or "*Folktandvård*" signs.

Sun Advice

The Gulf Stream dictates Sweden's temperate climate of warm sunshine during July and August. Although the sun is not fierce, good sun protection is necessary. Take precautions near the water.

Drugs

Prescription and nonprescription drugs and medicines are available from a pharmacy *(apotek)*. Information about the nearest all-night facility is posted at all pharmacies. A 24-hour service is available in most cities.

Safe Water

Tap water is safe to drink, and mineral water *(mineralvatten)* is widely available.

Restrooms

Public restrooms *(toalett)* are easy to find. There is a charge of 5SKr–10SKr to use some restrooms. Separate facilities for men *(Herrar)* and women *(Damer)* are always clean and modern.

Electricity

Sweden has a 220-volt power supply. Electrical sockets take plugs with two round pins. American appliances will need a plug adapter and will require a transformer if they do not have a dual-voltage facility.

National Transportation

Train *(Tåg)*

The Swedish rail network is operated by several companies: Statens Järnvägar (SJ), Tågkompaniet, Arriva Sweden and Inlandsbanan. It is an efficient and extensive system extending above the Arctic Circle. General information (timetables, prices, etc) is available from any station *(järnvägsstation)*. On some trains reservations are necessary. To obtain tickets for travel with SJ, the largest train operator, ☎ 0771 75 75 75; www.sj.se.

Bus *(Buss)*

There is an excellent, inexpensive bus network of express services between larger towns and cities in south and central Sweden and between Stockholm and the north. The largest bus operator is Swebus, ☎ 0771 218 218; www.swebus.se.

Ferry *(Färja)*

There are ferry services in Sweden, and you can get various island-hopping boat passes or coupons. Most depart from Stockholm. Passes are available from Waxholmsbolaget, on Strömkajen in Stockholm, ☎ 08 600 1000; www.waxholmsbolaget.se.

Driving

Drive on the right

Speed Limits

Police can impose on-the-spot fines, but cannot collect them. Pay particular attention to road signs as speed limits also are based on the quality and safety of the actual road.

 Limited-access highways
110 k.p.h. (68 m.p.h.)
Some parts of the E4 and E6 **120 k.p.h. (74 m.p.h.)**. Divided highways **90 k.p.h. (56 m.p.h.)**

 Main roads
70 k.p.h. (43 m.p.h.)

Urban areas
50 k.p.h. (31 m.p.h.), reduced to **30 k.p.h. (18 m.p.h.)** around schools

Seat Belts

Must be worn in front and rear seats at all times.

Driving (continued)

Blood Alcohol

The legal blood alcohol limit is 0.02%. Random breath tests on drivers are carried out frequently, especially late at night, and the penalties for offenders are severe.

Tolls

There are no highway tolls in Sweden except when crossing the Øresund Bridge between Sweden and Denmark, the Svinesund Bridge between Sweden and Norway, and smaller tolls on the Motalabron Bridge and the Sundsvall Bridge. Stockholm's and Gothenburg's inner city areas do have tolls that drivers of rental cars must pay. Check with your car-rental company that this is included in the price.

Car rental

The leading car-rental firms have offices at airports and train stations. Hertz offers discounted rates for AAA members (see page 15). For reservations:

	United States	Sweden
Alamo	(877) 222-9075	020 100531
Avis	(800) 633 3469	010 494 8050
Budget	(800) 218-7992	010 494 8010
Hertz	(800) 654-3001	08 629 2750

Fuel

Gas *(bensin)* is sold unleaded *(blyfri)* in 95 and 98 octane. Diesel also is available. Most gas stations are self-service, and on highways and in main towns they are open 24 hours. Major credit cards are accepted.

AAA Affiliated Motoring Club

Motormännens Riksförbund (M) Fridhemsgatan 32, Stockholm, ☎ 020 211 111; www.motormannen.se. Not all automobile clubs offer full services to AAA members.

Breakdowns and Accidents

There are 24 hour emergency phones at regular intervals on highways. If you are involved in an accident, ☎ 112 for police. If you break down while driving, contact Assistancekåren: ☎ 020 912 912 (toll-free) or 08 627 57 57; www.assistancekaren.se. Most car-rental firms provide a free rescue service; follow the instructions given in the documentation. Use of a repair service other than those authorized by your rental company may violate your agreement.

Other Information

The minimum age for driving a car is 18 (may be higher for some car-rental firms). An International Driving Permit (IDP) is recommended; some car-rental firms require it, and it can speed up formalities if you are involved in an accident.

Driving (continued)

A Green Card (international motor insurance certificate) is recommended if you are driving a private car; see page 15 for more information Dimmed headlights must be turned on year-round, even during daylight hours. Be aware of moose, roe deer and reindeer appearing on roads, especially at dawn or dusk.

Useful Words and Phrases

Any effort made to speak Swedish is appreciated although most Swedes also speak English. German, Danish and Norwegian are understood.

In Swedish, a vowel sound is usually long when it is the final syllable, and verbs are the same regardless of person. Definite articles are determined by the ending of the noun: -en and -et for singular nouns and -na or -n for plural. There are an additional three letters in the Swedish alphabet – å, ä and ö – which always appear at the end in alphabetical lists.

There are two words for "you": *du* and *ni*. *Ni* is the polite form, *du* is the familiar form. Unlike some other European countries, it is not necessarily impolite to address a complete stranger with the familiar form. In fact, many Swedes consider the polite form to be old-fashioned.

Do you speak English?	*Talar ni Engelska?*
excuse me	*ursäkta mig*
hello	*hej*
goodbye	*adjö/hej då*
yes/no	*ja/nej*
how much is it?	*hur mycket kostar den?*
I'd like	*Jag skulle vilja ha*
I don't understand	*Jag förstår inte*
please	*snälla, vänligen*
thank you	*tack*
the hotel	***hotell***
breakfast	*frukost*
lunch	*lunch*
dinner	*middag*
key	*nyckel*
room	*rum*
shower	*dusch*
the restaurant	***restaurang***
beef	*nötkött, oxkött*
beer	*öl*
bread	*bröd*
chicken	*kyckling*
coffee/tea	*kaffe/te*
dessert	*efterrätt*
fish	*fisk*
lamb	*lammkött*
pork	*fläsk*
wine	*vin*
please bring the check	*notan tack*

Switzerland

National Flag

Essential for Travelers

● Required ● Recommended ● Not required

Passport	●
Visa (check regulations before you travel)	●
Travel, medical insurance	●
Round-trip or onward airline ticket	●
Local currency	●
Traveler's checks	●
Credit cards	●
First-aid kit and medicines	●
Inoculations	●

Essential for Drivers*

Driver's license	●
International Driving Permit	●
Car insurance (for nonrental cars)	●
Car registration (for nonrental cars)	●

*see also *Driving* section

Important Addresses

Switzerland Tourism
Swiss Center, 608 Fifth Avenue
New York, NY 10020
☏ 1 800 794 7795 (toll free)
www.myswitzerland.com
Note: this office is not open to the public.

Schweiz Tourismus (Switzerland Tourism)
Toedistrasse 7
8027 Zürich, Switzerland
☏ 00800 100 200 29 (toll free)
www.myswitzerland.com

American Embassy
Sulgeneckstrasse 19
CH-3007 Bern, Switzerland
☏ 031 357 7011 (Mon.–Fri. 9–12:30 and 1:30–5:30)
or 031 357 7777 (after hours)
https://ch.usembassy.gov

Customs

✔ **Duty-free limits on goods brought in from non-European countries:**
250 cigarettes or cigars or 250g tobacco; 5 L. alcohol under 18% volume and 1 L. alcohol over 18% volume; plus any other duty-free goods (including gifts) to the value of SF300. These limits apply to visitors aged 17 and over.

There are no currency regulations but amounts worth SF10,000 (or equivalent) should be declared.

✗ No unlicensed drugs, weapons, ammunition, obscene material, counterfeit money or copied goods.

For customs limits for returning U.S. citizens see page 16.

Money

Swiss franc (SF)

Switzerland's currency is the Swiss franc (SF), which is divided into 100 centimes or "Rappen." The denominations of franc bills are 10, 20, 50, 100, 200 and 1,000.
There are coins of 5, 10, 20 and 50 centimes and 1, 2 and 5SF.

ATMs are plentiful and credit, debit and prepaid cards are accepted in hotels, large stores and upscale restaurants; check first in small or rural establishments. It is a good idea to carry a mix of large and small Swiss franc denominations.

Tips and Gratuities

Tips are welcomed but not expected, as a service charge is always included. A small tip is accepted for exceptional service.

Restaurants, cafés/bars (service included)	change
Taxis (usually includes service)	change
Porters, chambermaids	change
Hairdressers	change
Restroom/cloakroom attendants	change

Communications

Post Offices

Buy stamps *(timbres poste/Briefmarken)* at a post office *(bureau de poste/Postamt)*, Swisscom shops, at newsstands *(kiosque/ Zeitungsstand)* or from a hotel. Hours for out-of-town post offices may vary.

Telephones

You can use cash or a prepaid phone card *(télecarte/Kartentelefon)* to make a call in Switzerland. Most telephones have direct dialing for international calls. A Taxcard (phone card) can be bought from newsstands, gas stations, train stations and post offices for 5–20SF. Check that the phone booth is equipped with a Taxcard reader. Public phones are mainly found in post offices and train stations. Check overseas cell phone usage with your provider.

Phoning inside Switzerland
All Swiss telephone numbers in this book include an area code; dial the number that is listed. To call national information dial 1811.

Phoning Switzerland from abroad
The country code for Switzerland is 41. Note that Swiss numbers in this book do not include the country code; you will need to prefix this number if you are phoning from another country. To phone Switzerland from the United States or Canada, omit the first zero from the Swiss number and add the prefix 011 41. (Note that Swiss area codes are either one or two digits.) Example: 01 122 33 44 becomes 011 41 1 122 33 44.

Phoning from Switzerland
To phone the United States or Canada from Switzerland, prefix the area code and number with 00 1. Example: (111) 222-3333 becomes 00 1 111 222-3333. To call international information dial 1811.

Emergency Telephone Numbers

Police *(police/Polizei)* **117**
Fire service *(pompiers/Feuerwehr)* **118**
Ambulance *(ambulance/Krankenwagen)* **144**
General emergencies **112**
Emergency calls are free from phone booths.

Time Zones

Zurich: 12 noon
New York: 6 a.m. (-6 hours)
Chicago: 5 a.m. (-7 hours)
Denver: 4 a.m. (-8 hours)
Los Angeles: 3 a.m. (-9 hours)

Hours of Operation

Stores are open Monday to Saturday 9–6:30; some may close on Saturday afternoon at 4 or 5 p.m. and all are generally closed on Sundays. Some out-of-town stores now open seven days a week; some smaller stores may close for lunch (noon–1:30 p.m.).

The hours of operation for **banks** are generally weekdays 8:30–4:30. However, hours can vary depending on the town; ask at your hotel or a tourist office.

Post offices are open Monday to Friday 7:30–noon and 2–6:30 and to noon on Saturday morning except for some major offices in cities, which close later; small offices have briefer hours of operation.

Museums are open 10–6 and often close on Monday. Hours vary, so check locally.

Pharmacies operate Monday to Saturday 8–6.

National Holidays

Banks, businesses and most stores close on these days. Various cantons observe other national holidays such as Jan. 2, May 1, Corpus Christi and All Saints' Day.

Jan. 1	New Years' Day
Mar./Apr.	Good Friday
Mar./Apr.	Easter Monday
May	Ascension Day
May/Jun.	Pentecost Monday
Aug. 1	National Day
Dec. 25	Christmas Day
Dec. 26	St. Stephen's Day

Photography

Digital camera equipment and developing services are available in towns and cities. Photography is prohibited in some military areas. It is quite common to come across the Swiss army when you are walking, hiking or mountain biking. Some footpaths are closed during maneuvers, and temporary barriers set up by the army should be observed at all times. Photography may be forbidden in some churches and museums; ask before taking photographs if you need to obtain permission to do so. In particular, always ask permission before taking photographs of other people.

Health

Medical Insurance

Private medical insurance is recommended. U.S. and Canadian visitors will have to pay for all medical treatment, including emergency assistance, consultation or admittance to a hospital *(hôpital/Krankenhaus)*. If you are planning to take part in winter sports, special sports policies are widely available. For information on medical issues dial Anglo-Phone, ☎ 0900 576 444 (toll call), from anywhere in Switzerland.

Dental Services

A dentist *(dentiste/Zahnarzt)* will charge for any treatment; dental work is expensive so check whether it is covered by your medical insurance. Dentists are listed in the telephone directory. You also can ask for English-speaking dentists at your embassy, hotel or a tourist office.

Sun Advice

Conditions vary considerably; no country in Europe combines within so small an area such marked climatic contrasts. The sun can be deceptively strong in the mountains; protection is essential. The warmest part of Switzerland is south of the Alps, which is under the influence of the Mediterranean. Sun protection is needed; it is advisable to wear a hat and apply sunscreen.

Drugs

Pharmacies sell a range of medicines and drugs and dispense prescriptions. Many pharmacists speak English. At least one pharmacy in every town stays open late; check on store doors or at www.sos-pharmacie.ch.

Safe Water

Tap water is safe to drink throughout Switzerland. Mineral water *(eau minérale/ Mineralwasser)* is widely available.

Restrooms

Most toilets *(toilettes/Toiletten)* are clean and well maintained. They are indicated by a variety of signs, such as "WC" or *Toiletten*. Women's restrooms are designated *Damen, Frauen, Femmes, Dames, Signore* or *Donne;* men's as *Herren, Männer, Hommes, Messieurs, Signori* or *Uomini*.

Electricity

Switzerland has a 230-volt power supply. Electrical sockets take plugs with two round pins. American appliances will need a plug adapter and will require a transformer if they do not have a dual-voltage facility.

National Transportation

Train *(Train/Zug)*

Swiss Federal Railways is Chemins de Fer Fédéreaux (CFF) in French, Schweizerische Bundesbahnen (SBB) in German and Ferrovie Federali Svizzere (FFS) in Italian. It runs a fast, clean and efficient service. Express trains only stop at major cities. *Trains régionales/Regionalzuge* are slow trains usually running the same routes. To reach an English-speaking operator, ☎ 0900 300300 (toll call). There are various good-value rail passes available. Inquire at tourist offices, any large railroad station, or online at www.sbb.ch.

Bus *(Autobus/Bus)*

The bus service takes passengers to mountainous regions where railroads are unable to go. Mail bus routes *(Post Bus)* offer scenic routes, occasionally delivering the mail. There are special offers; passes and cards that combine train, bus and boat travel are available at reduced rates. Eurolines operates in Switzerland. Go online at www.eurolines.com for information.

Ferry *(Ferry/Fähre)*

There are many excursions and some scheduled services on Switzerland's lakes. Regional tourist offices in different cantons can offer information, and some take reservations.

Driving

Drive on the right

Speed Limits

Police can impose on-the-spot fines, for which a receipt is issued. Fines are severe.

 Limited-access highways *(Autobahn)*
120 k.p.h. (74 m.p.h.)
Expressways **100 k.p.h. (62 m.p.h.)**

 Main roads
80 k.p.h. (49 m.p.h.)

 Urban areas
50 k.p.h. (31 m.p.h.) or
30 k.p.h. (18 m.p.h.)

Seat Belts

Must be worn in front and back seats at all times. Children under 12 years or under 150cm in height must sit in a special child seat. Children over 12, or over 150cm in height, must wear a seat belt.

Lights It is mandatory to use headlights at all times, even during the day.

Driving (continued)

Blood Alcohol

The legal blood alcohol limit is 0.05% (0.01% for novice drivers). Random breath tests on drivers are carried out frequently, especially at night. Penalties for offenders are severe.

Tolls

An annual road tax of SF40 is levied on all cars and motorcycles using Swiss highways. Permits *(vignettes/Vignetten)*, available at border crossings, post offices and service areas, are valid for multiple reentry into Switzerland within the duration of the license period. To avoid border delays, it is advisable to buy the permit in advance from STC at www.swisstravelsystem.co.uk.

Car Rental

The leading car-rental firms have offices at airports and train stations. Hertz offers discounted rates for AAA members (see page 15). The minimum age for car rental is 23.
For reservations:

	United States	Switzerland
Alamo	(844) 354 6962	848 445 522
Avis	(800) 633 3469	848 81 18 18
Budget	(800) 218-7992	locations.budget. com/ch
Hertz	(800) 654-3001	www.hertz.co.uk/ rentacar/car-hire/ switzerland

Fuel

Gas and diesel are sold in liters. There are 24-hour gas stations on highways and in cities; many have refreshment facilities and stores. Credit cards are accepted for payment.

AAA Affiliated Motoring Club

Touring Club Suisse (TCS) Chemin de Blandonnet 4, CH-1214 Vernier/Geneva, Switzerland ☎ 0044 000 111; www.tcs.ch. If you break down while driving ☎ 0800 140 140 (TCS breakdown service). Not all automobile clubs offer full services to AAA members.

Breakdowns and Accidents

There are 24-hour emergency phones at regular intervals on highways. If you are involved in an accident ☎ 117 for police. Most car-rental firms provide a free rescue service; if your car is rented, follow the instructions given in the documentation. Use of a car-repair service other than those authorized by your car-rental company may violate your agreement. You must use a warning triangle in the event of an accident/breakdown; this must be kept within easy reach (not in the trunk).

Driving (continued)

Other Information

The minimum age for driving a car is 18 (may be higher for some car-rental firms). An International Driving Permit (IDP) is recommended; some car-rental firms require it, and it can speed up formalities if you are involved in an accident. A Green Card (international motor insurance certificate) is recommended if you are driving a private car; see page 15 for more information.

Dimmed headlights must be used when passing through tunnels. Yellow mail buses have priority at all times, as do vehicles ascending mountain roads. Many mountain pass roads are closed from October through June. For road conditions ☎ 163.

Useful Words and Phrases

There are four official languages spoken in Switzerland: German, French, Italian and Romansch. About 18 percent of the population in southwest Switzerland speak French. South of the Alps, Italian (12 percent) is predominant throughout Ticino and parts of the Grisons (also known as the Graubünden). Most Swiss (65 percent) speak German. A Swiss-German dialect with a variety of local variations is used in everyday conversation; traditional German is used for business purposes.

The fourth language is Romansch, an ancient hybrid of Celtic and Latin tongues spoken by about 50,000 people in the Surselva region of southeastern Switzerland.

This coexistence of distinct languages results in a true "European" nation. The Romansch area is probably the most "Swiss" part of the country. French influence is evident in Lausanne, while Lugano exhibits both Italian and Swiss influences.

Every Swiss child learns two or three languages. English is spoken throughout the country, but an attempt to say a few words in any of Switzerland's languages will always be appreciated.

See page 521 for French words, page 525 for German and page 541 for Italian.

European Distance Chart

Road distances, in kilometers (km), are calculated by the shortest or quickest routes (highways, main roads) from center to center and do not take into account seasonal weather conditions.

Km	Miles
1	0.62
10	6.2
20	12
30	19
40	25
50	31
100	62
200	124
300	186
400	249
500	311
1000	621
1500	932
2000	1243

Cities (diagonal labels):

Amsterdam (NL), Athens (Athína) (GR), Barcelona (ES), Bath (GB), Berlin (DE), Bruges (Brugge) (BE), Brussels (Bruxelles-Brussel) (BE), Budapest (HU), City of Luxembourg (LU), Cologne (Köln) (DE), Copenhagen (København) (DK), Dublin (IE), Edinburgh (GB), Florence (Firenze) (IT), Geneva (Genève) (CH), Ghent (Gent) (BE), Helsinki (FI), Innsbruck (AT), Lisbon (Lisboa) (PT), London (GB), Lyon (FR), Madrid (ES), Munich (München) (DE), Naples (Napoli) (IT), Nice (FR), Odense (DK), Oslo (N...)

Distance matrix (km):

```
Athens:              2819
Barcelona:           1531 3081
Bath:                 713 3317 1666
Berlin:               655 2337 1863 1277
Bruges:               247 2867 1319  463  825
Brussels:             203 2770 1335  548  765   97
Budapest:            1400 1472 1923 1908  875 1457 1358
City of Luxembourg:   405 2604 1149  762  763  317  212 1192
Cologne:              261 2565 1352  758  574  307  208 1152  206
Copenhagen:           788 2792 2133 1430  435  968  918 1331  950  748
Dublin:              1102 3706 2055  526 1664  850  935 2293 1154 1143 1816
Edinburgh:           1136 3740 2089  613 1698  884  969 2327 1188 1177 1849  444
Florence:            1378 2104 1079 1720 1233 1287 1188  949  972 1130 1714 2107 2138
Geneva:               989 2426  754 1102 1113  754  719 1257  509  741 1387 1489 1522  615
Ghent:                219 2827 1319  505  781   54   57 1414  276  264  932  892  925 1242  752
Helsinki:            2082 3404 3291 2705 1462 2243 2192 1943 2191 2000 1177 3092 3127 2589 2545 2207
Innsbruck:            929 2075 1357 1411  750  966  867  730  619  681 1234 1798 1838  485  567  920 2179
Lisbon:              2231 4233 1242 2359 2793 2020 2036 3078 2080 2213 2945 2746 2780 2233 1849 2020 4222 2412
London:               534 3137 1487  182 1095  281  367 1725  586  575 1247  560  645 1535  920  322 2524 1236 2178
Lyon:                 921 2547  634 1110 1226  762  727 1392  517  721 1500 1497 1530  713  147  762 2655  710 1697  932
Madrid:              1764 3665  612 1891 2325 1552 1568 2510 1612 1745 2477 2278 2313 1664 1365 1552 3754 1945  634 1713 1220
Munich:               824 2039 1341 1307  586  862  763  663  514  576 1099 1694 1726  625  588  816 2015  148 2434 1129  733 1926
Naples:              1846 1101 1552 2189 1702 1755 1650 1418 1440 1599 2182 2576 2609  474 1098 1714 3059  958 2704 2011 1184 2137 1098
Nice:                1384 2419  660 1577 1346 1229 1195 1264  985 1136 1742 1965 1999  419  534 1229 2775  700 1812 1399  471 1245  800  892
Odense:               761 2940 2116 1402  583  940  890 1479  922  720  165 1789 1821 1692 1370  904 1333 1216 2916 1224 1487 2449 1082 2163 1726
Oslo:                1383 3387 2727 2025 1030 1563 1512 1926 1544 1343  603 2412 2445 2304 1981 1527 1021 1827 3538 1847 2098 3071 1694 2775 2338  761
                      642 3246 1595  114 1204  390  475 1833  694  683 1356  500  584 1644 1028  431 2633 1344 2286   93 1036 1819 1232 2115 1505 1327 1951
                      502 2878 1031  632 1064  291  307 1491  358  484 1216 1019 1061 1146  537  291 2493  937 1730  454  463 1263  825 1617  932 1188 1811
                     2048 4049 1118 2175 2609 1836 1852 2894 1897 2029 2761 2563 2598 2049 1665 1836 4038 2229  311 1997 1515  564 2250 2522 1630 2733 3356
                      898 1989 1711 1461  349  999  902  527  736  696 1848 1878 1027  965  963 1721  549 2683 1283 1082 2216  384 1498 1198  952 1523
                     1656 1339 1362 1998 1511 1565 1460 1228 1250 1408 1992 2385 2415  284  908 1524 2869  768 2514 1820  994 1947  907  215  702 1975 2587
                      969 1904 1483 1468  731 1023  924  551  675  721 1244 1855 1889  674  730  977 2045  184 2571 1290  876 2069  147 1145  874 1227 1840
                     1973 3975 1080 2101 2535 1762 1778 2820 1822 1955 2687 2488 2522 1975 1591 1762 3964 2155  537 1923 1440  595 2176 2447 1556 2659 3282
                     2233 4068  995 2361 2795 2021 2038 2913 2082 2214 2946 2748 2783 2068 1769 2022 4224 2348  464 2183 1623  538 2354 2540 1649 2918 3542
                     1431 3435 2775 2073 1078 1611 1560 1974 1593 1391  651 2460 2493 2352 2029 1575  524 1875 3586 1895 2146 3119 1742 2823 2386  809  517
                      607 2406 1121  973  752  539  434 1061  224  359 1026 1360 1393  778  393  498 2181  465 2093  795  491 1626  353 1249  789 1009 1621
                       62 2835 1493  663  698  200  171 1423  376  287  832 1050 1084 1397  883  170 2127  959 2192  485  892 1725  847 1868 1360  804 1427
                     1307 1863 1230 1678 1132 1244 1139  707  929 1059 1612 2065 2098  252  579 1203 2349  388 2382 1500  700 1815  527  724  570 1595 2207
                     1142 1711 1754 1651  672 1200 1101  250  935  895 1252 2038 2069  844 1001 1154 1743  472 2883 1473 1146 2339  405 1315 1161 1275 1847
                      819 2347 1031 1161  845  728  623  983  413  572 1217 1548 1583  579  278  687 2274  283 2118  983  423 1616  312 1050  590 1200 1812
```

European Distance Chart

Oxford (GB)	Paris (FR)	Porto (PT)	Prague (Praha) (CZ)	Rome (Roma) (IT)	Salzburg (AT)	Santiago de Compostela (ES)	Seville (Sevilla) (ES)	Stockholm (SE)	Strasbourg (FR)	The Hague (Den Haag) (NL)	Venice (Venezia) (IT)	Vienna (Wien) (AT)	Zurich (CH)
560													
2103	1548												
1389	1034	2501											
1926	1439	2331	1311										
1396	988	2388	374	951									
2029	1474	230	2445	2253	2320								
2289	1733	603	2701	2346	2498	830							
2001	1858	3403	1447	2629	1887	3328	3589						
901	493	1910	605	1055	515	1835	2109	1669					
592	465	2010	918	1674	992	1934	2195	1475	598				
1606	1110	2199	813	530	445	2124	2218	2255	738	1330			
1579	1234	2700	324	1121	291	2624	2743	1895	803	1165	603		
1089	652	1935	698	856	456	1860	2019	1860	222	842	540	725	

A

AAA sightseeing tours 13
AAA Travel Agencies 14, 15
ABBA The Museum,
  Stockholm 439
Agorá, Athens 248
air travel 14, 16
Akershus slott og festning,
  Oslo 367
Akrópoli, Athens 248–249,
  250
Albertina, Vienna 29
Ålesund, Norway 359
Alexanderplatz, Berlin 219
Algarve, Portugal 372
Alte Pinakothek, Munich
  233
Altstadt, Zurich 458
Amalienborg Plads,
  Copenhagen 143
Amsterdam, Netherlands
  342–349, 484–485
Amsterdam Museum 345
Andersen, Hans Christian
  149, 151
Anne Frank Huis,
  Amsterdam 345
Aran Islands 270
Arc de Triomphe, Paris 178
Ardennes, Belgium 52
Ardennes, Luxembourg 324
Århus, Denmark 135
Asamkirche, Munich 233
Ashmolean Museum of Art
  and Archaeology, Oxford
  109
Assembly Rooms, Bath 115
Astrup Fearnley Museet,
  Oslo 367
Ateneumin taidemuseo,
  Helsinki 161
Athens, Greece 244–250,
  478–479
Austen, Jane 117
Austria 18–25, 26–47,
  463–465, 494–497
  Innsbruck 34–39
  map 20–21
  Salzburg 40–47
  Vienna 26–33

B

Bairro Alto, Lisbon 381
Baixa, Lisbon 381
Barcelona, Spain 410–417,
  488–489
La Barceloneta, Barcelona
  413
Barri Gòtic, Barcelona 413
Barrio Antiguo, Santiago
  420
Barrio de Santa Cruz, Seville
  427
Basilica di San Marco,
  Venice 317
Basilica di San Pietro, Rome
  296
Basiliek van het Heilig
  Bloed, Bruges 65, 68–69
Bath Abbey 115
Bath, Britain 112–117,
  469–470
Bauhaus-Archiv, Berlin 219
Bavaria, Germany 212–213
Begijnhof, Amsterdam
  345–346

Begijnhof, Bruges 65
Belfast, Northern Ireland
  271
Belfort, Bruges 65–66
Belgium 48–55, 56–75,
  465–467, 498–501
  Bruges 62–69
  Brussels 56–61
  Ghent 70–75
  map 50–51
Bergen, Norway 359
Bergischer Dom, Cologne
  229
Berlin, Germany 216–222,
  476–477
Berlin Wall 222
Berliner Dom, Berlin 219
Binnenhof, The Hague 353
BMW Museum, Munich
  233
Boqueria, Mercat de la,
  Barcelona 414
border controls 14
Brandenburger Tor, Berlin
  219–220
Brandts and Brandts 13,
  Odense 148
Britain 76–85, 86–117,
  467–470, 502–505
  Edinburgh 98–105
  London 86–97
  map 78–79
  Oxford 106–111
  Bath 112–117
British Museum, London 90
Bruges Beer Experience,
  Bruges 66
Bruges, Belgium 62–69, 466
Brussels, Belgium 56–61,
  465
Buckingham Palace, London
  97
Budapest, Hungary
  258–264, 479
Budai Vár, Budapest 261
Burano, Venice 321
Burg, Bruges 68–69
buses and coaches 13
  see also essential
  information

C

Ca' d'Oro, Venice 317
cable cars 13
Camino de Santiago, Spain
  422
Campanile, Venice 317
Canal Grande, Venice
  317–318
canals, Amsterdam 348–349
Cappelle Medicee, Florence
  305
Capri, Italy 313
car parking 16
car rental 15
  see also essential
  information
Carl Nielsen Museet,
  Odense 149
Casemates de la Pétrusse,
  Luxembourg 331
Castel Nuovo, Naples 311
Castell dell'Ovo, Naples 311
Castelo de São Jorge,
  Lisbon 381
Catedral, Barcelona 413

Catedral, Santiago 420
Catedral, Seville 427
Cathédrale Notre-Dame,
  Luxembourg 331
Cathédrale Notre-Dame,
  Paris 178
Cathédrale Notre-Dame,
  Strasbourg 203
Cathédrale Orthodoxe Russe
  St.-Nicolas, Nice 197
Cathédrale St.-Jean, Lyon
  189
Cathédrale St.-Pierre,
  Geneva 453
Cathédrale des Sts.-Michel
  et Gudule, Brussels 59
cell phones 12
Centre Belge de la Bande
  Dessinée, Brussels 59
Centre d'Histoire de la
  Résistance et de la
  Déportation, Lyon 189
Centre National d'Art et de
  Culture Georges-
  Pompidou, Paris 178–179
Certosa di San Martino,
  Naples 311–312
Champs-Élysées, Paris 179
Christ Church Cathedral,
  Dublin 277
Christ Church, Oxford 109
Christiansborg Slot,
  Copenhagen 143
Cimiez, Nice 197
Cité des Sciences et de
  l'Industrie, Paris 184
City of Luxembourg
  328–333,483–484
climate and seasons 9
Collezione Peggy
  Guggenheim, Venice 318
Cologne, Germany 224–229,
  477
Colosseo, Rome 296
Conciergerie et Ste.-
  Chapelle, Paris 179
Copenhagen, Denmark
  140–145, 471–472
Covent Garden, London 93
credit cards 11
Croix-Rousse, Lyon 189
currency exchange 11
customs regulations 14
  U.S. Customs 16
  see also essential
  information
Czech Republic 118–123,
  124–131, 470–471,
  506–509
  map 120–121
  Prague 124–130

D

Danmarks
  Jernbanemuseum,
  Odense 148–149
Dansk Jødisk Museum,
  Copenhagen 143–144
Danube Museum,
  Esztergom 265
Delft, Netherlands 355
Delphi, Greece 251
Delta Expo, Netherlands
  336
Den Blå Planet,
  Copenhagen 144

Den Fynske Landsby,
  Odense 149
Denkmal für die Ermordeten
  Jüden Europas, Berlin
  220
Denmark 132–139,
  140–151, 471–473,
  510–513
  Copenhagen 140–145
  map 134
  Odense 146–151
dental services see
  essential information
Design Museum Gent,
  Ghent 73
Deutsches Museum,
  Munich 233
disabilities, travelers with
  12
distance chart 570–571
  see also essential
  information
Dom, Salzburg 43
DomQuartier, Salzburg
  43
Dresden, Germany 211
drinking water 10
  see also essential
  information
driving 14–16
  see also essential
  information
Drottningholms Slott,
  Stockholm 439
Dublin, Ireland 274–281,
  479–480
Dublin Castle 277
Dublin City Gallery: The
  Hugh Lane 277, 279
Dublin Writers Museum
  279
Duomo, Battistero e
  Campanile di Giotto,
  Florence 305

E

eau de Cologne 226
Edinburgh, Britain 98–105,
  468–469
Edinburgh Castle 101
Eixample, Barcelona
  413–414
El Escorial, Monasterio de,
  Spain 409
electricity/electrical
  appliances 9
  see also essential
  information
emergency phone numbers
  see essential information
England 80–82, 86–97,
  106–117
  see also Britain
Englischer Garten, Munich
  233–234
EPIC The Irish Emigration
  Museum, Dublin 279
essential information
  493–569
Estadio Santiago Bernabéu,
  Madrid 405
Esztergom, Hungary 265
Ethnikó Archaiologikó
  Mouseío, Athens 249
Ethnikós Kípos, Athens
  249

F

F.C. Barcelona, Museu,
Barcelona 415
ferries 14
see also essential
information
Festspielhäuser, Salzburg 43
Festung Hohensalzburg,
Salzburg 43–44
Finland 152–157, 158–163,
473, 514–517
Helsinki 158–163
map 155
Fjordland, Norway 359, 369
flamenco 426
Florence, Italy 302–307,
481–482
Fondation Baur, Geneva 453
Fontana di Trevi, Rome 297
Foro Romano e Monte
Palatino, Rome 297
Fourvière, Lyon 189–190
Frammuseet, Oslo 367
France 164–173, 174–205,
473–476, 518–521
Lyon 186–193
map 166–167
Nice 194–199
Paris 174–185
Strasbourg 200–205
Franziskanerkirche,
Salzburg 44
Frauenkirche, Munich 234
Fraumünster, Zurich 458
Fundació Joan Miró,
Barcelona 414
Funen, Denmark 136, 149
funiculars 13

G

Galerie d'Art de la Ville de
Luxembourg 332
Galleria dell'Accademia,
Florence 305
Galleria Borghese, Rome 297
Galleria degli Uffizi, Florence
306
Gallerie dell'Accademia,
Venice 318
Gamla Stan, Stockholm
442–443
Gellért-hegy, Budapest 261
Gemeentemuseum Den
Haag, The Hague 353
Geneva, Switzerland
450–455, 491–492
Georgian House, The,
Edinburgh 101
Germany 206–215,
216–237, 476–478,
522–525
Berlin 216–222
Cologne 224–229
map 208–209
Munich 230–237
Getreidegasse, Salzburg 44
Ghent, Belgium 70–75,
466–467
Giant's Causeway, Ireland
271
Giralda, Seville 427
Goldenes Dachl, Innsbruck
37
Goulandris Mouseío
Kykladikís Téchnis,
Athens 249

Grand' Place, Brussels 61
Les Grandes Places,
Strasbourg 203
Graslei en Korenlei, Ghent
73
Greece 238–243, 244–251,
478–479, 526–529
Athens 244–250
map 240
Groeningemuseum, Bruges
66
Gross St. Martin, Cologne
227
Grossmünster, Zurich 458
Gruuthusemuseum, Bruges
66
Guinness Storehouse,
Dublin 279

H

Haags Historisch Museum,
The Hague 353
The Hague, Netherlands
350–354, 485
Halászbástya, Budapest 262
Haus der Kunst, Munich 234
Haus der Natur, Salzburg
44
H.C. Andersens Hus,
Odense 149
health 10
see also essential
information
health insurance 9
Helsingin kaupunginmuseo,
Helsinki 161
Het Gravensteen, Ghent 73
Het Huis van Alijn, Ghent 73
Hofbräuhaus, Munich 235
Hofburg, Vienna 29–30
Hofkirche, Innsbruck 37
Holyrood Park, Edinburgh
101–102
Ilősök tere, Budapest 262
hotels and restaurants
461–492
Houses of Parliament,
London 90–91
Hungary 252–257, 258–265,
479, 530–533
Budapest 258–264
map 254–255
Hungerburgbahn, Innsbruck
37

I

Igreja e Torre dos Clérigos,
Porto 389
Île de la Cité, Paris 179
Île St.-Louis, Paris 179–180
Imperial War Museum,
London 91
Innsbruck, Austria 34–39,
463–464
insurance 9
see also essential
information
International Driving Permit
(IDP) 15
Ireland 266–273, 274–281,
479–480, 534–537
Dublin 274–281
map 269
Isla Mágica, Seville 427

Italy 282–291, 292–321,
480–483, 538–541
Florence 302–307
map 284–285
Naples 308–312
Rome 292–299, 301
Venice 314–320

J

Jane Austen Centre
115–116
Jardin Anglais, Geneva 453
Jardin des Tuileries, Paris
180
Jardins do Palácio de
Cristal, Porto 389
Josefov, Prague 127
Joyce, James 278

K

Kafka, Franz 128
Kaiser-Wilhelm-
Gedächtniskirche, Berlin
220
Karlův most, Prague 127, 129
Kensington Palace, London
91
Kew Gardens, London 91
Kilmainham Gaol, Dublin 279
Kirche am Steinhof, Vienna
30
Kirche St. Peter, Zurich 458
Kölner Dom, Cologne 227
Kolonáki, Athens 249
Kon-Tiki museet, Oslo 367
Kortárs Művészeti Múzeum
– Ludwig Múzeum,
Budapest 262
Kostel svatého Mikuláše,
Prague 129
Kraanlei, Ghent 73–74
Kulturforum, Berlin 220
Kungliga Slottet, Stockholm
439–440
Kunsthaus, Zurich 458–459
Kutná Hora, Czech Republic
131

L

lace-making 63, 64, 321
Landesmuseum Zürich,
Zurich 459
Lenbachhaus, Munich 234
Létzebuerg City Museum,
Luxembourg 331
Lisbon, Portugal 378–384,
486–487
London, Britain 86–97,
467–468
London congestion
charging 16
London Eye, London 91–92
Loretánská kaple, Prague
129
Löyly, Helsinki 161
LUGDUNUM Musée &
Théâtres Romains, Lyon
190
Luonnontieteellinen museo,
Helkinsi 161
Luxembourg 322–327,
328–333, 483–484,
542–545
City of Luxembourg
328–333
map 325

Lykavittós, Athens 249
Lyon, France 186–193,
474–475

M

Madrid, Spain 402–408,
487–488
Magyar Állami Operaház,
Budapest 262
Magyar Nemzeti Múzeum,
Budapest 262–263
Maison des Canuts, Lyon
190
MAMCO (Musée d'Art
Moderne et
Contemporain), Geneva
454
map of Europe 6–7
le Marais, Paris 180
Markt, Bruges 66–67
Marmorkirken, Copenhagen
144
Mátyás-templom, Budapest
262
Mauritshuis, The Hague 354
medical treatment *see*
essential information
Mercat de la Boqueria,
Barcelona 414
Mergellina, Naples 312
Mesdag Collectie, De
Hague, 354
Mirabellgarten, Salzburg 44
Moderna museet,
Stockholm 440
Monasterio de las Descalzas
Reales, Madrid 405
Monastiráki, Athens
249–250
money 10–11
see also essential
information
Møntergården, Odense 149
Montjuïc, Barcelona 414
Montmartre, Paris 180, 182
Mosteiro dos Jerónimos,
Lisbon 382
motoring clubs 14–15
Mozart, Wolfgang Amadeus
31, 41, 44, 45, 46, 47
Mozarts Geburtshaus,
Salzburg 44
Mozarts-Wohnhaus,
Salzburg 46
Munch-museet, Oslo
367–368
Munich, Germany 230–237,
477–478
Murano, Venice 321
Musée Alsacien, Strasbourg
203–204
Musée Archéologique,
Strasbourg 204
Musée Ariana, Geneva 453
Musées des Arts Décoratifs,
Lyon 191
Musée d'Art et d'Histoire,
Geneva 453–454
Musée d'Art Moderne et
d'Art Contemporain
(MAMAC), Nice 197
Musée d'Art Moderne et
Contemporain (MAMCS),
Strasbourg 204
Musée d'Art Moderne de
la Ville de Paris, Paris 182

Musée départmental des Arts Asiatiques, Nice 197
Musée Barbier-Mueller, Geneva 454
Musée des Beaux-Arts, Lyon 190
Musée des Beaux-Arts, Strasbourg 204
Musée Carnavalet, Paris 182
Musée des Confluences, Lyon 190
Musées Gadagne, Lyon 191
Musée Horta, Brussels 59
Musée des Instruments de Musique, Brussels 59–60
Musée International de la Croix-Rouge et du Croissant-Rouge, Geneva 454
Musée du Louvre, Paris 182–183
Musée Magritte Museum, Brussels 60
Musée Matisse, Nice 197–198
Musée National d'Histoire Naturelle, Luxembourg 331–332
Musée National Marc Chagall, Nice 198
Musée de l'Oeuvre Notre-Dame, Strasbourg 204
Musée d'Orsay, Paris 183
Musée du quai Branly-Jacques Chirac, Paris 183
Musées royaux des Beaux-Arts de Belgique, Brussels 60
Musée des Tissus, Lyon 191
Musée de la Ville de Bruxelles, Brussels 60
Musei Capitolini, Rome 297
Musei Vaticani, Rome 297–298
Museo Arqueológico Nacional (MAN), Madrid 405
Museo Archeologico Nazionale, Naples 312
Museo d'Arte Contemporanea di Roma (MACRO), Rome 298
Museo de Bellas Artes, Seville 427
Museo Cerralbo, Madrid 405
Museo e Gallerie Nazionali di Capodimonte, Naples 312
Museo Nacional Centro de Arte Reina Sofía, Madrid 405–406
Museo Nacional del Prado, Madrid 406
Museo Nazionale del Bargello, Florence 306
Museo Nazionale Etrusco di Villa Giulia, Rome 298
Museo das Peregrinacións e de Santiago, Santiago 420, 423
Museo do Pobo Galego, Santiago 420–421

Museo de la Real Academia de Bellas Artes de San Fernando, Madrid 406–407
Museo di San Marco, Florence 306
Museo y Tesoro de la Catedral, Santiago 421
Museo Thyssen-Bornemisza, Madrid 407
Museu Calouste Gulbenkian, Lisbon 382
Museu Coleção Berardo, Lisbon 382
Museu d'Història de Barcelona, 415
Museu de Marinha, Lisbon 382
Museu Nacional d'Art de Catalunya (MNAC), Barcelona 415
Museu Nacional do Azulejo, Lisbon 382
Museu Nacional Soares dos Reis, Porto 389
Museu Picasso, Barcelona 415
Museum für Angewandte Kunst, Cologne 227
Museum de Gevangenpoort, The Hague 354
Museum Haus am Checkpoint Charlie, Berlin 220
Muséum d'Histoire Naturelle, Geneva 454
Museum of Bath at Work 116
Museum of Ireland – Archaeology, Dublin 280
Museum of London 92
Museum Ludwig, Cologne 227
Museum of Oxford 109
Museum Schnütgen, Cologne 228
Museum voor Schone Kunsten, Ghent 74
Muséum des Sciences Naturelles, Brussels 60
Museumsinsel, Berlin 221

N
Nagy Zsinagóga, Budapest 263
Naós tou Olympíou Diós, Athens 250
Naples, Italy 308–312, 482–483
Nasjonalgalleriet, Oslo 368
National Gallery, Dublin 280
National Gallery, London 92
national holidays *see* essential information
National Maritime Museum, London 92
Nationalmuseet, Copenhagen 144
Nationalmuseum, Stockholm 440
National Museum of Ireland – Archaeology, Dublin 280
National Museum of Scotland, Edinburgh 102

Natural History Museum, London 94
Netherlands 334–341, 342–355, 484–485, 546–549
Amsterdam 342–349
The Hague 350–354
map 337
Neue Pinakothek, Munich 234
Neues Rathaus, Munich 234
newspapers/magazines 10
Nice, France 194–199, 475
Nielsen, Carl 146, 149
Nieuwe Kerk, Amsterdam 346
Nordiska museet, Stockholm 440
Nordkettenbahn, Innsbruck 37
Norsk Folkemuseum, Oslo 368
Norsk Maritimt Museum, Oslo 368
Norsk Opera & Ballett, Oslo 368
Northern Ireland 270–271
Norway 356–363, 364–369, 485–486, 550–553
map 358
Oslo 364–368
Ny Carlsberg Glyptotek, Copenhagen 144–145
Nykytaiteen museo Kiasma, Helsinki 161–162

O
Odense Koncerthus, Odense 149
Odense, Denmark 146–151, 472–473
Odeonsplatz, Munich 236
Oktoberfest, Munich 235
Olympiapark, Munich 236
Onze-Lieve-Vrouwekerk, Bruges 67
opening hours *see* essential information
Országház, Budapest 263–264
Oslo, Norway 364–368, 485–486
Oude Kerk, Amsterdam 346–347
Oxford, Britain 106–110, 469
Oxford Castle & Prison 109–110
Oxford colleges 107–108
Oxford University Museum of Natural History 110

P
packing essentials 9–10
Padrão dos Descobrimentos, Lisbon 382, 384
Palace of Holyroodhouse, Edinburgh 102
Palácio da Bolsa, Porto 389
Palacio Real, Madrid 407–408
Palais Grande-Ducal, Luxembourg 332
Palais des Nations, Geneva 454
Palazzo Ducale, Venice 318

Pantheon, Rome 298
Park Güell, Barcelona 416
Paris, France 174–185, 473–474
Parque de María Luisa, Seville 428
Parque das Nações, Lisbon 384
Parque del Retiro, Madrid 408
Parthenón, Athens 248
passports and visas 8–9
Pécs, Hungary 254, 257
personal safety and security 11–12
Petite France, Strasbourg 204
Petřín, Prague 129
pharmacies 10
see also essential information
photography *see* essential information
Piazza Navona, Rome 298
Piazza San Marco, Venice 318
Piazza di Spagna e Scalinata della Trinità dei Monti, Rome 298, 301
pilgrimages 422
Pinakothek der Moderne, Munich 236
Piréas, Athens 250
Pitt Rivers Museum, Oxford 110
place Bellecour, Lyon 191
place du Bourg-de-Four, Geneva 454
place de la Concorde, Paris 184
place Masséna and Promenade de Paillon, Nice 198
place des Vosges, Paris 180
Pláka, Athens 250
Platéia Syntágmatos, Athens 250
Plaza de España, Seville 428
Plaza Mayor, Madrid 408
Plaza de Toros de la Maestranza, Seville 428
Plaza de la Villa, Madrid 408
Poble Espanyol, Barcelona 416
Pompeii, Italy 311
Ponte Dom Luís 1, Porto 389
Ponte Vecchio, Florence 306
Port Vell, Barcelona 416
Porto, Portugal 386–391, 487
Portugal 370–377, 378–391, 486–487, 554–557
Lisbon 378–384
map 373
Porto 386–391
post offices *see* essential information
Potsdam, Germany 223
Praça do Comércio, Lisbon 384
Praça da Ribeira, Porto 389
Prague, Czech Republic 124–130, 470–471
Praza do Obradoiro, Santiago 421

Pražský hrad, Prague
129–130
Prinzregentenstrasse,
Munich 237
Promenade des Anglais,
Nice 198
pubs 281, 468
Puerta del Sol, Madrid 408
Punta della Dogana, Venice
318–319
Pulteney Bridge, Bath 116
Pýli Adrianoú, Athens 250

Q
Le Quartier Latin, Paris 184

R
rack railways 13
La Rambla, Barcelona 416
Rathaus, Cologne 228
Reale Alcázar, Seville 428
Real Jardín Botánico,
Madrid 408
Residenz, Munich 236
Residenzplatz, Salzburg 46
restrooms see essential
information
return travel to the United
States 16
Rhine, River 210–211
Rialto, Venice 319
Rijksmuseum, Amsterdam
347
Roman Baths, Bath 116
Rome, Italy 292–299, 301,
480–481
Römisch-Germanisches
Museum, Cologne 228
Rosenborg Slot,
Copenhagen 145
Rossio, Lisbon 381
Rothenburg ob der Tauber,
Germany 213
Royal Crescent, Bath 116
Royal Botanic Garden
Edinburgh 103
Royal Mile, Edinburgh
104–105
Royal Yacht *Britannia*,
Edinburgh 103
Rundetårn, Copenhagen
145

S
Sacré-Cœur, Paris 180, 182
Sagrada Família, Temple
Expiatori de la, Barcelona
416
Ste.-Chapelle, Paris 179
St. Giles' Cathedral,
Edinburgh 103
St. Paul's Cathedral, London
94
St. Stephen's Green, Dublin
280
St. Ursula, Cologne 228
Salzburg 40–47, 464–465
Salzburg Festival 45
Salzburg Museum Neue
Residenz/Spielzeug
Museum, Salzburg 46
San Clemente, Rome 301
San Giorgio Maggiore,
Venice 319
Sankt Knuds Kirke, Odense
150

Sanssouci Palace, Potsdam
223
Santa Croce, Florence 306
Santa Maria Gloriosa dei
Frari, Venice 320
Santa Maria Maggiore,
Rome 301
Santa Maria del Mar,
Barcelona 416
Santa Maria dei Miracoli,
Venice 319
Santa Maria della Salute,
Venice 320
Santa Maria in Trastevere,
Rome 301
Santi Giovanni e Paolo,
Venice 320
Santiago de Compostela,
Spain 418–423, 489
Schloss Ambras, Innsbruck
37–38
Schloss Belvedere, Vienna
30
Schloss Charlottenburg,
Berlin 221
Schloss Nymphenburg,
Munich 236
Schloss Schönbrunn,
Vienna 30, 32
school vacations 9
Science Museum, London
94–95
Scotland 80, 82–83, 98–105
see also Britain
Scottish National Gallery,
Edinburgh 103
Scuola di San Giorgio degli
Schiavoni, Venice 320
Scuola Grande di San
Rocco, Venice 320
Sé, Lisbon 384
Se, Porto 390
Senaatintori, Helsinki 162
Setas de Sevilla (Metropol
Parasol), Seville 428
Seurasaaren ulkomuseo,
Helsinki 162
Seville, Spain 424–428,
489–490
Shakespeare, William 111
silk industry 193
Sintra, Portugal 385
Sint-Baafskathedraal, Ghent
74
Sint-Janshospitaal, Bruges
67
Sint-Salvatorskathedraal,
Bruges 67
Skansen, Stockholm
440–441
Spaccanapoli, Naples 312
Spain 392–401, 402–429,
487–490, 558–561
Barcelona 410–417
Madrid 402–408
map 394–395
Santiago de Compostela
418–423
Seville 424–428
Spanische Hofreitschule,
Vienna 32
Stadhuis, Bruges 67, 68
Stadmuseum Gent (STAM),
Ghent 74
Stadshuset, Stockholm 441
Stadtturm, Innsbruck 38

Staroměstská radnice,
Prague 130
Statens Museum for Kunst,
Copenhagen 145
Stedelijk Museum voor
Actuele Kunst, Ghent 74
Stephansdom, Vienna 32
Šternberský palác, Prague
130
Stiftskirche St. Peter,
Salzburg 46
Stockholm, Sweden
436–443, 490–491
Stockholms
Medeltidsmuseet,
Stockholm 441
Strahovský klášter, Prague
130
Strasbourg, France
200–205, 475–476
Stratford-upon-Avon, Britain
111
Strauss, Johann 31
subways (metro) 13
sun safety see essential
information
Suomen kansallismuseo,
Helsinki 162
Suomenlinna, Helsinki 162
Swarovski Kristallwelten,
Innsbruck 38
Sweden 430–435, 436–443,
490–491, 562–565
map 433
Stockholm 436–443
Switzerland 444–449,
450–460, 491–492,
566–569
Geneva 450–455
map 446–447
Zurich 456–459
Széchenyi Gyógyfürdő és
Uszoda, Budapest 264
Szent István Bazilika,
Budapest 264
Szépművészeti Múzeum 264

T
Tate Britain, London 95
Tate Modern, London 95
tax-free shopping 16
telephones 12
see also essential
information
television and radio 10
Tidens Samling, Odense 150
Tiergarten, Berlin 221
time see essential
information
tipping see essential
information
Tiroler Volkskunstmuseum,
Innsbruck 38
Tivoli, Copenhagen 145
Tivoli, Italy 300
Topographie des Terrors,
Berlin 221
Torcello, Venice 321
Torre de Belém, Lisbon 384
Tour Eiffel, Paris 184
tourist offices see essential
information
Tower of London 95–96
trains 13
see also essential
information

trams 13
transportation
between cities 13–14
in cities 13
see also essential
information
travel insurance 9
traveler's checks 8
Trelleborg, Denmark 136
Trinity College, Dublin 280
trolley buses 13
Tuscany, Italy 284, 286

U
Uhrenmuseum, Vienna 32
Ulster, Ireland 270–271
United Nations 454
University Church of
St. Mary the Virgin,
Oxford 110
University of Oxford Botanic
Garden, Oxford 110
Unter den Linden, Berlin 221

V
V&A Museum, London 96
Van Gogh Museum,
Amsterdam 347
Városliget, Budapest 264
Vasamuseet, Stockholm 441
Vatican, Rome 299
Venice, Italy 314–320, 483
Via Appia Antica, Rome 301
Vieille Ville, Luxembourg
332
Vieille Ville, Nice 198
Vienna, Austria 26–33, 463
Vieux Lyon 191
View From The Shard,
London 96
Vigelandsparken, Oslo 368
Vikingaliv 441
Vila Nova de Gaia, Porto 390
Villa Adriana, Tivoli 300
Villa Borghese, Rome 301
Villa d'Este, Tivoli 300
Villa Vauban, Luxembourg
332
Villette, La, Paris 184
Vondelpark, Amsterdam
347
Vredespaleis, The Hague
354

W
Wales 80, 82
see also Britain
Wallraf-Richartz-Museum
and Fondation Corboud,
Cologne 228
Weimar, Germany 211
Westminster Abbey,
London 96
winter sports 39, 429
World of Discoveries, Porto
390

Z
Zealand, Denmark 135,
136–137
Zoo Zurich 459
Zuiderzeemuseum,
Netherlands 336
Zurich, Switzerland
456–459, 492

Acknowledgments

The Automobile Association wishes to thank the following photographers and organizations for their assistance in the preparation of this book.

Abbreviations for the picture credits are as follows – (t) top; (b) bottom; (l) left; (r) right; (c) center; (AA) AA World Travel Library

3 AA/J Smith; 18 AA/J Smith; 22 Jon Arnold Images Ltd/Alamy; 23 AA/J Smith; 25 imageBROKER/Alamy; 29 AA/J Smith; 30 AA/D Noble; 31 AA/M Siebert; 32 AA/D Noble; 33 AA/J Smith; 34 Aivar Mikko/Alamy; 37 Kuttig - Travel/Alamy; 38 Andy Christiani/Alamy; 39 AA/M Jourdan; 43 AA/A Baker; 45 AA/J Smith; 47 AA/J Smith; 48 Chris Dorney/Alamy; 52 AA/A Kouprianoff; 53 Marc Hill/Alamy; 55 PCL/Alamy; 57 imagebroker/Alamy; 61 eye35.com/Alamy; 63 AA/A Kouprianoff; 65 Hideo Kurihara/Alamy; 66 Alexandre Fagundes/ Alamy; 68 AA/A Kouprianoff; 69 AA/A Kouprianoff; 71 Ian Dagnall/Alamy; 73 Arterra Picture Library/Alamy; 74 Riccardo Sala/Photolibrary; 75 age fotostock /Alamy; 76 eye35/Alamy; 81 AA/M Moody; 82 AA/J Smith; 85 AA/J Tims; 90 AA/J Tims; 93 AA/J Tims; 94 AA/N Setchfield; 95 AA/W Voysey; 97 Andy Myatt/Alamy; 101 AA/K Blackwell; 102 Colin Burn-Murdoch/Alamy; 104 Marco Secchi/Alamy; 105 AA/K Blackwell; 106 AA/J Tims; 110 AA; 111 AA/J Wyand; 112 Courtesy of Visit Bath; 115 marc zakian/Alamy; 116 Courtesy of Visit Bath; 117 Jane Tregelles/Alamy; 118 AA/T Woodcock; 121 AA/S McBride; 123 AA/L Noble; 126 AA/J Smith; 127 Nataliya Hora/Alamy; 128 AA/S McBride; 129 AA/J Wyand; 130 AA/S McBride; 131 AA/J Wyand; 132 AA/D Forss; 135 AA/J Wyand; 136 F1online digitale Bildagentur GmbH/Alamy; 137 Tibor Bognar/Alamy; 139 AA/D Forss; 144 Morten Svenningsen/Alamy; 148 AA/D Forss; 150 AA/D Forss; 151 The Art Archive/Alamy; 152 Layne Kennedy/Corbis; 154 Photoshot Holdings Ltd/Alamy; 155 AA; 157 Peter Lilja/Photolibrary; 158 PCL/Alamy; 163 Manfred Gottschalk/Alamy; 164 AA/I Dawson; 168 AA/J Edmanson; 169 AA/J Tims; 170 AA/C Sawyer; 171 AA/R Strange; 173 Manfred Gottschalk/Alamy; 176 AA/K Blackwell; 178 Hercules Milas/Alamy; 179 AA/K Paterson; 180 AA/K Blackwell; 181 AA/M Jourdan; 182 AA/J Tims; 185 Prisma Bildagentur AG/Alamy; 187 AA/J Wyand; 189 AA/J Wyand; 191 AA/J Wyand; 192 Hemis/Alamy; 193 Hemis/Alamy; 197 AA/J Tims; 198 AA/J Tims; 199 AA/J Tims; 201 Jon Arnold Images Ltd/Alamy; 203 AA; 205 AA/B Smith; 206 AA/A Kouprianoff; 211 AA/A Baker; 212 AA/C Sawyer; 213 AA/M Jourdan; 215 AA/A Kouprianoff; 219 Anne-Marie Palmer/Alamy; 222 AA/T Souter; 223 AA/A Kouprianoff; 224 AA/A Baker; 227 AA/A Hemmisen; 229 Bildarchiv Monheim GmbH/Alamy; 233 AA/M Jourdan; 235 AA/C Sawyer; 236 AA/T Souter; 237 Oliver Hoffmann/Alamy; 238 AA/Mockford & Bonetti; 243 AA/Mockford & Bonetti; 246 AA/Mockford & Bonetti; 247 Jan Wlodarczyk/Alamy; 248 AA/Mockford & Bonetti; 251 AA/R Surman; 252 AA/J Smith; 257 AA/J Smith; 260 AA/J Smith; 261 AA/J Smith; 262 AA/J Smith; 263 AA/J Smith; 265 AA/K Paterson; 266 AA/C Hill; 270 mauritius images GmbH/Alamy; 271 AA/K Blackwell; 273 AA/K Blackwell; 276 AA/K Blackwell; 277 AA/K Blackwell; 278 "; Phil Crean A/Alamy"; 279 EPIC Ireland CHQ Limited/Ros Kavanagh; 281 AA/K Blackwell; 282 AA/Mockford & Bonetti; 287 AA/J Tims; 288 AA/Mockford & Bonetti; 289 AA/Mockford & Bonetti; 291 AA/C Sawyer; 296 AA/Mockford & Bonetti; 298 AA/Mockford & Bonetti; 299 AA/Mockford & Bonetti; 300 AA/Mockford & Bonetti; 301 AA/Mockford & Bonetti; 305 AA/J Tims; 307 AA; 308 imageBROKER/Alamy; 312 AA/M Jourdan; 313 Jon Arnold Images Ltd/Alamy; 317 AA/Mockford & Bonetti; 319 AA/Mockford & Bonetti; 320 AA/S McBride; 321 AA/C Sawyer; 322 Jon Arnold Images Ltd/Alamy; 324 David Robertson/Alamy; 327 Travelshots.com/Alamy; 331 blickwinkel/Alamy; 332 Lana Sundman/Alamy; 333 David Robertson/Alamy; 334 AA/A Robinson; 336 AA/A Robinson; 338/39 AA/A Robinson; 339b AA/A Robinson; 341 Louise Heusinkveld/Alamy; 345 Paul Brown/Alamy; 346 AA/K Paterson; 347 AA/A Robinson; 348 AA/A Robinson; 349 AA/A Robinson; 351 CW Images/Alamy; 353 David R. Frazier Photolibrary, Inc./Alamy; 354 moodboard/Alamy; 355 AA/K Paterson; 356 David Robertson/Alamy; 360 AA; 361 imagebroker/Alamy; 363 Body Philippe/Photolibrary; 364 blickwinkel/Alamy; 369 AA/K Naylor; 370 AA/P Wilson; 372 AA/M Wells; 374 AA/M Wells; 375 AA/M Wells; 377 AA/M Wells; 381 AA/T Harris; 383 AA/M Wells; 384 AA/M Wells; 385 AA/T Harris; 388 AA/Mockford & Bonetti; 390 AA/Mockford & Bonetti; 391 AA/A Kouprianoff; 392 AA/M Bonnet; 396 AA/M Jourdan; 397 AA/P Wilson; 399 AA/M Chaplow; 401 AA/M Bonnet; 405 Glyn Thomas Photography/Alamy; 406 AA/M Jourdan; 407 AA/M Jourdan; 408 AA/R Strange; 409 AA/M Chaplow; 412 AA/M Bonnet; 413 AA/M Bonnet; 414 AA/M Jourdan; 415 AA/M Bonnet; 417 AA/M Bonnet; 418 imagebroker/Alamy; 421 BANANA PANCAKE/Alamy; 422 BANANA PANCAKE/Alamy; 423 Hemis/Alamy; 424 Jon Arnold Images Ltd/Alamy; 428 Karol Kozlowski/Alamy; 429 AA/C Sawyer; 430 BANANA PANCAKE/Alamy; 432 BANANA PANCAKE/Alamy; 435 AA/K Naylor; 438 AA/K Naylor; 439 Chalermchai Chamnanyon/Alamy; 440 Chad Ehlers/Photolibrary; 441 BANANA PANCAKE/Alamy; 442 Sweden And Swedish/Alamy; 444 Tibor Bognar/Alamy; 449 Eva Bocek/Alamy; 450 Hemis/Alamy; 455 Andre Jenny/Alamy; 459 Cosmo Condina Western Europe/Alamy; 460 Prisma Bildagentur AG/Alamy; 494t Central Intelligence Agency; 498t Central Intelligence Agency; 502t Central Intelligence Agency; 506t Central Intelligence Agency; 510t Central Intelligence Agency; 514t Central Intelligence Agency; 518t Central Intelligence Agency; 522t Central Intelligence Agency; 526t Central Intelligence Agency; 530t Central Intelligence Agency; 534t Central Intelligence Agency; 538t Central Intelligence Agency; 542t Central Intelligence Agency; 546t Central Intelligence Agency; 550t Central Intelligence Agency; 554t Central Intelligence Agency; 558t Central Intelligence Agency; 562t Central Intelligence Agency; 566t Central Intelligence Agency.

Every effort has been made to trace the copyright holders, and we apologize in advance for any unintentional omissions or errors. We would be pleased to apply any corrections in any following edition of this publication.